Early Rome and the Latins

Marble group of the Dioscuri found
in the Forum Romanum.

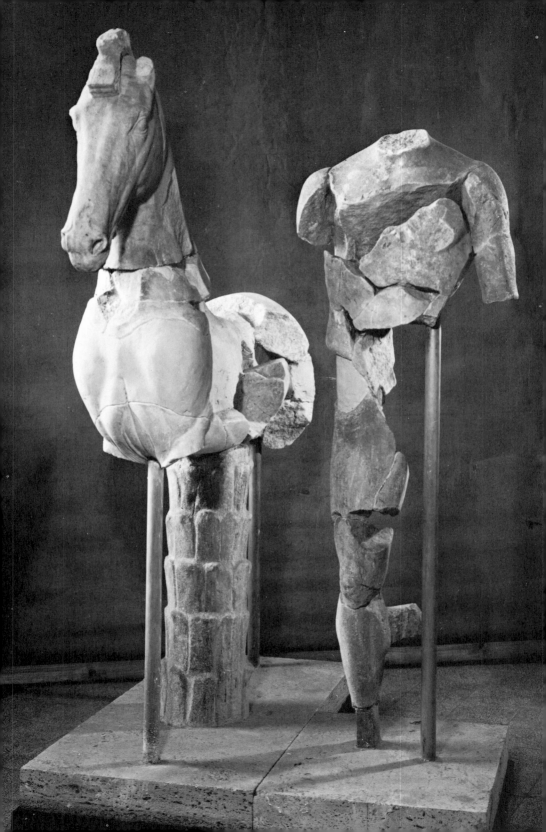

JEROME LECTURES   SEVENTH SERIES

Early Rome

and the Latins

by A. ALFÖLDI

Ann Arbor

THE UNIVERSITY OF MICHIGAN PRESS

All rights reserved
Library of Congress Catalog Card No. 63-8076
Published in the United States of America by
The University of Michigan Press and simultaneously
in Toronto, Canada, by Ambassador Books Limited
Printed in The Netherlands by E.J. Brill, Leiden

P. DE FRANCISCI

A. DEGRASSI

G. LUGLI

D. MUSTILLI

M. PALLOTTINO

P. ROMANELLI

VIRIS ILLUSTRISSIMIS

DE PRIMORDIIS URBIS ROMAE ELUCIDANDIS

OPTIME MERITIS

D. D. D.

Acknowledgments

This book is based on the Jerome Lectures given at the American Academy in Rome in the summer and at the University of Michigan in the fall of 1961. I wish to express my sincere gratitude to the Committee of the Jerome Foundation for the honor of appointing me Jerome lecturer and for publishing the lectures in their present enlarged form. I am particularly indebted to Dean Ralph A. Sawyer and to Professor Gerald F. Else for their many kindnesses. The generous hospitality of Harlan H. Hatcher, president of the University of Michigan, has made the weeks in Ann Arbor unforgettable.

Equally memorable were the two months which I spent with the staff and members of the American Academy in Rome. My special thanks go to Professor Thomas R. S. Broughton, director of Studies and Richard A. Kimball, director of the Academy, who spared no effort to make my stay agreeable and to facilitate my task.

The volume includes results of research undertaken prior to the preparation of the Jerome Lectures. This was made possible by an annual travel grant from the Institute for Advanced Study in Princeton—that unique retreat for humanists and scientists alike with which I have had the privilege to be associated since 1955.

This reconsideration of the birth and rise of Roman power in Latium could never have been attempted without the contributions of many dear Italian friends and colleagues. The book is dedicated

ACKNOWLEDGMENTS

to Pietro de Francisci, Attilio Degrassi, Giuseppe Lugli, Domenico Mustilli, Massimo Pallottino, and Pietro Romanelli, whose own work did much to pave the way for a new understanding of early Roman history. I gratefully acknowledge substantial help received from Ferdinando Castagnoli, Gianfilippo Carettoni, Lucos Cozza, Enrico Paribeni, and Carlo Pietrangeli (Rome), Guido Achille Mansuelli (Bologna), and Werner Johannowsky (Naples).

Lucy T. Shoe (Princeton) placed at my disposal her extensive knowledge of architectural moldings. Steven Foltiny advised me on all aspects of Iron Age civilization.

Denys E. R. Haynes (London), Ernest Nash and Helmut Sichtermann (Rome), Arthur Suhle (Berlin), Jacques Yvon (Paris), Attilio Stazio and Enrica Pozzi (Naples), and Enrico Leuthold (Milan) sent me photographs and plaster casts or allowed me to reproduce objects in important collections. Many of the photographs reproduced on the plates were made by András Alföldi, Jr.

Judith E. Sachs (Princeton), Mrs. Inez Longobardi, and Hans H. Voelker (Rome) provided me with books and bibliographical assistance.

The manuscript was read by J. Frank Gilliam (New York), Jacques Heurgon (Paris), and Otto Skutsch (London). Individual chapters were read by Frank E. Brown (New Haven), Jean Béranger (Lausanne), Konrad Kraft (Frankfurt a. M.), Herbert Nesselhauf (Freiburg i.B.), Hans-Georg Pflaum (Paris), Wolfgang Schmid and Johannes Straub (Bonn), and Lily Ross Taylor (Bryn Mawr). Naturally, they do not share with me the responsibility for my mistakes.

Last but not least I wish to thank my friends J. Frank Gilliam and Otto Skutsch, and Mrs. J. B. Greene, as well as Miss Elisabeth Horton, secretary of our School, who tried hard to render intelligible my Hungarian ways of expression dressed in English words, and Jean Béranger who had the great kindness to check the quotations from classical authors.

My debt of gratitude to all of those mentioned is very great.

Preface

The history of early Rome was not laid down in writing by contemporary observers. The ancient narratives that have come down
to us belong to a much later period and cannot be trusted implicitly.
The archaeological evidence represents but an infinitely small fragment
of the material once in existence. All we have to go on are heteroge-
neous odds and ends of information whose reliability must be checked
and rechecked before they can be used for the historical reconstruction.

This lack of ample documentation explains the difficulties inherent
in any attempt to write the history of that period. But these difficulties
are not as insurmountable as they appeared to the scholars who chose
to disregard the early stages and to begin their account with the
Gallic catastrophe.

Recent excavations in the Eternal City and in Latium have yielded
new documentary evidence. Improved methods in the evaluation
of both literary and monumental sources have made it possible for
us to rectify and complement the hazy picture created by the annalists.
New studies on architectural techniques and modern stratigraphical
excavations provide new data for the organization. The advance
in the typological and chronological classification of find-groups
opened up new insights into the cultural, economic, and political
developments. Art representations, coins, engraved gems, mostly
neglected, bring in some cases unexpected support, rounding off the

literary information. Religious rites reveal survivals of early political institutions. Social anthropology helps us to understand archaic social and political structures.

Pilgrimages to historical sites and walks along ancient highways of Latium played an essential part in the preparation of these lectures. It would be impossible for me to compete with the prodigious anthropo-geographical knowledge of Thomas Ashby and J. B. Ward Perkins, of Giuseppe Lugli and Ferdinando Castagnoli, or with Louise Holland's unique sense for hydro-geographical factors. But I hope that long years of military service in my youth taught me a lesson enabling me to see strategical possibilities and appreciate problems of wartime communications and commercial road networks.

In the 150 years since B. G. Niebuhr's days every generation has sifted the literary tradition over and over again and contributed to its correct interpretation. The comprehensive prosopographical surveys of Friedrich Muenzer and Matthias Gelzer have furnished scholars with a new tool with which to check the reliability of personal data. Two main trends, however, prevailed in the evaluation of the literary evidence. First, a radical scepticism, amounting almost to an obsession tended to make historians deny the reliability of every written statement concerning the early centuries. Then, the tide of pessimism receded, to be followed by a wave of optimism ready to accept everything that had been rejected before.

There were, of course, some few leading minds who were not caught in these two currents—above all the genius of Theodor Mommsen who combined penetrating logic with a sober common sense. Gaetano De Sanctis in Italy and some other historians whose names we shall have occasion to mention later also stood firm. But they were unable to check the prevailing trends. The present situation can be described with the words recently used by an able young scholar: "The full tide of critical history, represented perhaps by Ettore Pais, seems to be ebbing. We may be entering a new age of faith."

I have done my best to look at the problems without prejudice and to reexamine independently every scrap of the written tradition. The results obtained by this inquiry conflict with either or both of the opposing currents of thought. In some instances the rehabilitation of the traditional account goes beyond the beliefs of the believer, in others, more of it is discarded than the champions of "hypercriticism" would think possible. Apart from such extreme cases my investigation confirms a fact established long ago but sometimes disregarded in recent years, namely, that a true basis for Roman history may be found in the consular lists of the Republic only, whereas the annalist narrative on the regal period is without real foundation. Therefore, I have tried to save every bit of evidence after the flight of the Tarquins, but have not followed the picture of the Annals for the regal epoch— except some valuable information, preserved with the rubbish.

In lectures offered to a broader public one does not expect a discussion of every detail concerning the relations of early Rome with the outside world. But so as to clear the way for the historical reconstruction, more space was needed for preparatory chapters than for the account of the events. I also found it necessary to report on essential passages both in the ancient accounts and in modern authors of merit, partly to support my own arguments, partly to give an idea of trends and progress in research.

One of the major difficulties in preparing a survey of this kind is the excessive amount of printed studies on our subject. Many older treatises have been superseded by more recent contributions and numerous modern publications simply repeat what has been said many times before. In order to give a general idea of the scope of the publications to be examined, I refer to a statement of R. Werner, whose voluminous book on the same subject will soon appear in Munich. According to Dr. Werner, his critical bibliography will include some 630 treatises on the transition from the Monarchy to the Republic alone. If we add the studies on archaeology, numismatics, inscriptions, ethnology, prehistory, and history of religions which had to be considered for the present book, the number of publications examined comes close to a thousand. One's views develop and mature as the work progresses, and so it may happen more than once that a passage expressing a similar point of view is overlooked if the paper in which it occurs was checked in early stages of the project. I can only hope that omissions of this kind are not too frequent. Books and articles which proved of no value for our investigation were passed over in silence. Some old books, however, often forgotten elsewhere, are quoted systematically—above all others A. Schwegler's Roman history (published from 1853 on), which offers the first complete, thorough compilation of the source materials handed down to us in Greek and Roman literature.

Finally, I should like to give a brief advance outline of the results. Regal Rome, the ruling power of Central Italy according to the Annals, turns out to be no more than a vigorous vassal of some southern Etruscan states which tried to snatch this important transfer place from each other. Fifth-century Rome, on the other hand, vastly underestimated, becomes the scene of a spectacular development. During this crucial period, Rome grows in size and striking power and overshadows gradually the other Latin states. Even the shock of the Gallic catastrophe cannot halt its ascent.

This may be a disappointment to those who still believe in the hegemonial position of Rome in the seventh and sixth centuries B.C. But the fact that her rise started later than the annalists would have us believe has no bearing on the greatness of the Eternal City as the ruler of the Mediterranean world.

> *Haec est in gremium victos quae sola recepit,*
> *humanumque genus communi nomine fovit,*
> *matris, non dominae ritu.*
>
> (Claudian *De cons. Stil.* 3, 150 sqq.)

Princeton
The Institute for Advanced Study   *Easter 1963*

Contents

LIST OF ILLUSTRATIONS   XVI

ABBREVIATIONS   XVIII

Chapter I

NOMEN LATINUM: THE PECULIAR STRUCTURE OF THE LATIN
LEAGUE AND ITS HISTORICAL EVOLUTION   1

> General Considerations, 1. The Thirty Units of the *Prisci
> Latini*, 10. The Sacred Banquet of the Thirty Peoples on the
> Holy Mountain of the Latins, 19. Changed Aspects, New De-
> velopments, 25. The Latin Festival, 29. The Meetings of the
> Latins in the Meadows under the Alban Mountain, 34. Con-
> stitution and Management of the Latin League, 36. The
> Executive Organs of the Latin League, 42.

Chapter II

AT THE CROSSROADS OF TRUTH AND FICTION:
THE LAST DECADE OF THE SIXTH CENTURY IN LATIUM   47

> The Reorganized Latin League Against Porsenna, and Its Center
> in Aricia, 47. The Chronicle of Cyme and the Roman Historio-
> graphy, 56. Porsenna in Rome, 72. The Federal Sanctuary
> of the Latin Cities in the Aventine Precinct of Diana and Its
> Local Successors, 85.

Chapter III

THE LATINS AS ROMAN SUBJECTS UNDER THE KINGS:
THE ANNALIST FICTION   101

The Characterization of the Invented Roman Superiority, 101.
The Written Alliances of Rome with the Latins, 111. The *Foe-
dus Cassianum* in the Annals, 113. The Evidence Against the
Annalist Doctrine, 117.

Chapter IV

THE PROJECTION OF THE ROMAN CONQUEST OF MIDDLE
ITALY BACK INTO THE DARK AGES BY FABIUS PICTOR   123

The Manipulation of Figures and Dates, 125. The Characteristic
Features of the Pretended Expansion Under the Kings, 131.
The Alleged Conquest of Entire Nations by the Kings, 135.
The Leitmotif of Hegemony, 141. The Legalistic Machinery of
the Annals, 145. Hellenistic Mannerism in Pictor's Concept:
His Female Characters, 147. Prejudice in Pictor, as Reflected
in his Hatred of the Claudii, 159. The Responsibility of Fabius
Pictor, 164

Chapter V

THE ETRUSCAN RULE IN LATIUM AND ROME   176

The Etruscan Occupation of Campania, 182. The Etruscan
Encroachment upon the Latin Communities, 186. The Etruscan
Domination in Rome, 193. Etruscan Powers Struggling for the
Possession of Rome, 202. The Etruscan States which, in Succes-
sion, Dominated Rome: a) Tarquinii, 206. b) Caere, 209. c)
Vulci, 212. d) Veii, 231. e) Clusium, 234.

Chapter VI

ALBA LONGA AND LAVINIUM:
THE OLD CAPITALS OF THE LATIN TRIBE   236

Alba Longa, 236. Lavinium, 246. The Belief in Trojan Des-
cent, and the Ritual of the "Trojan" Divinities in Lavinium, 250.
The New Archaeological Evidence of the Federal Sanctuary in
Lavinium, 265. The *Penates* as Dioscuri in Lavinium and
Rome, 268. The Myth of the Sow with the Thirty Piglets and
Its Transformations, 271. Trojan Legend and Etruscan Domi-
nation in Latium, 278.

Chapter VII

TOPOGRAPHICAL AND ARCHAEOLOGICAL REALITIES VERSUS
LITERARY INVENTION   288

The Etruscans at the Mouth of the Tiber, 288. The Sacred
Boundary of the *Ager Romanus*, 296. The Rural Districts Within

and Beyond the Sacred Boundary of the *Ager Romanus*, 304. The Dream of the "Grande Roma Dei Tarquinii," 318.

Chapter VIII

THE ASCENT OF ROME DURING THE EARLY REPUBLIC   336

Southern Etruria and Rome after the Kings, 337. The Beginnings of Roman Sea Power, 347. The First and Second Treaties between Carthage and Rome, 350. The Celtic Invasions, 355. The Wars of the Early Republic with the Volscians and Aequians, 365. The Latin City-States and the Roman Republic Until the Conquest of Latium in 338 B.C., 377. Some Associates and Rivals of the Rising Roman Power: Gabii and Tusculum, Praeneste and Tibur, 378. The Latin League from the Battle at Lake Regillus to Its Dissolution (338 B.C.), 391. The Roman Ascendancy over Latium, 398. The Relations of the Latins with Rome During the Early Republic: Political, Legal, and Social Aspects, 414.

APPENDIX. L'OCCUPAZIONE ETRUSCA DI CAMPANIA,
BY W. JOHANNOVSKY   420

INDEX   425

Illustrations

(Plates after p. 433)

FRONTISPIECE   Marble group of the Dioscuri found in the Forum Romanum.

PLATE I   1-2: The cult image of Diana in Aricia on denarii of the year 43 B.C.—1: Vienna, 2: Vienna, 3: Winterthur.

PLATE II   Marble group of the Dioscuri, found at the Lacus Iuturnae on the Forum Romanum.

PLATE III   1: Roman silver coin from the last decades of the third century B.C., Coll. W. Niggeler, Baden bei Zürich. 2: Terracotta herm. Tarquinia, Museo nazionale. 3: Roman silver coin (as no. 1), private coll. in Italy. 4: Bronze coin struck in Capua under Hannibal, Berlin. 5: Gold coin, 2nd half of the 3rd Cent. B.C., Paris. 6: Reverse of the same type, Florence. 7: Heavy cast coin, found in the Lago di Nemi (after Haeberlin). nos. 1, 3-5, 6 enlarged; 2 and 7 reduced in size.

PLATE IV   1-2: Denarii of C. Sulpicius, about 100 B.C. 3: Bronze coin of Tuder in Umbria, late third century B.C. Paris. 4: Denarius of Vespasian in London. 5: Relief sculpture in Rome.

PLATE V   Marble group of the sow with the thirty piglets. Vatican.

PLATE VI   1-3: Bronze medallions of Antoninus Pius. Paris.

PLATE VII   1-4: Bronze coins and medallions of Antoninus Pius—1, Mus. Capitol; 2, Berlin; 3-4, Vienna. 5: Denarius of a Cornelius Cetegus in Paris. 6: Intaglio, Coll. Arndt, Munich. 7: Glass paste in Berlin. 8: Bronze coin in commerce. All specimens enlarged.

PLATE VIII   Wall painting from the "tomba François" in Vulci: Mastarna frees Caeles Vibenna.

PLATE IX   Wall painting from the same tomb: Larth Ulthes stabs Laris Papathnas.

PLATE X   Wall painting from the same tomb: Rasce kills Pesna Arcmsnas.

PLATE XI   Wall painting from the same tomb: Aulus Vibenna kills Venthi Caules

PLATE XII   Wall painting from the same tomb: Marce Camitlnas kills Cneve Tarchunies.

PLATE XIII   1-4: Engraved gems and glass pastes—1-2, 4, London; 5-6, After Ad. Furtwängler, Ant. Gemmen, pl. 22, 13-14; 7, Geneva; 8-11, 13-14, Berlin; 15-18 denarii of L. Papius Celsus, 12, Paris.; 15, Vatican; 16-18, after Schweiz. Numism. Rundschau, 36, 1954, pl. 24. All enlarged.

PLATE XIV   1-11: Engraved gems and glass pastes—1, Paris; 2, Geneva; 3, London; 4-7, after Ad. Furtwängler, *op. cit.* pl. 21; 8-11: after Ad. Furtwängler, Beschreibung der geschnittenen Steine im Antiquarium (Berlin), pl. 8. All enlarged.

PLATE XV   1-4: Carthaginian tetradrachms struck in Magna Graecia —1, A. Hess, Lucerne; 2-4, New York. 5-7: Roman didrachms, Private coll., Italy.

PLATE XVI   The great altars outside Lavinium. Reconstruction of F. Castagnoli.

PLATE XVII   The cista Pasinati in the British Museum.

PLATE XVIII   1: Roman bronze coin, private coll., Italy. 2: Bronze coin of Capua, after L. Forrer, Weber Coll. 1, 1922, no. 300. 3: Etruscan silver coin, Paris. 4: Roman ingot money, after E. J. Haeberlin, Aes grave 1910, pl. 59, 2. 5: Archaic Latin dedication from Lavinium.

PLATE XIX   Drawings of a Caeretane earthenware jug, found at Tragliatella near Caere.

PLATE XX   1: Drawings from the same jug. 2: Wall painting from the "Tomba Campana" in Veii, after G. Dennis. 3: Bronze fibula from Marzabotto. 4: Tarquinia. 5: Bologna. 6: Another from Este. 7: Gold ornament from Marsiliana.

PLATE XXI-XXII   The Tragliatella jug.

PLATE XXIII   Attic red figure vase in Boston.

PLATE XXIV   Attic black figure vase in Hamburg.

PLATE XXV   Etruscan red figure vase from Vulci in Munich.

MAPS

Ancient Latium. (After plates)

The Roman Territory in the Sixth and Fifth Centuries B.C., p. 297

Abbreviations

AJA	American Journal of Archaeology
Ant. cl.	Antiquité classique (Bruxelles)
Arch. Anz.	Archaeologischer Anzeiger (printed with the Jahrbuch des deutschen archaeologischen Institutes)
Arch. cl.	Archaeologia classica (Roma)
Athen., n. s.	Athenaeum (Pavia), nuova serie
BEFAR	Bibliothèque des Ecoles Françaises d'Athènes et de Rome
K. J. Beloch, RG	*Idem*, Römische Geschichte (Berlin-Leipzig 1926— only the first vol. published)
T. R. S. Broughton, MRR	*Idem*, The Magistrates of the Roman Republic (Philological Monographs, publ. by the Amer. Philol. Assoc. XV 1-2, New York 1954 and 1952)
Bull. Com.	Bulletino della Commissione Archaeologica comunale (Roma)
CAH	Cambridge Ancient History
CIL	Corpus Inscriptionum Latinarum (Berlin)
Cl. Phil.	Classical Philology (Chicago, Ill., 1906—)
Cl. Q.	Classical Quarterly (London-New York)
CRAI	Comptes-Rendus de l'Académie des Inscriptions et Belles-Lettres (Paris)
A. Degrassi	cf. ILLRP

A. Degrassi, Inscr. It. XIII 1	*Idem*, Inscriptiones Italiae XIII 1, *Fasti consulares et triumphales* (Roma 1947)
G. De Sanctis, St. d. R. 1¹	*Idem*, Storia dei Romani 1 (Firenze 1907)
G. De Sanctis, St. d. R. 1²	*Idem*, Storia dei Romani 1, reimpression, somewhat shortened, of the same work (Firenze 1956)
G. De Sanctis, St. d. R. 2¹	*Idem*, second vol. of the same work (Firenze 1907)
G. De Sanctis, St. d. R. 2²	*Idem*, second vol., reimpression, somewhat shortened (Firenze 1956)
G. De Sanctis, St. d. R. IV 2, 1	*Idem*, vol. 4, part 2, first half (Firenze 1953)
H. Dessau	Cf. ILS
DH	Dionysi Halicarnassensis Antiquitatum Romanarum quae supersunt, ed. C. Jacoby, vol. 1-4 and suppl. (Lipsiae 1885-1925). (The passages translated in English are quoted from the edition of E. Cary, Loeb Classical Library)
Dict. d. ant.	Dictionnaire des antiquités grecques et romaines, réd. par Ch. Daremberg et Edm. Saglio (Paris 1877—)*s.d.* in 5 vols.
F. Gr. Hist.	Die Fragmente der griechischen Historiker, hrsg. von F. Jacoby (Berlin and Leiden 1926—)
GGA	Göttinger gelehrte Anzeigen
J. Heurgon, Rech.	*Idem*, Recherches sur l'histoire, la religion et la civilisation de Capoue préromaine des origines à la deuxième guerre punique (Paris 1942)
J. Heurgon, La vie quotid.	*Idem*, La vie quotidienne chez les Etrusques (Paris 1961)
H.R.Rel. 1²	Historicorum Romanorum reliquiae, ed. H. Peter, second ed., vol. 1 (Leipzig 1914)
ILLRP	Inscriptiones Latinae liberae rei publicae, fasc. prior, cur. A. Degrassi (Firenze 1957)
ILS	Inscriptiones Latinae selectae, ed. H. Dessau (Berlin 1892-1916)
JdI	Jahrbuch des deutschen archaeologischen Institutes (Berlin)
JHS	Journal of Hellenic Studies (London)
JRS	Journal of Roman Studies (London)
J. Marquardt, St.-V.	*Idem*, Die römische Staatsverwaltung (Leipzig, vol. 1², 1884; vol. 2², 1884; vol. 3², 1885)

ABBREVIATIONS

S. Mazzarino, Dalla mon.	*Idem*, Dalla monarchia allo stato repubblicano (Catania 1945)
Ed. Meyer, GdA 2²	*Idem*, Geschichte des Altertums, vol. 2, second ed. (Stuttgart 1893)
Mél.	Mélanges d'archéologie et d'histoire de l'Ecole Française de Rome (Paris)
Mommsen, RF 1-2	Th. Mommsen, Römische Forschungen 1 (Leipzig 1864); 2 (Leipzig 1879)
Mommsen, Ges. Schr.	*Idem*, Gesammelte Schriften, 8 vols. (Berlin)
Mommsen St. R. 1³.2³.3	*Idem*, Das römische Staatsrecht (Leipzig), vol. 1, third ed., 1887; vol. 2, third ed., 1887; vol. 3, 1888
Mommsen, RG	*Idem*, Römische Geschichte, vol. 1, seventh ed. (Berlin 1888)
Mon. Ant.	Monumenti antichi (Milan 1890—)
Mus. Helv.	Museum Helveticum (Basel 1944—)
K. O. Müller-W. Deecke	*Idem*, Die Etrusker (Stuttgart 1877), vol. 1-2
N. Chron.	The Numismatic Chronicle (London 1866—)
B. G. Niebuhr, RG 1²	*Idem*, Römische Geschichte, vol. 1, second ed., 1823
H. Nissen, It. Lk. II 1; II 2	*Idem*, Italische Landeskunde, vol. II 1 and II 2 (Berlin 1902)
N. Sc.	Atti della R. Accademia dei Lincei, Notizie degli Scavi di antichità (Milan 1876—)
E. Pais, St. crit. 1	*Idem*, Storia critica di Roma, vol. 1 (Roma 1913)
E. Pais, St. d. R. 1³	*Idem*, Storia di Roma, third ed., vol. 1 (Roma 1926)
PBSR	Papers of the British School at Rome
L. Pareti, St. d. R.	*Idem*, Storia di Roma, vol. 1 (Roma 1952)
Philol.	Philologus (Berlin 1846—)
RE	Pauly's Realencyclopaedie der classischen Altertumswissenschaft, in neuer Bearbeitung, von G. Wissowa, W. Kroll, and others (Stuttgart 1893—)
RVV	Religionsgeschichtliche Versuche und Vorarbeiten (Giessen 1903—)
Rend. Pont. Acc.	Rendiconti della Pontificia Accademia Romana di Archeologia (Rome 1921-23—)
R. Et. Gr.	Revue des études grecques (Paris 1888—)
R. Et. Lat.	Revue des études latines (Paris 1928—)
Rh. Mus.	Rheinisches Museum für Philologie (Bonn and Frankfurt 1827—)

RM	Deutsches Archäologisches Institut. Römische Abteilung. Mitteilungen (München, 1886—)
A. Schwegler, RG 1-3	*Idem*, Römische Geschichte (Tübingen) vol. 1, 1853; vol. 2, 1856; vol. 3, 1858
A.-N. Sherwin-White, R. Citiz.	*Idem*, Roman Citizenship (Oxford 1939)
SBBayr. Ak.	Sitzungsberichte der bayerischen Akademie der Wissenschaften
SB Heid.	Sitzungsberichte der Heidelberger Akademie der Wissenschaften
SDHI	Studia et documenta historiae et Iuris (Rome 1935—)
St. Etr.	Studi etruschi (Firenze 1927—)
Stud. Rom.	Studi Romani (Rome 1953—)
SMSR	Studi e materiali per lo studio della storia degli religioni (Roma)
W. Schulze, ZGLEN	*Idem*, Zur Geschichte lateinischer Eigennamen (Abh. Ges. Wiss. Göttingen n. F. 5, 5, 1904)
L. R. Taylor, Vot. Distr.	*Ead.*, The Voting Districts of the Roman Republic (Papers and Monographs of the American Academy in Rome, vol. 20, 1960)
TAPA	Transactions and Proceedings of the American Philological Association (Hartford 1871—)
Varro, *LL*	M. Terenti Varronis De lingua Latina quae supersunt, rec. G. Goetz et Fr. Schoell (Lipsiae 1910)
Varro *RR*	M. Terenti Varronis Rerum rusticarum libri tres, post H. Keil iterum ed. G. Goetz (Lipsiae 1912)
G. Wissowa, RuK²	*Idem*, Religion und Kultus der Römer, second ed. (München 1912)

Chapter I

NOMEN LATINUM:
THE PECULIAR STRUCTURE OF THE LATIN
LEAGUE AND ITS HISTORICAL EVOLUTION

The organization of the Latin tribe,[1] such as we see it in historical times, is commonly supposed to have grown as naturally as a plant, which needs little more than sun and rain to spring up from a tiny seed; and it is believed to have sprung up first in the soil of Latium, as though these tribes had shared no experience and had undergone no political and social evolution before they entered Italy.

Illustrious scholars think [2] that the seeds from which the confedera-

---

[1] A. Schwegler, RG 2, 288 sqq., has collected the source material.

[2] We mention only a few distinguished scholars of our century: G. De Sanctis, St. d. R. 1[2], 370, 376 sqq. ; 2[2], 85. L. R. Taylor, Local Cults in Etruria (Papers and Monographs of the Am Ac Rome 2) 1923, 13 sq. L. Homo, L'Italie primitive, Paris 1925, 92, 111. K. J. Beloch, RG 180 sq., 193. H. Last, CAH 7, 1928, 348. M. Gelzer, RE 12, 948. A. N. Sherwin-White, R. Citiz., Oxford 1939, 8, 11 sqq., 17. G. Giannelli, La repubblica romana,[2] Milano 1955, 23. P. De Francisci, Primordia civitatis, Roma 1959, 131, 479, with further juridical literature in n. 325, etc.

tion of the Latins germinated after a long and agitated period of troubles in their country were small village communities, "each a tiny *populus*," grouped together in various religious leagues, each of which had a cult center of its own. These little federations of villages —it is maintained—grew successively in a rectilinear evolution to fully conscious political units of considerable city-states. It is supposed that until the process of synoecism had made considerable progress, there could be no large and important political leagues, no unified group embracing all the *populi* of Latium; and that the spontaneous impulse of the *populi Latini* toward unification around cult centers finally called into existence the overall union of the Latins in the League of the Alban Mount. The meetings on this mountain and the gatherings in a large meadow below it are regarded as the manifestations of two different associations, whereas in truth they were only different items on the agenda of the great annual Latin conventions. We shall come back to that later.

The analogies on which this picture is based are the Ionian League and the Amphictyonic League of Delphi. Admittedly, there are common features between the life of Greek state federacies and that of the Latin League: individual wars between member-states and individual pacts between them; and, later, the gods' peace on the days of the common annual sacrifices and games. But these Greek confederations had already left the period of migrations and the tribal stage of their development behind them a millennium before; they long ago had become fixed in geographical areas, settled in separated units, becoming autonomous states as early as in the Mycenaean age in their *poleis*. It is not they, but the Dorians, more recent intruders in Greece, who are comparable in many respects to the Italic cattle-rearers and warriors, because they also preserved remnants of the mobilized life of their migrations and of their old social and political structure.

In Latium, those common religious celebrations of cities which did not have any political significance were in truth no primary phenomena of the earliest phase of an incipient coalescence, but on the contrary, they were the religious survivals of political organisms of an ancient past.

The neglect of the phases of national history previous to the data of our literary information involved another misconception. All the different fusions, unions, conventions of the Latin states are regarded today as different Leagues.[1] This, even at best, is only half of the truth. The concrete situation had, of course, varying elements on every occasion. When Rome was entrusted with the care of the Latin Festival on the *mons Albanus* in the middle of the fifth century B.C. (and not under the last king, as the Roman Annals pretend),[2] it certainly mirrored the growing importance of her power but it meant no new foundation, nor did it imply her hegemony. Or: when Ardea obtained the honorable task of maintaining the federal sanctuary of Venus, discharged before by Lavinium, this was a late development, involving no political initiative or advantages; besides this, Ardea did not otherwise replace Lavinium, where the federal sacrifices to the ancestral gods continued to be celebrated until the end of antiquity.[3] Or again: when the grove of Diana in Aricia became the political center of the Latins, this was a completely new development, but the states rallied around Aricia were again the same Latins, with the exception of one or two cities which were at that moment under the sway of a foreign conqueror.[4] Later, when Rome tried to substitute the grove of Diana at the Lago di Nemi by another grove of the same goddess on the Aventine, this was an attempt to replace Aricia in the leadership of the Latins—of all the Latins if possible; and the confederation mentioned in this connection is not a newly created formation but the alliance of Latin states—of all of them on principle. Quite generally, I do not know of any such federal organization which would not have intended to include the *nomen Latinum*, i.e., the totality of the Latins. The cults, around which every such federation was constituted, were not abandoned when their political background vanished and they continued to be an obligation of the Latin peoples— they are for the historian most valuable petrifacts of early developments, even if important Latin *populi* would not or could not participate in their foundation [5] or if some such states let themselves be

---

[1] A few examples for this generally expressed view : G. De Sanctis, St. d. R. 2¹, 1907, 90 sq. E. Täubler, Imperium Romanum 1, 1913, 304 sqq. H. Last, CAH 7, 1928, 348. A. N. Sherwin-White, *op. cit.* 11 sqq. L. Pareti, St. d. R. 1, 1952, 237 sq. F. W. Walbank, A Historical Commentary on Polybius 1, Oxford 1957, 345.

[2] Cf. below, p. 31 sqq.

[3] Cf. below, p. 260 sqq.

[4] Cf. below, p. 47 sqq.

[5] Rome was absent when the *lucus Dianensis* of Aricia was founded, but participated nevertheless, later, in the celebration of the annual festival of the *Diana Aricina* cf. below, p. 85 sqq., and AJA 64, 1960, 137 sqq.

represented only by the common sacrifices of the Latin peoples on the Alban Mountain, in Lavinium or elsewhere, but were absent in the ensuing political deliberations.[1]

Naturally, the political focus or focuses of the nation were shifting. The numbers of participants and of absentees in the actions and celebrations of the League were changing with the times and situations, just as the number of official cults of the League was increased and their political significance could vanish or overshadow the others; as also the leading powers and the League itself were subject to such fluctuations. But behind these manifold appearances and oscillations there stood—we repeat—only a single reality: the nation.

There were only a few scholars who did not forget that the backbone of the Latin League was nothing other than the primeval tribal organization;[2] that the bounds connecting originally the *nomen Latinum* were not written treaties but sprang from the notion of

---

[1] Concerning Tibur and Praeneste in the early Republican Age see below, p. 385 sqq. Our sources on the structure of the Latin confederation have been vitiated by the annalist fiction, pretending that some Volscian states and all the Hernicans were included in the Latin sacrifices on the Alban Mountain (DH VIII 62, 3 ; 63, 2 ; 68, 1. Liv. II 30, 8 ; 40, 12 ; 41, 1). It is impossible that foreign elements participated in the sacred acts carried out for the welfare of the *nomen Latinum*, and we know in fact that the Hernicans preserved their own national federation still in later times (cf. Liv. VI 10, 7. IX 42, 11.). A. N. Sherwin-White, *op. cit.* 24 sq., realized this already ; we think, however, that the Hernican League made its alliance with the Latin League in the fifth century (as Mommsen, St. R. 3, 612, assumed), and not with Rome, as A. N. Sherwin-White believes ; cf. our last chapter on the role of the League at that time. The whole story of the admission of foreign peoples to the Latin League belongs, I am sure, to the fictitious assertion of the Annals that the Alban League was the creation of the last Roman king (DH IV 49, 1) whose great power is illustrated by this increase. Cf. also G. De Sanctis, St. d. R. 2[1], 1907, 9, 102 sq. M. Gelzer, RE 12, 955, etc.

[2] Mommsen, St. R. 3, 608 sq., clearly perceived the facts and consequences of the tribal organization ; he erred only in reprojecting their validity "back, far beyond of all historical recollections." E. Täubler, Imperium Romanum 1, Leipzig 1913, 302 sq. *Idem*, Tyche, Leipzig 1926, 198 sqq. Br. Paradisi, Atti d. Congr. int. di dir. rom. 1948, vol. 4, Milano 1953, 3 sqq. P. Frezza, Corso di storia del diritto romano, Roma 1954, 11 sqq. M. Gelzer, RE 12, 944. G. I. Luzzatto, Per un ipotesi sulle origini e la natura delle obbligazioni romane, Milano 1934, 32 sqq. A. N. Sherwin-White, in spite of his reliance on the theory of "religious leagues," fully recognizes (op. cit. 14) that the memory of the preurban, tribal organization in Latium was kept alive by intercommunal festivities and councils ; cf. *ibid.* 30 sqq. M. Coli, Studi in onore di P. De Francisci 4, Milano 1956, 520 sq. For tribal antecedents in the structure of the Greek Leagues : E. Kornemann, RE Suppl. 4, 918 sqq. (with literature). Cf. also H. U. Instinsky, Klio 30, 1937, 121. A. Steinwenter, RE 10, 1263 sqq.

kinship; and also that this social configuration reached back to prehistoric ages, many centuries before the city-state came into being in
Italy and before Rome was founded. In fact, tribal ties were a living
reality of which everybody was aware in Latium: the common
language; the common annual sacrifices to the ancestral gods; the
common myth of origin from the female boar who, by guidance of
the divinity, lured the ancestor of the tribe to follow her to Alba
Longa, his future seat as King of the Latins;[1] the exclusive community
of legal marriage and of business arrangements between all the Latins
kept them alive. Nor did the Latins forget their old tripartite organization of thirty units.[2] The existence of a tribal king in olden times was
still palpable in the fifth century B.C. in the continuation of his function
as the *dictator Latinus*, even if in an attenuated form restricted to the
use of sovereign power (*imperium*) during one year only.[3]

The Roman historians of the Late Republic liked to explain the
peculiar combination of manifestations and actions of the Latin
League as the imitation of refined Greek institutions. The Greek
tribes had common sanctuaries, writes Dionysius of Halicarnassus,[4]
"where they assembled with their wives and children at the appointed
times, joined together in sacrificing and celebrating their festivals,
engaged in various contests . . . and made joint offerings to the
gods. After they witnessed the spectacles and celebrated the festival,
and also received the other evidences of goodwill from one another,
if any difference had arisen between one city and another, arbiters sat
in judgment and decided the controversy; and they also consulted
together concerning the means both of carrying on war against
foreigners and maintaining their mutual accord."

Yet the roots from which all these features, common to the Greek
and Roman assemblies, originated can be traced more exactly in ob-
serving the same characteristics in another environment where the
archaic structure of the old Indo-European stock-breeder societies,
inherited by Ougrian, Turkish, and Mongolian peoples, was preserved
almost intact until the eighteenth century, isolated from the southern
world of culture: I mean the mounted shepherds of northern Asia.[5]

[1] Cf. below, p. 236 sqq.
[2] Cf. below, p. 10 sqq.
[3] Cf. A. Schwegler, RG 2, 1856, 291.
[4] DH IV 25, 4-6.
[5] I have been drawing the attention of the scholars to this source of cultural
morphology of the Indoeuropean tribes since 1931, and I hope to go into

NOMEN LATINUM

Here it can be easily observed that the single domains of common life in primitive societies are not yet differentiated and isolated from each other as in our own time. On the contrary, they are linked with each other, united in an inseparable complex. The sacred concepts of their rituals, the forms of social organization, the economic activities with their products and protection, the character of warfare and the forms of government, are all included in this complex, anchored emotionally by a theriomorphic myth of origin and by the dramatic revival of this myth at the great annual gatherings of the peoples, when sacrifices are made and games arranged, when the youths look for life-partners; and when at the same time the distribution of grazing grounds between the clans is discussed and consultations on peace and plans for raids are made. The study of these cattle-rearer and warrior societies teaches us one more lesson. When their state-organization fell apart because of a crushing defeat in war, the conqueror could reshape it again on the platform of a mythical concept. The new union was based on the common descent from a cosmic giant, or the ruler's family tree was started from the creation of heaven and earth, being the same sacred fiction as previous foundations. In consequence of this, violent breakdowns could not delete this mythical anchorage of the organizatory pattern in Eurasia until the last century. This exchangeability of actual elements and the perseverance of the scheme give us the key to the explanation of how the "thirty peoples" of the Alban League remained—at least on principle—always thirty. The sacred pattern did not lose its validity when the old framework was upset by recent growth, as in the parallel cases of the three gentile tribes of the *comitia curiata* and of the thirty *curiae* of the Roman citizens, simple organizatory schemes, conceived for small groups, which were maintained until Rome became the capital of the world.

The cohesion of the Latin nation was founded, as we contend, a good deal on such archaic tribal bonds although the tribal unity was

details in a book on the earliest forms of the Roman state and society (now in preparation). For the time being see my remarks in the following papers : Die theriomorphe Weltbetrachtung in den nordasiatischen Kulturen (Arch. Anz. 1931, 393 sqq.). The origin of the dignity of the *tarchan* (Magyar Nyelv 28, 1932, 205 sqq., in Hungarian). Bear Cult and Matriarchal Structure in Eurasia (Nyelvtudományi Közlemények 50, 1936, 5 sqq. in Hungarian). Königsweihe und Männerbund bei den Achaemeniden (Schweizer. Archiv für Volkskunde 47, 1951, 11 sqq.).

due to fall apart after the beginnings of a sedentary life in Latium. The common features of the tribal epoch did not vanish when the mobile units of the migrating tribe became stationary settlements, or when city-states replaced the village agglomerations. The consciousness of the common origin, the use of a common language, the old rites and the unwritten laws of ancestral customs and habits enabled the politicians of the day in historically known times to exploit these old components for new purposes of fusion.

Quite naturally both aspects had their role in the historical developments: the prehistoric elements with their antiquated features of tribal life, as well as the ever-changing factors introduced by new situations. Though the tribal metropolis lost its power, disintegrated by new urban centers of political gravitation, its force of attraction was maintained spiritually by the continuance of its religious significance. And the centrifugal trend of particularism yielded again, if only partially, to the need of a united front when outward pressure enforced it. Further on, though the aspirations of rising powers in Latium itself disrupted the tendencies of reamalgamation, and though Roman supremacy replaced the sovereign alliance of the Latins thereafter, the tribe remained a compact reality and obtained a significant share in the conquest and government of the Mediterranean world—a conquest which never could have taken place without the superb accumulation of energies, physical and mental alike, of that nation. We shall follow all stages of these developments in this book, from the seventh century B.C. onward, when the bare outlines of real history show up for the first time, until 338 B.C., when Latium was forced to serve the interests and purposes of the Roman state.

The disregard of tribal cohesion and of the pre-Italic phase of Latin history in recent works, as I see it, is due not least to a general tendency in prehistorical research—a new branch of historical science with imposing achievements in the factual knowledge of excavated materials, but still exposed to the danger of contaminating exact typological and stratigraphical results with preconceived theories. The new trend in this field is to deny the role of migrations in prehistoric epochs, or to reduce their importance to naught.[1]

---

[1] A thorough typologist, with an imposing command over his material, denied in his communication at the International Congress of Prehistoric and Protohistoric Sciences in Rome (August 1962) the fact of the Dorian migration and tried to explain its consequences by psychological reasons.

This new concept cannot be refuted by direct proofs in vast regions of Europe where the light of written history penetrated too late to uncover the identity of the peoples living there before. But there is a region on the fringe of the radiation-range of Greek culture where identification of all the waves of newly intruding peoples can be ascertained from the Iron Age onward. This area is the basin of the Carpathians in southeastern Europe. It is possible here to discriminate the legacy of the Cimmerians arriving in the eighth century from northern Asia; that of the Scythians coming from the same environment in the sixth century; and to discern the burial grounds and habitats of the Celts, inundating the Danube valley from the West at the time when they captured Rome, and more permanently a hundred years later, when Delphi was also ransacked. In the Late Hellenistic Age, Iranian nomads battled their way to this area, arriving from the East along the Danube valley. They were the Sarmatian Rhoxolani and Iazyges, who seized the fertile plains of present Rumania and Hungary. In the time of the Empire, Teutonic tribes arrived, moving down in stages from Scandinavia. After them came the Huns, Avars, Kutrigur-Bulgars, Slavonic peoples, Hungarians, and still others after them from Siberia, the Caucasus, northern Europe, and southern Russia.

The tide of migrating hordes of course did not arrive the first time with the Cimmerians on that crossroad of peoples. Newcomers from every direction saturated its rich soil with the blood of settlers installed there, but also mingled with them long before those mounted archers intruded. The finds unequivocally testify to this from the Neolithic age on. But whoever would like to suppose that in Western Europe no such convulsions occurred needs only to read the commentaries of Caesar on his Gallic wars to see the incredible ease with which peoples established there decided to quit, if circumstances deteriorated. It is therefore preposterous to deny the fact of the migrations, even if they were much more rare in the Appenine Peninsula than in southeastern Europe, which was ever suffering from them.

The desire to minimize the influence of migrations [1] encouraged historians to look for other reasons for the presence of the ancient peoples of Italy. An eminent scholar of outstanding merit, M. Pallot-

---

[1] This tendency arose partly as a justifiable reaction against the over-simplified and biassed racial theory, based on migrations, denying amalgamations with the autochthonous population.

tino, now explains the origin of the Latins as the product of the amalgamation of several local groups, which process of fusion would have produced the *cultura di Lazio*, the material culture of the Iron Age in Latium. This assumption was facilitated by the untenable view that Latin immigration occurred as early as about 2000 B.C. and by the hypothesis that they infiltrated in small groups.

The truth is, I am convinced, that the Latins occupied their home-country Latium as much as a thousand years later, arriving from beyond the Alps. Their immigration could well have had intermediate stages, but it was one coherent process also in this case.[1] Their new home-country is a clearly defined quadrilateral unity situated between Etruria and Campania, and between the high ridges of the Apennines and the sea.[2] The affinities as well as the individual character of the Italic dialect, which was their language, demonstrate, on one hand, that the conquerors completely absorbed the scarce Bronze-Age population of their territory and, on the other, that their geographical separation from their Italic relatives lasted long enough before the age of writing to permit crystallization of this vernacular idiom. If their name became here *Latinus*, "man from the flat land," this does not mean that their collectivity did not exist before,[3] even if it ripened and was transformed in the new environment. Their case has an analogy in that of the Samnites who, much later, descending from their mountains, occupied the territory of Capua with the fertile plain south of Latium and from it were called *Campani*.In these new surroundings the Greek atmosphere, the Etruscans subjugated by

---

[1] An excellent critical bibliography of the problem of the Italic migration is to be found in the work of Ernst Meyer, Römischer Staat und Staatsgedanke[2], Zürich-Stuttgart 1961, 448 sqq. The latest studies and statements to be added to this are : R. Bloch, CRAI 1958 (1959) 294. H. Riemann, GGA 214, 1960, 16 sqq. M. Pallottino, St. Etr. 2. ser. 28, 1960, 11 sqq. *Idem*, Arch. cl. 12, 1960, 1 sqq. A. Piganiol, Journal des Savants, 1961, 21 sqq. H. Riemann, Gnomon 33, 1961, 382 sqq. (a review of S. M. Puglisi, La civiltà appenninica, Firenze 1959). S. Ferri, Studi class e orient. 9, 1960, 161 sqq. R. Chevallier, Latomus 21, 1962, 99 sqq. R. Pittioni, RE Suppl. 9, 241 sqq. F. Oelmann, Germania 37, 1959, 205 sqq., and B. Stjernquist, Simris 2 (Acta Arch. Lund., ser. in 4⁰, no. 5) 1961, 45 sqq., give the latest contributions to the problem of the house-urns. The volume "Civiltà del Ferro," Bologna 1960, contains many essential contributions to this problem. Cf. also R. Peroni, Riv. di Scienze Preistoriche 16, 1961, 125 sqq., esp. 192 sq. A. Boëthius, Etruscan Culture, Land and People, Malmö 1962, 22, 29, 34 sq.

[2] Cf. K. J. Beloch, RG 144 sqq.

[3] As A. N. Sherwin-White, R. Citiz. 30, thinks.

them, and the experiences of their autonomous existence fused them into a new nationality. In both cases a given anthropological and cultural complex, transplanted in a new geographical frame and encircled by new neighbors, gains its final stature; its mixture with the populations found there could color their character but did not create it.

ℰ

THE THIRTY UNITS OF THE *PRISCI LATINI*

The name of the "old Latin peoples" (*prisci casci populi Latini*, as Ennius calls them [1]), *prisci Latini*, as they are called usually, is a vague notion. It means sometimes the most ancient Latins in general,[2] sometimes those cities which were thought to be the foundations of the ruling city Alba Longa.[3] Again, in other cases, this is the designation of the cities of Latium, which were conquered by Rome in 338 B.C.,[4] in order to distinguish these "original Latins" from the new "Latin colonies" of Rome founded subsequently outside Latium proper. This gives the clue to the epithet *prisci*: they are the "old ones" as opposed to the new ones, in the same way as the older King Tarquin of the Annals was designated *Priscus*, as contrasted with the younger one.

This expression has nonetheless a peculiar corollary: the cities of the *prisci Latini* are always thirty in number—not just an agglomerate but an organized confederacy, either opposing Rome or serving her.[5] In truth, as we shall discuss later,[6] Rome was one of the thirty members of the League; she was set apart and above the League only by the annalist fiction with the intention of pushing Roman supremacy as far back as possible to the dawn of history; nor did

---

[1] Enn., *Ann.* fr. 24 Vahlen = Varro, *LL* 7, 28 : *cascum vetus esse significat Ennius, quod ait : 'quam prisci casci populi tenuere Latini.'*

[2] Verg., *Aen.* 5, 596 sqq. Schol. Bob. ad. Cic., *Pro Planc.* 9,23 (p. 128 Hildebr.). Paul. Fest., p. 253, 1 L.

[3] Liv. I 3, 7, and elsewhere.

[4] Plin., *N.h.* XXXIV 5, 20 : *antiquior (sc. celebratio columnarum), sicuti C. Maenio, qui devicerat priscos Latinos.*

[5] Cf. below, p. 17 sqq.

[6] E.g., Liv. I 32, 11. 13 ; 33, 3 ; 38, 4 ; 52, 2 sq. II 18, 3. DH III 31, 4 ; 34, 3. VI 63, 4 ; 74, 6 ; 75, 3.

The Thirty Units of the Prisci Latini

Alba found thirty colonies in her position as a ruling city,[1] from whom Rome is supposed to have taken over the domination of all the Latins. She, too, was but one of the thirty units, even if once the seat of the tribal king of the Latins.

The Roman historians of the late Republic tried several times to reconstruct the list of the thirty members of the Latin alliance. Unfortunately, the obligation of thorough and exact inquiry did not then exist,[2] and the lists they produced are nothing but superficial compilations. Nevertheless, precious crumbs of relevant information are included in them.[3]

The lost source used by Dionysius of Halicarnassus [4] pretended that the peoples sharing in the festival of Juppiter Latiaris on the

---

[1] DH III 31, 4 : ἡ μὲν δὴ τῶν ’Αλβανῶν πόλις . . . ἡ τὰς τριάκοντα Λατίνων ἀποικίσασα πόλεις καὶ πάντα τὸν χρόνον ἡγησαμένη τοῦ ἔθνους, ὑπὸ τῆς ἐσχάτης ἀποκτίσεως καθαιρεθεῖσα, ἔρημος εἰς τόδε χρόνου διαμένει. The "last colony" of Alba, Rome, is consequently one of her thirty colonies. Dionysius did not realize that in this way Rome cannot be put asunder from the thirty peoples ; but when he enumerated (V 61, 3) twenty-nine Latin cities without Rome (mentioning erroneously Lavinium and Laurentum as two of them), he did it with the afterthought that they were thirty with Rome. Cf. also VI 20, 3 : τὴν ’Αλβανῶν πόλιν, ἐξ ἧς αὐτοί τ’ἀπῳκίσθησαν καὶ Λατίνων ἅπασαι πόλεις.

[2] Cf. our third and fourth chapters, pp. 101 sq.

[3] Every scholar discussing the *feriae Latinae* was inevitably involved in dealing with these lists of peoples. We quote for *both* these problems R. H. Klausen, Aeneas und die Penaten 1, 1839, 798 n. 1482. A. Schwegler, RG 2, 296 sq., 322 sqq. A. Bormann, Altlatinische Chorographie und Städtegeschichte, Halle 1852, 33 sqq., 57 sqq. Mommsen, RF 2, 1879, 103. *Idem*, Ges. Schr. 5, 69 sqq. M. Zoeller, Latium und Rom, Leipzig 1878, 128 sqq. J. Beloch, Der italische Bund, Leipzig 1880, 177 sqq. *Idem*, RG 144 sqq. O. Seeck, Rh. Mus. n. F. 37, 1882, 20 sq. Christian Werner, De feriis Latinis, Diss. Leipzig-Köln 1888. H. Nissen, It. Lk. II 2, 581. Mommsen, St. R. 608, 611, 613 sq. C. Jullian, D.-S. 4, 1067. G. Wissowa in J. Marquardt, St. V. 3², 1885, 296 sqq. J. Binder, Die Plebs, Leipzig 1909, 295 sq. G. De Sanctis, St. d. R. 1¹ 171. A. Samter, RE 6, 2213 sqq. E. Täubler, Imperium Romanum 1, Leipzig 1913, 290 sqq. G. Wissowa, RuK², 39 sqq. H. Rudolph, Stadt und Staat im alten Italien, Leipzig 1935, 82 sqq. A. Rosenberg, Hermes 54, 1919, 121 sqq. A. N. Sherwin-White, R. Citiz. 1939, 8 sqq. M. Gelzer, RE 12, 952. A. Piganiol, Histoire de Rome 1³, Paris 1949, 50. J. Carcopino, Virgile et les origines d’Ostie, Paris 1919, 228 sqq. A. Brelich, Ant. cl. 20, 1951, 335 sqq. M. Rambaud, R. Et. Lat. 37, 1959 (1960), 107 sqq. R. Merkelbach, Mus. Helv. 18, 1961, 89. L. Pareti, St. d. R. 1, 1952, 222 sqq., 418 sqq. P. De Francisci, Primordia civitatis, Roma 1959, 131 sqq. P. Frezza, Corso di storia del diritto romano, Roma 1954, 11 sqq. Cf. also G. Tomasetti, La Campagna romana, 4 Roma 1926, 506 sqq. G. Lugli, Mem. Pont. Acc. 3. ser. 1, 1923, 251 sqq. M. Pallottino, Relazioni del X. Cogr. Intern. di Scienze Storiche 2, Firenze 1955, 47 sqq., and often elsewhere.

[4] DH IV 49, 1 sqq.

NOMEN LATINUM

Alban Mountain were forty-seven. This was, I am convinced, freely invented to illustrate the might of the last Roman king, who succeeded by his trickery and also by his prestige—so it is pretended—to induce all the Hernican cities and the two most powerful Volscian cities, Ecetra and Antium, to join forever his newly formed (!) Latin League: these alien communities are also included in that number of forty-seven. This statement is taken seriously by modern scholars.[1] The true nature and character of the Italic national confederacies, however, denies *a priori* the possibility to admit foreigners to the sacrifices performed for the welfare of the nation. We know, further, that the Hernicans never gave up their own tribal gatherings (connected, no doubt, with a corresponding ritual). On the other hand, Antium was in all probability still in Latin hands in the time of that king, because the Volscians intruded only when Etruscan rule collapsed some time after his rule in Latium;[2] and, furthermore, the sovereignty of the Tarquins over Latium is not historical.[3] Also unhistorical is the pretension of the Roman Annals that the Latin festival on the Alban Mountain was founded by the last Roman king. Though we do not know the exact number of the members of the Hernican League, the basis of the freely invented figure of 47 states, which are said to have participated in the Alban League of Superbus, must have included 15 Hernican communities to add to the 30 Latin and 2 Volscian cities.

Dionysius inserted in his account of Roman history at the beginning of the fifth century B.C. the list of the member-states of the Latin League [4] then preparing war against Rome. He copies this list from an annalist source, the intention of which was to illustrate the superior-

---

[1] Mommsen, Gesammelte Schriften 5, 76 n. 3, declined to accept this fiction. He wrote : "Dass er (DH) das Latiar zu einem Internationalfest der Latiner, der Herniker und zweier Volskerstädte umschafft, ist seine Schuld." But his statement was mostly overlooked. Curiously enough, Mommsen tried to save the number 47 as authentic, though he recognized that the basis of these mathematics is unsound.

[2] Cf. below, p. 365 sqq.

[3] Cf. below, p. 101 sqq.

[4] DH V 61, 3 : οἱ δ᾽ ἐγγραψάμενοι ταῖς συνθήκαις πρόβουλοι καὶ τοὺς ὅρκους ὀμόσαντες ἀπὸ τούτων τῶν πόλεων ἦσαν ἄνδρες, Ἀρδεατῶν, Ἀρικηνῶν, Βοϊλλανῶν, Βουβεντανῶν, Κορανῶν, Καρυεντανῶν, Κιρκαιητῶν, Κοριολανῶν, Κορβιντῶν, Καβανῶν, Φορτινείων, Γαβίων, Λαυρεντίνων, Λανουινίων, Λαβινιατῶν, Λαβικανῶν, Νωμεντανῶν, Νωρβανῶν, Πραινεστίνων, Πεδανῶν, Κορκοτουλανῶν, Σατρικανῶν, Σκαπτηνίων, Σητίνων, Τιβουρτίνων, Τυσκλανῶν, Τοληρίνων, Τελληνίων, Οὐελιτρανῶν.

ity of Rome over *all* the Latins by the complete specification of their strength;[1] the author of that source also counted Rome among the thirty Latin states, because he gave the names of twenty-nine of them without Rome—even erroneously taking Laurentum and Lavinium for two different units. Nobody has doubted, since it was recognized by Mommsen, that this list is an artificial product, conflated by an annalist. But this man was still aware of the number of units of the League, and some of the names he compiled are relevant.

Another list, assembled by Pliny the Elder in his *Natural History*,[2] recounts the names of the thirty peoples as those governed once by Alba Longa (*populi Albenses*),[3] manifestly in the strange belief that all of them vanished with the old capital, and not realizing that this is the core of the Latin nation. This roll also is a "learned" construction.[4] It contains, nevertheless, important archaic elements besides the mention of cities which played a part in early history but then decayed (*Alba Longa, Aefulae, Bola, Carventum, Corioli, Fidenae, Long[ul]a, Castrimoenium, Nomentum, Pedum, Politorium, Sassula,* and *Vitellia*); some geographical names introduced by mistake (*Hortenses, Sicani, Velienses*),[5] and finally some of totally unknown provenience,

---

[1] The original author of this list supposed that the Volscians were already in possession of Southern Latium (DH V 62, 3 ; cf. VI 7, 4), yet he enumerates Setia, Norba, Velitrae, Satricum, and Circei as Latin cities—in all probability in the knowledge of their occupation by the Latin League of the early Republic, when they became federal colonies ; cf. below, p. 394 sqq.

[2] Plin., *N.h.* III 5, 68-70 : *In prima regione praeterea fuere in Latio clara oppida . . . et cum iis carnem in monte Albano soliti accipere populi Albenses* : *Albani, Ae(fu)lani, Accienses, Abolani, Bube(n)tani, Bolani, C(arven)tani, Coriolani, Fidenates, For(c)ti, Hortenses, Latinienses, Longani, (S)anates, Macnales, Munienses, Numin(t)enses, Olliculani, Octulani, Pedani, Poletaurini, Querquetulani, Sicani, S(a)solenses, Tolerienses, Tutienses, Vimitellari, Velienses, Venetulani, Vitell(i)enses. ita ex antiquo Latio LIII populi interiere sine vestigiis.* We follow the analysis of A. Rosenberg, Hermes 54, 1919, 121 sqq., with some reservations and passing over some unwarranted suppositions. Cf. also F. Ribezzo, Onomastica 2, 1948, 29 sqq.

[3] That the *Albenses* do not belong to the list of the thirty is the well-founded opinion of B. G. Niebuhr and of L. Ian-C. Mayhoff, in their edition of Pliny the Elder 1, 1906, 259, and that of M. Pallottino, Arch. cl. 12, 1960, 27, etc. Niebuhr was rebuked in vain by A. Schwegler, RG 1, 348 and 2, 299, as well as by Mommsen, Ges. Schr. 5, 75 sq.

[4] K. J. Beloch, RG 149 sqq.

[5] We shall see (cf. p. 193 sqq.) that Rome was a united organization as early as in the seventh century B.C., including the *montes* of the Palatine-city and the *colles* of the Quirinal, so that the Velia of the list cannot be the village between Palatine and Esquiline ; A. Rosenberg, *op. cit.* 125 sq. thought more reasonably of the erroneous intrusion of Velia. *Contra* : F. Ribezzo, *l.c.* and M. Pallottino, Arch. cl. 12, 1960, 27.

which would be relevant if they came from southern Latium, occupied since the flight of the Tarquins by the Volscians (*Accienses, Abolani, Macnales, Olliculani, Octulani, Vimitellari, Venetulani*).[1] The high interest of this list lies in the core of little districts without an urban center, such as the *Tolerienses* and *Tutienses* in the valleys of the rivers Tolerus and Tutia,[2] and perhaps of the *Bubentani*, if they were of the same sort. Among these tiny rural areas those around Rome are the most revealing because their independent existence must, of course, precede their subjugation by the Romans. Their membership in the League as autonomous communities beside Rome could emerge only at a time when Roman power was in its embryonic stage, still hidden in the crowd of small surrounding communities in the eighth and seventh centuries B.C. The little *populi* to which we refer, mentioned in the list of Pliny, are the *Forcti* and the *Sanates*,[3] whose existence is attested about 450 B.C. by a provision of the Twelve Tables regulating their juridical position within the Roman state; the *Latinienses*, established opposite the Vatican Hill on the Latin bank of the Tiber,[4] and, finally, the *Querquetulani*, the Κορκοτουλανοί of Dionysius, who cannot be sought on the Caelian Hill with the Roman antiquarians but only outside Rome in the direction of the *porta Querquetulana*,[5] somewhere not far away.

The inclusion of these tiny little *populi* in the member-list of the tribal organization not only illuminates the earliest stage of Roman history but also illustrates the important fact that the original members of the Latin League were not urban communities but groups of shepherd-warriors located in an area distributed to them by the king of the tribe. The names of some of these groups were not forgotten even after they had an urban center: designations such as 'Ardea of

[1] Mommsen, Ges. Schr. 5, 79 sq., supposed that an official list of the *populi* who were entitled to participate in the Latin festival existed ; though we cannot admit that all the 30 names of Pliny's list are authentic, the few names discussed above could well have come from such an old source.

[2] Cf. A. Rosenberg, *op. cit.* 133 and 137.

[3] The emendation of the *Foreti* and *Manates* of the list was proposed by Chr. Huelsen, in SB Heid., phil.-hist. Kl. 1916, Abh. 14, 53 (O. Gradenwitz), accepted by A. Rosenberg, *op. cit.* 127 sqq., and M. Lejeune, R. Et. Lat. 29, 1951, 43 sqq.

[4] A. Rosenberg, *op. cit.* 133.

[5] Cf. *ibid.* p. 136 and above, 13 n. 5 on *Velia*. H. Jordan, Topographie der Stadt Rom im Altertum I 1, 1878, 227 sq. The existence of an oak forest on the Caelian Hill has little bearing on this problem ; such forests were to be found everywhere.

15

The Thirty Units of the Prisci Latini

the Rutuli," "Suessa of the Pometini," and perhaps also "Lavinium of the Laurentes" exemplify this.[1]

In addition to these lists of the thirty peoples, some of them are specially mentioned or attested as belonging to the sacred union of the Latin tribe: Rome,[2] Ardea,[3] Laurentum-Lavinium,[4] Lanuvium,[5] Labici, Gabii, Bovillae,[6] Cabum,[7] and Caenina.[8]

It is a deplorable loss for us that the count of the Latin states closing their ranks against the menace of Porsenna about 505 B.C.[9] has been mutilated by the same grammarian who saved part of it from oblivion. The names of Tusculum, Aricia, Lanuvium, Laurentum-Lavinium, Cora, Tibur, Pometia and Ardea only are preserved. Though Rome and eventually also some more cities of Northern Latium, overrun by the invader, could not be represented at the conclusion of this alliance, the aspiration of its originators was evidently to include all the Latins in it. And indeed the center of this rally, Aricia, was regarded as the metropolis of all the Latins; when Rome induced her conationals to transfer their federal sanctuary

[1] The transformation of the subdivisions of Italic tribes in stationary units gradually urbanized has often been observed and discussed. Cf., e.g., Ad. Schulten, Philol. 53, 1894, 631 sqq. E. Kornemann, Klio 5, 1905, 78 sqq. *Idem*, Klio 14, 1915, 190 sqq. A. Rosenberg, Der Staat der alten Italiker, Berlin 1913, *passim*. St. Weinstock, Klio 24, 1931, 235 sqq. G. De Sanctis, Riv. di filol. 60, 1932, 433 sqq. V. Basanoff, Rev. arch., ser. 6, 9-10, 1937, 43 sqq. G. Devoto, Gli antichi italici, Firenze 1931,[1] 262 sqq. Fr. Leifer, Zur Vorgeschichte des römischen Führeramtes (Klio, Beiheft 23) 1931, 100 sqq., etc. E. Kornemann, RE 18, 2318 sqq. (with further literature). P. De Francisci, Primordia civitatis, Roma 1959, 135 sqq.
[2] Varro, *LL* 6, 25. On the *Lares grundules* cf. below, p. 277 sq.
[3] Liv. XXXII 1, 9. ILLRP 188.
[4] Liv. XXXVII 3, 4.
[5] Liv. XLI 16, 1-2.
[6] Cic., *Pro Planc.* 9, 23.
[7] The official corporation of the *Cabenses sacerdotes feriarum Latinarum montis Albani* (CIL VI 2173 = XIV 2228 with the note of Dessau ; cf. VI 2174. 2175). K. Latte, Röm. Religionsgeschichte, München 1960, 405.
[8] The *sacerdotes Caeninenses*, another corporation of equestrian rank in imperial times (cf. the epigraphical evidence quoted by K. Latte, *op. cit.* 405 n. 5), certainly officiated primarily on the site of Caenina as did their prototype Romulus (Fab. Pictor fr. 5 b = H. R. Rel. 1², p. 12 Peter : ῾Ρωμύλος μὲν οὖν τὸν χρόνον τοῦτον ἐτύγχανεν ἅμα τοῖς ἐπιφανεστάτοις τῶν κωμητῶν πεπορευμένος εἴς τι χωρίον Καίνιναν ὀνομαζόμενον ἱερὰ ποιήσων ὑπὲρ τοῦ κοινοῦ πάτρια) ; but K. Latte must be right in supposing that they represented Caenina also on the Latin festival of the Alban Mountain : nobody else was there to do this for that decayed community.
[9] Cf. my remarks in : AJA 64, 1960, 137 sqq., and below, p. 49 sqq.

of Diana from Aricia to Rome, her purpose was to replace her rival in this role.[1] The federal character of both these cults of Diana was maintained in fact also in much later times,[2] i.e., they were performed by all and every Latin state.

At this juncture, a question arises. If the Latin League embraced all the Latin communities, and if, on the other hand, the fixed number of its members was thirty, what happened to the new states founded by the League (*coloniae Latinae* in the original sense of this designation) in the fifth and fourth centuries B.C.? They were also part of the *nomen Latinum*, like the old states, and it would be hardly possible to exclude them from the sacred community of the nation. In the list of Dionysius, Cora, Norba, Setia, Satricum, Velitrae, and Circeii were such federal foundations of the fifth and early fourth centuries. As the list is a relatively late compilation, their names are certainly not those of the old pre-Volscian communities on these sites, but just the newly populated colonies of the League. As the Volscian conquest of southern Latium around 500 B.C. must have abolished a relevant part of the thirty, the gap in this total could have prevented for a long time the sacred number of member-states from going beyond it. Nor was the old pattern disrupted by the rise of new leading powers. We have already touched upon the fact that when Lavinium replaced Alba, the confederation remained that of the thirty; and also that after the leadership shifted first to Aricia and then to Rome, the old centers continued their secular life, reduced *ad sacra*. Also the structural scheme did not die at once with the new developments. It is not by mere chance that the number of Roman colonies with "Latin" status was still in 209 B.C. exactly thirty.[3] In the epoch of the second Punic war, it was only a symbolic gesture of Roman politics to adhere to this pattern of the venerable Latin past; it nevertheless demonstrates its continuity, even if vanishing at last, long ago outmoded in a new world. This living force of the old framework in the late third century B.C. implies that the number

---

[1] Liv. I 45, 3. DH IV 26, 2 : Ῥωμαίους δὲ τὴν ἁπάντων Λατίνων ἔχειν προστασίαν. Further details below, p. 85 sqq.

[2] Cf. my remarks in SMSR 32, 1961, 21 sqq.

[3] Liv. XXVII 9, 7. Cf. the detailed discussion by E. Pais in : Mem. Acc. Linc., cl. scienze mor., 5. ser. 17, 1924, 312 sqq. It is important to retain that Rome in 209 B.C. was not any more one of the thirty, but she was the ruling city above them. This is the real base of the annalist fiction, pushing back this state of affairs arbitrarily to a remote epoch.

thirty of the member-states of the Latin League was maintained [1] before Rome's final conquest of Latium in 338 b.c., even if members of no consequence were obliged to cede, under some pretext, the high command of the federal army to the major powers when they were to take it over in rotation.

The same tenacious adherence to this obsolete structural pattern in a completely changed state of things can be illustrated by the corresponding development in Rome. For the correct appraisal of this parallelism we must premise that for the archaic mentality the idea of unity is not that of our modern science, trying to reveal the fundamental laws of Nature through their function, but a unity of a permanent pattern: the world is for the primitive societies like a crystal (I borrow this definition from E. Cassirer) [2] which can be split in small and still smaller units, yet the smallest particles preserve the same characteristic forms of organization as the largest specimens. In this way the organizatory scheme of totemist societies is reproduced exactly in their subdivisions. This applies also for our comparison.

The thirty Latin units were unquestionably articulated in a tripartite organization [3] in the same way as Rome, where the thirty *curiae* of the citizen clans were the subdivisions of the three gentile tribes.

They were the cadre of recruitment of the legion of 3000 infantrymen and 300 cavalrymen. The senate, the colleges and fraternities of the ancient priesthoods, were coordinated to this tripartite system; the early colonies still reflect this pattern. The thirty *curiae* still decided on vital matters of the state in the time of the Late Republic, maintaining their old constitution with equal rights for every member, disregarding class differences with their common meals and common sacrifices to *Juno Quiritis*.

There was the same organizatory type, of course, in other Latin communities—though we have information only for a few of them, no one doubts their general validity—and it existed, too, in other

---

[1] As A. Schwegler, RG 2, 1856, 302, maintained it already ; cf. Mommsen, Ges. Schr. 5, 80.

[2] E. Cassirer, Die Begriffsform des mythischen Denkens (Studien der Bibliothek Warburg 1) 1922, 34 sqq.

[3] A faint remainder of this is the legend in DH I 73, 3 : ἄλλοι δὲ λέγουσιν Αἰνείου τελευτήσαντος Ἀσκάνιον ἅπασαν τὴν Λατίνων ἀρχὴν παραλαβόντα νείμασθαι πρὸς τοὺς ἀδελφοὺς Ῥωμύλον τε καὶ Ῥῶμον τήν τε χώραν καὶ τὴν δύναμιν τὴν Λατίνων τριχῇ.

NOMEN LATINUM

Italic nations.[1] The roots of this kind of social and political formation are, however, much older than the immigration of the Latins into Italy, and their expansion is by far greater than the sphere of the Indo-European family of peoples.[2] This point must be stressed against the opinion of illustrious scholars who think it came into being only as a relatively late development in Latium itself. They overlook or disregard the traces of a prehistoric past still apparent in the manifestations of the federal organism of the thirty Latin peoples in the epoch of Roman supremacy.

These survivals constitute a coherent complex consisting of the myth of origin, justifying the common cult of the Latins by their common descent, and of the rites intended to foster and reinforce the ties of origin; both based on and performed in the same distribution of thirty units. We have already stressed that the political dealings, the business transactions, and marriages concluded at the great annual gatherings were corollaries of the cult-acts and common rejoicings.

The myth of origin,[3] explaining how the Latins arrived in their actual homeland, is not preserved in its genuine form; but we know the pattern of it in Italy and elsewhere well enough to recognize its original features. A female white boar, messenger of the divinity,

[1] In my study on the oldest structure of the Roman state, now in preparation, I shall give all the details on the tripartite system and I shall discuss the modern views on this topic.

[2] I hope to have shown in my study "Bear Cult and Matriarchal Form of Organisation in Eurasia" (Nyelvtudományi Közlemények 50, 1936, 5 sqq., in Hungarian ; to be reprinted in the volume mentioned in the previous note) that the tripartite social system arose among the Indo-European and other peoples alike as a matriarchal formation. Since then G. Dumézil investigated some aspects of this structure among the Italic tribes (Cf. his studies : Rev. Hist. d. Rel. 118, 1938, 188 sqq. Mythes et Dieux des Germains, Paris 1939. Juppiter Mars Quirinus, Paris 1941, 45 sqq., 129 sqq. Horace et les Curiaces[5], Paris 1942, 50 sqq. Iuppiter Mars Quirinus IV Paris 1948. Latomus 13, 1954, 129 sqq. L'idéologie tripartite des Indoeuropéens, Bruxelles (Coll. Latomus 31) 1958. R. Et. Lat. 39, 1961, 257 sqq.) with many important observations, the value of which is not diminished even if we cannot accept his main thesis on the "functional" differentiation of the tripartition in soldiers, priests and cultivators of the soil as in Iran and India. The great difficulty in this complex problem is that the tripartition (of matriarchal origin as I think) was coupled in Rome and in many other states with a (patriarchal) bipartition. Iuppiter Mars Quirinus represent, in my opinion at least, the supreme god with the two divine protectors of a bipartite system, or in other words : Iuppiter presiding over both the Palatine and the Quirinal communities.

[3] Cf. below, p. 271 sqq. for details.

lured the ancestor of the migrating tribe to follow her. At the place where she stopped to give birth to thirty piglets the ancestor and king of the Latins established his seat and assigned dwelling places to the thirty subdivisions all around it. In the original version of this account, the sow halted on her flight at the site of Alba Longa. Later, as we shall see, when Lavinium became the Latin metropolis instead of the first royal headquarters, the Laurentes pretended that the sow was directed by divine guidance not to Alba but to their city; and a Greek historian reported that he saw there, toward the end of the fourth century B.C., the bronze statue of the sow with the thirty little suckling pigs. The thirty *populi* of the Latins, assembled annually on the Alban Mountain and sending their representatives also to the solemnities in the sacred precinct of Lavinium, celebrated the memory and venerated the divinity of their first king and ancestor, keeping alive this myth of their common existence. The primeval antecedents of their reunions are nowhere as conspicuous as in a rite to which we now turn our attention.

❧

THE SACRED BANQUET OF THE THIRTY PEOPLES ON THE HOLY MOUNTAIN OF THE LATINS

The divinity to whom the common cult of the Latins on the Alban Mountain was offered was Juppiter Latiaris.[1] But it is not correct to imagine the peculiar character of this primeval divinity to be like that of the Zeus of classical Greece or like that of Juppiter in the sense of republican Rome. In an antiquarian account not biased by annalist tendentiousness and explaining a popular practice displayed on the Latin festival, it is said that this solemnity honored the memory of the ancestral kings Aeneas and Latinus; and, furthermore, that Latinus became Juppiter Latiaris.[2] This account is not to be discarded

[1] DH IV 49, 2. Fest., p. 212, 15 sqq. L. CIL XIV 2227 (29 A.D.). Further details in the article of Aust in Roscher's Lex. II 1, 686 sqq.

[2] Schol. Bob in Cic., *Pro Planc.* (p. 128, 25 sqq. Hildebrandt) : *Nam quidam id* (sc. sacrificium Latinorum anniversarium) *initum ex imperato Fauni contendunt, nonnulli post obitum Latini regis <et> Aeneae, quod ii nusquam comparuerant. Itaque ipsis diebus ideo oscillare instituerunt, ut pendulis machinis agitarentur : quoniam eorum corpus in terris non erat repertum, ut animae velut in aëre quaererentur.* Fest., p. 212, 15 sqq. L. : *Oscillantes, ait Cornificius, ab eo quod os celare sint soliti personis propter verecundiam, qui eo genere lusus utebantur. Causa autem eius iactationis proditur (. . . . .)*

offhand. Though the original forefather belonging to Alba was not Aeneas but Silvius—we shall enlarge upon this whole theme in our sixth chapter—and although Latinus was attached to Lavinium, not to Alba, the connection between the progenitor of the nation and Juppiter Latiaris will prove itself to be an old and organic concept, which must have existed already when Alba Longa flourished. Further on, the identification of the First King and the Supreme God is reaffirmed not only in the myth but also in the practice of the second federal cult of the Latins in Lavinium, dedicated again in the first instance to Aeneas and Latinus.[1] It is extremely unlikely that the religious basis of tribal worship in Alba differed from that in Lavinium, where it becomes tangible for us at least from the sixth century on. The worship of the divine ancestor, we need hardly add is just what we must expect in a tribal religious manifestation.

Propitiatory rites, dedicated to deified ancestral kings, and a hilarious agitation, bustling the awakening of Nature, were connected at the Latin festival in the same way as in the *Lupercalia* of the Romans. The Holy Mountain was sprinkled with milk by the presiding authorities to promote fertility.[2] All those present were entertained at a banquet, to which each city was obliged to contribute something; some brought lambs, some cheese, milk and the like.[3] On the last

Latinus rex, qui praelio, quod ei fuit adversus Mezentium, Caeritum regem, nusquam apparuerit iudicatusque sit Iuppiter factus Latiaris. Itaque scit eius dies feriatos liberos servosque requirere eum non solum in terris, sed etiam qua videtur caelum posse adiri per oscillationem, . . . Atque ideo memoriam quoque redintegrari initio acceptae vitae per motus cunarum lactisque alimentum, quia per eos dies feriarum et oscillis moveantur, et lactata potione utantur. These accounts coming from a common source were rejected by K. Latte, Röm. Religionsgeschichte, München 1960, 145 sqq. The interrelation of the traditions on Alba and Lavinium as the first Latin centers is, however, not artificial, but emerged from an actual competition between the two ; cf. below, p. 247 sqq. See also R. Merkelbach, Mus. Helv. 18, 1961, 89 sqq.

[1] Cf. below, p. 246 sqq.

[2] Cic. *De div.* I 11, 118 (: *De consulatu suo l. II)* : *Tu quoque, quum tumulos Albano in monte nivales lustrasti et laeto mactasti lacte Latinas.*

[3] DH IV 49, 1 : ἵνα συνερχόμενοι καθ'ἕκαστον ἐνιαυτὸν εἰς τὸν ἀποδειχθέντα τόπον πανηγυρίζωσι καὶ συνεστιῶνται καὶ κοινῶν ἱερῶν μεταλαμβάνωσιν. 49, 2 : θυσίας τε συντελεῖσθαι κοινὰς τῷ καλουμένῳ Λατιαρίῳ Διὶ καὶ συνεστίασεις, τάξας ἃ δεῖ παρέχειν ἑκάστην πόλιν εἰς τὰ ἱερά καὶ μοῖραν, ἣν ἑκάστην δεήσει λαμβάνειν. 49, 3 : ταύτας τὰς ἑορτάς τε καὶ τὰς θυσίας μέχρι τῶν καθ'ἡμᾶς χρόνων ἐπιτελοῦσι ῾Ρωμαῖοι Λατίνας καλοῦντες, καὶ φέρουσιν εἰς αὐτὰς αἱ μετέχουσαι τῶν ἱερῶν πόλεις αἱ μὲν ἄρνας, αἱ δὲ τυρούς, αἱ δὲ γάλακτός τι μέτρον, αἱ δὲ ὁμοιῶ τι τούτοις (πελάνου γένος). ἑνὸς δὲ ταύρου κοινῶς ὑπὸ πασῶν θυομένου μέρος ἑκάστη τὸ τεταγμένον λαμβάνει. Fest., p. 212, 30 sq. L. : *quia per eos dies feriarum . . . lactata potione utantur.*

day of those *feriae* the solemn sacrifices were performed for the welfare of all the Latins. The women of the neighboring cities led the victims to the altars at the top.[1] Several bulls were slaughtered,[2] among them a white one,[3] the meat of which was solemnly distributed among the member-states.[4] This was the highlight of the ceremonies, observed with painstaking care: if the organizers forgot to give to one of the Latin communities the little portion due it, the whole feast was likely to be repeated.[5]

To request that portion of meat from the white bull immolated on the *mons Albanus* (*carnem petere*) was regarded, in the time of the Later Republic, as a manifestation of the elevated position of the Latins in the new empire of the Romans, as a juridically conceived privilege. It was not forgotten, however, that its base was religious, *vetus superstitio*.[6] Pliny the Elder calls the peoples entitled to share in this sacred act as those dependent on Alba (*carnem in monte Albano soliti accipere populi Albenses*). Varro defines the same more correctly as *Latini populi*, and, indeed, the cities mentioned accidentally as having this right in common with Rome—Ardea, Lavinium, Lanu-

---

[1] Cic., *Att.* I 3, 1 : *Aviam tuam scito desiderio tui mortuam esse et simul, quod verita sit ne Latinae in officio non manerent et in montem Albanum hostias non adducerent.* O. Skutsch - H. J. Rose, Cl. Q. 36, 1942, 18 sq. On the sacred grove on the top cf. Liv. I 31, 3 : *visi etiam* (sc. in monte Albano) *audire vocem ingentem ex summi cacuminis luco, ut patrio ritu sacra Albani facerent.* See H. Nissen, It. Lk. II 2, 1909, 580. G. Lugli, Boll. d'Arte 10, 1930, 162 sqq.

[2] Liv. XLI 16, 1-2.

[3] Arnob. 2, 68 : *in Albano antiquitus monte nullos alios licebat, quam nivei tauros immolare candoris.*

[4] Cic., *Pro Planco* 9, 23 and Schol. Bob. (p. 128, 25 sqq. Hild) ad *l.l.* : *Quod vero mentionem petendae carnis fecit, pertinet ad consuetudinem sacri anniversarii ... Feriarum Latinarum sacrificio solebat hoc observari, ut de hostia civitates adiacentes portiunculas carnis acciperent ex Albano monte secundum veterem superstitionem. Verum tam exiguum in illis civitatibus numerum hominum significat, ut desint etiam, qui carnem petitum de sollemni more mittantur.* Varro, *LL* 6, 25 : *Latinae feriae dies conceptivus dictus a Latinis populis, quibus ex Albano monte ex sacris carnem petere fuit ius cum Romanis, a quibus Latinis Latinae dictae.* DH IV 49, 2 : τάξας ἃ δεῖ παρέχειν ἑκάστην πόλιν εἰς τὰ ἱερά, καὶ μοῖραν ἣν ἑκάστην δεήσει λαμβάνειν. 49, 3 : ἑνὸς δὲ ταύρου κοινῶς ὑπὸ πασῶν θυομένου μέρος ἑκάστη τὸ τεταγμένον λαμβάνει. Plin., *N.h.* III 5, 69 : *carnem in monte Albano soliti accipere populi Albenses.* Serv., *Aen.* 1, 211 : *ut in Albano Latinis visceratio dabatur, id est caro.*

[5] Liv. XXXII 1, 9 : *Feriae Latinae pontificum decreto instauratae sunt, quod legati ab Ardea questi in senatu erant sibi in monte Albano Latinis carnem, ut adsolet, datam non esse* (199 b.c.). XXXVII 3, 4 : *Latinaeque instauratae, quod Laurentibus pars carnis, quae dari debet, data non fuerat* (190 b.c.).

[6] Schol. Bob. *l.c.* (n. 4 above).

NOMEN LATINUM

vium, Labici, Gabii, and Bovillae[1]—are exactly the Latin states of the region of the Alban hills.

It is a relevant feature of this ritual of the meat-distribution that each city received her appointed share (μέρος τὸ τεταγμένον), the share that every one of them was due (μοῖραν ἦν ἑκάστην δεήσει λαμβάνειν).[2] We assume, and this is an obvious supposition, that these *portiunculae* assigned to each community were not just bits in equal weight, but well-defined parts of the white bull—the more savory and the less edible allotted according to precedence and power.

The type of such ceremonial banquets and their magico-religious purpose is well known to everybody who has studied social anthropology.[3] They were in their most primitive forms the participation of a social group in the vital forces of the zoomorphic ancestor by absorbing some part of his body, and renewing thereby the ties of relationship. Such a coordination of the sacred banquets with the subdivisions of a tribal organization, as we observed in the Latin festival, are to be found also in the shepherd-warrior culture of Eurasia. The clearest instance of this is the case of the Oghuz-Turks, as described by the medieval Persian scholar Rashid al-Din.[4] The Oghuz had 24 clans, arranged again in six subdivisions, conceived as the offspring of six sons of the ancestral king. Each of these six tribal groups had a bird-of-prey as a special guardian spirit. At festivals and banquets of the Oghuz each of these six groups always had to eat the same part of the ox consumed by the tribe on the occasion; these parts were specially assigned to each of the six detachments, composed of four clans.

The origin of this apportioning of meat among the clans is obvious in that part of the world. In the hard life of the steppe or in the desert, the participation of relatives and neighbors in the meat of an animal

[1] Cf. above, 20 n. 3; 21 n. 1-5

[2] DH *l.c.* (p. 20 n. 3).

[3] For an introduction to this problem, see W. Robertson Smith, Lectures on the Religion of the Semites, Edinburgh 1889. E. Reuterskiöld, Die Entstehung der Speisesakramente (Religionswissenschaftliche Bibliothek, hrsg. v. W. Streitberg u. R. Wünsch, 4) Heidelberg 1912. M. P. Nilsson, Geschichte der griechischen Religion 1², München 1955, 156 sq., 572 sqq.

[4] Rashíd al-Din, cf. M. T. Houtsma, Wiener Zeitschrift für die Kunde des Morgenlandes 2, 1888, 219 sqq. Z. v. Gombocz, Our Turkish Personal Names from the Age of the Arpad Dynasty, (in Hungarian) Budapest 1916, 6. A. N. Maksimov, Contributions to the Problem of Totemism among the Peoples of Siberia (in Russian). Moscow 1928, 3 sqq.

The Sacred Banquet of the Thirty Peoples

killed by a hunter or slaughtered by its owner was vitally important for the community and therefore was sanctioned by use and habit and regulated by strict ceremonies.[1] Besides this, in the epic poetry of these peoples the eating of the meat of the same animal makes friends and allies of deadly enemies;[2] the distribution of the meat served on solemn occasions is connected with manifestations and declarations of peace and fraternity.[3]

This is the atmosphere which must be postulated also for the mentality and experience of the Indo-European tribes immigrating in Italy. A close analogy to the distribution of meat between the members of the Latin confederation is provided by the prescriptions of the priestly corporation of the *fratres Atiedii* in Umbrian Iguvium: the twenty subdivisions of this primeval brotherhood obtained the same amount of meat at their ceremonial banquets.[4] The analogous usages of the thirty Roman *curiae* must be also adduced because, as we saw, the subdivisions had the same social and religious structure as the major units comprising them. The *curiae* had not only their own religious duties but also their common meals, compared already by the ancients with the συσσίτια of the Dorians.[5] "The common meals of Italos," mentioned by a Syracusan historian of the fifth century B.C.,[6] point to the fact that this sort of political and religious practice was widespread among the Italic peoples. Nor are the traces of the primordial meaning of those collective repasts totally absent in the Ancient World. The bestial act of the Bacchants, devouring the raw

---

[1] M. Shieroshevski, Journal Anthrop. Inst. 31, 1901, 65 sqq. A. A. Kaufmann, Der gemeinsame Bodenbesitz Moskau 1908, übers. R. Augustin (Masch-. Schr.) 65 sqq. W. Schmidt-W. Koppers, Völker und Kulturen (Der Mensch aller Zeiten 3, Regensburg 1924), 226 sqq. G. M. Potanin, Očerki sěvero-zapadnoi Mongolii, St. Petersburg 4, 1883, 39. W. Radloff, Aus Sibirien 1, Leipzig 1884, 301 sqq. R. Thurnwald, Anthropos 14-15, 1919-20, 505 sqq. A. R. Brown, Anthropos 9, 1914, 627. W. Robertson Smith, Die Religion der Semiten, Leipzig, 1899, 212 sq., 239 sqq. S. M. Shirokogoroff, The Social Organisation of the Northern Tungus, Shanghai, 1929, 195 sqq. Sir James Frazer, Totemism and Exogamy 1, London 1910, 30 sq., 46, 58 sq.; 2, 1910, 520 ; 3, 1910, 40, 55, 67, 92, 97, 124, 267, 326. M. A Castrén, Reiseerinnerungen aus den Jahren 1838-1844, St. Petersburg 1853, 286. G. M. Potanin, ARW 25, 1927, 100.

[2] W. Radloff, Proben aus der Volksdichtung der türkischen Stämme Süd-Sibiriens 4, St. Petersburg 1872, 63.

[3] M. Shieroshevski, Journ. Anthrop. Inst. 31, 1901, 82 sqq.

[4] Cf. U. Coli, Il diritto pubblico degli Umbri, Milano 1958, 55 sq., 87 sq. J. Heurgon, JRS 49, 1959, 164.

[5] DH II 23, 2.

[6] Antiochos of Syracuse quoted in Aristot., *Pol.* 7, 10 = 1329 b.

meat of the animals that they have torn to pieces in their frenzy, meant their sacramental participation in the essence of their god.[1] The belief that whoever tastes the meat of the human victim offered to Zeus Lykaios—once the ancestral god of an Arcadian wolf-clan— also becomes a wolf shows the primeval concept of the assimilation to the theriomorphic ancestor-giant by eating in a cult communion.[2] The ritual meals of archaic fraternities in Rome at the festival of the *Lupercalia* and of Hercules at the *ara maxima* were connected with the dramatic revival of the myth of origin—a correlation which must be postulated in some form also for the Latin festival. The constitution of a secret society of men by the magic ceremony of drinking each other's blood is another variety of the same primitive concept: it is still apparent in the ritual initiation of the accomplices of Catilina.[3]

The idea of tribal totality is apparent also in the notion of the *nomen Latinum*. The thirty cities—even if Alba and Rome are purposefully exempt from this category by annalist fiction—mean, for our authorities, the totality of the Latins;[4] they offer on the Alban Mountain their annual sacrifices for the welfare of all the Latins.[5] Only the existence of the tribal complex can explain why a treaty with the Latin states embraced "every person of Latin origin." [6] The original significance of the term *nomen Latinum* is the tribe, comprising in itself every collectivity and every individual of Latin descent, in the same way that *nomen Etruscum*, *nomen Hernicum*, or *nomen Volscum* included the whole of those nations.[7] The high antiquity of this

---

[1] E. Reuterskiöld, *op. cit.* 126 sqq. M. P. Nilsson, Geschichte der griechischen Religion 1², München 1955, 45 sqq., 156 sq., 572 sq.

[2] S. Reinach, Cultes, Mythes et Religions 1, Paris 1908, 16.

[3] J.Heurgon,Mélanges Charles Picard 1, Paris '48 (Rev. arch. 6. sér. 29), 438 sqq.

[4] Liv. I 52, 2 sq., calls the thirty cities *omnes Latini*.

[5] DH IV 49, 3 : θύουσι δ'ὑπὲρ ἀπάντων.

[6] DH V 50, 4 : γεγραμμένον ἐν ταῖς συνθήκαις ἁπάσας παρεῖναι τὰς πόλεις ταῖς κοιναῖς ἀγοραῖς, ὅσαι τοῦ Λατίνων εἰσὶ γένους. V 61, 2 : ὅσοι τοῦ Λατίνων μετεῖχον γένους. In the same way *ibid*. VI 18, 1.

[7] Some examples of this terminology in Livy will suffice to illustrate this : Liv. I 38, 4. III 8, 10. VII 17, 6 ; 28, 2. VIII 3, 8 ; 4, 12 ; 11, 10. IX 19, 2 ; 41, 6 ; 42, 11 ; 45, 5. X 11, 12 ; 34, 7. XXII 27, 11 ; 38, 1 ; 57, 10. XXIII 12, 16 ; 17, 8 ; 22, 5. XXVI 15, 3 ; 16, 6 ; 34, 7 ; XXVII 9, 1. XXIX 19, 9 ; 24, 14 ; 27, 2. XXX 41, 5 ; 44, 13. XXXI 5, 4. If the antiquarian Cincius (in Festus, p. 276, 24 sq.) uses the expression *Commune Latium* instead of *nomen Latinum*, this is an adoptation of the Greek τὸ κοινὸν τῶν Λατίνων ; cf. DH V 52, 2 ; 54, 5 ; 61, 5 ; 76, 2 etc. Cf. Mommsen, St. R. 3, 608 sq., 611 sq. P. Frezza in : Scritti in onore di C. Ferrini 1, Milano 1947, 275 sqq. *Contra* : A. N. Sherwin-White, R. Citiz. 19. P. De Francisci, Primordia civitatis, Roma 1959, 130 sqq.

concept is patent in the terminology of the Umbrian tablets of Igu-vium. They call down the wrath of Heaven upon their hostile neigh-bors, intending to wipe them out entirely, calling these peoples *tuscom, naharcom, iabuscom nomen*.[1] All these traits, dating back to time immemorial, warrant the assumption that the organization of the thirty peoples was not the result of a secondary evolution, but the survival of an obsolete system. On the other hand, the spectacular ascent of Rome during the first centuries of the Republic, though it did not suppress the antiquated forms of the Latin confederation, perverted their actual contents. A clear instance of this is the *nomen Latinum*, the meaning of which was subjected to a violent reinter-pretation in 338 B.C. Rome, victorious over her conationals, remained further on in the frame of the *populi Latini* on the Latin Festival only because Alba Longa was no longer a political organism which could cast a shadow on her new sovereign status. But otherwise she detached herself from the notion of the *nomen Latinum*: the ruling power could no longer remain at the same level with the subjugated. From then on, the *nomen* was valid [2] only for the *socii nominis Latini*, becoming a privileged but inferior entity vis-à-vis the sovereign community. The number of thirty members was still respected, but Rome was not included in it any longer.

✢

CHANGED ASPECTS, NEW DEVELOPMENTS

The evolution remodeling the Latin League was due partly to the gradual transformation of common life from tribal groups to city states, partly to the effect of the Etruscan occupation of Latium and the impact of Etruscan culture following the conquest. The adapta-tion of the Latin tribal collectivity to the requirements of a league

---

[1] Tab. Iguv. VI b 54. 58. VII a 12. 47 (p. 275 ed. Devoto²).

[2] As it occurs in the *Senatus consultum de Bacchanalibus*, in the *lex de repetundis*, the earliest legal texts we have (Fontes iuris Romani 1, Firenze 1941, 240 sqq. ; *ibid.* 84 sq.). This changed meaning lurks, of course, in the whole of the Annal-ist tradition : the Romans of a later epoch did not like the idea that they were not the rulers over the Latins from the beginning.

26

NOMEN LATINUM

of city-states was achieved on the pattern of the constitution of the Etruscan confederation.[1]

The League of the Twelve Etruscan Cities was brought, so we must assume, from Asia Minor,[2] where it was modeled on the lines of the Ionian League,[3] serving in Italy as a base for the conquest of the bulk of the peninsula, and also as a frame for the foundation of the network of two more *dodekapoleis* in the Po valley and in Campania. It was originally governed by a king, and later by an annual *sacerdos* or *praetor*, a magistrate who inherited the religious as well as the profane duties and powers of the monarch,[4] although his function was restricted to one year. The comprehensive authority of the national kingdom was also reflected still later in the fact that the League had an overall boundary line of its whole territory.[5]

The twelve cities gave the powers of chief executive to their confederation in annual rotation: this procedure was also followed by the Latins.[6] The representatives of the member-states, and with them a large crowd, assembled annually in a sacred precinct of central situation, the *fanum Voltumnae*,[7] in the same way as in Latium. The Etruscan states as well as the Latins offered solemn sacrifices for the welfare of the nation to their supreme god; they also elected their governing magistrates, discussed matters of common interest, held a market, and arranged public games. In cases of emergency, extra-

[1] As observed already by Mommsen, St. R. 1³, 666 n. 3 and 3, 617, and demonstrated by A. Rosenberg, Der Staat der alten Italiker, Berlin 1913, 76 sqq. (cf. *idem*, Hermes 54, 1919, 114), and E. Kornemann, Klio 14, 1914, 200 sqq. See also K. O. Müller-W. Deecke, 1, 319 sqq. E. Bormann, Archäologisch-epigraphische Mitteilungen aus Österreich-Ungarn 11, 1887, 103 sqq. A. Rosenberg, *op. cit.* 60 sqq. L. R. Taylor, Local Cults in Etruria (Papers and Monographs 2) 1923, 22 sqq. M. Pallottino, St. Etr. 2. ser. 24, 1955-56, 67 sqq., and the papers quoted below, p. 177 sqq.
[2] P. Ducati, Etruria antica 1, Torino 1925, 131. Ed. Meyer, G. d. A. 5, 1902, 123, stresses the point that the federation of the twelve cities is in the fifth century already in full decadence. *Contra* : L. R. Taylor, *op. cit.* 14. L. Pareti, Rend. Pont. Acc. 3, ser. 7, 1929-31, 89 sqq. G. Camporeale, La parola del passato 13, 1958, 8 sqq., contradicted by M. Sordi, Le rapporti romano-ceriti, Roma 1960, 19 n. i. For further details cf. below, p. 176 sqq.
[3] As suggested by J. Heurgon, Rech. 77.
[4] Cf. e.g., M. Pallottino, Etruscologia³, Milano 1955, 181, and below, p. 42 sqq.
[5] S. Mazzarino, in : Iura 12, 1961, 33 sqq.
[6] A. Rosenberg, *op. cit.* 55.
[7] Cf. below, p. 204 sqq.

ordinary meetings were held, also connected with a market.[1]

It was not the result of the vague influence of a common cultural atmosphere that the Latin states reshaped their national assembly according to the Etruscan pattern. It was rather the inevitable conse- quence of Etruscan domination which lasted about one and a half centuries. Without the permission and supervision of their overlords the survival of this assembly would be hardly imaginable. The Etruscan city-kings of Latium could not be absent from the Latin Festival—so said the Roman Annals of Tarquinius Superbus. The Etruscan stamp on the federal cult of the Latins is clearly reflected by the reinterpretation of the ancestral god *Indiges* as the Trojan hero Aeneas discussed in our sixth chapter. Such a thorough assimilation was certainly not restricted to the sphere of religion.

The most important consequence of the adaptation of the Latin federal organization to Etruscan ways and means was the transition from custom and habit to written agreements and a precise legislation. The mutual concessions and privileges of Latin individuals and states among themselves, anchored previously by the emotional and ritual bonds of their relationship, became the "Latin" rights. What we know as the *ius Latii* in a late and perverted form, warranted in the fifth century B.C. the equal rights of all the members of the nation including Rome. It is impossible for us to prove this in detail, because our sources of information desert us. But the political relationship of the Latin states, struggling against the aggressive mountain tribes in the fifth century, presupposes the existence of this *ius aequum*, as we shall see.

An illustration of the deep penetration of the Etruscan pattern in the Latin federal machinery is provided by the adoption of the insignia of power. It is known [2] that the rulers of the Twelve Cities were preceded in public by a *lictor*, bearing an axe encompassed in a bundle of rods. Whenever the twelve states undertook a joint military action, the twelve axes of the twelve kings (or republican executives in later times) were handed over to the man who was invested with

---

[1] Liv. IV 23, 5 : *Igitur cum duae civitates legatis circa duodecim populos missis impetrassent, ut ad Voltumnae fanum indiceretur omni Etruriae concilium* . . . 24, 2 : *Itaque cum renuntiatum a mercatoribus esset negata Veientibus auxilia*, etc. IV 61, 2. V 17, 6 sqq. VI 2, 2. IX 41, 6. DH III 59, 4 : συναχθέντες εἰς μίαν ἀγορὰν περὶ καταλύσεως τοῦ πολέμου διαλέγεσθαι πρὸς αὐτὸν ἐψηφίσαντο. IX 1, 2. Diodor. XX 44, 9.

[2] DH III 61, 2-3, etc.

the supreme power. When the Romans became powerful enough to subdue Latium and to compete with the prestige of the Etruscan League, they introduced the twelve *fasces* of the chiefs of the Etruscan League as the symbol of power of their own consuls. This polemical parallelism emerged, I think, only in the fourth century B.C.; but it shows nevertheless that even at that time the Etruscan federal machinery was still the coveted prototype for the ruling power of Latium.

This development was, of course, not an isolated phenomenon. The Sabines had annual gatherings, too, held in the sacred precinct of Feronia, luckily discovered not long ago. It is situated on a plateau large enough to take tens of thousands of people, with a most opportune and unobstructed view in every direction, fit also for an assembling army to spot approaching enemies or hostile movements.[1] In this precinct not only was the worship of Feronia absolved but great masses flocked together for the purpose of trafficking — merchants, artisans, and husbandmen alike; these "fairs" (ἀγοραί) of Feronia were famous.[2] It goes without saying that military and political consultations also took place on the same occasion. Similarly the Hernicans had a *concilium populorum Hernicorum omnium*, gathering every year in a meeting place suitable for games (called *circus*); there they held their political discussions and made decisions — certainly in much earlier times than the late fourth century B.C., when it is accidentally mentioned.[3] The assemblies of the Volscians and Aequians were again of the same sort, religious, political and commercial conventions;[4] nor did the Samnites and other peoples of the same Italic group lack this institution.[5] All these annual meetings show the same complex character as that of the Latins.

---

[1] Strab. V 2, 9 (C. 226). Varro, *LL* 5, 74. DH II 49. L. R. Taylor, JRS 10, 1920, 29 sqq. *Eadem*, Local Cults in Etruria (Papers and Monographs 2) 1923, 47 sqq., 54 sq. R. Bloch-L. Foti, Rev. philol. 3. ser. 27, 1950, 65 sqq. R. Bartoccini, L'autostrada del Sole si ricollega all' antico nodo stradale di Lucus Feroniae (Etratto dalla Rivista "Autostrada" n. 8, Agosto 1961).

[2] DH III 32, 1-2.

[3] Liv. IX 42, 11.

[4] Liv. IV 25, 7-8. DH VIII 58, 1 : ἀλλὰ τὸ ἔθνος ἅπαν εἰς τὸν ἔννομον ἀγορὰν συναχθέν, εἰς ἣν ἔθος ἦν αὐτοῖς, ὅτε περὶ τῶν μεγίστων βουλεύεσθαι μέλλοιεν ἐξ ἁπάσης πόλεως προβούλους ἀποστέλλειν.

[5] Liv. VII 31, 11, and elsewhere.

THE LATIN FESTIVAL

We have already referred to the tendentious effort of the Annals to conceal the tribal origin of the *feriae Latinae*, thereby separating Rome from the Latin tribesmen over whom she had already been ruling for quite a while when the writing of the Annals was first begun.[1] Hence the false pretension that Roman kings, Tarquin the Elder, or the last Tarquin founded this festival for the Latins designed to give the impression that they were already subjects of Rome.[2] The antiquarians, less prejudiced than the historiographers, attribute the origin of this common festival to the primeval Latins or to some of the mythical figures of their legendary prehistory.[3]

The *Latiar*, as the ritual performances on the *mons Albanus* were called,[4] was held evidently in the early spring. After Rome took over its supervision, or in any case after 338 B.C., its date depended on the entering of office of the Roman consuls[5] who fixed it by edict.[6] It is not unlikely that in the archaic epoch the festivities, meetings, and rejoicings lasted three days, as they did in 168 B.C.[7] The end of the celebrations was signalized by a great bonfire, kindled on the peak of the mountain when darkness fell.[8]

[1] Cf. Mommsen, St. R. 3, 613 sq. J. Binder, Die Plebs, Leipzig 1909, 329 sqq., 344 sqq. E. Täubler, Imperium Romanum 1, Leipzig 1913, 290, 293 sqq.

[2] DH VI 95, 3-4. Schol. Bob. ad Cic., *Pro Planc.* 9, 23 p. 128, 25 sqq. Hild. (Tarquinius Priscus). DH IV 49, 1-3. *Vir. ill.* 8, 2 (Superbus). Livy is certainly not reticent by chance.

[3] Schol. Bob. *l.c.*: *Nam Latinae feriae a quo fuerint institutae, dissentiunt plerique auctores. Alii ... existimant ... a Latinis priscis. Atque inter hos ipsos causa sacrificii non convenit. Nam quidam id initum ex imperato Fauni contendunt, nonnulli post obitum Latini regis (et) Aeneae.* Cic., *Pro Mil.* 31, 85. Serv., *Aen.* 12, 135. Cf. also Strab. V 3, 4 (C. 231).

[4] Cic., *Ad Q. fr.* II 4, 2. Macrob., *Sat.* I 16, 16. The *feriae* and the *sacrum in monte Albano* were different: Liv. V 17, 2-3. In the same way *ibid.* XXII 1, 6 : *Latinis feriis actis, sacrificio in monte perfecto*, and DH IV 49, 2 ἑορταί and θυσίαι specified. Chr. Werner, *op. cit.* 29 sq., may be right that *Latiar* meant the sacrifices especially. The *feriae* in contrast to the rites, meant all the profane items, including the serious business before 338 B.C.

[5] Mommsen, RF 2, 1879, 104. Chr. Werner, *De feriis Latinis*, Diss. Leipzig 1888, 36 sqq. A. Samter, RE 6, 2213 sq.

[6] Liv. XLI 16, 5 ; XLII 10, 15 ; XLV 3, 2. Cic., *Fam.* VIII 6, 3. Varro, *LL* 6, 25. Macrob. *l.c.*

[7] Liv. XLV 3, 2. The statements of DH VI 95, 3-4, and Plut., *Camill.* 42, 6, are distorted by annalist fiction ; cf. Chr. Werner, *op. cit.* 17, 23., and Suet., *Claud.* 4. Tac., *Ann.* IV 36, 1.

[8] Lucan. 1, 550 sq.: *ostendens confectas flamma Latinas.* 5, 400 sqq.: *nec non Iliacae numen quod praesidet Albae, haud meritum Latio sollemnia sacra subacto, vidit flammifera confectas nocte Latinas.*

After the close of the festival, two more days were *dies religiosi* when no action could be taken by the executives of the Latin states [1]—primarily to enable the gathering to dissipate undisturbed. This was a reasonable prolongation of the God's peace, obligatory in Latium during the days of these solemnities. This prohibition of hostilities is defined by our authorities as a religious ban—one more indication of the fact that this custom originated in a remote epoch when only superstitious fear could bridle bad intentions, and long before laws took over the regulation of interstate relations in Latium.[2] In those early days, and especially after the disintegration of the tribal kingdom, war was the normal state of things in Latium; otherwise the proclamation of the sacred armistice would have had no sense.[3] Until the end of Latin independence, the League had no rule that prohibited any Latin state to make war against whom it wished.[4]

In the later centuries of the Republic, with which period our information on the working of the machinery of the *feriae Latinae* begins, this feast was arranged by the Romans for the Latin.[5] The Roman Annals would have us believe, as we have seen, that this hegemonial role of Rome was already established under the Etruscan kings. In reality it was not Rome but Lavinium who took over from Alba Longa the leadership of the Federation; and, again, it was not Rome but Aricia with Tusculum who first replaced Lavinium as the leading powers. Roman aspirations for preeminence in Latium started only after the fall of the Tarquins, when the might of Alba had already vanished completely, as we shall hope to demonstrate in this book. As **A. N.** Sherwin-White has observed,[6] the control

[1] Cic. *Ad Q. fr.* II 4, 2 : *Dies erant duo, qui post Latinas habentur religiosi. Ceterum confectum erat Latiar.*

[2] Macrob., *Sat.* I 16, 16 : *nam cum Latiar, hoc est Latinarum sollemne, concipitur, item diebus Saturnaliorum, sed et cum mundus patet, nefas est proelium sumere.* DH IV 49, 2 : καὶ ἐκεχειρίας εἶναι πᾶσι πρὸς πάντας. (The Greek word is explained in Gell. I 25, 9 ; cf. *ibid.* 4 : *bellum enim manet, pugna cessat*). DH VI 95, 3. Nic. Dam., *Vita Caes.* 5. Cass. Dio XXXIX 30, 4 (56 B.C.) : οὐκ ἐπὶ τὰς ἀνοχὰς τὰς Λατίνας ... ἐς τὸ Ἀλβανὸν ἀφίκοντο. XLI 14, 4. XLIII 48, 4. XLIV 4, 3. XLVI 33, 4. XLVII 40, 6. XLIX 16, 2 ; 42, 1. LIV 6, 6 ; 17, 2. LV 2, 5. This truce is erroneously denied by A. Rosenberg, Hermes 54, 1919, 169 sq.

[3] The God's peace explains also the presence of foreign merchants on the fairs of the *Latiar* and other federal meetings. A local instance for such a truce on the days of public games in Rome is given by Liv. IV 35, 3 (425 B.C.).

[4] This was the rule until the conquest of Latium by Rome ; cf. Liv. VII 38, 1 and VIII 2, 13, and also below, p. 36. 121 sq. 414 sq.

[5] DH IV 49, 3 : τὴν ἡγεμονίαν τῶν ἱερῶν ἔχουσι Ῥωμαῖοι.

[6] As A. N. Sherwin-White, R. Citiz. 11, expresses this.

of the *Latiar* in these circumstances gave no political hegemony in Latium, only an increase of its prestige.

If we must lower the date of Roman ascendancy in Latium so much, Mommsen's observation [1] that the list of the Roman prefects of the *feriae Latinae* starts only with 451 B.C. gains a new importance. This is just the moment when Roman expansion reaches southward to the region of the Alban Hills; [2] and therefore we must assume, with A. Degrassi, that indeed the Roman supervision of the Latin Festival started only with the decemvirate.

Further changes in the management of the festival could be expected in 338 B.C., when the victorious Romans completely reshaped their relations with the Latin states. But on the soil of Alba Longa, where no actual political power overshadowed the annual gatherings, Rome made concessions to the piety of her tribesmen toward the cradle of the nation. First of all, she closed the ring of the participating states in the Festival: from that year on, those obtaining "Latin" status were not admitted. More surprising is the fact, overlooked hitherto, that the sacrifices on the mountain were accomplished also after 338 B.C. by the magistrates of the member-cities in rotation, and not by the Roman consuls, as in Lavinium. The cogent proof for this is the case of Lanuvium in 176 B.C. when this city not only furnished the bulls for the sacrifice but its executive also performed the ritual, praying for the welfare of all the Latins.[3]

This admission of the Latin states to the propitiation of Jupiter Latiaris in 338 B.C. in continuation of the previous practice is rather remarkable because the Roman state took it for granted that its welfare depended as much on the god of the Alban Mountain as on its own Juppiter Capitolinus and Juppiter Indiges of Lavinium. This belief is manifest in the painstaking care with which Rome watched over

---

[1] Mommsen, RF 2, Berlin 1879, 100 sqq. (with a different evaluation of this fact). CIL I² p. 56. A. Degrassi, Inscr. It. XIII 1, 1947, 143 sqq. Mommsen, St. R. 3, 607 sqq. A. Rosenberg, Hermes 54, 1919, 118. M. Gelzer, RE 12, 947 sqq.

[2] Cf. below, p. 245 sqq.

[3] Liv. XLI 16, 1-2. The Lanuvian magistrate was imprudent enough to forget to mention the welfare of the ruling city besides that of all the Latins ; thus this city was due to pay the expenses of the repeated sacrifices once more. Mommsen, St. R. 3, 613 sq., writes : "wie die Stadt Rom (since the fall of Alba) Herrin des Bodens ist, so tritt sie auch als eigentliche Festgeberin auf." But we shall see that the territory of Alba did not belong to the rural districts of Rome prior to 338 B.C.

NOMEN LATINUM

the flawless fulfillment of the solemnities on the mountain.

The consuls had to provide for the welfare of the Roman State by the three religious acts just mentioned: the *votorum nuncupatio* on the Capitol, the performance of the *Latiar* on the Alban Mountain,[1] and the state sacrifices in Lavinium. All three of these religious obligations had high priority before the profane agenda: the consuls were not allowed even in times of emergency to depart to the provinces before they had fulfilled these three ritual duties.[2] Not only the consuls but every other magistrate of the Romans was bound to be present at the celebration on the Alban Mountain; not even the tribunes of the *plebs*, who were otherwise not allowed to quit the town in the year of their office, were excepted;[3] if the elections were delayed for some reason, and there was no one to arrange the *feriae Latinae*, a dictator was created *ad hoc* for this purpose.[4] The magistrates of all the Latin cities were also obliged to join the Roman magistrates on that occasion.[5]

The awe inspired by the ancestral god of Alba must have been tremendous even in the later Republic. Prodigies which occurred during the festivities were regarded as most sinister.[6] So as not to enrage the Juppiter of the Latins, every detail of the arrangements for the *Latiar* was observed by the Romans with meticulous care. If, for example, the Festival was announced by magistrates whose appointments were invalidated by some formal fault, their legitimate successors were compelled to repeat the whole celebration at

---

[1] DH VIII 87, 6 : πρὸς ἕνα καιρόν, ἐν ᾧ πᾶσαι θύουσιν αἱ τῆς πόλεως ἄρχαι κοινὴν ὑπὲρ τοῦ Λατίνων ἔθνους τῷ Διὶ θυσίαν ἐπὶ τὸ Ἀλβανὸν ὄρος ἀναβαίνουσαι. Cf. IV 49, 3. Liv. XXI 63, 5. XXII 1, 6, etc.

[2] Liv. XXV 12, 1-2 : *Romae consules praetoresque usque (ad) ante diem quintum Kal. Maias Latinae tenuerunt. eo die perpetrato sacro in monte in suas quisque provincias proficiscuntur* (212 B.C.). XLII 35, 3 : *Quo maturius in provincias magistratus proficiscerentur, Latinae Kalendis Iuniis fuere : eoque sollemni perfecto C. Lucretius praetor . . . Brundisium est profectus* (171 B.C.). XLIV 21, 3 ; 22, 16 (168 B.C.).

[3] DH VIII 87, 6. Strab. V 3, 2 (C. 229). CIL I² p. 58. Inscr. It. XIII 1, 147. The consuls were accommodated in a house on the mountain, built for this purpose. Cass. Dio LIV 29, 7.

[4] *Fasti Capitol.* a. 257 a. Chr. n. (CIL I² p. 58. Inscr. It. XIII, 1, p. 43. : *dictator Latinarum feriarum caussa.*

[5] Liv. XLI 16, 1-2 (Lanuvium). CIL XIV 2231 = ILS 2990 = ILLRP 188 (official dedication of the Ardeates). Lucan., *Phars.* 3, 87 : *Quaque iter est Latiis ad summam fascibus Albam.* But it is obvious, too, that the people who came *e municipiis . . qui carnem Latinis petant* (Cic., *Pro Planc.* 9, 23) were no others than the local magistrates.

[6] Cic., *De div.* I 11, 18 (= *De cons. suo*, l. II).

once.[1] Even Caesar, personally free from superstitious inhibitions, when hastening to push through in eleven days the most urgent state business before beginning his operations against Pompey, found it necessary to perform the Latin Festival.[2] And no wonder: it was firmly believed that omissions of this kind in the past had brought terrible dangers.[3] For everything improperly done in connection with the *Latiar* its repetition was ordered by the senate.[4] All these precautions of the Roman state, which naturally were also exhibited to strengthen the allegiance of the Latins, testify to tribal coherence in historical times, reinforced by the religious prejudices just revealed.

During the *feriae Latinae* joyous celebrations were held everywhere in the cities of the Latins—though we are informed of them only in Rome.[5] Here, a chariot race was arranged on the Capitoline Hill, with a curious archaic ceremonial honor for the victorious charioteer.[6] Juppiter Latiaris was propitiated on that occasion in Rome with a human sacrifice.[7] These odd features attest the prehistoric origin

[1] Liv. V 17, 2 : *inventumque tandem est ubi neglectas caerimonias intermissumque sollemne di arguerent : nihil profecto aliud esse quam magistratus vitio creatos Latinas sacrumque in Albano monte non rite concepisse.*

[2] Caes., *B.c.* 3, 21.

[3] Liv. XXI 63, 5. Cass. Dio XLVI 33, 4-5. XLVII 40, 6. XLIX 16, 2.

[4] Details given by Chr. Werner, *op. cit.* 35 sq. A. Samter, RE 6, 2215, 46 sqq.

[5] Chr. Werner, *op. cit.* 35 sqq. A. Samter, *op. cit.* 2215, 46 sqq. The confront-ation of the Capitoline cult with the *Latiar*, made by G. Wissowa, RuK², 39 sqq., is erroneous ; the two cults were basically different, and no temple on the Alban hills existed in early times ; cf. G. Lugli, I Santuari celebri del Lazio antico, Roma 1932, 16 sqq.

[6] Plin., *N.h.* XXVII 7, 45-6 : *Absinthii genera plura sunt :... multoque Italicum amarius. ... herbae facillimae, ... praeterea sacris populi Romani celebratae peculiariter, siquidem Latinarum feriis quadrigae certant in Capitolio victorque absinthium bibit.* This was rejected by K. Latte, Römische Religionsgeschichte, München 1960, 146, n. 1. ; but we know that other games were held on the *area Capitolina* (cf. below, p. 327 sqq.), and so there is no reason to doubt the statement of Pliny. The drinking of the victorious charioteer recalls the soma-drink of the Vedic king after his symbolic chariot-race ; cf. G. Dumézil, R. Et. Lat. 36, 1958 (1959) 130 sqq., on a similar parallelism between the ritual of the *equus October* and the Indian *aśvamedha*. It is certainly a very archaic treat.

[7] Tertull., *Apol.* 9, 5 : *Ecce in illa religiosissima urbe Aeneadarum piorum est Iuppiter quidam, quem ludis suis humano sanguine proluunt. 'Sed bestiarii', inquitis.* Min. Fel. 30, 4. Cypr., *De spect. 3.* Tatian. 29. Firm. Mat., *De err.* 26, 2. Prudent., *Contra Symm.* 1, 396. Paulin. Nolan. c. 32, 109 sqq. Athanas., *Contra gentes* 25, 42 (Migne PGr 25, 50). Porphyr., *De abstin.* 2, 56. These data are dismissed as false inventions by H. J. Rose, Mnemos. 55, 1927, 273 and K. Latte, *op. cit.* 144 n. 3. But general considerations do not suffice to discard such a concrete evidence, at least in my opinion.

of the accompanying manifestations of the main festival, which was itself not more recent.

THE MEETINGS OF THE LATINS IN THE MEADOWS UNDER THE ALBAN MOUNTAIN

A reliable author reported that before 340 B.C. the envoys of the Latin states held their annual meetings regularly at the spring of the brook Ferentina at the foot of the Alban Mountain.[1] The exact site of this meeting place has not yet been discovered. However, G. De Sanctis has brought forward strong arguments for a localization to the south of the *Mons Albanus* where a depression of the *Via Appia* offered a favorable area to accommodate a large crowd.[2]

The ancients connected the gatherings held *ad caput aquae Ferentinae* with Romulus,[3] Tullus Hostilius,[4] Tarquinius Priscus,[5] and Superbus,[6] which means only that they were an old institution. The moderns take them either as a new Latin League in its own right or connect them with the League reshaped under the leadership of Aricia at the end of the sixth century B.C. Neither suggestion is quite correct.

If these meetings belonged to a new, individual confederation, the cult of the goddess Ferentina would have become a federal worship and would doubtlessly have been preserved carefully as such after

---

[1] Cincius *op*. Festus, p. 276, 19 sqq. L. : *Alba deinde diruta usque ad P. Decium Murem consulem populos Latinos ad caput Ferentinae, quod est sub monte Albano, consulere solitos, et imperium communi consilio administrare.*

[2] G. De Sanctis, St. d. R. 2¹, 1907,91 = 2², 86 n. 1, supported by Liv. II 38, 1 : *praegressus . . . ad caput Ferentinum, ut quisque venerit, primores eorum excipiens . . . et eos ipsos sedulo audientes . . . et per eos multitudinem aliam in subiectum viae campum deduxit,* the *via* in question being the *Appia* heading towards the Volscian territory. Other opinions are to be found in J. Beloch, Der italische Bund unter Roms Hegemonie, Leipzig 1880, 187, 193. H. Nissen, It. Lk. II 2, 558. K. J. Beloch, RG 1926, 182, 185, 186. H. Last, CAH 7, 1928, 405, 487 sq. G. Lugli, I santuari celebri del Lazio antico, Roma 1932, 25. C. Daicoviciu, Ephemeris Dacoromana 4, 1930, 37 sqq. A. N. Sherwin-White, R. Citiz. 12 sqq. L. Pareti, St. d. R. 1, 1952, 234 sqq. G. Gianelli, La repubblica romana² 1955, 24, 157, etc.

[3] Plut., *Rom*. 24, 2 (after the murder of Titus Tatius in Lavinium) καὶ καθαρμοῖς ὁ ʽΡωμύλος ἥγνισε τὰς πόλεις, οὕς ἔτι νῦν ἱστοροῦσιν ἐπὶ τῆς Φερεντίνης π(ηγ)ῆς (mss. : πύλης, emended by Cluver) συντελεῖσθαι.

[4] Fest., p. 276, 17 sqq. L., quoted above in n. 1. DH III 34, 3.

[5] DH III 51, 3.

[6] DH IV 45, 3. Liv. I 50, 1 ; 51, 9 ; 52, 5.

the political eclipse of the supposed special organization, as were all the other federal cults of the ancient past. But this did not happen. The ritual performed here, known from a cursory mention in a legendary context, had nothing to do with the *nomen Latinum*: it may have been only an annalist invention.[1] Though there must have been a sacred grove around the spring,[2] no religious celebrations of the League are referred to in the accounts of the reunions *ad caput Ferentinae*, which speak only of the concentration of armies there,[3] of markets and political meetings.[4] We might suppose, with Mommsen, that the army had congregated there already in very early times when the religious duties of the Latin assemblies were performed at other places. The geographical situation of the *caput Aquae Ferentinae* speaks against such an early date, however; it corresponds rather to that of a postern gate on the arterial road leading toward the Volscians, the wars with whom belong to the fifth century B.C. and not to the regal age. The same date can be established by a consideration of the political conventions held there. The leading statesmen of the Latins, electing their functionaries, deciding on peace and war, and on diplomacy, had no need of extensive fields to provide room for their reunions. It cannot be doubted that as long as the old centers —Alba, Lavinium, Aricia, Tusculum—had the leadership, political consultations were held in their own territories along with the religious performances. So the role of the *caput Ferentinae* could have started only when they declined and when they were reduced *ad sacra*, i.e., after the birth of the Republic. In that epoch filled by Volscian

---

[1] Plut., *Rom.* 24, 2, quoted above, 34, n. 3.

[2] Liv. I 50, 1 : *ad lucum Ferentinae*, as also I 52, 5, and VII 25, 5. Plut., *Rom.* 24, 2.

[3] Liv. I 52, 5 (under King Superbus) : *indictumque iunioribus Latinorum, ut ex foedere die certa ad lucum Ferentinae armati frequentes adessent.* In truth, this was the given place for uniting the Latin contingents only when preparing war against the Volscians, i.e., from the early fifth century on.

[4] Dionysius uses always the word ἀγορά, "market," for the political conventions of the national leagues. Cf. DH III 34, 3 : αἱ δὲ τῶν Λατίνων πόλεις ἰδίᾳ μὲν οὐδὲν ἀπεκρίναντο πρὸς τοὺς πρέσβεις, κοινῇ δὲ τοῦ ἔθνους ἀγορὰν ἐν Φερεντίνῳ ποιησάμενοι ψηφίζονται μὴ παραχωρεῖν Ῥωμαίοις τῆς ἀρχῆς καὶ αὐτίκα αἱροῦνται δύο στρατηγοὺς αὐτοκράτορας εἰρήνης τε καὶ πολέμου. III 51, 3 : Οἱ λοιποὶ Λατῖνοι . . . εἰς τὴν ἐν Φερεντίνῳ συνελθόντες ἀγορὰν ἐψηφίσαντο κτλ. IV 45, 3 : προεῖπε δι'ἀγγέλων ἥκειν εἰς τὴν ἐν Φερεντίνῳ γενομένην ἀγορὰν τοὺς εἰωθότας ὑπὲρ τοῦ κοινοῦ τῶν Λατίνων συνεδρεύειν. IV 45, 5 : οἱ πρόεδροι τῶν Λατίνων are present. V 50, 2. 3. 4 ; 61, 1. Cincius in Festus, p. 276, 17 sqq. Liv. I 50, 1. VII 25, 5 : *concilia populorum Latinorum ad lucum Ferentinae habita* (349 B.C.). Cf. VIII 14, 10.

wars, when Rome (as we shall see), though already thrusting into prominence but still far from the hegemony of Latium, was nothing more than an important member-state of the confederation, the political center of the League was shifted to that neutral area, the *lucus Ferentinae*, which also had become the habitual starting-point for offensive operations of the Latin federal army.

We must assume that the meetings at the *caput aquae Ferentinae* were regularly summoned on the eve of spring coinciding, as before, with the time of the common sacrifices of the Latins on the Alban Mountain or with those in Lavinium, and separated from them only geographically. This severance of the religious and the profane parts of the tribal gatherings is a basically new stage of the historical evolution. Instead of the primary role of emotional factors, political and juridical considerations motivate the League from now on.

℘

CONSTITUTION AND MANAGEMENT OF THE LATIN LEAGUE

When the Latins immigrated in Latium the basis of their common existence was the natural cohesion of a related human group. Custom, habit, and relative strength coordinated their common existence, not written alliances. Hereafter, when tribal units all over the country put down roots in their respective geographical sites, their new, individual existence was due to a factual growth rather than to a constitutional development. Still later, when these settlements became urbanized centers, Latium was subjected to the Etruscans, who could hardly concede to the Latin cities a full political autonomy. But the Etruscan League at least exhibited a prototype for future developments in Latium. As in Etruria, individual freedom of action of the member-states was conspicuous in Latium in the period from 505 to 338 B.C. As in Etruria, local wars between the Latin states were the order of the day, along with special treaties between them.[1] Also in Latium the participation of a city in a concerted action of the League depended on the actual decision of every one of them.[2]

Even the annual executive officers of the Latin confederation were

[1] Mommsen, St. R. 3, 615, and below, p. 121, 377 sqq.
[2] E.g., Liv. VII 27, 5.

not chosen by the League but given to the cities in rotation. They were elected by the local authorities of the city next in turn, who also legalized their choice by exploring the will of the gods by *auspicium and augurium*, the ritual bird-watching of Etruscan type; finally, they were recognized as legitimate leaders by the *acclamatio* of the federal army,[1] in the same way that early Roman (and certainly also other Latin) magistrates were appointed by their predecessors, confirmed by *auspicium*, and acknowledged as lawful leaders by the gentile assembly *comitia curiata* of the citizenry. A modification of this rotation-system was introduced when the League got two praetors as annual leaders instead of the previous one-man management, because the two principals were taken from different cities.[2]

The organization of the League in the epoch in which the *lucus Ferentinae* was its meetingplace reflects the same sort of governmental body and officials as those of the individual cities. Besides her executive magistrate(s), the League was directed by a federal council (*concilium Latinorum*), which met in every year[3] but could be summoned any time when an important decision had to be taken.[4] The members of this council were leading aristocrats of the Latin states.[5] Theoretically every unit of the *nomen Latinum* was supposed

[1] Cincius in Fest., p. 276, 17 sqq. L., and below, p. 119 sqq. In contrast with the reliable statement of Cincius, DH V 50, 2 writes : καὶ γένεται κοινὴ τῶν συναγομένων εἰς Φερεντῖνον ἀγορά . . ., ἐν ᾗ ψῆφον ἐνεγκεῖν ἔδει τὰς πόλεις . . . καὶ στρατηγοὺς ἀποδεῖξαι κτλ. If historical, this could only concern the decision on which city should give the exicutive.

[2] DH III 34, 3 (The collegiality reprojected in the time of Tullus Hostilius, but the *modus procedendi* certainly authentic) : καὶ αὐτίκα αἱροῦνται δύο στρατηγοὺς αὐτοκράτορας εἰρήνης τε καὶ πολέμου,"Αγκον Ποπλίκιον ἐκ πόλεως Κόρας καὶ Σπούσιον Οὐεκίλιον ἐκ Λαουϊνίου. A similar anachronism, but valid as a pattern of the subsequent period is the statement in DH V 61, 3, that Octavius Mamilius of Tusculum and Sextus Tarquinius of Gabii were elected as leading officers of the League. In 340 B.C. the two chiefs of the League are L. Annius from Setia and L. Numisius from Circei.

[3] Liv. I 50, 2 ; 51, 8 ; III 2, 3 ; VI 10, 7. VII 25, 5. VIII 3, 2. 10 ; 14, 10. DH III 34, 3 ; 51, 3. IV 45, 3 ; 46, 1 ; 48, 3. V 50, 2 ; 61, 1. Plut., *Rom.* 24, 2. Fest., p. 276, 20 L.

[4] DH V 50, 4 : γεγραμμένον ἐν ταῖς συνθήκαις ἁπάσας παρεῖναι τὰς πόλεις ταῖς κοιναῖς ἀγοραῖς, ὅσαι τοῦ Λατίνων εἰσὶ γένους, παραγγειλάντων αὐταῖς τῶν προέδρων.

[5] *Principes Latinorum* (Liv. VIII 3, 2. 8), *Latinorum proceres* (Liv. I 45, 2 ; 50, 1), *primores populorum* (Liv. I 51, 4), *capita nominis Latini* (Liv. I 52, 4). The *decem principes Latinorum* summoned by the Roman senate to appear before him may be historical for the last years of the existence of the League ; but this may be an anachronistic invention ; cf. Brandis, RE 4, 2254 sq.

to join the League and be present at its sessions;[1] in practice, however, powerful cities separated themselves from the League and became rivals.

The *concilium* assembled at the *Lucus Ferentinae* decided upon vital matters of common interest and, above all, on war and peace.[2] In this concern, and in this one only, the League interfered in the period between 505 and 338 B.C. with the sovereign rights of her member-states. As Mommsen[3] observed, the recruitment and composition of the federal army was based on a common system of assessment of property (*census*), prescribed by the League. This is manifest from the parallelism between the methods of assessment in Rome before the segregation of the censorial office from the normal magistrature on one side, and the procedure valid in the cities with a "Latin" status until much later times. This timocratic base, we must add, is nothing else than the so-called Servian constitution, which consequently is not a specifically Roman but a federal institution, a coordination vitally important for the organization and mobilization of the federal army in an epoch when the nation could survive only by such a concentration of its forces. The broad horizon and political wisdom of the Latin parliament is palpable for us in the systematic build-up of a network of federal colonies in the epoch of the Volscian wars, discussed in Chapter VIII.[4]

Some remnants of the federal legislation, passed in all likelihood in the fifth century B.C., demonstrate the superior significance of the League above the individual city-states in that epoch. The *ius exilii* proves that the Latin federal territory had a precise circumscription, like the overall area occupied by the Twelve Cities of Etruria. The *ius sedis mutandae* attests that in the period in question there was a sort of federal citizenship. The basic rights of all the Latins, the *conubium* and the *commercium*, illustrate the equality of the juridical position of all the Latins, Rome included. Some comments on these basic notions must be added.

The privilege of every Latin man to change his domicile inside

---

[1] Cf. DH V 50, 4 (quoted above 34, n. 4).

[2] Cincius, cf. Festus 276, 20 sqq. L. : . . . *usque ad P. Decium Murem consulem populos Latinos ad caput Ferentinae, quod est sub monte Albano, consulere solitos, et imperium communi consilio administrare.* Cf. also the passages of Dionysius and Livy quoted above 35, n. 4.

[3] Mommsen, St. R. 3, 615.

[4] Cf. below, p. 392 sqq.

Latium at will (*ius sedis mutandae*) will be revealed in the course of our inquiry as the main obstacle for a free man of Latin origin to accept Roman citizenship voluntarily before 338 B.C.: we shall see in the account of events that the freedom to choose which Latin city one wished to live in still meant much more than "to become a Roman." [1]

How the basic Latin rights could be perverted when their original political foundations collapsed is conspicuous in the case of the *ius exilii*, which was originally anything rather than "exile." [2] The possibility offered by the *ius sedis mutandae* was open, of course, to persons who were forced to leave their home-city for political reasons, or were striving to escape from punishment. This opportunity is one of the roots of the provision of the federal legislation. In such an eventuality the *ius sedis mutandae* enabled any Latin, endangered at home, to settle without harm in another Latin city and with undiminished rights. But the *ius exilii* also had roots in federal criminal legislation. "An old and venerable legal custom of the Latin tribe," as Mommsen put it,[3] "prescribed that nobody should be enslaved in the state where he was a free citizen. If he was to lose his freedom and citizenship as a punishment, he could become a slave only somewhere outside his place of origin. This rule was now extended to the whole territory of the *nomen Latinum*: no former citizen of a Latin state could be enslaved inside the federal boundary. An application of this prescription was inserted in the Twelve Tables [451 B.C., an important *terminus ante quem* for the federal law, preceding the Roman legislation] viz. that the insolvent debtor could be sold by the creditor only beyond the Tiber, i.e. outside the federal territory; another application of it is the clause of the second treaty between Rome and Carthage [343 B.C.] that a Latin ally of Rome, taken prisoner by Carthaginians, must regain his freedom when going ashore in a Roman harbour."

Common privileges of all the Latins were originally also the right to

---

[1] The latest study on this topic is : C. Castello, Il cosidetto ius migrandi dei Latini a Roma, in : Bull. dell' Ist. di diritto romano 61-62, 1958, 209 sqq. G. Tibiletti, Athen., n.s. 28, 1950, 213 sqq. Cf. Mommsen, St. R. 3, 367 sq. J. Binder, Die Plebs 356 sq. H. Kornhardt, SDHJ 19, 1953, 4 sqq.

[2] A recent study on this subject is that of G. Crifò, Ricerche sull' "exilium" nel periodo repubblicano, parte prima (Fondazione G. Castelli 32), Milano 1961, which contains the references to the ancient evidence and to its modern evaluations. We differ from this valuable work in an essential point, maintaining that the *exilium* was originally not a Roman, but a Latin federal institution.

[3] Mommsen, RG 1⁷, 102 sqq.

conclude legally valid business transactions (*ius commercii*) [1] and legal marriages (*ius conubii*) [2] between individuals of different Latin states.

After the disintegration of the tribal organization, when feuds between individual groups became endemic, the main opportunities for Latins of different provenance to conclude business were the tribal festivals, which still continued. The armistice on these days enabled even foreign merchants [3] to make commerce with the assembled Latin people. We have no knowledge of the process whereby business relations between all the Latins were extended to the whole of a calendar year; nor do we know how and when the general validity of these normalized relations was restricted to the Latin tribesmen. But it is obvious that the juridical fixation of this *ius commercii* in Latium could be achieved only by a superior instance, and that this authority could not be other than the *concilium Latinorum*, meeting at the grove of Ferentina.

The *ius conubii* developed on the same lines. In the tribal period intermarriage between the different subdivisions was certainly controlled by superstitious prohibitions, sanctified by myth—as true of all peoples at the same stage of evolution. The legend of the rape of the Sabine women attests that the two-clan system, which connected the Quirinal with the Palatine, had the custom of exogamic intermarriage; this may reflect the structure once existent for all the

---

[1] B. G. Niebuhr, RG 2², 77. J. Beloch, Der italische Bund 153. G. De Sanctis, St. d. R. 1², 376 sq. Mommsen, St. R. 3, 628 sqq., 632 sq. P. De Francisci, Storia del diritto romano II 1, 1944, 11. A. N. Sherwin-White, R. Citiz. 14, 30 sq. E. Manni, Per la storia dei municipii fino alla guerra sociale, Roma 1947, 31 sqq. M. Kaser, Das römische Privatrecht (Handb. d. Altertumswiss.) München 1955, 27, 29 n. 17 (literature). F. De Martino, Storia della costituzione Romana 2, Napoli 1960, 65.

[2] A. Schwegler, RG 1, 453 sq., and the studies quoted in the last footnote ; further on : E. De Visscher, Jura 2, 1951, 140 sqq. *Idem*, Revue intern. d. droits de l'antiquité 1, 1952, 403 sqq., 411 sqq. E. Volterra, in : Studi in memoria di E. Albertario 2, Milano 1953, 347 sqq.

[3] Liv. IV 24, 2 : *cum renuntiatum a mercatoribus esset negata* (sc. ad fanum Voltumnae) *Veientibus auxilia*. VI 2, 2 : *hinc Etruriae principum ex omnibus populis coniurationem de bello ad fanum Voltumnae factam mercatores adferebant.* Liv. I 30, 5 : *Tullus* (rex) *ad Feroniae fanum mercatu frequenti negotiatores Romanos comprehensos querebatur.* DH III 32, 1 (in the *lucus Feroniae*) πολλοὶ δὲ χρηματιζόμενοι διὰ τὴν πανήγυριν ἔμποροι τε καὶ χειροτέχναι καὶ γεωργοί, ἀγοραί τε αὐτόθι λαμπρόταται ... ἐγίνοντο. As already noticed, Dionysius calls all the annual assemblies 'common markets' (κοινὴ ἀγορά). If the story in Liv. V 8, 2-3 should be authentic, it would illustrate a drastic change in the course of the fifth century B.C.

Latins.[1] After that the tribal unity was politically disrupted, inter-marriage between individuals of two different home-cities was still possible at the annual gatherings.[2] The marriage-form of the so-called *coëmptio*, closed as a sale-transaction, reaches back certainly to this epoch. In this respect, too, the transition to the practice of concluding such intermarriages throughout the year, as well as a legal codification instead of custom and habit, is palpable for us only in its final results. It seems, at least to me, that in 451 B.C., when the *conubium* between patricians and plebeians in Rome was severed by an enactment of the Twelve Tables, the regulation of the intermarriage of the Latins was already established by the League.[3]

In 338 B.C. when Rome dissolved the League, the former federal privileges of the Latins were restricted to Roman citizens. The parliament was abolished, the *commercium* and the *conubium* were granted only to those cities which were willing to bear the burden of the Roman citizenship, which was not so attractive then as it became later. An exception was made with the few states which were still strong enough to assert some sort of independence, such as Tibur and Praeneste, or were emotionally important enough for the nation to be treated with respect, such as Lavinium.[4]

---

[1] In my book on the oldest structure of the Roman state, now in preparation, I shall enlarge on this subject.

[2] Our source information is useful only in confirming the obvious fact that the *conubium* between Latin cities (including Rome) was untimely old. Cf. Diod. VIII 25, 4 (on Alba Longa and Rome) : οἱ δὲ δῆμοι πρὸς ἀλλήλους ἐπιγαμίας ἔχοντες καὶ φιλίαν. Strab. V 3, 4 (C 231) : Ἀλβανοὶ δὲ κατ᾽ ἀρχὰς μὲν ὡμονόουν τοῖς Ῥωμαίοις ὁμόγλωττοί τε ὄντες καὶ Λατῖνοι . . . ἐπιγαμίαι τε ἦσαν πρὸς ἀλλήλους καὶ ἱερὰ κοινὰ τὰ ἐν Ἄλβᾳ καὶ ἄλλα δίκαια πολιτικά. DH VI 1, 2 (497 B.C., before the battle at Lake Regillus) : ἐτύγχανον δὲ πολλαὶ πάνυ γυναῖκες εἰς τὰς ἀλλήλων πόλεις ἐκδεδομέναι καὶ διὰ τὸ συγγενὲς καὶ διὰ φιλίαν.

[3] A very different picture of the historical evolution, as sketched above, is given by Pl. Fraccaro, *Opusc.* 1, 1956, 104 sqq., whose generous person and splendid work I greatly admire : no wonder that so eminent a scholar was followed by many others. But the rich harvest of his devoted life remains unimpaired, even if the reader can be persuaded by our study that his concept of the oldest Roman history was not right.

[4] Liv. VIII 14, 2-10 : *relatum igitur de singulis* (sc. populis) *decretumque. Lanuvinis civitas data. . Aricini Nomentanique et Pedani eodem iure, quo Lanuvini, in civitatem accepti, Tusculanis servata civitas, quam habebant . . . in Veliternos . . . graviter saevitum . . in agrum senatorum coloni missi . . . et Antium nova colonia missa . . . Tiburtes Praenestinique agro multati . . . . ceteris Latinis populis conubia commerciaque et concilia inter se ademerunt.* Cf. Liv. IX 43, 23. Discussions of this passage are noted in J. Binder, Die Plebs, Leipzig 1909, 353 sqq. A. N. Sherwin-White, R. Citiz. 107, and elsewhere.

ॐ

THE EXECUTIVE ORGANS OF THE LATIN LEAGUE

It is a remarkable fact that the Latins were able to continue at least the usual religious celebrations of their tribal organization throughout the seventh and sixth centuries B.C., along with their annual gatherings on the Alban Mountain and in Lavinium, in spite of Etruscan domination, which held their country in its grip through most of these two centuries. The tribal structure thus was kept alive though the tribal kingship had no chance of survival under Etruscan rule; on the contrary, we must ascribe the eclipse of the royal seat of Alba Longa—a natural fortress in a governing position—and the establishment of a new center, Lavinium, in the plain, to the pressure of the new situation.

If the tribal organization worked under the Etruscans, it must have had some sort of an executive organization even if the activity of the persons in charge had not much to do with politics, but was restricted to the announcement of the *feriae Latinae* and to the performance of the federal sacrifices. We know that a federal functionary of this type existed in Etruria, which could be adapted to a similar role in Latium. The chief magistrate of the Etruscan League was not only the *praetor* but also the *sacerdos Etruriae*, the chief priest of the confederation.[1] We also know that the executive of the Latin League who consecrated the federal grove of Diana at Aricia was called originally not *dictator*, but *dicator Latinus*,[2] again an official with religious duties. So we are entitled to assume that the annual leader of the Latin League was created under the Etruscan domination in imitation of the *sacerdos Etruriae*.[3] At the very moment when the Latin League regained her freedom of action in the last decade of the sixth century, the *dicator-dictator* of the Latin League could take up political and military functions in the same way as the *sacerdos-praetor* of the Etruscans.[4]

[1] Liv. V 1, 5 (403 B.C., speaking of the man who afterwards became the last king of Veii) : *cum ob iram repulsae, quod suffragio duodecim populorum alius sacerdos ei praelatus esset*, etc.

[2] Cato, *Orig.* fr. 58 (H. R. Rel. 1², p. 72 Peter) ; cf. H. Rudolph, Stadt und Staat im römischen Italien, Leipzig 1935, 12 sq. Against the interpretation of Rudolph cf. the studies quoted below in n. 4 and our discussion p. 53 sqq. A linguistic analysis of the word *dictator* is given by G. B. Philipp, in : Gymnasium 66, 1959, 97 sqq.

[3] Cf. A. Rosenberg, Der Staat der alten Italiker, Berlin 1913, 66 sq.

[4] Mommsen, St. R. 3, 618 sq., denied this, because he misinterpreted the

Executive Organs of the Latin League

The priority of the federal dictatorship being established, the dictature in individual Latin cities [1] can only be a copy of the federal one. Likewise, it is a reasonable supposition that in Rome also, when the Republican magistracy started around 504 B.C., the first pairs of names of the *fasti* were in fact not those of two consuls but those of an annual *dictator* and of his *magister equitum*; in other words, the extraordinary office of the Roman dictators of later times is only a subsequent stage of evolution, presupposing the existence of the normal office of an annual *dictator*.[2]

The archaic name of the Roman dictator was *magister populi*, i.e., he was the master of the *populus*, of the totality of the Romans, including the aristocracy.[3] His powers were unrestricted and undifferentiated in an immediate continuation of the regal powers. That his office was older than all the rest of the Roman functionaries is demonstrated by the fact that the employment of the others was called cumulatively *magistratus*, derived from the term of the *magister*

statement of Cincius in Festus, p. 276, 17 sqq. L. Cf. A. Rosenberg, *op. cit.* 65, 69 sq., 80 sqq. E. Kornemann, Klio 14, 1915, 196 sqq. The discussion of this problem was intensified by the acute reasonings of H. Rudolph, *op. cit.* 11 sq ; cf. G. De Sanctis, Scritti in onore di B. Nogara, Città del Vaticano 1937, 147 sqq. F. Altheim, Römische Geschichte 2, Frankfurt 1953, 414 sq. (who erroneously speaks of the collegiality of the Latin dictators). S. Mazzarino, Dalla mon. 157, 189 sqq., 203 sq., 261 n. 164 (with further quotations). A. N. Sherwin-White, R. Citiz. 59 sqq.

[1] K. J. Beloch, Der italische Bund unter Roms Hegemonie, Leipzig 1880, 130. *Idem*, RG 1926, 230 sqq. W. Liebenam, Städteverwaltung im römischen Kaiserreiche, Leipzig 1900, 254. *Idem*, RE 5, 388 sqq. J. Marquardt, St. V. 1², 1881, 148. Mommsen, St. R. 2, 170 sqq. A. Rosenberg, *op. cit.* 71 sqq. H. Rudolph, *op. cit.* 7 sqq. M. Gelzer, RE 12, 944 sqq. A. N. Sherwin-White, R. Citiz. 59 sqq. E. Manni, Per la storia dei municipii fino alla guerra sociale, Roma 1947, 93 sqq.

[2] W. Ihne, Forschungen auf dem Gebiet der römischen Verfassungsgeschichte, Frankfurt/M. 1847, 42 sqq. A. Schwegler, RG 2, 92 sq. G. De Sanctis, St. d. R. 1¹, 1907, 421 sqq. 2¹, 1907, 96 sqq. A. Rosenberg, *op. cit.* 77-79. E. Kornemann, Klio 14, 1915, 190 sqq. K. J. Beloch, RG 230 sqq. Pl. Fraccaro, Rivista di filol. class. n.s. 6, 1928, 551 sqq. A. Momigliano, Bull. Com. 58, 1930 (1931) 29 sqq. W. Soltau, Hermes 49, 1914, 357 sqq. More juridical literature is given by U. v. Lübtow, Das römische Volk, Frankfurt 1955, 166 sqq. A. Bernardi, Athen., n.s. 30, 1952, 3 sqq. (The 12 *fasces* are not earlier, I am sure, than the fourth century B.C., and their duplication for extraordinary dictatorship could only follow the twice 12 *fasces* of the consuls). U. Kahrstedt, Symb. Osl. 30, 1953, 69 sqq. D. Cohen, Mnemosyne 4. ser. 10, 1957, 300 sqq., would isolate the Roman dictatorship from the Latin one, a phenomenon *sui generis* that is impossible in my mind.

[3] R. Stark, Res publica, Diss. Göttingen 1937, 9 sqq., 12 sqq. P. De Francisci, *op. cit.* 599, 608 n. 251, 736 sqq.

(*populi*).[1] For the same reason, the appointment to the dictatorship was never bound to the previous holding of another office,[2] because it existed before the other offices were created. This is also reflected by the fact that only a dictator was entitled to drive the annual nail in the wall of the *cella Minervae* in the Capitoline temple,[3] no doubt because the annual dictator took over this duty after the flight of the last king. And superstition prohibited changing the qualification of the performer of this ritual act, also if in case of a plague the same magic ceremony was prescribed to nail down the disease.

An excellent scholar, followed by others,[4] has assumed that the Roman dictatorship started earlier, as a democratized form of the kingship. But we shall see that the Etruscan monarchy in Rome was interrupted again and again by violent changes: there was no peaceful evolution which could have produced such a temperate autocracy. The sovereign power of the dictator, the *imperium*, was, as we have seen, an unrestricted regal power, taken over ca. 504 B.C. by the 300 horsemen of the noblemen-bodyguard, who constituted then the patriciate, i.e., the closed circle of the potential holders of the *imperium*. This group monopolized from then on the royal privilege of the legalization of their acts by *augurium* and *auspicium*, ascertaining the approval of divinity.

The appointment of the federal dictator, as described by a learned antiquarian, was not quite the same as the *creatio* of the early magistrates of Rome by their predecessors.[5] After his designation, the *dictator Latinus* needed only the approval of the gods explored by the *augur*, as was the case with the Roman king, described in the investiture of Numa in Livy; after the consent of the divinity was established, he was presented to the federal army, whose acclamation validated his election in the same way as the acknowledgement of the creation of the Roman executives was approved originally by the cheering shouts of the *comitia curiata*.[6]

The powers of the federal dictator are barely mentioned in our

[1] *Contra* : J. Vogt, Die römische Republik[2], Tübingen 1951, 41.
[2] P. De Francisci, *op. cit.* 604, on the basis of Mommsen, St. R. 2[3], 145 sqq., 173.
[3] Cf. below, p. 78 sq. 167. 325. 351.
[4] S. Mazzarino, Dalla mon. 76 sqq., 86 sqq. J. Heurgon, Historia 6, 1957, 75 sqq. De Francisci, *op. cit.* 599 sqq.
[5] As my honored friend, P. De Francisci, *op. cit.* 600 sqq., assumed.
[6] A. Rosenberg, Hermes 54, 1919, 149.

sources but they certainly were of the same kind as those of the Roman executive. This is suggested by a number of parallels. The federal authority convoked the assembly,[1] as the Roman executive convoked the Senate. The triumphal procession of the victorious Roman general had the same Etruscan features as the procession of the federal high commander, paying his homage to Juppiter Latiaris, etc.[2]

We have no reference to the date at which the federal dictatorship was transformed to the collateral function of two *praetors*.[3] The same change must have already been achieved in Rome in the decade when the *Fabii* and the *Quinctii* were in power year by year, in the same way as the same two clans were entrusted by the state to preside jointly at the festival of the *Lupercalia*, or at any rate in the same epoch.[4] On the other hand, the normal dictature was continued much longer in other Latin cities, so that the date of change in the management of the League cannot be determined by such parallels.

The Latin League was prominent in the first century of the Republic. It saved the nation from subjugation by the mountain tribes, which conquered the southern part of Latium. Rome was then not yet the hegemonial power, though she was already beginning her

---

[1] DH V 50, 4.

[2] G. De Sanctis, St. d. R. 2¹, 1907, 100. G. Lugli, La via trionfale a Monte Cavo = Mem. Pont. Acc. R. di arch. 3. ser. 1, 1923, 251 sqq. Cf. the Roman imitations of the Latin triumph by Roman generals since 231 B.C. : *fasti triumphales* p. 79 Degrassi. The Praenestine cista published by A. Michaelis, Mon. ined. 10, 1876, 105 sqq., and reproduced, e.g., in Roscher's Lex. 2, 695 by Aust, is not a Latin triumph, as it is believed to be, but that of Aeneas. The standard in the hand of Ascanius with the sea-eagle on top is the badge of a city. Cf. E. J. Haeberlin, Aes grave, Frankfurt 1910, pl. 64, 4-5. I shall return to this problem elsewhere.

[3] When the Latins αἱροῦνται δύο στρατηγοὺς αὐτοκράτορας εἰρήνης τε καὶ πολέμου in DH III 34, 3, already under Tullus Hostilius, this is an evident anachronism ; the πρόεδροι τῶν Λατίνων in DH IV 45, 5, and the προεστηκότες τῶν Λατίνων DH V 52, 3, are certainly the two Latin federal praetors of later times. Cf. also DH V 61, 3 ; 76, 3 ; VI 2, 1 ; 4, 1 ; 5, 2. 3. 4. 5. Liv. VIII 3, 9. W. Ihne, RG 1, Leipzig 1868, 128 sq. Mommsen, St. R. 3, 617. A. Rosenberg, Der Staat der alten Italiker 77. K. J. Beloch, RG 188 sq. M. Gelzer, RE 12, 961 sqq. S. Mazzarino, Dalla mon. 168 sqq. L. Pareti, St. d. R. 1, 1952, 359. Pl. Fraccaro, Athen., n.s. 12, 1934, 54 sqq., has shown how the collegiality is reflected in the "Servian" constitution. But this timocratic system belongs to the fifth century B.C. in my conviction.

[4] We shall try to demonstrate in the book mentioned above (18 n. 1) that the *Lupercalia* were originally connected with the double kingship in pre-Etruscan Rome ; but the assignment of state cults to princely clans belongs to the fifth century B.C.

ascent in the League, being protected by the shield of the united Latins, until the time had come for her to take over the place for which she had matured under this protection. This evolution will be illustrated in all detail in the following chapters, each of which tries to examine its problems from a different angle.

Chapter II

AT THE CROSSROADS OF TRUTH AND FICTION: THE LAST DECADE OF THE SIXTH CENTURY IN LATIUM

THE REORGANIZED LATIN LEAGUE AGAINST PORSENNA, AND ITS CENTER IN ARICIA

In a recent study[1] I discussed the archaic statuary group reproduced on the reverse of the denarius struck by *P. Accoleius Lariscolus*, a scion of the local aristocracy of Aricia (pl. I, 1-2). His career in Rome, starting with the office of a *IIII vir monetalis* or of a *quaestor* in 43 B.C., he certainly owed to his clan's relations with Octavian. It has been demonstrated that the three divinities (the threefold unity of which

---

[1] A. Alföldi, AJA 64, 1960, 137 sqq. An important confirmation of my results came from E. Paribeni, AJA 65, 1961, 55 sqq. A much later representation of the same group of three divinities is to be found on a silver ring in the Benaki Museum at Athens ; B. Segall, Katalog der Goldschmiede-Arbeiten des Museum Benaki, Athens 1938, no. 157 with pl. 36. Another member of the same family appears on the inscription Année epigr. 1933, 391 no. 84 : *C. Iulio Roeme(talci) regi ... M. Acculeius M. f. Vol., amico bene merito f.c.*

is also expressed in a primitive way by the horizontal bar on their necks) represent Hecate, in the center, with the huntress Diana holding a bow, on her right, and (in all likelihood) the moon-goddess with a poppy in her hand on her left. This combination, we think, is not the result of the syncretism of religious ideas at the end of the Republic, but emerged in archaic Greece. The cypress grove behind the group is doubtless the famous *nemus Dianae* in Aricia, whose festival on August 13 was called in imperial times *Hecateides idus*. The Latin Diana, and specifically the Diana of Aricia, was also characterized as a three-fold unity by expressions such as *tria virginis ora Dianae*, and she was invoked as *tergemina Hecate, diva triformis, potens Trivia, Diana triplex*, i.e., she was the Greek Ἑκάτη τριοδῖτις.

The existence of this archaic image in Aricia—as we have indicated further on—may have been responsible for the late literary legend concerning its origin: Orestes brought it from Tauris, hence Diana's savage rites. Its real iconographical basis, reestablished by us in our inquiry, also points toward Greece; but the stylistic details reveal unmistakably that the original artist was an Etruscan. Especially important for the dating of the group is the hairdress of Diana-Hecate, which is clearly rendered on the obverse, but it is present also on the three goddesses of the reverse: the two rows of round curls, also framing the short hairs around the neck, never occur in this combination without hairplaits in Greek art. This special variety is, however, fairly frequent in the last phase of the archaic Etruscan sculpture and painting, from the very end of the sixth century B.C. on. This date proves to be very significant, as we shall see, and must therefore be kept in mind. This Greek trinity, reaching Latium by Etruscan mediation, must also have had an early *interpretatio Latina*: whereas the temple of the *Diana Nemorensis*, which much later replaced the cult under the open sky in the sacred grove, was mainly dedicated to the divine tutor of the female life, the *Diana triformis* in the archaic Latin religion seems to have been the heavenly protagonist of a warlike society of men, divided into three parts.

This statuary group owes its special historical interest to the fact that by a unique chance, the dedicatory inscription of the sacred grove where it was erected was preserved, or at least the most relevant part of it. This inscription, evidently set up in the holy precinct at the same time as the cult image, speaks of the establishment of a federal cult of Diana at Aricia—of a political act, involving heavy consequences for the fate of Latium as well as for Etruria and Campania. This famous inscription was preserved in the *Origines* of Cato, who copied it on the spot. His text has been transmitted by the grammarian Priscian,[1] who wrote out this passage twice with the same wording. It reads:

Cato Censorius ibidem (sc. *in II Originum*): *Lucum Dianium in nemore Aricino Egerius Baebius*[2] *Tusculanus dedicavit dictator*[3] *Latinus. hi populi communiter*: *Tusculanus, Aricinus, Lanuvinus, Laurens, Coranus, Tiburtis, Pometinus, Ardeatis Rutulus.*

A reminiscence of the text transmitted by Cato is also to be found in the quasi-scientific explanation of a proverb in Festus:[4] *Manius Egeri<us lucum> Nemorensem Dianae consecravit, a quo multi et clari viri orti sunt, et per multos annos fuerunt*; *unde proverbium 'Multi Mani Ariciae.'*

The date of the document, saved from oblivion by Cato, has often been discussed. One group of scholars has put it in the regal period of Rome, at the latest under Servius Tullius.[5] Others wished to

---

[1] H. R. Rel. 1[2], 72 frg. 58 (= Priscian. 4 p. 129 Hertz and 7, p. 337 Hertz).

[2] The mss. have : *Laebius* (H), *Lebius* (Par. R A(miens) B(ern), *Baebius*(S), *Bebius*(K), etc. F. Altheim, Italien und Rom[2], Frankfurt 1942, 415, prefers the reading *Laevius*, but S. Mazzarino, Dalla mon., 250 n., advocates with sound arguments *Baebius*.

[3] The codex R has *dicator* ; on this cf. below, p. 53.

[4] Fest., p. 128, 15 L. Cf. also Ps.-Acro, ad. Hor., *Serm.* II 3, 228. Flor. I 5, 8.

[5] H. Jordan, Die Könige im alten Italien, Berlin 1887, 46. But Mommsen, CIL I[2] p. 298 sqq., has already observed that Diana is not represented in the oldest cycle of festivals in the Roman calendar. This fact makes it impossible to date the Roman cult of Diana in the regal epoch and eliminates the combinations based on the invented annalist tale which claims the priority of Diana's sanctuary on the Aventine. A. Schwegler, RG 2, 291, bases his dating on the presence of Pometia. However, this city was not yet in the possession of the Volscians under the reign of Superbus, but only after the battle near the Lake Regillus. G. De Sanctis, St. d. R. 2[1], 104 sqq. H. Horn, Foederati, Diss. Frankfurt 1930, 90, thought that the foundation of a new federal cult was a revendication of the cult center of Diana for Aricia from the Aventine grove : we shall return to this point later (cf. p. 85 sqq.). A. Rosenberg, Hermes 54, 1919, 158 sq. stresses the absence of Signia from the list : but we do not think that this list is complete. A. N. Sherwin-White, R. Citiz., 12, supposes that Cato was dealing in the second book of the *Origines* only with the earliest history of Latium. But fr. 44 mentions the organization of the Celts in Italy. H. Last, CAH 7, 1928, 350, was fully aware of the date of Cato's document, but guesses that "if the precinct of Diana entered on a new period of its history as a federal center towards the beginning of the fifth century, it seems to have served this

advance this date, sometimes as far forward as the fourth century B.C.[1] Other scholars, however, were led to the conclusion that the composition of the allies best fits the political situation of Latium at the end of the sixth century.[2] The plausibility of this can be demonstrated through the account of the life of the Cymean tyrant Aristodemos the Effeminate, which sheds light on the chain of events that led the Latins to enter into that alliance. As will be shown later, we possess on this topic a Hellenistic version of the local chronicle of Cyme, which is prior to and independent of the Roman annalists, but was also used by them or rather by some of their Greek sources.[3] The relevant features of this tale, preserved in a digression of Dionysius of Halicarnassus (VII 3-11), are as follows: In the twentieth year after the Etruscan invaders were defeated by the Cymeans under the walls of their city in 524 B.C., envoys of Aricia arrived in Cyme asking for help against an Etruscan host which was besieging them. Aristodemus, the hero of the previous victory, had been sent by sea to assist the Aricians with a small Cymean force. He arrived

purpose before." Yet the *consecratio* of the grove clearly means a new start and we shall see that this was due to a special political situation. S. Mazzarino, Dalla mon. 156 sqq., dates this consecration in the year 524 or a little after it, owing to a chronological confusion of the events of 524 and 504 B.C. discussed below, p. 71 sq. G. Giannelli, La repubblica romana[2], Milano 1955, 188 n. 2, accepted the tradition that the Aventine cult of Diana was founded by Servius Tullius (against this cf. below, p. 85 sq.), but he also accepted the conclusions of Wissowa on the priority of Aricia over the Aventine. He tried to predate the former to the latter; his date for Aricia is far too high ("prima della metà del VI. sec."). A. Momigliano, Rendinc. Acc. Linc., cl. mor. 1962, 387 sqq., argues against Wissowa and the present writer unconvincingly.

[1] Ed. Meyer, G. d. A. 5, Stuttgart 1902, 137 (about 450 B.C.). A. Piganiol, La conquête romaine, Paris 1927, 124 (at the beginning of the fourth century). K. J. Beloch, RG, 187 sq. (389 B.C. or not much later). F. Schachermeyr, RE 4 A, 2365 (after the fall of the Tarquins).

[2] K. J. Beloch, Der italische Bund, Leipzig 1880, 179 sqq. G. De Sanctis, St. d. R. 2, 93. M. Gelzer, RE 12, 953 (whom we do not follow in the early date for the first treaty with Carthage, which mirrors, as we think, a completely different situation) with H.U. Instinsky, Klio 30, 1937, 12. Hugh Last, *loc. cit.* (cf. 49, n. 5 above), followed by A. E. Gordon, TAPA 63, 1932, 178. G. Giannelli, Trattato di storia romana 1, Roma 1953, 182, supposed a restoration of the Arician League about 500 B.C. A. Momigliano, Bull. Com. 58, 1930 (1931) 31. We are giving only some characteristic opinions of scholars and no exhaustive survey of the modern literature. Cf. also G. De Sanctis, St. d. R. 1[2], 409 sqq. G. Bloch, La république romaine, Paris 1913, 68. F. Schachermeyr, RE 4A, 2365, etc.

[3] Cf. below, p. 56 sqq., where all the relevant quotations are reproduced *in extenso*.

in good time and though the Aricians were pushed inside their walls in the ensuing battle, Aristodemus again killed the Etruscan commander-in-chief and gained an overwhelming victory, as in 524 B.C. If the date of the first battle is accepted—and nobody rejects it—it is a great mistake to reject the second, which is clearly based on the reliable account of the life of the tyrant of Cyme. Even the distorted late version of his biography clearly reveals, as do the annalists, that it was in his early youth that Aristodemus distinguished himself in the first battle and that he earned the second success in his mature manhood, at the height of his political career.

A great scholar and many others following his lead [1] thought that the second of these two dates was a result of a contamination of the Cymean chronology with that of Roman historiography. This supposition has no foundation at all.[2] Both dates are Cymean, both are to be accepted as historical.[3] The annalists also recounted those events, as we have already stated, shifting them back some years— apparently to bring them in some accord with the year of the inauguration of the Capitoline sanctuary, which is identified with the first year of the Republic. In the annalistic version the commander of the defeated Etruscan army was the son of King Porsenna, and we have no right to deny the historicity of these persons, or the approximate date of their successes and setbacks, to be discussed later on.[4]

This evidence clarifies the purpose of the renewal of the Latin federation to reorganize in a new center in the sacred grove of Aricia. The absence of Rome from that reorganized tribal league is not due

---

[1] G. De Sanctis, St. d. R. 1¹, 456 sq. Pl. Fraccaro, Opuscula 1, Pavia 1956, 13. G. Giannelli, La repubblica romana 1², 90 n. 28, 100 sqq. L. Pareti, St. d. R. 1, 314. H. Last, CAH 7, 1928, 395 sqq. (with some restrictions). A. E. Gordon, The Cults of Aricia, Berkeley 1934, 2. This theory seems to have been the starting point of the inadmissible hypothesis that Mastarna and Porsenna were the same. Cf. L. Pareti, St. Etr. 5, 1931, 154 sqq.

[2] In view of the fundamental importance of this question we treat it fully below, p. 56 sqq.

[3] The Roman chronology is in general inclined to advance by some few years the dates reckoned lower by the Greeks. Cf. O. Leuze, Die römische Jahrzählung, Tübingen 1909, 377 sq. E. Kornemann, Internationale Monatsschrift 14, 1920, 491. E. Pais, St. crit. 1, 1913, 371, gives correctly 504. A. Piganiol, La conquête romaine, Paris 1927, 67, sets the date in view to the annalist datings in the year 506, as does F. Altheim, Römische Geschichte 2, Frankfurt 1953, 104. Older views in Leuze, *op. cit.* 378.

[4] Cf. below, p. 64 sqq.

AT THE CROSSROADS OF TRUTH AND FICTION

to the effort of the Latins to shake off the yoke of Rome: [1] this yoke had not yet been imposed upon them.[2] Nor was this alliance a local religious confederation, as often supposed: the new alliance was due to an acute political crisis.[3] Rome was then in the hands of the king of Clusium, whose aggression also threatened the whole of Latium. The decision of the Latins to shift their religious and political center must have happened just after Porsenna captured Rome, and before the defeat of his army under the walls [4] of Aricia. Rome, only 26 kilometers north of Aricia, was the strategic base for those operations against the Latins.

Also the question of the number of Latin cities included in the Arician confederation, and of the number of those absent, depends not on local politics and local balance of power, but on a war situation. Cato's list of the participating cities is considered by the majority of historians [5] to be complete, but excellent scholars [6] agree with the present writer that the list is incomplete. The impression of completeness was enhanced by the exact repetition of it in Priscian. But even in our days, when an absent-minded scholar uses twice a quotation he mutilated when copying it, the repetition does not make it better. The confused fragments 25 and 141 of the *Origines* [7] show that Priscian's repetitions are based not on repeated inspections of original texts, but on his own excerpts. It is probable that he stopped copying

[1] As G. De Sanctis, *op. cit.* (above 49, n. 5) 2, 90, thought. J. Beloch, Der italische Bund 135, 186 sqq., 194 sqq., sought the reason for the absence of Rome in the misrepresentation of the annalists, who pretend that Rome stood outside and above the Latin League even before 338 B.C. This is incorrect. Cf. below, p. 53 sqq.

[2] Cf. below, p. 72 sqq.

[3] As S. Mazzarino, *op. cit.* (above 49, n. 2,) 156 sqq., realized it.

[4] The archeological evidence was studied by Gr. Florescu, Ephem. Dacorom. 3, 1925, 6 sqq.

[5] J. Beloch, Der italische Bund 179 sqq. E. Täubler, Imperium Romanum 1, 1913, 303 sqq. G. De Sanctis, *op. cit.* (above 49 n. 5) 92. Ed. Meyer, G. d. A. 5, 1902, 137. F. Altheim, Griechische Götter im alten Rom (Religionsgesch. Vers. u. Vorarb. 22, 1) 1930, 94, 98, 131 sqq. M. Gelzer, RE 12, 953. L. Pareti, *op. cit.* (above 51 n. 1) 1, 234.

[6] O. Seeck, Rh. Mus., n. f. 37, 1882, 15 sqq. K. J. Beloch, RG 1, 1926, 187 sqq. H. Dessau, CIL XIV p. 204. The document is also carefully analyzed by M. Zoeller, Latium und Rome, Leipzig 1878, 228 sq. Jahrbücher f. Philol. 127, 1883, 169 sqq. E. Pais, St. crit. 1, Roma 1913, 372 sq. T. Frank, An Economic History of Rome, Baltimore 1927, 45 sq. G. Wissowa, RuK², München 1912, 247 sq.

[7] Cf. the note of H. Peter in his edition of the H. R. Rel. (vol. 1², p. 63) on these extracts.

with *Ardeatis Rutulus* because he was interested only in the form of the adjective *Ardeatis*.[1] Furthermore, the Roman historians after Cato reported that all the Latins ὅσοι τοῦ Λατίνων μετεῖχον γένους,[2] rose against (Porsenna and) Rome. Livy,[3] having in mind the ancient Latin tribal confederation, the *populi Albanenses, carnem in monte Albano soliti accipere*,[4] expresses the same idea in his *triginta iam coniurasse populos*, the thirty peoples rising against Rome. The enumeration of these cities by Dionysius [5] in the same context is, of course, a late compilation—he gives 29 cities,[6] thus understanding the absence of Rome—but attesting to the opinion of the ancients that the whole of Latium, in so far as it was not taken by Porsenna, sided with Aricia. This is the confederation which was overcome by Rome—I think not without Etruscan backing—in the battle on Lake Regillus, Cicero's *Latini omnes* (Pro Balb. 23, 53). Also the dedicatory inscription means the League, the head of which was the *dictator Latinus*,[7] who represented the *nomen Latinum*.[8] It is true [9] that the best manuscript of Priscian reads not *dictator* but *dicator Latinus*; this, however, does not detract at all from the federal character of this official.[10] We can admit with S. Mazzarino that the original title was *dicator*, in the same way as the ζιλαϑ, the magistrate presiding over the Etruscan League, was translated in Latin first as *sacerdos*[11] and later as *praetor Etruriae*.

It may be mere chance that the *dictator* of the inscription Egerius Baebius comes from Tusculum, for the annual head of the League was chosen from all the cities, each in turn.[12] The prominence of

---

[1] As already observed by K. J. Beloch, RG 1, 187.

[2] DH V 61, 2.

[3] Liv. II 18, 3.

[4] Plin., *N.h.* III 5, 69. Cf. above, 10 sqq. 19 sqq.

[5] DH V 61, 3. Cf. O. Seeck, Rh. Mus., n.F. 37, 1887, 18 sqq. H. Nissen, It. Lk. II 2, 558 sqq., 590 sqq. G. De Sanctis, St. d. R. 2, 100 sqq.

[6] DH V 20, 2 : πλὴν μιᾶς τῆς ῾Ρωμαίων πόλεως ; cf. V 50, 4 : an involuntary confession of the fact that Rome was included in the original League and did not rule over it.

[7] In this sense, M. Gelzer, RE 12, 953. Cf. above, p. 42 sqq.

[8] Cf. C. G. Lorenz, *De dictatoribus Latinis ac municipalibus*, Progr. Grim. 1841, 24, 30 sqq.

[9] H. Rudolph, Stadt und Staat im römischen Italien 11 sqq.

[10] As recognized by H. U. Instinsky, Klio 30, 1937, 122. F. Altheim, RG 2, 1953, 415 sqq. S. Mazzarino, *op. cit.* (49 n. 5) 154 sqq., 250 sqq. Cf. also p. 42 above. On Egerius Baebius see F. Münzer, RE 5, 1981 sq. H. Dessau, CIL XIV p. 204.

[11] A. Rosenberg, Der Staat der alten Italiker 61 sqq.

[12] Cf. below, p. 119 sqq.

Tusculum in those days is stressed, however, by our literary sources.[1]
In any case the placing of the sanctuary on Arician territory was the
consequence of political ascendancy which had shifted from Alba
Longa and Lavinium.[2] The annalists, though they extol the leadership
of a Tusculan (king or general) in the Latin camp, stress equally
the primary role of Aricia in those days,[3] enhanced by the significant
victory of Aristodemus under her walls.[4] Of the other cities named in
the dedication, Lavinium, Ardea, Lanuvium, further on Cora and
Pometia behind Aricia, and finally Tusculum, as H. Last observes,
"lay in a continuous line round the frontiers of Roman territory
from a point near Ostia as far as Gabii." [5] He has seen also that the
ring would be broken and Tibur would be cut off if Praeneste with
Labici and Pedum were absent, and that there would be a gap between
the western boundaries of Tibur and the river if Nomentum and Crustumerium did not fill it. The situation of the highly important Praeneste, however, would be dangerous if it stood aloof. The interior
line of Etruscan communications with Campania, which runs via
Tiber-Anio-Tibur-Praeneste and through the valleys of the rivers
Tolerus and Liris, would be cut and Praeneste would be isolated from
the allies of Porsenna by Tibur if Praeneste were to take the side of the
king. The better choice for Praeneste was therefore to join Cyme with
the Arician alliance. And, in all probability, Praeneste belonged in
those years to the Latin League: Livy [6] has the notice under the year
499 B.C.: *Praeneste ab Latinis ad Romanos descivit*. Therefore we believe
she was in fact with the Latins until then, along with Labici and
Pedum [7] and with other cities which are more difficult to specify

---

[1] Cic., *Att.* IX 10, 3. *Idem, De nat. deor.* II 2, 6. DH IV 45, 1. 4; 47, 4. V
61, 1. 4-5 ; 62, 1 ; 76, 3. VI 2, 2 ; 4, 1 ; 5, 3 sqq. 11, 2-3 ; 12, 1. Liv. I 49, 9. II
19, 7 sqq. ; 20, 8-9 etc. Cf. G. McCracken, RE 7 A, 1464 sqq.

[2] Livy adds (I 45, 3) to a popular fable, told on the occasion of the transfer
of the federal cult-center to the Aventine, the remark : *ea erat confessio caput
rerum Romam esse* (details given below, p. 85 sqq). The same is true for Aricia.

[3] Liv. I 50, 1-52, 5. The person of Turnus Herdonius remains obscure (DH
IV 45, 4, says he was a native of Corioli), but the preponderance of Aricia
illustrated by it is historical. DH V 51, 1. 2 ; 61, 1. 2. 4-5 ; 62, 1. VI 21, 2.
Flor. I 5, 8.

[4] K. J. Beloch, Der italische Bund 187, thought that Aricia was the permanent center of the Latin League : this is certainly a misconception.

[5] H. Last, CAH 7, 1928, 488.

[6] Liv. II 19, 2.

[7] G. De Sanctis, St. d. R. 2, 92. *Ibid.* on *Velitrae*. On *Ardea* : M. Gelzer,
RE 12, 944.

individually than to indicate as a group. Dionysius mentions [1] particularly Antium with Cyme and Tusculum as allies of Aricia against Lars Arruns: the connivance of Antium surely made the landing of the Cymean craft easier.

Aricia did not long remain the focus of the Latin League; the balance of power in Latium soon shifted again, this time toward Rome, Praeneste, and Tibur.[2] In 495 B.C. the Romans defeated the Auruncans near Aricia.[3] If, as seems likely, the report is true, other Latin *populi* may have helped the Aricians too. But some decades later the Romans appear as masters over Aricia and its neighbor, Ardea,[4] turning the quarrel between the two to their own advantage. The sanctuary of *Diana Nemorensis* remained famous but its political significance vanished forever.[5]

The battle of Aricia in the last decade of the sixth century was, as often stated, a decisive blow to the Etruscan domination over Latium.[6] But did it really bring the end of the Etruscan domination? It is frequently overlooked that over the head of the Latins *two Etruscan groups* were fighting each other: the Tarquins and southernmost Etruria, siding with Cyme and the Arician alliance on one hand, and Porsenna, reconciled after his severe defeat with the captured Rome, on the other. The Campanian settlements of the Etruscan League had not yet been destroyed, and Etruscan bridgeheads across Latium were bitterly needed between them and the mother country. We must suppose that Rome was one of them. And is it not remarkable, as E. Gabrici [7] pointed out, that Aristodemus preferred a clandestine infiltration by sea with his army for the relief of Aricia, rather than risking a march across the country? This move seems to imply the presence of Etruscan or pro-Etruscan forces between his

[1] DH V 36, 1-4.

[2] T. J. Dunbabin, The Western Greeks, Oxford 1948, 344, is right in speaking of this as "a short-lived Latin alliance to resist Etruscan attempts at reconquest."

[3] Liv. II 26, 4-6. DH VI 32, 3.

[4] Liv. III 71, 1-5.

[5] H. Rudolph, *op. cit.* (above 53 n. 9) 14 n. 1, calls attention to official dedications of Latin colonies in the sanctuary of Diana at Nemi ; cf. CIL XIV 4269 (Ariminum) and CIL VI 133.

[6] E.g., Ed. Meyer, GdA 5, 1902, 122. W. Hoffmann, Rom und die griechische Welt im IV. Jahrhundert v. Chr. (Philol., Suppl. 27, 1) 1934, 1 sqq. L. Homo, L' Italie primitive, Paris 1925, 151 sqq. G. Giannelli, Trattato (above, 50 n. 2) 1, 161, 169 sq.

[7] E. Gàbrici, Mon. ant. 22, 1913, 580 sqq.

home city and the goal of his expedition. One generation later, in 474 B.C., the Etruscans made a similar move, turning round Latium by sea for the attack on Cyme—evidently because in the meantime they had lost their Latin allies.

The blow at Aricia was hard but it was the overture to the independence of Latium rather than the sudden liberation of the Latins from their Etruscan overlords.

℘

THE CHRONICLE OF CYME AND THE ROMAN HISTORIOGRAPHY

Anyone reading with care the first books of Dionysius and Livy is struck by the lack of a sound geographical foundation in the account of events under the kings. This geographical basis was already missing in the historical works on which the narrative of these Augustan writers is based. Except for a few old Latin settlements close to Rome, even the scarce geographical data of the regal epoch belong to pseudo-history, as will be set forth in the next chapters of our investigation.[1] Nothing can be more sure, consequently, than the fact that the Greek city of Cyme lay far outside the narrow horizon of the pontifical annals which was restricted to the vicinity, and also that the oral tradition or written family records of the aristocratic clans at the disposal of Fabius Pictor and his followers contained no information on the history of that Campanian city. The question, therefore, is how the biography of the Cymean tyrant Aristodemus the "Effeminate" came to be inserted into the historical accounts of the Late Roman Republic.

The existence of a local chronicle of Cyme was recently denied by the eminent philologist F. Jacoby.[2] He incorporated in his great collection only such fragments as contained the name of a local author. The anonymous ones were omitted. This is a questionable departure, because forged names of such writers occur—as Jacoby himself was well aware—and fragments not bearing the name of their original author can have derived from such a local source. Jacoby

---

[1] Cf. p. 101 sqq. 135 sqq.
[2] F. Gr. Hist. I B no. 576 (p. 678 sq. with the commentary, p. 606 sqq., and the footnotes, pp. 333 and 352 sqq.).

incorporated three allegedly Cymean fragments in his great work: the first referring to the degenerate delicacy and wantonness of the Cymeans, the second to the Sibyl of Cyme, and the third to the Greek origin of the Romans. We reproduce their text in the original because their wording enables the reader at once to form a judgment on their data and character. They are:

fr. 576, 1 : καὶ Κυμαῖοι δὲ οἱ ἐν ᾿Ιταλίᾳ ὥς φησιν ῾Υπέροχος ἢ ὁ ποιήσας τὰ εἰς αὐτὸν ἀναφερόμενα Κυμαϊκά, διετέλεσαν χρυσοφοροῦντες καὶ ἀνθιναῖς ἐσθῆσι χρώμενοι καὶ μετὰ γυναικῶν εἰς τοὺς ἀγροὺς ἐξιόντες ἐπὶ ζευγῶν ὀχούμενοι. (Athen., Deiphnosoph. 12, 37, p. 528 D-E).

fr. 576, 2 : Τὴν δὲ ἐπὶ ταύτῃ χρησμοὺς κατὰ ταὐτὰ εἰπούσαν ἐκ Κύμης τῆς ἐν ᾿Οπικοῖς εἶναι, καλεῖσθαι δὲ Δημὼ συνέγραψεν ῾Υπέροχος ἀνὴρ Κυμαῖος. χρησμὸν δὲ οἱ Κυμαῖοι τῆς γυναικὸς ταύτης ἐς οὐδένα εἶχον ἐπιδείξασθαι, λίθου δὲ ὑδρίαν ἐν ᾿Απόλλωνος ἱερῷ δεικνύουσιν οὐ μεγάλην, τῆς Σιβύλλης ἐνταῦθα κεῖσθαι φάμενοι τὰ ὀστᾶ. (Pausan. X 12, 8).

fr. 576, 3: <*Hyperochos*> *historiae Cumanae compositor Athenis quosdam profectos Sicyonem Thespiasque; ex quibus porro civitatibus, ob inopiam domiciliorum, conpluris profectos in exteras regiones, delatos in Italiam, eosque multo errore nominatos Aborigines; quorum subiecti qui fuerint* † *caeximparum* † *viri, unicarumque virium imperio montem Palatium, in quo frequentissimi consederint appellavisse a viribus regentis Valentiam: quod nomen adventu Euandri Aeneaeque in Italiam cum magna Graece loquentium copia interpretatum, dici coeptum Rhomen* (Fest., p. 328, 5 Linds.).

On the basis of such fragments attributed to "Hyperochos" Jacoby [1] establishes the fact that this Cymean author flourished later than has been believed: his dubious name and the character of the first quotation show that, in this case we are dealing not with an old chronicle of Cyme, whose free existence ended in 421 / 20 B.C., but with a literary product in the style of Amelesagoras and Cephalon, a work which tried to win authority through the suggested antiquity of the Apollinic name of Hyperochos. Jacoby sees his judgment reinforced by the contents of the fragments. The Sibyl of Cyme is the last in the series of these legendary prophetesses. The *Aborigines* and the Arca-

[1] *Op. cit.* (56 n. 2) 607.

dians, and the explanation of the name of 'Ρώμη as the translation of an original *Valentia* suggest some knowledge of the Latin language and they prove that the work was intended for the Roman public. The Romans are the focus of interest; over and above their Trojan and Arcadian forefathers, their origin is also embellished by Attic ancestors—conceived in the same way as the descendence of Tarquinius Priscus from the Corinthian noble Demaratos, which was already known to Polybius from the early annalists.

Though these penetrating remarks of Jacoby reveal some important facts, the verdict of this illustrious scholar is weakened by his disregard of all the other Cymean data transmitted without an author's name; all these anonymous fragments concern the life and character of the tyrant Aristodemus the "Effeminate" and can have had their source only in the Cymean tradition.

From the same source as "Hyperochos" came another story, also describing the debilitating luxury of the Cymeans, which tells of the heroic Xenokrite, mistress of Aristodemus and helper of his slayers, which is found in Plutarch's *De mulierum virtutibus* (ch. 26). The tyrant is said to have deliberately encouraged effeminacy in the Cymean boys: he had them wear long hair and golden ornaments, and at the same time he compelled the girls to cut their hair and to wear boys' clothes and a short undergarment. In this passage also the salient feature is the absence of real historical details, though the knowledge of them is manifest in the picture of Aristodemus, his hair long like a child's, making himself conspicuous by his valor and his forethought in (unidentified) "wars against the barbarians." And as in the reliable version of the abridged biography (DH VII 3-11) the second great opportunity for Aristodemus to distinguish himself comes twenty years after his first great exploits, so in the Xenokrite episode of Plutarch the first exploits of Aristodemus in war are achieved on the eve of manhood, and his second great victory is earned when he is at the peak of his career. What is relevant for the writer is the picturesque, sensational, and piquant tale of the τρυφή of the tyrant, who pays with a dreadful end for his happy years of ruthless autocracy. This conception, so lively in Athens in the days of the Persian menace as mirrored in classical tragedy,[1] became in this novel in Plutarch a

---

[1] Cf. my sketch in: Late Classical and Mediaeval Studies in Honor of A. M. Friend, Jr., Princeton 1955, 15 sqq.

frivolous tale—of course a tale extremely popular to the readers of the age of Hellenism.[1]

This total suppression of historical details in exchange for fanciful stories, characteristic also of "Hyperochos," is not the original version of the Κυμαικά: the comparison with the incomparably more valuable story of the life of Aristodemus, inserted in the seventh book of Dionysius of Halicarnassus, will make this evident at the first glance. The version used by Athenaeus and Plutarch had already been influenced by the Roman annalists: in the Xenokrite chapter of Plutarch, Aristodemus is sent not to assist the Latins, but to help the Romans; the Etruscans do not attack the Latins in Aricia, but are trying to bring back the Tarquins to Rome. As we shall see in the next chapter, this is based on an illogical presumption of the annalists, who begin the description of the attack of Porsenna with the false assertion that he was incited by the Tarquins to make war, but abandoned their cause, siding with Rome. They can motivate this illogical turn of events only by the miraculous effect of Roman *virtus* on the conqueror, which led him to drop Superbus, his alleged protégé. The fact that Cyme was with the Latins against Porsenna and harbored their ally the Roman king, pleads strongly against such a volte-face on the part of the king of Clusium, by whom expelled Superbus took refuge in the south.

Furthermore, we know that the annalists also exploited the Κυμαικά. They mention the intervention of Aristodemus in the following contexts:

1) Aristodemus defeats the Etruscans besieging Aricia: Liv. II 14, 5-9 (508 B.C.): *Omisso Romano bello Porsinna, ne frustra in ea loca exercitus adductus videretur, cum parte copiarum filium Arruntem Ariciam oppugnatum mittit. Primo Aricinos res necopinata perculerat; arcessita deinde auxilia et a Latinis populis et a Cumis tantum spei fecere ut acie decernere auderent. Proelio inito, adeo impetu se intulerunt Etrusci ut funderent ipso incursu Aricinos; Cumanae cohortes arte adversus vim usae declinavere paululum, effuseque praelatos hostes conversis signis ab tergo adortae sunt. Ita in medio prope iam victores caesi Etrusci. Pars perexigua, duce amisso, quia nullum propius perfugium erat, Romam inermes et fortuna et specie supplicum delati sunt. Ibi benigne excepti divisique in hospitia. Curatis volneribus,*

---

[1] A brilliant survey of this topic is given by H. Herter in the *Reallexikon für Antike und Christentum* (s.v. *effeminatio*), Stuttgart 1959, 620.

ali profecti domos, nuntii hospitalium beneficiorum; *multos Romae hospitium urbisque caritas tenuit*: *hic locus ad habitandum datus, quem deinde Tuscum vicum appellarunt.*

Dion. Hal. V 36, 1-4 (506 B.C.):

Οἱ δὲ τὸν τέταρτον ἐνιαυτὸν ἄρξαντες ὕπατοι Σπόριος Λάρκιος καὶ Τίτος Ἑρμίνιος ἄνευ πολέμου τὴν ἀρχὴν διετέλεσαν. ἐπὶ τούτων ῎Αρρονς ὁ Πορσίνου τοῦ Τυρρηνῶν βασιλέως υἱὸς τὴν ᾿Αρικηνῶν πόλιν δεύτερον ἔτος ἤδη πολιορκῶν ἐτελεύτησεν. εὐθὺς γὰρ ἅμα τῷ γενέσθαι τὰς Ῥωμαίων σπονδὰς τὴν ἡμίσειαν τῆς στρατιᾶς μοῖραν παρὰ τοῦ πατρὸς λαβὼν ἐστράτευσεν ἐπὶ τοὺς ᾿Αρικηνοὺς ἰδίαν κατασκευαζόμενος ἀρχὴν καὶ μικροῦ δεήσας τὴν πόλιν ἑλεῖν, ἐλθούσης τοῖς ᾿Αρικηνοῖς ἐπικουρίας ἔκ τε ᾿Αντίου καὶ Τύσκλου καὶ τῆς Καμπανίδος Κύμης. παραταξάμενος ἐλάττονι δυνάμει πρὸς μείζονα τοὺς μὲν ἄλλους ἐτρέψατο καὶ μέχρι τῆς πόλεως ἤλασεν, ὑπὸ δὲ Κυμαίων, οὓς ἦγεν ᾿Αριστόδημος ὁ Μαλακὸς ἐπικαλούμενος, νικηθεὶς ἀποθνήσκει, καὶ ἡ στρατιὰ τῶν Τυρρηνῶν μετὰ τὴν ἐκείνου τελευτὴν οὐκέτι ὑπομείνασα τρέπεται πρὸς φυγήν. πολλοὶ μὲν δὴ αὐτῶν διωκόμενοι ὑπὸ τῶν Κυμαίων διεφθάρησαν, ἄλλοι δὲ πλείους σκεδασθέντες ἀνὰ τὴν χώραν εἰς τοὺς ἀγροὺς τῶν Ῥωμαίων οὐ πολὺ ἀπέχοντας κατέφυγον ὅπλα τ᾿ἀπολωλεκότες καὶ ὑπὸ τραυμάτων ἀδύνατοι ὄντες προσωτέρω χωρεῖν. οὓς ἐκ τῶν ἀγρῶν οἱ Ῥωμαῖοι κατακομίζοντες εἰς τὴν πόλιν ἁμάξαις τε καὶ ἀπήναις καὶ τοῖς ἄλλοις ὑποζυγίοις ἡμιθνῆτας ἐνίους, καὶ φέροντες εἰς τὰς ἑαυτῶν οἰκίας τροφαῖς τε καὶ θεραπείαις καὶ ταῖς ἄλλαις φιλανθρωπίαις πολὺ τὸ συμπαθὲς ἐχούσαις ἀνελάμβανον. ὥστε πολλοὺς αὐτῶν ταῖς χάρισι ταύταις ὑπαχθέντας μηκέτι τῆς οἴκαδε ἀφίξεως πόθον ἔχειν, ἀλλὰ παρὰ τοῖς εὐεργέταις σφῶν βούλεσθαι καταμένειν. οἷς ἔδωκεν ἡ βουλὴ χῶρον τῆς πόλεως, ἔνθα οἰκήσεις ἔμελλον κατασκευάσασθαι, τὸν μεταξὺ τοῦ τε Παλατίου καὶ τοῦ Καπιτωλίου τέτταρσι μάλιστα μηκυνόμενον σταδίοις αὐλῶνα, ὃς καὶ μέχρις ἐμοῦ Τυρρηνῶν οἴκησις ὑπὸ Ῥωμαίων καλεῖται κατὰ τὴν ἐπιχώριον διάλεκτον. . . .

2) Tarquinius Superbus found a last refuge with Aristodemus: Cic., *Tusc.* III 12, 27: *Tarquinio vero quid imprudentius, qui bellum gereret cum iis, qui eius non tulerant superbiam? Is cum restitui in regnum nec Veientium nec Latinorum armis potuisset, Cumas contulisse se dicitur inque ea urbe senio et aegritudine esse confectus.* Liv. II 21, 5 (495 B.C.): *Insignis hic annus est nuntio Tarquini mortis. Mortuus Cumis, quo se post fractas opes Latinorum ad Aristodemum tyrannum contulerat.*

Dion. Hal. VI 21, 3: Ταρκύνιος δ'ὁ βασιλεύς . . . οὔτε Λατίνων

Cyme and the Roman Historiography

ὑποδεχομένων αὐτὸν ἔτι ταῖς πόλεσιν, ... εἰς τὴν Καμπανίδα Κύμην
ᾤχετο πρὸς Ἀριστόδημον τὸν ἐπικληθέντα Μαλακὸν τυρρανοῦντα τότε
Κυμαίων. παρ'ᾧ βραχύν τινα ἡμερῶν ἀριθμὸν ἐπιβιοὺς ἀποθνήσκει
καὶ θάπτεται ὑπ αὐτοῦ. τῶν δὲ σὺν ἐκείνῳ φυγάδων οἱ μὲν ἐν τῇ Κύμῃ
κατέμειναν, οἱ δὲ εἰς ἄλλας τινὰς πόλεις σκεδασθέντες ἐπὶ ξένης τὸν
βίον κατέστρεψαν. Cf. also VIII 64, 2 and *De viris ill.* 8, 6.

3) Rome stricken by famine in 492 b.c., tries in vain to obtain
corn in Cyme:

Livy II 34, 3-5: *Ventumque ad interitum servitiorum utique et plebis
esset, ni consules providissent, dimissis passim ad frumentum sectandum, non
in Etruriam modo dextris ab Ostia litoribus laevoque per Volscos mari
usque ad Cumas, sed in Siciliam quoque: adeo finitimorum odia longinquis
coegerant indigere auxiliis. Frumentum Cumis cum coemptum esset, naves pro
bonis Tarquiniorum ab Aristodemo tyranno, qui heres erat, retentae sunt;
in Volscis Pomptinoque ne emi quidem potuit: periculum quoque ab impetu
hominum ipsis frumentatoribus fuit; ex Tuscis frumentum Tiberi venit: eo
sustentata est plebs.* Dion. Hal. VII 1, 3 : ταῦθ'ἡ βουλὴ μαθοῦσα πρέσβεις
διεπέμπετο πρὸς Τυρρηνοὺς καὶ Καμπανοὺς καὶ τὸ καλούμενον Πωμεντῖνον πεδίον σῖτον ὅσον ἂν δύναιντο πλεῖστον ὠνησομένους. 2, 1-4 :
Οἱ μὲν οὖν ἐπὶ Σικελίας πλέοντες πρέσβεις ... μετὰ θέρος ἐπανῆλθον
εἰς Ἰταλίαν πολλὰς κομίζοντες ἀγοράς. οἱ δ'εἰς τὸ Πωμεντῖνον ἀποστα-
λέντες πεδίον ὀλίγου μὲν ἐδέησαν ὡς κατάσκοποι πρὸς τῶν Οὐλούσκων
ἀναιρεθῆναι διαβληθέντες ὑπὸ τῶν ἐκ Ῥώμης φυγάδων, χαλεπῶς δὲ
πάνυ διὰ τὴν προθυμίαν τῶν ἰδιοξένων αὐτὰ διασῶσαι δυνηθέντες τὰ
σώματα, δίχα τῶν χρημάτων ἀνέστρεψαν εἰς τὴν Ῥώμην ἄπρακτοι.
ὅμοια δὲ τούτοις συνέβη παθεῖν καὶ τοῖς εἰς τὴν Ἰταλιῶτιν ἀφικομένοις
Κύμην. καὶ γὰρ αὐτόθι πολλοὶ Ῥωμαίων διατρίβοντες, οἱ σὺν τῷ βασιλεῖ
Ταρκυνίῳ διασωθέντες ἐκ τῆς τελευταίας μάχης φυγάδες, τὸ μὲν πρῶτον
ἐξαιτεῖσθαι παρὰ τοῦ τυράννου τοὺς ἄνδρας ἐπεχείρησαν ἐπὶ θανάτῳ,
ἀποτυχόντες δὲ τούτου ῥύσια κατασχεῖν ταῦτα τὰ σώματα παρὰ τῆς
ἀπεσταλκυίας πόλεως ἠξίουν, ἕως ἀπολάβωσι τὰς ἑαυτῶν οὐσίας, ἃς
ἔφασαν ὑπὸ Ῥωμαίων ἀδίκως δεδημεῦσθαι, καὶ ταύτης ᾤοντο δεῖν τῆς
δίκης τὸν τύραννον αὐτοῖς γενέσθαι κριτήν. ὁ δὲ τυραννῶν τότε τῆς
Κύμης Ἀριστόδημος ἦν ὁ Ἀριστοκράτους, κτλ. (The next sentences
on the origin of the nickname correspond to Plutarch, *De mulier.
virt.* 26) 12, 1-3 : Ἐπὶ δὲ τοῦτον δὴ τὸν Ἀριστόδημον ἔτος ὁμοῦ τι
τεσσαρεσκαιδέκατον ἤδη τυραννοῦντα Κύμης οἱ σὺν Ταρκυνίῳ φυγάδες
καθιστάμενοι τὴν κατὰ τῆς πατρίδος ἐβούλοντο συντελέσασθαι δίκην.

AT THE CROSSROADS OF TRUTH AND FICTION

οἱ δὲ πρέσβεις τῶν Ῥωμαίων τέως μὲν ἀντέλεγον, ὡς οὔτ'ἐπὶ τοῦτον ἥκοντες τὸν ἀγῶνα οὔτ'ἐξουσίαν ἔχοντες, ... ὡς δ'οὐθὲν ἐπέραινον, ἀλλ' ἐγκεκλικότα τὸν τύραννον ἑώρων ἐπὶ θάτερα μέρη διὰ τὰς σπουδὰς καὶ τὰς παρακλήσεις τῶν φυγάδων, αἰτησάμενοι χρόνον εἰς ἀπολογίαν, καὶ διεγγυήσαντες τὰ σώματα χρημάτων ἐν τῷ διὰ μέσου τῆς δίκης οὐθενὸς ἔτι φυλάττοντος αὐτοὺς ἀποδράντες ᾤχοντο. θεράποντας δ'αὐτῶν καὶ τὰ ὑποζύγια καὶ τὰ ἐπὶ τῇ σιτωνίᾳ κομισθέντα χρήματα ὁ τύραννος κατέσχε. ταύταις μὲν οὖν ταῖς πρεσβείαις τοιαῦτα παθούσαις ἀπράκτοις ἀναστρέψαι συνέβη, ἐκ δὲ τῶν ἐν Τυρρηνίᾳ πόλεων οἱ πεμφθέντες κέγχρους τε καὶ ζέας συνωνησάμενοι ταῖς ποταμηγοῖς σκάφαις κατεκόμισαν εἰς τὴν πόλιν. αὕτη βραχύν τινα χρόνον ἡ ἀγορὰ Ῥωμαίους διέθρεψεν. (Cf. also Plut., *Poplic.* 3, 1-2).

As has long been recognized, the more concise Livy and the loquacious Dionysius have drawn from the same annalist sources. A. Klotz [1], for instance, considered Tubero to be their common source. But it is unlikely that the latter was the first to exploit the Cymean chronicle. On the other hand, the Xenokrite story of Plutarch is post-annalistic; it distorts the role of Aristodemus, making him an ally of the Roman Republic instead of the Tarquins; and as the three fragments of "Hyperochos" admitted by F. Jacoby are void of almost all factual content known to the Roman historians, they cannot derive from the source of the annalists. The use of the real Cymean history is more apparent in the latter than in the "Hyperochos" of F. Jacoby.

A third version of these events stands much nearer to the original Cymean source than either the author of the romantic Κυμαικά or the contamination of the Cymean information on Aristodemus with the meager stuff of the Roman annalists. This oldest variation is preserved in the aforesaid digression of Dionysius. Fortunately enough, this report of the spectacular rise and tragic eclipse of the tyrant was inserted into the annalistic account of the Roman history by Dionysius in such a careless way that the beginning and end of it, as well as the extent and style of the foreign substance included, can be immediately perceived. This was realized long ago by W. Christ, who made the following points: [2] Dionysius describes (VII 2 and 12) in more detail the aggressiveness of the exiles against the Roman

[1] A. Klotz, Livius und seine Vorgänger (Neue Wege zur Antike 2, 11) 1941, 218 sqq., esp. 234.
[2] W. Christ, SBBayrAK, phil.-hist. Kl. 1905, 62 sqq.

envoys than does Livy;[1] on the other hand, Dionysius does not mention the seizure of the cargo ships. But his narrative corresponds on the whole with Livy's. His report on these events begins in the second chapter of book VII and is continued only after an interval in the twelfth chapter (so that chapter 12 takes up the narrative exactly where chapter 2 broke off). Between the two is interpolated the biography of Aristodemus (VII 3-11). Dionysius himself draws the attention to and apologizes for his long diversion (VII 2, 5). It becomes evident at the first glance that this narrative of the fate of the tyrant, though rich in relevant details, has no bearing on Roman history. It is clear that it cannot have been taken from the Roman sources of Dionysius. The text copied by Dionysius was Greek [2] and his consultation of Greek sources is evident in his blame of Macer, Gellius, and the other Roman annalists (VII 1, 4-6) for their neglect of the Greek historical literature οὐκέτι μὴν παρὰ τῶν Ἑλληνικῶν ἐξετάσαι συγγραφέων—manifestly in the proud feeling that he himself is able to do so.

There is no trace of the presumptuous but empty loquacity of the rhetor of Halicarnassus in this interlude, the smoothly running, attractive style of which gives a sample of true Hellenistic narrative art. The cruelty of the tyrant is not yet submerged in the horrors of later stories and the conventional picture of the tyrant, and the account of his attempt to spoil the youth through luxury (VII 9, 3), though exaggerated, are still not extravagant. The Cymean origin of this tale is obvious. It contains precious data even if colored by local pride: the size of the first invading Etruscan army is enormously exaggerated to enhance the brilliance of the Cymean success in defeating it with a tiny contingent (VII 3, 2); on the other hand, the size of the relieving force sent with Aristodemus against the Etruscans besieging Aricia is reduced to a minimum, to underline again the splendor of the victory over such a huge host (VII 5, 3). The protest of the rivers near Cyme, miraculously reversing themselves (VII 3, 2-3) to show the indignation of their gods against the invaders, certainly mirrors popular Cymean tale.

The memory of the greatness of Cyme and the satisfaction of the reestablished aristocrats permeates this recital. The colorful report of sudden upheavals and sensational changes in the city, lifting

---

[1] Cf. the quotations above, p. 61 sq.
[2] W. Christ, *op. cit.* (above 62 n. 2) 69.

AT THE CROSSROADS OF TRUTH AND FICTION

Aristodemus to the highest peak of human success and then plunging him into the abyss of misfortune has the flavor of Alexandrine art. Yet it is conspicuous by a total indifference to Roman affairs: the world around and north of Cyme is that of the barbarians.

Eduard Meyer recognized long ago [1] that this account is based ultimately on a local chronicle of Cyme; but I am convinced he misjudged the reliability of the time element in it and the high importance of the essential data. The report concerning the history of Latium runs as follows:

VII 3, 1. "In the sixty-fourth Olympiad, when Miltiades was the archon at Athens, the Tyrrhenians who had inhabited the country lying near the Ionian gulf, but had been driven from thence in the course of time by the Gauls, joined themselves to the Umbrians, Daunians, and many other barbarians, and undertook to overthrow Cyme, the Greek city in the country of the Opicans founded by Eretrians and Chalcidians, though they could allege no other just ground for their animosity than the prosperity of the city [2]. For Cyme was at that time celebrated throughout all Italy for its riches, power, and all the other advantages, as it possessed the most fertile part of the Campanian plain and was mistress of the most convenient havens round about Misenum. The barbarians, accordingly, forming designs upon these advantages, marched against this city with an

[1] Ed. Meyer, GdA 2², 809 ; he reviles this report quite undeservedly, but I feel obliged to reproduce his verdict : "Der eingehende Bericht bei Dion. Hal. VII 3-12 ist so elend, dass die Annahme, er stamme aus Timaeus, wahrscheinlich erscheinen könnte ; aber die Motivierung des Etruskerzuges durch den Kelteneinfall können wir ihm doch nicht zutrauen. Eher kann die verwandte, aber nicht identische Erzählung bei Plut., virt. mulier. 26 mit der albernen Etymologie aus Timaeus stammen : auch Diod. VII fr. 10 ist wohl Timaeus. Die ursprüngliche Grundlage bildet eine einheimische Chronik wie die Κυμαϊκά des Hyperochus (FHG IV 434) ; aber die Erzählung ist in unseren Quellen so arg entstellt, dass sie nur mit schweren Bedenken benutzt werden kann." W. Christ, op. cit. 122 sq., thinks the story by DH VII 3-11 was transmitted from the Cymean tradition by Diocles of Peparethos, which is a mere guess like the thought of Ed. Meyer on Timaeus. E. Ciaceri, Storia della Magna Grecia 2, Milano-Roma-Napoli 1927, 272 n. 1, joins Ed. Meyer in referring the tale to Hyperochos, as do others. The independence of the Cymean evidence from the Roman historiography is also underlined in a short statement by Ernst Meyer, Mus. Helv. 9, 1952, 180. The story of Aristodemus by Diodorus VII fr. 10 may have derived from the same work as preserved by Dionysius VII 3-11, in so far as it is possible to form a judgment from the meager extract. W. Christ, op. cit. 65 sqq., connects directly DH VII 3-11 with Plut., De mulier. virt. 26, which cannot be accepted.

army consisting of no less than 500,000 foot and 18,000 horse. While they lay encamped not far from the city, a remarkable prodigy appeared to them, the like of which is not recorded as ever having happened anywhere in either the Greek or the barbarian world. 3. The rivers namely, which ran near their camp, one of which is called the Volturnus, and the other the Glanis, leaving their natural channels, turned their streams backwards and for a long time continued to run up from their mouths towards their sources. 4. The Cymeans, being informed of this prodigy, were then at least encouraged to engage with the barbarians, in the assurance that Heaven designed to bring low the lofty eminence of their foes and to raise their own fortunes, which seemed at low ebb. And having divided all their youth into three bodies, with one of these they defended the city, with another they guarded their ships, and the third they drew up before the walls to await the enemy's attack. These consisted of 600 horse and 4.500 foot. And so few in number, they sustained the attack of so many myriads.

4, 1. When the barbarians learned that they were ready to fight, they uttered their war-cry and came to close quarters, in the barbarian fashion, without any order, the horse and foot intermingled, in the expectation of utterly annihilating them. The place before the city where they engaged was a narrow defile surrounded by mountains and lakes, a terrain favourable to the valour of the Cymeans and unfavourable to the multitude of the barbarians. 2. For they were knocked down and trampled upon by one another in many parts of the field, but particularly around the marshy edges of the lake, so that the greater part of them were destroyed by their own forces without even engaging in the battle line of the Greeks. Thus their huge army of foot defeated itself, and without performing any brave action dispersed and fled in every direction. The horse, however, engaged and gave the Greeks great trouble; yet being unable to surround their enemies by reason of the narrow space, and Heaven also rendering the Greeks some assistance with lightning, rain and thunder, they were seized with fear and turned to flight. 3. In this action all the Cymean horse fought brilliantly, and they were allowed to have been the chief cause of the victory: but Aristodemus, nicknamed 'Malakos' distinguished himself above all the rest, for he alone sustained the attack of the enemy and slew their general as well as many other brave men. When the war was at an end, the Cymeans had offered sacrifices to the gods in thanksgiving for their victory and had given a splendid burial to those who had been slain in the battle, they fell however, into great strife concerning the prize for valour, disputing to whom they ought to award the first crown. 4. For the impartial judges wished to bestow this honour upon Aristodemus, and the people were all on his side. But the men in power desired to confer it upon Hippomedon, the commander of the horse, and the whole council championed his cause. The Cymeans were governed at that time by an aristocracy, and the people were not in control of many matters. And when a sedition arose because of this strife, the older men, fearing, that the rivalry might proceed to arms and bloodshed, prevailed on both parties to consent that each of the men should receive equal honours. 5. From this beginning Aristodemus became a champion of the people, and having cultivated proficiency in political oratory, he seduced the mob by his harangues, improved their condition by popular measures, exposed the powerful men who were appropriating the public property, and relieved many of the poor with his own money. By this means he became both odious and formidable to the leading men of the aristocracy.

5, 1. In the twentieth year after the engagement with the barbarians, ambassadors from the Aricians came to the Cymeans with the tokens of suppliants to beg their assistance against the Tyrrhenians who were making war upon them. For, as related in an earlier book, Porsenna, king of the Tyrrhenians, after making peace with Rome, had sent out his son Arruns with one half of the army when the youth desired to acquire a dominion for himself. Arruns then, at the time in question was besieging the Aricians, whom he had forced to take refuge inside their walls, and he expected to capture the city soon by famine. 2. When this embassy arrived, the leading men of the aristo-cracy, who hated Aristodemus and feared he might do some harm to the established government, thought they had got a very fine opportunity to get rid of him under a specious pretence. They accordingly persuaded the people to send 2,000 men to the aid of the Aricians and appointed Aristodemus as general, ostensibly because of his brilliant military achievments; after which they took such measures as they supposed would result in his either being destroyed by the Tyrrhenians or perishing at sea. 3. For being empowered by the Council to raise the forces that were to be sent as auxiliaries, they enrolled no men of distinction or reputation, but choosing out the poorest and the most unprincipled of the common people from whom they were under continual apprehension of some uprisings, they made up out of these the complement of men who were to be sent upon the expedition. And launching ten old ships that were most unseaworthy and were commanded by the poorest of the Cymeans, they embarked the forces on board of these ships, threatening with death anyone who would fail to enlist.

6, 1. Aristodemus, merely remarking that he was not ignorant of the purpose of his enemies, namely, that in word they were sending him to the assistance of the Aricians, but in fact to manifest destruction, accepted the command, and hastily setting sail with the ambassadors of the Aricians, and accomplishing the voyage over the intervening sea with great difficulty and danger, came to anchor at points along the coast nearest to Aricia. And leaving a sufficient number of men on board to guard the ships, on the first night he made the march, which was not a long one, from the sea to the city, and appeared unexpectedly to the inhabitants at dawn. 2. Then, encamping near the city and persuading the citizens who had fled for refuge inside the walls, to come out into the open, he promptly challenged the Tyrrhenians to battle. And a sharp engagement ensuing, the Aricians after a very short resistance all gave way and fled inside the walls. But Aristodemus with a small body of chosen Cymeans sustained the united shock of the enemy, and having slain the general of the Tyrrhenians with his own hand, put the rest to flight and gained the most glorious victory."

To make the evaluation of this priceless piece of evidence easier for the reader, we reproduce it below in Greek. The original text clearly illustrates the "tragic" style of Hellenistic historiography,[1] in which it was conceived, with a richly embroidered picture of unheard-of features; with unexpected, sudden shifts in the fortune of the hero, trampled down by Tyche after he indulged in effrenate luxury and criminal cruelty at the peak of his power. The original wording also shows, moreover, that this baroque writing was not yet obfuscated by the epidemic growth of school declamation: it is an early, still unbiased example of its genre.

F. Jacoby,[2] who passionately denied the Cymean provenience of

[1] B. L. Ulmann, TAPA 73, 1942, 25 sqq. F. W. Walbank, Cl. Q. 39, 1945, 8 sqq., and below, p. 150 sqq.

[2] F. Gr. Hist. 3 B vol. of notes to the commentary 1955, 333 n. 325 (against J. Geffcken and W. Schur).

AT THE CROSSROADS OF TRUTH AND FICTION

this account, was manifestly preoccupied with the literary form, and was of course justified in that this text is anything but a dry chronicle in the version just under discussion. In its present shape it is rather a novel, possibly extracted by Dionysius from Timaeus, whose inclination for the sensational *mise en scène*, and theatrical exploitation of the superstitious awe of his contemporaries and of the impressive painting of gorgeous luxury, was severely censored by Polybius;[1] the more so, as Timaeus was indeed used as a source by Dionysius.[2] But whether this account is borrowed from him or from another historical work of the same epoch, it is based on the local tradition of Cyme.[3] We can simply disregard at this time the exact definition of the literary form of that ultimate Cymean source, lost forever, because only the facts contained in its preserved Hellenistic adaptation are relevant for us. The text of the original Greek version runs as follows:

VII 3, 1-6, 2 : Ἐπὶ τῆς ἑξηκοστῆς καὶ τετάρτης ὀλυμπιάδος ἄρχοντος Ἀθήνησι Μιλτιάδου Κύμην τὴν ἐν Ὀπικοῖς Ἑλληνίδα πόλιν, ἣν Ἐρετριοῖς τε καὶ Χαλκιδεῖς ἔκτισαν, Τυρρηνῶν οἱ περὶ τὸν Ἰόνιον κόλπον κατοικοῦντες ἐκεῖθέν, θ' ὑπὸ τῶν Κελτῶν ἐξελασθέντες σὺν χρόνῳ, καὶ σὺν αὐτοῖς Ὀμβρικοί τε καὶ Δαύνιοι καὶ συχνοὶ τῶν ἄλλων βαρβάρων ἐπεχείρησαν ἀνελεῖν οὐδεμίαν ἔχοντες εἰπεῖν πρόφασιν τοῦ μίσους δικαίαν ὅτι μὴ τὴν εὐδαιμονίαν τῆς πόλεως. ἣν γὰρ Κύμη κατ'ἐκείνους τοὺς χρόνους περιβόητος ἀνὰ τὴν Ἰταλίαν ὅλην πλούτου τε καὶ δυνάμεως ἕνεκα καὶ τῶν ἄλλων ἀγαθῶν γῆν τε κατέχουσα τῆς Καμπανῶν πεδιάδος τὴν πολυκαρποτάτην καὶ λιμένων κρατοῦσα τῶν περὶ Μισηνὸν ἐπικαιροτάτων. τούτοις ἐπιβουλεύσαντες τοῖς ἀγαθοῖς οἱ βάρβαροι στρατεύουσιν ἐπ'αὐτήν, πεζοὶ μὲν οὐκ ἐλάττους πεντήκοντα μυριάδων, ἱππεῖς δὲ δυεῖν χιλιάδων

[1] Polyb. XII 24, 1-6. Cf. the excellent sketch of the Athenian spiritual life about 300 B.C. as a background of Timaeus' work in the study of A. Momigliano, Rivista storica ital. 71, 1959, 529 sqq., 545 sq.

[2] E. Gabba, Athen., n.s., 38, 1960, 183 (against F. Jacoby). Cf. also G. De Sanctis, Rivista di filol. 63 (n.s. 13) 1935, 297 sqq. A. Klotz, Rh. Mus. 87, 1938, 35 sq. The early date of the Celtic migration in this excursus is based on the same ultimate literary source as Liv. V 33, 5 ; 34, 1. Cf. G. A. Mansuelli, CRAI 1960 (1961) 80 sqq. F. Jacoby, F. Gr. Hist. 1 F 58, Komm. H. Homeyer, Historia 9, 1960, 349 sq.

[3] F. Jacoby, F. Gr. Hist. 3 B Kommentar 606, goes much too far in denying the existence of such local chronicles with the statement that the Κροτονιατῶν ὑπομνήματα in Iamblichus, *Vita Pyth.* 262 and the Τυρίων ὑπομνήματα in Timaeus, F. Gr. Hist. 566 F 7, were official documents found in archives and no historical accounts.

Cyme and the Roman Historiography

ἀποδέοντες εἶναι δισμύριοι. ἐστρατοπεδευκόσι δ'αὐτοῖς οὐ μακρὰν ἀπὸ τῆς πόλεως τέρας γίνεται θαυμαστόν, οἷον ἐν οὐδενὶ χρόνῳ μνημονεύεται γενόμενον οὔθ᾽ Ἑλλάδος οὔτε βαρβάρου γῆς οὐδαμόθι. οἱ γὰρ παρὰ τὰ στρατόπεδα ῥέοντες αὐτῶν ποταμοί, Οὐολτοῦρνος ὄνομα θατέρῳ, τῷ δ'ἑτέρῳ Γλάνις, ἀφέντες τὰς κατὰ φύσιν ὁδοὺς ἀνέστρεψαν τὰ νάματα καὶ μέχρι πολλοῦ διετέλεσαν ἀπὸ τῶν στομάτων ἀναχωροῦντες ἐπὶ τὰς πηγάς. τοῦτο καταμαθόντες οἱ Κυμαῖοι τότ᾽ ἐθάρρησαν ὁμόσε τοῖς βαρβάροις χωρεῖν ὡς τοῦ δαιμονίου ταπεινὰ μὲν τἀκείνων μετέωρα θήσοντος, ὑψηλὰ δὲ τὰ δοκοῦντα εἶναι σφῶν ταπεινά. νείμαντες δὲ τὴν ἐν ἀκμῇ δύναμιν ἅπασαν τριχῇ, μιᾷ μὲν τὴν πόλιν ἐφρούρουν, τῇ δ᾽ ἑτέρᾳ τὰς ναῦς εἶχον ἐν φυλακῇ, τῇ δὲ τρίτῃ πρὸ τοῦ τείχους ταξάμενοι τοὺς ἐπιόντας ἐδέχοντο. τούτων ἱππεῖς μὲν ἦσαν ἑξακόσιοι, πεζοὶ δὲ τετρακισχίλιοι καὶ πεντακόσιοι. καὶ οὕτως ὄντες τὸν ἀριθμὸν ὀλίγοι τὰς τοσαύτας ὑπέστησαν μυριάδας.

Ὡς δὲ κατέμαθον αὐτοὺς οἱ βάρβαροι μάχεσθαι παρεσκευασμένους, ἀλαλάξαντες ἐχώρουν ὁμόσε τὸν βάρβαρον τρόπον ἄνευ κόσμου πεζοί τε καὶ ἱππεῖς ἀναμὶξ ὡς ἅπαντας ἀναρπασόμενοι. ἦν δὲ τὸ πρὸ τῆς πόλεως χωρίον, ἐν ᾧ συνέμισγον ἀλλήλοις, αὐλὼν στενὸς ὄρεσι καὶ λίμναις περικλειόμενος, τῇ μὲν ἀρετῇ τῶν Κυμαίων σύμμαχος, τῷ δὲ πλήθει τῶν βαρβάρων πολέμιος. ἀνατρεπόμενοι γὰρ ὑπ᾽ ἀλλήλων καὶ συμπατούμενοι πολλαχῇ μὲν καὶ ἄλλῃ, μάλιστα δὲ περὶ τὰ τέλματα τῆς λίμνης, οὐδ᾽εἰς χεῖρας ἐλθόντες τῇ φάλαγγι τῶν Ἑλλήνων αὐτοὶ δι᾽αὐτῶν οἱ πλείους διεφθάρησαν. καὶ ὁ μὲν πεζὸς αὐτῶν στρατὸς ὁ πολὺς περὶ ἑαυτῷ σφαλείς, ἔργον δὲ γενναῖον οὐδὲν ἀποδειξάμενος, ἄλλος ἄλλῃ διασκεδασθεὶς ἔφυγεν. οἱ δὲ ἱππεῖς συνῆλθον μὲν ὁμόσε καὶ πολὺν τοῖς Ἕλλησιν οὗτοι παρέσχον πόνον. ἀδύνατοι δ᾽ὄντες κυκλώσασθαι τοὺς πολεμίους διὰ στενοχωρίαν, καί τι καὶ τοῦ δαιμονίου κεραυνοῖς καὶ ὕδασι καὶ βρονταῖς συναγωνισαμένου τοῖς Ἕλλησι, δείσαντες εἰς φυγὴν τρέπονται. ἐν ταύτῃ τῇ μάχῃ πάντες μὲν οἱ τῶν Κυμαίων ἱππεῖς λαμπρῶς ἠγωνίσαντο, καὶ τῆς νίκης οὗτοι μάλιστα ὡμολογοῦντο αἴτιοι γενέσθαι, ὑπὲρ ἅπαντας δὲ τοὺς ἄλλους Ἀριστόδημος ὁ Μαλακὸς ἐπικαλούμενος. καὶ γὰρ τὸν ἡγεμόνα τῶν πολεμίων οὗτος ἀπέκτεινε μόνος ὑποστὰς καὶ ἄλλους πολλοὺς καὶ ἀγαθούς. . .

Εἰκοστῷ δ᾽ὕστερον ἔτει τῆς πρὸς τοὺς βαρβάρους μάχης ἦλθον ὡς τοὺς Κυμαίους Ἀρικηνῶν πρέσβεις σὺν ἱκετηρίαις ἀξιοῦντες αὐτοὺς βοηθῆσαι σφίσιν ὑπὸ Τυρρηνῶν πολεμουμένοις. μετὰ γὰρ τὰς διαλλαγάς, ἃς ἐποιήσατο πρὸς τὴν Ῥωμαίων πόλιν ὁ βασιλεὺς τῶν Τυρρηνῶν Πορσίνας, τὸν υἱὸν Ἄρροντα δοὺς τὴν ἡμίσειαν τῆς στρατιᾶς ἔπεμψεν ἰδίαν ἀρχὴν κτήσασθαι βουλόμενον, ὡς ἐν τοῖς πρὸ τούτου δεδήλωκα

AT THE CROSSROADS OF TRUTH AND FICTION

λόγοις. ὃς ἐπολιόρκει τότε τοὺς Ἀρικηνοὺς καταπεφευγότας εἰς τὸ τεῖχος καὶ οὐ διὰ μακροῦ λιμῷ τὴν πόλιν αἱρήσειν ᾤετο. ταύτης τῆς πρεσβείας ἀφικομένης οἱ προεστηκότες τῆς ἀριστοκρατίας μισοῦντες τὸν Ἀριστόδημον καὶ δεδιότες, μή τι κακὸν ἐξεργάσηται περὶ τὴν πολιτείαν, κάλλιστον ὑπέλαβον εἰληφέναι καιρὸν ἐκποδὼν αὐτὸν ποιήσασ-θαι σὺν εὐσχήμονι προφάσει. πείσαντες δὴ τὸν δῆμον ἀποστεῖλαι Ἀρικη-νοῖς δισχιλίους ἄνδρας ἐπὶ συμμαχίαν, καὶ στρατηγὸν ἀποδείξαντες τὸν Ἀριστόδημον ὡς δὴ τὰ πολέμια λαμπρόν, τὰ μετὰ ταῦτ'ἔπραττον, ἐξ ὧν ἢ κατακοπήσεσθαι μαχόμενον ὑπὸ τῶν Τυρρηνῶν αὐτὸν ὑπελάμβανον ἢ κατὰ πέλαγος διαφθαρήσεσθαι. γενόμενοι γὰρ ὑπὸ τῆς βουλῆς κύριοι καταλέξαι τοὺς ἐπὶ τὴν συμμαχίαν ἐξελευσομένους τῶν μὲν ἐπισήμων καὶ λόγου ἀξίων οὐδένα κατέγραψαν, ἐπιλέξαντες δὲ τοὺς ἀπορωτάτους τε καὶ πονηροτάτους τῶν δημοτικῶν, ἐξ ὧν ἀεί τινας ὑπώπτευον νεωτερισ-μούς, ἐκ τούτων συνεπλήρωσαν τὸν ἀπόστολον. καὶ ναῦς δέκα παλαιὰς κάκιστα πλεούσας καθελκύσαντες, ὧν ἐτριηράρχουν οἱ πενέστατοι Κυμαίων, εἰς ταύτας αὐτοὺς ἐνεβίβασαν θάνατον ἀπειλήσαντες ἐάν τις ἀπολειφθῇ τῆς στρατείας.— Ὁ δ' Ἀριστόδημος τοσοῦτον εἰπὼν μόνον, ὡς οὐ λέληθεν αὐτὸν ἡ διάνοια τῶν ἐχθρῶν, ὅτι λόγῳ μὲν ἐπὶ συμμαχίαν αὐτὸν ἀποστέλλουσιν, ἔργῳ δ'εἰς πρόϋπτον ὄλεθρον, δέχεται μὲν τὴν στρατηγίαν, ἀναχθεὶς δ'ἅμα τοῖς πρέσβεσι τῶν Ἀρικηνῶν διὰ ταχέων καὶ τὸ μεταξὺ πέλαγος ἐπιπόνως καὶ κινδυνωδῶς διανύσας ὁρμίζεται κατὰ τοὺς ἔγγιστα τῆς Ἀρικείας αἰγιαλούς. καὶ καταλιπὼν ἐν ταῖς ναυσὶ φυλακὴν ἀποχρῶσαν ἐν τῇ πρώτῃ νυκτὶ τὴν ἀπὸ θαλάσσης ὁδὸν οὐ πολλὴν οὖσαν διανύσας ἐπιφαίνεται τοῖς Ἀρικηνοῖς περὶ τὸν ὄρθρον ἀπροσδόκητος. θέμενος δὲ πλησίον αὐτῶν τὸν χάρακα καὶ τοὺς καταπεφευγότας εἰς τὰ τείχη πείσας προελθεῖν εἰς ὕπαιθρον προὐκαλεῖτο τοὺς Τυρρηνοὺς εὐθὺς εἰς μάχην. γενομένου δ'ἐκ παρατάξεως ἀγῶνος καρτεροῦ οἱ μὲν Ἀρικηνοὶ βραχὺν πάνυ διαμείναντες χρόνον ἐνέκλιναν ἀθρόοι, καὶ γίνεται πάλιν εἰς τὸ τεῖχος αὐτῶν φυγή· ὁ δ' Ἀρι-στόδημος σὺν τοῖς περὶ αὐτὸν λογάσι Κυμαίων ὀλίγοις οὖσι πᾶν τὸ τοῦ πολέμου βάρος ὑποστὰς καὶ τὸν ἡγεμόνα τῶν Τυρρηνῶν αὐτοχειρίᾳ κτείνας τρέπει τοὺς ἄλλους εἰς φυγὴν καὶ νίκην ἀναιρεῖται πασῶν λαμπροτάτην.

The fundamental importance of this account for Roman historio-graphy cannot be exaggerated. When Fabius Pictor undertook to make the Greek world believe that the Roman people were not a barbarian horde but had a long record of past glories,[1] he had no

[1] M. Gelzer, Hermes 68, 1933, 129 sqq., and 69, 1934, 46 sqq., with the previ-ous literature quoted. Cf. below, Chapter IV.

Cyme and the Roman Historiography

reliable sources for the oldest epoch of Roman history. The Greek world ignored early Rome almost completely; yet there was one Greek city whose sphere of interest reached Latium in the preclassical epoch: Cyme. It is obvious that the Greek helpers [1] of Pictor put at his disposal the unique data of the Cymean chronicle—in the adaptation we have just quoted or in another—enabling him to assign a real time limit to the end of the monarchy and to shed some light on the birth of the Republic.[2] It is likely that Greek historians—Timaeus and others who had an interest in Rome's past [3]—paved the way. Yet the essential thing is that the Cymean chronicle became the real backbone of the chronology of events in Latium at the end of the sixth century.

The date of the Cymean victory over the invading Etruscans in 524 B.C. is not evaluated in the same way in the more recent discussions of this subject. Some scholars,[4] like us, take it as an established fact. Others think the whole story, including the date, uncertain.[5] Some of them hold that the battles attributed to 524 and to 504 in the Cymean report adduced by Dionysius actually represent only one victory [6]—a view to be rejected for methodical considerations. The original author of the digression in the seventh book of Dionysius dates the battle of Aricia εἰκοστῷ δ'ὕστερον ἔτει τῆς πρὸς τοὺς βαρβάρους μάχης (VII 5, 1). In the same sense the Xenokrite story (Plut., De mulier. virt. 26) depicts Aristodemus as a mere boy at the time of his first exploits against the barbarians and places his appointment as the leader of the expedition to relieve the Aricians at the height of his career, after he had held the highest offices of his native city. When Dionysius says that the Roman legation to Aristodemus

---

[1] Cf. e.g., M. Gelzer, Hermes 82, 1954, 346.

[2] The capture of Cyme in 421 B.C. in the annalistic tradition seems to have been transmitted by the same source. Cf. F. Altheim, Lex sacrata, Amsterdam 1940, 13 sq.

[3] Cf. my remarks in : Die trojanischen Urahnen der Römer (Rektoratsprogramm Basel 1956) 1957, passim.

[4] G. De Sanctis, St. d. R. 1², 430. J. Heurgon, Rech. 64 sq., 79 sq. E. Ciaceri, Storia della Magna Grecia 2, Milano-Roma-Napoli 1927, 272 sqq. The previous literature is given by B. Niese, RE 2, 922 no. 8. The archeological research in Cyme is reviewed by B. Combet Farnoux, Mél. 69, 1957, 7 sqq.

[5] T. J. Dunbabin, op. cit. 344. L. Homo, L'Italie primitive 149 sqq., does not take seriously the date of the event "pour ne pas être dupe d'une chronologie qui n'a de précis que les apparences."

[6] A. Piganiol, Essai sur les origines de Rome, Paris 1916, 66. L. Homo, op. cit. 150 sq. J. Heurgon, op. cit. 72.

asking for corn supply (492 B.C. in the annalistic tradition) occurred in the fourteenth year after the battle of Aricia (VII 12, 1), he again follows the chronology which emerges from the identification of the second Etruscan leader killed by Aristodemus with the son of King Porsenna. The discrepancy of three to four years between the Greek and the Roman chronology and the individual modifications of it cannot upset the basic correctness of the date and interrelation of the two distinct warlike events in question. We have four kinds of different and independent evidence mutually corroborating this result:

1) The stylistic date of the cult image in the *lucus Dianius* of Aricia.[1]

2) The inscription, set up with this statue, copied by Cato the Elder.[2]

3) The dedication of the Capitoline temple, the year of which, in the time of Appius Claudius Caecus, was calculated as 509 B.C. by counting the nails driven annually in its wall.[3]

4) The beginning of the *fasti consulares* implies the end of the rule of the Tarquins. The reexamination of the names given for the first decade of the Republic in these lists will show us that the data are in accord with the chronology of Aristodemus. This convergence demonstrates that not only the battle of Aricia but the military and political references connected with it are based on reality. King Porsenna, even if his figure is colored by legend, belongs not to the world of fiction but to history. Further proofs of this are offered by the following considerations.

❧

PORSENNA IN ROME

As I have shown, the defeat of the Etruscans under the walls of Aricia by Aristodemus was also known to the earliest Roman historians, who owed this date in last analysis to the Cymean chronicle.

---

[1] Cf. my paper in AJA 64, 1960, 137 sqq.
[2] Cf. above, p. 48 sqq.
[3] Kr. Hanell, Das altrömische eponyme Amt, Lund 1946, *passim*, and below, p. 78 sq.

They connect it quite reasonably with the attack of the Etruscan king of Clusium, Lars Porsenna,[1] who subjugated Rome.

His conquest, followed first by a bitter oppression and later by a reconciliation, was well known to the Romans even under the early Empire. Two blunt admissions of this conquest have often been noticed. *In foedere, quod expulsis regibus populo Romano dedit Porsina, nominatim comprehensum invenimus ne ferro nisi in agri cultu uteretur,* states Pliny the Elder;[2] *sedem Jovis Optimi Maximi,* writes Tacitus,[3] ... *quam non Porsenna dedita urbe nec Galli capta temerare potuissent.* Even the Roman historiography, whose purpose was to present a glamorous picture of the might and glory of the City from the earliest possible epoch on, has not been able to pass over this fact in silence. It freely admits the extreme gravity of the danger,[4] as also the heavy defeat which enabled Porsenna to capture the bridgehead of the city on the Janiculum.[5] The annalists also acknowledge the siege of the city and the famine to which it was reduced,[6] the humiliating armistice,[7] which forced the Romans to deliver the children of the nobility as hostages,[8] and the necessity of providing the victorious enemy with food and equipment for the next stage of the offensive south of Rome.[9] The loss of the *Septem pagi* north of the Tiber to the Veientanes is also stated.[10] Another kind of admission of the lasting annexation of Rome to the realm of the king of Chiusi is given in the tale of Dionysius,[11] when he states that the Roman senate offered Porsenna the seat of ivory, the sceptre, the triumphal robe and golden wreath — the symbols of royalty by which also the rule of Tarquinius Priscus over Etruria should have been recognized by the Tuscan League.

[1] The sources are quoted by A. Schwegler, RG 2, 52 sqq., and by W. Ehlers, RE 22, 315 sqq. For their evaluation by recent research cf. also H. Volkmann, RE 8A, 185.

[2] Plin., *N.h.* XXXIV 14, 139.

[3] Tac., *Hist.* III 72.

[4] Sallust., *Hist.* 1, fr. 11 (p. 6 Maur. : *bellum grave cum Etruria.* Liv. II 9, 5: *Non unquam alias ante tantus terror senatum invasit.* Liv. VI 40, 17. DH V 54, 5 : πόλεμον . . . ἁπάντων βαρύτατον. VI 12, 1.

[5] Liv. II 10, 1 sqq. DH V 22, 3 ; 23, 2-3 ; 37, 2 ; 39, 4.

[6] Liv. II 11, 1 sqq. 12, 1. DH V 65, 3.

[7] Liv. II 13, 3. DH V 65, 3.

[8] Liv. II 13, 4 ; 13, 6. DH V 65, 3, etc.

[9] DH V 65, 3 : ἀγορὰν καὶ ὅπλα καὶ τἆλλα ὅσων ἐδέοντο Τυρρηνοὶ παρασχεῖν ἐπὶ τῇ καταλύσει τοῦ πολέμου.

[10] Liv. II 13, 4 ; 15, 6. DH V 36, 4 ; 65, 3. Cf. H. Philipp, RE 2 A, 1551.

[11] DH V 35, 1.

AT THE CROSSROADS OF TRUTH AND FICTION

Although the plight of the Romans could not be denied, the cata-
strophy was camouflaged by heart-warming stories concerning the
heroic opponents of the conqueror: *tunc illa tria Romani nominis
prodigia atque miracula, Horatius Mucius Cloelia, qui nisi in annalibus
forent, hodie fabulae viderentur*.[1] But the fact that the annalists could not
avoid bringing up the disaster, and their attempt to cloak the capture
of Rome with romantic embellishments,[2] make it manifest that Pictor
and his followers found the victorious campaign of Porsenna in
their Greek literary sources, and were unable to skip them.

In the annalistic account the last Roman king and his partisans have
two contradictory and inconsistent roles in the war of Porsenna
against Rome. Porsenna starts his expedition, it is said, to reinstate
Superbus in his realm as *eiusdem sanguinis nominisque*.[3] If this were true,
nothing would have been easier for Porsenna after the capture of
Rome than to reinstall the Tarquins.[4] Instead, for psychological
reasons, an attempt is made to make the reader believe that Porsenna,
deeply impressed by the heroism of the Romans, gave up his design,
abandoning the Tarquins who fled to the Latins. This dramatic
turn of events is a literary invention, flattering the patriotic emotions
of later generations. The facts are different. In the historical tradition
based upon the Cymean chronicle, Superbus joined the Latins,
particularly Tusculum, their leading city with Aricia, and found
refuge in Cyme after Rome overcame the Latin confederation.[5] This
reveals through coherent inner logic the real course of events. Porsenna never made common cause with the Tarquins. The idea of the
late Roman historiographers that both kings represented the Etruscan

---

[1] Flor. I 4 (10) 3.

[2] These are not brought about by "la fulgida vena della poesia popolare",
as G. De Sanctis, St. d. R. 2¹, 128, thinks ; the *Horatii*, *Cloelii*, and *Mucii* may
have cherished such stories, but the decisive feature of those fabulous tales is
the tendentious literary fiction.

[3] Liv. II 9,1 sqq ; 13, 3 ; 15, 1-6 ; Cic., *Att.* IX 10, 3. DH V 21, 1-2 ; 33, 3 ;
34, 2 ; 54, 5 ; 65, 3. VI 74, 5. Flor. I 4 (10) 1-2. *Vir. ill.* 8, 5-6. Plut., *Poplic.*
16, 1 sqq.

[4] Th. Mommsen, RG 1⁸, Berlin 1888, 246. Ed. Meyer, GdA 2², 811. More
literature quoted by F. Schachermeyr, RE 4A, 2367. An opposite view is
advocated by G. De Sanctis, St. d. R. 2¹, 94.

[5] Liv. II 13, 4 ; 19, 4-20, 10 ; 21, 5 ; 34, 4. DH IV 45, 1 sqq. V 21, 3 sqq.
50, 1 ; 51, 1-2 ; 52, 1 sqq. ; 58, 2. 4 ; 61, 1 ; 76, 3. VI 12, 1 sqq. ; 21, 2 ; 74, 6.
VII 71, 2. Cic., *De nat. deor.* II 2, 6 ; *Att.* IX 10, 3. Flor. I 4 (10) 8 ; 5 (11) 1,
etc. More details on the sources in A. Klotz, *op. cit.* 228 sqq. On Octavius
Mamilius see F. Münzer, RE 14, 954 sqq.

nation is erroneous: two Etruscan groups oppose each other here. Superbus fled from the victorious ruler of Clusium, his enemy; he was harbored by the opponents of Porsenna, the Arician confederation and Cyme.

Another, really dramatic turn of events came about in consequence of the heavy setback under the walls of Aricia. The utter defeat of the host of Porsenna makes it plausible that he really made concessions to the subjugated Romans, nay more, that he even made an alliance with them. Rome, certainly aspiring to a more modern and independent self-government, could build its new political structure with this backing and at the same time face the menace from its Latin opponents; but also the king must have derived advantages from this southern outpost of his realm. Therefore it is reasonable to suppose that it was with his support that the Romans got a quantity of millet and spelt from Etruria[1] in a famine of the following decade.

Everything points to a more than momentary connection between Rome and Clusium: *Romanis pax fida ita cum Porsenna fuit.*[2] A remarkable feature of the literary tradition, the full sympathy and admiration of the vanquished Romans for the dreadful enemy, could be explained by a lasting alliance between the king and the young Republic.[3] The assertion that a statue of Porsenna stood in Rome beside the *curia* in later epochs [4] has not, of course, been substantiated but is not wholly impossible. The authentic popular legend explaining the origin of the state auctions by the act of *bona Porsennae vendere* starting with the rejoicing after the siege of Rome testifies to the gratitude of the Romans toward him.[5] It is quite credible, at least to me, that his tomb monument near Clusium was really known to the Romans.[6] We cannot doubt the belief of the Romans that he was king of Clusium,[7]

---

[1] DH VII 12, 3. Liv. II 34, 5.

[2] Liv. II 15, 7. Strab. V 2, 2 (220 C.). DH V 34, 4. Serv., *Aen.* 11, 133.

[3] Liv. II 13, 9 : *apud regem Etruscum non tuta solum, sed honorata etiam virtus fuit*, as the anecdotes on Cloelia, Scaevola, Cocles illustrate it. Plut., *Poplic.* 16, 1 ; 19, 9-10, etc.

[4] Plut., *Poplic.* 19, 10.

[5] Liv. II 14, 1-4. DH V 34, 4-5. Plut., *Poplic.* 19. Porsenna became a mythical figure in the imagination of the Romans (Cf. Calpurnius Piso, *Ann.* fr. 10 = H. R. Rel. 1², 124 Peter), as the Vibenna-brothers, cf. below, p. 228 sqq.

[6] Varro in Plin., *N.h.* XXXVI 13, 91. Cf. F. Messerschmidt, in:Das neue Bild der Antike 2, Leipzig 1942, 53 sqq.

[7] Liv. II 9, 1. DH V 34, 5. Plut., *Poplic.* 16, 1. Cass. Dio 3, fr. (= vol. 1, p. 39 Boiss.). The guess of E. Pais, St. crit. 2, 97 sqq., has been rejected by J. Heurgon, Rech., 70 n. 2.

AT THE CROSSROADS OF TRUTH AND FICTION

and we can with some confidence believe that he was the head of the Etruscan league.[1]

There emerges one more remarkable fact. If we disregard the invented consulates of the first years of the Republic—to which we shall return below—we find two Etruscans in charge of Roman affairs at the head of the *fasti*: they are *Sp. Larcius* and with him *T. Herminius*.[2] As the descendants of the *Larcii* did not continue to play any role in Roman politics and as we find in the *fasti* only one more *Herminius* (consul, 448 B.C.), their existence, as well as that of T. Larcius, dictator four years later, cannot be a fictitious invention. Just after the expulsion of the Tarquins they seem to have been confidants of Porsenna. Perhaps there were also other exponents of Porsenna in Rome: the Etruscan *Volumnii, Aquilii, Manlii* who are all at the head of the Roman state in the next decades can only be explained either by the earlier immigration of these clans from southernmost Etruria or by their more recent arrival from Vulci or Clusium. And also, if the cultural influence of Etruria did not end in the first half of the fifth century, this is not due to a supposed continuity of kingship,[3] but to the ties linking Clusium with Rome.

A rather essential question must remain unsolved concerning the antecedents of Porsenna's capture of Rome. Our Roman sources pretend that, before this attack was launched, Veii and Tarquinii sent

[1] Cf. J. Heurgon, *op. cit.* 70 sq. The doubts on the historicity of Porsenna and the attempts to identify him with Mastarna (cf. G. Giannelli, La repubblica romana[2], 101. J. Bayet, Tite-Live 2, Paris 1954, 24 n. 3. L. Pareti, St. Etr. 5, 1931, 154 sqq., etc.) are not justified. Against the explanation of the name given by S. P. Cortsen, Die etruskischen Standes- und Beamtentitel, Kopenhagen 1925, 126, cf. M. Pallottino, Etruscologia[3], Milano 1955, 180. Even if Livy does not know anything about it, the fact that Clusium asked for help of Rome hundred years later points to this old indebtedness of the Romans toward their ancient overlord.

[2] The literary tradition seems to be irresponsible in the statement that the two were commanders of the Roman army *against* Porsenna (DH V 22, 5. Plut., *Poplic.* 16, 6. Liv. II 11, 7-10) and that *they* brought cereals from the Pomptine plain during the siege (DH V 26, 3-5). These assumptions seem to have been spun without any foundation out of the names, coupling them with events transmitted without names, a procedure which often recurs in the historical works on early Rome. On the other hand, the Etruscan first name *Lars* of the Herminius, consul in 448, illustrates that this family is not yet romanized, which fits to the immigration two generation prior to that date.

[3] As E. Gjerstad, Bull. Com. 73, 1949, 50 (1953) 25 sq. and in : Legends and Facts of Early Roman History, Lund 1962, *passim* supposes it. Essential remarks to this problem in R. Bloch, R. Et. Lat. 37, 1959, 118 sqq.

an army to restore the throne of the Roman king.[1] That Superbus was dependent on Veii, in politics as well as in matters of art and religion, is likely enough and has been rightly assumed.[2] On the other hand, a move of Tarquinii and Veii would be possible only in opposition to Porsenna, and this seems to be hardly credible in the light of subsequent events. There is a curious feature in the annalistic tradition which is inconsistent with the idea of a national rebellion against alien rule: the liberators Brutus and Collatinus are said to belong to the Etruscan dynasty itself. This, if true, would mean a palace-revolution before the northern invasion arrived. In reality, however, Brutus' role is literary invention.

In any case, the "liberation" of Rome from the Tarquins was due to Porsenna, as was already observed by K. O. Müller and by Ed. Meyer.[3] We do not need to review all the divergent opinion on the reasons and events which led to the overthrow of the monarchy in Rome.[4] All the widely diverging views contain some essential elements of truth. When, for instance, G. de Sanctis [5] saw in the fall of the monarchy the effects of a long political evolution, or G. Giannelli [6] with many others a *coup d'état* of the aristocracy, they are only stressing different factors, of internal policy, aiming at the same result. National independence was, however, not the primary cause,[7] but the last consequence of this political chain-reaction in Rome. It was a general trend everywhere in Central Italy at that moment

---

[1] Cic., *Tusc.* III 12, 27, Liv. II 6, 1-7, 3 ; 13, 4 ; 15, 6. DH V 3, 1 sqq. ; 14, 1 sqq. VI 74, 4. Plut., *Popl.* 9, 1-10 ; cf. 13, 1. Zonar. 7, 12. Val. Max. I 8, 5. *Fasti Capit.* a. 509 ; cf. A. Degrassi, Inscr. It. XIII 1, 1947, 535.

[2] J. Gagé, Apollon romain (BEFAR 180) 1955, 57 sqq.

[3] K. O. Müller-W. Deecke, 1, 116 sqq. Ed. Meyer, GdA 2², 1893, 811 : "Es ist nicht undenkbar, dass in Wirklichkeit Porsenna die Tarquinier bekriegt und ihnen Rom abgenommen hat, sodass der Wegfall des Königtums mit dem Sturz der Herrschaft Porsennas gegeben war." The second half of this sentence does not correspond to our views. Cf. also A. Piganiol, Essai sur les origines de Rome, Paris 1916, 264 sqq. W. Hoffmann, Rom und die griechische Welt im IV. Jahrhundert v. Chr. (Philol. Suppl. 27, 1) 1934, 1 sqq.

[4] The literature is given, e.g., by F. Schachermeyr, RE 4 A, 2365 sqq., and by U. v. Lübtow, Das römische Volk, sein Staat und sein Recht, Frankfurt 1955, 176 sqq.

[5] G. De Sanctis, St. d. R. 1², 403 sqq. S. Mazzarino, Dalla mon. 104 sqq. A. v. Gerkan, Rh. Mus. n. F. 100, 1957, 91.

[6] G. Giannelli, La repubblica romana², 1955, 105 sqq. J. Gagé, Huit recherches sur les origines italiques et romaines, Paris 1950, 119 sqq.

[7] As my friend, E. Kornemann, imagined (Hist. Zeitschr. 145, 1931, 295) like many others of the previous generation.

for the rule of the aristocracy to replace that of kings: once the throne became vacant, the warlike nobility seized their opportunity.

It is most important for the solution of these vexed questions that by now we possess the stepping stones which enable us to wade through the mud of the perverted tradition concerning the dates of the reconstitution of the Latin League and of the annihilation of the army of Porsenna at Aricia. The reliability of the date of the flight of the Tarquins from Porsenna and of the establishment of a new regime in Rome is also confirmed by our acquaintance with the year in which the Capitoline temple was dedicated. A famous passage of Pliny the Elder [1] reveals to us that in the year 304 B.C. the aedile Cn. Flavius counted 204 years backward to the year of its dedication. Mommsen [2] perceived that the Roman year-reckoning started not from the foundation of the Republic and the liberation from the autocracy of the kings but from that religious date. But on the other hand, Kr. Hanell [3] recognized that not only were the annual nails in the wall of the Capitoline temple counted by Cn. Flavius but somebody after his nail-counting also added together the number of pairs of eponymous magistrates in the consular *fasti*. By this second procedure a gap was revealed *at the beginning* of the Republican era, since the nails in the Capitol's wall yielded a somewhat higher date than the pairs of magistrates listed in the *fasti*. The discovery of this gap by the pontiffs who were in charge of taking care of the *fasti* explains why just the *first* years at the top of the consular list were filled by forged names: the number of the 204 nails was taken for granted, the pairs of executives were completed arbitrarily by some more of them, with the gentile names of an important clan of the new plebeian nobility, and of that of the old patrician *gens* of the Valerii. To these names was also added the name of M. Horatius, on the supposition that he must have dedicated the sanctuary and driven the first nail in its wall. In fact, he only rededicated the temple after

---

[1] Plin., *N.h.* XXXIII 1, 19 (on *Cn. Flavius, Anni f., scriba* of *Appius Claudius Caecus* who was elected *aedilis curulis* by the people in opposition to the aristocracy) : *Flavius vovit aedem Concordiae . . . et, cum ad id pecunia publice non decerneretur, ex multatitia faeneratoribus condemnatis aediculam aeream fecit in Graecostasi, . . inciditque in tabella aerea factam*̣*eam aedem CCIII annis post Capitolinam dedicatam.*

[2] Th. Mommsen, Römische Chronologie², Berlin 1859, 198 sqq.

[3] Kr. Hanell, Dragma M. P. Nilsson dedicatum, Lund 1939, 256 sqq. *Idem*, Das altrömische eponyme Amt 198 sqq., and the necessary corrections noted by Ernst Meyer, Mus. Helv. 9, 1952, 177.

the Celtic storm, as we shall see later: it was the last Tarquin who consecrated his construction in 509 B.C. By discarding all these inter-polated names, we must bring the flight of the Tarquins with the Cymean chronology down to 505 B.C., and the battle at Aricia with the ensuing reconciliation between Porsenna and the Romans to 504 B.C.

Some further clarification is needed in the case of M. Horatius. We know that the ancients read his name on the architrave under the pediment of the sanctuary [1] and they thought that his name, replacing the name of the last king by an annual magistrate, was the result of a *damnatio memoriae*. Our authorities [2] diverge as to the date of the con-secration of the Capitol, placing it between the first and the third year of the Republic: Fabius Pictor dated it with Antias in the year corresponding to 509 B.C., Piso and Macer in the following year.[3] This hesitation must be due not to general chronological considera-tions but to different attempts to harmonize it with the conquest of the city: these men *knew* that Rome was occupied by the enemy and tried to shift the act of consecration to a time either before or after the capture of it. In the years after 509 there were as yet no magistrates but a lacuna covered after 304 B.C. by fictitious names and triumphs. The earliest Roman historians assumed that in the first year after the expulsion of the Tarquins there was an attempt on the part of Veii and Tarquinii to restore them and therefore the fight against Porsenna was put in the second and in the third year of the new era.[4]

How reliable are these lists in general? A series of respectable

---

[1] DH V 35, 3. Cf. Cic., *De domo* 54, 139. *Consol.* fr. 15. Val. Max. V 10, 1. Seneca, *Ad Marc.* 13, 5. Symm., Ep. III 6, 3.

[2] Polyb. III 22, 1. Liv. II 8, 6-8. VII 3, 8. Val. Max. V 10, 1. Plut., *Popl.* 14, 2 and 5. DH III 69, 2. IV 61, 3. Tac., *Hist.* 3, 72. Cass. Dio, fr. 13, 3. Cf. O. Leuze, Die röm. Jahrzählung 1909, 160 sqq., 298, 326 sqq. E. Kornemann, Hist. Zeitschr. 145, 1931, 296 n.l. C. Koch, Der römische Juppiter, Frankfurt 1937, 122. A. v. Gerkan, Rh. Mus., n. F. 100, 1957, 91.

[3] Fr. Münzer, *De gente Valeria*. Diss. Berlin 1891, 24 sqq. It was Pictor and not Livy who put the event in the first year, as A. Klotz, Livius und seine Vorgänger, 23, thought.

[4] For these calculations and the criticism of the sources cf., e.g., O. Leuze, *op. cit.* 325 sqq. Fr. Cornelius, Beiträge zur frühen römischen Geschichte, München 1940, 42 sqq. A. Klotz, *op. cit.* 211 sqq. G. Perl, Kritische Unter-suchungen zu Diodors römischer Jahrzählung (Berl. Akad., Schriften d. Sektion f. Altertumswiss. 9) 1957, 26. J. P. V. Balsdon, Gnomon 30, 1958, 296 sqq. J. Bayet, Tite-Live, vol. 1⁶, 1958, pp. CXIII sqq. H. Volkmann, RE 8 A, 183 sqq. H. Peter, H. R. Rel. 1², p. LV sqq., LXXXIII, CVIII sqq.

AT THE CROSSROADS OF TRUTH AND FICTION

scholars [1] deny the authenticity of the early part of the *fasti consulares*. Others defend them.[2] In any case, far-reaching manipulations must be admitted, manifest from the inclusion of a series of plebeian names in the early consular lists when no plebeian was yet eligible for the consulate.[3] Since it was demonstrated [4] that the patriciate was nothing

---

[1] Fr. Münzer, *op. cit.*, *passim*. B. Niese-E. Hohl, Grundriss der römischen Geschichte[5], (Handbuch d. Altertumswiss. III 5) München 1923, 13. J. Beloch, RG 232 sqq. E. Kornemann, Intern. Monatsschrift f. Wissenschaft, Kunst und Technik 14, 1920, 480 sqq. *Idem*, RG 1[3], bearbeitet durch H. Bengtson, München 1954, 73, 75, 79. Kr. Hanell, Das altrömische eponyme Amt 95 sqq., 118 sqq., 147 sqq., 165 sqq., 256 sqq. A. Klotz, Rh. Mus. n. F. 86, 1937, 219. A. Piganiol, Essai sur les origines de Rome, 237 sqq. *Idem*, Histoire de Rome[3], Paris 1949, 44 sq.

[2] Fr. Cornelius, *op. cit.* 50 sqq. A. Bernardi, Athen., n.s. 30, 1952, 11 sqq. S. Mazzarino, Dalla mon. 197 sq. L. R. Taylor, C. Ph. 41, 1946, 1 sqq. *Ibid*, 45, 1950, 84 sqq. *Ead.*, Proc. Am. Philos. Soc. 94, 1950, 511 sqq. L. R. Taylor and T. R. S. Broughton, Mem. Am. Ac. in Rome 19, 1949, 3 sqq. A. Degrassi, Inscr. Ital. XIII 1, 17 sqq.

[3] A. Enmann, Rh. Mus. 57, 1902, 517 sqq. K. J. Neumann, Strassburger Festschrift zur 46. Versammlung von Philologen und Schulmännern 1901, 309 sqq. G. De Sanctis, St. d. R. 1[2], 394 sqq. E. Kornemann, Der Priesterkodex in der Regia und die Entstehung der altrömischen Pseudogeschichte (Doktorenverzeichnis d. Philos. Fak, d. Univ. Tübingen 1910) Tübingen 1912, esp. 49 sqq., with the previous literature. W. Schur, Hermes 59, 1924, 452. A. Rosenberg, Einleitung und Quellenkunde zur römischen Geschichte, Berlin 1921, 113 sqq. W. Schur, RE Suppl. 5, 357, 359, 366 sqq. *Contra* : Pl. Fraccaro, La storia romana arcaica, Milano 1952, 11 sqq. The whole tradition was properly collected by A. Degrassi, Inscr. It. XIII 1, 348 sqq., and by T. R. S. Broughton, MRR 1, 1 sqq. Fr. Cornelius, *op. cit.* 100 sqq., tries to maintain the authenticity of the early plebeian consuls, but his argumentation is not convincing. If the early *Minucii* are called *Augurini (ibid.* 10*)*, it is illogical to admit (*ibid.* 50) on the one hand that the surname was a fake, given in reality much later to one of the first plebeian augurs, and to maintain on the other that the same *gentilicium* belonged to an extinguished patrician *gens*. Cic., *Brut.* 16, 62 : *Quamquam his laudationibus historia rerum nostrarum est facta mendosior. Multa enim scripta sunt in eis, quae facta non sunt, falsi triumphi, plures consulatus, genera etiam falsa et ad plebem transitiones, quum homines humiliores in alienum eiusdem nominis infunderentur genus : ut si ego me a M'. Tullio esse dicerem, qui patricius cum Servio Sulpicio consul anno decimo post exactos reges fuit.* This passage is often quoted, but it is more often forgotten, that it is valid also for the Annals which were written by the same sort of men as the *laudationes funebres* who distorted the historical truth for the same purpose and in the same manner. Cf. also Liv. II 21, 4 : *Tanti errores implicant temporum, aliter apud alios ordinatis magistratibus, ut nec qui consules secundum quos, nec quid quoque anno actum sit, in tanta vetustate non rerum modo, sed etiam auctorum digerere possis.* VIII 40, 4-5: *vitiatam memoriam funebribus laudibus reor falsisque imaginum titulis, dum familiae ad se quaeque famam rerum gestarum honorumque fallenti mendacio trahunt. inde certe et singulorum gesta et publica monumenta rerum confusa ; nec quisquam aequalis temporibus illis scriptor extat, quo satis certo auctore stetur.* Cf. also VI 1, 1-2. XXI 25, 4.

more than the noblemen-cavalry constituted as the bodyguard of the Etruscan kings and restricted to the families of those horsemen (in the same way as with the ruling aristocracy of the Aeolian Cyme), it becomes impossible to assume the existence of a transitional period in which plebeians still could be admitted to the annual leadership of the state. The qualification of the *equites* as such for the election, their exclusive right to explore the will of heaven by the *auspicia* and to obtain the *imperium*, is simply the usurpation of these royal monopolies by a clique, imaginable only immediately after the expulsion of the king and his family. The movement of the *plebs*, led by the heads of influential clans excluded from this *numerus clausus*,[1] began soon afterward for the purpose not of regaining but of obtaining these royal privileges. The plebeian names in the earliest part of the list must consequently be the result of later manipulations. Other traces of such alterations can be suspected. It is very likely that the king was replaced first by the *magister populi*, i.e., the dictatorship as a normal magistracy.[2] But as the *dictator* was coupled with the military and political representative of the nobleman-cavalry, the *magister equitum*, these two names also went in pairs. Such couples could have been interpreted by later generations as pairs of consuls, their original character obscured. On the other hand, the role of the *magister equitum*, the representative of the patriciate besides the magister of the whole *populus* including the senate, shows the post-monarchical origin of the institution.

In spite of these and other possible interpolations, the core of the list is old and sound, as Mommsen long ago realized. C. Cichorius [3] picked out from the earliest part of the consular *fasti* a considerable group of eponymous magistrates, whose families either died out or sank into obscurity; he demonstrated by this selection that nobody was on hand later when the lists were interpolated who would have had an interest in smuggling in such unknown or forgotten names into the *fasti*. Such names are the already mentioned *Larcii* and the

---

[4] A. Alföldi, Der frührömische Reiteradel und seine Ehrenabzeichen, Baden-Baden, 1952, *passim*.

[1] And not by aliens, freedmen, workmen, etc., as the generation of the Gracchi imagined.

[2] Kr. Hanell, *op. cit.* 175, 183. The latest literature is given by U. v. Lübtow, *op. cit.* (77 n. 4.) 166 sqq., 182 sqq. On the prototype of the *dictator Latinus* cf. above, p. 42 sq.

[3] C. Cichorius, *De fastis consularibus antiquissimis*, Diss. Leipzig 1886, 177.

Herminius in 506, 501, 498, 490 B.C., besides a much larger group of personalities listed mainly in the two decades before the decemvirate. But as Ed. Meyer [1] stressed, there is one point where instead of minor arbitrary alterations a real forgery can be detected. This is the beginning of the eponymous list where in the first three years besides M. Horatius, whose case we have already discussed, spurious names were smuggled in, to bridge the gap between the last king and the first officials of the Republican state.

The character and time of this forgery can be clarified to some extent. First, it is clear that it was committed by plebeian redactors of the pontifical annals because they were known to the earliest annalist writers who clothed those imaginary plebeian names of early officials with invented outstanding achievements; just as they also embellished their meager source materials with other stories, legendary and newly made fiction alike. The title *Brutus* of a *fabula praetexta* of Accius illustrates that the liberator was then a universally known figure in Rome; the sentimental story of Lucretia connected with Brutus was narrated by Fabius Pictor; [2] Horatius Cocles seems to be glorified by Ennius [3] and Pictor; Cloelia [4] also belongs to this old inventory.

Long before the annalists, when the plebeian *Iunii Bruti* became prominent in the Middle Republic, the name of their invented ancestor was smuggled into the list and also that of the first Valerius. [5] But then came "the father of great lies," Valerius Antias, to whom we must ascribe most of the three continuous consulates of Valerius Poplicola in the first three years of the Republic, the consulate of his brother in the fourth year, that of himself again in the fifth, as well as the heroic deeds of Valeria as a hostage of Porsenna. [6] Very helpful for the recognition of spurious names in the *fasti* is also the discovery

[1] Ed. Meyer, Kleine Schriften 2, Halle 1924, 301 sqq.

[3] F. Schachermeyr, RE 4A, 235, 2391. Vl. Groh, Athen., n.s. 6, 1928, 297. G. De Sanctis, St. d. R. 2, 46 sqq., thinks of an invention of popular poetry; I see in it Hellenistic motives and behind it family interests. Cf. M. Schanz-C. Hosius, Geschichte der römischen Literatur 1⁴, München 1927, 168 sqq., for the general outlines and Chapter IV.

[3] W. Soltau, Die Anfänge der römischen Geschichtsschreibung, Leipzig 1909, 97, on the basis of Polyb. VI 55, 1-3.

[4] Plin., *N.h.* XXXIV 6, 29. Fr. Münzer, RE 4, 110 sq.

[5] As Fr. Münzer, RE 8, 2403 sqq., supposed it.

[6] K. W. Nitsch, Rh. Mus. n. F. 23, 1868, 622 sq.; 24, 1869, 158 sqq. Th. Mommsen, RG 2, 132 sqq. Fr. Münzer, *op. cit.* (79 n. 3) 9 sqq. 54 sqq. W. Schur, RE Suppl. 5, 366. H. Volkmann, RE 8A, 187 sqq. A. Klotz, *op. cit.* (79 n. 3) 277. G. De Sanctis, St. d. R. 2¹, 113. Fr. Cornelius, *op. cit.* (79 n. 4) 19 sqq.

of Mommsen,[1] further developed by other scholars,[2] that the *cognomina* of the early consuls in our lists are additions of the Later Republic. For the history of the Free State, this observation can be coupled with the results of a new inquiry of the present writer.[3] It has been demonstrated in this study that the *cognomina* of our lists were originally nicknames of the magistrates, very often with a comical or derogatory touch. Such slanders, of course, had nothing to do with the names given in childhood by the parents, and they were in those early times not subjected to the will or decision of the clans, but were attributed by the masses to the leading personalities in the forum and in the field. Later, of course, when the warlike shepherds of the settlements around the Palatine and the Quirinal became the decisive power in Central Italy, the coarse surnames of the leading clans were gilded by age and glory in spite of their disreputable significance and these *cognomina* assumed a very honorable ring, as did the queer animals of mediaeval heraldry; so it came about that the princely *gentes* could use the *cognomina* of this epoch to distinguish the various branches of the clan.

One of those surnames was *Brutus*, the "Stupid," emerging apparently in the second half of the fourth century B.C. and inserted surreptitiously in the *fasti* either in 304 B.C. or not long afterward. Later on, especially after the wars with Hannibal, the nobility was no longer the kernel of the army but a ring of princely families ruling over the Mediterranean world. There was then a general tendency to obliterate the derisory meaning of those disreputable surnames of the leading clans by pious euphemistic explanations, resembling nursery fables. One such is the annalist tale of Brutus, which stresses the point that he was not stupid but that he hid his wisdom behind a simulated foolishness for the sake of saving himself from the suspicions of the cruel tyrant. How by such behavior he could become a *magister equitum*, the right hand of the king and the second-ranking man in the state, we do not grasp.[4]

---

[1] Th. Mommsen, RG 1, 45 sqq. ; cf. *ibid.* 2, 65 sqq.

[2] C. Cichorius, *op. cit.* (81 n. 3) 177 sqq. H. Dessau, Lateinische Epigraphik (Gercke-Norden, Einleitung 1, 1925, fasc. 10) 24. Fr. Cornelius, Untersuchungen zur frührömischen Geschichte, München 1940, 8 sqq., 14 sqq., etc. Cf. the remarks by G. Costa, I fasti consolari romani I 2, Milano 1910, 130 sqq.

[3] To be published soon.

[4] For a discussion of the problem and for the sources cf. C. J. Neumann, *op. cit.* (80 n. 3) 309. Vl. Groh, Athen. n.s. 6, 1928, 292 sqq. W. Schur, RE

AT THE CROSSROADS OF TRUTH AND FICTION

The case is similar to that of Valerius Poplicola.[1] It is impossible to decide when the surname of this most illustrious clan really arose; what is certain is only that its insertion in the *fasti* must be late. There can be no doubt that the explanation that the name was obtained *populi colendi causa* is wrong. The common people were not called *populus* in those early times: the archaic title magister *populi*, the frequent occurrence of this conception on the Eugubine tables, etc., show that *populus* in old Latin and other related idioms meant the totality of a people including the Senate. So the fable based on that name, which is interpreted as *plebicola*, is also a forgery.

A short digression on those ideal figures of the first years of the Republic, so attractive to the enthusiastic youth, is not out of place. Since Niebuhr, every historian must be prepared to discount them. Nor must teachers who wish to inspire high morality in their pupils have any scruples about dismissing their stories: they are only faint echoes of the real greatness of the Romans. The younger Balbus, who penetrated the camp of Pompey at Dyrrachium to pave the way for the new imperial state, carried out at least as daring an enterprise as the legendary Scaevola, who intruded into the camp of Porsenna. Scaeva and many more of the centurions of Caesar accomplished deeds far more hazardous than the lonely fight of Cocles against odds. And how much superior in military valor are men of flesh and blood, like the Cunctator, the Elder Africanus, or Caesar, than the bloodless novel-hero Brutus! Yet towering high above all of these men of amazing achievements appears the adamant firmness of the Roman people in face of the torrential invasion of Hannibal, which ravaged everything far and wide in Italy.

All that web of legend and fiction filled a gap between the inauguration of the Capitol and the real beginning of the rule of the annual functionaries in Rome. That this gap could be realized by the annalists explains the knowledge of the Etruscan moves and the Latin reactions upon them in the Cymean chronicle. These dates used before Pictor by Greek historians, we repeat, furnished us with a real basis for the reconstruction of the transition from the monarchy to the Republic.

Suppl. 5, 356 sqq. (no. 46 a). Ed. Meyer, GdA 2², 809 sqq. K. J. Beloch, RG 1 sqq., 8 sqq., 18 sqq. Cf. also DH V 18, 1-2.

[1] Cf. Fr. Münzer, *op. cit.* (79 n. 3) 54 sqq. H. Volkmann, RE 8A, 180. H. Peter, H. R. Rel. 1², 1914, p. LII sqq.

THE FEDERAL SANCTUARY OF THE LATIN CITIES IN THE AVENTINE PRECINCT OF DIANA AND ITS LOCAL SUCCESSORS

Aventinum aliquot de causis dicunt, says Varro (*De 1. Lat.* 5, 43), . . . *alii A<d>ventinum ab adventu hominum, quod com<m>une Latinorum ibi Dianae templum sit constitutum*. The Roman historians attribute the foundation of this federal sanctuary, like that of so many other beneficent institutions, to the good old king Servius Tullius, whose diplomacy was supposed to persuade the Latin peoples to transfer their annual conventions to the Aventine and to build a temple there to the goddess.[1] The existence of such a federal sanctuary has never been questioned and cannot be doubted; but the alleged date of its foundation is in line with the general tendency of the Roman historians to shift back in time so far as possible the hegemony of Rome over Latium.[2] The lesson to be taught by the pretended early foundation of this religious center of the Latins is expressed by Livy in the following words: *ea erat confessio caput rerum Romam esse* (I 45, 3). Dionysius [3] states that in his youth he saw the pillar with the inscription in archaic characters "once used in Greece." This stele actually stood in the temple of Diana on the Aventine, as is proved by the quotation of this document by Roman antiquarians.[4] Mommsen [5] argues plausibly

---

[1] Liv. I 45, 2-3. DH IV 26, 3-5. *Vir. ill.* 7, 9-13. Cass. Dio 1, p. 24 Boiss. = Zon. VII 9, 11.

[2] Cf. our detailed survey on this topic below, 101 sqq.

[3] DH IV 26, 5 (Servius Tullius): στήλην κατασκευάσας χαλκῆν ἔγραψεν ἐν ταύτῃ τά τε δόξαντα τοῖς συνέδροις καὶ τὰς μετεχούσας τῆς συνόδου πόλεις. αὕτη διέμεινεν ἡ στήλη μέχρι τῆς ἐμῆς ἡλικίας ἐν τῷ τῆς Ἀρτέμιδος ἱερῷ κειμένη γραμμάτων ἔχουσα χαρακτῆρας οἷς τὸ παλαιὸν ἡ Ἑλλὰς ἐχρῆτο. To give the oldest Roman institutions a civilized Greek taint belongs to the favorite patterns, with which the Greek rhetorician served the ambitions of his Roman patrons. My much regretted friend H. Last (CAH 7, 1928, 350 sqq.) thought that the words in which this stele is described by Dionysius point to an alphabet as early as that found on the *cippus* beneath the *lapis niger*, which may be dated in the sixth century. This suggestion gives too much credit to Dionysius and his annalist sources : even if it is based on reality, a script could strike a contemporary of Augustus as archaic, even if it came from the fourth century. We do not agree, on the other hand, with those who take the inscription as "eine Flunkerei des Dionysios," as W. Ihne, RG 1, Leipzig 1868, 59. A. Stein, Römische Inschriften in der antiken Literatur (78. Bericht der Lese- und Redestelle der deutschen Studenten in Prag 1929) Prag 1930, 19. J. Binder, Die Plebs, Leipzig 1909, 38 sqq., etc.

[4] Fest., p. 164, 1 Linds. : *Nesi pro sine positum <est in lege dedicationis arae> Dianae Aventinen<sis>*. The completion of the lacune is a well-founded conjecture of Scaliger.

AT THE CROSSROADS OF TRUTH AND FICTION

that the ritual prescriptions of the *ara Dianae in Aventino*, taken over by so many Diana-sanctuaries in the Roman world, were copied from this *lex dedicationis arae Dianae Aventinensis*. The name of the legendary king certainly did not stand at the head of this text, on which the curiosity of old Cato could have discovered the name of another *dictator Latinus*, just as he caught the name of *Egerius Baebius* on the document in the grove of Aricia.[1]

In any case the federal character of this foundation, which concerns us, is established above any suspicion.[2] Even the naive anecdote that the sacrifice [3] of a bull of exceptional strength to Diana on the Aventine by a Roman instead of a Latin would warrant the Roman rule over Latium by the will of fate sounds like a preliterary echo of a Roman effort to draw the political center of the Latins from the *nemus* of Aricia to that on the Aventine. The date of the foundation of this new federal sanctuary can be safely established from a brilliant observation of E. Pais and G. Wissowa. We reproduce the summary of the deductions of the latter in his own words: [4] "It is the unanimous opinion of our sources that this sanctuary (on the Aventine) was created by the Latin peoples and Rome at their common expense, as proposed by King Servius Tullius . . . . The striking fact that Diana has been selected to be the divine patron of the League is explained in our tradition by the supposition that the sanctuary of Artemis in Ephesos was the seat of the Ionian League. It is likely that this belief inspired the Romans later on, when they felt the need to have an image of the goddess in the Aventine temple, to choose for this purpose the type of the Ephesian Artemis, viz., that of her derivative,

[5] Th. Mommsen, St. R. 3, Leipzig 1888, 614 sq. I cannot understand why the document should be the fruit of a revision, undertaken *after the dissolution* of the League, as he supposed.

[1] K. J. Beloch, RG 192 sqq.

[2] Cf., e.g., G. Wissowa, RE 5, 331 sq. Hugh Last, *op. cit.* (85 n. 3), etc.

[3] The earliest extant evidence of this is the denarius of A. Postumius Albinus from about 80 B.C. (Th. Mommsen, Geschichte des römischen Münzwesens, Berlin 1860, 617 n. 442. H. A. Grueber, BMC Rep. 1, 1910, 351 sq., nos. 2836 sqq.). This monetary type reflects the version of the story, concerning the issue between Latins and Romans, as given also in *Vir. ill.* 7, 9-13, and Cass. Dio 1, p. 24 Boiss. Zon. = VII 9, 11; whereas Juba and Varro (in Plut., *Quaest. Rom.* 4) with Liv. I 45, 3-7, and Val. Max. VII 3, 1, gave it as a Sabine-Roman competition for superiority.

[4] G. Wissowa, RE 5, 332 sqq. *Idem*, Religion und Kultus der Römer[2], München 1912, 39 (the second quotation); cf. *ibid.* 247 sqq., and E. Pais, St. d. R. I 1, Torino 1898, 332.

the Artemis of Massalia (Strab. IV 180).—The real reason for this choice was, however, a different one: it was due to the fact that the sanctuary on the Aventine was an offspring ("Filiale") of the Arician one and its foundation meant that the ritual center of the Latins has been shifted from Aricia to Rome . . . With Diana also the cult of Egeria, originally tied up with the environments of Aricia, migrated to Rome . . . [1] The anniversary of the foundation of the Aventine sanctuary was celebrated on the day of the festival of the goddess in Aricia (Stat., *Silv.* III 1, 60), viz., the 13th of August, . . . and this day was sacred to Diana in the whole of Italy (Stat., *Silv.* III 1, 59 sq.: *omnisque pudicis Itala terra focis Hecateidas excolit idus*). The primary importance of this sacred precinct emerges also from the fact that the statutes of this temple (*lex dedicationis*, cf. Festus, p. 165 b 25), in all likelihood the oldest known, became the model for all subsequent cult foundations of this kind: the general prescriptions of those later creations habitually repeated the formula *ceterae leges huic arae titulisq. eaedem sunto, quae sunt arae Dianae in Aventino* (CIL XII 4333, etc.). . ."

"Therefore we can be sure that the transfer of the (Arician) cult of Diana to the Aventine implied the predominance of Rome in the religious duties of the Confederation . . .: the reception of the hitherto not venerated Diana in Rome mirrors the beginnings of the absorption of the Latins in the Roman state,—in the same way as in general the extension of the circle of the cults in Rome progressed in parallel with the conquest." [2]

The conclusions of Wissowa have been accepted by most of the modern historians of Rome who, with a very few exceptions,[3] believe also in the historicity of the traditional date of origin of the Aventine sanctuary under Servius Tullius.[4] Some of them, suspecting

---

[1] We may add also Anna Perenna : Ovid., *Fast.* 3, 523 sqq. 647 sqq.

[2] Cf. now in general : J. Bayet, Histoire politique et psychologique de la religion romaine, Paris 1957, 122 sqq. The most archaic ritual forms of this religious imperialism were, however, restricted to Southern Etruria and Latium ; cf. G. Rohde, Die Bedeutung der Tempelgründungen im Staatsleben der Römer, Marburg 1932, 9 sqq.

[3] J. Binder, Die Plebs, Leipzig 1909, 331. A. Merlin, L'Aventin dans l'Antiquité, Paris 1904, 215. A. Piganiol, La conquête romaine, Paris 1927, 120.

[4] E.g., G. De Sanctis, St. d. R. 1, 31, 375, 388. E. Täubler, Imperium Romanum, 1, 1913, 306 sqq. A. Rosenberg, Hermes 54, 1919, 151. K. J. Beloch, RG 192. L. Homo, L'Italie primitive 146. H. Last, CAH 7, 1928, 350 sqq. M. Gelzer, RE 12, 948. C. Bailey, Phases in the Religiosity of Ancient Rome (Sather Lectures 10), Berkeley 1932, 118. S. Mazzarino, Dalla mon. 149 sqq.

AT THE CROSSROADS OF TRUTH AND FICTION

that the Arician precinct was founded at a more recent date than the epoch of that king, tried to reverse the interrelation between the two cults, regarding the Aventine as the primary and the elder one; [1] this attempt, however, has been successfully disproved [2] and the results of Wissowa once more stabilized.

The priority of Aricia as a center of the Latin League under the auspices of Diana over the Aventine being thus firmly established, it remains to correct a small but all-important detail in view of the interrelations of the federal cult in Aricia and Rome. Wissowa, as we have seen, takes the Aventine precinct as a succursal of that of Aricia. This would be the most obvious conclusion in the world if the Roman institution were a local, municipal branch or descendant of the ritual center in Aricia. But the Aventine was a *comune Latinorum Dianae templum* as well as its mother-cult, and the League could have had only one such center at one time for the federal celebrations. Only in one city could the representatives of the allied cities and the annual magistrates of the League fulfill their ritual obligations on the day of the festival of Diana, which was also the solemn day of celebration for the Latin municipal Diana-cults in every city. This has most important implications. It is obvious that the Aventine could have been the focus of the Latin League only at a later time than Aricia. As the rise of the original *lucus Dianius* was due to a temporary political preponderance of Aricia, so its replacement by a rival institution of the same kind was also due to political reasons. It could happen only when the primary organization had been overcome by a competitor. And as we know now that the rise of Aricia to leadership belongs to the last decade of the sixth century, the substitution of it by Rome is later than this date. Rome could replace Aricia in this role only after the victory at Lake Regillus, and not in the middle of the sixth century; not under Servius Tullius, as the annalists would have us believe. "La construction du temple de Diane," wrote A. Merlin in 1906, [3]

A. E. Gordon, TAPA 63, 1932, 179. Pl. Fraccaro, Opuscula 1, Pavia 1956, 12. L. Pareti, St. d. R. 1, 1952, 318. A. Bernardi, Athen., n.s. 30, 1952, 18 n.i. G. Giannelli, La repubblica romana[2] 46, 49. S. Ferri, Studi class. e orient. 1953, 79 sqq. P. De Francisci, Primordia civitatis 666 sqq.

[1] G. De Sanctis, St. d. R. IV 2, 1, 1953, 160 sqq. M. Gelzer, RE 12, 953, line 32 sqq. F. Altheim, Griechische Götter im alten Rom (RVV 22, 1) 1930, 137 sqq., and repeatedly elsewhere. G. Pasquali, La nuova antologia 386, 1936, 415.

[2] A. E. Gordon, TAPA 63, 1932, 180 sqq.

[3] A. Merlin, *op. cit.* (87 n. 3) 215.

"commémorait les premiers progrès des armes romaines, prélude des triomphes futurs; elle proclamait la soumission des Latins, reconnaissant la souveraineté [we would say "prépondérance" only] de la République, mais non pas encore leur conquête et leur absorption."

The abundant archaeological discoveries in the Eternal City have demonstrated that a temple from the middle of the sixth century would not be an abnormality in Rome. But the Aventine was located outside the sacred boundary line, not within it, and this constitutes a different situation for a highly official, politically prevalent cult. As we established the defeat of the Latins as a *terminus post quem*, and as we shall see that the Aventine could become a federal center only before 456 B.C., the date of its foundation is well defined inside the time limits of that victory and the decemvirate—presumably nearer to the first event than to the second. We do not think the sanctuary as a building was erected there at once: the replacement of the *lucus Dianius* of Aricia with a cult-image in the open air could be achieved by the consecration of another grove; the building seems to me a subsequent addition.[1]

The location of a federal sanctuary on the Aventine is the first reason why the hill remained outside the gates of the city: the federal center needed exterritorial rights. The federal cult of Diana on the hill of *Corne* near Tusculum,[2] which seems to have been one more attempt to challenge the leadership in the League, perhaps somewhere in the second half of the fifth century, was situated also outside the city proper. In the same way the row of 13 big archaic altars, discovered recently outside Lavinium,[3] can be regarded confidently as the remains of the federal sanctuaries of Lavinium, dating from the sixth century B.C.[4]

The late date of origin of the Aventine precinct has momentous

---

[1] DH IV 26, 3 relates that Servius Tullius persuaded the Latins to constitute a ἱερὸν ἄσυλον, which is first of all a precinct; Emperor Claudius thought the same when he provided for some *sacra ex legibus Tulli regis piaculaque apud lucum Dianae per pontifices danda* (Tac., *Ann.* XII 8, 1).

[2] Plin., *N.h.* XVI 91, 242: *Est in suburbano Tusculani agri colle, qui Corne appellatur, lucus antiqua religione Dianae sacratus a Latio.* In this case the same is true as for the Aventine: a *federal* sanctuary cannot be duplicated, as, e.g., G. De Sanctis, *op. cit.* (87 n. 4) 2, 43, or E. Täubler, *op. cit.* 307 sqq., thought.

[3] F. Castagnoli, Dedica arcaica Lavinate a Castore e Polluce (SMSR 30, 1959).

[4] Cf. A. Alföldi, Die trojanischen Urahnen der Römer 9 sqq., and p. 265 sqq. below.

AT THE CROSSROADS OF TRUTH AND FICTION

historical consequences. This hill was in the coming centuries the seat of the peculiar religious and political organization of the *plebs*. This organization did not originate under Servius Tullius. The federal phase of the Diana precinct occurred no doubt prior to the plebeian occupation on the Aventine. Luckily enough, the time of this latter event, the first great adventure of the plebeian revolution,[1] born after 505 B.C. and growing in strength ever since, was preserved in the memory of the Romans because it was connected with fundamental developments on which the political struggle depended until 287 B.C. In spite of all inaccuracies and uncertainties of our literary evidence, the decisive facts still emerge from the dull sea of oblivion.

The plebs seized the Aventine as a stronghold against the ruling patriciate some few years before the middle of the fifth century, and the possession of the lots distributed by this revolutionary organization was officially recognized soon afterwards by the state, when the plebeian leaders were reconciled with the aristocracy.[2] Then, and only then, did the Aventine become the seat of the plebeian revolution, transforming itself into a political organism, admitted step by step within the frame of the patrician state and finally amalgamated with it.[3] The Aventine, seized about 456 B.C. as the military basis of the

---

[1] G. De Sanctis, St. d. R. 2¹, 30 sqq., and A. Momigliano, Bull. Com. 59, 1931, 166, realized that the names of the earliest tribunes of the *plebs* are a fictitious multiplication of the really known names of heroes from the years with which we are concerned.

[2] See the penetrating remarks on the sources and the clear summary of facts by J. Bayet in the appendix of his Tite-Live 3, 1954, 126 sqq. and 145 sqq.

[3] Liv. III 31, 1 : *Deinde M. Valerius Sp. Verginius consules facti . . . . De Aventino publicando lata lex est.* 32, 7 (*C. Menenio P. Sestio Capitolino coss.*) : *Placet creari decemviros . . . Admiscerenturne plebeii controversia aliquamdiu fuit* ; *postremo concessum patribus modo ne lex Icilia de Aventino aliaeque sacratae leges abrogarentur.* Cic., *in Cornelianam* (Ascon. p. 77 Clark) : *Tum interposita fide per tris legatos amplissimos viros Romam armati revertuntur. In Aventino consederunt* ; *inde armati in Capitolium venerunt* ; *decem tr.pl. <per> pontificem, quod magistratus nullus erat, creaverunt.* Diod. XII 24, 5 (The army in the Algidus, instigated by Verginius) : πάντων δ' ἐπὶ βοηθεῖν τοῖς ἠτυχηκόσιν ὁρμησάντων, μετὰ τῶν ὅπλων νυκτὸς εἰς 'Ρώμην εἰσέπεσον. οὗτοι μὲν οὖν κατελάβοντο λόφον τὸν ὀνομαζόμενον 'Αουεντῖνον. DH X 31, 2 : (ὁ 'Ικίλλιος ὁ δήμαρχος) . . . εἰσέφερε γάρ τι καὶ οὗτος πολίτευμα καινὸν ἀξιῶν ἀπομερισθῆναι τοῖς δημόταις τόπον εἰς οἰκιῶν κατασκευὰς τὸν καλούμενον Αὐεντῖνον, . . . ὃς οὐχ ἅπας τότε ᾠκεῖτο, ἀλλ' ἦν δημόσιός τε καὶ ὕλης ἀνάπλεως. 32, 2-4 : μετὰ τοῦτο . . . . ἐν τῇ λοχίτιδι ἐκκλησίᾳ συναχθείσῃ ὑπὸ τῶν ὑπάτων ὁ νόμος ἐκυρώθη, ὅς ἐστιν ἐν στήλῃ χαλκῇ γεγραμμένος, ἣν ἀνέθεσαν ἐν τῷ 'Αὐεντίνῳ κομίσαντες εἰς τὸ τῆς 'Αρτέμιδος ἱερόν. Cf. 32, 5. B. G. Niebuhr, RG 1², 379. K. W. Nitsch, Rh. Mus., n. F. 24, 1869, 155 sqq. ; 25, 1870. 88 sqq. In addition to the works of Merlin, *op. cit.* 34 sqq., J. Bayet, *loc. cit.*, G. De

plebs, was transformed gradually into its administrative center after its existence had been acknowledged and legalized.

For a better understanding of the *coup d'état* of 456 we must of course look back to the roots of the "popular" movement. This was a violent reaction against the constitution of the patriciate,[1] which, as we have already stated, appropriated for its closed circle the privileges of the *auspicium* and *imperium*, the exclusive claim to the magistracy, after the flight of the Tarquins. This reaction, though fostered by the aspirations of the men of the street, was not brought about by foreigners, rich merchants, or freedmen and workers, all of them still despised and politically disregarded in much later centuries:[2] we must completely forget the menace of the urban proletariat of the Late Republic, which colors the narrative of our relatively late sources and of their modern followers; this menace did not exist in the archaic Rome. The rising of the lower strata was in reality organized and directed by the descendants of those powerful Roman clans,[3] which were excluded from the closed ring of the patriciate, but who aspired nevertheless to the leadership of the state. The ordinary citizen supporting them had also, of course, some advantages or some protection from those patrons, but even our late evidence betrays the crucial fact that the main concern of the plebeian movement was the gradually successful admission of its leaders to the government. We see no demolition of social barriers, nor the participation of the masses in the benefits and privileges of the aristocracy when the *plebs* achieved its goal; we see only the recognition of the *tribuni plebis* and later on [4]

Sanctis, St. d. R. 1, 13, 24, see also A. Schwegler, RG 1, 598 sqq. O. Gilbert, Geschichte und Topographie der Stadt Rom im Altertum 2, Leipzig 1885, 144 sqq. Chr. Hülsen-H. Jordan, Topographie der Stadt Rom I 3, 1907, 153. O. Richter, Topographie der Stadt Rom (Handb. d. Altertumswiss. II 3, 2), München 1901, 204. J. Binder, Die Plebs, 87 sqq. E. Pais, St. d. R. 3³, Roma 1926, 222 sqq. S. B. Platner, Th. Ashby, A Topographical Dictionary of Ancient Rome, London 1929, 65 sqq. G. Niccolini, Il tribunato della plebe, Milano 1932, 44 sqq. For a different interpretation cf. D. Van Berchem, Mus. Helv. 17, 1960, 30 sqq.

[1] A. Alföldi, Der frührömische Reiteradel und seine Ehrenabzeichen, Baden-Baden 1952.

[2] We shall return to this problem in another study, dealing with the right of association in the early centuries, the results of which are briefly given in the Schweizer Münzblätter 5, 1954, 25 sqq.

[3] The same was considered by G. Giannelli, La repubblica romana², Milano 1955, 119 and 124.

[4] A. Momigliano, Bull. Com. 60, 1932 (1933), 222.

of the *aediles*, as state officials and the successive incorporation of the leading social stratum of the *plebs* in the noblemen-cavalry. The reaction of this important social group against the patriciate certainly did not wait through half a century to manifest itself. The reconciliation under the decemvirate shows them already garnering the ripe fruits of their political struggle. At the start of the new régime under and after Porsenna, the *equites* had the double advantage of a superior military efficiency and of a firmly established social recruiting-ground for their retinue, whereas the exact forms and tactics of the pedestrian reaction had still to be worked out in the next decades. When the permanent occupation of the Aventine occurred, this evolution had already matured.

In later times, with which we are better acquainted, the political and administrative center of the *plebs* was not the temple of Diana but that of Ceres, Liber, and Libera on the Aventine. The literary tradition placed the vow of the *dictator* Postumius Albus to build a temple to Ceres in the year 496, and the dedication of the sanctuary in the year 493 B.C. This date has been accepted by many scholars,[1] but at the same time others have supported a contrary view with weighty arguments.[2] It did not escape their attention [3] that A. Postumius Albus, a leading figure of the new ruling aristocracy, was the least likely personality for the role of creating a permanent center for the revolutionary opposition. The victory at Lake Regillus, won by him,

---

[1] G. Wissowa, Religion und Kultus der Römer[2], München 1912, 297 sq. *Idem*, RE 3, 1973. I. G. Scott, Mem. Am. Acad. in Rome 7, 1929, 107 n. 5. G. Pasquali, La nuova antologia 386, 1936, 410. Kr. Hanell, *op. cit.* 174. A. Mazzarino, Dalla mon. 149, 251 sq. n. 133. J. Vogt, Die römische Republik[2], Freiburg 1951, 43 sqq. Fr. Altheim, RG 2, Frankfurt 1953, 52, 114. 139 sqq., 182. R. Bloch CRAI 1954, 203 sqq. H. Le Bonniec, Le culte de Cérès à Rome, Paris 1958, 213 sqq. (with more literature). R. Bloch, R. Et. Lat. 37, 1959, 125 sqq. *Idem*, Revue de Philol. 3. ser. 34, 1960, 185 sqq. R. Schilling, Hommages à G. Dumézil (Coll. Latomus 45) 1960, 190 sq. D. Van Berchem, Mus. Helv. 17, 1960, 30. Some good observations in a paper by H. Wagenvoort, Mnemos. 4. ser. 13, 1960, 111 sq.

[2] E. Pais, St. d. R. 3[3], Roma 1927, 152 sqq. K. J. Beloch, RG 63 sqq. W. Hoffmann, Rom und die griechische Welt im IV. Jahrhundert v. Chr. (Philol. Suppl. 27, 1) 1934, 98 sqq. W. Schur, RE 13, 71. E. Kornemann, Internat. Monatschrift 14, 1919-20, 491 sq. A. Bruhl, Liber pater, Paris 1953, 32 sqq. G. Giannelli, *op. cit.* 125, G. De Sanctis, St. d. R. 1, 37 sqq., and especially with a detailed discussion, *idem*, St. d. R. IV 2, 1, Firenze 1953, 194 sqq. The arguments brought forward by these scholars are not superseded by H. Le Bonniec, *op. cit.* 235 sqq.

[3] E. Pais, Italia antica 1, Bologna 1922, 84 sqq. W. Hoffmann, *op. cit.* 99.

was the ordeal which proved the fitness of the cavalry class for ruling in the state. The *Dioscuri*, to whom on the battlefield he vowed a temple on the Forum, were indeed the heavenly patrons of the nobleman-cavalry and, moreover, the archaeological evidence strongly supports the traditional date of the foundation of this sanctuary.[1] The statuary group of the divine youths with their horses, which stood near the temple at the *Lacus Iuturnae* on the Forum, has been recovered by excavations (Frontispiece and pl. II). It is the work of a Greek artist from Magna Graecia, and we agree with W. Amelung that it dates from the fifth century B.C.; the palm-trunk supports under the horses are later additions. Consequently the legend of their appearance, announcing the great victory of Postumius Albus, is almost contemporary. But the idea that a protagonist of the *equites*-patricians would have vowed and built the temple of Ceres, i.e., cared for a safe refuge for the most dangerous opponents, situated outside the sphere of supervision [2] of the patrician magistrates, is unbelievable. As De Sanctis pointed out long ago, this foundation could only have been conceived by the *populares*, not by their adversaries.

The same objections apply to the assignment in the fifth century of a legal and administrative role to the temple of Ceres. This would anticipate the practice of later epochs. Of course, before this sanctuary was built, indeed before the political movement of the *plebs* started, the fines and expropriations conceived as a *sacratio* to Ceres existed in the archaic juridical practice of the Romans.[3] But this time-honored practice has nothing to do with the erection of the temple, dedicated to a foreign triad. The expropriation of the goods of Spurius Cassius for Ceres in the form of a cult-statue of the goddess was suspect even

---

[1] On the early temples of Rome cf. : I. Scott Ryberg, An Archaeological Record of Rome from the VIIth to the IInd Century B.C. (Studies and Documents, ed. by K. and S. Lake 13) London 1940, and E. Gjerstad, Early Rome 3, Lund 1960, *passim*. The cult of the Greek Dioscuri in archaic Latium is now established by F. Castagnoli, *op. cit.* (89 n. 3) 109 sqq. As in Rome and in Tusculum, *Castor* and *Pollux* were also in Lavinium certainly connected with the ruling aristocracy. For further details see below Chapter VI.

[2] Cf. below, p. 99 sq.

[3] Plin., *N.h.* XVIII 3, 12. Plut., *Rom.* 22, 3. Cf., e.g. W. W. Fowler, JRS 1, 1911, 57 sqq. K. J. Beloch, RG 246. K. Latte, Zeitschr. Sav.-Stiftung 67, 1950, 50 sqq. W. Kunkel, Zeitschr. Sav.-Stiftung 68, 1951, 562. G. De Sanctis, St. d. R. IV 2, 1, 1953, 194 n. 259. B. Perrin, Studi in memoria di E. Albertario 2, Milano 1953, 400 sqq. H. Le Bonniec, *op. cit.* 165 sqq.

to the common source of Livy and Dionysius.[1] In the same way the *iuris interpretes* [2] refused to believe in the alleged prescription of the *leges Valeriae-Horatiae* of 449 B.C., protecting the inviolability of the tribunes of the plebs *sanciendo ut qui tribunis plebis aedilibus* (the latter did not yet exist in my mind) *iudicibus decemviris nocuisset, eius caput Iovi sacrum esset, familia ad aedem Liberi Liberaeque venum iret*: [3] it cannot be doubted, in fact, that the *sacrosanctitas* of the tribunes was defended in those early days not by legal provisions of the patrician state, but by the curse of the totality of the plebeians on offenders, who became victims of the lynchjustice of the revolution.[4] Another prescription of the same legislative action concerning the temple of Ceres, is an obvious forgery: *Institutum etiam ab iisdem consulibus, ut senatus consulta in aedem Cereris ad aediles plebis deferrentur, quae antea arbitrio consulum supprimebantur vitiabanturque.*[5] The idea that the Senate before 287 B.C. would entrust its archive to the supervision and control of its opponents, who where not yet acknowledged as organs of the administration, and who had their seat *extra pomerium*, is extravagant. As late as 304 the publication of such documents by the aedile Cn. Flavius caused consternation; and the vitiation of those protocols by the consuls continued, as e.g., the arbitrary emendations in a politically crucial decision implemented by Pompey in 52 shows. Over and above this the *senatus consulta* did not yet play the part of vehicles of the administration that they played later: the senatorial jurisdiction certainly did not yet overpower the actual orders of the governing functionaries in the fifth century B.C. And the legal texts, relevant for the *plebs*,

---

[1] Cf. Liv. II 41, 10 (Plin., *N.h.* XXXIV 4, 15. Val. Max. V 8, 2) with DH VIII 79, 4. On the source : A. Klotz, Livius und seine Vorgänger 243 sqq. On the fiction : Th. Mommsen, RF 2, 1879, 174. G. De Sanctis, St. d. R. 2¹, 11 n. 4, and IV 2, 1, 194 n. 259.

[2] Liv. III 55, 8-10.

[3] Liv. III 55, 6-7. DH VI 89, 3.

[4] Cf. G. De Sanctis, St. d. R. 2¹, 28 n. 3. J. Bayet, Tite-Live 3, 1954, 145 sqq., and the following notes. *Contra* : A. Momigliano, Bull. Com. 60, 1932 (1933) 221. H. Le Bonniec, *op. cit.* 347 sqq.

[5] Liv. III 55, 13. Cf. among others Th. Mommsen, RF 2, 164 sqq. G. De Sanctis, *op. cit.* 2, 28 sqq., 51 sqq. J. Beloch, RG 1, 328 sqq. G. Giannelli, *op. cit.* 125, 130. Pl. Fraccaro, Opuscula 1, Pavia 1956, 19. A. Guarino, in the *Festschrift für F. Schulz*, Weimar 1951, 458 sqq. P. De Francisci, Storia del diritto romano 1, Milano 1943, 350. More juridical literature given by U. v. Lübtow, Das römische Volk 104 n. 483. *Contra* : G. Niccolini, Il tribunato della plebe, Milano 1932, 42 sqq. E. Manni, Il mondo classico, 9 1939, 263. F. Altheim, RG 2, 181. H. Le Bonniec, *op. cit.* 344.

were not yet preserved in the sanctuary of Ceres, but in the precinct of Diana, where the *lex Icilia de Aventino publicando* was there still later.[1] In other words: the temple of Ceres was not in existence in the years of the decemvirate. Furthermore, the peculiar ritual of this sanctuary yields another *terminus post quem* for the date of its erection.

The cult of Ceres in Rome has evidently very old indigenous roots.[2] But the triad Ceres-Liber-Libera belonged to the *peregrina sacra*[3] and it was never forgotten that it came from the Greeks. The way by which Ceres arrived has been clarified by I. Scott Ryberg,[4] who documented it by the small terracotta *arulae* in early Roman finds. They emerge first as a typical offering in the Sicilian sanctuaries of Demeter, and spreading thence across *Magna Graecia* to Campania and Rome.[5] The continuous series[6] of Greek priestesses officiating in that sanctuary, praying in Greek and providing the *Graecus ritus* for the cult, can only be taken as an uninterrupted chain going back to the very act of the first regulations. Livy notes on the year 428 B.C.:[7] *datum inde negotium aedilibus, ut animadverterent ne qui nisi Romani di NEU QUO ALIO MORE QUAM PATRIO COLERENTUR.* If this were a reliable

---

[1] DH X 32, 4 (quoted above 93 n. 3). Cf. A. Rosenberg, Der Staat der alten Italiker, Berlin 1913, 2. A. Momigliano, Bull. Com. 60, 1932 (1933) 222, etc. *Contra* : H. Le Bonniec, *op. cit.* 357, *perperam omnino.*

[2] G. Wissowa, RuK², 192 sq. Th. Mommsen, CIL I², p. 283 sqq. G. De Sanctis, St. d. R. IV 2, 1, 191 sqq. D. Sabbatucci, L'edilità romana (Mem Acc naz Lincei, cl. sc. morali, ser. 8, vol. 6, 3) Roma 1954, 277 sq. R. Bloch, CRAI 1954, 203 sqq. H. Le Bonniec, *op. cit.*, 15 sqq., 108 sqq. Cf. also J. Marquardt, St. V. 3², 362 n. 7. N. Turchi, La religione di Roma antica, Bologna 1939, 83 sqq. *Contra* : F. Altheim, Terra mater, Frankfurt 1931, 111.

[3] Fest., p. 268, 27 Linds. : *Peregrina sacra appellantur, quae aut evocatis dis in oppugnandis urbibus Romam sunt co(ac)ta, aut quae ob quasdam religiones per pacem sunt petita, ut ex Phrygia Matris Magnae, ex Graecia Cereris, Epidauro Aesculapi : quae coluntur eorum more, a quibus sunt accepta.* Cic., *Pro Balbo* 24, 55, is explicit in this matter : *Sacra Cereris . . ., cum essent adsumpta de Graecia, et per Graecas curata sunt sacerdotes et Graeca omnino nominata. Sed cum illam, quae Graecum illud sacrum monstraret et faceret, ex Graecia deligerent, tamen sacra pro civibus civem facere voluerunt, ut deos immortales scientia peregrina et externa, mente domestica et civili precaretur. Has sacerdotes video fere aut Neapolitanas aut Velienses fuisse, foederatarum sine dubio civitatum.* It is important that the Carthaginians hired Greek priestesses for the same cult in their city in 396 B.C., just about the time in which the Greek goddess was introduced in Rome ; cf. Diod. XIV 77, 2.

[4] I. Scott Ryberg, *op. cit.* (93 n.i.) 154 sqq.

[5] J. Heurgon, Rech. 55, 74. L. Banti, St. Etr. 17, 1943, 196 sqq. R. Bloch, R. Et. Lat. 37, 1959, 126. G. De Sanctis, St. d. R. IV 2, 1, 195 sqq. H. Le Bonniec, *op. cit.* 288 sqq.

[6] Details given by H. Le Bonniec, *op. cit.*, 397 sqq.

[7] Liv. IV 30, 11.

AT THE CROSSROADS OF TRUTH AND FICTION

report, the aediles, the guardians of the temple of three foreign divinities, would be obliged first to wipe out the religious basis of their
own political organization. Yet, not Ceres and her companions, but
Apollo must have been the first Greek divinity brought into Rome
on grounds of the consultation of the Sibylline books.[1] His temple
was vowed in 433 and dedicated in 431 B.C. Even in 399 B.C., when
the Greek divinities admitted officially as patrons of the Roman state
were honored for the first time with a *sellisternium*,[2] Ceres, Liber,
and Libera were not among them: this first choice of six pairs of
Olympian gods may have prevented the inclusion of Ceres in the
sellisternia until 217 B.C. Just at this time, about 400 B.C., a fresh wave
of Greek influences penetrated Rome.[3] *Juno Regina* brought to Rome
by *evocatio* from Veii and transferred to the Aventine, was worshipped
by the *Graecus ritus* [4] from 396 B.C. The construction of the temple
of our triad could not have taken place much later,[5] but no definite
year before or after the Celtic catastrophe can be suggested for it.

The temple of Ceres was built in "Tuscanic" style,[6] but the use of
this style was continued in Latium until Hellenism finally succeeded in
replacing it.[7] If the temple of Ceres, Liber, and Libera was a younger
contemporary of the Capitoline temple, its decoration would probably
have been entrusted to artists of Veii or Vulci. But we know that it
was decorated by two Greek artists, Damophilos and Gorgasos;

---

[1] G. Wissowa, RuK², 293. E. Kornemann, *op. cit.* (92 n. 2) 490 sq. G. Pasquali, *op. cit.* (92 n. 1) 410. (If he states on p. 413 that "le importazioni di divinità
greche cessano dal 484 fino niente meno che al 293, l'anno dell'introduzione
del culto di Esculapio," this is a slip of pen which happens to occur even in
the case of such a great scholar.) A. Piganiol, Histoire de Rome³, Paris
1949, 58. G. De Sanctis, St. d. R. IV 2, 1, 194 sqq. J. Gagé, Apollon romain
(BEFAR 182) 1955, 17 sqq. Also the dedication of other temples is offuscated
by spurious details ; cf. Fr. Münzer, Adelsparteien und Adelsfamilien, Stuttgart
1920, 90.

[2] G. Wissowa, RE 3, 1976 and 12, 1101 with all details.

[3] W. Hoffmann, *op. cit.* (92 n. 2) 68 sqq.

[4] G. Wissowa, RuK², 191.

[5] A. Kirsopp Michels, TAPA 80, 1949, 346, stressed the fact that all festivals
of Ceres are associated with the temple in the calendar. This means that the
temple was erected before the final redaction of the annual celebrations was
achieved.

[6] Vitruv. III 3, 5 ; cf. IV 7.

[7] This will become evident from the comprehensive work of Lucy Shoe on
architectural moldings. I am indebted to her for acquainting me with her
materials. Cf. A. Boethius, in : Palladio (Rivista di Storia dell'Architettura)
1958, 1, 1 sq.

their employment together with the introduction of a Greek ritual, which was entrusted to Greek priestesses brought from the south,[1] is no mere coincidence.

In our case the introduction of a Greek cult with all its Greek paraphernalia has a very special and very relevant reason: its connection with the *plebs*. As the corn supply was first of all vital for the poor, the corn goddess seemed to modern scholars [2] the most obvious patroness of the plebeians. But why was the old Roman agrarian divinity, Ceres with Tellus, not selected for this purpose instead of an alien triad with a foreign ritual? We understand this choice at once when we know the political background. It will be demonstrated in a study on the right of association in the Republican Rome,[3] that spontaneous and self-supporting political organization outside the official machinery was never granted there, though the contrary has been generally believed since Mommsen. The most outstanding consequence of this absolute lack of opportunity to build up free unions forced all the people to whom the privileges of the ruling aristocracy were denied to create organizations for the realization of political aims and social dreams under the cover of religious fraternities, which were, if not welcomed, yet not prohibited. The autochthonous cults being from the beginning controlled by the magistrates and official state priests, the foreign cults, also attracting the masses by their strange character and secretiveness, enveloped them with mysterious awe. As some divinities from Asia Minor, Syria, Egypt, and Persia were later found suitable for this purpose, so, to begin with, Greek cults were available to serve as camouflage and as the focus of forbidden political and social aspirations. The difference between the first experiment and the later ones is that in the first instance the revolutionary group, using the cult of Ceres, Liber, and Libera as a basis of organization, was successful, while the

---

[1] Plin., *N.h.* XXXV 12, 154 : *Plastae laudatissimi fuere Damophilus et Gorgasus, iidem pictores, qui Cereris aedem Romae ad Circum maximum utroque genere artis suae excoluerant, versibus inscriptis Graece, quibus significarent ab dextra opera Damophili esse, ab laevo Gorgasi. Ante hanc aedem Tuscanica omnia in aedibus fuisse auctor est Varro, et ex hac, cum reficeretur, crustas parietum excisas tabulis marginatis inclusas esse, item signa ex fastigiis dispersa.* The copious modern discussion of this famous passage is given by H. Le Bonniec, *op. cit.* 255 sqq.

[2] G. Wissowa, RE 3, 1975. H. Le Bonniec, *op. cit.* 243 sqq.

[3] The results of this treatise are summarized in a note on the cult of Isis in Rome and its connections with the revolution, in : Schweizer Münzblätter 5, 1954, 25 sqq.

98

later attempts taking advantage of the cultual associations of Bacchus, Sabazios, Bellona, and Isis were successively suppressed by the state. The real discrepancy between these later focuses of social dissatisfaction and the plebeian cult-centers on the Aventine, however, lies in the fact that the initiates of Bacchus and the Hellenized oriental gods just mentioned first gathered in secrecy with the faithful and their fanatics, and that they grew to a political danger only successively with the increasing size of their cult societies. The movement of the *plebs*, on the contrary, was not a product of this sort of hidden religious ferment, but burst into flame as reaction to the assumption of power by the mounted guards of the Tarquins. It was a part of the army which revolted, and its political strength was gaining fresh ground with the new military importance of the armored infantry in the last decades of the fifth century B.C.[1] The sheltering of the opposition under the auspices of a foreign cult is in this case a relatively late phase of the evolution—perhaps a lesson taught by the *popularis* movements of other cities.

In any case, the introduction of the new cult of Ceres, Liber and Libera on the Aventine was still the act of a revolutionary corporation,[2] and the cult never lost its markedly plebeian character.[3] Its institution shows an imitative opposition to the patrician state-cult, just as the political management of the *plebs* mirrors the polemical parallelism with the patrician administration. It is enough to recall briefly the main features of this intentional, competitive assimilation, already recognized by the modern historians. The original number of the tribunes of the *plebs*, like that of the consuls, was two.[4] The plebeian gatherings and their methods of polling were copied after the pattern of that of the state.[5] Correspondingly to the Capitol, the stronghold of the Etruscan kings and their patrician successors, the Aventine stronghold of the *plebs* was exempt from the voting districts

[1] A. Piganiol, Histoire de Rome[3], Paris 1949, 49.
[2] G. De Sanctis, Rivista di filol., n.s. 10, 1932, 444. The creation of the functionaries of the *plebs* must not be confused with the creation of the cult: these two are different manifestations.
[3] Details given by H. Le Bonniec, *op. cit.* 342 sqq. The traditional plebeian banqueting on the day of the *Cerealia* was imitated in a competitive manner by the patrician dinner-circles feasting on the *Megalensia*. Cf. Gellius XVIII 2, 11 with Plaut., *Men.* 100 sq.
[4] E.g., F. Altheim, RG 2, 199. More quotations in U. v. Lübtow, Das römische Volk 98 sqq.
[5] Th. Mommsen, RG 2, 179.

of the tribes, as L. R. Taylor reminds me. In the same way the triad on the Aventine with two female divinities besides a paternal god copied the Capitoline triad, in defiance of the state religion of the ruling aristocracy.[1] The *epulum Iovis* of the *ludi plebeii* copied the same celebration at the *ludi Romani*,[2] as the *ludi Ceriales* did with the "Roman" games.[3]

Topographical features are also revealing. The temple was situated at the foot of the Aventine hill, opposite the *Circus maximus*. The choice of this site may have been influenced by the fact that agrarian cults had their homes in the *vallis Murcia*,[4] but this was certainly not the decisive consideration. Though virtually below the hill, the *templum Cereris* was still excluded with the hill from the sacred boundary of the city.[5] This makes it evident that the military preparedness of the plebeians against the patricians was over when the site was selected for the construction: the revolution had been already tolerated officially—i.e., after the decemvirate—but carefully avoided placing its center within the city proper.

The Aventine, covered with woods [6] in the early fifth century B.C., still lay outside the city. That is the only possible explanation for its selection as the seat of the Latin League, which needed extraterritoriality.[7] But if the hill, which was included in the so-called Servian walls after the Gallic invasion,[8] remained exempt from the juridical sphere *intra pomerium*, this is due to the regard for the seat of the plebeian "state in state." The freedom of association being prohibited in the

[1] A. Pestalozza, I caratteri indigeni di Cerere, Milano 1897, 48. A. Bruhl, Liber pater, Paris 1953, 39. R. Bloch, CRAI 1954, 210. H. Le Bonniec, *op. cit.* 293 sqq.

[2] D. Sabbatucci, *op. cit.* (95 n. 2) 269 sqq. (with references).

[3] *Ibid.*, 266.

[4] As H. Le Bonniec, *op. cit.* 185 sqq., 270, thinks.

[5] The ancients forgot the reason for this ; cf. Gell. XIII 14, 4-7. On the site : A. Merlin, *op. cit.* (87 n. 3) 53 sqq. S. B. Platner-Th. Ashby, *op. cit.* (90 n. 3) 109 sq. H. Le Bonniec, *op. cit.* 254 sqq.

[6] The memory of the *Lauretum* on the Aventine seems not to have been invented by DH III 43, 1 ; on the contrary, the transfer of the populations of Tellenae and Politorium to the Aventine under Ancus (*ibid.* 1-2) cannot be accepted as historical. Cf. Chr. Huelsen in H. Jordan's *Topographie der Stadt Rom* 1³, Berlin 1907, 151 sqq. J. Binder, Die Plebs 82. A. Merlin, *l.c.* for details.

[7] In this sense, E. Täubler, Imperium Romanum, 311 n. 2.

[8] G. Säflund, Le mura di Roma repubblicana (Skrifter, utgivna av Svenska Institutet i Rom 1) Lund 1932. A. v. Gerkan, Rh. Mus. 100, 1957, 82 sqq. Details and divergent opinions will be discussed below, p. 320 sqq.

city, as we have already mentioned, the only possible way the state could tolerate an *illicita coitio* was to locate it outside the sphere of the coercive rights of its functionaries. The political wisdom of Rome manifests itself once more in this clever half-way solution: the antagonists theoretically banished can remain practically protected by the walls and their center was also unmolested because it was not inside the sacred boundary line.

Chapter III

THE LATINS AS ROMAN SUBJECTS
UNDER THE KINGS:
THE ANNALIST FICTION

THE CHARACTERIZATION OF THE INVENTED
ROMAN SUPERIORITY

If we believe the annalists, Rome was mistress of the Latins since the hour of her birth. Strabo's source stated that the "Latins" were the subjects (ὑπήκοοι) of Rome from the time of Romulus and his successors.[1] Plutarch [2] thought that they (all the Latins as a unit) made an alliance with Rome's founder. The idea that Rome *alone* and the Latins in their *totality* were partners or two opponents since that time remains the fundamental tenet in the pseudo-history of regal Rome. Romulus had already been the potential sovereign over the old capital of the Latin tribe—we are told—though he did not wish to take over the heritage of Numitor but gave the annual dictatorship to the Albans instead.[3]

---

[1] Strab. V 3, 4 (C. 231).
[2] Plut., *Rom.* 23, 6.
[3] Plut., *Romul.* 27, 1.

THE LATINS AS ROMAN SUBJECTS

The claim of supremacy over all the Latins is not based on a pretended primeval conquest but on a shrewd, though transparent, juridical fiction. This original deceit, a πρῶτον ψεῦδος of the Roman annals of history, was extended like a spider's web over all struggles of the Latins with Rome for independence until their final subjugation. This spider's web is, however, like a thread of Ariadne in our hands enabling us to find our way through that labyrinth of forged history. The theory of Roman rule over the Latins since Romulus and his first successors, though a much simplified one, is not a patchwork but a consistent doctrine coherently documented. The hegemonial position of the rising Roman power in the Republic is projected by it back into the epoch of the kings.

In order to understand this theory, we have to clarify the notion on which it is mainly based, i.e., that Rome as well as all the other Latin cities were *coloniae* of Alba Longa, founded by that city. It is, of course, well established that the tombs of the Early Iron Age on the Alban mountain belong to the same cultural group as those in Rome;[1] yet this means only that both of them are Latin, not that Rome was founded by Alba. It is also true that Alba once was the seat of the Latin tribe's ruler. But her role belonged to the pre-city epoch in Latium; the single groups of his tribe, constituted in a fixed number of thirty units—a number which was sanctified by religion, habit, and practical usefulness alike—were certainly in existence at the time of the Latin immigration. The oldest settlements of the Latin shepherds were still parts of a strategic whole and not *coloniae* sent out from a center, as were later the Roman colonies. They did not begin at all as urban communities.

The annalist concept of the *coloniae Albenses* is therefore unhistorical. Yet the history of the Latin-Roman relations in the regal epoch is based entirely on this fiction: Rome was a regular colony of the Albans,[2] the Annals pretend, as were all thirty cities of the *prisci Latini* who were therefore the *populi Albenses*.[3] According to Dionysius,

[1] Inez G. Scott, Mem. Am. Ac. 7, 1929, 24 sqq. M. Pallottino, Arch. cl. 12, 1960, 1 sqq.

[2] Lic. Mac. *fr.* 3 Peter (H. R. Rel. 1² p. 299 = Censorin, De die natali 20, 2). DH I 71, 5 ; 73, 3 ; 85, 1 sqq. II 2, 1 ; 36, 2 ; 62, 1 ; III 2, 3 ; 3, 1 ; 5, 1 ; 7, 5 ; 8, 2 ; 10, 3 ; 11, 7 sqq. 23, 19 ; 28, 4 ; 31, 4. VI 20, 3. Liv. I 6, 3 sqq. ; I 23, 1 ; 52, 2. XXVI 13, 16. Plut., *Rom.* 9, 1 sqq., and elsewhere. Further details in A. Schwegler, RG 1, 452 sqq.

[3] Liv. I 3, 7 ; 52, 2. DH III 31, 4 ; 45, 2. III 1, 2 ; 31, 4. VIII 19, 1. *Origo*

Rome was more powerful already under King Tullus than her mother-city and extended her supremacy over her. In the third generation of her existence, Rome became so mighty that many Latin cities preferred to be ruled by the Romans instead of their Alban progenitors.[1] In Rome's war with the Latins under Tullus all *populi Albenses* together faced Rome standing alone,[2] as always henceforward in that pseudo-history and as was the case later in the reality of the fourth century. Livy—though much more sober and concise—drew this concept from the same source [3] as the tedious rhetor of Halicarnassus.

The annalist fiction maintains that the sovereignty over the Latins was not achieved by a cruel victory over them and, above all, over their capital, Alba Longa, but by a symbolic fight of the Roman and Alban triplets, by a duel of mythical pattern and some legendary embellishment. *Cupido imperii duos cognatos . . . populos ad arma stimulat.[4] . . . Ineamus aliquam viam*, is the theme, *qua utri utris imperent sine magna clade . . . decerni possit.*[5] And before the triple combat, it was agreed that sovereignty over the city of the defeated group will be the price of valor: *Priusquam dimicarent, foedus ictum inter Romanos et Albanos est his legibus ut cuiusque populi cives eo certamine vicissent, is alteri populo cum bona pace imperitaret.*[6] Indeed, the Roman king does with the Albans after that contest as he pleases,[7] in the same way as the Romans do later with their subject *socii* allies.[8] Varro [9] already uses this account. The alleged transfer of Alba's citizens to Rome affirmed once more the legal character of the succession of Rome as the ruling power superseding Alba Longa, a succession which never happened in fact; in the middle of the fifth century B.C.[10] when the Romans extended their sway up to the Alban region, the old capital had already shrunk to an insignificant settlement. Rome is said to have had an

---

gent. Rom. 17, 6, etc. Cf. H. Nissen, It. Lk. II 2, 551 sqq. 555 sq. K. J. Beloch, RG 148 sqq., 161 sq. L. Pareti, St. d. R. 1, 1952, 231 sqq. and above, p. 10 sq.

[1] DH III 9, 4. 6. 7 ; 11, 5. 9.

[2] DH III 33, 1 sq. 34, 4 sq.

[3] Liv. I 22, 3 ; 23, 7. 9 ; 24, 2 sq. 25, 2. 12. 13 ; 26, 11 ; I 32, 3. For details on the sources see Fr. Münzer, RE 7, 107 no. 1.

[4] Liv. I 23, 7.

[5] *Ibid.* I 23, 9.

[6] Liv. I 24, 2-3. 25, 2. 12 sq. ; 26, 11.

[7] Liv. I 26, 1 ; 27, 4 sqq.

[8] Liv. I 28, 5 sq.

[9] Varro, *Rer. human.* l. 8 (= Fest., p. 476, 5 L.)

[10] Cf. below, p. 244 sqq.

THE LATINS AS ROMAN SUBJECTS

army of *socii* of the later type already in her war with the Albans under Tullus and, of course, later under Tarquinius Priscus and Superbus.[1]

The rather sophisticated juridical fiction underlying this pseudo-documentation, however, emerges most clearly from the account of Dionysius.[2] He writes: the cities of the Latins were at odds with the Romans for the first time under King Tullus, because after the razing of the Albans' city they were unwilling to yield the leadership to the victors. Fifteen years after the destruction of Alba, the Roman king sent envoys to the thirty cities which were once the colonies and subjects of Alba (εἰς τὰς ἀποίκους τε καὶ ὑπηκόους αὐτῆς) summoning them to obey his orders, since the Romans succeeded the Albans' supremacy over the Latin race and therefore laid claim to everything the Albans had possessed. He pointed out that there are two methods of acquisition by which men are able to become masters of what belonged to others. One of these possibilities is compulsion, the other choice; the Romans had acquired by both methods the supremacy over the cities the Albans held before. For, when the Albans became the enemies of the Romans, the latter conquered them by arms, and, after they lost their home city, the Romans gave them a share in their own commonwealth; it was but reasonable that the Albans both perforce and voluntarily yield to the Romans the sovereignty they exercised over their subjects.

The ultimate author of this forged concept had forgotten but one thing: Rome was meant as one of the thirty colonies and nevertheless she aspired to the rule over *all the thirty*, not over twenty-nine!

This theory was, of course, not invented by Dionysius. Livy, too, knew it and resumed it by putting the following words in the mouth of King Superbus:[3] *Posse quidem se vetusto iure agere quod, cum omnes Latini ab Alba oriundi sint, in eo foedere teneantur, quod ab Tullo res omnis Albana cum colonis suis in Romanum cesserit imperium; ceterum se utilitatis id magis omnium causa censere ut renovetur id foedus, secundaque potius fortuna populi Romani ut participes Latini fruantur quam urbium excidia vastationemque agrorum, quas Anco prius patre deinde suo regnante perpessi sint, semper aut exspectent, aut patiantur.*

And in 340 B.C. Livy refers to this ancient alliance: *Haecine foedera*

---

[1] DH III 4, 1 ; 23, 2 ; 27, 3 ; 33, 3 ; 57, 3 ; 65, 4. 6 ; IV 3, 2 ; 50, 1.
[2] DH III 34, 1 sq.
[3] Liv. I 52, 2 sq. Cf. Varro, *Rer. human.* l. 8. in Fest., p. 476, 5 L.

The Invented Roman Superiority

*Tullus, Romanus rex, cum Albanis, patribus vestris, Latini, haec L. Tar-
quinius vobiscum postea fecit?* [1]

All ensuing wars of Rome with the Latins are consequently treated
as if the superior Roman might had to face the united group of the
Latins. So, for instance, under King Ancus [2] who, of course, reduced
them to obedience, and under Tarquin the Elder who again subdued
the League, though five mighty Etruscan cities helped them; the
Romans ravaged their territory: [3] Rome—this is what the original
source of our tradition wished to point out—has already outgrown the
combined forces of Central Italy, not only those of her Latin kinsfolk.

Apparently forgetting that he previously had implied the existence
of a Latin confederation, Dionysius [4] describes the action of King
Servius Tullius who, animated by noble Greek examples, succeeded
in uniting all the cities belonging to the Latin race in a League,[5] the
center of which was the grove of Diana in Rome, under the sovereign
leadership of this city: *Ea erat confessio caput rerum Romam esse*, as
Livy states. The consequences of this statement are twice overlooked
in the same way: first, we find the Latins assembling under Superbus
not on the Aventine but at the *caput aquae Ferentinae* under the Alban
mountain; [6] second, the alleged submission of the Hernicans and of
the two most important Volscian cities is said to have brought into
existence a "new" center on the *mons Albanus* under the leadership
of Rome, where the Latins met along with those new dependent
allies.[7] The "new" center was, however, in fact very old then. Another
tradition would attribute to Servius Tullius [8] the foundation of the
Capitol as a *federal* sanctuary—which it never was.

The last king is described as ruling over the whole body of the
Latins, over *omne nomen Latinum* [9]—though *nomen* includes all the
parts of the tribe, Rome as well. The Latins elected Superbus to be

---

[1] Liv. VIII 5, 9. Cf. Th. Mommsen, St. R. 3, 618 n. 2.
[2] DH III 37, 2 sqq. 38, 1 sq. 39, 1 sq. 40, 5. Liv. I 32, 3 : *Igitur Latini, cum
quibus Tullo regnante ictum foedus erat, sustulerant animos.*
[3] DH III 50, 7 ; 54, 3 ; 57, 3 ; IV 3, 2. Liv. I 35, 7 ; 38, 4. *Vir. ill.* 6, 8. Plin.,
N.h. III 5, 70 (Valerius Antias).
[4] DH IV 25, 3 sqq.
[5] Cf. above, p. 85 sqq. Liv. I 45, 3.
[6] DH IV 45, 3. Cf. above, p. 34 sqq.
[7] DH IV 49, 1-3.
[8] Tac., *Hist.* 3, 72 : *mox Servius Tullius sociorum studio, dein Tarquinius Superbus
capta Suessa Pometia hostium spoliis extruxere* (sc. Capitolium).
[9] Liv. I 50, 3.

THE LATINS AS ROMAN SUBJECTS

their lifelong ruler,[1] as they had done with Tarquin the Elder and King Servius, under the most solemn formalities.[2] The notion that Rome was one of the members of the League of the Latins, and the other notion that she stood isolated, over and above the Latins, constantly oscillate in this account.[3]

Also, King Superbus does not deal with single Latin cities in the Annals, but with the *Latinorum gens*. His son-in-law from Tusculum is *longe princeps Latini nominis*, and he commands the tribe as his servants: *Latinorum proceres in diem certam ut ad lucum Ferentinae conveniant, indicit.* He has the audacity to make a game of all the Latins, *ludificari . . . omne nomen Latinum*—the League which is obeying him like a servant. The only man who dares to oppose him is murdered by the treacherous tyrant.[4] The superiority of Rome is demonstrated by the order of the king to mix his own troops with the Latin contingents at his will: *indictum . . . iunioribus Latinorum, ut ex foedere die certa ad lucum Ferentinae armati frequentes adessent. qui ubi ad edictum Romani regis ex omnibus populis convenere, ne ducem suum neve secretum imperium propriave signa haberent, miscuit manipulos ex Latinis Romanisque, ut ex binis singulos faceret binosque ex singulis; ita geminatis manipulis centuriones imposuit.*[5] But the Latins had then in reality their complete autonomy also in the army organization and were, even much later, still fighting in their own contingents,[6] making war with whom they liked.[7] The military organization of the archaic epoch, which distributed systematically the enrolled men of the Roman gentile tribes in the tactical units of the legion,[8] also contradicts categorically such a mingling of Romans and Latins. The whole dream of a Roman power haloed by antiquity is in strange contrast even with the annalists' own account: the king, who is said to be the unquestioned overlord of so many peoples, conducts a seven-year "frog and mice" war with an

---

[1] DH IV 48, 3 : τὸν δὲ Ταρκύνιον . . . . ἡγεμόνα ποιοῦνται τοῦ ἔθνους ἐπὶ τοῖς αὐτοῖς δικαίοις ἐφ' οἷς Ταρκύνιόν τε τὸν πάππον αὐτοῦ πρότερον ἐποιήσαντο καὶ μετὰ ταῦτα Τύλλιον. Cf. *ibid.* 46, 1-3 ; 48, 3 ; 49, 1. Liv. I 50, 4. Cf. 49, 8 ; 50, 1 sqq.

[2] *Ibid.* 48, 3 : συνθήκας τε γράψαντες ἐν στήλαις καὶ περὶ φυλακῆς τῶν συγκειμένων ὅρκια τεμόντες.

[3] *Ibid.* 5, 1 (cf. 50, 4) ; 51, 2.

[4] Liv. I 49, 8-9 ; 50, 1 sqq; 57 sqq. DH IV 45, 3-49, 1.

[5] Liv. I 52, 5-6. Cass. Dio fr. 11, 6 Zon. VII 10, 5 (vol. I, 27 Boiss.).

[6] Liv. III 22, 5.

[7] Liv. VIII 2, 13 and below, p. 377. 392.

[8] Th. Mommsen, St. R. 3, 104 sqq. For details see U. v. Lübtow, Das römische Volk, Frankfurt 1955, 48 sq.

immediate neighbor, Gabii (the only basis for which tale is the existence of an old *foedus Gabinum*) without being able to conquer this small city.[1]

The fiction that Rome ruled over the Latins on the legal base of an ancient *foedus* is maintained in the Roman literary tradition also in the story of the events after the flight of the Tarquins.[2] The Romans, without the slightest hope of help from outside, entered alone—we are told—upon a dangerous war and won it brilliantly [3] against τὸ κοινὸν τῶν Λατίνων, the *triginta populi*. The Latins, vanquished, no longer dispute the supremacy (περὶ τῆς ἀρχῆς), or strive for equality (περὶ τῶν ἴσων), but are ready for all future time to be allies as well as subjects (συμμάχους δὲ καὶ ὑπηκόους), reminding the Senate of their unswerving services in the past.[4] The subjugation is stated to be a complete success: *numquam alias ante publice privatimque Latinum nomen Romano imperio coniunctius fuit*,[5] for a very long time, *numquam ambigua fide*.[6]

The ways and means of persuading the reader are rather transparent. The narrative of the great conflict of Latium with the Volscians and Aequians in the fifth century B.C., dying down after the Celtic attack, shows the steady use of a few devices and motifs, enlivening the dry catalogue of wars, which Pictor found in the *annales maximi* of the pontiffs. These are:

a) The Latins or the Hernicans, or both these peoples, report to the Romans a Volscian or Aequian attack, often combined; Rome acts for them, protects them, and retaliates the blows of their enemies, so in the years

495 B.C. DH VI 27, 2. Liv. II 22, 4; 24, 1. In the same year Rome
defeats also the Auruncans near Aricia, Liv. II 26, 4 sqq.

---

[1] F. Schachermeyr in his valuable survey, RE 4A, 2364, 37 ff., thinks that the hegemony of the Tarquins in Latium is good pre-annalistic tradition : "Das ergibt sich aus der sekundären Aufteilung auf Priscus und Superbus, welche dem echten Überlieferungsstocke eigen ist." Cf. 2362. The truth is, I think, that Pictor has split the data of a written summary on the reign of the last king of Rome who built the Capitol, in the rules of two Tarquins ; but the historical value of that source concerning the rule of the Tarquins over Latium is more than dubious, cf. Chapter VII.

[2] DH V 21, 3 ; 22, 4 ; 26, 3-4 ; 50, 1 sqq.

[3] DH V 62, 1 sqq. VI 17, 1. Liv. II 18, 3 sqq.

[4] DH VI 18, 1 sqq. 20, 5. VII 71, 2.

[5] Liv. II 22, 7.

[6] *Ibid.* VI 2, 3.

494 B.C. DH VI 34, 3 sq.; 36, 3. Liv. II 30, 8.

489 B.C. This time Rome is unable to fulfill her duties.

482 B.C. DH VIII 83, 4.

481 B.C. DH IX 1, 2.

479 B.C. DH IX 14, 1. Liv. II 48, 4.

474 B.C. DH IX 35, 6. Liv. II 53, 4-5.

466 B.C. DH IX 60, 2 sq. 7. Liv. III 2, 1.

464 B.C. DH IX 62, 1 sqq. Liv. III 4, 10 sq.

463 B.C. Rome is this time unable to help her allies. DH IX 67, 4. Liv. III 6, 4 sqq.: . . . *socii pro tristi nuntio tristiorem domum referentes, quippe quibus per se sustinendum bellum erat quod vix Romanis fulti viribus sustinuissent.*

462 B.C. Liv. III 8, 6; cf. 7, 3-5. DH IX 70, 3.

458 B.C. DH X 22, 4 sqq.

457 B.C. DH X 26, 4.

455 B.C. DH X 43, 1 sqq. Liv. III 31, 3.

450 B.C. DH XI 23, 2.

449 B.C. Liv. III 57, 8. The Romans also recuperate the lost mobile property of their subject-allies for them, Liv. III 63, 4; cf. IV 29, 4 (431 B.C.).

424 B.C. Liv. IV 36, 4.

418 B.C. Liv. IV 45, 6.

413 B.C. Liv. IV 51, 7-8.

409 B.C. Liv. IV 55, 1.

386 B.C. The Latins and Hernicans interpellated *cur per eos annos militem ex instituto non dedissent,* Liv. VI 10, 6. The complete subordination of the *socii* is often stressed, until the great upheaval of 340 B.C., as in Livy VII 42, 8.

353 B.C. Liv. VII 19, 6 sqq.

We have a special reason for giving this list: it shows that in the minds of the annalists there was no rotation of command within the League or even an alternation between the League and Rome in subsequent years; the Latins have nothing to say, nothing to undertake. They report only the approach of an enemy; Rome acts.

b) In those wars the Romans have at their free disposal—so the Annals report—besides their own army the auxiliary forces of the Latins and Hernicans, e.g., in the years

491 B.C. DH VI 91, 1.

480 B.C. The Latin and Hernican subjects of Rome offer double the number of soldiers called for by the Romans. Rome dismisses with thanks half of their contingent. DH IX 5, 2; cf. 13, 1.

478 B.C. The *socii* mobilize a force equal to the Roman army, taking the field with this. DH IX 16, 3-4.

475 B.C. The consuls march out against Veii *accitis Latinorum Hernicorumque auxiliis*, Liv. II 53, 1. Cf. DH IX 34, 3.

468 B.C. The auxiliary forces (τά συμμαχικά) present themselves in Rome of their own accord even before they were notified of the expedition. DH IX 57, 1. Cf. Liv. II 64, 8 sqq.

467 B.C. The Aequi must also furnish auxiliary troops on request. DH IX, 59, 5. Cf. Liv. III 1, 8; 2, 2 sq.

464 B.C. Liv. III 5, 8: *venissetque in periculum summa rerum, ni T. Quinctius peregrinis copiis, cum Latino Hernicoque exercitu subvenisset. Ibid.* 5, 15: *Cohortes inde Latinae Hernicaeque ab senatu gratiis ob impigram militiam actis remissae domos.*

460 B.C. A similar case as in 464: Liv. III 19, 8.

459 B.C. The obligation of the allies is based on their treaty of alliance: *Hernici et Latini iussi milites dare ex foedere, duaeque partes sociorum in exercitu, tertia civium fuit.* (Liv. III 22, 4).

450 B.C. The allies send the same number of warriors to Rome as the Roman citizen army. DH XI 23, 2.

431 B.C. Liv. IV 26, 12: *Hernicis Latinisque milites imperati: utrimque enixe oboeditum dictatori est.*

349 B.C. Rome again does *imperare milites* to her allies, Liv. VII 25, 5.

   c) In addition to and beyond the notion just surveyed, namely that the annual contingents of the Latin allies were simply the normal complement of the Roman army—which in fact they became much later—the Annals pretend that the Latins were *not* allowed to make war on their own initiative: after Lake Regillus *tutius visum est defendi inermes Latinos, quam pati retractare arma* (Liv. II 30, 9). We give as examples:

495 B.C. The Senate does *not* accept the offer of the Latins to assist Rome in a war: "the proper forces are sufficient to punish those in revolt." DH VI 25, 3 sqq.

489 B.C. In a grave situation Rome allows the Latins exceptionally to enroll their youth in a Latin army under their own generals:

"For by the treaty of alliance these things were forbidden."
DH VIII 15, 2.

474 B.C. The Latins take the initiative and defeat their enemies without Roman help. DH IX 35, 6. The proud words in Livy II 53, 4-5, explaining why the Romans also took action, though the Volscians and Aequians are beaten, *mos, credo, non placebat, sine Romano duce exercituque socios propriis viribus consiliisque bella gerere*, may come from Valerius Antias,[1] but the underlying concept is older.

460 B.C. After the *coup d'état* of Appius Herdonius we read in Livy III 19, 8: *et qui antea Latinos ne pro se quidem ipsis, cum in finibus hostem haberent, attingere arma passi sumus, nunc, nisi Latini sua sponte arma sumpsissent, capti et deleti eramus.*

340 B.C. One of the leaders of the Latins in their revolt is said by Livy VIII 4, 8 to have stated: *qui ne nostrorum quidem finium nobis per nos tuendorum ius antea dabant.*

d) In order to stress the sovereign power of Rome over the *socii* since olden times it was assumed that Superbus mingled Latins and Romans in the maniples, as we saw.[2] The same thing is imagined to have continued until 340 B.C., when Livy, VIII 6, 15, writes: *curam acuebat quod adversus Latinos bellandum erat, ... institutis ante omnia militaribus congruentes: ... collegaeque iisdem in praesidiis, saepe iisdem manipulis permixti fuerant.* The absolutely superior position of the ruling power is also exemplified for 459 B.C. by the assertion that the Latin contingents are entirely at the disposal of the Roman general. Liv. III 22, 4-5: *duae ... partes sociorum in exercitu, tertia civium fuit. Fabius non permixtam unam sociorum civiumque sed trium populorum tres separatim acies ... instruxit.* DH X 22, 2 expresses the same: the consuls μερισάμενοι τριχῇ τάς τε οἰκείας καὶ τὰς παρὰ τῶν συμμάχων δυνάμεις, etc.[3] His statement is based again upon the same source used by Livy.

e) To this imaginary conquest of the Latins since King Tullus belongs the qualification of the early *coloniae Latinae* as a category of inferior status—as it became after 340 B.C. when the League was dissolved and the Latin cities degraded. But the colonies of the League

[1] Cf. K. W. Nitzsch, Rh. Mus. n. F. 24, 1869, 173 sqq.
[2] Cf. above, p. 104 sqq.
[3] Cf. K. W. Nitzsch, Rh. Mus. n. F. 25, 1870, 99 sqq.

in the archaic epoch were not all inferior to the Roman ones, as we shall see in their survey.[1]

The intentions of the source which has backdated the inferior position of the early Latin colonies from after 340 B.C. to the period of King Tullus are revealed by the fact that the dependence of the Latins in 340 is expressly claimed not to be due to recent subjugation but to go back to the old superiority of Rome under the kings: *Haecine foedera*—we read in the speech of the consul—*Tullus, Romanus rex, cum Albanis, patribus vestris, Latini, haec L. Tarquinius vobiscum postea fecit? Non venit in mentem pugna apud Regillum lacum? Adeo et cladium veterum vestrarum et beneficiorum nostrorum erga vos obliti estis?* (Liv. VIII 5, 9-10). And a *praetor Latinus* mentions (*ibid.*, 4, 7 sqq.): *quis dubitat exarsisse eos, cum plus ducentorum annorum morem solveremus?* [2]

༄

THE WRITTEN ALLIANCES OF ROME WITH THE LATINS

The community of the Latin tribe was founded on prehistoric ante-cedents: on common origin, common language, the same world of thought, on common ancestral institutions—and not on political documents and written conventions. The Roman Annals pretend, however, that Rome was independent of tribal ties already at the time of her foundation and that she subjugated the Latin nation under her third king, though not being able to deny her own Latin origin or to conceal completely her membership in the archaic tribal organi-zation. Striving to persuade us that Rome's supposed ancient superio-rity was legalized by solemn treaties, the Annals postulate also for those *foedera* of high antiquity, which are partly mythical, partly historical alliances, two partners: the totality of the Latin cities on the one hand, and Rome on the other.

This arbitrary division, which cannot be correct for the remote period in consideration and which simply projects the balance of power at the time of the peace treaty of 338 B.C. back into the dark

[1] A. N. Sherwin-White, R. Citiz., 34 sqq. E. T. Salmon, Phoenix 7, 1953, 94, and below, p. 391 sqq. 416.

[2] The battle at Lake Regillus was interpreted as only a rebellion against a long-established supremacy, Liv. VI 2, 3 ; 28, 7 ; 33, 2.

THE LATINS AS ROMAN SUBJECTS

ages, emerges first on the *aurei* struck by a Veturius in the Second Punic War, with the double head of the *Penates* on the obverse and the representation of the ritual conclusion of an alliance on the reverse (pl. IV, 5-6). As shown elsewhere,[1] the two acting persons of the scene are old King Latinus, embodying the *nomen Latinum*, and Aeneas, ancestor of the Romans.[2] This is a version known to Vergil, whose Aeneas comments on this alliance [3] as a *foedus aequum*:

> ... *paribus se legibus ambae*
> *invictae gentes aeterna in foedera mittant.*
> *sacra deosque dabo*; *socer arma Latinus habeto,*
> *imperium sollemne socer.*

The lesson taught to the Latins in revolt by these gold coins was conceived in the midst of the struggle for existence against Hannibal, as to remind them of their obligations under the time-honored alliance. This serious and solemn, highly official admonition on sacred obligations is the more remarkable in that it does not refer to the *foedera* of the Roman kings or to the treaty of the year 493 B.C. with the Latins, on which the annalists base their claim of Roman supremacy, but to a mythical pact. It seems to me, therefore, that the claim of the Annals was not yet formulated but was made only in the Greek work of Pictor written in the next decades.

The first treaty introduced in the Annals is anything but an equal pact, a *foedus aequum*. In fact it is meant as a subjugation against which the Latins rise in rebellion: *igitur Latini, cum quibus Tullo regnante ictum foedus erat, sustulerant animos, et, cum incursionem in agrum Romanum fecissent, repetentibus res Romanis superbe responsum reddunt.*[4] The same treaty is described in other words as *cum res omnis Albana cum coloniis suis in Romanum cesserit imperium*,[5] and as dictated by Rome: *in eo foedere superior Romana res erat.*[6] This does not really sound like a *foedus aequum*!

The much debated *foedus Cassianum* of 493 B.C. is in the Annals

---

[1] A. Alföldi, AJA 63, 1959, 20 sqq.

[2] *Idem*, Die trojanischen Urahnen der Römer (Rektoratsprogramm der Universität Basel für das Jahr 1956), Basel 1957.

[3] Verg., *Aen.* 12, 190 sqq.

[4] Liv. I 32, 3 ; *ibid.* 33, 3 sqq.

[5] Liv. I 52, 2.

[6] *Ibid.* 4.

nothing but a reconfirmation of the Roman hegemony,[1] granted as an unexpected and special favor to the vanquished.[2] And Livy, speaking of the "old treaty" with the Latins, renewed in 358 B.C., means nothing else but the fictitious primeval act of submission.[3] He realizes, of course, the discrepancy between the two pretensions of an "equal" alliance and, at the same time, a subordination of the Latins. He puts these words in the mouth of a leader of the Latins during the war of 340 B.C.: *si . . . sub umbra foederis aequi servitutem pati possumus.*[4] And again:[5] *si foedus, si societas aequatio iuris est.* The original "equality" meant of course something very different; it was the same juridical position of all the Latins, including Rome; it still manifested itself in the fifth century B.C. in the equal division of booty and in their share in the foundation of federal colonies. These are not to be confused with the reduced rights of the later Latin colonies founded by Rome.[6] But even in those later so-called Latin colonies the concession of the same jurisdiction by the Romans as for their own citizens is a remnant of the original and real *aequatio iuris*; [7] and this is reflected also in the admission of the aristocracy of the Latin allies to the curule magistrature in Rome.[8]

℘

THE *FOEDUS CASSIANUM* IN THE ANNALS

After the victorious war with the Latins at Lake Regillus a new arrangement was necessary. To find a *modus vivendi* with Rome, the

---

[1] DH VI 21, 2 : ἀνθ' ὧν εὕροντο παρὰ τῆς βουλῆς τὴν ἀρχαίαν φιλίαν καὶ συμμαχίαν καὶ τοὺς ὅρκους τοὺς ὑπὲρ τούτων ποτὲ γενομένους διὰ τῶν εἰρηνοδικῶν ἀνενεώσαντο.

[2] DH VI 95, 1. Liv. II, 25 ; 30, 9.

[3] Liv. VII 12, 7 : *sed inter multos terrores solacio fuit pax Latinis petentibus data et magna vis militum ab his ex foedere vetusto, quod multis intermiserant annis, accepta.* Cf. also Polybius II 18, 5 (between the Gallic catastrophe and the new Celtic invasions) : ἐν ᾧ καιρῷ Ῥωμαῖοι τὴν τε σφετέραν δύναμιν ἀνέλαβον καὶ τὰ κατὰ τοὺς Λατίνους αὖθις πράγματα συνεστήσαντο. The war ending with the victory at Lake Regillus is, for Livy, only an interruption of the old *foedus*, VI 2, 3 : *novus quoque terror accesserat defectione Latinorum* (cf. VII 12, 7) *Hernicorumque, qui post pugnam ad lacum Regillum factam per annos prope centum nunquam ambigua fide in amicitia populi Romani fuerant.* Cf. also M. Gelzer, RE 12, 959, 61 sqq.

[4] Liv. VIII 4, 2.

[5] *Ibid.* 4, 3. Cf. E. Täubler, Imperium Romanum, Leipzig 1913, 284 sq., who stresses the incongruence, but does not detect its real source.

[6] Cf. A. N. Sherwin-White, R. Citiz. 22, 34.

[7] Th. Mommsen, St. R. 3, 1887, 629 sqq.

[8] A. N. Sherwin-White, *op. cit.* 34.

THE LATINS AS ROMAN SUBJECTS

Latin bloc grouped around Aricia and Tusculum had to renounce the sheltering of the Tarquins. The readmission of Rome to the League was of supreme importance in view of common enemies east of Latium. But the undisputed sovereignty of Rome, which the Annals would like to suggest, was yet far from being achieved. What is the actual truth in the face of the distortion by our Roman informants? [1]

The treaty of 493 B.C. is said to have been concluded by Spurius Cassius, then consul for the second time. The *Cassii* of historical rimes were plebeians who could not be consuls in the fifth century; but as Mommsen [2] pointed out, the plebeian Cassii appear on the political stage only after 171 B.C., a date too late for smuggling imaginary ancestors into the old list of magistrates, as the *Junii* and *Marcii* did a century earlier. Consequently, we cannot exclude the possibility that the treaty was briefly mentioned in the pontifical annals under the heading of the year in question; [3] even if the name of Sp. Cassius alone appeared on the treaty,[4] this could well be due to the fact that

---

[1] Some characteristic opinions of modern scholars are to be found in the following works : A. Schwegler, RG 2, 18, 56, 307 sqq. W. Ihne, RG 1, 1868, 81 n. 5, 90, 129 sq. n. 6 ; 130. K. W. Nitzsch, Rh. Mus. n. F. 24, 1869, 150 sqq. M. Zoeller, Latium und Rom, Leipzig 1878, 190 ff. Th. Mommsen, RF 2, 158 sq.; cf. 113 sqq. J. Beloch, Der italische Bund, Leipzig 1880, 194 sqq. Th. Mommsen, St. R. 3, 1887, 611 n. 1 ; 618 n. 2. Ed. Meyer, GdA 5, Stuttgart 1902, 136 sq. E. Täubler, *op. cit.* 276 sqq. J. Binder, Die Plebs, Leipzig 1909, 332 sqq. G. De Sanctis, St. d. R. 2, 1907, 96 sqq. E. Pais, St. d. R. 1², 1926, 324 sqq. W. Soltau, Wiener Studien 35, 1913, 257. G. De Sanctis, Atti del I⁰ Congresso di Studi Romani, Roma 1929, 231 sqq. A. Rosenberg, Hermes 55, 1920, 337. Ed. Meyer, Kleine Schriften, 2, Halle 1924, 301. L. Homo, L'Italie primitive, Paris 1925, 176 sqq. K. J. Beloch, RG 1, 189 sqq., 193 sq. A. Oltramare, Bull. de la Soc. d'Hist. et d'Arch. de Genève, 5, 1925-34, 268 sqq. H. Last, CAH 7, 1928, 489 sqq. M. Gelzer, RE 12, 954. 956, 63 ; 958, 9. A. Momigliano, Bull. Com. 58, 1930 (1931) 32 sqq. H. Horn, Foederati, Diss., Frankfurt 1930, 87 sqq. A. N. Sherwin-White, *op cit.* 19 sqq. Kr. Hanell, Das altrömische eponyme Amt, Lund 1946, 172 sqq. A. Piganiol, Histoire de Rome³, Paris 1949, 54. J. Vogt, Die römische Republik², Tübingen 1951, 42, L. Pareti, St. d. R. 1, 1952, 414 sq. G. Giannelli, Trattato di Storia romana 1. Torino 1953, 183. F. Altheim, RG 2, 1953, 118. Pl. Fraccaro, Opuscula 1, Pavia 1956, 105. F. Hampl., Rh. F. Mus. n. 100, 1958, 68 sqq.

[2] Th. Mommsen, RF 2, 153 sqq.

[3] Cic., *Pro Balbo* 23, 53. Liv. II 33, 3-4. 9. DH VI 19, 4 ; 20, 1 ; 21, 2 ; 95, 2. Cf. also Th. Mommsen, St. R. 3, 1887, 611 n. 1. Fr. Münzer, RE 3, 1749 ff. E. Pais, St. d. R. 3, Roma 1927, 143 sqq. E. Täubler, *l.c.* Ed. Meyer, Kleine Schriften 1924, 300. H. Horn, *op. cit.* 94 sqq. H. Last, *op. cit.* 490 sq., and others.

[4] M. Zoeller, *op. cit.* 192 sqq.

the dictatorship as a *normal* annual office was then still not replaced by the consulship. But as the whole activity of Cassius in the Annals is a mere literary invention, and has not even any elements of genuine "legend," so the contents of the treaty also must be regarded with caution. No doubt Cicero had seen one of the old treaties with the Latins inscribed on bronze;[1] but he also had known the Annals, attributing such a document to Spurius Cassius.[2] And the *foedus Latinum* quoted by Verrius Flaccus[3] can only come from a faulty transcription or résumé in a literary text: it contains the word *pecunia*, though the Romans had no coinage before 269 / 268 B.C.,[4] and its mention, therefore, excludes even the reference to the *foedus* of 338 B.C., let alone that of 493! Moreover, the text given in Dionysius VI 95, 2, must be a later addition to the notes which were appended to the names of the eponymous magistrates in the genuine *fasti*, as assumed by Mommsen: Dionysius mentions previously the renewal of the Latin alliance under the dictatorship of A. Postumius Albus, which cannot have been so soon repeated and duplicated in the same political situation. He writes: VI 21, 2: ἀνθ' ὧν εὕροντο παρὰ τῆς βουλῆς τὴν ἀρχαίαν φιλίαν καὶ συμμαχίαν καὶ τοὺς ὅρκους τοὺς ὑπὲρ τούτων ποτὲ γενομένους διὰ τῶν εἰρηνοδικῶν ἀνενεώσαντο.

The provisions of the treaty of Spurius Cassius in Dionysius VI 95, 2, do not deserve the credit they receive from historians. They bear the imprint of an epoch later than the fifth century. They are as follows:

(1) "Let there be peace between the Romans and all the Latin cities as long as the heaven and the earth shall remain where they are. Let them neither make war upon one another themselves, nor bring in foreign enemies, nor grant a safe passage to those who shall make war upon either." We know,[5] however, that in fact there was nothing in the Latin *foedus* which would prohibit the members of the League from making war against whom they wished. Concerning the sentence forbidding the use of foreign armies against other members of the

---

[1] Cf. C. Cichorius, *De fastis consularibus antiquissimis*. Diss. Leipzig 1886, 173 sq.

[2] Cf. also A. Andrén, Hommages à L. Herrmann (Coll. Latomus 44) Bruxelles 1960, 88 sqq. G. Pasquali, La nuova antologia 386, 1936, 416, stresses the point that the text of DH is "non integro e in rielaborazione annalistica."

[3] Fest., p. 166, 29 L. : *Nancitor in XII nactus erit, prenderit. Item in foedere Latino 'pecuniam quis nancitor, habeto', et 'si quid pignoris nanciscitur, sibi habeto'.*

[4] Cf. my remarks in R M 68, 1961, 64 sqq.

[5] From Liv. VIII 2, 13 ; cf. below, p. 121 sq.

League, such a clause would have made sense a century later when the Latins tried to shake off the Roman yoke with Volscian, Hernican, and even Celtic assistance, or after 348, when Rome, in fact, did invite the Carthaginians to maltreat her mutinous allies.[1] Such a provision would suit, consequently, the treaties of 358 or of 338 B.C., but not the agreement concluded after the victory at Lake Regillus.

(2) "Let them assist one another, when warred upon, with all their forces, and let each have an equal share of the spoils and booty taken in their common wars." The mutual assistance of Romans and Latins, however, was not dependent on a *foedus* in the fifth century, but on actual decisions of the League, as will be apparent soon. Such bilateral aid must have been agreed upon in 338 B.C. The same applies to the equal sharing of booty between Rome and the Latin League, pre-supposing the Roman supremacy, which was established gradually after the struggle against Volscians and Aequians was won and defi-nitely stabilized in 338.[2] Rome's predominance became overwhelming about 400 B.C., as we shall see.[3] The balance of power in 493 B.C. was however still far from being so favorable for Rome.

(3) "Let suits relating to private contracts be determined within ten days, and this in the city, where the contract was made." Such highly developed forms of litigation, affording special judges and tribunals, are thinkable only much later—later even, than the Twelve Tables.[4] The underlying concepts of *commercium* and *connubium*, based in this clause on internal peace as the normal state of things, looked very different in the archaic epoch.[5] Interurban trade and marriages between citizens of different Latin states were then possible solely at the great annual gatherings of the tribe, on the days of which a sacred peace was granted to all tribesmen.[6] We are therefore convinced

---

[1] Cf. below, p. 409; cp. 350 sqq.

[2] Cf. M. Zoeller, *op. cit.* 206. E. Täubler, *Imperium Romanum* 281 sqq. The revolutionary agitation of Spurius Cassius is exemplified by his intention to give the common people and the allies shares in the war booty and the captured enemy territory : Liv. II 41, 1. DH VIII 69, 4 ; 76, 2 ; 77, 2-3. Cf. Plinius, *N.h.* XXXIV 5, 20, with the commentary of Th. Mommsen, RF 2, 163 n. 22, who still based his reasonings on the "von Haus aus bestehenden römischen Hege-monie" (*ibid.*, n. 23).

[3] Ed. Meyer, Kleine Schriften 2, 1924, 299 sqq.

[4] J. Binder, Die Plebs, 350. E. Täubler, *op. cit.* 281 sqq. A. Rosenberg, Her-mes 54, 1920, 132.

[5] Cf. above, p. 38 sqq.

[6] Cf. above, p. 29 sqq.

that the attempts of Beloch and others [1] to lower the date of the treaty failed only because they tried to transfer the person of Sp. Cassius into the fourth century instead of leaving untouched his name as well as the historicity of the reconciliation between Rome and the Latins after the battle at Lake Regillus. There are also some anachronisms in Dionysius' text which point to its later origin.

༉

THE EVIDENCE AGAINST THE ANNALIST DOCTRINE

With his sovereign perspicacity, Mommsen realized the falsifying tendency of the Annals which projected Rome's ruling power over Italy in their own times back into ages immemorial. He expressed his views on this point with the same precision of mind and clarity which we admire in all his grandiose life's work.[2] But why did he not

---

[1] K. J. Beloch, RG 1, 1926, 193 sqq. A. Oltramare, *op. cit.* 268 sqq. Cf. H. Horn, *op. cit.* 90 sqq. A. Rosenberg, Hermes 55, 1920, 337. A. Piganiol, Histoire de Rome[3], 54. H. Last, *loc. cit.*

[2] Th. Mommsen, St. R. 3, 609 : "Was hieraus sich zu ergeben scheint, dass auch die Stadt Rom einst wie Alba und Praeneste eine der Städte 'latinischen Namens' gewesen ist, das weist die römische Auffassung entschieden ab. Nicht bloss steht in der gesamten conventionellen Vorgeschichte Rom nicht in, sondern neben Latium, sondern es ist auch die sehr alte Gründungslegende ausdrücklich darauf gestellt, neben dem Festhalten der gemeinschaftlichen Nationalität in scharf tendenziöser Haltung die Zugehörigkeit zu der latinischen Staatengemeinschaft auszuschliessen. Allem Anschein nach hat schon die römische Logographie sich bemüht, in der Legendengestaltung die der späteren hegemonischen Rolle Roms nicht angemessene ursprüngliche Gleichstellung im latinischen Stammbund zu verleugnen und auch die Erinnerung daran zu vertilgen ; und es ist ihr dies vollständig gelungen. Von dem latinischen Stammbund, wie er bis zu seiner Auflösung im Jahre 416 der Stadt neben und unter Rom stand, berichten die römischen Annalen allerdings ; aber das Bild, welches sie uns von der Gestaltung der römisch-latinischen Ordnungen vorführen, ist ungefähr vergleichbar dem des römischen Königtums : es weist nicht bloss im Einzelnen zahlreiche Unklarheiten und Widersprüche auf, sondern die uns vorliegenden Erzählungen entbehren vielfach der realen Grundlage und erweisen sich pragmatisch wie staatsrechtlich als Construction relativ später Darsteller . . .". See also p. 610 sq. : "Die römische Logographie kennt den latinischen Stammbund nicht anders als in Abhängigkeit von Rom und Roms Hegemonie über Latium wird von ihr nicht so sehr entwickelt, als vorausgesetzt. Ihr gelten die Städte der Latiner sämtlich als von Alba aus gegründet und übt dieses bei Beginn der Stadt Rom über Latium das Regiment etwa in der Weise, wie in historischer Zeit es Rom geführt hat ; indem dann Rom unter dem vierten seiner Könige durch die Kampfwette die Hegemonie über Alba gewinnt und bald darauf die Stadt incorporiert, fällt ihm vom Rechts

draw the consequences of his clear insight and why did he accept the anachronistic doctrine of the imaginary Roman supremacy for his reconstruction of the political relations between Rome and Latium? The answer to this question is not difficult. Mommsen thought that the epoch of the tribal coherence of the Latins was over, long before the birth of Rome; therefore he did not realize the chronological absurdity of the pretended early date of the Roman domination over Latium, and did not seriously consider evidence against the annalistic doctrine.

The Latin migration was one of the consequences of the Illyrian inroads toward the south of Europe; its traces survived not only in the myths and in certain religious institutions of the Republic but also in the inventory of the Iron Age findings in Latium, which strongly suggest a common origin of some Central European, Middle Italian, and Balkan find-groups. Still more relevant to our problem is the fact that the Latin tribal League survived as a political organization with various reshuffles, with shifting centers of diverse significance until 340 B.C., continuing to have a shadowy existence even after this date on annual solemnities. On the other hand, we can follow step by step how the primeval tribal organization, along with the aspirations of other political centers of the Latins, vanished in face of the fast-growing might and pressure of the Eternal City. This development also demonstrates, however, that the flourishing little Rome of the Tarquins did not yet have her later autonomous, sovereign historical role in Latium. The superiority of Lavinium in archaic Latium, illustrated in one of our next chapters,[1] points to the same fact.

wegen diejenige über ganz Latium zu. Die latinischen Städte sind oftmals säumig in Erfüllung ihrer Pflichten und versuchen auch verschiedene Male das Glück der Waffen ; aber die Verträge, die die drei letzten Könige und sodann Sp. Cassius mit ihnen schliessen, sind im Wesentlichen nur erneuernder und bestärkender Art. Die Abhängigkeit des latinischen Bundes, wie sie unter Tullus festgestellt war, bleibt unverändert, bis der Bund selbst gesprengt wird, und sie damit sich auf die einzelnen Städte überträgt. Es ist das nicht Geschichte, wohl aber die staatsrechtliche Darlegung des Verhältnisses, welches der Auflösung des latinischen Bundes unmittelbar vorherging, der Hegemonie Roms über die übrige in foederativen Geschlossenheit neben ihr stehende Nation." Cf. also *ibid*. 616 n. 4., 617 sqq. (on the equivocal application of the *foedus aequum*). See also J. Binder, Die Plebs 331 sqq. E. Täubler, *op. cit.* 286 sq., 293 sq., 316 sq., 330 sq. Rosenberg, Hermes 54, 1919, 150 sq. K. J. Beloch, RG 1, 1926, 180. A. Piganiol, Mél. 38, 1920, 297 sqq.

[1] Cf. Gymnasium 67, 1960, 193 sq., and below, p. 246 sqq.

Evidence against the Annalist Doctrine

Priceless information concerning the structure and function of the Latin League during the earlier Republic is given in a fragment of Cincius,[1] an antiquarian of the early Augustan Age. The main points of his statement are as follows:

1) The Latin *populi* had their regular annual meetings outside the Roman territory, *sub monte Albano*, until 340 B.C. The context unmistakably reveals that Rome is one of those *populi*.[2]

2) At these meetings there were discussions on problems of common interest (*populos Latinos . . . consulere solitos*), of course, mainly on matters of political and military nature.

3) They had common magistrates (*imperium communi consilio administrare*). As we saw, these magistrates were first the *dictator Latinus*, later two federal Latin *praetors*.

4) The magistrates of the League were chosen by the League in rotation from the member-cities, among which was also Rome: *quo anno Romanos imperatores ad exercitum mittere oporteret iussu nominis Latini*, etc. This fundamental passage has been rightly interpreted by M. Zoeller and A. Rosenberg in the sense that Rome's turn to give the annual leader for the League ensued before 340 B.C. in a normal

---

[1] Fest., p. 276, 15 L.: *Praetor ad portam nunc salutatur is qui in provinciam pro praetore aut consule exit ; cuius rei morem ait fuisse Cincius in libro de consulum potestate talem* : "*Albanos rerum potitos usque ad Tullum regem ; Alba deinde diruta usque ad P. Decium Murem consulem populos Latinos ad caput Ferentinae, quod est sub monte Albano consulere solitos, et imperium communi consilio administrare, itaque quo anno Romanos imperatores ad exercitum mittere oportet iussu nominis Latini, complures nostros in Capitolio a sole oriente auspiciis operam dare solitos. Ubi aves addixissent, militem illum, qui a communi Latio missus esset, illum quem aves addixerant, praetorem salutare solitum, qui eam provinciam optineret praetoris nomine*. Concerning the person of the writer (as different from the annalist Cincius Alimentus) cf. H. Peter, H. R. Rel. 1², 1914, p. CIV sq. M. Schanz-C. Hosius, Geschichte der lateinischen Literatur 1⁴, München 1927, 175 sqq. Cincius the Antiquarian is quoted by Liv. VII 3, 7, and used also without indicating the source. About the fragment in question cf. B. G. Niebuhr, RG 1², Berlin 1827, 282 : "denn es sind Fragmente aus ihm, die allein mit klaren Worten das frühere Verhältnis von Rom und Latium darstellen, welches in allen Annalen der Nationalstolz verfälscht hat." A. Schwegler, RG 2, 343. M. Zoeller, *op. cit.* 205. E. Pais, St. crit. 3, 364, n. 1. Th. Mommsen, St. R. 3, 619 n. 2. G. De Sanctis, St. d. R. 2¹, 99. A. Rosenberg, Hermes 54, 1919, 148 sqq. M. Gelzer, RE 12, 955 sqq., 961, 56. A. N. Sherwin-White, R. Citiz. 13.

[2] Cf. also DH V 50, 2 and 4 : Rome belongs to the League, though it was notified to be present in the case in question, in spite of written agreement : γεγραμμένον ἐν ταῖς συνθήκαις ἁπάσας παρεῖναι τὰς πόλεις ταῖς κοιναῖς ἀγοραῖς, ὅσαι τοῦ Λατίνων εἰσὶ γένους, παραγγειλάντων αὐταῖς τῶν προέδρων. Cf. V 54, 5.

sequence among the other cities. This fact disposes of the fiction that the entire Latin group depended on Rome and that Rome ruled over it as she did later. A. Schwegler and G. De Sanctis tried to interpret the sentence as referring to an alternation between the commune Latium on one side and Rome on the other. But there is no indication of this in the passage just quoted. Nor have the Romans control of allied forces which are, on the contrary, administered *communi consilio, iussu nominis Latini*. Mommsen and Gelzer do not see here any rotation at all, but they think that the above-mentioned eventuality of changing management (*quo anno*) means that Rome was sending a commander to the federal army in the event of war—Rome alone and always a Roman one. However, the supreme decision did not depend on Rome according to Cincius, but on the *nomen Latinum*. The federal army was organized by the whole Latium, *a communi Latio missus*.[1] The *imperium* administered *communi consilio* was a normal federal magistrature which convoked the League, presided at the consultations, made sacrifices to the federal gods and also commanded the armed forces. The restriction of this office to the case of war by Mommsen is mistaken. Exceptional federal officials such as the Roman *dictator* in emergency cases did not exist for the *nomen Latinum*. Nobody can believe that the magistrates of the League always came from Rome; since they possessed the federal *imperium*, they were allowed to act in war and in peace.[2] The names of the Latin dictators and praetors who achieved victories for the League were suppressed by the Roman Annals because they would contradict and disturb the account given by the annalists.[3]

Since Rome considered the *auspicia* taken in the territory of the

---

[1] A confirmation of my views is given by O. Skutsch, Cl. Q. 11, 1961, 251, who translated this sentence "when it was the turn of the Romans to provide a general for the Latin League"—having no axe to grind and paying no attention whatsoever to the historical problem. *Contra*: J. Pinsent, Class. Journal 55, 1959, 83 sqq.

[2] Cf. DH III 34, 3 : at the time of King Tullus the 30 Latin cities αἱροῦνται δύο στρατηγοὺς αὐτοκράτορας εἰρήνης τε καὶ πολέμου, Ἄγκον Ποπλίκιον ἐκ πόλεως Κόρας καὶ Σπούσιον Οὐεκίλιον ἐκ Λαουϊνίου. The two *praetors*—instead of a *dictator*—are anachronistic, but the definition of their power *(imperium)* is not. A strange idea of Beloch is (RG 190 sq.) that the command was given to the city, the territory of which was the scene of military operations. But Cincius does not speak of a danger or emergency when the federal army arrives at Rome.

[3] A. Piganiol, Mél. 38, 1920, 306 sq. F. Münzer, Adelsparteien und Adelsfamilien, Stuttgart 1920, 44 sq. M. Gelzer, RE 12, 961.

Evidence against the Annalist Doctrine

Latin cities as legal,[1] this implies that federal magistrates invested with federal *imperium* in all those cities were recognized by the Romans.

This antiquarian source, disregarding the surreptitious theory of the Annals, reveals that Rome did not face the Latin League as a separate unit, but was one of its members. The ritual obligations of the Romans in different federal centers show the same ties, the same coordination with the Latin cities, as we shall see later. Even in Rome, Varro [2] correctly described the federal sanctuary on the Aventine as *commune Latinorum Dianae templum*.

The confederation of the Latins was much looser and granted much more freedom to its members than the annalistic tradition suggests.[3] The proclamation of a Truce of God for the days of the great annual convention [4] shows clearly that members of the League sometimes made war with each other; and in a tense moment of Roman history the Annals confess the plain truth: *in foedere Latinos nihil esse quod bellare cum quibus ipsi velint, prohibeantur (sc. a Romanis)*.[5]

A special case of such local wars is attested by Livy [6] for the first half of the fifth century B.C.: *Aricini atque Ardeates de ambiguo agro cum saepe bello certassent, multis in vicem cladibus fessi iudicem populum Romanum cepere*. Such particular wars correspond, on the other hand, to the peculiar treaties between the Latin cities, as for instance the old *foedus* between Rome and Gabii [7] or that between Ardea and Rome; [8] in 348 B.C. the first treaty with Carthage still distinguishes the Latin cities having a special *foedus* with Rome from the other cities, which do not have such a treaty: ἐὰν δέ τινες Καρχηδονίων λάβωσί τινας, πρὸς οὓς εἰρήνη μὲν ἐστιν ἔγγραπτος ῾Ρωμαίοις, μὴ ὑποτάττονται δέ τι αὐτοῖς (Polyb. III 24, 6).[9] We agree with Täubler that these local wars and agreements might have helped the process, by which Rome—proving herself to be the most vigorous Latin state after the

---

[1] Varro, *LL* 5, 33, with comments by Th. Mommsen, St. R. 3, 629.

[2] *LL* 5, 43.

[3] Cf. E. Täubler, *op. cit.* 316 sq. The incompatibility between the *foedus Latinum* and individual alliances between single members of the League, as postulated by Beloch, *op. cit.* 187, did not exist.

[4] Cf. above, p. 19 sqq.

[5] Liv. VIII 2, 13.

[6] Liv. III 71, 2.

[7] DH IV 58, 4. Fest., p. 48, 19 L. Hor., *Epist.* II 1, 24 sq. E. Babelon, Description historique et chronologique des monnaies de la République romaine 1, Paris 1885, 149 no. 17, and 151, no. 2-21.

[8] Liv. IV 7, 4. 10. 11. 12.

[9] Cf. F. Walbank, A Historical Commentary on Polybius 1, Oxford 1957, 345.

long struggle with Volscians and Aequians—brought under her sway the other Latin cities, one by one, until their final subjugation in 340 B.C. This Roman ascendency is, however, not the renewal of an old supremacy, but a completely new achievement.

F. Münzer's judgment on the reliability of our source material for the early history of Rome holds good also in this special case. "Our scruples," he writes,[1] "are not based on the improbability of the things reported, but rather on the narrow-mindedness of the accounts. Things are considered only from one definite angle: concerning the relations between Rome and the outside world, all views—except the Roman—were suppressed. The Romans, who proved themselves at last to be superior to all their enemies, took this superiority as well as the inferiority and subordination of all the non-Romans as given *a priori* . . . We must not be mesmerized by this view . . . In general the whole Roman tradition has the tendency of concealing as far as possible the role of the Latins and of other allies in the ascendancy of Rome." [2] The same scholar has also revealed that as late as in the fourth century B.C.—and, of course, to a still larger extent before this time—the nobility of the other Latin cities was considered by the Roman governing class as its equal.[3] But after the conquest, the Romans only reluctantly admitted even the most outstanding men of the neighboring cities to equal rights and status.[4] The contempt for the municipal nobles, reflected in the Annals, mirrors the Roman attitude after the conquest no less clearly than do the words of the Consul T. Manlius of 340 B.C., concerning the demands of the Latins: [5] *qui adeo non tenuit iram, ut, si tanta dementia patres conscriptos cepisset, ut ab Setino homine leges acciperent, gladio cinctum in senatum venturum se esse palam diceret et quemcumque in curia Latinum vidisset sua manu interempturum. Et conversus ad simulacrum Iovis 'audi, Iuppiter, haec scelera' inquit; 'audite Ius Fasque. Peregrinos consules et peregrinum senatum in tuo, Iuppiter, augurato templo captus atque ipse oppressus visurus es?'* Cicero, an offspring of an old municipal aristocracy, was scorned by the oligarchy as *inquilinus urbis Romae*, "bondman of the city of Rome." But this contempt is a late development. It is not the attitude of the fifth century B.C.

[1] Fr. Münzer, Adelsparteien und Adelsfamilien der römischen Republik, 46.
[2] *Ibid.*, 66.
[3] *Ibid.* 50, 64 sq., and *passim*.
[4] *Ibid.* 47.
[5] Liv. VIII 5, 7-8.

Chapter IV

THE PROJECTION OF THE ROMAN CONQUEST OF MIDDLE ITALY BACK INTO THE DARK AGES BY FABIUS PICTOR

"The most difficult virtue required by the historian of early Rome," wrote the regretted Pl. Fraccaro not long ago,[1] "is that of being able to renounce the greater part of the information the ancients have handed down to us; next comes that of knowing how to interpret and to illuminate the rest." It is only with utmost reluctance that we leave out of consideration the bulk of our written evidence; but we do it with a clear conscience. There has been no doubt since Niebuhr that the alleged conquests by the kings are for the most part evident forgeries or that they must at least be regarded with suspicion. If, notwithstanding this fundamental insight revealing the unreliability of our sources, so many vain attempts have lately been made to save a good deal of their account for the historical reconstruction of that remote epoch, this was due, I think, to an erroneous approach to the literary tradition.

[1] Pl. Fraccaro, JRS 47, 1957, 65.

The habitual way of dealing with the account of continuous victories and no setbacks since Romulus is to select the apparently more reasonable items for use and to discard—silently or explicitly—what looks silly. This procedure would obviously be all right if our source material were something like the natural remnants of the life of Early Latium, washed down by the torrent of Time from the hills of the Historical Past along with countless pebbles and mud into the Lowland of our Age; and if the dried-out riverbed of Antiquity had preserved this invaluable material along with the stones and sand, to be simply picked up by the Historian from the useless mass of dull debris. Yet the real essence of these tales is far from being such a spontaneous, haphazard agglomeration. It is, rather, like a skillfully conceived mosaic pavement with a pattern, purposely imitating ancient art, but containing only a few little authentic mosaic stones and distorting completely the original design by a fictitious new one. Therefore, before trying again to comb out the small bits of reliable facts from the rubbish, we must attempt to grasp the outlines of the fictitious pattern. Thus a schematical concept will reveal itself, based on theoretical assumptions. This tale of conquest is not built on known facts but on a preconceived scheme, marking out the stages of a rapid growth and expansion. It is not the work of a clumsy scribbler but a shrewd doctrine forged by a far-sighted politician. This man was the first historian of Rome, writing in Greek for the Greeks, and trying to make them believe that his people were no barbarian horde, recently risen to power by rude force, but a highly civilized community of a most glorious past, the mistress of Middle Italy for centuries. The subsequent annalists did not inquire into the past themselves but tried to shape his concept in a more attractive way, prolonging the narrative, amplifying the number of the slain enemies found in Pictor's account, and adding fanciful details. They criticized particular points of his work, added new perspectives to his picture, but used the frame he created for the earliest Roman past. Even Livy who protested against the lies and distortions of his predecessors did not do this as a research worker wishing to establish what really happened, but out of sheer honesty. He tried to come as near as possible to the truth by going back in doubtful cases to the *scriptorum longe antiquissimus Fabius*, but not a step further. Therefore what we need to do is to uncover the pattern established by Fabius, which became the canonical account of the rise of the Roman power. The

figures illustrating the growth of Early Rome give us the first opportunity to grasp the means used by that creative mind in shaping the
pseudo-history of his home city.

᠌

THE MANIPULATION OF FIGURES AND DATES

The registration of the annual magistrates governing the state was
the duty of the *pontifices* ever since the beginning of the Republic.
The management of public affairs and private business alike needed
the dating method which gave the exact designation of each and every
year by those names. The pontiffs therefore annually added the new
names to the ever-growing list of magistrates, inserting more and
more detail on the events of each year; but a systematic historical
survey was outside the scope of those priestly officials, nor did they
ever think of fitting the eponymous list into the frame of Greek
chronology. This was not their job, but was achieved subsequently
by historians and antiquarians.[1]

The notion that Rome was founded by the hero Aeneas, fleeing to
the West after the fall of Troy, or by his son or grandson, is at least
as old as the sixth century B.C.[2] The various versions of this event
were already recorded by Greek historians before the birth of the
Roman Annals.[3] As F. Jacoby has demonstrated, the most important
Greek precursor of Roman history, Timaeus of Tauromenium, in
his general history linked up the foundation of the city with the flight
of Aeneas from Troy, but in his books on Pyrrhus he put Rome's
foundation in correlation with that of Carthage and consequently
fixed the date of both events in 814 / 13 B.C.; by this artifice and its
dramatic exploitation he created a romantic primeval basis for the
great struggle for power between Rome and Carthage in the Mediterranean world, a struggle the beginning of which he saw with his
own eyes.[4] A generation after Timaeus, Fabius Pictor finished his

[1] O. Leuze, Die römische Jahrzählung, Tübingen 1909, 275 sq., 277 sq.

[2] Cf. my study, Die trojanischen Urahnen der Römer (Rektoratsprogramm
der Universität Basel für das Jahr 1956) 1957.

[3] F. Gr. Hist. 566 F 59-61 and vol. 3 B Kommentar 536, 574 sq. ; Noten
zum Kommentar 1955, 331 n. 309-11.

[4] The inconsistency of giving two different dates could have been covered
by the fiction of a renewal of the foundation, occurring several times in the
tradition. Timaios F 60 (= DH I 74, 1) mentioned indeed τὸν δὲ τελευταῖον

FABIUS PICTOR

work, basing his chronological speculations on the synchronism invented by Timaeus. The date of 814 / 13 fixed the time of Rome's birth more than three and a half centuries after the fall of Troy: Rome could no longer be the immediate foundation of Aeneas, but had to be founded by one of his remote descendants.

This had two important consequences for the fictitious chronology. Pictor tried to make the length of the regal age (from Timaeus' date of foundation to that of the birth of the Republic) agree with the total of the seven kings' regnal years. The rather mythical concept of seven rulers, when transferred into history, provided seven generations; therefore Pictor shortened the chronology of Timaeus by two generations. His date was 747 B.C. given in the manner of the Greek chronographs as Ol. 8, 1.[1]

It is to be stressed that previously no such date was fixed: the poets Naevius and Ennius, though later than Pictor, still connected the origins of Rome directly with Aeneas and his family and the subsequent annals correct and change without any restraint or inhibition the date given by Pictor.[2] There was no obstacle, no fixed traditional date before him.

These mathematics, based on Timaeus' newly established chronology, brought about a big gap between the sack of Troy in the twelfth century B.C. as given by Hellenistic chronographers and the arbitrary date of the birth of Rome in the eighth century B.C. To bridge this hiatus and to connect nevertheless the founders of Rome with the Trojan hero, Pictor invented the dynasty of the Aeneads ruling in Alba Longa, the last "colony" of which would be Rome. Cato the Elder and others concocted more names and more dates for this list, but the groundwork of this house of cards was laid down by the first writer of the Annals.[3]

γενόμενον τῆς 'Ρώμης οἰκισμὸν ἢ κτίσιν. But already Antiochus of Syracuse spoke (in the last third of the fifth century) of a Rome founded before the Trojan war, in DH I 73, 5 (F. Gr. Hist. 555 F 6) : κατὰ μὲν δὴ τὸν Συρακούσιον συγγραφέα παλαιά τις εὑρίσκεται καὶ προτεροῦσα τῶν Τρωϊκῶν 'Ρώμη. Further details given in A. Schwegler, RG 1, 350 n. 5.

[1] Cf. Th. Mommsen, Römische Chronologie², Berlin 1859, 137. O. Leuze, Die römische Jahrzählung, Tübingen 1909, 47 sq., 79 sq., 281 sq. F. W. Walbank, A Historical Commentary on Polybius 1, Oxford 1957, 665 sq.

[2] DH I 74, 1-2. Solin. 1, 27, etc. Cf. F. Gr. Hist. 809 F 3 a-b. 810 F 1.

[3] Th. Mommsen, Röm. Chron.² 152 sq. A. Schwegler, RG 1, 343 sqq. Fr. Leo, Gesch. d. röm. Lit. 1, 1913, 63 sq. O. Leuze, op. cit. 88 sqq., 266 sqq. (who assumes 13 names in the original list). Fr. Münzer, RE 6, 1839. Th.

Manipulation of Figures and Dates

He also was striving to make the exactness of his dates believable and therefore parallelled his invented regnal years with Greek events.[1] He simulated an extreme precision: the rape of the Sabine women by Romulus' men happened, e.g., in the fourth month after the foundation ceremony,[2] being counted evidently from April 21 to August 21, i.e., from the festival of the *Palilia* to that of the *Consualia*. There is no doubt that he was conscious of his deceit, as well as when he asserted[3] that the Roman territory was divided into 26 *tribus* by Servius Tullius, which made a total of 30 tribes with the four urban *tribus*. Livy[4] instead says under 495 B.C.: *Romae tribus una et viginti factae*, and even this date is too early, since his statement presupposes the incorporation of territories acquired a century later.

In dealing with the epoch of the kings, we have to bear in mind the fact that the account we possess never had a chronological backbone and that therefore the quasi-exact dates presented to us cannot be true. Livy[5] was exasperated by the wild exaggerations of the later annalists who tried to outbid Pictor: *audet tamen Antias Valerius*

Mommsen, RF 2, 1879, 268 n. 62, 288 sqq., thought that the dynasty of the *Silvii* is "eine der spätesten Erdichtungen." But he was not able to refute H. Peter's observation (H. R. Rel. 1², p. LXXXVII) that in the account of Pictor Romulus is the son of Numitor's daughter. Thus the *last* kings of Alba were connected with the founders of Rome : Τῶν ἀπ' Αἰνείου γεγονότων ἐν "Αλβῃ βασιλέων εἰς ἀδελφοὺς δύο, Νομήτορα καὶ 'Αμούλιον, ἡ διαδοχὴ καθῆκεν (fr. 5 a). Cf. also L. Holzapfel, Römische Chronologie, Leipzig 1885, 259 sqq., 276 sqq. G. De Sanctis, St. d. R. 1², 200 sq. Pl. Fraccaro, Studi Varroniani, Padova 1907, 216 sqq.

[1] P. Bung, Q. Fabius Pictor, Diss. Köln 1950, 197, n. 5.

[2] Plut., *Rom.* 14, 1.

[3] H. R. Rel.² fr. 9 = F. Gr. Hist. 809 F 8 (DH IV 15, 1).

[4] Liv. II 21, 7. Cf. L. R. Taylor, Vot. Distr. (MemAmAc Rome 20) 1960, 5 sqq. with n. 9-10 and 6 n. 11 and 36. Dionysius mentions definitely that Fabius Pictor called these 26 divisions *tribus* (φυλάς in his words) ; Pictor also said that (including the four city-tribes) there were thirty *tribus* already under King Tullius. Further on he compares this statement with that of Vennonius who pretended that under this ruler the rural tribes numbered 31, and with the four urban tribes they already reached the final figure of the 35 *tribus*. Varro, *De vita pop. Rom.* in Non. p. 62 L. *et extra urbem in regiones XXVI agros viritim liberis adtribuit* (sc. Servius Tullius ; cf. Pap. Oxy 17, 1927, no. 2088), depends on Fabius Pictor. I do not see any possibility to discard this statement by supposing that the 26 districts of Pictor were *pagi*. E. Gabba, Athen., n.s. 39, 1961, 102 sq., 103 sq. with n. 21, 106 and 115, already realized the responsibility of Pictor who witnessed the constitution of the last *tribus* in 241 and must have been aware of the previous foundations' chronology, to which we return in Chapter VII.

[5] Liv. III 5, 12-13.

concipere summas . . . . exsequendo subtiliter numerum. But: is the difference in figures between an early annalist asserting that when Romulus defeated Veii 8000 Etruscans died on the battlefield, and the later ones recording 14,000 really relevant? [1] Or is it not all the same whether, as Pictor has it, 40 talents were invested from the booty of Pometia in the foundation of the Capitol or 40,000 pounds of silver,[2] as Piso more grandly suggests, since the more modest amount is no less fictitious than the larger? The tendency is the same in both cases: to invest the alleged stupendous growth of the city with the semblance of reality. The initiative of Pictor was the decisive factor even for the most impossible subsequent overstatements. Essential is the fact that truth was distorted intentionally. We read in the annals of 494 B.C. that the Romans alone, without their allies, mobilized ten legions for the first time.[3] The inventor of this statement knew, no doubt, that such a huge army could be mustered first in 349 B.C. Even then this size of armed forces seemed enormous: [4] . . . *senatus anxius . . . contendere omnes imperii vires consules dilectu habendo iussit: . . . decem legiones scriptae dicuntur . . . quem nunc novum exercitum, si qua externa vis ingruat, hae vires populi Romani, quas vix terrarum capit orbis, contractae in unum haud facile efficiant.*

Instead of adding further individual examples, we may more conclusively discuss continuous chains of figures revealing the system according to which the deceit was practised: the statistical data on the rapid increase of the population. The assumption of the common source of Dionysius and Livy that the census was introduced by King Servius Tullius and remained the basis of the social and military structure of the Republic must have originated from Pictor. *Census in civitate . . . non erat; ab Servio Tullio est facta,* writes Livy (IV 4, 2); τιμήσεις δ'ἐγένοντο τῶν βίων καὶ τάξεις τῶν εἰς τοὺς πολέμους εἰσφορῶν, ὡς Τύλλιος ὁ βασιλεὺς ἐνομοθέτησε, says Dionysius (V 20, 1).[5]

It is relevant to observe that even before the alleged introduction of the census, precise statistics were given for all the period since Romulus. Dionysius [6] informs us that Romulus founded the city with

---

[1] Plut., *Rom.* 25, 3-4.
[2] Liv. I 53, 2-3 ; 55, 7-9.
[3] Liv. II 30, 7. DH VI 42, 1.
[4] Liv. VII 25, 7-9.
[5] Cf. also DH V 75, 3.
[6] DH I 87, 3 ; II 2, 4 ; 16, 2. Lyd., *De mag.* 1, 9. Cass. Dio fr. 5, 8 (vol. 1, 9 Boiss.).

3000 foot soldiers and 300 horsemen. Plutarch [1] gives the number of 1000 hearths, but we are told that Romulus transferred the population of the cities conquered by him to Rome, giving them shares of property and full citizenship. The new city grew like a wild fire in a forest. When the Romans were reconciled under him with the Sabines, their combined strength amounted to 6000 infantrymen and 600 cavalry.[2] After Antemnae and Caenina were captured, their inhabitants were treated the same way; 2500 persons were brought over from Fidenae [3] to Rome on "April 1." Cameria had the same fate after its conquest: 4000 citizens were immediately enrolled in the Roman *tribus* and *curiae*.[4] Even the Etruscans of Veii are stated to have been dealt with in this generous manner: a huge number of their war prisoners who preferred to stay in Rome were granted citizenship and plots of land.[5]

In this way the army was soon doubled by the founder [6] and the city grew further at an amazing pace. In his Sabine war Romulus already had 20,000 foot soldiers and 800 horsemen.[7] When he died, the Roman armed forces counted 46,000 legionaries and 1000 horsemen.[8] Again new legions and squadrons of cavalry were organized by King Tullus after the conquest of Alba Longa.[9] Ancus Marcius allegedly transplanted the population of some more Latin cities,[10] and the rate implied is breathtaking. Thus it was possible for the inventor of these statistics to raise the number of the citizens under Servius Tullius to more than 80,000.

Under this ruler, Eutropius (1, 7) mentions 83,000 and Dionysius 84,700 citizens (IV 22, 2). Livy records about the first census[11] by that king: *adicit scriptorum antiquissimus Fabius Pictor, eorum qui arma*

---

[1] Plut., *Rom.* 9, 3.

[2] Plut., *Rom.* 20, 1. Liv. I 13, 5. Cf. DH II 47, 1. Lyd., *De mag.* 1, 16 etc.

[3] Plut., *Rom.* 23, 7.

[4] DH II 50, 5.

[5] DH II 55, 6.

[6] DH II 35, 1 sqq. Plut., *Rom.* 20, 1, mentions erroneously the doubling of each legion. Cf. Liv. I 13, 5.

[7] DH II 37, 5.

[8] DH II 15, 1-16, 3. Since B. G. Niebuhr, RG 1², 1827, 243, this figure was attributed to Valerius Antias.

[9] Liv. I 30, 3. DH III 27, 1 ; 29, 7-30, 1. 3-4 ; 31, 1-3. Val. Max. III 4,1.

[10] Politorium, Tellenae, Ficana : DH III 37, 4 ; 38, 2-3 ; 43, 2. Liv. I 33, 2 sq.

[11] Liv. I 44, 2: Fab. Pictor fr. 10, H. R. Rel. 1², p. 22 = F. Gr. Hist. 809 F 9. Th. Mommsen, RF 2, 398, 400 sqq. M. Gelzer, Hermes 68, 1933, 151 n. 2. P. Bung, *op. cit.* 161 n. 1.

FABIUS PICTOR

ferre possent, eum numerum fuisse. This boastful pseudo-precision proves that the construction of these ever-increasing figures was the work of that *scriptorum antiquissimus* who started these mathematical acrobatics with Romulus, managed to arrive at this enormous amount under Servius Tullius, and continued his fictitious display in the same style. The census figures of the early Republic have already been collected by J. Beloch.[1] According to him we have the following evidence:

508 B.C. 130,000 DH V 20, 1. Plut., *Poplic.* 12, 4.
503 B.C. 120,000 Hieron., Chron., Ol. 69, 1.
498 B.C. 150,700 DH V 75, 3; cf. VI 63, 4 (where 130,000 is reported).
493 B.C. 110,000 DH VI 96, 4; cf. IX 25, 2.
474 B.C. 103,000 DH IX 36, 3.
465 B.C. 104,714 Liv. III 3, 9.
459 B.C. 117,319 Liv. III 24, 10; cf. 22, 1; Eutr. 1, 16, 3.
392 B.C. 152,573 Plin., *N.h.*, XXXIII 1, 16, 3.

"It is obvious that these figures are greatly exaggerated," observed Beloch;[2] but the purpose of this exaggeration is transparent only when we realize that it was built up by the continuous amplification of the 80,000 citizens given under Servius Tullius. For the assessment of the whole manipulation with the early census figures, it is important to know that even the census figures recorded for the first half of the third century B.C. are not reliable,[3] although they are not as grotesquely distorted as those for the earliest period. It is a sheer impossibility that the size of the population remained stationary in those years of unparalleled expansion between 293 and 264 B.C., when the territory of the Roman state was tripled. This alleged standstill is a consequence of the overstressed growth of the population in the earliest phase of Rome's life: Pictor was constrained to slow down in order to tally his imaginary figures with the really known data of his own epoch.[4]

---

[1] J. Beloch, Die Bevölkerung der griechisch-römischen Welt, Leipzig 1886, 340. *Idem*, RG 216 and also in : Der italische Bund, Leipzig 1880, 89 sqq.
[2] K. J. Beloch, RG 216.
[3] *Ibid.* and Der italische Bund 84 sqq. with details.
[4] Beloch has shown, Griech. Gesch. III 1, 1904, 677 n. 1. (cf. A. Rosenberg, Einleitung und Quellenkunde zur röm. Geschichte, Berlin 1921, 124 and Hermes 57, 1922, 127 sqq.) that Pictor exaggerated also the strength of the fleet at the beginning of the First Punic War, and that he falsified the account of the Celtic War between 225-22.

He himself gave the reliable figures of the combatants of Italy in 225 B.C.,[1] which must have been the starting point for building up his imaginary statistics illustrating the pretended growth of Early Rome in this pseudo-rational manner.

༃

THE CHARACTERISTIC FEATURES OF THE PRETENDED EXPANSION UNDER THE KINGS

"From the very beginning, immediately after her founding," writes Dionysius, "[Rome] began to draw to herself the neighboring nations, which were both numerous and warlike, and continually advanced, subjugating every rival." This ambitious announcement was not invented by Dionysius of Halicarnassus.[2] For Livy, too, Rome's might emerged with her birth: *iam res Romana adeo erat valida, ut cuilibet finitimarum civitatum bello par esset.*[3] Not only were the captured Latin cities treated with the utmost clemency by Romulus, but even the Sabines and the Veientanes of Etruscan origin were immediately enrolled in the tribes of the citizens.[4] We know [5] that the myth of foundation in the Annals went back to Pictor: all the evidence suggests that the pattern of the prodigious growth belongs in essence to the same author.

Some of Romulus' alleged conquests were spun out of just the names of small ancient cities of the neighborhood,[6] well known to the man who first employed them in the picture of Romulus' rule. One

[1] F. Gr. Hist. 809 F 19. Th. Mommsen, RF 2, 1879, 382 sqq. J. Beloch, Der italische Bund 78, 80 sqq. J. Beloch, Die Bevölkerung, etc., 355 sqq. For a detailed bibliography see F. W. Walbank, A Historical Commentary on Polybius 1, Oxford 1957, 196 sqq.

[2] DH I 3, 4 ; cf. I 4, 1 sqq.

[3] Liv. I 9, 1.

[4] DH II 16, 2 ; 55, 6.

[5] DH I 79, 4.

[6] The references are to be found in A. Schwegler, RG 1, 528 sqq. A. Degrassi, Inscr. Ital. XIII 1, 1947, 534 sqq., and elsewhere. If clans of the patriciate had possessions in *Collatia, Medullia, Cameria, Amentum, Mugillum,* as their cognomina prove it, this does not mean that those localities were conquered under the kings, as K. J. Beloch, RG 166 sqq., supposed. *Antemnae* and *Ficana* along the Lower Tiber could have preserved their autonomy, because Ostia did not exist ; this speaks against J. Beloch, *loc. cit. Cameria* and *Antemnae* are reported to have revolted against Rome in 507 B.C. (DH V 21, 3). This means, if historical, that they still existed at the time of the early Republic.

of these was Caenina, the special cults of which were attended by the Roman *sacerdotes Caeninenses*;[1] as this ritual performance is woven in the foundation myth [2] as told by Pictor, we must infer that this fiction also goes back to the first author of the annals. Among the other names of cities, the capture of which is imputed to the founder, some mark the start of the expansion toward Etruria. The case of Crustumerium is revealing. Its conquest by Romulus,[3] by Tarquin the Elder,[4] and again in 499 B.C.,[5] are altogether fictitious: since it was situated to the north of Fidenae, it could have been captured only after the latter in the last decades of the fifth century, not much before the fall of Veii.[6] No less characteristic is the treatment of two neighboring towns just south of Crustumerium, Fidenae and Ficulea.[7] Fidenae, about 8 kilometers to the north of Rome along the ancient route of salt-transport coming from the mouth of the Tiber, was a bridgehead of Veii, stopping the Roman expansion toward Etruria. The annalists assert that this stronghold was conquered under Romulus, but they repeat its conquest under Tullus Hostilius, Ancus Marcius, and Tarquinius Priscus; and even say it was subjugated once more in 498 B.C.—an impossible assertion on the eve of the great clash of Rome with the Latin League of Aricia. In fact, as De Sanctis observed long ago, the story about the catastrophe of the Fabii at the Cremera (a brook reaching the Tiber from the west, opposite to the city in question) presupposes that Fidenae was not yet in Roman possession two decades after that date. Its subjugation by King Ancus is clearly copied from the scheme of the historical capture of Veii by digging mines under its walls. This sort of fiction—the reprojected repetition—may reveal the methods of Pictor. He knew the estates of his clan around the Cremera; he must have equally known when Fidenae fell. Ficulea lost its independence in the same years as Fidenae,[8] and not under King Tarquinius Priscus.

---

[1] G. Wissowa, RE 3, 1279.

[2] Pictor, fr. 5 b. H. R. Rel. 1², 12 = F. Gr. Hist. 089 F 4 = DH I 79, 13: ῾Ρωμύλος μέν οὖν τὸν χρόνον τοῦτον ἐτύγχανεν ἅμα τοῖς ἐπιφανεστάτοις τῶν κωμητῶν πεπορευμένος εἴς τι χωρίον Καίνιναν ὀνομαζόμενον ἱερὰ ποιήσων ὑπὲρ τοῦ κοινοῦ πάτρια.

[3] Liv. I 11, 3. DH II 36, 1 ; III 49, 6. Plut., *Rom.* 17, 1-2.

[4] Liv. I 38, 4. DH III 49, 6.   [5] Liv. II 19, 2.

[6] Ed. Meyer, GdA 5, 1902, 140. K. J. Beloch, RG 159, 175 sqq.

[7] All data collected by A. Schwegler, RG 1, 529, and also by G. De Sanctis, St. d. R. 2¹, 128 sqq. Cf. O. Richter, Hermes 17, 1888, 433 sqq. A. Degrassi, *op. cit.* 534, etc.

[8] K. J. Beloch, RG 160 and 175 sqq.

The Pretended Expansion under the Kings

The most grotesque distortion of truth, however, is the assertion that Romulus already was victorious over Veii, the power of which city was still superior to that of Rome in the first half of the fifth century B.C., as we shall see in the following chapters; in fact it was in 396 B.C., and then only after a heavy struggle that this Etruscan stronghold could be overcome by Rome. As a prelude to the alleged conquest of all the Etruscans under the kings Priscus and Servius Tullius, Veii is said to have been defeated under Ancus again. In the 'first year of the Republic' when in fact King Superbus was in power, and five years later again when Porsenna was holding Rome in his iron grasp, fictitious triumphs over the Veientanes were recorded in the Annals. Then, corresponding to the case of Fidenae just mentioned, the long siege of Veii about 400 B.C. is predated to 483-74 B.C.[1] in order to balance with a success the historical defeat of the Fabian army at the Cremera.

These predatings and the duplication of historical events combined with them, have often engaged the attention of modern scholars. However, they are not a capriciously applied device, to fill up the lacunae of the meager entries of the *Annales maximi* of the pontiffs, but the result of a rather systematic procedure within the frame of a carefully contrived plan. A few characteristic examples can illustrate this.

It was recognized long ago [2] that the account of the two Tarquins either tells the same exploits twice or splits them in such a way as to let the younger finish what the elder has begun. The most striking instance of the latter procedure is the building of the Capitoline temple, discussed later on in this study, and also the construction of the *cloaca maxima*.[3] We know that Fabius Pictor's work already contained the concerted picture of the deeds of the two Tarquins. Moreover, it was Pictor who identified Mastarna, the Vulcentane

[1] G. De Sanctis, St. d. R. 2¹, 125 sq., 133 sqq., whose results were accepted also by L. Pareti, Atene e Roma, n.s. 12, 1931, 218. The evidence for all forged victories is quoted in the works mentioned p. 131 n. 6 ; cf. especially A. Degrassi, *op. cit.* 65 sqq. and 534 sqq.

[2] E. Pais, St. d. R. I 1, 1898, 347, 466. *Idem*, St. crit. I 2, 154 sq. G. De Sanctis, Klio 1902, 102. *Idem*, St. d. R. 1¹, 371. A. Rosenberg, Einleitung und Quellenkunde zur römischen Geschichte, Berlin 1921, 116, writes that this duplication was made "by the legend" ("Sage") : though very critical otherwise, he was not aware at that time that we have to do with an intentional fiction. F. Schachermeyr, RE 4 A, 2376.

[3] For the latter cf. Cass. Hemina fr. 15 with the commentary by H. Peter.

FABIUS PICTOR

conqueror of Rome, with the good old king of the authentic Roman legend, Servius Tullius. He evidently combined the Etruscan report on Mastarna, who replaced a Tarquin on the throne of Rome, with the short introduction of the consular lists first published in 304 B.C., containing the main headings of the acts of the last king. As he did not have any information on the predecessor of Mastarna other than his name,[1] he distributed the items of the *res gestae* of the last king between the two; and as he did not find any other place in the list of the seven legendary kings for the contaminated figure of Servius Tullius-Mastarna, he inserted it between his two Tarquins.

The same sort of arbitrary construction is apparent also in the duplication of the decemvirate, to which we shall turn below, and further on in the repetition of Roman successes and achievements found in the pontifical Annals recorded for the years about 400 B.C.; they are transferred and make a second appearance in the reign of the last king, and the beginnings of the Republic. Such items are the beginnings of the colonization, the constitution of the rural districts with gentile names, along with a copious series of forged victories.

The same uninhibited recourse to fiction is apparent also in the chronology of the first stage of Roman history. We have seen that Pictor daringly brought the foundation date of Rome proposed by Timaeus two generations down,[2] so as to gain the proper length of time for the rule of seven kings; further, that the gap opened up by Timaeus, when he lowered this date from Aeneas down to 814-13 B.C., was filled in by Pictor, who inserted between the arrival of Aeneas and the birth of his home-city the dynasty of Alba Longa. His freely invented arithmetic reveals a play with the magic of numbers: Aeneas ruled 3 years in Lavinium, Alba was founded after 30 years by his son; the reign of the Alban kings lasted 300 years. The first epoch of legendary history, the reign of the antithetical

---

[1] Cf. Cic., *De re publ.* II 18, 33 : *sed temporum illorum tantum fere regum inlustrata sunt nomina.*

[2] Cf. above, and also : G. F. Unger, Rh. Mus. 35, 1880, 1 sqq. A. Schwegler, RG 1, 343 sqq. Fr. Münzer, RE 6, 1839, 20 sqq. F. Jacoby, F. Gr. Hist. 3 B, Kommentar, 1955, 564 (on fr. 59-61). 574 sq., and in the vol. of notes to the commentary 314. Kr. Hanell, *op. cit.* 166 sqq. S. Mazzarino, Stud. Rom. 8, 1960, 388 sqq. R. Van Compernolle, Hommages à L. Herrmann (Coll. Latomus 44), 1960, 750 sqq. All the scholars who try to harmonize the date of foundation in Pictor with the archeological evidence are not aware of the fact that before him this date was put centuries earlier. Cf. M. Pallottino, Arch. cl. 12, 1960, 8 sqq.

pair of Romulus and Numa, was figured out by him in such a way as to fill exactly an Etruscan *saeculum*.[1] If he has selected the year 747 B.C. as his date of the foundation of Rome, he was relying again on a *saeculum*: namely, on the date of the *ludi saeculares* in 348 B.C.[2] For the integration of the rise of Rome with the history of the civilized world, he synchronized the events of her dawn with remarkable happenings in Greece, in the manner of Timaeus.[3] The fruit of his irresponsible speculation, however, became the backbone of Roman chronology. Later the four dictatorial years were interpolated in the consular list of the fourth century B.C. and also added to his foundation date; Polybius defines the date as 751 B.C., the Augustan *fasti* as 752 B.C., and Varro as 753.[4]

꒳

THE ALLEGED CONQUESTS OF ENTIRE NATIONS BY THE ROMAN KINGS

The conquests of the last four kings reached prodigious proportions in the narrative of the annalists. To inflate their significance and at the same time to camouflage the lack of geographical data, those conquests do not mention cities, but whole populations: the totality of the Latins, Sabines, Volscians—even that of the Etruscans. One exception is made: if we disregard the names of some irrelevant places mentioned in order to mark Rome's supremacy over the Latins, it is the old capital, Alba Longa. If a rather carefully compiled list of the Latin strongholds is given,[5] the purpose is to show that the whole nation was united against Rome and the latter, superior to their combined strength, did not have to share the glory of her victory with anybody. All thirty Latin cities waged war against the Roman king Tullus who made a truce with all the Latins after his

---

[1] A. Schwegler, RG 1, 557 sq. On additional combinations of the same character cf. J. Hubaux, Rome et Véies, Paris 1958, 60 sqq. M. Sordi, I rapporti romano-ceriti, Roma 1960, 32, 173 sqq.

[2] A. Piganiol, Histoire de Rome[1], 1939, 43 sqq.

[3] A. Schwegler, RG 1, 675 sqq. E. Pais, Studi storichi 2, 1893, 328. G. F. Unger, Römisch-griechische Synchronismen vor Pyrrhos, S. B. Bayr. Ak. 1876, 531 sqq. Kr. Hanell, *loc. cit.*

[4] A. Piganiol, *loc. cit.*

[5] DH V 61, 3. Cf. above, p. 10 sqq.

victory.[1] King Ancus was also superior to all the Latins,[2] as was his successor, the first Tarquin,[3] to whom all Latins surrendered, and who treated them with noble moderation when they did everything he wanted. Servius Tullius did not even need to use weapons: his prestige and diplomacy were sufficient to transfer the center of the Latin League to the Aventine hill: [4] *ea erat confessio caput rerum Romam esse*.[5] The ultimate source of Livy and Dionysius, in describing how King Superbus oppressed the League of the Latins by shrewd devices and menace, may be the oldest annalist; but Cicero followed another version,[6] saying: *omne Latium bello vicit*.

Even after the kings the absolute supremacy of Rome over the *triginta populi* of the Latins is maintained by the Annals in the first decades of the Republic, when only the survival could be the aim in the bitter struggle with them.[7] Our last chapter will show how the light of real history begins to penetrate this veil in the second half of the fifth century, and how the names of the Latin opponents also emerge with the facts.[8]

In the same way as the Annals claim the subjugation of the Latins, the Romans are said to have mastered the Sabines, a process beginning with Romulus.[9] Tullus fought against the Sabine nation and not against single cities,[10] and of course he won the contest, as did after him Ancus,[11] Tarquin the Elder,[12] and Superbus.[13] The "Sabines" are

[1] DH III 33, 1 sqq. Liv. I 32, 3.

[2] Liv. I 32, 3.33, 6. DH III 38, 4-39, 4. The conquest is illustrated by the capture of cities, but Politorium, Medullia, and Ficana are not really important and their role is without any historical foundation.

[3] Liv. I 35, 7 ; 38, 4 : *omne Latinum nomen domuit*. DH III 49, 1 sqq. Fasti triumph. p. 65 Degrassi. Flor. I 1, 5. *Vir. ill.* 6, 8. Cf. Plin., *N.h.* III 5, 70. Plut., *Rom.* 16, 8. Zon. 7, 8. The place-names: Apiolae (= Pometia), Crustu-merium, Nomentum, Collatia, Corniculum, Ficulea, Cameria were picked at will from later accounts, in order to give the impression that the report was based on detailed information. The important cities were left out again.

[4] Liv. I 45, 1 sqq. Val. Max. VII 3, 1. DH IV 25, 3 sqq.

[5] Liv. I 45, 3.

[6] Cic., *De re p.* II 24, 44.

[7] Liv. II 18, 3. DH VI 17, 2. Liv. II 20, 13; 21, 3. Inscr. It. XIII 3, no. 10, etc.

[8] Cf. below, p. 377 sqq.

[9] DH II 38, 3 ; 39, 1 ; 40, 2. III 1, 2. Macrob. I 8, 1. *Fasti Capitol.*, cf. A. Degrassi, Inscr. It. XIII 1, 534.

[10] DH III 32, 1 sqq. 4 sq. 33, 1 sq. Macrob., *l.c. Fasti Capitol.*, *l.c.*

[11] DH III 40, 2 sqq. 5, speaks also of the victorious attack on a "great and prosperous city" and "on some other cities of the Sabine people." *Fasti Capitol.*, *op. cit.* pp. 65 and 535.

The Alleged Conquests of Entire Nations

said to have become Roman citizens paying tribute.[1] At the beginning of the Republic, from 504 B.C. on, the subjugation of the "Sabines" is mentioned again and again,[2] and they always surrender most solemnly.

The most puzzling invention among these antedated conquests is the alleged subjugation of the Etruscans. The fact that not the Romans but the Etruscans were the conquerors is completely suppressed: Lucumo, a stranger and immigrant is magnanimously admitted to the highest positions in the city. He is made king as a reward for his merits as is his successor; not even the widely known capture of Rome by Porsenna is admitted. If Livy suppressed the puzzling invention of Etruria's conquest by King Priscus,[3] this happened because he did not believe it; but, since this event is mentioned by Ennius,[4] it must have come from Pictor, on whom Ennius' text concerning the regal epoch seems to be mainly based. The talkative report by Dionysius on these alleged exploits [5] mirrors the tendency smuggled into that remote past by Fabius Pictor. The Etruscans voted that all their cities should wage joint war against the Roman king, but they were decisively beaten.[6] Later on the king broke the spirit

[12] DH III 55, 1 sqq.; 59, 1 sqq. 63, 1 sqq. Liv. I 36, 1 sqq. *Vir. ill.* 6, 8. Macrob. I 6, 8. *Fasti Capitol.* pp. 65 and 535.

[13] Liv. I 55, 8 sqq. 53, 3. DH IV 45, 2 ; 50, 1 sq. The conquest of the "Sabines" exemplified by the capture of the Volscian city of Suessa Pometia. *Fasti Capitol. l.c.* Hor., *Ep.* II 1, 24 sqq.

[1] DH IV 52, 2. Cf. G. De Sanctis, St. d. R. 2, 1907, 123 sqq.

[2] DH V 37, 1 sqq. 4 ; 38, 1 sqq. ; 40, 1 ; 41, 1 ; 42, 1. 4 ; 44, 1 sqq. 5 ; 45, 1 sq. 46, 1 sq. 3 sq. 48, 2 ; 49, 1 sq ; VI 31 sq. ; 34, 1 ; 42, 1 sq ; IX 59, 3. Plut., *Poplic.* 20, 1 sq. Eutr. 1, 11. *Vir. ill.* 15, 1. For further details : A. Degrassi, *op. cit.* pp. 65 and 536. Cf. also A. Klotz, Livius und seine Vorgänger, Berlin 1941, 225 sqq.

[3] A slight trace of this is left in his account on Servius Tullius' exploits after Priscus' death, I 42, 2 : *bellum cum Veientibus—iam enim induantiae exierant—aliisque Etruscis sumptum.* Cf. also I 55, 1 : *foedus cum Tuscis renovavit.* A successor of Pictor went even further and let the Etruscans be vanquished already by Tullus Hostilius. Cf. Cicero, *De re p.* II 17, 31. Plin., *N.h.* IX 39, 136. Macrob., *Sat.* I 6, 7. Hieron., *Chron.*, p. 164. Schoene.

[4] Ennius 3, fr. 6 v. 152 Vahlen : *Hac noctu filo pendebit Etruria tota.*

[5] DH III 51, 1-4, records an alliance between Clusium, Arretium, Rusellae, Vetulonia, and Volaterrae with the purpose of aiding the Latins against Tarquin the Elder. But archaeology has revealed that these more northern cities of Etruria could not interfere much with Latium. And we know that the Romans did not advance north of the forest around Viterbo before 310 B.C. : *Silva erat Ciminia magis tum invia atque horrenda, quam nuper fuere Germanici saltus, nulli ad eam diem ne mercatorum quidem adita* (Liv. IX 36, 1).

[6] DH III 57, 1 sqq. VI 75, 3.

FABIUS PICTOR

of all Etruscans by a glorious victory, and their general assembly decided to ask for peace and acknowledged defeat. They accepted any terms they could get from the victor. Tarquinius, who graciously permitted them to enjoy their own laws and government, enjoyed complete sovereignty over all Etruscan states.[1] Obtaining from them the *insignia* of sovereign power, he did not avail himself of these honors as conferred upon himself; he left it to the Senate and the people to decide whether he should accept them or not. And he wore the attributes of power over the Etruscans [2] only after they unanimously approved this. This absurd tale was found by Dionysius in most of the earlier Roman historical works: ὡς οἱ πλεῖστοι γράφουσι τῶν ʽΡωμαϊκῶν συγγραφέων (DH III 62, 1).

Such an enormous lie should serve as a *memento* for everybody who wishes to consider the conquest of the Latins by Rome since the seventh century B.C. as historical: the juridical reasoning and the legalistic coloring of the fictitious tale is the same here as it is in the annalist's story of Rome's rule over the Latins from the time of the first kings.

After the death of Priscus, as Dionysius relates it,[3] the Etruscan cities rose in revolt against Rome, but after twenty years of war without respite, they all were forced to surrender to Servius Tullius.[4] The last Roman king also ruled over all the Etruscans [5]—the common source of Dionysius and Livy assumed that not only Etruria but even Campania was subjected to Rome.[6]

A more difficult instance of such distortions is offered by the Volscians and the Aequians, tribes not as far away as all the states of Central and Northern Etruria; but the vague reference to *Volsci* and *Aequi* for alleged conquests by the kings are the results of the same

---

[1] DH III 58, 1 sqq. Flor. I 5, 5. Oros. II 4, 11. *Fasti Capitol.* p. 65 Degrassi. Cf. the remarks by B. G. Niebuhr, RG 1², 1827, 39. See also L. Pareti, Atene e Roma, n.s. 12, 1931, 213 sq., 217 sq.

[2] *Ibid.* III 60, 1 sqq. IV 3, 2 ; 27, 1. Vergil applied the same procedure to the legendary prehistory when he sent the royal insignia by Tarchon to Euander, *Aen.* 8, 505 sqq.

[3] DH IV 27, 1 sqq. *Fasti Capitol., l.c.*

[4] DH IV 27 sqq. Cic., *De re p.* II 21, 38. *Vir. ill.* 7, 6. Zon. VII 9, 10. Liv. I 42, 2-3. Oros. II 4, 11.

[5] DH IV 65, 2. Cf. Liv. I 55, 1 : *Tarquinius . . . foedus cum Tuscis renovavit.*

[6] DH VI 50, 2 ; 75, 3. The πόλις ἡ ʽΡωμαίων ἡ τοσούτων ἄρχουσα ἀνθρώπων of Dionysius (VI 71, 3) has its equivalent in Livy I 59, 9 : *Romanos homines, victores omnium circa populorum.*

tendency: [1] these peoples were subdued by the Etruscans, as we shall see, not by Rome.[2] In the annalist fiction, King Ancus has already defeated the Volscians,[3] King Priscus vanquished them and the Aequians,[4] and under Superbus they were depending completely on Rome [5] after losing the best part of their territory.

Another way to illustrate the progress of Roman expansion was found by the first annalist in predating later colonization. The strategically conceived occupation by the 30 units of the immigrating Latins was seen by him as a systematic colonization implemented by Lavinium and Alba Longa—as the Roman kings are said to have founded colonies around these cities. But the whole concept of an actual colonization emerged, I am sure, not as a Roman device for controlling her subjects, but as a strategic network of the Latin confederacy in its struggle against the mountain peoples of the Volscians, Aequi and Sabines in the fifth century, when the grip of the Etruscans on Latium and on those mountain shepherds was loosened.[6]

If the colonization under the kings is completely invented, the last items deserve some attention. Fabius Pictor, it seems to me, wished to prove Roman occupation of Latium down to the boundary of Campania by the assertion that King Superbus founded colonies in Suessa Pometia, Signia, and Circeii. Concerning the first of these cities, he had before his eyes a written summary of the *res gestae* of the last king, mentioning that this monarch financed the building of the Capitoline temple from the booty of Pometia.[7] But he duplicated the story of Superbus, repeating it with slight modification as the *res*

---

[1] This speaks against V. Arangio-Ruiz, Scritti giuridici raccolte per il centenario della casa editrice Jovene, Napoli 1954, 124.

[2] Cf. below, p. 193 sqq, and G. De Sanctis, St. d. R. 2, 1907, 116 sq.

[3] DH III 41, 5.

[4] Cic., *De re p*. II 20, 36. Strab. V 3, 4 (C. 231).

[5] Liv. I 53, 2 sqq. DH IV 49, 1 ; 52, 3. V 62, 3. *Fasti Capitol*. pp. 65 and 535 Degrassi.

[6] E. Pais, Mem. Lincei ser. 5, 17, 1924, 315, is unsatisfactory, as is K. J. Beloch, RG 295 sqq. : "Natürlich haben die Gründungsdaten nicht den geringsten Wert, aber an der Colonisation selbst kann kein Zweifel sein." Cf. F. Schachermeyr, RE 4A, 2385. Cf. our Chapter VIII.

[7] Liv. I 55, 8 sq.; cf. 53, 3 = Pictor fr. 13 Peter (H. R. Rel. 1², 25). Cic., *De re p*. II 24, 44 ; Strab. V 3, 4 (C. 231). I accept the results of G. De Sanctis, St. d. R. 2, 1907, 104 sqq. F. Schachermeyr, RE 4 A, 2385.

gestae of Priscus,[1] in which the same city is called Apiolae,[2] a simple translation of Pometia into Greek.

But this is not the invention of the much scorned Valerius Antias, as Niebuhr thought it was: the Greek translation of the Latin name Pometia makes it more likely that it was the Greek annals of Pictor that introduced this fiction [3] and that he was the author of the duplication just mentioned. Since a Roman breakthrough to the Pomptine plain at such an early date, when the cities of the Arician League (Pometia was one of them) were not yet conquered must be unhistorical; [4] the same applies to the statement that Pometia became a *colonia Latina* in 505 B.C.[5]

The colonization of Signia and Circeii by Superbus is likewise unhistorical. The Volscian Signia,[6] near the Etruscan lifeline toward Campania across the Tolerus-Liris valleys, may not have been Roman at such an early date. Gabii, much closer to Rome, was conquered according to the annalist tradition only by the deceit of the tyrant—*minime arte Romana, fraude et dolo*—in reality, not at all yet.[7] Nor could Signia have become a Roman colony in the second year of the Republic,[8] before the victory over the Latin League. More absurd still is the alleged early colonization of Circeii in the gate from Latium to Campania; this city was conquered only in 393 B.C. when the Latins could no longer resist Rome and the Volscians had collapsed.[9] Nor is the siege of Ardea by Superbus historical: Pictor needed[10] it for the Lucretia novel as well as for the preposterous display of Roman might.

---

[1] Cf. above, p. 132, 139.

[2] Valerius Antias fr. 11 Peter (H. R. Rel. 1², 242). Liv. I 35, 7. DH III 49, 1. Strabo V 3, 4 (C. 231). Cf. B. G. Niebuhr, RG 1², 1827, 525.

[3] For an analogous case cf. Pictor's explanation of the *instauratio ludorum* below, p. 155 sq., 171.

[4] Cf. G. De Sanctis, *l.c.*

[5] Liv. II 16, 8. In 495 B.C. Pometia is Volscian in Liv. II 22, 2 ; it is said nevertheless to have been captured by the Volscians in the same year : *ibid.* II 25, 5 sqq. Cf. E. Pais, *op. cit.* 314 sqq.

[6] Liv. I 56, 3. DH IV 63, 1. Cic., *De re p.* II 24, 44. G. De Sanctis, St. d. R. 2, 1907, 106 n. 2. E. Pais, *op. cit.* 314 sqq. Philipp, RE 2A 2347 sqq.

[7] Liv. I 53, 4 sqq. DH IV 52, 3-58, 4.

[8] DH V 20, 1. Plut., *Popl.* 16, 3.

[9] Diod. XIV 102, 4. Cf. Liv. VI 5, 2 ; 12, 6 ; 17, 7 ; XXIX 15, 5. G. De Sanctis, *op. cit.* 108 sqq.

[10] F. Gr. Hist. 809 F 12 (= DH IV 64, 2 sqq.).

ॐ

THE LEITMOTIF OF HEGEMONY

The aspiration of the Romans to become a leading power in Latium
was born in the fifth century B.C. [1] With the subjugation of all the
Latins in 340-38 B.C., it reached its goal. In this first stage, Rome as
caput rerum [2] meant the leadership in Latium. An echo of this still
modest early claim was preserved by Pictor.[3] The story of the human
head which was found unharmed when the foundations of the
Capitol were dug and which foretold the future greatness of the city
must be as old as the popular explanation of the word *Capitolium* as
Caput Oli, i.e., the head of the Vulcentan hero of Etruscan Rome,
Aulus Vibenna. Another, even clearer, instance of this first concept
of Roman imperialism is the rustic anecdote of the horned cattle of
exceptional size, the sacrifice of which in the precinct of Diana on
the Aventine promised the leadership over the Latins (or Sabines)
by the will of the gods: *cuius civitatis eam civis Dianae immolasset, ibi
fore imperium.*[4] The limited local ambitions of the Romans in the last
decades of the fifth century B.C. are clearly mirrored in the account
of the prodigy of the terra-cotta quadriga, prepared in Veii for the
Capitoline temple, which was swelling in the furnace, betraying to
the experts the future superiority of Rome in the competition with
Veii.[5] There was no ideological basis to this concept of "hegemony"
in early Rome, nothing corresponding to the classical Greek ἀριστεία
καὶ πρωτεία, or the Roman *virtus* as the vehicle of conquest proclaimed
by Livy and others in the Augustan age; [6] its basis was the law of
the stronger which rules archaic societies: *se in armis ius ferre*, as the
Gauls say in Livy,[7] *et omnia fortium virorum esse.*

[1] Cf. Chapter VIII, p. 336 sqq.

[2] Liv. I 55, 5 sqq. V 54, 7 sqq.

[3] Pictor fr. 12 Peter. All pertinent passages are collected in H. R. Rel. 1²,
p. 23 sq.

[4] Liv. I 45, 3-7. *Vir. ill.* 7, 10. The duped owner of the *bos* is a Sabine in
Livy, a Latin in the *viri illustres*.

[5] Details in : A. Schwegler, RG 1, 772 n. 4 and 773 n. 1, and K. O. Müller-
W. Deecke 2, 252. Plin., *N.h.* VIII 42, 161. Fest., p. 340, 31 L. Serv., *Aen.* 7,
158. Plut., *Poplic.* 13, 1-5. This quadriga was one of the *septem pignora imperii*,
but in 296 B.C. it had already disappeared and was replaced by a bronze
statuary group. Cf. Liv. X 23, 12 and A. Andrén, Rend. Pont. Acc. 32, 1960, 45.
This illustrates the age and the genuineness of the legend.

[6] H. Hoch, Die Darstellung der politischen Sendung Roms bei Livius.
Diss. Frankfurt am M. 1952, 34 sqq.

[7] Liv. V 36, 5.

FABIUS PICTOR

Quite different from this primeval indigenous idea of power is the contest for the primacy as conducted by the Roman kings according to Dionysius, who repeats this tale *ad nauseam*.[1] From the time of Tullus Hostilius none of the Latin cities can dispute the supremacy over the nation.[2] The Latins under Priscus are still rivals of Rome for the sovereignty, but are reduced to obedience along with the most powerful of her neighbors, the Etruscans, and with the Sabines.[3] Supremacy is the aim of the city under Servius Tullius.[4] The Etruscan League was not willing to yield him the sovereignty, but after a hard and long struggle they were humbly begging to be pardoned for their revolt and accepted the Roman yoke.[5]

Some years after the crushing defeat by Porsenna, we are told, the Roman commonwealth regained its strength and aimed again at the hegemony. The Sabines, elated by a victory, demanded that Rome yield the leadership to them, but were forced to surrender once more.[6] These boastful claims are made again and again, concerning the Latins [7] and the Sabines.[8] All wars are conducted for supremacy ὑπὲρ ἀρχῆς καὶ δυναστείας.[9] The war against the Auruncans is said to be such a contest of valor,[10] entered into for the sake of hegemony. The vocation of Rome was remembered even when greatly menaced by the Volscians: to rule over the ruling and to command those who command others.[11]

Overworked by Dionysius, the idea of hegemony was greatly reduced in Livy, but is nevertheless manifest in his work. The Romans always fought *pro libertate et imperio*: liberty means their own freedom and *imperium* is the yoke for their neighbors. The existence of a common source in both writers is apparent. In the duel between the Alban and Roman triplets, the ἀγὼν τῆς ἡγεμονίας of

[1] This fiction is sometimes taken seriously. Cf. H. Horn, Foederati. Diss. Frankfurt am Main 1930, 88.
[2] DH III 11, 5.
[3] DH IV 9, 2.
[4] DH IV 23, 4 ; 26, 2.
[5] *Ibid.* IV 27, 2. Cf. *ibid.* 3 sqq.
[6] *Ibid.* IV 39, 4 ; 45, 2.
[7] *Ibid.* V 50, 4 ; 65, 4.
[8] *Ibid.* VI 49, 1.
[9] *Ibid.* VI 6, 2 ; VIII 70, 2 ; IX 9, 1. 4 ; 43, 2 ; 46, 2.
[10] *Ibid.* VI 32, 2.
[11] *Ibid.* VIII 17, 1 ; 25, 4 ; 32, 3 ; X 5, 5 ; 14, 1. XI 9, 6 ; 59, 2. XII *fr.* 13, 2. *fr.* 14, 1.

Dionysius (III 14, 2) corresponds to the *ut Romanus Albano imperet* in Livy (I 25, 12), viz., *ibi imperium fore, unde victoria fuerit* (I 24, 2). The tyrannical government of the decemvirate is described by Livy (III 38, 2) *contemni coepti erant a finitimis populis, imperiumque ibi esse, ubi non esset libertas, indignabantur.* The same story is drawn out to a lengthy tirade in Dionysius (XI 3, 1): καὶ τὸ ἐλεύθερον (ἐν 'Ρώμῃ) ἅπαν ἀπολωλεκυίας ἀφορμὴν κρατίστην ὑπολαβόντες ἔχειν οἱ πολέμῳ κρατηθέντες ὑπ'αὐτῆς τάς τε ὕβρεις ἅς ὑβρίσθησαν ἀποτίσασθαι καὶ τὰ ἀπολωλότα ἀναλαβεῖν. It is evident that the arrogant rhetor and the discreet historian had the same ultimate source, Pictor.

The great struggle with the mountain tribes in the fifth century when Rome gradually became prominent was not yet an enterprise which could have been called with Livy (IV 37, 5) *de imperio certare*. Survival was at stake, not supremacy. But after the Celtic storm when Rome strove to subjugate all neighbors, this slogan approached reality: *cum externis pro imperio certare.*[1] Some decades later, when the envoys of the Campanians asked the Senate for help against the Samnites, they told the truth:[2] *subactis his gentibus quae inter nos vosque sunt, quod propediem futurum spondet et virtus et fortuna vestra, continens imperium, usque ad nos habebitis.* And in 340 B.C., the Roman rule over the Latins was in fact *pro imperio agere*.[3] *De imperio certare*[4] was the war against Samnium, indeed. Times changed.

The views of the annalists on early Rome were conceived while they looked back with one eye into the past and with the other at the future glory of the leading power of the Mediterranean world, as was observed long ago.[5] The new Empire needed an old pedigree,[6] a justification of its prodigious growth.[7] This was given by the lofty idea of the *princeps terrarum populus*,[8] which from the very beginning

[1] Liv. VI 18, 11.
[2] Liv. VII 30, 8.
[3] *Ibid.* VIII 5, 3.
[4] *Ibid.* VIII 23, 9.
[5] F. Münzer, Adelsp. 1920, 4 : "Bei den ältesten Berichterstattern ist vor allen festzuhalten, dass sie die Vergangenheit nur im Hinblick auf die Gegenwart darstellten, die Entstehung der vorhandenen Zustände erklären, ihre künftige Erhaltung oder Umgestaltung historisch begründen wollten, als Politiker an die Aufgabe des Geschichtsschreibers herantraten."
[6] L. Homo, L'Italie primitive, Paris 1925, 18 sqq.
[7] H. Hoch, *op. cit.* (p. 141 n. 6) with a bibliography of specialized literature on p. 7, n. 1.
[8] Liv. I, praef. 3.

FABIUS PICTOR

began to draw to herself the nearest neighboring nations, subjugating every rival [1] as the divinity had ordered.[2] The founder—a divine being himself—selected the best possible site, the heart of the whole of Italy; [3] Ancus built the harbor of Ostia for the future center of the world,[4] just as long before that time Hercules founded his cult on the site of Rome for the people who would once rule the *oikumene*.[5] The city walls were not built for a handful of men but for a large population by Romulus,[6] aware of the great destiny of his posterity.[7] The gods reveal the coming greatness of the Roman Empire to the builder of the Capitol: [8] *movisse numen ad indicandam tanti imperii molem traditur deos*: we have already seen that this originated from Pictor, together with the *perpetuitatis auspicium*.[9]

The census is instituted by Servius Tullius in view of great things to come: *rem saluberrimam tanto futuro imperio*.[10] Under the Tarquins the Romans are *victores omnium circa populorum*.[11] And, after the last king has disappeared, there is no change in the Annals which continue to announce, from time to time, the great events to come.[12] The high platform, on which the annalists stood to proclaim their version of Rome's beginnings, was the conquered Mediterranean world; they were unable to descend from it, when Rome's real history, starting with the Republic, began to dissipate the fog of mystification.

Though these facts themselves were underlined more than once, it was necessary to be reminded of them. They help to make it clear that Early Rome's history in the Annals is not the product of chance

---

[1] DH I 3, 4.

[2] Liv. I 12, 2 sqq. ; 16, 7. DH IV 26, 2.

[3] Liv. V 54, 4. Cic., *De re p.* II 3, 5 sqq.

[4] Flor. I 1, 4.

[5] Liv. I 7, 3 sqq.

[6] Liv. I 8, 4.

[7] Liv. I 9, 3 : *urbes quoque, ut cetera, ex infimo nasci ; dein, quas virtus ac di iuvent, magnas opes sibi magnumque nomen facere ; satis scire origini Romanae et deos adfuisse et non defuturam virtutem.* Cf. I 9, 9 ; 38, 7 ; V 3, 10.

[8] Liv. I 55, 3. DH IV 59, 1-61, 2. Tac., *Hist.* 3, 72.

[9] Fabius Pictor *fr.* 12 Peter (H. R. Rel. 1², p. 23). Liv. I 55, 2-4 ; 56, 5-7. DH III 69, 5-6. IV 61, 2.

[10] Liv. I 42, 5, cf. 14, 4 : the *Fidenates* also foresee the danger arising on their horizon when Rome is founded.

[11] Liv. I 59, 9.

[12] Liv. IV 4, 4 : *Quis dubitat, quin in aeternum urbe condita, in immensum crescente nova imperia sacerdotia, iura gentium hominumque instituantur?* DH VIII 26, 4 : ἐνθυμοῦ τὸ μέγεθος τῆς πόλεως καὶ τὴν λαμπρότητα τῶν ἐν τοῖς πολέμοις πράξεων καὶ τὴν ἐκ τοῦ θείου παροῦσαν αὐτῇ τύχην, δι' ἥν ἐκ μικρᾶς τοσαύτη γέγονε.

but was based on a systematic plan. In its essential features this plan was already followed by Ennius, a younger contemporary of Fabius Pictor, as may be seen from Fr. Leo's [1] description of his "Annals": "this poem is not a mere chronicle, i.e., a versified sequence of haphazard events. It is rather a constant and irresistibly mounting ascent of the nation, starting from modest beginning. The arrangement follows a definite scheme: the first half told, in three triads of the foundations of the future Empire laid by the kings, of the spread of the Roman name over Italy, and of the defence of the Italic Empire against the rival power and the overthrow of the enemy. The second half dealt with the establishment of empire over the world."

Romulus' statement in Livy that *mea Roma caput orbis terrarum sit* seems to be based on Ennius [2] but the concept comes from Pictor. Even the form and the title *Annales* of the poem may have been suggested by the first "Annals."

୧

THE LEGALISTIC MACHINERY OF THE ANNALS

For the understanding of the treatment of the Latin League in our literary tradition we must notice that the juridical elaboration of the theme which we previously tried to elucidate is not restricted to this people alone. The Sabines defeated by King Tullus wrote the terms of the peace treaty on stelai set up in their temples.[3] A schematical motif of the narrative is the employment of general assemblies as vehicles of actions and developments. The Volscians, e.g., meet in order to adopt a common plan for the war against Rome.[4] The magistrates of every city meet together with a great multitude of common people. The vote is taken after many speeches. The Hernicans have a juridical argument with the Senate on the validity of the treaty between them and King Tarquinius.[5] The same parliamentary procedures as those concerned with the Latins are described in reference to Etruria's general assembly.[6] This gives a quasi-legal character

---

[1] Fr. Leo, Geschichte der römischen Literatur 1 (Leipzig 1913) 172.
[2] Liv. I 16, 6 sq. Cf. H. Hoch, *op. cit.* 62.
[3] DH III 33, 1.
[4] DH VIII 4, 3-4.
[5] DH VIII 64, 2.
[6] DH IX 18, 2-4.

to the fiction, as does the *donatio Constantini* and many other forged enactments of later times; the intention is to lend more exactness, more stress, and more credibility to the political theory, with painstaking descriptions of the lawful forms in which Rome obtained her hegemony at the dawn of her history. For this purpose the fifth century center of the Latin League on the Aventine is put back into the age of Servius Tullius, whereas the oldest tribal center on the *Mons Albanus* is considered as the creation of Superbus.

There are other facets to this tendency.[1] The disproportionate growth of the city is explained by the wise and humane policy of the kings since Romulus, who transferred the populations of the conquered cities in bulk to Rome and permitted them to retain all their mobile possessions, built them new homes, and incorporated them into the body of the citizens. They admitted their aristocracy to the patriciate (as the example of the *familiae Albanae* shows). This procedure is, of course, in complete contrast to the rude habits of those ancient days when the conquered lost not only their possessions but their freedom or lives. *Exemplo maiorum augere rem Romanam victos in civitatem accipiendo*[2] was certainly invented for those early days, as to inspire respect in the Greeks: *materiam crescendi per summam gloriam suppeditat.*

Another feature of this trend is the use of alliances as proofs of authenticity. Romulus makes a *foedus* with Titus Tatius,[3] a non-

---

[1] Cf. E. Gabba, Athen., n.s. 38, 1960, 187 sq., on DH II 15, 1 sq.

[2] Liv. VIII 13, 16. Some examples are given above, p. 129 sqq. Livy and Dionysius depend on common sources, e.g., Liv. I 33, 2 sq. = DH III 43, 2, etc. The fiction was maintained as a Roman practice even in the early Republic : DH VI 2, 2. On the other hand, we have to remember the fact that this procedure of transfer of entire city-populations was indeed a practice of Sicilian tyrants (cf. for instance Ad. Holm, Geschichte Siziliens 1, Leipzig 1874, 98 sq., 130 sqq. K. F. Stroheker, Dionysios I., Wiesbaden 1958, 151). This is important, because the Sicilian Greeks, who served the interests of Carthage against Rome during the first and the second Punic wars, were those opponents by whom Fabius Pictor was constrained to produce an antithetical picture to their own on the growth of the Roman power (as Kr. Hanell, Histoire et historiens dans l'antiquité, Vandoeuvres-Genève 1956, 149, rightly stressed) ; and every polemical parallelism leads to mutual borrowings and to assimilation of ideals and practice. Beside this, the alleged liberalism of the ancient Romans in admitting aliens to their citizen-body was a very attractive aspect for the Roman propaganda, as Philipp V of Macedon's letter shows : IGr IX 2, 517 = F. Schroeter, *De regum Hellenisticorum epistulis*, Leipzig 1932, 78 sqq. n. 31.

[3] Cic., *De re p.* II 7, 13.

aggression pact with the metropole of the Latins, Alba Longa.[1]

Romulus developed a legislation incorporated in the collection of the *leges regiae*.[2] Numa organized the religious institutions *ex commentariis regiis*.[3] This tendency reached the heights of absurdity, when it engendered the notion that the Republic had its written legalization by the prescripts of a king: *duo consules inde comitiis centuriatis a praefecto urbis ex commentariis Servi Tulli creati sunt, L. Junius Brutus et L. Tarquinius Collatinus*.[4] This curious assertion is explained in Livy,[5] writing on Servius Tullius: *id ipsum tam mite ac tam moderatum imperium tamen, quia unius esset, deponere eum in animo habuisse quidam auctores sunt, ni scelus intestinum liberandae patriae consilia agitanti intervenisset.*

The desire for constitutional authorization manifested itself in the transference of the regal attributes of the Etruscans to Priscus and in the offer of the same symbols by the Senate to Porsenna.[6]

We need not go into the question of the ultimate source of these legal fictions. It will be sufficient in this connection to stress the fact that the later annalists, whose accounts of the Latin League are preserved to us, apply the same invented features in their reports of Rome's other neighbors in the regal epoch. We know that Fabius Pictor already described the political reforms of Servius Tullius;[7] and I have proved recently that in relation to the coinage he consciously distorted a statement by Timaeus and intentionally antedated the Roman bronze coinage—which began only in his parents' lifetime— as a creation of that legendary king.[8] Thus I must suppose that the kernel of this whole legalistic fiction is his creation.

༄

HELLENISTIC MANNERISM IN PICTOR'S CONCEPT: HIS FEMALE CHARACTERS

Livy's art of writing is always delightful but rarely are the personal touches so heart-warming as in the anecdote in which the admission

---

[1] DH III 3, 1.

[2] Cf. the bibliography in Peter, H. R. Rel. 1², 1914, p. VI n. 1., and E. Gabba, Athen., n.s. 38, 1960, 175 sq., 201 sqq.

[3] Liv. I 31, 8 ; 32, 2. DH III 36, 4. Plut., *Marcell.* 8, 9. Plin., *N.h.* XXVIII 2, 14. Cic., *Pro C. Rabir.* 5, 15.   [4] Liv. I 60, 4.   [5] Liv. I 48, 9.

[6] DH V 35, 1. In the area of private law, Verginia's fate brought great opportunity for fictitious juridical dealings. Cf. P. Noailles, *Fas et ius*, Paris 1948, 187 sq.   [7] DH IV 15, 1.   [8] A. Alföldi, RM 68, 1961, 64 sqq.

of the plebeians to the consulate, an epoch-making turning point of Roman history, is derived from a petty domestic occurrence. He writes:[1]

"Marcus Fabius Ambustus was a very influential man, not only among his fellow-patricians but with the plebs as well, for the members of that class felt that he was far from looking down upon it. He married his two daughters, the elder to Servius Sulpicius, the younger to Caius Licinius Stolo, a man of mark, albeit a plebeian. And the very fact that he did not reject such an alliance had won regard for Fabius with the common people. It happened by chance that the two Fabiae sisters were whiling away the time in chatting in the house of Servius Sulpicius, then consular tribune, as women will do. Then the lictor of Sulpicius, who was returning from the Forum, rapped on the door, in the usual manner with his rod. At this the younger Fabia, being unused to the custom, went white, which made the elder laugh with surprise at her sister's ignorance. But that laugh rankled in the other's mind, for a woman's feelings are influenced by trifles. I suppose, too, that the crowd of people who attended the magistrate and was anxious to fulfill his orders, made her look upon her sister's marriage as a fortunate one and to regret her own—with that erroneous judgment which makes us all so very loath to be outdone even by our nearest relatives. She was still suffering from the smart of wounded pride when her father, happening to see her, asked if anything was wrong. She would fain have concealed the reason for her grief, which was too little consistent with sisterly affection and did no great honor to her husband. But he brought her by tender inquiries to confess that she was unhappy in being coupled to one beneath her, having married into a house where neither high honors nor influence could enter. Ambustus then comforted his daughter and bade her be of good cheer: she would see ere long in her own home the same distinctions she beheld at her sister's. From that moment he began to make plans with his son-in-law, . . ." Then follows the story of how Fabius Ambustus obtained by his political activity, aided by C. Licinius and L. Sextius, the admission of the plebeians to the consulate.

This intimate story has the ring of truth. But if authentic it could have been preserved only within the narrow circle of the Fabian

[1] Liv. VI 34, 5-11.

family. We have therefore sound reason to assume that it was a member of this clan, Fabius Pictor, who brought it into literary circulation—to be sure, not in the charming form given it by Livy but with all its basic features. We suppose this with more confidence because Pictor assessed the admission of the plebeians to the consulate as one of the great turning points of Roman history and gave its special date as 22 years after the sack of the city by the Gauls.[1]

As a preamble to the story just recounted, Livy remarked: [2] *parva ut plerumque solet, rem ingentem moliundi causa intervenit,* "a trivial cause, as so often happens, set on foot a tremendous change." This short sentence,[3] which is the philosophical motivation of the affair in question, must have belonged already to the account of Pictor. Livy uses it elsewhere,[4] of course, but he inherited this argument along with its context from his predecessors.

Greek thinkers from Solon onward tried hard to elucidate the forces which brought about the decisive changes in their governmental systems.[5] The grandiose concatenations of cause and effect which they discovered were replaced in the Hellenistic Age by insignificant occurrences and subjective motifs—in the same way in which in sculpture and painting the majestic revelation of divine greatness vanished before the well-observed humble features of daily life. Spirituality, a possession of the few, gave way to the shallow mentality of the man of the street.

Historians were encouraged to take up this new attitude by concessions which even the philosophers were prepared to make. Plato admits [6] that if the body of the state is in bad health, albeit only in that case, a little impulse from outside can release the avalanche of

---

[1] We know only the old Latin translation of this passage (in Gell. V 4, 1 sqq. F. Gr. Hist. 809 F 33) : *quapropter tum primum ex plebe alter consul factus est duovicesimo anno postquam Romam Galli ceperunt.*

[2] Liv. VI 34, 5.

[3] Liv. VI 34, 5.

[4] Liv. III 27, 7 : *puncto temporis maximarum rerum momenta verti* XXVII 9, 1 : *ceterum transportati milites in Siciliam ... prope magni motus causa fuere ; adeo ex parvis saepe magnarum momenta rerum pendent.* XXXII 17, 9 : *ad summam universi belli pertinere ratus, ... quod ex momentis parvarum plerumque rerum penderet.* Cf. Tac., *Ann.* IV 32, 2 : *non tamen sine usu fuerit introspicere illa primo aspectu levia, ex quis magnarum saepe rerum motus oriuntur.*

[5] Cf. H. Ryffel, Μεταβολὴ πολιτειῶν, der Wandel der Staatsverfassungen (Noctes Romanae 2) Bern, 1949. K. v. Fritz, The Theory of the Mixed Constitution in Antiquity, New York 1954, 414 sqq.

[6] Platon, *Resp.* 8, 556 e.

revolution. Aristotle after him also mentions among all the many different reasons for the upturn of governments, love-affairs and other private doings of important persons. His motivation [1] is already that which we found in Livy: Γίγνονται μὲν οὖν αἱ στάσεις οὐ περὶ μικρῶν, ἀλλ'ἐκ μικρῶν, στασιάζουσι δὲ περὶ μεγάλων.

If in the ensuing epoch of Hellenism such trivialities are seized upon with preference by historians as the causes of violent changes in the public life, this was due to the fact that they followed from now on the entertaining features of the contemporary belles-lettres instead of applying high scientific and moral viewpoints. The reader no longer was to be raised to the lofty atmosphere of contemplation, but dragged down into the agitated scenery of the events recounted, and to experience the emotion and excitement aroused by them.

It was pointed out long ago by P. Scheller [2] that the technical machinery and the tricks created by the tragic poets, and exploited by contemporary rhetoric, were taken over also by the Hellenistic historiographers. "This style of writing," as F. W. Walbank puts it,[3] "Polybius calls 'tragic' and it certainly shared many of the characteristics of tragedy, though indeed it contained several other ingredients, for instance the marvellous and the monstrous (τὸ τερατῶδες) which Aristotle specifically excluded from tragedy, as well as the trivial, the meretricious and the sentimental night scenes, detailed descriptions of clothing, love-interest, and so on."

Here and there, as scholars have not failed to notice, this dramatized style appears also in the Roman Annals.[4] A. Momigliano quite recently observed and cautiously commented on these novelistic features in the Roman Annals: [5] "I know that it may seem 'una

[1] Aristot., *Polit.* V 4, 1 sqq. (1303 b, 17).

[2] P. Scheller, *De hellenistica historiae conscribendae arte*, Diss. Leipzig 1911, 57 sq., 67 sqq., 78 sqq.

[3] F. W. Walbank, Historia 9, 1960, 216. Cf. Ch. Brink, Proceed. Cambr. Philol. Soc. no. 186, 1960, 14 sq.

[4] G. Sigwart, Klio 6, 1906, 352, wrote on the episode of Verginia : "Die ganze Erzählung Diodors macht vielmehr den Eindruck einer griechischen Novelle als einer römischen Sage. Das ganze Motiv entspricht vollständig dem Geschmack der Alexandrinerzeit ; schon im 4. Jahrhundert wurde es Sitte, Umwälzungen im Staatsleben durch erotische Legenden zu motivieren."

[5] A. Momigliano, Secondo contributo alla storia degli studi classici, Roma 1960, 84. The new book of R. Krayer, Frauenlob und Naturallegorese, 1960, was not yet accessible to me. So I do not know whether this author paid attention to the Greek antecedents of this Hellenistic theme which through lack of space could not be discussed here, though W. Marg has urged me with good

pedanteria appena credibile' (to repeat De Sanctis' words) to point out that our sources speak only of *gesta virorum*, while women prominently figure in our legends.[1] But this is what is stated in our sources, and I do not consider it impossible that in men's banquets the convention was to leave women out. If so, Cloelia, Lucretia and Virginia are excluded from the world of ballads." And indeed these genre-paintings of female virtue have nothing to do with genuine epics of the Latin past. Rather, they exhibit the Roman application of Alexandrine romance, painted over with national colors of heroism, gratifying the reader with a political lesson and with moral satisfaction.

Most important, in my view, however, is the fact that all these emotional stories are not scattered over the narrative in a haphazard way, but fitted in systematically on the sore spots of early Roman history, where episodes spun around repulsive or attractive women, as with the case of the two Fabiae, serve to introduce radical changes and frightening events. This procedure can be documented with the following instances:

1. *Tarpeia.*

There was in Rome an old tradition [2] that the Capitoline Hill was occupied by the Sabines "under Romulus." Fabius presented this affair in such a way that the Sabine conquest was not due to the inferiority of the Roman warriors but to the treachery of a girl, who was seduced by the golden ornaments worn by the Sabines and promised to her by them. Pictor painted in this fragment the ruinous effects of covetous greediness with the colors of the classical trage-

reason to do this. He kindly reminds me of the intimate talks of Dareios with Atossa (Herod. 3, 134) which stimulated the expedition against Hellas, as well as of Odysseus' fate, influenced so much by Circe, Calypso, Nausica, Penelope, etc. Yet these cases are still bound to profoundly human aspects of real life. Those women are companions of the men, not angels or demons, and the men with whom they are associated are not yet blind tools of their influence, nor true devils. Nor is their role a mechanically applied trick to move ahead the narrative. For the general atmosphere cf. also H. Strasburger, Festschrift für P. Kirn, Frankfurt 1962, 13 sqq.

[1] It would be more correct, I think, if we were not to call these stories "legends" any longer.

[2] The historical background will be discussed in my study on the *Lupercalia*, the old royal festival of the Romans.

dy.[1] Demonike, seduced by a golden bracelet, may be the prototype of the treason of Tarpeia. It must attract our attention that Pictor ascribes to the Sabines a degenerate luxury, and this is not the only time; [2] warriors making the display of golden ornaments were in the eyes of the ancients effeminate barbarians, whereas this rustic people was otherwise regarded to be the prototype of uncorrupted simplicity and probity. Already Cato the Elder attributed their old-fashioned manners to their alleged Spartan origin.[3] It is clear, therefore, that the denigration of the Sabines in Pictor must be intentional. A clue to this prejudice seems to be his hatred against a princely Roman family of Sabine origin, the Appii Claudii, an emotion, to which, as we shall see, he gave vent in his work.[4]

The role of Tarpeia shows how Pictor enlivened with exciting stories in the Hellenistic manner popular traditions that were fading away.[5] But it also becomes manifest that he had not much respect for objectivity. There may have been some justification for Piso Censorius [6] to censure him for the misrepresentation of the fate of Tarpeia, even if he could not replace it by a more reliable account.

2. Tullia.

The frightful outrage committed by the wicked daughter of the good old king is a Hellenistic short story,[7] characterized as such by Livy (I 46, 3) with the words: *tulit et Romana regia sceleris tragici exemplum.*

---

[1] Fab. Pict., F. Gr. Hist. 809 F 6 (DH II 38, 3) : Καὶ αὐτὴν (τὴν Τάρπειαν) ὡς μὲν Φάβιός τε καὶ Κίγκιος γράφουσιν, ἔρως εἰσέρχεται τῶν ψελλίων, ἅ περὶ τοῖς ἀριστεροῖς βραχίοσιν ἐφόρουν, καὶ τῶν δακτυλίων ; χρυσοφόροι γὰρ ἦσαν οἱ Σαβῖνοι τότε καὶ Τυρρηνῶν οὐχ ἧττον ἀβροδίαιτοι. Cf. also DH II 40, 2 : οἱ δὲ περὶ τὸν Φάβιον ἐπὶ τοῖς Σαβίνοις ποιοῦσι τὴν τῶν ὁμολογιῶν ἀπάτην, κτλ.

[2] Fab. Pictor, F. Gr. Hist. 809 F 27 (= Strab. V 3, 1 p. 228: φησὶ δ᾽ ὁ συγγραφεὺς Φάβιος ῾Ρωμαίους αἰσθέσθαι τοῦ πλούτου τότε πρῶτον, ὅτε τοῦ ἔθνους τούτου (=τῶν Σαβίνων) κατέστησαν κύριοι.

[3] Cato, Orig. fr. 50 (H. R. Rel. 1², 68 sq.) Cf. E. Gabba, Athen., n.s. 38, 1960, 185 sqq.

[4] Cf. below, p. 159 sqq.

[5] Cf. the bibliography in the paper of A. Momigliano, Secondo contributo 85 n. 59.

[6] DH II 40, 3. Further objections of Piso against Pictor : DH IV 7, 5. Liv. I 55, 8 sqq. Cf. K. Latte, Römische Religionsgeschichte 111 n. 2.

[7] Cf. the source material of A. Schwegler, RG 1, 707 sqq. Cf. also Mommsen, St. R. 2³, 717. Ed. Meyer, Rh. Mus. 37, 1882., 618 n. 1. F. Schachermeyr, RE 4 A, 2381, 34 sqq.

The convergency between Diodorus, Dionysius, and Livy [1] betrays its provenience from the early Annals, even if only in its general outlines. The role of a woman bringing about an upturn in the life of the state is indicated in a way corresponding to that of the two Fabiae. The murderer acts *muliebribus instinctus furiis*,[2] and there is a pointer in Livy: *initium turbandi omnia a femina ortum est.*[3]

3. *Lucretia.*[4]

In the Annals the violation of Lucretia causes the downfall of the Tarquins and the end of the kingship. A connoisseur of the sources, as profound as Fr. Muenzer, still assumed that this tale contained a kernel of truth.[5] However, it has, I hope, become evident in our second chapter that the last king was not overthrown by a civilian rising, but was chased away by a foreign power:[6] every attempt to save Lucretia for history is, therefore, a priori condemned to failure. The events framing the rape of Lucretia, such as the siege of Ardea by King Superbus and the nocturnal visit of the greedy prince in the house of his chaste victim,[7] were contained in Pictor's Annals: the culminating point of this literary composition, the tragedy of Lucretia, could not be lacking in them. There is little purpose in trying to trace a poetic treatment of the same subject in Greek literature, as does W. Soltau.[8] It suffices to bear in mind that this propensity to dramatic fashioning is a prevalent tendency in Greek historiography, since this style was first conceived in the circle of Isocrates.[9]

4. *Verginia.*

Here again, as with Lucretia, we find an emphatic use of the motif that

---

[1] Ancient and modern data collected by F. Schachermeyr, RE 13, 1692 sqq. *Idem*, RE 4 A, 2351, 2381, 2388. Cf. A. La Penna, Studi class. e orientali 6, 1956, 112 sqq. G. Devoto, St. Etr. 2. ser. 26, 1958, 17 sqq.

[2] Liv. I 47, 7.

[3] Liv. I 46, 7.

[4] Details in : Fr. Münzer, RE 13, 1692 sqq. no. 38.

[5] *Op. cit.* 1695. *Contra* : L. Pareti, Atene e Roma n.s. 12, 1931, 215.

[6] I have already given a resumé of my results in : Gymnasium 67, 1960, 193 sqq.

[7] F. Gr. Hist. 809 F 12 (DH IV 64, 2 sqq.).

[8] W. Soltau, Die Anfänge der römischen Geschichtsschreibung, Leipzig 1909, 36, 40, 70 sq., 95 sqq. *Idem*, Preussische Jahrbuecher 155, 1914, 459.

[9] W. Schur, RE Suppl. 5, 358.

154

lustful greed may upset a whole governmental system: *sequitur aliud in urbe nefas ab libidine ortum, haud minus foedo eventu quam quod per stuprum caedemque Lucretiae urbe regnoque Tarquinios expulerat, ut non finis solum idem decemviris qui regibus, sed causa etiam eadem imperii amittendi esset.*[1] The same motivation returns in Dionysius,[2] thus demonstrating their common source: Ποιήσομαι δὲ τὸν περὶ αὐτῶν (*scil.* τῶν δέκα) λόγον οὐκ ἀπὸ τῶν τελευταίων ἀρξάμενος, ἃ δοκεῖ τοῖς πολλοῖς αἴτια γενέσθαι μόνα τῆς ἐλευθερίας, λέγω δὲ τῶν περὶ τὴν παρθένον ἁμαρτηθέντων ᾽Αππίῳ διὰ τὸν ἔρωτα.

We shall see below [3] that the decemvir Appius Claudius was painted with the colors of the Greek literary convention, as a voluptuous and cruel tyrant, because he and all the Claudii of early Roman history were denigrated by Fabius Pictor, the two princely houses being fiercely opposed to each other in his own lifetime. How far Pictor could go in disregarding objective facts is revealed by the manipulation of the chronology of the Decemvirate. So as to be able to enlarge upon the emotional details of his hostile picture of the decemvir Appius, he extended the office of the ten men by a second year.[4] This fictitious second Decemvirate is older than the younger annalists and therefore the repetition of the story of Superbus and Lucretia in that of Appius Claudius and Verginia is not, as has been supposed,[5] an invention of those younger writers.

One more judicious remark of A. Momigliano [6] must be inserted here: "Coriolanus, the ferocious patrician, belongs to the *gens Marcia*, which was plebeian in historical times; Virginia is patrician, but her fiancé is plebeian. The majority of the other 'poetic' stories is not colored by the political passions that one would naturally attribute to the Romans of the fifth and fourth centuries B.C. This is not decisive, but it makes a date as late as the third century more probable for the present form of the legends." The "peaceful coexistence" of patricians and plebeians observed by Momigliano is the same as the

---

[1] Liv. III 44, 1. He had his doubts about the truth of the story ; cf. III 47, 5.
[2] DH XI 1, 6.
[3] Cf. below, p. 162 sq.
[4] G. Sigwart, Klio 6, 1906, 283 sqq. E. Täubler, Untersuchungen zur Geschichte des Dezemvirats und der Zwölftafeln (Historische Studien Heft 148), Berlin 1921. K. J. Beloch, RG 244, and others.
[5] W. Soltau, Die Anfänge 99 sqq. E. Burck, Die Welt als Gesch. 1, 1935, 446 sqq.
[6] A. Momigliano, Secondo contributo 84.

atmosphere in the episode of the two Fabiae. The liberal attitude of the Fabii propagated by Pictor colored all the emotional stories under discussion.

5. *Cloelia.*

The lovely episode of the courageous Roman maiden and of the chivalrous king of Clusium [1] was invented along with its concomitant stories,[2] "in order to veil with them the disgrace of the subjugation of Rome" by Porsenna.[3] This camouflage was conceived by the first annalist for the use of his Greek readers. It is not mere chance that the bravery of Cloelia is painted again with the technical means and motives of Hellenistic literature.[4]

6. *The mother of Coriolanus.*

In his classical essay [5] on Coriolanus Mommsen writes [6] as follows: "The whole narrative is pervaded by a romantic and humane atmosphere, but before all other things, it exalts the female virtue to a degree which may have no equal in the whole ancient tradition." "If otherwise the Roman Annals confirm the rule that women have their place not in the citizen-body and the State, but in the household; and if they apply this rule elsewhere so completely that even the names of ladies are completely lacking, this tale was on the contrary created by a Roman panegyrist of women (Frauenlob)." The name of the man who said this unique homage to the fair sex is attested by Livy: [7] he found this narrative *apud Fabium longe antiquissimum auctorem.*

It is recounted in this same context how and why the habit was introduced to arrange the Roman Games more than once in a given year. This was already to be found in the Annals of Pictor.[8] His explanation was that before the festival began a slave was whipped across the circus with the cross of torment on his shoulder. This unpleasant prelude provoked the anger of the Supreme God and he

[1] Details given by Fr. Münzer, RE 3, 110 sqq.
[2] Cf. above, Chapter II.
[3] Fr. Münzer, *loc. cit.*
[4] W. Soltau, Die Anfänge 97.
[5] Mommsen, RF 2, 113 sqq.
[6] *Ibid.* 143.
[7] H. R. Rel. 1² fr. 17, p. 32. F. Gr. Hist. 809 F 14 (Liv. II 40, 10).
[8] Cic., *De div.* I 26, 55.

could only be propitiated by the repetition of the games. Mommsen,[1] who realized that this belongs to the original substance of the Annals, also observed that "the starting-point here is, as it is so often, an etymological aetiology. The author who fabricated this, in trying to find a historical motivation of the *instauratio ludorum* (as the repetition was called) and at the same time to give the meaning of the word *instauratio*, stated that it came ἀπὸ τοῦ σταυροῦ." [2] The childish etymological play *stauros-instaurare* was invented for a work written in Greek, *i.e.*, for the Greek Annals of Fabius Pictor.

The same great historian to whom we owe this diagnosis also proved that the story of Coriolanus was forcibly inserted in the meager skeleton of the Pontifical Chronicle [3] by some pontiff of the *gens Marcia*.[4] No plebeian, of course, could gild his family tree by such a swindle before the beginning of the third century B.C. when such men were first admitted to the pontificate. But the terrible havoc wrought by the Volscians must be historical nevertheless. The Romans never invented disasters offuscating their own glory; and just at that time, about 480 B.C., the offensive power of the Volscians was at its height.[5] The fiction of the Annals with which they contaminate the account of the facts can be well grasped. It is pretended here that the Volscians would never have been able to humiliate Rome had they not had the chance to win over a great Roman general to their side. It was this Roman commander-in-chief who brought them into the position of capturing Rome without resistance. But at the last minute a Roman matron threw her unique moral qualities into the scales, and the nightmare of utter destruction vanished.

There emerges a serious possibility that the sublime role of a Roman mother was suggested to Fabius Pictor by an Alexandrine writer. Among the scholiast's summaries of Callimachus' poem, the Αἴτια, there appears the theme of the moral and patriotic superiority

[1] Mommsen, RF 2, 145 sq. More recent studies noticed in : A. Momigliano, Secondo contributo 83 sq.

[2] *Expressis verbis* in Macrob., *Sat.* I 11, 5.

[3] Mommsen, *op. cit.* 137.

[4] *Ibid.* 149 sqq.

[5] Cf. *ibid.* 126 sq. The pilgrimage of the matrons to Coriolanus is invented, so as to explain the location of the sanctuary of *Fortuna muliebris* outside the city, and this at a time when the original meaning of the cult was already forgotten (cf. G. Wissowa, RuK² 257 sq.). It could have been hinted at by the pontiff, who smuggled into the *annales maximi* the story of Coriolanus ; but its elaboration belongs certainly to Pictor.

of a Roman matron over her own son, who is invested with *imperium* in a critical situation.[1] It may be that the late Johannes Stroux was right in supposing [2] that Callimachus found this "aition" already existing in the historical work of Timaeus, which was also accessible to Pictor.

7. *The wife of Arruns of Clusium.*

Dionysius motivates the incursion of the Gauls into Italy by the following story: [3] A certain Lucumo, a prince of the Tyrrhenians, being about to die, entrusted his son to a loyal man named Arruns, who was to act as guardian. Upon the death of the prince, Arruns, taking over the guardianship of the boy, proved diligent and just in carrying out his trust, and when the boy came to manhood Arruns turned over to him the entire estate left by his father. For this service he received no similar kindness from the youth. It seems that Arruns had a beautiful young wife of whose society he was extremely fond and who, up to that time, had always shown herself chaste. But the young man, becoming enamored of her, corrupted her mind as well as her body and sought to hold converse with her, not only in secret, but openly as well. Arruns, grieving at the seduction of his wife and distressed by the wanton wrong done him by them both, but unable to take vengeance upon them, prepared for a sojourn abroad ostensibly for the purpose of trading. When the youth welcomed his departure and provided everything that was necessary for trading, Arruns loaded many skins of wine and olive oil and many baskets of figs on the wagons and set out for Gaul.

The Gauls at that time had no knowledge either of wine made from grapes or of oil such as is produced by our olive trees, but used for wine a foul-smelling liquor made from barley rotted in water, and for oil stale lard, disgusting both in smell and taste. Accordingly, on that occasion when for the first time they enjoyed fruits which they had never before tasted, they got wonderful pleasure out of each. And they asked the stranger how each of these articles was produced and among what men. The Thyrrhenian told them that the country producing these fruits was large and fertile and that it was inhabited

---

[1] Callimach., *Dieges*. col. 5, 25 (F 106-107 Pfeiffer). Cf. J. Stroux, Philol. 89, 1934, 304 sqq. G. De Sanctis, Rivista di filol. 63 (n.s. 13) 1935, 299 sq.

[2] Cf. also G. Pasquali, Studi ital. di filol. class. n.s. 16, 1939, 70 sqq.

[3] DH XIII 10 (14) sqq.

by only a few people who were no better than women when it came to warfare. He advised them to purchase these products from others no longer, but to drive out the present owners and enjoy the fruits as their own. Persuaded by these words, the Gauls came into Italy and to the Tyrrhenians, known as the Clusians, from whence had come the man who persuaded them to make war.

This story is also preserved in other sources [1] quite independently of Dionysius. Mommsen thought that it stemmed from the more recent annalists—manifestly because he found it not serious enough. H. Peter demonstrated,[2] however, that Cato already knew it and J. Heurgon inferred correctly from a passage of Polybius [3] that this historian was also acquainted with it. Behind both of them stands a common source, Pictor. We cannot exclude the possibility that the latter did not invent this frivolous story but found it in some Greek author. But the idea that the thirst for revenge of a deceived husband should release such a disaster fits well into the frame of mind of the first writer of Roman history who dramatized every turning point of the national history by smuggling in such motives of turbulant emotions and reckless passions.

He employed such elements in his account even to dramatize recent happenings. W. W. Tarn [4] and F. W. Walbank [5] have observed in his work some miraculous occurrences and amazing female characters [6] attesting this. His interest in female excellence was not due or not only due to his personal disposition. It was also a sign of the times. Nothing could illustrate this better than the fact that the Roman state had the head of her Trojan ancestress, Ilia or Rhome, put on coins struck during the First Punic War (pl. XV, 5-7). This act was merely a reply to the enemy, a polemical antithesis to the representation of Dido on coins of Magna Graecia under Carthaginian rule, struck one or two generations before (pl. XV, 1-4).[7] This solemn confrontation

[1] Liv. V 33, 2-4. Gell. XVII 13, 4. Plut., *Camill.* 15, 3-6. Zonar. 7, 23 (vol. 2, 153 Dind.). Cf. also Plin., *N.h.* XII 1, 5. G. F. Unger, SBBayr. Ak. 1876, 548 sqq. Mommsen, Hermes 13, 1878, 517 sq. *Idem*, RF 2, 301 sq. J. Bayet, Tite-Live 5, Paris 1954, 156 sqq.

[2] Cato, *Orig.* fr. 36 (H. R. Rel. 1², 65), with the remarks of H. Peter.

[3] Polyb. II 17, 3 ; cf. J. Heurgon, La vie quotid. 310.

[4] W. W. Tarn, JHS 27, 1907, 51 n. 19.

[5] F. W. Walbank, Cl. Q. 39, 1945, 12.

[6] Polyb. II 4, 8 ; 8, 12. Cf. also J. Gagé, Revue de philol. 3. ser. 35, 1961, 29 sqq.

[7] Cf. my remarks, in : Die trojanischen Urahnen der Römer (Rektorats-programm der Universität Basel 1956) 1957, 31 sq.

of Dido with Ilia-Rhome by the Roman government, challenging Carthage, could well inspire poets to embroider further on this theme. Another basis for this polemical opposition was established about the same time by Timaeus who synchronized the foundation date of the two antagonists. But poets disregarded his date and pushed back the mythical origins of the great clash for the domination of the Mediterranean world to the sack of Troy. It may have been Naevius who conceived the poetic encounter of the Trojan hero Aeneas, ancestor of the Romans, with Dido, founder and queen of Carthage. He did not need an historical fabrication, as did Pictor, when focusing the tremendous conflict upon a sentimental love story.

ॐ

PREJUDICE IN PICTOR, AS REFLECTED IN HIS HATRED OF THE CLAUDII

The scoundrel who drove Verginia to her death was an Appius Claudius. And not only he, but all the members of his clan are painted in the darkest colors in the Annals. This persistent defamation begins with the immigration of Attius Clausus, the ancestor of the Claudii, from his Sabine native land, reported as having occurred in 504 B.C.[1] He is described as a deserter, *transfuga*,[2] who sees better chances for the Romans in a forthcoming clash and deserts his own people in their need. He goes over to the enemy with a considerable host of his clients; the old agrarian district named after him *tribus Claudia* would have been the territory assigned to this group. G. Wissowa thought [3] that the immigration of the Claudii was originally handed down without a specific date—so far we agree—and that it was only later connected with the date of the establishment of the Claudian tribe. Fr. Muenzer [4] tried to save the historicity of this account, though he admits a difficulty which it involves. Namely, the *Quirina* and the *Palatina* were the *tribus* to which the patrician Claudii belonged,

---

[1] The source material was collected by A. Schwegler, RG 2, 57 sq.

[2] Liv. II 16, 5. DH V 40, 5. K. J. Beloch, RG 173 sqq. L. R. Taylor, Vot. Distr. (Mem. Am. Acad. Rome 20) 1960, 35 sq., accepts the historicity of this story, but she stresses correctly that the organization of the *tribus Claudia* in DH V 40, 5, happened only σὺν χρόνῳ, a long time after the immigration of the Claudii.

[3] G. Wissowa, RE 3, 2650.

[4] Fr. Münzer, RE 3, 2663.

FABIUS PICTOR

and not the *Claudia*. We must add to this that the urban tribe of the *Palatina* lost entirely its original social composition in historical times and sheltered mainly the descendants of slaves, so that the inclusion of patricians in the *Palatina* voting district could have happened only in a remote epoch.

Mommsen had a clearer insight into the background of this story. He realized [1] that since the Claudii belonged to those princely clans from which a series of agrarian districts in the immediate neighborhood of the city got their names, and since they obtained the consulate as early as 495 B.C., it is practically impossible for them to have been received into the citizen body so late. We can now go a step further. In Chapter VII it will be demonstrated that the gentile tribes—and with them the *tribus Claudia* north of the Anio—were constituted only some years after 426 B.C., and not in 495 B.C. [2] Further, the contention of the Annals that Attius Clausus became a leading man of the aristocracy immediately after his arrival—*haud ita multo post in principum dignationem pervenit* [3]—is to be rejected. A nonpatrician could never become a member of this class in the Republican epoch; [4] as not only the first Appius Claudius known to us became consul in 495 B.C., but also his sons in 471, 460, and 451 B.C., they evidently belonged to the original kernel of patricians whose ring must have been closed about 504 B.C.

We hope to have proved in an earlier study that the patriciate was constituted when the Tarquins fled and the 300 horsemen of their bodyguard took over the government along with the religious and legal sanction of the *imperium*: the exclusive right to consult the gods and to legalize the annual functionaries by *augurium* and *auspicium*. [5] Even some branches of the same families who became qualified for magistrature were excluded from this new caste: the acceptance of newly arrived strangers would have been out of the question.

We also have proof of the fact that the Claudii belonged at this

[1] Mommsen, RF 1, 1864, 293. *Idem*, St. R. 3, 1886, 26 n. 1.

[2] Consequently, this story is no "old historical tradition", as Fr. Münzer *loc. cit.* supposed, and historical only in so far as the Appii Claudii must have belonged to the Sabine component of the pre-Etruscan bipartite organization of the Roman State. The family tradition was in fact that Attius Clausus immigrated under "Romulus"; cf. Suet., *Tib.* 1, and Verg., *Aen.* 7, 707 sqq.

[3] Liv. II 16, 5.

[4] Mommsen, RF 1, 173 sq.

[5] A. Alföldi, Der frührömische Reiteradel und seine Ehrenabzeichen, Baden-Baden, 1952.

juncture to the old leading class. One branch, which was much later still entitled to inherit the property of the patrician Claudii if there were no direct descendants, did not obtain the patriciate when its circle was closed; [1] this means that in 504 both the plebeian and the patrician branches of the Claudii were Romans and both belonged to the prominent social group. Finally, Mommsen again has shown [2] that the bulk of the patrician families, the so-called *gentes minores*, could never have climbed so high as to reach the position of a *princeps senatus*. This was reserved for the highest aristocracy, the *gentes maiores*, to which, besides the Aemilii, Fabii, Manlii, and Valerii, the Claudii, already a leading clan in 504, also belonged.[3]

This misrepresentation of the *gens Claudia* in the Annals is intelligible when originated by somebody whose family was involved in political rivalry with it, and who tried to lower their prestige by picturing them as late immigrants, Sabine refugees and not truly blue-blooded princely persons. In addition to this, the first Claudius is already denigrated as an extremely stubborn enemy of the simple citizen.

Mommsen demonstrated a hundred years ago [4] that this gloomy picture is not based on realities. Attius Clausus is said to be a ruthless enemy of the common man. The *insita superbia animo*,[5] the *natura inmitis et efferatus hinc plebis odio, illinc patrum laudibus*, his *horrida et atrox sententia* in the Senate [6] characterize him as the arrogant and insolent pitiless leader of the diehards. The expressions quoted and some variants on them, were employed for almost every Claudius in the Annals. Already their ancestor is shown as a violent man, *vehementis ingenii vir*; his alleged repulsiveness is still further underlined

---

[1] Mommsen, RF 1, 293.

[2] *Ibid.* 258. The *gentes minores* attained leading positions already in the fifth century B.C., as the case of the Papirii attests, and they must therefore have belonged to the leading class of the regal age. Cf. Cic., *De re p.* II 20, 35. *Idem, Fam.* IX 21, 2. Liv. I 35, 6. Tac., *Ann.* 11, 25.

[3] The judgement of K. J. Beloch, RG 338, is therefore correct (disregarding his unjustified sarcasm): "Ein reicher Mann, der in seiner Heimat politischen Einfluss besitzt, wandert doch nicht aus, um in der Fremde ἀτίμητος μετανάστης zu werden. Nur als Verbannter verlässt er die Vaterstadt ... Oder glaubt M. etwa, die Römer hätten solchen Verbannten neuen Grundbesitz gegeben, wie das von Ap. Claudius erzählt wird? Und glaubt er überhaupt an der Sage der Einwanderung der Claudier?"

[4] Mommsen, RF 1, 285 sqq. Fr. Münzer, RE 3, 2863 no. 321, with all the details.

[5] Liv. II 27, 1.

[6] Liv. II 29, 9.

FABIUS PICTOR

by contrasting with him his colleague in the consulate, Servilius, as moderate, *lenibus remediis aptior*.[1]

His son C. Claudius, consul in 460 B.C., is also painted as an obstinate enemy of the *plebs*,[2] ἔμφυτον τὸ πρὸς τοὺς δημοτικοὺς ἔχοντα μῖσος,[3] though he is not defamed as thoroughly as his brother, the decemvir Appius Claudius, who is the *carnifex*, the executioner of the Roman people, the peak of insolence, lawless lust and wickedness.[4] The colorful account of his monstrousness was conceived for the denigration of his entire clan, the *familia superbissima et crudelissima*.[5]

The misdeeds of this alleged malefactor culminate in the second year of the decemvirate. "The unfair sentence, passed to serve his private interest and not the common good," writes Mommsen,[6] "the compliancy of the subservient go-between, the inordinate desire from which the honest maid finds no other way of salvaging her honour than death, all these are habitual features of the classical picture of a tyrant—thus Livy incriminates the members of the second decemvirate in general expressly and consistently with usurpation and tyranny."

The great historian just quoted still thought that the second year of the decemvirate was historical and blamed the late annalists for adding this calumny to their account of it.[7] However, it has been recognized since then [8] that this second year was inserted for the purpose of obtaining space for the story of Verginia, created with the conventional means of literary invective for the denigration of the Claudii. With this discovery the very roots of this campaign of calumniation emerge, reaching back to the beginnings of the Roman historiography; it shows, too, how uninhibited must have been the man who invented this little novel.

The son of the decemvir Appius is not handled with kid gloves in the Annals either. He is stigmatized as *inde ab incunabulis inbutus odio*

---

[1] Liv. II 23, 15.
[2] DH X 9, 2.
[3] Details in : Fr. Münzer, RE 3, 2863 no. 322.
[4] Details in : Fr. Münzer, RE 3 2698 sqq. n. 123.
[5] Liv. II 56, 7-8, cf. 5.
[6] Mommsen, RF 1, 299.
[7] Also Fr. Münzer, *loc. cit.*, follows him in the conviction that we have to do with a genuine saga. But cf. Ed. Meyer, Kleine Schriften 1, 1910, 375.
[8] E. Täubler, Untersuchungen zur Geschichte des Dezemvirats und der Zwölftafeln (Histor. Studien Heft 148) Berlin 1921, and K. J. Beloch, RG 242 sqq.

tribunorum plebisque (Liv. IV 36, 5). Again the grandson of the decemvir is presented as seething with hatred and overbearing. [1] This sort
of wholesale condemnation was hardly possible with the venerable
figure of Appius Claudius Caecus.[2] Nonetheless, an attempt was made
in the Annals to bring him into discredit. He is a flatterer of the mob
and an enemy of the Senate, a revolutionary who πολλὰ τῶν πατρῴων
νομίμων ἐκίνησε.[3] The sacrilegious changes made by him in the cult
of Hercules at the *Ara maxima*; the unheard-of admission of sons
of freedmen to the Senate; the improper by-passing of the same
venerable corporation committed by him in financial matters; his
illegal candidacy for the consulate during his censorship—these are
the main points of the accusations against him. Inconsistently enough,
the list of his wrongdoings is supplemented with alleged animosity
against the *plebs*, as is typical for every Claudius: he—the champion
of the freedmen—is said to have opposed the admission of plebeians
to the magistrature.

It did not, as I have mentioned, escape the keen perception of
Mommsen that this general attack against the Claudii is a literary
invention. He ascribed this mischief to some demagogical annalist
of the post-Gracchan period.[4] What he was scorning, however, was
rather the full exploitation of a tendency already in existence, because
he speaks of the "distortion and fiction directed against the Claudii,
with which the entire older annalistic literature is impregnated." [5]
And after him it was revealed by H. Peter[6] that this machination was
perpetrated by Fabius Pictor; Peter also realized that it was rivalry
of the two princely houses which gave rise to this indirect attack.

The tension between these two clans may have had very old antecedents. To us it becomes apparent first in the opposition of Quintus
Fabius Rullianus [7] to the liberal reforms of Appius Claudius Caecus.
This clash may have had repercussions even a generation later in the
house of the parents of Fabius Pictor. But in the lifetime of the latter

[1] Details in : Fr. Münzer, RE 3, 2697 no. 122.
[2] Details in : Fr. Münzer, RE 3, 2681 sqq. no. 91. Cf. Mommsen, RF 2,
284 sqq.
[3] Diod. XX 36, 1.
[4] Mommsen, RF 1, 287 sqq., 314 sqq.
[5] *Ibid.* 313 ; cf. 299 sqq., 307 n. 41.
[6] H. Peter, H. R. Rel. 1², p. XLVII sq. L sq. XC. P. Bung, Quintus Fabius
Pictor, Diss. Köln 1950, 157 sqq.
[7] Cf. Fr. Münzer, RE 3, 2684, 33 sqq. O. Schoenberger, Hermes 88, 1960,
220 sqq.

there was a Claudius whose unpleasant personality and disastrous failures offered all the repellent features that could be ascribed to a Claudius we find in the Annals. This arch-villain was P. Claudius Pulcher,[1] consul in 249 B.C., who angered all Romans by his crushing defeat in a naval battle, and still more by his arrogant behavior after it. The insolence of this man and his ruthless severity is censured not only by Diodorus.[2] Naevius [3] has a fragment with the words *superbiter contemptim conterit legiones,* in which C. Cichorius [4] recognized the reference to Pulcher. It has been thought [5] that the words of the poet reflect the bitterness against an outrage endured by the poet himself. The reports concerning this Claudius, however, breathe the same animosity as does the literary portraiture of his ancestors. His cynical disregard of the divine warning when the hens refused to feed before the unfortunate battle; the haughtiness of his sister; the intrigues designed to defeat the process against him; the insult to the ancestral customs (*mores maiorum*) when he appointed to the office of dictator a dependent follower socially disqualified for this highest public distinction: all these features were stressed so as to stir up antipathy and disrespect toward the Claudii. They were conceived by Fabius Pictor.[6]

☙

THE RESPONSIBILITY OF FABIUS PICTOR

The memory of the kings was still alive in Rome in the fifth century B.C. They belonged to the generations of the fathers and grandfathers of the living. But there was nobody who would care to perpetuate

---

[1] Cf. Fr. Münzer, RE 3, 2857 no. 304. Cf. H. H. Scullard, Roman Politics 220-150 B.C., Oxford 1951, 31 sqq., 36 sqq., 56 sqq., 61 sqq.

[2] Diod. XXIV 3.

[3] Naev., fr. 45 Morel=47 Marmorale.

[4] C. Cichorius, Römische Studien, Leipzig 1922, 45 sqq.

[5] E. Marmorale, Naevius poeta[2], Firenze 1953, 36 sqq.

[6] F. Altheim, Festschrift für J. Friedrich, Heidelberg 1959, 11, thinks that Diodorus' source was Philinus and also believes in the priority of Naevius over Pictor. I do not see valid proofs for his opinions. E. Marmorale, *op. cit.* 43 sqq., maintains that the *probra in principes civitatis de Graecorum poetarum more dicta* (Gell. III 3, 15) in Naevius are spontaneous manifestations of Naevius' sense of independence. But these attacks may be directed against the opponents of his patrons. It was hardly possible in Rome to indulge in that *Graecorum mos* for the common man ; cf. Cic., *De re p.* IV 10, 11.

their memory in writing.[1] But for contemporary events at least some provision was made. Rolls of the annual magistrates were started, and with them some basic facts of public interest were recorded. Rome was certainly not the only nor the first city to introduce such an annual protocol. Therefore, the combination of the list of eponymous officers with short remarks on wars, triumphs, hunger, pestilence, and on prodigies, etc., is likely to imitate usage established in other (Etruscan or Latin) communities.

These files with the names of magistrates and the items added in annotation to them were not prepared for publication, but filed for the convenience of the governing persons and their class,[2] i.e., for the patricians alone, in the fifth century B.C. These files were the kernel of the original *annales maximi*, entrusted to the *pontifex maximus*. [3] The style of their laconic notes had a great influence on the beginnings of historiography. The short entries in Naevius on the war operations in the years 263, 257, and 241 B.C. still reflect it.

---

[1] Cic., *De orat*. II 12, 52 says that the *annales maximi* (i.e., the names of the governing magistrates and the few facts registered with them by the *pontifex maximus*) began *ab initio rerum Romanarum*. But in truth the annual protocol in question started only with the annual magistrates. Cicero evidently confused the published *annales maximi* edited in the Gracchan age by the high pontiff P. Mucius Scaevola with the original Annals kept by the high pontiffs, which were the consular lists, accompanied by some notes, the *tabulae dealbatae* (Serv., *Aen*. 1, 373) of the young Republic. The same confusion is obvious in the statement (DH I 74, 3. *Origo gentis Rom*. 17, 3. 5 ; 22, 2) that the pontifical Annals, as well as the others told the story, that Numa was the pupil of Pythagoras. Nor was the date of the foundation of the city stabilized in the original *fasti*, kept up to date by the pontiffs (DH I 73, 1 ἐν ἱεραῖς δέλτοις). The canonical authority of these lists would have prohibited the chaos of arbitrary datings; cf. DH I 74, 3 who writes concerning this date : οὐδ' ἐπὶ τοῦ παρὰ τοῖς ἀρχιερεῦσι κειμένου πίνακος, ἑνὸς καὶ μόνου τὴν πίστιν ἀβασάνιστον καταλιπεῖν in the conviction that the original *tabulae* included it ; this is a manifest error. Nor could the annotated eponymous list be identical with the *pontificii libri*, which *provocationem etiam a regibus fuisse declarant*.

[2] Mommsen, RF 2, 242 n., says that before Pictor "das römische Stadtbuch noch mehr zu den Urkunden gehörte, als zu der Literatur." Cf. also Kr. Hanell, Histoire et historiens dans l'antiquité, Vandoeuvres-Genève 1956, 149.

[3] Cic., *De orat*. II 12, 52 : *erat enim historia nihil aliud nisi annalium confectio ; cuius rei memoriaeque publicae retinendae causa ... usque ad P. Mucium pontificem maximum res omnes singulorum annorum mandabat litteris pontifex maximus referebatque in album et proponebat tabulam domi, potestas ut esset populo cognoscendi ; itaque etiam nunc annales maximi nominantur*. It is of course out of the question that the man of the street *(populus)* had access to the office of the high pontiff. Cicero mentions, *De leg*. I 2, 6, that before the annalists started with their historical works, there was nothing but the *annales pontificum maximorum, quibus nihil*

The specific character of the things registered in this chronicle, besides wars and colonies founded, can be illustrated by some examples:

426 B.C.: A. Cornelius Cossus earns the *spolia opima*, killing the Veientane king.[1]

458 B.C.: The Capitol seized by banished men supported by slaves, but promptly reoccupied.[2]

From 436 B.C. onward: Prodigies forecasting bad harvest and pestilence.[3] Solemn prayers to the gods registered.[4]

From 399 B.C. on: The banquets arranged for the divinities (*lectisternia*) entered on record.[5]

During the fifth century the building of temples was noted down too. Unfortunately, some of these entries (such as those of the Sanctuaries of Diana and Ceres) are spurious, but others are unquestionable.

The eclipse of June 21, 400 B.C., was determined.[6]

potest esse ieiunius. A similar statement has been made by Cato the Elder : *Orig.* fr. 77 (H. R. Rel. 1², 77 Peter = Gell. II 28, 6): *Verba Catonis ex originum quarto haec sunt : non lubet scribere, quod in tabula apud pontificem maximum est, quotiens annona cara, quotiens lunae aut solis lumine caligo aut quid obstiterit*. Sempron. Asellio fr. 1-2 (H. R. Rel. 1², 179 = Gell. V 18, 7) scorns the dry style of the *annales libri* in general. Cf. also Serv., *Aen.* 1, 373. Quintil. X 2, 27.

[1] Details are given by Fr. Münzer, RE 4, 1289 sq. no. 112.

[2] For details, cf. R. Bonghi, La nuova antologia 2. ser. 19, 1880, 399 sqq. Fr. Münzer, RE 8, 618 sqq.

[3] Details are given, e.g., in L. Wülker, Die geschichtliche Entwicklung des Prodigienwesens bei den Römern, Diss. Leipzig 1903.

[4] Liv. IV 21, 5, etc. Cf. G. Wissowa, RE 4 A, 942 sqq. A. Kirsopp Lake, in : Quantulacumque, Studies presented to Kirsopp Lake, London 1937, 243 sqq.

[5] Liv. V 13, 6. G. Wissowa, RE 12, 1108 sqq.

[6] Enn., *Ann.* fr. 163 Vahlen³ (Cic., *De re p.* I 16, 25). Cicero says that this event was recorded *apud Ennium et in maximis annalibus consignatum*. But the date *anno quinquagesimo et CCC fere post Romam conditam* makes it difficult if it is in this form ascribed to Ennius : the *fasti* began in 504 B.C., so that events of the regal age were not comprised in them. Furthermore, Ennius still connected the foundation of the city with the flight of Aeneas from Troy and with the fate of his family ; and the low dates for the year of the foundation simply did not exist before Timaeus and Pictor. All in all, the 350 years from the foundation could be reckoned only by somebody who combined the consular year of the eclipse, given in the pontifical Annals and probably in Ennius, with the Polybian date for the founding of the city, i.e. by Cicero himself. This will be demonstrated in the forthcoming commentary of Ennius by O. Skutsch, who kindly allowed me to read his manuscript (to be published in Oxford by Clarendon Press).

Responsibility of Fabius Pictor

These specimens show that the original text was not lost during the Gaulish storm, and also that it was already annotated. Apart from such testimonies, the preservation of this earliest part of the *annales maximi* is attested also by later consultation of them, as e.g., in 331 B.C., when somebody found a remedy for public trouble in the driving of a nail into the wall of a sanctuary. The Annals recorded that this was done during a secession of the *plebs* in the fifth century.[1] Another such inspection in 252 B.C. revealed the vicissitudes of the men sent with a precious gift to Apollo in Delphi immediately after the capture of Veii.[2] The size of the annual notes was growing in the fourth century, and still more so in the third. By 296 B.C. it had been found worth while to mention the erection of an art monument by the aediles.[3] In the first two centuries of the Republic only the aristocracy had had access to this chronicle. The indignation and wrath of the patricians in 304 B.C., when it was made public by Cn. Flavius,[4] demonstrates that until then it had been their privilege to use it.

After the publication of these annotated consular lists in 304 B.C., copies could be made for the convenience of everybody who was interested in them. It could hardly be doubted that along with the *Fasti* the notes added to them were contained in the transcripts circulating among the public. It seems to me that the *res gestae* of the last king, used by Fabius Pictor, were appended to the beginning of the *fasti*, together with the forged names of the first years of the Free State, for the Chronicle as published in or soon after 304. Such a complement is intelligible if it was prepared for the lists for sale to the public, but difficult to understand if it was only to be found in the archives of the high pontiff. In the same way the plebeian consulates of the early Republic were certainly forged in the early third century B.C. in order to display in public these alleged glories, and not keep them hidden in the archives.[5] Such a revised redaction of the

---

[1] Liv. VIII 18, 11-12: *neque de veneficiis ante eam diem Romae quaesitum est. prodigii ea res habita . . . ; itaque memoria ex annalibus repetita in secessionibus quondam plebis clavum ab dictatore fixum alienatasque discordia mentes hominum eo piaculo compotes sui fuisse, dictatorem clavi figendi causa creari placuit.*

[2] Diod. XIV 93, 3 sq. Liv. V 15, 3 ; 18, 2 sqq. Val. Max. I 1 ext. 4. Plut., *Camill.* 8, 3 sqq. App., *Ital.* 8.

[3] Liv. X 23, 12.

[4] Cf. my study : Der frührömische Reiteradel und seine Ehrenabzeichen, Baden-Baden 1952, 21 sqq.

[5] Liv. VIII 40, 4-5 : *vitiatam memoriam funebribus laudibus reor falsisque imaginum titulis, dum familiae ad se quaeque famam rerum gestarum honorumque fallenti mendacio*

annales maximi has already been postulated by scholars.[1] The transcripts of this version of the pontifical Annals circulating among the nobility in a restricted number were not produced for general consumption.[2]

It has been supposed by serious historians [3] that this pre-Fabian chronicle already contained a short description of the rule of the seven kings. It may be that just the number of the kings was mentioned in it, because Pictor operated with this round figure as though it were a definite one, but hardly anything more than the number could have existed in it. This is because a chronological framework for the epoch before Porsenna's incursion was completely absent before Pictor. As, prior to him, the founding of the city was connected with years immediately after the sack of Troy, each king would thus have ruled for almost a century until the sixth century B.C.[4] The pontiffs had no reason to create such a pseudo-history: their duty was only the annual registration of current events, *memoriae publicae retinendae causa*. The purpose of their files changed, however, when these became accessible outside of their office. The stimulus for secretly adding supplements was still rooted in internal politics only: the

---

trahunt. inde certe et singulorum gesta et publica monumenta rerum confusa ; nec quisquam aequalis temporibus illis scriptor extat, quo satis certo auctore stetur. As W. Weissenborn-H. J. Müller observed in their commentary long ago, Livy hinted at the corruption of the consular and triumphal lists with the expression *publica monumenta rerum*. But the forgery penetrated into the consular lists before Pictor : cf. Mommsen, RF 2, 151 sq., and the studies quoted in the next note.

[1] Cf. A. Enmann, Rh. Mus. n. F. 57, 1902, 517 sqq. E. Kornemann, Der Priesterkodex in der Regia, Tübingen 1912. *Idem*, Klio 11, 1911, 245 sqq. W. Soltau, Die Anfänge der römischen Geschichtsschreibung, Leipzig, 1909, 217. L. Cantarelli, Studi romani e bizantini, Roma 1915, 145 sq. G. De Sanctis, St. d. R. 1², 16 sqq. E. Pais, St. crit. 1, 61 sqq. O. Leuze, Die römische Jahrzählung, Tuebingen 1909, 168 sq., 197 sq. H. Peter, H. R. Rel. 1², p. XX sqq. K. J. Beloch, RG 87 sqq. C. W. Westrup, Danske Vid. Selskab, hist.-fil. medd. XVI 3, 1929. M. Gelzer, Hermes 69, 1934, 46 sqq. F. Schachermeyr, Klio 23, 1930, 278 sqq. Fr. Klingner, Die Antike 13, 1937, 1 sqq. G. Pasquali, Studi ital. di filol. class. n.s. 16, 1939, 73 sq. F. Boemer, Symb. Osl. 29, 1952, 34 sq., 50 sqq. L. Pareti, St. d. R. 1, Torino 1952, 13 sqq., 677 sqq. I have more confidence in the pontifical chronicle of the first century of the Republic than does the much regretted Pl. Fraccaro, JRS 47, 1957, 60 sq.

[2] Cf. R. Chr. W. Zimmermann, Klio 26, 1933, 257 sq.

[3] E.g., A. Rosenberg, Einleitung und Quellenkunde zur römischen Geschichte, Berlin 1921, 113 sqq., 116 sq.

[4] The confusion persisted even much later ; cf. Solin. 1, 27. Besides Naevius and Ennius even Sallustius, *Catil.* 6, connected the foundation of Rome with the arrival of the Trojans.

interest of the new plebeian nobility provided it. The relations of the state with the outside world, however, still lay outside the scope of these powerful new arrivals. And who would have believed in Rome about 300 B.C. that the Latins had been Roman subjects for centuries, or that Etruria had been conquered by the Romans in the sixth century B.C.? But in the course of the third century the political horizons of Rome embraced more and more of the entire Mediterranean World, and the stage was set for a completely new political outlook—and for Fabius Pictor.

This man was an offspring of the oldest Roman aristocracy.[1] It seems to me that he must have been born about 260 B.C.[2] It is likely that in the war against the Celts of Northern Italy he was already a military tribune (225-22 B.C.). After the catastrophic defeat at Cannae he was sent by the Senate to Delphi to ask for the advice of Apollo in their precarious situation.[3] It has been suggested that he was selected for this mission because he was an expert in matters of religion and one of the *decemviri sacris faciundis*.[4] But it seems to me that his task was rather a diplomatic exploration of the actual state of things in the Hellenistic East than a religious investigation; and that the qualification for this was his knowledge of Greek literature and mentality. Though naturally he carried out the consultation of the oracle with an ostentatious piety, as he himself reported, the information he brought back from his voyage about the anti-Roman trend among the Greeks, fostered by the Greek historians of Hannibal, was certainly much more important to the governing body. The whole outlook and tendency of his work suggest that his Annals, written in Greek for the Greeks, were planned as an answer to the propaganda of the mortal enemy in Greece and the Hellenistic realms. They had meaning only when published as Pictor's own contribution

---

[1] Mommsen, Hermes 13, 1878, 322 sqq. The references to his personal data are collected in H. R. Rel. 1², p. LXIX sqq., by H. Peter, and in the RE 6, 1836 sq. (no. 126) by Fr. Münzer. His fragments are now printed also in F. Gr. Hist. 809 F 1 sqq.

[2] As A. Klotz, Hermes 80, 1952, 327, thought. K. J. Beloch, RG 95, would like to lower this limit to 240 B.C., but Pictor was certainly more than 16 years old when he fought against the Celts. And his mission to Greece in 216 B.C. was an important one, very likely to be entrusted to somebody of maturity; cf. Fr. Münzer, RE 6, 1837, 10 sqq.

[3] Liv. XXII 57, 5. XXIII 11, 1 sqq. Plut., *Fab.* 18, 3. App., *Hann.* 27, Cf. F. Gr. Hist. 809 T 3.

[4] H. Diels, Sibyllinische Blätter, Berlin 1890, 11, 106. Fr. Münzer, *loc. cit.*

170

to the war effort as soon as possible after his return from Greece, and not later when the war was over.[1]

Pictor's account was based on the years from the beginning of the Republic.[2] The authority of the *Annales maximi* was such that any other arrangement was out of the question: even the epic poets of his age, Naevius [3] and Ennius [4] gave consulates, briefly mentioned wars, prodigies, and the rest of the items of the pontifical chronicle. For the history of the kings Pictor did not possess the background of the pontifical Annals, but adapted his narrative to their succinct style.[5]

This sort of laconic wording was regarded as poor by the great masters of style, such as Cicero and his friends,[6] just as earlier old

[1] K. Latte and Kr. Hanell, Histoire et historiens dans l'antiquité, Vandoeuvres-Genève 1956, 176 sqq. It was until recently generally believed that the Annals of Pictor were published only after the war with Hannibal. Cf. e.g., K. J. Beloch, RG 96. Fr. Leo, Geschichte der römischen Literatur, 1913, 87. F. Boemer, Symb. Osl. 29, 1952, 37. M. Gelzer, Hermes 82, 1954, 352. W. Hoffmann, Historia 9, 1960, 317 n. 22. I would like to stress here the point that many statements of Pictor on contemporary events are much more easily understood when it is realized that they were written in the heat of the gigantic struggle, and not when it was over. The detailed statistics of the able-bodied men ready for military service in Roman Italy by the outbreak of the Celtic war in 225 B.C., boasting the huge amount of 800,000 potential soldiers, is intended certainly as a warning for those who expected the imminent collapse of Rome after Cannae and Trasimenus. The Latin Annals of Pictor must be a translation of the Greek text, as is assumed by many scholars, e.g., M. Schanz-C. Hosius, Geschichte der römischen Literatur 1, München 1927, 172. R. Chr. W. Zimmermann, Klio 26, 1933, 251 sqq. K. J. Beloch, RG 98 sq. F. W. Walbank, Cl. Q. 39, 1945, 16 n. 2. Kr. Hanell, *op. cit.* 161 sqq. K. Latte, *ibid.* 171 sq. *Contra*: Fr. Münzer, RE 6, 1843, and others.

[2] Mommsen, RF 2, 363. F. W. Walbank, *op. cit.* 17 sq. P. Bung, Quintus Fabius Pictor, Diss. Köln 1950, 148 sqq. M. Gelzer, Hermes 82, 1954, 348. Kr. Hanell, *op. cit.* 168 sq.. etc.

[3] F. Boemer, *op. cit*, 39 sq.

[4] Fr. Leo, *op. cit.* 163.

[5] DH I 6, 2.

[6] Cic., *De leg.* I 2, 5-6 : *abest enim historia litteris nostris . . . Nam post annales pontificum maximorum, quibus nihil potest esse ieiunius, si aut ad Fabium aut . . . Catonem aut ad Pisonem aut ad Fannium aut ad Vennonium venias, quamquam ex his alius alio plus habet virium, tamen quid tam exile quam isti omnes?* It becomes plain how to understand this statement if we compare it with his *De orat.* II 12, 51. 53: *atqui, ne nostros contemnas, inquit Antonius, Graeci quoque ipsi sic initio scriptitarunt, ut noster Cato, ut Pictor, ut Piso . . . Hanc similitudinem scribendi* (sc. annalium maximorum) *multi secuti sunt, qui sine ullis ornamentis monumenta solum temporum, hominum, locorum gestarumque rerum reliquerunt. Itaque qualis apud Graecos Pherecydes, Hellanicus, Acusilas fuit aliique permulti, talis noster Cato et Piso, qui neque tenent, quibus rebus ornetur oratio—modo enim huc ista sunt importata—et,*

Cato had similarly scorned the *annales maximi* as meager and dull. This simple, factual style was, however, not at all dry, *sine ullis ornamentis*. The colorful narrative of the foundation myth and of the *pompa circensis* [1] reveal a really entertaining literary talent in Pictor; his ability for allover planning and dramatic *mise-en-scène* also stands out.

That he wrote in Greek and used the modern technique of Hellenistic historiography was not a superficial or irresponsible decision. "The writing of history in Rome"—I quote Kr. Hanell [2]—"sprang into existence as an immediate consequence of the terrific struggle of Rome with Carthage. This conflict was at the same time a controversy between the Romans and the Greeks of Magna Graecia. The Roman historiography emerged as a reply to the Greeks of Sicily in the First Punic War." One of those Sicilian writers paid more attention to Roman developments than the rest and his work paved the way for Pictor: he was Timaeus of Tauromenium. [3]

Timaeus turned twice to the illustration of the past and the character of the Romans: once in his general work and once in his books on Pyrrhus which were appended to his great work at the end of his long life. [4] He certainly enlarged upon the origins of Rome. His

dum intelligatur quid dicant, unam dicendi laudem putant esse brevitatem. Despising this manner, Cicero characterized even the speeches of the great orator of the generation before himself, P. Rutilius Rufus (F. Gr. Hist. 815 T 10), as *orationes ieiunae*, though admitting that Rutilius was a *vir doctus et Graecis litteris eruditus . . ., prope perfectus in Stoicis, quorum peracutum et artis plenum orationis genus scis tamen esse exile* (!). Cornelius Nepos (Cato 3) says that the *Origines* of Cato are written *nulla doctrina*, which likewise means only "without rhetorical embellishments." On problems of style cf. E. Burck, Die Erzählungskunst des Livius (Problemata ii), Berlin 1934. U. Knoche, Neue Jahrbücher 1939, 139 sqq., 289 sqq. J. P. V. Balsdon, Cl. Q. 47, 158 sqq. A. Klotz, Hermes 80, 1952, 341. *Idem,* La nouvelle Clio 5, 1953, 238. F. Boemer, Historia 2, 1953-54, 189 sqq. A. Momigliano, Rendic. Accad. Lincei 8. ser., classe sc. mor. 15, 1960-61, 310 sqq.

[1] F. Gr. Hist. 809 F 13 (DH VII 71, 3 sqq.).

[2] Kr. Hanell, *op. cit.* 149.

[3] The state of research on Timaeus until 1936 is excellently presented by R. Laqueur, RE 6 A, 1076 sqq. Cf. further : F. Jacoby, F. Gr. Hist. III B Kommentar, 1955, 529 sq., 536 sq., 565 sq., and *ibid.* Notenband 319 n. 82; 322 n. 121 ; 330, 331 n. 308. Kr. Hanell, *op. cit.* 150 sqq. A. Momigliano, Rivista storica ital. 71, 1959, 549. T. S. Brown, Timaeus of Tauromenium (Univ. Calif. Publ. in Hist. 55) Berkeley-Los Angeles 1958.

[4] DH I 6, 1 : τὰ μὲν ἀρχαῖα τῶν ἱστοριῶν ἐν ταῖς κοιναῖς ἱστορίαις ἀφηγησαμένου, and Gell. XI 1, 1 : *Timaeus in historiis, quas oratione Graeca de rebus populi Romani composuit.* Cf. F. Gr. Hist. 566 T 9. F. Jacoby (in his commentary 540 sq. and in the vol. of notes appended to it 311 sq. n. 7) thinks that Varro (the source of Gellius) meant by the *historiae de rebus populi Romani* the books on Pyrrhus.

account of the arrival of Hercules at the site where Rome was later founded,[1] and his description of the strange contest at the festival of the *equus October*[2] illustrate his vivid interest in the mythical pre-history and in curious usages, as do his inquiry in Lavinium concerning the Trojan relics preserved there[3] and his descriptions of Etruscan peculiarities.[4] Yet he did not produce a history of the Roman kings, nor did any other Greek historian who made occasional remarks on the foundation or on the vicissitudes of this city. It is even possible that Timaeus did not mention any Roman king other than Romulus.[5] The "history" of the kings was to be written by a Roman.

We have already seen that Fabius Pictor wrote his Annals first to counter the propaganda of the Greek historiographers of Hannibal, Silenus, Chaereas, Sosylus, and the rest. The hatred aroused against Rome by such hostile agitation was a powerful weapon indeed.[6] A Roman counterattack was urgently needed[7] to show the Greeks that the respectable institutions and the great achievements of the Roman people equaled those of the Greeks, or even that the Romans were in fact Greeks.[8] Pictor was prepared to demonstrate this at any cost.

A recent investigation of later developments in Pictor's narrative has demonstrated that he was a politician of real stature.[9] He justified in a clear and suggestive way, on the basis of the experience acquired during the great war, Roman imperialism *ex eventu*: all the steps of the Roman government since Messana were expounded by him as a

---

[1] Diod. IV 19, 4-21, 1, traced back to Timaeus by R. Laqueur, RE 6 A, 1177 and G. Pasquali, Studi ital. di filol. class., n.s. 16, 1939, 71 sq. Cf. J. Bayet, Recherches sur l'origin d'Hercule romain (BEFAR) 1926.

[2] F. Gr. Hist. 566 F 36.

[3] F. Gr. Hist. 566 F 59. His words πυθέσθαι δὲ αὐτὸς ταῦτα παρὰ τῶν ἐπιχωρίων clearly imply either the presence of Timaeus in Lavinium, or his acquaintance with men from this city.

[4] F. Gr. Hist. 566 F 1 with the remarks of F. Jacoby in his commentary 547 sq.

[5] Cf. my paper in RM 68, 1961, 64 sqq.

[6] Cf. Polyb. IX 37, 7 sq. Liv. XXXI 29 sqq., etc.

[7] H. Peter, Wahrheit und Kunst, Geschichtsschreibung und Plagiat im klassischen Altertum, Leipzig 1911, 273 sq. M. Gelzer, Hermes 68, 1933, 129 sqq. *Idem*, Hermes 69, 1934, 49 sqq., and 82, 1954, 342 sqq. A new study is announced by A. Momigliano, Rivista storica ital. 71, 1959, 555 n. 78. *Contra*: F. W. Walbank, Cl. Q. 39, 1945, 15. Kr. Hanell, *op. cit.* 175. P. Bung, *op. cit.* 1 sq. F. Boemer, Symb. Osl. 29, 1952, 42 sq.

[8] M. Gelzer, Hermes 69, 1934, 54 sq. Fr. Münzer, RE 6, 1840.

[9] A. Heuss, Histor. Zeitschr. 169, 1949, 473 sq.

consistent course of action. Rome was forced to act—so he pretended—because she was threatened. But even the ancients observed that
he did not refrain from distorting the truth in advocating the Roman
cause.[1] Free invention and arbitrary construction had, however,
much more room in the dark epoch between the foundation of the
city and that of the Republic than in a report on recents events. He
gave, as we saw, a political and juridical documentation of the growth
of the Roman power, as being in accordance with the will of the gods,
pointing from the hour of its birth toward its future greatness.[2] The
inherent superiority of Rome over the Latins, beginning with Romulus, belonged to this program and was set forth and illustrated
without much regard to realities.

What he made out of the Roman past can be compared to a certain
degree with the accomplishment of a man who, six hundred years
later, compiled the so-called Historia Augusta, also for a national
purpose, though on a much lower level and with much less talent
than Fabius Pictor. The scribbler in question had for the first half of
his narrative a coherent and solid account at his disposal. As far as
this reached he applied free inventions only occasionally, together
with some distortions of the original version. But in the second half
of his compilation, where he based his account on sparsely worded
chronicles alone, he filled the many lacunae with conversational fiction,
which was, however, not without a marked purpose. In the case of
Pictor the fiction prevailed in the first half of his Annals, where he
had barely any sources to follow. The spurious matter is much
reduced after the beginning of the *fasti consulares*, where he could
rely on a sound chronological base, and where the historical facts
were known to him.

Different circumstances combined to lend his work a tremendous
importance. He became "by far the oldest" Roman historian, *longe
antiquissimus auctor*, παλαιότατος γὰρ ἀνὴρ τῶν τὰ Ῥωμαϊκὰ συνταξα-
μένων. [3] Having no predecessors, his possibilities for free invention
were unlimited. Every annalist after him based his work directly
or ultimately on that of Pictor. His picture of Early Rome became

---

[1] Polyb. I 14, 1 ; 15, 2. III 9, 6 sqq. K. J. Beloch, RG 98. H. Peter, Wahrheit
und Dichtung (p. 172 n. 7) 289, 331 sqq. P. Bung, *op. cit.* (above p. 163 n. 6) 33 sq.
[2] The story of the head, found in the foundation-pits of the Capitoline
temple, is discussed below, p. 218 sqq.
[3] Liv. I 44, 2 ; Cf. 55, 8. II 40, 10. VIII 30, 7. Cic., *De leg.* 1, 6. DH VII 71, 1.

the backbone of every subsequent account.[1] As J. Heurgon put it,[2] "qui, le premier, donna de l'histoire romaine un récit que ses successeurs purent bien développer, rectifier ou déformer selon leur tempérament et leur passions, mais qu'il avait fixé *ne varietur* dans ses cadres chronologiques et ses données essentielles."

His responsibility for the distortion of early Roman history is heavy, but it is mitigated by special circumstances. The art of rhetoric, encroaching everywhere upon the spiritual life of Hellenism, cultivated fiction as an intellectual weapon of the orator, the lawyer, the politician, and of course as a vehicle for belles-lettres. Unfortunately, history was also regarded as a branch of rhetoric, and even as such *par excellence*.[3] Besides this, partiality for one's own country did not seem abnormal to the ancients.[4] Moreover, the playful and romantic stories in Timaeus' work depicting the beginnings of so many peoples certainly added wings to the vivid imagination of Pictor; and an attractive literary setting was an inescapable requirement when writing for a Greek public.[5]

Writing as he did under the pressure of a deadly menace, Pictor did not have the leisure of old Cato to look for forgotten documents of the past, to make pilgrimages to historical places of Latium. He was forced to act quickly. It is possible, too, that it was not entirely his own decision to write his Annals. He could have been encouraged or even ordered by the Senate to do it when he reported on the situation abroad on his return from Delphi.

What he produced was no dishonest forgery. He constructed, from what little legend and far-off memories had to offer, an imaginary but worthy childhood for the new leading power of the Mediterranean World. Some distortion of truth in his work resulted from

[1] A. Momigliano, Secondo contributo, Roma 1960, 86. F. Boemer, Historia 2, 1953-54, 200, 204 sq.

[2] J. Heurgon, La vie quotid. 311. Cf. also E. Pais, Studi storici 2, 1893, 338 sq.

[3] Cic., *Brut.* 11, 42 : *historia est opus oratorium maxime . . . concessum est rhetoribus ementiri in historiis, ut aliquid dicere possint argutius.* If Plin., n.h. XXXV, 2, 8 thinks that *etiam mentiri clarorum imagines erat aliquis virtutum amor*, we feel that the distortions of truth in Pictor had at any rate a much more honorable excuse.

[4] Cf. e.g., P. Scheller, De Hellenistica historiae conscribendae arte, Diss. Leipzig 1911, 35 sq. H. Peter, Wahrheit und Dichtung 289.

[5] He could think what Livy writes V 21, 9 : *sed in rebus tam antiquis si quae similia veri sint pro veris accipiantur, satis habeam.* But Livy distantiates himself from this kind of fiction : *haec ad ostentationem scaenae gaudentis miraculis aptiora quam ad fidem neque adfirmare neque refellere est operae pretium.*

personal bias; but primarily, distortion was a *pia fraus* committed in the interest of the state, with which the fate of his family had been allied for many centuries. It was not his fault that his presentation of Early Rome became canonical. "If the people accept Roman rule," announces Livy in the preface to his great work, "they must also accept the divinity of Romulus." Plutarch, just before making a similar statement,[1] mentions that he relied on the narrative of Diocles and Pictor in recounting the origins of Rome. Was it not Pictor, then, who first struck this high-sounding note? He did it on another occasion when he inserted the story of the head found in the foundation-holes of the Capitol and made it forecast the future greatness of the place. But in any case, who would dare to contradict him after the victory over Hannibal? Even the Latins were impeded by fear and respect from exposing the forgery.

His face picture of the beginnings of Rome has survived the centuries, but now it must deceive us no longer: we can now try to build up from the scraps of evidence we possess the outlines of the true evolution in Latium, from the dawn of history to the conquest of the Latins.

---

[1] Liv. 1 *praef.* 7 : *Datur haec venia antiquitati ut miscendo humana divinis primordia urbium augustiora faciat ; et, si cui populo licere oportet consecrare origines suas et ad deos referre auctores, ea belli gloria est populo Romano ut, cum suum conditorisque sui parentem Martem potissimum ferat, tam et hoc gentes humanae patiantur aequo animo quam imperium patiuntur.* Plut., Rom. 8, 9 : ὧν τὰ πλεῖστα καὶ Φαβίου λέγοντος καὶ τοῦ Πεπαρηθίου Διοκλέους . . . ὕποπτον μὲν ἐνίοις ἐστὶ τὸ δραματικὸν καὶ πλασματῶδες, οὐ δεῖ ἀπιστεῖν τὴν τύχην ὁρῶντας οἵων ποιημάτων δημιουργός ἐστι, καὶ τὰ Ῥωμαίων πράγματα λογιζομένους, ὡς οὐκ ἂν ἐνταῦθα προῦβη δυνάμεως, μὴ θείαν τιν᾽ ἀρχὴν λαβόντα καὶ μηδὲν μέγα μηδὲ παράδοξον ἔχουσαν.

Chapter V

THE ETRUSCAN RULE IN LATIUM AND ROME

Tuscorum ante Romanum imperium late terra marique opes patuere: "far and wide reached the might of the Etruscans on land and sea before the Roman supremacy came into existence," says Livy.[1] *Tuscos autem omnem paene Italiam subiugasse manifestum est*: "it is an obvious fact that the Etruscans subjugated almost the whole of Italy," comments Servius on a passage of Vergil.[2] These and other statements of the same kind not only go back to a reliable source, viz., the *Origines* of the Old Cato,[3] but they are fully verified by the results of the archaeological researches of our age.

This great nation of sailors and warriors, of craftsmen and merchants, of splendid organizers and technicians, so utterly different from the Indo-European cattle-rearers, arrived not long after these latter in the Apennine Peninsula from Asia Minor,[4] settling in present-

---

[1] Liv. V 33, 7 ; cf. I 2, 5.
[2] Serv., *Aen.* 10, 145.
[3] H. Peter, H. R. Rel 1¹, 1870, 71 ad Cat., *Orig.* fr. 67.
[4] The origin of the Etruscans is still hotly debated. Cf., e.g., K. O. Müller-W. Deecke, Die Etrusker 1, Stuttgart 1877, 65 sqq., and the latest contributions : F. Altheim, Der Ursprung der Etrusker, Baden-Baden 1950. F. Schachermeyr, Etruskische Frühgeschichte, Berlin 1929, esp. 89 sqq. M. Pallottino, L'origine

176

day Tuscany, the rich hilly country which has borne their name ever since. Deeply penetrated by Greek culture but also contesting the Greeks of Southern Italy and Sicily for the rule of the sea,[1] the Etruscans owed the amazingly easy success of their rapid expansion to their overwhelming technical skill and superior strategical planning,[2] which found no worthy match in the inferior iron-age civilization and decaying tribal structure, the primitive fortification systems of the shepherd villages of the Indo-European peoples established in these regions.

The subjugation of the peoples in Etruria proper was a great warlike enterprise,[3] achieved by the whole nation; it must have been such a common effort also that led to the conquest of Campania and after this, to that of the Po valley as well. It is impossible to imagine achievements of this magnitude without a wholesale coordination, though, curiously enough, this has been emphatically denied by excellent scholars,[4] who thought that the expeditions into the Po valley or the seizure of the Campanian plain were the enterprise of individual cities or chieftains with their dependents.

Of course, before and after such enormous common undertakings particularism prevailed, just as in Greece before and after the Persian wars, or in the Latium of the fifth century, where federal actions and local wars between the Latin cities alike were the order of the day. The history of Rome under Etruscan rule will show us that bloody

---

degli Etruschi, Roma 1947. *Idem*, Arch cl 7, 1956, 109 sqq. A. Piganiol, Studies in Roman Economic and Social History, Princeton 1951, 79 sqq. *Idem*, Cahiers d'Histoire Mondiale 1, 1953, 238 sqq. *Idem*, A Ciba Foundation Symposium on Medical Biology and Etruscan Origins, London 1959, 56 sqq. G. Säflund, Historia 6, 1957, 10 sq. A. W. Byvanck, V. Türk Tarih Kongresi, 1956 (1960), 164 sqq. S. Mazzarino, Iura 12, 1961, 36. J. Heurgon, La vie quotid., Paris 1961, 9 sqq. A. Boëthius, in : Etruscan Culture, Land and People, Malmö 1962, 34 sq. 50 sq. 63.

[1] Cf. K. O. Müller-W. Deecke, *op. cit.* 1, 78 sqq., 174 sqq., 271 sqq. R. A. Fell, Etruria and Rome, Cambridge 1924, 36 sqq. J. Heurgon, *op. cit., passim.*

[2] Ed. Colozier, Mél. 64, 1952, 6 sqq. ; *ibid.* 65, 1953, 65 sqq. (with the previous contributions quoted).

[3] Plin., *N.h.* III 14, 112 : *Umbrorum gens antiquissima Italiae existimatur . . ., trecenta eorum oppida Tusci debellasse reperiuntur.*

[4] Ed. Meyer, GdA 2, 1902, § 435. G. De Sanctis, St. d. R. 1², 423. R. A. L. Fell, Etruria and Rome, Cambridge 1924, 39. L. Pareti, Rend. Pont. Acc. 7, 1929-31, 89 sqq. G. Camporeale, La parola del passato fasc 13, 1958, 5 sqq. *Contra* : J. Heurgon, Rech. 67 sqq. R. Lambrechts, Essai sur les magistratures des républiques étrusques (Études de philol., d'arch. et d'hist. anc. publ. par l'Inst. Hist. Belge de Rome 7) 1959, 27 sqq. with some relevant details.

wars between Etruscan states were raging again and again as early as the sixth century B.C.; the great exploits of the heroes of Caere and of Vulci, as reflected in a new *elogium* and in the slaughters illustrated in the burial chambers of the "tomba François" of Vulci, mirror the same state of affairs.[1] But these moments of dissolution were followed by concerted actions, and the helplessness of the central organs in the epoch of Roman preponderance must not induce us to under-estimate their role in the time of Etruscan domination.

The confederation of the twelve Etruscan states survived even the loss of its power, and at the great annual gatherings, besides the solemn sacrifices and the display of all sorts of games, political deliberations by the leading men of their cities were still held under Roman rule—even if their decisions were reduced to honors and flattering decrees for their conquerors.[2] But before that epoch of decay the confederation "was at least able to undertake a military action, to control the policies of the cities, to take coercive measures against them, and also to bring them help if needed. We grasp (in the sources) how this League expressed its political and military principles concerning the whole nation in its resolutions. Besides this, it should be remarked that, in spite of the defective functioning of this federal organism in the realization of a policy of its own, the existence of the *nomen Etruscum*, of a national unity of the Etruscans, was acknowledg-ed and given consideration by their enemies."[3] It was certainly a sudden if only short revival of great concerted actions of the League—the role of which must be taken for granted—in a glorious past, when it coordinated the contributions of single Etruscan states in equipping an invasion fleet in 205 B.C. for the Elder Scipio, providing timber, masts, wooden ship-structures, canvas, iron accessories, weapons, and supplies of wheat and other foodstuffs (Liv. XXVIII 45, 14-18).

Nobody today questions the statement of our sources that this national federation was governed originally by lifelong kings; nor can it be doubted that their overwhelming successes were won while the unity was strong, and that the decline was due to the disintegration of the central power, torn asunder by the strife of its mem-

[1] Cf. J. Heurgon, Rech. 68 sq. *Idem*, La vie quotid., 315 sqq.
[2] K. O. Müller-W. Deecke, *op. cit.* 1, 320 sqq. J. Heurgon, Historia 6, 1957, 86 sqq. R. Lambrechts, *op. cit.* 25 ff.
[3] R. Lambrechts, *op. cit.* 27 sq., with the quotations attesting this.

bers.[1] But even in that later period the shadowy image of the kingship was maintained by the religious representative and at the same time executive chief of the nation, the *sacerdos* or *praetor Etruriae*. Elected annually in rotation from the twelve *lucumones*, the heads of the member-states, he presided at the *concilium omnis Etruriae*, the national council, which met once or, if needed, several times a year.[2] An appropriate and striking expression of the once regal might of the *zilath mechl rasnal*—this was the original name of the *praetor Etruriae*— was the display of twelve executioners, marching before him when he appeared in public, with their axes fastened in a bundle of rods. They represented the united power of the twelve cities.[3]

The time-honored organization of the twelve cities,[4] continued in existence until the close of Antiquity, although their number was increased to fifteen in Roman times. Though its function was restricted to the annual sacrifices for the welfare of the Etruscan nation and the Roman Empire, to the traditional celebration of games and official manifestations of loyalty, the federal tradition was preserved unbroken, carried on to posterity by the same old aristocracy which stood once beside its cradle. The memories of the glorious past of the League were not forgotten. Consequently the assertion of our sources that by the conquest and colonization of Campania [5]—we shall return to this below—as well as by the taking possession of the Po valley,[6] each of the twelve states founded a daughter-city in the

---

[1] Strab. V 2, 2 (p. 219 C.) on the early epoch of Etruscan history : τότε μὲν οὖν ὑφ'ἑνὶ ἡγεμόνι ταττόμενοι μέγα ἴσχυον, χρόνοις δ'ὕστερον διαλυθῆναι τὸ σύστημα εἰκὸς καὶ κατὰ πόλεις διασπασθῆναι βίᾳ τῶν πλησιοχώρων εἴξαντας. Cf. Liv. I 8, 3 : *ex duodecim populis communiter creato rege.*

[2] Cf. for details K. O. Müller-W. Deecke, *l.c.* J. Heurgon, Historia 6, 1957, 83 sqq., 99 sqq. R. Lambrechts, *op. cit.* 95, 102 n. 5, 103, and M. Pallottino, St. Etr. 24, 1955-56, 68 sqq.

[3] Diod. V 40, 1. DH III 61, 2 ; cf. 59, 4. Liv. I 8, 3, etc. The twelve lictors of the Roman executive illustrate the competition with the *whole* of Etruria, an ambition which could not have existed before ca. 400 B.C. at the earliest. Prior to this date, I think, only one bunch of *fasces* were carried before the leading magistrates of the Roman State.

[4] Strab. V 2, 2 (p. 219 C.).

[5] Strab. V 4, 3 (p. 242 C.) : ἄλλοι δὲ λέγουσιν οἰκούντων Ὀπικῶν πρότερον καὶ Αὐσόνων, οἱ δ'ἐκείνους κατασχεῖν ὕστερον Ὄσκων τι ἔθνος, τούτους δ'ὑπὸ Κυμαίων, ἐκείνους δ'ὑπὸ Τυρρηνῶν ἐκπεσεῖν. διὰ γὰρ τὴν ἀρετὴν περιμάχητον γενέσθαι τὸ πεδίον. Δώδεκα δὲ πόλεις ἐγκατοικίσαντας τὴν οἷον κεφαλὴν ὀνομάσαι Καπύην.

[6] Liv. V 33, 9 : *Et in utrumque mare vergentes incoluere urbibus duodenis terras, prius cis Appenninum ad inferum mare, postea trans Appenninum totidem, quot capita*

ETRUSCAN RULE IN LATIUM AND ROME

newly occupied territory, cannot be brushed aside as a mythical tale or a literary fiction. Moreover, such a reasonable distribution of risk and advantage was the right way to achieve such huge tasks, planned and implemented by the Confederation. The imposing proportions of those two enterprises became clear in the light of recent archaeological discoveries concerning the latter, planned on the basis of the rich experiences gained in the former adventure and carried out with a refined technical machinery.

The seizure and immediate urbanization of present-day Lombardy [1] was indeed based on a comprehensive strategical scheme and executed with an amazing technical efficiency—features quite unthinkable without a central direction and coordination.

One of the main archaeological proofs attesting the creation of the new cities in the north at a given moment, ex novo, is the site of modern Marzabotto.[2] "Her plan of urbanization is, it seems, total, because the sanctuaries show the same exact orientation towards the North (as the residential area): the same religious prescriptions defined the location of the sacred citadel of the city, as that of the places for the houses of men, though the difference in level between the plain of Misano and the terrace of the temples is one of *ca.* 14

---

originis erant, coloniis missis, quae trans Padum omnia loca,—excepto Venetorum angulo qui sinum circumcolunt maris,—usque ad Alpes tenuere. Diod. XIV 113, 2 (on the Etruscans in the Po Valley) : τούτους δ'ἔνιοί φασιν ἀπὸ τῶν ἐν Τυρρηνίᾳ δώδεκα πόλεων ἀποικισθῆναι. Verg., *Aen.* 10, 198 sqq. Schol. Veron., *Aen.* 10, 200 : *Item Caecina .... (Ta)rchon, inquit, eum exercitu Appeninum transgressus primum oppidum constituit, quod tum (Mantuam) nominavit (vocatumque Tusca lingua) a Dit(e patre) est nomen. Deinde undecim dedicavit Diti patri ..... ibi constituit annum et item locum consecravit, quo duodecim oppida (condere ...).* Serv. auct., *Aen.* 10, 198 : *alii a Tarchone Tyrrheni fratre conditam dicunt : Mantuam autem ideo nominatam, quod Etrusca lingua Mantum Ditem patrem, appellant, cui cum ceteris urbibus, et hanc consecravit.* The ultimate source of these statements is the *Origines* of Cato ; cf. Serv., *Aen.* 10, 179 : *Cato originum qui Pisas tenuerint ante adventum Etruscorum, negat sibi compertum ; sed inveniri Tarchonem, Tyrrheno oriundum, postquam eorundem sermonem ceperit, Pisas condidisse.* Plut., *Camill.* 16, 1-3 : Οἱ δὲ (Γαλάται) ἐμβαλόντες εὐθὺς ἐκράτουν τῆς χώρας ὅσην τὸ παλαιὸν οἱ Τυρρηνοὶ κατεῖχον, ἀπὸ τῶν Ἄλπεων ἐπ' ἀμφοτέρας καθήκουσαν τὰς θαλάσσας, ... καὶ πόλεις εἶχεν ὀκτωκαίδεκα καλὰς καὶ μεγάλας καὶ κατεσκευασμένας πρός τε χρηματισμὸν ἐργατικῶς καὶ πρὸς δίαιταν πανηγυρικῶς, ἃς οἱ Γαλάται τοὺς Τυρρηνοὺς ἐκβαλόντες αὐτοὶ κατέσχον. Cf. also K. O. Müller-W. Deecke, *op. cit.* 1, 125 sqq., 154 sq.

[1] G. A. Mansuelli, CRAI 1960, 65 sqq.

[2] A. Grenier, Bologne villanovienne et étrusque (BEFAR 106), Paris 1912, 116. J. Heurgon, La vie quotid. 168 sqq.

meters . . . The entire plan shows distinctly [1] a relationship with the Greek methods of urbanisation. But at the same time it also illustrates the religious base of the Etruscan urbanism, as opposed to the political foundations of the urbanism of the Greek world . . . The creator of the city plan of Marzabotto imposed a perfectly abstract scheme upon the terrain, subordinating the private initiative to the regulations required by the whole pattern, i.e., to the requirements of the public interest. Private persons could buy in the new city lots in the measure of their economic means; therefore, the interior of the great *insulae* (house-blocks) is not symmetrically divided, as the trenches marking the limits of the individual possessions illustrate. The regularity of the general plan of the town enforced, of course, a regularity in the disposition of the houses, but every lot has been used in a different manner." "The alignment of the buildings of industrial character along the route from north to south . . . proves that the man who conceived this urbanistic design has foreseen a functional differentiation between the different quarters when delineating his concept of the future settlement."[2]

The same impression emerges from the newly discovered elements of the urbanistic pattern of Spina, the big Etruscan trading center at the mouth of the Po, with the axial lay-out of her rectilinear streets.[3] A salient feature of this grandiose project is the regulation of the waterways. Spina was built on lagoons as was Venice later and ships could unload beside the storehouses.[4] Canalization, drainage of marshland, regulation of water-courses and of the level of lakes accompanied everywhere the Etruscan occupation in Italy; in the Po region such hydrotechnical provisions were of special importance and were certainly projected by the League before she embarked upon this great adventure.

---

[1] F. Castagnoli, Ippodamo di Mileto e l'Urbanistica a pianta ortogonale, Roma 1956.

[2] G. A. Mansuelli, *op. cit.* 72, 73.

[3] N. Alfieri, in N. Alfieri-P. E. Arias, Spina. Guida al museo archeologico in Ferrara, Firenze 1960, 21 sqq. (49 sqq. a useful bibliography of all the special contributions is given). Cf. G. A. Mansuelli, *op. cit.* 77 sqq.

[4] Plin., *N.h.*, III 16, 120 : *hoc ante Eridanum ostium dictum est, ab aliis Spineticum ab urbe Spina, quae fuit iuxta, praevalens, ut Delphicis creditum est thesauris.* Strab. V 1, 7 (p. 214 C.) : μεταξὺ δὲ . . . ἡ Σπῖνα, νῦν μὲν κωμίον πάλαι δὲ Ἑλληνὶς πόλις ἔνδοξος. θησαυρὸς γοῦν ἐν Δελφοῖς Σπινητῶν δείκνυται, καὶ τἄλλα ἱστορεῖται περὶ αὐτῶν ὡς θαλασσοκρατησάντων. Cf. N. Alfieri, *l.c.*, G. A. Mansuelli, *l.c.*, J. Heurgon, La vie quotid., 130 sqq.

182

The immense masses of sediment brought down from the mountains year by year by the waters feeding the Po covered the site of Spina, cutting her off from the sea already in the Augustan age,[1] and prohibiting her identification until the age of aerial photography. This also is the reason why we do not yet know the sites of all the twelve Etruscan cities, south and north of the Po; there is no reason whatsoever to doubt their existence.[2] Some of them however, were, not founded on virgin soil as were Marzabotto and Spina; at Felsina, for instance the Etruscans imposed their rule on a flourishing Villanovan community. This latter method of subjugation was the prevailing type of earlier Etruscan colonization—in Etruria proper as well as in Latium and elsewhere—in the first phase of their conquest.

THE ETRUSCAN OCCUPATION OF CAMPANIA

The history of Latium in the epoch when the Etruscans extended their sway over this part of Italy is obscured no less by the lack of information than by the deliberate forgery of Fabius Pictor. This real father of the lies of early Roman history was, of course, reticent about the overwhelming superiority and rapid expansion of the Etruscans because the imaginary Roman conquest of Central Italy under the Tarquins, invented by him, would reveal itself as nonsense in the face of the massive evidence illustrating the Etruscan ascendancy over the whole Apennine peninsula.

In spite of this failure of our sources of information, there exists, luckily enough, the possibility to grasp at least the bare outline of the developments which involved the Etruscan occupation of the homeland of the Latins. Namely, we can use the date and peculiar circumstances of the seizure of Campania by the Etruscans to clear up the question of when and how Latium became subjected to them.

Modern scholarship, since Niebuhr, has never lost sight of the

[1] Strab., *l.c.*: ἡ Σπῖνα ... νῦν δ' ἐστὶν ἐν μεσογαίᾳ τὸ χωρίον περὶ ἐνενήκοντα τῆς θαλάττης σταδίους ἀπέχον. Cf. K. O. Müller-W. Deecke, 1, 208 sqq.
[2] G. A. Mansuelli, a very competent scholar, *op. cit.* 67 and 79 sqq., questioned the existence of all the twelve cities; but in August 1962 he mentioned (orally) his recent experience with Roman settlements found by himself, in this region, under a layer of sediment over ten meters thick, a circumstance which may cause him to reconsider his view just quoted.

simple truth that from the time when the new Etruscan *dodekapolis* arose on the Campanian plain the conquerors were forced to keep open the passage from their more northern country to their southern colonial territory; and that this passage was just the soil of Latium, the natural bridge between Etruria and Campania. This geographical link between the two territories was due to become the common playground of political forces radiating from both, once the new "Twelve cities" were established south of it.

We do have a literary report on the arrival of the Etruscans in Campania. However, it is transmitted in a biased form and hitherto there was no reliable archaeological evidence to check the alternative chronological possibilities emerging from it. The report is that of old Cato, discussed by Velleius Paterculus [1] on the foundation date of Capua, the capital city of the new *dodekapolis*. Leading authorities of the last one and a half centuries maintained hopelessly diverging views on this date; a few examples will suffice to illustrate this. M. Pallottino would put the event in the year 471 B.C.; [2] T. J. Dunbabin thinks that the Etruscans reached the farthest point of their push toward the south at Fratte near Salerno little before 530 B.C.; [3] B. G. Niebuhr and, more recently, J. Heurgon place the great conquering expedition in the year 524 B.C.; [4] a considerable group of renowned scholars—in the greatest detail the theory is, I think, presented by A. Boëthius—consider the date for this to be about 600 B.C.; [5] G. De Sanctis and F. Castagnoli maintain that the conquest

[1] Cato fr. 69 (H. R. Rel. 1², p. 74 Peter = Vell. I 7, 2): *Quidam huius* (sc. Hesiodi) *temporis tractu aiunt a Tuscis Capuam Nolamque conditam ante annos fere octingentos et triginta. quibus equidem adsenserim: sed M. Cato quantum differt! qui dicat Capuam ab eisdem Tuscis conditam ac ... Nolam* ; *stetisse autem Capuam, antequam a Romanis caperetur, annis circiter ducentis et sexaginta. quod si ita est, cum sint a Capua capta ducenti et quadraginta, ut condita est, anni sunt fere quingenti. ego pace diligentiae Catonis dixerim, vix crediderim tam mature tantam urbem crevisse, floruisse, concidisse, resurrexisse.* Cf. H. Peter, ad l. l.—Polyb. II 17, 1 (F. Gr. Hist. 706 F 17 a) writes that the conquest of Campania happened at the same time as that of the Po Valley—no doubt erroneous information. J. Heurgon reminds me of the serious possibility that the parallel with Hesiod could hint at a synchronism implemented by Timaeus.

[2] M. Pallottino, La parola del passato, fasc. 47, 1956, 84 sqq.

[3] T. J. Dunbabin, The Western Greeks, Oxford 1948, 346.

[4] B. G. Niebuhr, RG 1², 1827, 75 sqq. J. Heurgon, Rech. 59 sq., 62 sqq., 71. M. Combet-Farnoux, Mél. 69, 1957 (1958), 12.

[5] A. v. Gutschmid, Kleine Schriften 5, Leipzig 1894, 343. J. Beloch, Campanien, Breslau, 1890, 8 sqq. H. Diels, Hermes 22, 1897, 216 sq. Ed. Meyer, GdA 3³, Stuttgart 1954, 653. Chr. Hülsen, RE 3, 1555 sq. Cf. also K. O.

was achieved already in the second half of the seventh century B.C.[1] Finally, L. Pareti is inclined to push back the origins of Capua to ca. 680 B.C.[2] Recent excavations—to the results of which we shall return immediately—reveal the surprising fact that the highest estimates come nearest to the truth.

Velleius Paterculus read in his source that in the opinion of Cato Etruscan Capua had existed for 260 years before she became part of the Roman Empire; her foundation would belong, consequently, to 471 B.C. As the Samnites wiped out the old governing class of the city as early as in 423, or possibly even in 437 B.C., the Roman writer could not believe that a city of such magnitude could develop and reach her size in only 34, or 48 years respectively. On the other hand, L. Pareti is right in stressing the point that Cato, a real connoisseur of the history of the origin of Italian cities, could hardly have written such an absurdity; and further that the source of Velleius must have distorted his original statement. The simplest supposition is that Cato counted back 260 years to the foundation of Capua not from the Roman, but from the Samnite occupation. This would mean that Capua was founded in 683 B.C., and Pareti was able to cite archaeological materials from the site, pointing in the same direction: local imitations of Etruscan *bucchero* pottery found along with protocorinthian sherds of the first half of the seventh century B.C. The same scholar also rightly underlined the circumstance that on later products of the local *bucchero* Etruscan inscriptions appear, testifying that with the models of that earthenware the Etruscans also arrived there.

Since 1947 when Pareti's statement was made, new finds came to light, confirming it. Recent excavations in Campania clearly show the two currents [3] arriving here, with a marked interval in the course

---

Müller-W. Deecke, 1, 165 sqq. H. Nissen, It. Lk. 2, 696 sqq. P. Ducati, Etruria antica 2, 1925, 10 sq. A. Boëthius, *Symbolae philologicae O. A. Danielsson octogenario dicatae*, Uppsala 1932, 1 sq.

[1] G. De Sanctis, St. d. R. 1², 430 sqq., 437. F. Castagnoli, Bull. Com. 74, 1951-52, 49 sqq.

[2] L. Pareti, La tomba Regolini-Galassi, Città Vaticano 1947, 498 sq.

[3] The difficulty in distinguishing the archeological material of these two groups, the Villanovan people and the Etruscans in Tuscany itself, is well known. But in Campania their remains become distinct. In general, the fundamental difference between the two ethnic groups and their respective archeological materials can be well realized if we compare the situation in Etruria with the early Iron Age civilization north of the Alps, in the mountainous country of present day Austria as well as in the plains of the Carpathian Basin, closely related to the Villanovan. The striking parallelism of the two environments in

of the Iron Age: first the Villanova civilization of Italic tribes sweeping down as far to the South as Salerno,[1] perhaps in flight before the Etruscan invaders of Tuscany who made them homeless. Then, toward the end of the eighth century, Greek, Phoenician, and Etruscan ware was streaming in, as G. Buchner has illustrated by the concrete example in his research work on the isle of Ischia,[2] reflecting the clash of Greek, Carthaginian, and Etruscan interests in this region. Some decades after this interlude, the presence of the Etruscans can already be ascertained. In Capua, W. Johannowsky found a great number of burials, reaching back to the seventh century in which the fine imported Etruscan *bucchero leggero* precedes the mass of local *bucchero* imitations and—a very significant feature—no Greek imports, though the flourishing city of Cyme had been in existence in the neighborhood since about 750 B.C. The same situation can be seen in Cales.[3] The beginnings of the uninterrupted stream of imports

the ninth and eighth centuries B.C. suddenly stops thereafter. The Transalpine sphere continues to preserve further on its prehistoric character developing in a straight line from its previous phase of evolution, whereas in Italy the sudden inundation of Oriental and Greek wares, the transition from the villager's life to urbanized culture is accompanied by a change in social structure, a hitherto unknown religious world, a revolutionizing military technique, new industrial and commercial concepts, a new style in the political thought. What is the reason for this abrupt bifurcation of two related civilizations within two related groups of the Indoeuropean tribes? The housewife who has once forgotten to put yeast or baking powder in her cake will easily grasp this: the Etruscan ferment was absent to the north of the Alps, but present in the south. The Etruscan settlement besides the Villanovan *oppidum* in Bologna: e.g., R. A. L. Fell, Etruria and Rome, Cambridge 1924, 15 sqq., 25 sqq. The same situation has been revealed in San Giovenale, as A. Boëthius kindly informs me; cf. the English edition of the Swedish excavation-report. See also H. Hencken, J. B. Ward Perkins, and R. Bloch in the Ciba Symposium volume, 29 sqq., 50 sqq. Finally, J. Heurgon kindly informed me that R. Bloch excavated a Villanovan settlement which was alongside an Etruscan one in Casalecchio di Reno near Bologna. *Contra*: M. Pallottino, Gnomon 34, 1962, 597.

[1] The preparation of the Sixth International Congress of Prehistoric and Protohistoric Sciences in Rome (August 29-September 3, 1962), organized with great skill and competence by M. Pallottino, with the accompanying regional exhibits, greatly enlivened the Iron Age research in the provinces of Italy considered in this book. Important new materials for the Early Iron Age in Campania have been made accessible in the work of M. Napoli- V. Panebianco-Br. d'Agostino, Mostra della Preistoria e della Protostoria nel Salernitano, Salerno 1962.

[2] In an impressive report, given at the aforesaid Congress August 29, 1962, to be published in the *Atti*. Cf. J. Heurgon, Rech. 73 sqq.

[3] The new excavations in Capua and Cales are still unpublished. I owe cordial thanks to Dr. W. Johannowsky for showing me his finds as well as for his

are of course only the second step: the warlike occupation preceded them.

As a seagoing people, the Etruscans certainly realized the importance of Campania on their piratical and commercial expeditions to the south along the coast. It is a sound guess that they already had a foothold in the Gulf of Naples before their armies captured the important sites in the interior.[1] By this same reasoning their invasion was conceived also to counteract and stop the Chalcidean colonization. They succeeded indeed in restricting the agrarian territory of Cyme and in prohibiting the foundation of additional Greek settlements there.[2] Their coastal towns in Campania remained the stepping stones of their rule over the Tyrrenian Sea through the two and half centuries of their free existence. However, their communication lines with their mother country on land became even more vital for them, involving the necessity of a firm hold upon the strongpoints of Latium.

℣

THE ETRUSCAN ENCROACHMENT UPON THE LATIN COMMUNITIES

There is a basic difference between the Etruscan rule in Campania and in Latium. The meager soil of the Latin cattle-rearers did not invite the establishment of a new colonial Etruria, as in the South. In Latium the safe passage of goods and armies was to be made sure— a secondary aim as compared with the efforts made in the Po Valley and in Campania. The Etruscans always remained a minority here, superimposed on the indigenous population at key points, which also explains the ease with which the Latins got rid of them at the time of Porsenna.

contribution to this book printed in the Appendix, and to Prof. A. De Franciscis for further information. But not in the last instance, I am greatly indebted to the generous help of Prof. D. Mustilli.

[1] L. Pareti, *op. cit.* 499 sq., 503 sqq.

[2] Strab. V 4, 3 (p. 242 C.) on the successive waves of conquerors of Campania: ἄλλοι δὲ λέγουσιν... Σιδικίνους κατασχεῖν ὕστερον Ὄσκων τι ἔθνος. τούτους δ'ὑπὸ Κυμαίων, ἐκείνους δ'ὑπὸ Τυρρηνῶν ἐκπεσεῖν. The earliest migratory movements, not quoted here, may be learned combinations without much real background (cf. the note of F. Jacoby on F. Gr. Hist. 555 F 7, Komm. n. 48), but the sentence quoted is historical. Cf. K. O. Müller-W. Deecke, 1, 160 sqq. L. Pareti, *op. cit.* 45, 496 sq., 503 sq., and others.

Etruscan Encroachment upon the Latin Communities

There were two equally important lines of communication running across Latium from the north to the south. An internal route descended with wares from Central Etruria on the Tiber, continuing the transport on the Anio via Tibur and Praeneste, soon reaching down the valley of the Tolerus and Liris rivers, and ending in Cales, Capua, and Nola.[1] As Capua was the metropolis of the new daughter-cities in the south, the priority of the highway directed toward her over the coastal road becomes evident; archaeological facts, to be mentioned immediately, support this assumption. Whereas this continental route brought the products of Central Etruria down the Tiber to the interior of Campania, the other artery of traffic and commerce ran near the coast, being the natural outlet for the wares of Tarquinia and Caere but also discharged the cargo of riverboats to Antium, Circeii, and Tarracina. The key points of the internal route were Gabii, Tibur and Praeneste; of the coastal route, Rome and Lavinium.

The safety of the internal line was enhanced by the fact that not only Picenum,[2] but also the original territory of the Volscians [3] on the north-eastern flank of this line were under Etruscan control. At the junction of the river valleys provided by Nature to form the track of this route, the stronghold of Praeneste [4] was already in the second half of the seventh century the seat of Etruscan rulers. The fabulous riches of their tombs—the dates given by different scholars are either

[1] L. Pareti, *op. cit.* 497, assumes three main arteries. Tusculum certainly did not belong to the Praenestine one. Cf. also H. Nissen, It. Lk. II 2, 1902, 620 sq. Th. Ashby, St. Etr. 3, 1929, 177. G. Lugli, La Nuova Antologia, 16. apr. 1937. L. A. Holland, TAPA 80, 1949, 305 sq. *Contra*: Ed. Meyer, GdA 2, 1902, § 436, who erroneously considers Praeneste a cul-de-sac with no approach to the sea as Rome had ; a similar view is maintained by A. N. Sherwin-White, R. Citiz. 15.

[2] Plin., *N.h.* III 5, 70. Steph. Byz. s.v. Πικεντία. K. O. Müller-W. Deecke 1, 138 sq., 163.

[3] Cato fr. 62 (H. R. Rel. 1², 73 Peter = Serv., *Aen.* 11, 567; cf. 581): *Licet* (sc. Metabus) *Privernas esset, tamen, quia in Tuscorum iure paene omnis Italia fuerat, generaliter in Metabum omnium odia ferebantur. nam pulsus fuerat a gente Volscorum, quae etiam ipsa Etruscorum potestate regebatur, quod Cato plenissime exsecutus est.* Cf. also *ibid.* fr. 7. (: Priscian. 5, p. 182 H.) : *Cato. in I originum* : *Agrum quem Volsci habuerunt, campestris plerus Aboriginum fuit.* We know that after 504 B.C. Etruscan rule no longer existed in this region; we also know that the Volscian sweep to Southern Latium came only in this later epoch. On the other hand, the Etruscan rule over this people cannot be doubted ; it is evident that it belonged mainly to the sixth century.

[4] Cf. A. Boëthius, *op. cit.* 5. F. Schachermeyr, RE 4 A, 2355. H. Besig, RE Suppl. 8, 1257 sqq.

near to the middle or near the end of the century [1]—presuppose an earlier stabilization because such treasures are not accumulated from one day to the other. On the other hand, these masses of precious objects were not the overflow of local resources; the poor stony soil of Praeneste did not produce them. They were won by the exploitation of the new communication line across the country opened after the foundation of Capua. The beginnings of the Etruscan rule in Praeneste must therefore go back as far as some time in the first half of the seventh century. Etruscan tombs contemporary with those of Praeneste were found also on the outskirts of Gabii,[2] a station on the same route, and more such traces south of Praeneste will certainly come to light some time in the future.

The archaeological data hitherto available along the second great artery of communications traversing Latium vertically are a little later than those just reviewed, as far as the Etruscan element goes, with which we are here concerned. But they also must reach back into the seventh century B.C. We shall pay more attention to them when we turn to the history of Lavinium and Rome in that epoch.

The Etruscan rule left its traces everywhere in Latium. We must refrain from enlarging upon them; a few data, already noticed by others, must suffice to testify to this.[3] We shall discuss below the genuine popular legend of King Mezentius of Caere, which shows that the Latins of a later epoch still remembered the old times when they were exploited and oppressed by the Etruscans.[4] The Greeks of Hellas also heard of the Etruscan occupation of Latium in the sixth century B.C.: if the last lines appended to the Theogony of Hesiod [5]

---

[1] The older literature over the archaic tombs of Praeneste is to be found in H. Besig, *ibid.* Cf. A. Della Seta, Boll. d'Arte 3, 1909, 161 sqq. C. Densmoore Curtis, Mem. Am. Ac. Rome 3, 1919, 25 sqq. *Idem*, The Bernardini Tomb : Diss. d. Pontif. Acc. Rom. di Arch. 2. ser. 14, 1920, 113 sqq. *Idem*, Mem. Am. Ac. Rome 5, 1925, 9 sqq.—Date : L. Pareti, *op. cit.*, 511, pleads for 610-600 B.C. ; P. J. Riis, Gnomon 1951, 68 for 640-635 B.C. Cf. also D. Randall MacIver, Villanovans and Early Etruscans, Oxford 1924, 228 sq. R. Pittioni, RE Suppl. 9, 282. The archaic jewelry of the Praenestine rulers presumably of Caeretane origin : G. Pinza, Materiali per la etnologia antica toscano-laziale, Milano 1915, 377 sqq. L. Pareti, *op. cit.* 456 sqq., 518 sqq. D. Randall MacIver, *op. cit.* 204.

[2] G. Pinza, Bull. Com. 1903, 321 sqq. *Idem*, Mon. Linc. 15, 1905, 394. L. Pareti, *op. cit.* 461.

[3] Cf. F. Schachermeyer, Etruskische Frühgeschichte, Berlin 1929, 203 sq.

[4] Cf. below, p. 209 sqq.

[5] Hesiod., *Theog.* 1011 sqq.

confuse the conquerors and the subjugated, this gross error reveals the fact that the statement cannot be a late insertion. A concrete survival of the Etruscan domination over the Latins, attesting the submission and loyalty of the latter toward the former, will be dealt with in the chapter on Lavinium: this is the identification of Aeneas—a founder-hero of south Etruscan cities—with the divine ancestor of the Latin tribe in the sixth century B.C., and his uninterrupted worship at the annual gatherings in Lavinium thereafter.

The international conflict which burst into flames in the great naval battle of Alalia a little while after 540 B.C.[1] involved—from the time that the Phocaeans settled in Corsica around 564 B.C.—Latium with the whole west coast of Italy. Whereas the Etruscans gave a free hand to Carthage in Sicily and Spain, the Carthaginians regarded Campania, along with all the Etruscan coastal points of support on the Latian coast, as the sphere of interest of their ally, both of them hostile to Cyme. In 524 B.C., when an Etruscan army of vast size pushed across Latium towards Cyme and again homeward after its crushing defeat,[2] international complications are again seen to affect things in Latium. How many times this occurred will remain forever unknown to us.

Imports of mobile goods, historically relevant only in great masses or in peculiar circumstances, could not in themselves testify to a domination. But the religious architecture, totally Etruscan in Latium,[3] combined with numerous traces of Latino-Etruscan divinities,[4] shows not only a profound influence but an amalgamation, which could not happen without the presence of the fertilizing factor in the territory of the receptive medium. The cultural *koiné*, in archaic Italy so acutely grasped by Santo Mazzarino,[5] was only a secondary consequence of the Etruscan conquest. Though we possess information enough only in the case of Rome to realize that the sudden influx of Etruscan culture in Latium was the direct consequence of the

[1] Herod. 1, 165-167. Diod. V 13, 4. Sen., Ad Helv. matr. 7, 8. Steph. Byz. *s.v.*
[2] Cf. above, p. 56 sqq., and below, p. 231.
[3] A. Andrén, Architectural Terracottas from Etrusco-Italic Temples. Lund 1939-1940. R. Bloch, R. Et. Lat. 37, 1959, 128 sqq. L. Shoe's volume on the moldings will soon clear up further this all-important Etruscan influence.
[4] L. R. Taylor, Local Cults in Etruria (Papers and Monographs of the Am. Ac. in Rome 2) 1923, 8 sqq. R. Schilling, La religion romaine de Vénus. (BEFAR 178) Paris 1954, 76 sq. Cf. my remarks on the Diana of Aricia, AJA 64, 1960, 137 sqq. and below, p. 251 sqq. on Aeneas in Latium.
[5] S. Mazzarino, Fra Oriente e Occidente, Firenze 1947.

ETRUSCAN RULE IN LATIUM AND ROME

Etruscan occupation, the same decisive change in the life of the other Latin communities at the same moment cannot have been brought about by a different impulse. The occupation also explains the uniformity of their cultural advance. The Latin alphabet, for example, though derived in the last resort from a Greek prototype, was transmitted by the Etruscans.[1]

Besides such general symptoms, the rule of the Etruscans also left its stamp in one way or another upon each and every Latin city. A few indications, already noticed, will suffice to illustrate this. In Solonium, southwest of Rome, near the twelfth milestone of the road to Ostia, an Etruscan king was once in power—a genuine trait, even if preserved in a freely invented story.[2] In a similar way, Tarchetios, a mythical king of Alba Longa, is an Etruscan figure and Etruscan features are also woven into the narrative which contains his name and is another variant of the Roman myth of origin.[3] By her name Tusculum betrays her Tuscan antecedents;[4] the same is true of Turnus, King of the Ardeates—an ally of Caere in a genuine old tale to which we will return soon—whose name is a shortened form of Tyrrhenus.[5] The tombs of Ardea show, even in the fourth and third centuries B.C., the profound Etruscanization of this city.[6] The fundamental Etruscan influence, political and spiritual alike, which manifested itself in the tribal worship of all the Latins in Lavinium, will be discussed in our next chapter.[7] The flourishing of Praeneste under Etruscan conquerors gave rise to the rich industrial art of this city, which was still in full bloom during the middle Republic. A considerable proportion of the prominent local families here as well as in

[1] G. Buonamici, Epigrafia etrusca 1932, 111 sq. G. Février, Histoire de l'écriture², Paris 1959, 440 sq. M. Lejeune, R. Et. Lat. 35, 1957, 28 sqq.

[2] Fest., p. 296, 15 L. DH II 37, 2. Propert. IV 1, 31. M. Fluss, RE 3A, 981 sq. Cf. below, p. 302 n. 3.

[3] Details in F. Altheim, Griechische Götter im alten Rom (RVV XXII 1, 1930) 51 ff. W. F. Otto, Archiv f. lat. Lexicographie 15, 1908, 118. F. Marbach, RE 4 A, 2294 sq. (further lit.). On Promathion cf. the interesting hypothesis of S. Mazzarino, Stud. Rom. 8, 1960, 387 sq. I hope to return to this topic in my forthcoming study on the structure of the pre-Etruscan state.

[4] B. G. Niebuhr, RG 4², 1827, 182 and many others after him repeated this fact. *Contra* : K. J. Beloch, RG 229 sq. ; yet cf. 147.

[5] B. G. Niebuhr, RG 1², 200 sqq. A. Schwegler, RG 1, 331. Cf. below, p. 210.

[6] A. Boëthius, Atti del 3. Congresso nazionale di Studi Romani 1, Bologna, 1935, 147. *Idem*, in the review "Roma," 12, 1934, 297 sqq.

[7] Cf. below, p. 209 sqq.

Etruscan Encroachment upon the Latin Communities

Tibur were Etruscan.[1] In Satricum, Etruscan inscriptions have been found.[2] The names of Velitrae (*Velathri*) and Privernum are also Etruscan. Nor are archaeological remnants of the Etruscan period missing in this region of the Pomptine marshes; the most essential of them are the traces of the hydrotechnical engineering works established for the drainage of this fertile swampy district. Again, both the names of Anxur-Tarracina are Etruscan.[3] The last lines of the Theogony of Hesiod, reporting that Latin kings ruled over the Etruscans, though reversing the conqueror and the conquered, are based on wrongly reproduced but originally correct information about Etruscan rule over Latium.

The most relevant characteristic of Etruscan domination, and the real clue to its amazing success, is the fact that the conquerors aspired to create a symbiosis with the conquered. Being a small minority, imposing itself upon masses many times superior to their own numbers, a lasting control would be impossible otherwise. Though inhumanly cruel during hostilities, they indeed managed to amalgamate the conquered peoples with themselves without constraining them to give up their national life. Consequently the subjects formed a sense of loyalty toward their new overlords, aspiring to their superior form of life. It was not an idle guess when Varro stated that the Romans learned the methods of colonization from the Etruscans: the rule of the latter appears as a providential preparation of the peoples of Italy for higher civilization and more advanced political thinking, a lesson retained even after they shook off the foreign patronage, and preparing the way toward the unification of the Mediterranean world under the leadership of Rome.

For this, ample illustrations could easily be adduced but a few examples will suffice. In the geographical prolongation of Latium toward the north, the Capenates, Faliscans, and Fidenates were settled, being branches of the same Latin stock. When they became subjects of Veii, they identified their political concepts and human ideals with those of their conquerors but at the same time they preserved their national character, along with their language, religion, and so forth, developing a refined culture of their own on Etruscan and

---

[1] St. Weinstock, RE 6A, 820 sq.

[2] M. Pallottino, St. Etr. 13, 1939, 427 sqq.

[3] L. Pareti, La tomba Regolini-Galassi, 1947, 497 sqq. M. Hoffmann, RE Suppl. 8, 1147 sqq., and others.

Greek lines. The same happened in Latium. We shall see that the tribal League of the Latins continued under the Etruscans to convene every spring in Lavinium, to propitiate by solemn sacrifices their common ancestor and to discuss matters of common interest. Manifold aspects of this Etrusco-Roman merger which concern Rome will be apparent below. Nor was the effect of the Etruscan domination different in Praeneste. Either from the Bernardini Tomb, where the Etruscan rulers displayed their prodigious wealth, or, if not found in it, at any rate coming from the same place and from another tomb of the second half of the seventh century B.C. [1], a golden serpentine fibula is known which bears the earliest Latin inscription known to us: *Manios med fhefhaked Numasioi*, "Manios made me for Numasios." An even more impressive manifestation of this Etrusco-Latin co-existence is offered by a recent observation of J. Heurgon concerning another object of the same Bernardini Tomb. [2] On a large silver cup of this funeral treasure the name of the female owner, *Vetusia*, is inscribed, thus exhibiting, as on precious vases of other rich Etruscan tombs, the right of property of a woman—a matriarchal feature as characteristically Etruscan as it is un-Latin. But in the Praenestine case, the name of the queen who possessed the cup is Latin: *Vetusia*, which would later be spelled *Veturia*, a member seemingly of the same clan as the patrician *Veturii* in Rome. Consequently, the queen, surrounded with all the splendor of Etruscan magnificence by her Etruscan husband, was an offspring of the local Praenestine aristocracy. This may be a typical case of alliances between the conquerors and the leading groups of the conquered, not only in Latium but also all over the Peninsula where the Etruscans extended their sway.

This interpenetration of Etruscan and Latin components also accounts for the considerable common element in the Etruscan and Latin name systems, which shows that the borrowing was reciprocal; [3] and also for the deep Etruscan influence on Latium, which is more manifest in Rome than elsewhere in the country only because the historical tradition of the other Latin cities is lost.

---

[1] Cf., e.g., D. Randall-MacIver, Villanovans and Early Etruscans, Oxford 1924, 216 sqq. CIL I[2], p. 717. A. Ernout, Textes latins archaïques, Paris 1957, no. 1. A. Degrassi, ILLRP 1, etc.

[2] J. Heurgon, La vie quotid. 112 sq. Cf. Q. G. Giglioli, Arch. cl. 2, 1950, 85.

[3] W. Schulze, ZGLEN, *passim*. E. Lattes, Klio 12, 1912, 377 sqq. G. Herbig, Idg. Forsch. 26, 1909, 357 sqq. R. A. L. Fell, *op. cit.* 39 sq.

THE ETRUSCAN DOMINATION IN ROME

Rome's greatness has been very often explained as the direct consequence of her advantageous geographical position. Mommsen, for example, forcefully stresses this point: [1] situated at a strategically important juncture of the Latin maritime and fluvial commerce, also a stronghold of Latium toward the sea, Rome was due to rise high, he says. Yet we now know that the Etruscan river did not much interest the Latin cattle-rearers of the archaic period; still less was their concern with the sea trade. And whereas many Etruscan cities were natural citadels, almost impregnable to direct attack, Rome's site is open to aggression from all quarters and has none of the geographical advantages of Veii, Praeneste, and other neighboring places. This vulnerability explains why Rome became the victim of a series of Etruscan invasions, as we shall prove. The Servian wall, which made her a formidable stronghold, was not yet in existence in the sixth century, nor would there yet be a full complement for such a huge enceinte in this epoch when Rome was still a city of moderate size. She was hemmed in from the north, east and south by Veii, Tusculum, Aricia, and Lavinium; in the west, threatened rather than protected by the sea, she had no elbow-room for growth and might.

In general, a geographical situation in itself can never be the key for the historical growth of a settlement. A site is like the Sleeping Beauty who could slumber until the end of time if the noble Prince did not awaken her. Places become of outstanding importance only when a lifeline of communications of great significance for peace and war bisect them. The river-crossing at the *Isola Tiberina*, controlled by Rome, obtained its importance only in a larger connection when the transportation of the output of the Veientane saltworks at the mouth of the river necessitated the transversal communications toward the Sabines; and still more so when the vertical artery of commerce and troop movements toward Campania was opened up by the Etruscans along the coastal track of their approach to the new province. We have already seen that the central importance of Capua in the Campanian conquest brought the interior line of access to that new focus in the foreground; hence also the priority of the vital fortresses protecting this line in Latium over the principal junctures

[1] Mommsen, RG 1[8], 46.

of the coastal road to Campania in the same territory: hence, the earlier chance for the efflorescence of Gabii, Tibur, and Praeneste surpassing that of Rome. The precedence of those natural strongholds in the hills over the port of transshipment near the coast is also the obvious result of the natural sequence of events: the military bases in Etruscan hands were important from the first decades of the occupation; the emporium of the transit-commerce developed after consolidation. The efflorescence of Rome as an Etruscan base of transport and communications engendered, however, fateful complications: rival Etruscan powers equally needed this unloading place at the lowest reaches of the Tiber and each in turn snatched it away from its previous conqueror.[1]

The abundant proofs of Etruscan domination over Rome are of course in irreconcilable contrast with the annalist fiction of a Roman superiority, nay a Roman supremacy over the Etruscans in the epoch when the latter were sweeping down across Latium toward the Straits of Sicily. Nevertheless, the rising tide of credulity—plainly a reaction to the hypercriticism of earlier generations—has encouraged scholars of distincti on to try to reconcile the annalist tale of Roman ascendancy over the Etruscans with the tangible reality of the Etruscan rule over Rome.[2] Relying on the fact that Rome emerged as a Latin-speaking community after the Etruscan period, attempts have been made to palliate her previous dependence by the vague notion that she became included in the Etruscan "sphere of interest."[3] Others advanced still further on this slippery ground, maintaining that Rome was not conquered at all by the Etruscans.[4]

We have seen already that the preservation of the Latin character of Latium under the Etruscans was due to the fact that the small group of conquerors could not assimilate the proportionately large mass of the conquered; Rome was no exception to this rule. For the same reason it became easy to shake off the ruling minority when the

---

[1] We are developing here a theme, the basis of which is anticipated in a remark of De Sanctis, St. d. R. 1², 437 : "Ora in Campania non era dato pervenire agli Etruschi senza che traversassero liberamente il basso corso del Tevere ; e questo non potevano senza dominare in Roma ; quindi il dominio etrusco in Roma ebbe principio almeno nella seconda metá del VII. secolo, nè probabilmente è anteriore."

[2] Cf. Vl. Groh, Rend. Pont. Acc. 3, 1924-25, 215 sqq.

[3] E.g., G. Gianelli, La repubblica romana, 1955, 49, and others.

[4] E. Gjerstad, Opusc. Rom. 3, 1960, 101 ; but cf. *idem*, Legends and Facts of Early Roman History, Lund 1962, 33.

The Etrucan Domination in Rome

Latins acquired the skill and technique needed to maintain a "modern" state in those days. Consequently the unbroken continuation of the Latin idiom and nationality [1] does not invalidate the numerous proofs of the Etruscan domination in Latium—in the same way, for example, as the survival of the Hungarian language in the basin of the Carpathians does not disprove the one hundred and sixty years of subjugation of Hungary by the Turks, or its long affiliation to the Habsburg Empire.

One of the consequences of the Etruscan occupation was urbanization, a new order, disturbing the rights of property by imposing by the will of a conqueror a general plan on the capriciously shaped, irregular agglomerations of iron-age settlements. We must stress the point that this crucial change was not a spontaneous conversion of the Roman population to a new way of life, without precedence in its previous evolution, but a *tour de force*, imposed upon it by a foreign power—a surgical intervention with good final results, but a hard time for the patient.

Whereas the way of life of the Italic tribes did not necessitate or imply urbanization, the Etruscans promoted and implanted it everywhere. Though their methods of town-planning at the time of the capture of Rome were not yet at the technical level of their later great colonial enterprises, the urbanization of this Latin agglomeration of small villages was nevertheless a wholesale undertaking, the precepts and instructions for which were certainly laid down already in writing—not in scientific treatises but in sacred books which preceded them.[2] The report in the Annals that the foundation-works of the Capitoline temple and the drainage system of the Forum valley were achieved by the forced labor of the citizens imposed upon them by the Tarquins [3] seems to me to be based on factual

---

[1] M. Pallottino, Le origini dei popoli italici nell' antichità (10. Congr. intern. di scienze storiche, Roma 1955, vol. 2) 47 sqq.

[2] Fest., p. 358, 21 L.: *Rituales nominantur Etruscorum libri, in quibus perscriptum est, quo ritu condantur urbes, arae, aedes sacrentur, qua sanctitate muri, quo iure portae, quomodo tribus, curiae, centuriae, distribuantur, exercitus constituant <ur>, ordinentur ceteraque eiusmodi ad bellum ac pacem pertinentia.* Cf. Varro, LL 5, 143: *oppida condebant in Latio Etrusco ritu multi, . . . et ideo coloniae et urbes conduntur* (further passages noted, e.g., in the edition of G. Goetz-F. Schoell, Leipzig 1910, 43 sq.).

[3] Cic., *Verr.* V 19, 48: *et enim vel Capitolium, sicut apud maiores nostros factum est, publice coactis fabris operisque imperatis, gratis exaedificari atque effici potuit.* Liv. I 56, 1-3 (Superbus) *intentus perficiendo templo, . . . usus . . . operis etiam ex plebe. qui cum haud parvus et ipse militiae adderetur labor, minus tamen plebs gravabatur*

memories of the Romans. We must also suppose, I am sure, that this compulsory participation of the population was the real basis of the entire city building program and was not applied only in the cases mentioned in our sources.

The radical changeover to urban life, brought about by Etruscan concepts and dictates, will be more readily intelligible to the reader if he will remember the completely different social and political structure—manifest also in topography—which gave form to the village-like settlements spreading out on the hills of Rome before that foreign intervention. It can be demonstrated (this will be the subject of another study of the present writer) that pre-Etruscan Rome was a double community of Latins on the Palatine and Sabines on the Quirinal, united by an archaic state pattern, embracing all aspects of life—religious, political, economic, and social. The common center of this double unit at the time when the Etruscans were laying hands on it was already situated at the sloping fringe of the later Forum valley, because the sacred hearth of Vesta, the Eternal Fire of which was supposed to warrant the existence and welfare of its community, was posted here, outside both areas. If these areas were not linked together, this cult—vital to each of them—would not have been left outside, in an ever threatened no-man's-land. The new masters did not touch the location of the State-Hearth. We have archaeological evidence for its existence there from the beginning of their domination, from about 600 B.C.[1] Inseparably linked with the fire of Vesta since time immemorial was the House of the Two Kings, the *regia*. This, too, was left untouched by the foreign rulers.

se templa deum exaedificare manibus suis, quam postquam et ad alia ut specie minora sic laboris aliquanto maioris traducebantur opera, foros in circo faciendos cloacamque maximam . . . sub terra agendam, etc. Vir. ill. 8, 3 (Tarquinius Superbus) *(foros) in circo et cloacam maximam fecit, ubi totius populi viribus usus est, unde illae fossae Quiritium sunt dictae.* Cass. Hemina fr. 15 (Serv., *Aen.* 12, 603 = H. R. Rel. 1²
p. 103 Peter) : *Cassius Emina ait, Tarquinium Superbum, cum cloacas populum facere coegisset et ob hanc iniuriam multi se suspendio necarent, iussisse corpora eorum cruci affigi.* Plin., *N.h.* XXXVI 15, 107 : *cum id opus Tarquinius Priscus plebis manibus faceret, essetque labor incertum maior an longior, passim concita nece Quiritibus taedium fugientibus, novum, inexcogitatum ante posteaque remedium invenit ille rex, ut omnium ita defunctorum corpora figeret cruci spectanda civibus simul et feris volucribusque laceranda, etc.*
    [1] A. Bartoli, Mon. ant. 45, 1961, 2 sqq. The date is furnished by a great quantity of potsherds, defined by the author as Italo-Geometric, Subgeometric and as Bucchero fine (leggero) ; the "Bucchero pesante" is completely lacking. The date given by E. Gjerstad, Early Rome 3, Lund 1960, 359 sqq., 372 sqq. (575 B.C. and thereafter), is too late ; cf. H. Riemann, GGA 214, 1960, 16 sqq.

The Etruscan kings, however, did not perform their duties in the *regia* but transferred their residence, as well as the center of public activity, to the *arx*, the fortress of the Capitoline Hill, used before only as a refuge in wartime.[1] Though we know only that it was on the citadel that the king announced to the people on the kalends and the nones the festivals and market days of every month on the citadel, this also implies that other proclamations and orders were given on the same spot.[2] The Etruscan name of one of the three gateways of this stronghold, the *porta Ratumenna*, was still known to later generations.[3] In the heart of the new city, between the Capitol and the Palatine, the retinue of the foreign ruler settled down; the name of the *vicus Tuscus* [4] preserved its memory until the end of antiquity. Also, the *Caelius mons*, a hill inside the oldest city, was regarded by the Romans as a settlement of Etruscan soldiery; [5] although this was only a vague reminiscence of times in which no written history existed, the basic truth of this notion can hardly be doubted. These same recollections gave rise to the speculations concerning the manner in which the Etruscan groups could have been joined to the Latin and Sabine elements of the citizen-body: though the notion that the tribe of the *Luceres* [6] was Etruscan has no foundation at all, the underlying belief that one-third of the population of the primeval city was Etruscan deserves attention. *Quippe cum populus Romanus Etruscos, Latinos Sabinosque sibi miscuerit et unum ex omnibus sanguinem ducat, corpus fecit ex membris et ex omnibus unus est*: [7] "The Roman people having received within itself Etruscans, Latins, and Sabines, and being of one blood drawn from them all, has made one body of the members and out of them all has become one." These are the words of a Roman writer of imperial times; the ideas underlying them are decidedly detrimental to the national pride and cannot therefore be false inventions. Furthermore, this claim is not at all extravagant: the researches of W. Schulze and Fr. Münzer long ago proved that a group of the families of the

[1] L. A. Holland, TAPA 80, 1949, 313.

[2] See for details, e.g., W. Kroll, RE 17, 1467 sqq. A. Kirsopp Michels, TAPA 80, 1949, 323 sq.

[3] Fest., p. 340 L. Plut., *Popl.* 13, 4. Plin., *N.h.* VIII 42, 161. Solin. 45, 15.

[4] The evidence is given, e.g., by K. O. Müller-W. Deecke 1, 110 sqq.

[5] Varro, *LL* 5, 46. Serv., *Aen.* 5, 560. Fest., p. 38, 26 ; 486, 12 L. Tac., *Ann.* 4, 65. CIL XIII 1668. DH II 36, 2. Cf. Liv. II 14, 9.

[6] The evidence collected by A. Schwegler, RG 1, 1853, 499 n. 6. Cf. W. Strzelecki, RE 9 A, 766 sq.

[7] Flor. II 6, 18, 1.

old Roman aristocracy is of Etruscan origin, as attested by their names. A Latin city, governed by Etruscan overlords, could well be termed a Τυρρηνὶς πόλις, an "Etruscan city," as many Greek historians called Rome.[1]

To the coordinated Etruscan planning of the city belonged the comprehensive subterranean drainage system of the Forum valley, which dried out the marshes and made possible its transformation into a civic and commercial center,[2] and further on the design of the *sacra via* crossing it.[3] Also Etruscan is the creation of the four urban regions and, with them, the four administrative districts.[4] This new topographical structure of the urbanized settlement replaced the clans, united in the three gentile tribes, which had been the basis of organization in the previous epoch. The flourishing of this new city is indicated most clearly by the remains of an impressive number of archaic Tuscan temples, even if some of them were built only in the first century of the Republic. Architectural terra-cotta reliefs, which once decorated these sanctuaries, have been found on the Velia, on the Cispius, on the Capitoline Hill, in the *comitium* and other parts of the marketplace, and in the *Forum Boarium*.[5]

We have already seen that the rule of the Tarquins ended in Rome in 505 B.C. For the beginnings of the Etruscan domination the ever-growing amount of exact archaeological observations will one day yield more specific information than can be offered at this time; the general situation is, however, reflected clearly enough by the present state of research. The importation of subgeometric Greek pottery had already begun at the end of the eighth century B.C.;[6] but the continuous influx of the fine early Etruscan *bucchero* vases, along with the products of the Italo-geometric, proto-Corinthian, Ionian, Laco-

[1] DH I 29, 2.

[2] E. Gjerstad, Early Rome 3, 1960, 292. J. Heurgon, La vie quotid. 130 sq., 165 sq. L. A. Holland, Janus and the Bridge, Rome 1961, 44 sq.

[3] E. Gjerstad, *op. cit.*, 3, 334 sq., 354 sq., 358. A. Piganiol kindly informs me that he is shortly going to publish a special investigation of the origins of the *sacra via*.

[4] L. R. Taylor, Rend. Pont. Acc. 27, 1952-54, 225 sqq. *Idem*, Vot. Distr. 71 n. 12 (lit).

[5] I. Scott, Mem. Am. Ac. 7, 1929, 95 sqq. E. Gjerstad, *op. cit.* 78 sqq., 134 sqq., 139 sq., 189, 195 sq., 201 sq., 250 sq., 256 sq., 262, 287 sq., 378 sq. Cf. also A. v. Gerkan, Rh. Mus. 100, 1957, 82 sq. M. Pallottino, Arch. cl. 12, 1960, 22.

[6] E. Paribeni, Bull. Com. 76, 1959, 4 sqq. and 21, and the following note.

nian, and Attic potters,[1] began only with the conquest of Campania, when the two main lines of communication toward the south also made these goods easily available in Latium. Simultaneously the earthenware made in Rome itself was assimilated to the Etruscan ware.[2]

We have seen that the connection of the new southern province with the Etruscan mother-country needed to be guarded by strong-points across Latium; and also that Rome was necessarily enmeshed in the network of these Etruscan military bases. When did this happen? We can approach the problem by the following considerations. The earliest Greek importations in the votive deposits of the archaic temples in the Forum Boarium are dated to the late seventh century B.C.; from ca. 600 B.C., Greek vases (as well as Etruscan ones, of course) were offered continuously to the deities worshipped here throughout the sixth century, as E. Paribeni demonstrated quite recently.[3] Consequently, the older of these temples cannot have been built later than about 600 B.C. when the continuous flow of offerings started. The building of Tuscan temples, of course, was not among the first acts of urbanization. Before that, considerable time was to elapse, from armed subjugation to the planning and realization of a "modern" city building program. Nor is it an established fact or even likely that the temples in question were the earliest ones in Rome. The *Capitolium vetus* on the Quirinal, obviously older than the temple of Jupiter on the Capitoline Hill, for example, is a more likely candidate for priority.

On the other hand, the early imported pottery reached Rome when the iron age civilization still prevailed there; if the village settlements of Villanovan type were transformed into an up-to-date city in two

---

[1] I. Scott Ryberg, An Archaeological Record of Rome from the Seventh to the Second Century B.C. (Studies and Documents ed. by K. Lake and S. Lake 13, 2), London-Philadelphia 1940, 5 sqq., 37 sqq. E. Gjerstad, Early Rome 1, 1953, Figs. 31, 57, 73, 102, and p. 148 sqq. *Ibid.* 2, Lund 1956, figs. 120, 126-27, 132-33, 139-40, 169, 188, 201, 219-21, 223, 230-32, 246-47. Cf. P. Romanelli, Gnomon 31, 1959, 434 sqq. H. Müller-Karpe, Von Anfang Roms (RM, 15. Ergänzungsheft) 1959, 14 sqq. Many reports on new excavations could be quoted ; e.g., P. Romanelli, Stud. Rom. 1, 1953, 3 sqq. B. Andreae, Arch. Anz. 1957, 127 sqq. A. Wotschitzky, Anz. f. Alt.-Wiss. 9, 1956, 193 sqq ; 10, 1957, 1 sqq. M. Pallottino, Stud. Rom. 5, 1957, 256 sqq. A. v. Gerkan, Rh. Mus. n. F. 104, 1961, 143 sq.

[2] H. Riemann, GGA 214, 1960, 16 sqq.

[3] E. Paribeni, Bull. Com. 77, 1962, 25 sqq.

generations in 600 B.C., it was an amazingly quick evolution. The question is only whether the Etruscan occupation is one generation earlier than the date of origin of the sanctuaries just discussed or must be pushed back still further, to about the middle of the seventh century B.C. The present writer does not believe that we have the means to decide this. In any case, Etruscan domination in Rome lasted not much less than one hundred fifty years. Looking back upon this epoch of foreign domination from the culmination of Roman power after the conquest of the Ancient World, it seems to be the preparation of the Latins for the great tasks of the future, something like the higher education of a child marked by Providence for a resplendent career. Certainly it left its seal on the Roman state and Roman society forever, as it did on the whole of Latium.[1]

In the memory of the Romans the name of the ruler was not only *rex*, but also *lucumo*,[2] the Etruscan name for a city-king. The Etruscan concept of *imperium*, the absolute supreme power entrusted to a person if approved by the gods, and governing in steady consultation with the divinity, was inherited by the Republic,[3] as was its symbol, the spear.[4] The Etruscan origin of the insignia and costume of the kings and republican magistrates was never forgotten in Rome.[5] Important Etruscan elements are manifest also in the organization and equipment of the army in Early Rome,[6] as well as in the calendar

[1] Cf. in general : K. O. Müller-W. Deecke, *op. cit.* G. De Sanctis, St. d. R. 1², 440 sq. R. A. L. Fell, *op. cit.* 39 sqq. R. Enking, RM 66, 1959, 65 sqq. M. Pallottino, Etruscologia³, Milano 1955. J. Heurgon, La vie quotid.

[2] The Etruscan designation for the local ruler became the personal name of the first Etruscan king in the legendary tradition. Details in e.g. : Fr. Münzer, RE 13, 1706 sq. Cf. F. Gr. Hist. 706 F 24.

[3] A. Rosenberg, Der Staat der alten Italiker, Berlin 1913, 51 sqq. E. Kornemann, Klio 14, 1915, 190 sqq. A. Momigliano, Bull. Com. 59, 1931, 42 sq. S. Mazzarino, Dalla mon. 1945, 215 sq. P. De Francisci, St. Etr. ser. 2, 24, 1955-56, 19 sqq. (with the special literature listed in n. 103-4) is certainly right in supposing that the concept of *imperium* has pre-Etruscan beginnings. H. Wagenvoort, Roman Dynamism, London 1947, has shown this. But preceding the Etruscan conquest Rome had two chieftains at the same time, as I hope to show soon ; the real monarchy is Etruscan, not Roman. Cf. also U. Coli, Regnum, Roma 1951. P. De Francisci, Primordia civitatis, Roma 1959, 361 sqq.

[4] S. Mazzarino, *op. cit.* 58 sqq., 78. A. Alföldi, AJA 63, 1959, 1 sqqq. Cf. the picture in E. Paribeni, St. Etr. 12, 1938, pl. 19, 1.

[5] Liv. I 8, 3. Flor. I 1, 5, etc. Cf. K. O. Müller-W. Deecke, 1, 341 sq. A. Alföldi, Der frührömische Reiteradel, Baden-Baden 1952.

[6] Cf. E. McCartney, Mem. Am. Ac. in Rome 1, 1917, 121. R. A. L. Fell, *op. cit.* 73 sqq., and my study quoted in the foregoing note.

The Etruscan Domination in Rome

system,[1] the method of reckoning the years,[2] and in the sphere of legal procedure.[3] Public games with the preliminary, solemn parade imitated Etruscan habits and institutions.[4] A broad stream of Etruscan influence inundated the state religion as well as private religiosity.[5] The cult of Jupiter, Juno, and Minerva, in which the state religion was focused, was an Etruscan pattern.[6] The Trojan Aeneas, venerated in some cities of Southern Etruria as their founder-hero, was identified by the Latins with their own tribal ancestor and was venerated also as such a divinity by the Romans, whose ancestral cult of the *Lares* also bears an Etruscan name.[7] Instead of multiplying examples we shall mention only that a series of Greek divinities were transmitted to Rome by Etruscan mediation, such as *Hercules-Hercle*-Herakles,[8] *Frutis*-Aphrodite,[9] and others. The intensity of this Etruscan impact is clearly perceivable in the close relationship of the Etruscan system of nomenclature to the Roman one.[10] The education of the noble youth of Rome was not Greek but Etruscan during the early Republic.[11] Etruscan inscriptions, scratched on vases, were found on the slope of the Capitol and on the Palatine,[12] demonstrating the use of this

[1] K. O. Müller-W. Deecke 2, 302. A. Kirsopp Michels, TAPA 80, 1949, 323 sqq., 331 sqq.

[2] Liv. VII 3, 5-8 ; cf. above, p. 179 n. 6. J. Heurgon reminds me of Schol. Veron., *Aen.* 10, 200 on Caecina : *constituit annum.*

[3] S. Mazzarino, Jura 12, 1961, 24 sqq.

[4] A. Piganiol, Recherches sur les jeux romains, Strasbourg-Paris 1923, 15 sqq. R. A. L. Fell, *op. cit.* 75 sqq. J. Heurgon, La vie quotid. 241 sq.

[5] For general orientation cf. C. Clemen, Die Religion der Etrusker, Bonn 1936. K. Latte, Röm. Religionsgeschichte, München 1960, 111. J. H. Waszink, Gnomon 34, 1962, 447.

[6] Serv., *Aen.* 1, 422 : .... *prudentes Etruscae disciplinae aiunt apud conditores Etruscarum urbium non putatas iustas urbes, in quibus non tres portae essent dedicatae et tot viae, et tot templa, Iovis Iunonis Minervae.* Cf. P. Ducati, Etruria antica 1, Torino 1925, 95 sqq.

[7] Cf. below, p. 250 sqq.

[8] J. Bayet, Herclé, étude critique des principaux monuments relatifs à l'Hercule étrusque, Paris 1926.

[9] R. Schilling, La religion romaine de Vénus (BEFAR 178) 1954, 76 sq.

[10] K. O. Müller-W. Deecke 1, 434 sqq. G. Herbig, Indogermanische Forschungen 26, 1909, 357 sqq. W. Schulze, ZGLEN, *passim.* E. Lattes, Klio 12, 1912, 377 sqq.

[11] Cf. above, p. 197 sqq, and Liv. IX 36, 3: *habeo auctores volgo tum Romanos pueros, sicut nunc Graecis, ita tum Etruscis litteris erudiri solitos,* to which J. Heurgon kindly called my attention, mentioned already by J. Marquardt, St. V. 3, 394 sq. Mommsen, St. R. 3, 588. *Idem*, RG 1⁷, 226. J. Heurgon, La vie quotid. 286 sq.

[12] M. Pallottino, Bull. Com. 69, 1941, 101 sqq. *Idem*, St. Etr. 22, 1952-53, 309 sqq. Arch. cl. 12, 1960, 35 sqq.

language in archaic Rome. Etruscan art and architecture prevailed in Rome in the sixth century B.C. and also under the early Republic, along with Etruscan engineering and techniques.[1]

We have also seen that the Etruscans understood perfectly how to assimilate alien peoples without stripping them of their original character.[2] At the same time that Etruscans living in Rome were writing in their own idiom, the indigenous population here was already writing in its own letters—the Latin alphabet developed from a Greek prototype by Etruscan mediation—and in their own tongue. The playful contents of the lines scratched on the so-called Duenos vase [3] and the solemn prescriptions of the Forum cippus (so-called *lapis niger*) [4] both illustrate this. The dawn of history after the end of the Etruscan rule reveals a development bearing on this view: the individuality of the Roman state and its people was not suppressed by Etruscan domination but, on the contrary, it advanced with a new impetus, a new vigor, in which we may see the beneficent effect of Etruscan patronage.

❧

ETRUSCAN POWERS STRUGGLING FOR THE POSSESSION OF ROME[5]

We have already observed that the wares descending from Central Etruria on the Tiber did not reach, but skirted Rome on their way to Capua; on the other hand Rome was ideally situated to become the main transshipping and reloading point toward the south for coastral southern Etruria. The consequences of this constellation were economic as well as political. "The commercial relationship [of Rome] with

---

[1] Cf., e.g., A. Boëthius, The Golden House of Nero, Ann Arbor 1960, 10 sqq. L. Shoe in her forthcoming volume on the moldings. F. Schachermeyr, RE 4A, 2359 sq.

[2] Cf. K. O. Müller-W. Deecke 1, 102 sqq., 106 sq. H. Hencken, Ciba-Symposium 44 (for early Etruscan antecedents).

[3] A. Degrassi, ILLRP 2. E. Gjerstad, Early Rome 3, 1960, 161 sqq. *Idem*, Septentrionalia et Orientalia (Studia B. Karlgren dedicata, K. Vitt. Hist. och Ant. Ak. Handl., Del 91) 1960, 133 sqq. (with previous literature).

[4] A. Degrassi, ILLRP 3. Cf. G. Carettoni, JRS 50, 1960, 195 sqq. G. Dumézil, R. Et. Lat. 36, 1958, 109 sqq.

[5] Cf. for general information the useful survey of F. Schachermeyr, RE 4A, 2348 sqq.

Etruria," writes Inez Scott Ryberg,[1] "which is attested by archaeological evidence is limited for the most part to a small area, including only the southernmost neck of Etruria, between the Faliscan region and the sea. Study of Etruscan finds shows that the sites in this southern section form a closely interrelated group, while the material from the rest of Etruria is quite different in character. This relatively small cultural circle, of which Caere and Tarquinii were the chief centers, extends northward to include Pitigliano, Vulci and Marsiliana. On its eastern fringe the Faliscan district might be called an outpost, always maintaining its native character, even though affected by close contact and a lively trade with southern Etruscan centers. Veii forms a kind of bridge between Etruscan and Faliscan sites, more Etruscanized than the latter but definitely more Italic than Caere and Tarquinii. Rome was an outpost rather of the Etruscanized Faliscan culture than of the Etruscan circle. At the same time Rome maintained some relationship with the more distant centers of Etruria. A number of bronzes, as has been noted, bear witness to trade with Vetulonia. Vetulonia may also have been the source of amber objects found in Rome . . ."

This overall picture emerging from the statistical analysis of the finds can be verified and differentiated by historical data. These data prove once more that Rome was depending politically on Etruscan powers in the very region from which she imported wares. Moreover, they demonstrate that Etruscan Rome was not permitted to grow and prosper in a stable and continuous political evolution, but was upset again and again by violent convulsions when a city of Southern Etruria other than that ruling her took control. This state of affairs did not escape the attention of some distinguished historians,[2] but —so far as I can see—no one followed up its consequences, which are of decisive importance. First of all, the dependence of Rome on a series of Etruscan powers, supplanting each other in every generation, leaves no room for the sovereign Rome of the annalists, already ruling over the neighboring peoples and expanding her sway even over the same Etruscans who subjugated her.

The historical reality of Etruscan supremacy over Rome and the

---

[1] I. Scott Ryberg, An Archeological Record of Rome, 46 sqq.
[2] Cf., e.g., G. De Sanctis, St. d. R. 1², 437. I. G. Scott, Mem. Am. Ac. 7, 1929, 78 sqq. L. Homo, L'Italie primitive 140. J. Heurgon, Rech. 68 sq. *Idem*, La vie quotid. 316 sqq. L. Pareti, La tomba Regolini-Galassi 57.

ETRUSCAN RULE IN LATIUM AND ROME

annalist fiction of a Rome at the same time victorious in every direction are mutually exclusive. The obvious contradiction was obscured by the supposition that the invaders of Rome, wrenching this important crossroad from each other in turn, were not the Etruscan states from which they came but self-supporting leaders with their private armies, like the *condottieri* of the Renaissance who made politics on their own account: thus their Etruscan origin would not hinder them in pursuing their own imperial aims as independent Roman monarchs.

There was indeed one instance, and one only—we shall enlarge upon it later—which came near to this notion: three leading men of Vulci, allied with others from other Etruscan states, when prohibited by their political opponents from returning to their home city, succeeded in killing the previous Etruscan king of Rome along with his chief allies and took over his realm. Yet all the other cases are different: not individual adventurers [1] but Etruscan states took hold of Rome so as to extend their sway or to secure the free passage toward the south: Tarquinii and Caere, Veii and Clusium. Besides these separate states, however, the sovereign Etruscan League also was represented in Rome by means of two cults, both referring to the same divinity.

The divine patron of the Etruscan League under whose auspices the federal assembly held its meetings outside of Volsinii [2] was *Voltumna*, an otherwise not usual designation for the supreme god *Tinś*.[3] *Voltumna* was also worshipped in Rome, where the Latin tongue transformed his name to *Vortumnus* or *Vertumnus*.[4] His statue, appa-

---

[1] The impression that individual leaders and not states conquered Rome may have been enhanced by the old epic style of the glorification of great warriors, in which the role of the armies completely vanishes and the valiant deeds of princely figures are exalted. This style is reflected on the single combat scenes of the "tomba François" (here pl. VIII-XII) and on the Late Republican *denarii* (H. A. Grueber, Coins of the Roman Republic in the British Museum, London 1910, pl. 30, 4-5 ; 32, 4 ; 56, 1-2) or in the narrative of Livy (II 6, 7-9 ; 20, 8-9, etc.) ; it governs also the new elogia of Tarquinia (P. Romanelli, N. Sc. 1948, 260 sqq.).

[2] R. Bloch, Mél. 59, 1947, 9 sqq ; 62, 1950, 53 sq.

[3] Cf. W. Eisenhut, RE 9A, 852 sqq. ; cf. *ibid.* 8A, 1669 sqq.

[4] W. Schulze, ZGLN 252, 272. G. Wissowa, RuK², 1912, 287 sqq. G. Herbig, Mitt. d. Schles. Ges. f. Volkskunde 23, 1922, 13 sqq. A. Ernout-A. Meillet, Dict. etymol. ³ 1951, 1285. J. Carcopino, Virgile et les origines d'Ostie (BEFAR 116) 1919, 117 sq. L. R. Taylor, Local Cults in Etruria, Roma 1923. R. Pettazzoni, SMSR 4, 1928, 207 sqq. F. Altheim, Griechische Götter im alten Rom (RVV 22, 1) 1930, 8 sqq., 159. A. E. Gordon, TAPA 63, 1932, 187. J. Heurgon, R. Et. Lat. 14, 1936, 109 sqq. G. Devoto, St. Etr.

rently protected by a little *aedicula*,[1] stood at the corner of the "Etruscan quarter" (*vicus Tuscus*), where it met the *Sacra via*,—i.e., in the Forum Romanum beside the Temple of Castor. This location in the very heart of the city demonstrates in itself that the god must have arrived before the Republic, when foreign divinities were excluded from the territory of the city proper. There are also other reasons, however, which have already convinced most scholars that the reception of *Voltumna* occurred in the time of the Etruscan kings.[2]

The identity of *Vortumnus* with the supreme god of the Etruscan confederacy cannot be doubted. Varro characterizes *Vortumnus* as *deus Etruriae princeps*,[3] and Propertius [4] not only informs us that he came from Etruria, but also that his original home city was Volsinii, putting in the mouth of the god the words *Tuscus ego et Tuscis orior, nec paenitet inter proelia Volsinios deseruisse focos*. In Etruria *Voltumna* had no other function than to watch over the national assembly outside Volsinii.[5]

The setting of the statue of *Vortumnus* and the lack of an official character of his worship make it almost certain that the god was transplanted to Rome by the Etruscans settled in the *vicus Tuscus*. The Romans themselves did not even realize or care about the fact that he was the same divinity previously adopted by their state under the slightly different but evidently identical name *Volturnus*.[6]

Volturnus had a *flamen*, a state-priest in Rome, as did the supreme ruler of heaven and the two divine protectors of the pre-Etruscan double community, *Juppiter*, *Mars*, *Quirinus*, and as did a series of divinities—*diva Palatua*, *Furrina*, *Falacer pater*, for example—which

14, 1940, 275. J. Heurgon, Rech. 1942, 71 sqq. Y. Basanoff, Rev. d'hist. des rel. 126, 1943, 5 sqq. J. Heurgon, St. Etr. 2. ser. 24, 1955-56, 103. G. Campo-reale, La parola del passato 13, 1958, 5. K. Latte. Röm. Religionsgesch. 1960, 191 n. 3. A. J. Pfiffig, Gymnasium 68, 1961, 55 sq.

[1] Porphyrio's commentary to Hor., *Epist.* I 20, 1, mentions the *sacellum* of Volturnus which suggests such a chapel. Cic., *Verr.* II 1, 154, and Liv. XLIV 16, 10, have *signum Vertumni* (cf. Prop. IV 2, 2 *Vertumni signa paterna dei* in poetic plural, as W. Eisenhut, RE 8A, 1671, explains it).

[2] The temple of *Vertumnus* on the Aventine, outside the *pomerium* can well be a later importation, after the conquest of Volsinii by the Romans. Cf. CIL I² p. 325. Fest., p. 228, 21 L.

[3] Varro, *LL* 5, 46 ; repeated by Serv., *Aen.* 5, 560.

[4] Propert. IV 2, 3 sq.

[5] Liv. IV 23, 5 ; 25, 7 ; 61, 2. V 17, 6. VI 2, 2.

[6] References to ancient sources and modern discussions are collected by W. Eisenhut, RE 9A, 849 sqq.

were obsolete relics of early Rome in historical times.[1] The day of his annual festival (August 25) was included in the oldest cycle of Roman festivities, conceived in the Etruscan epoch.[2] It was a renowned French scholar, J. Heurgon,[3] who revealed the historical background of the identity of this god with the river-god of Capua and the Etruscan name of the same city, capital of the new dodecapolis in the south: *Volturnum*. If the federal god *Volturnus*—a river-god and also a universal cosmic being, as was the Latin *Indiges* discussed below —was brought to Rome when Capua was founded, as J. Heurgon supposed and as, following in his footsteps, the present writer assumes, then his cult reflects the authority of the Etruscan League in the seventh century on that new crossroad of Etruscan long-distance traffic in Latium, which some hundred years later became the Queen of the Mediterranean World.[4]

༜

THE ETRUSCAN STATES WHICH, IN SUCCESSION, DOMINATED ROME

The cities which extended their sway over Rome were the following:

Tarquinii (?)

The Roman Annals knew two kings called *Tarquinii*, as everyone

[1] Enn., *Ann.* 122 sqq. Vahlen[3]. Varro, *LL* 7, 45 ; cf. 6, 21. Paul. Fest., 519 L.

[2] Mommsen, CIL I[2] pp. 240, 298, 327. A. Degrassi, Inscr. It. XIII 1, 318. Cf. W. Schulze, ZGLEN 260. G. Wissowa, RuK[2] 224 sq. G. Herbig, Philol. 84, 1917, 450 sq. M. Pallottino, Elementi di lingua Etrusca, Firenze 1936, 104. K. Latte, Röm. Religionsgesch. 1960, 37 n. 5, 137, 148. Cf. above p. 204 n. 4, and the following note.

[3] J. Heurgon, R. Et. Lat. 14, 1936, 109 sqq. *Idem*, Rech. 71 sq., where he summarizes the results of his research in the following words : "Or justement, un lien tenu nous invite à chercher aux environs de Clusium et de Volsinii, en même temps qu'à Vulci, l'une des bases de départ de l'expédition, qui devait soumettre la Campanie aux Étrusques. Ce n'est pas que, pour ressaisir le détail des événements, nous soyons singulièrement démunis. Il y a toutefois un fait certain : c'est que Rome a été une étape dans la marche en avant des conquérants. La preuve en est dans l'existence à Rome et à Capoue d'un dieu Volturnus qui sous ce nom du moins est inconnu ailleurs ; dieu universel, mais qui, en tant que dieu fluvial, valut au Tibre un de ses noms passagers et au Volturne son nom durable. Ce culte commun, antérieur à toute influence religieuse de la Campanie sur Latium, et qui par conséquent remonte à l'époque de l'hégémonie étrusque, semble bien démontrer qu'il y a eu anciennement entre les deux villes des relations religieuses, qui ne peuvent s'expliquer qu'en

knows. But it was recognized long ago that the written source from which the narrative of the acts of these two rulers was drawn reported only the deeds of the last king. And we shall see below that it was Fabius Pictor who copied this story and divided the achievements of the last ruler between the two.[1] The source in question used by Pictor was presumably nothing else than the introduction to the consular lists, compiled by some pontiff not earlier than the early third century. Besides this, the paintings of a tomb in Vulci (pl. VIII-XII), to which we shall return shortly, have preserved for us the reference to a Roman king, *Cneve Tarchu[nies]*, who was another member of the same Etruscan clan, not the last monarch. This independent evidence establishes the historicity of this dynasty, which may have given more than two sovereigns to Rome.

The family name of these kings, *Tarchna* in Etruscan, *Tarquinius* or *Tarquitius* in Latin, occurs rather frequently in Southern Etruria.[2] It could be due to mere chance that the most ample documentation for this name has been preserved for us in Caere; nothing prevents us, therefore, from accepting the Roman tradition, according to which the first king of this house was a native of Tarquinia. On the other hand, the ascendancy of other Etruscan states over Rome, discussed below, leaves no room for the capture of Rome by Tarquinii, except in the earliest phase of the Etruscan expansion toward the south. And indeed, in those early days Tarquinii was the leading Etruscan power. The Etruscans themselves believed that it was their earliest center in Italy, founded by the hero-ancestor of the nation, by *Tarchon* himself; the archaeological evidence confirms the importance and the splendor of Tarquinii in those early days.[3] The newly discovered laudatory inscriptions, *elogia*, from Tarquinii commemorating the heroic exploits of the ancestors [4] attest that the great past

admettant p.ex. qu'elles ont eu un certain temps les mêmes maîtres ou que les fondateurs de Capoue se sont arrêtés à Rome avant de pousser plus loin."

[4] The geographical situation of Volsinii is so central that she came to be the seat of the League even before she reached a real prominence among the Twelve States.

[1] For details see A. Schwegler, RG 1, 1853, 668 sqq. F. Schachermeyr, RE 4A, 2348 sqq., 2375 sq. and p. 222 sqq. below.

[2] Cf. the data, e.g., in W. Schulze, ZGLEN 95 sqq. F. Schachermeyr, RE 4A, 2348 sqq., 2372 sq. R. A. L. Fell, *op. cit.* 46 n. 4.

[3] Cf. K. O. Müller-W. Deecke 1, 67 sqq., 112 sqq., 470 sq., 494 sqq. G. Dennis, The Cities and Cemeteries of Etruria 1³, London 1883, 301 sqq. M. Pallottino, Etruscologia⁵, Milano 1963, 177 sqq.

[4] P. Romanelli, N. Sc. 1948, 260 sqq. J. Heurgon, Mél. 63, 1951, 119 sqq.

ETRUSCAN RULE IN LATIUM AND ROME

of this state was not obliterated even in Roman imperial times.

One of these unfortunately fragmentary inscriptions may speak of the conquest of nine Latin cities by a king or magistrate of Tarquinii, if the complement of a mutilated word, proposed as an alternative solution by M. Pallottino [1] and accepted by J. Heurgon,[2] is correct —and the present writer is inclined to believe that it is. The partial restoration of this *elogium*, registrating victories of a Tarquinian king or general born in an Etruscan city of less importance (Orclanum?), over the great rival of Tarquinii, Caere, as well as over Arretium, would run in this case:

> (praenomen)]*s* *S*[(nomen) . . . *ur*
> (affiliation)] *Orgol*[ani]*ensis*
> C]*aeritum regem vi*[cit
> A]*rretium bello* [. .
> de La]*tinis novem o*[ppida (?)
> cepit]

One more letter would relieve us of all uncertainty! In any case, the odds are not unfavorable for the supposition that Tarquinii was in fact the original home of a royal house governing in Rome. The rule of this dynasty was twice interrupted, so far as we know: once around the middle of the sixth century by a Vulcentan army, and again by Porsenna in 505 B.C. It can be assumed with some confidence that the Vulcentans were displaced in 524 B.C., when a powerful Etruscan army, advancing on Cyme, passed through Rome on its way to the south.[3] The reestablishment of the Tarquinii in 524 could not have happened without the consent of Veii, then at the height of her prosperity and vitally interested in the control of this region for the free passage of her imports and exports on water and on land. This also meant that the Tarquins no longer depended on their original home city but on their immediate neighbor to the

---

Idem, La vie quotid. 314 sqq. M. Pallottino, St. Etr. 21, 1950-51, 147 sqq. E. Vetter, Glotta 34, 1954-55, 59 sqq. F. Della Corte, St. Etr. 24, 1955, 73 sqq.

[1] M. Pallottino, St. Etr. 21, 1950-51, 164 sqq. (= P. Romanelli, N. Sc. 1948, 266 n. 77.) Cf. J. Heurgon, La vie quotid. 120.

[2] J. Heurgon pointed out (La vie quotid. 316) that the mentioning of *Arretium* in line 4 precludes the repetition of this city-name in line 5 ; in this way the restoration of the latter designation to *Latinis* becomes very likely.

[3] Cf. above, p. 47 sqq. The participation of the Umbrians and of the Daunians (DH VII 3, 1) points to the fact that the enterprise was one of the Etruscan League, and not that of some Etruscan cities.

Etruscan Domination over Rome

north. They must by then have coalesced with the local aristocracy so as to have a party on which to rely. If they came indeed from Tarquinii in the seventh century, as we believe, they must have given more than one king to the Romans before *Cneve Tarchu[nies]-Cnaeus Tarquinius* was superseded by the Vulcentan group of warriors.

Caere

Cato the Elder preserves for us the priceless memory of a historical fact in his account of the vintage-festival of the Latins; [1] namely,

[1] Cato, *Orig.* fr. 12 (H. R. Rel. 1², 59 Peter = Macrob. Sat. III 5, 10): *Veram huius contumacissimi hominis* (sc. contemptoris divom Mezentii) *causam in primo libro originum Catonis diligens lector inveniet. ait enim Mezentium Rutulis imperasse, ut sibi offerrent quas dis primitias offerebant, et Latinos omnes similis imperii metu ita vovisse :* 'Iuppiter, si tibi magis cordi est nos ea tibi dare potius quam Mezentio, uti nos victores facias.' Other excerpts of Cato vary in details. Verr. Flacc., *Fasti Praen.* (CIL I² p. 236, 316) to April 23 : *(Vini omnis novi libamentum Iovi) consecratum (est cum Latini bello premere)ntur ab Rutulis, quia Mezentius rex Etrus(co)rum paciscebatur, si subsidio venisset, omnium annorum vini fructum.* Fest., p. 322, 14 L. : *Rustica vinalia appellantur mense Augusto XIIII Kal. Sept. Iovis dies festus, quia Latini bellum gerentes adversus Mezentium, omnis vini libationem ei deo dedicaverunt.* Varro, in Plin., *N.h.* XIV 12, 88 : *M. Varro auctor est Mezentium Etruriae regem auxilium Rutulis contra Latinos tulisse vini mercede quod tum in Latino agro fuisset.* Plut., *Quaest. Rom.* 45 : "Διὰ τί τῶν Οὐιναλίων τῇ ἑορτῇ πολὺν οἶνον ἐκχέουσιν ἐκ τοῦ ἱεροῦ τῆς ᾿Αφροδίτης" ; Πότερον, ὡς οἱ πλεῖστοι λέγουσι, Μεζέντιος ὁ Τυρρηνῶν στρατηγὸς ἔπεμψε πρὸς Αἰνείαν σπενδόμενος ἐπὶ τῷ λαβεῖν τὸν ἐπέτειον οἶνον ; ἀρνησαμένου δ'ἐκείνου, τοῖς Τυρρηνοῖς ὑπέσχετο κρατήσας μάχῃ δώσειν τὸν οἶνον. Αἰνείας δὲ τὴν ὑπόσχεσιν αὐτοῦ πυθόμενος τοῖς θεοῖς τὸν οἶνον καθιέρωσε, καὶ μετὰ τὸ νικῆσαι συναγαγὼν τὸ καρπευθὲν ἐξέχεε πρὸ τοῦ ἱεροῦ τῆς ᾿Αφροδίτης. Ovid., *Fast.* 4, 877-895 : *cur igitur Veneris festum Vinalia dicant, quaeritis, et quare sit Iovis ista dies? Turnus quo Aeneas Latiae gener esset Amatae, bellum erat : Etruscus Turnus adoptat opes. clarus erat sumptisque ferox Mezentius armis .... quem Rutuli Turnusque suis adsciscere temptant partibus ; haec contra dux ita Tuscus ait : .... qui petis auxilium, non grandia, divide mecum praemia, de lacubus proxima musta tuis !...'adnuerant Rutuli, Mezentius induit arma ; induit Aeneas adloquiturque Iovem :* 'hostica Tyrrheno vota est vindemia regi ; Iuppiter, e Latio palmite musta feres !' *vota valent meliora ; cadit Mezentius ingens, etc.* DH I 65, 1-5 : Αἰνείου δ'ἐξ ἀνθρώπων μεταστάντος .... παρέλαβε τὴν Λατίνων ἡγεμονίαν ὁ ...... ᾿Ασκάνιος ... τοῦ δὲ βασιλέως τῶν Τυρρηνῶν τά τε ἄλλα ὡς δεδουλωμένοις ἀφόρητα ἐπιτάσσοντος καὶ τὸν οἶνον ὅσον ἂν ἡ Λατίνων γῆ φέρῃ Τυρρηνοῖς ἀπάγειν ἀνὰ πᾶν ἔτος, οὐκ ἀνασχετὸν ἡγησάμενοι τὸ πρᾶγμα τῆς μὲν ἀμπέλου τὸν καρπὸν ἱερὸν ἐψηφίσαντο τοῦ Διὸς εἶναι γνώμην ἀγορεύσαντος ᾿Ασκανίου, αὐτοὶ δὲ ... ἐξῆλθον ἐκ τῆς πόλεως ... καὶ αἱροῦσιν εὐπετῶς τὸ ὀχύρωμα ... Μεσέντιος δὲ .. ἀπῆλθεν ὑπόσπονδος ... καὶ .. πρὸς τοὺς Λατίνους βέβαιος φίλος ἦν. The same version in *Origo gentis Rom.* 15, 1-4 with the addition : *ut docet Lucius Caesar libro primo, itemque Aulus Postumius in eo volumine, quod de adventu Aeneae conscripsit atque edidit.* The struggle of Aeneas and the Latins with Mezentius, king of Caere is also mentioned by Cato, *Orig.* fr. 9 (Serv., *Aen.* 1, 267). fr. 10 (Serv., *Aen.* 4, 620). fr. 11 (Serv., *Aen.* 6, 760 ; cf. Serv., *Aen.* 9, 742.). He is the ultimate

ETRUSCAN RULE IN LATIUM AND ROME

the King of Caere, Mezentius, in the legendary tale Cato reports, is said to have imposed on the Latins the humiliating obligation to deliver to him each year the wine they produced. Cato, though quarrelsome and opinionated, was animated by an affectionate love for his native Latin countryside and he perpetuated its past with tender care in his *Origines*. The popular traditions and antiquarian data recorded in his writings deserve our full confidence, except if he uses Fabius Pictor or another distorting author of the same sort. This story, certainly reflecting Etruscan domination in Latium, unfavorable to national pride, embarrassing for the tendentious misrepresentation of early Latin history in the Annals, is above suspicion. The setting of the story is sixth-century Latium. The neighbors of Lavinium, where it is staged, are the Rutuli of Ardea, whose king not by chance is called Turnus, i.e., Tyrrhenus, "the Etruscan"; the ruler of Privernum, Metabus, is also Etruscan.[1] The story, motivating the offerings of the new wine to Juppiter and Venus,[2] concerns the whole of Latium, comprising, naturally, Rome. But there also exists another variant of this legendary tale, which gives the reasons for the tithe consecrated to Hercules at the *ara maxima* in Rome,[3] recalling the tithe paid to the Etruscans by the Latins.

Such tributes in kind were the basis of the taxation in the Persian Empire;[4] Carthage imposed a tithe on natural products upon her subjects in Libya as well as in Sicily;[5] the Messenians were constrained

source of Liv. I 2, 3 ; 3, 4. Fest., p. 212 15 L. *Origo gentis Rom.* 14, 1-2 Schol. Veron., *Aen.* 7, 485. Iustin., *Epit.* XLIII 1, 12-13. Verg., *Aen.* 8, 1 sqq. 478 sqq. App., *Basil.* 1, 2. Tzetz., ad Lycophr. 1232. Cf. A. Schwegler, RG 1, 288. 329 sqq. K. O. Müller-W. Deecke 1, 343. J. Carcopino, D.-S. 5, 893 sq. M. Sordi, I rapporti romano-ceriti e l'origine della civitas sine suffragio, Roma 1960, 13, has some good remarks on the version of Vergil on Mezentius ; but the connection of Mezentius with Caere (and not with Veii) cannot be interpreted away, nor can the date of origin for this tradition be lowered from the sixth century to the fourth.

[1] Verg., *Aen.* 11, 539 sqq. Serv., *Aen.* 11, 567.

[2] Cf. for a detailed discussion : G. Wissowa, RuK², 289. F. Bömer, Rh. Mus. n. F. 90, 1941, 30 sqq. R. Schilling, La religion romaine de Vénus (BEFAR 178) 1954, 100 sqq., 137 sq. G. Dumézil, Latomus 20, 1961, 524 sqq. *Idem*, R. Et. Lat. 39, 1961, 261 sqq. K. Latte, Römische Religionsgeschichte, München 1960, 74 sqq.

[3] Plut., *Quaest. Rom.* 18 : Διὰ τί τῷ Ἡρακλεῖ πολλοὶ τῶν πλουσίων ἐδεκάτευον τὰς οὐσίας ; Πότερον ὅτι . . . Ῥωμαίους ὑπὸ Τυῤῥηνῶν δεκατευομένους ἀπήλλαξεν.

[4] Ps.-Aristot., Oecon. VI 1, 4 (1345 b 31 sqq.).

[5] Cf., e.g., W. Ensslin, Rom und Karthago, Leipzig 1943, 266 sq. K. F. Stroheker, Dionysios I., Wiesbaden 1958, 166 (with details).

to deliver up a great part of their crop to the Spartans: in short, before the general diffusion of currency, we find this system of exploiting subject peoples everywhere. The natives of Corsica were obliged to furnish to their Etruscan overlords resin, wax, and honey;[1] the Latins certainly had to deliver to them other products besides shipmasts and wine.

Around the middle of the sixth century B.C., when Carthage and Etruria succeeded in stopping the colonial expansion of the Greeks in their spheres of interest, and the Etruscan supremacy in Italy was considerably strengthened,[2] Caere was playing a considerable role in these developments; her supremacy in Latium must be connected in all likelihood with this culmination of her power. In the great naval battle at Alalia at the coast of Corsica, the Caeretane fleet bore the brunt of the fight with Carthage against the Phocaeans;[3] but at the same time Caere was in close commercial contact with other Greek states. She had a treasure-house of her own in Delphi, and if the Greek writers sometimes exempt her from the wholesale condemnation of the rest of the Etruscans for their reckless piracy and barbarous cruelty,[4] this is not because they were more humane and less given to piracy, but only because of those rewarding business relations. The main harbor of Caere was known abroad under its Greek name of *Pyrgi*; for the Carthaginians, however, she had another anchorage, *Punicum*.[5] The unceasing influx of Greek pottery into Latium arrived, no doubt, mainly via Caere,[6] along with intellectual imports from the Graeco-Etruscan civilization, the traces of which, of course, are not as conveniently and exactly ascertainable as are the potsherds.[7]

[1] Diod. V 13, 4.

[2] G. De Sanctis, St. d. R. I², 327 sq. T. J. Dunbabin, The Western Greeks, Oxford 1948, 342 sqq. J. Bérard, La colonisation grecque de l'Italie méridionale², 1957, 67, 222.

[3] Herod. 1, 166 sqq. Thucyd. I 13, 5. Cf. H. Meltzer, Geschichte der Karthager 1, Berlin 1879, 170 sqq.

[4] Strab. V 2, 3 (p. 220 C.). Serv., *Aen.* 10, 184.

[5] L. Pareti, in : Idea 1950, no. 6, 4.

[6] Cf. L. Pareti, La tomba Regolini-Galassi, Roma 1947, 5 sqq., 24 sq., 39 sq., 48 sq., 52 sqq. B. Schweitzer, RM 62, 1955, 95 sqq. O. W. v. Vacano, Die Etrusker, Hamburg 1957, 120. M. Pallottino, Etruscologia³, Milano 1955, 102 sqq., 136 sq., 145 sq. M. Guarducci, Archeologia classica 4, 1952, 241 sqq. A. Andrén, Rend. Pont. Acc. 32, 1960, 41 etc.

[7] Solin. 2, 7, mixes up Pelasgians and Etruscans: *Agyllam* (sc. nominatam esse) *a Pelasgis, qui primi in Latium litteras intulerunt.*

Fregenae, ten miles north of Ostia on the coast, still belonged to the Caeretanes in imperial times. If Caere's territory, in the East, did not extend to the Tiber, it would seem to be the consequence of the growth of the Veientan power, which drove a vertical wedge west of the lowest reaches of the Tiber between Rome and the district of Caere. But this was a subsequent development to which we shall return later.

Vulci

The source material on the Vulcentane occupation of Rome is well known. It has been discussed many times.[1] But a tiny piece of this evidence has been overlooked—a small detail which proves to be of crucial importance. The entire picture changes by complementing our information with it.

The learned Emperor Claudius, pleading in his speech to the Senate for the admission of the Gallic aristocracy to the public dignities of the Roman state, brought forward examples from the past to show that such a liberal concession was in accord with ancestral usage. One of the proofs he used [2]—others had already adduced some examples long before him [3]—was the amazing career of one of the Roman

---

[1] K. O. Müller-W. Deecke 1, 110 sqq. A. Schwegler, RG 1, 506 sqq., 511 sqq., 718 sqq. M. Zoeller, Latium und Rom, Leipzig 1878, 173 sq. V. Gardthausen, Mastarna oder Servius Tullius, Leipzig 1882. G. Körte, JdI 12, 1897 (1898) 57 sqq., 69 sqq. E. Petersen, JdI 13, 1899, 128. F. Münzer, Rh. Mus. 53, 1898, 607 sqq. G. De Sanctis, Klio 2, 1902, 96 sqq. O. Gilbert, Topographie der Stadt Rom, Leipzig, 1886, 39 sqq., 264 sqq. E. Pais, St. crit. 1, Roma 1913, 511. F. Messerschmidt, Nekropolen von Vulci (JdI Ergänzungsheft 12) 1930. *Idem*, Die Antike 4, 1928, 103 and JdI 45, 1930, 62. I. G. Scott, Mem. Am. Ac. 7, 1929, 75 sqq. L. Pareti, St. Etr. 5, 1931, 147 sqq. A. Momigliano, L'opera dell'imperatore Claudio, Firenze 1932, 30 sqq. M. Pallottino, St. Etr. 13, 1939, 456 sqq. S. Mazzarino, Dalla mon., 184 sqq. J. Heurgon, Rech. 68. J. Gagé, Huit recherches sur les origines italiques et romaines, Paris 1950, 135 sqq. F. Altheim, RG 2, Frankfurt 1953, 109 sq. F. Schachermeyr, RE 4A, 2362. J. Bayet, Tite-Live 5, Paris 1954, 126 sqq. G. Giannelli, La repubblica romana² 1955, 49. E. St. Staveley, Historia 5, 1956, 101 sqq. P. De Francisci, Primordia civitatis, Roma 1959, 639. G. Radke, RE 8A, 2454 sqq., etc.

[2] *Orat. Claud.* (CIL XIII 1668 = ILS 212) 1, 17 sqq.: *Huic* (sc. Tarquinio Prisco) *quoque et filio nepotique eius (nam et hoc inter auctores discrepat) insertus Servius Tullius, si nostros sequimur, captiva natus Ocresiá, si Tuscos, Caeli quondam Vivennae sodalis fidelissimus omnisque eius casus comes, postquam variá fortuna exáctus cum omnibus reliquís Caeliáni exercitus Etruria excessit, montem Caelium occupavit et a duce suo Caelio ita appellita(vit), mutatóque nomine (nam Tusce Mastarna ei nomen erat) ita appellatus est, ut dixi, et regnum summa cum rei p. útilitate optinuit.*

[3] Cf. Liv. IV 3, 12, in a corresponding context: *Servium Tullium . . ., captiva Corniculana natum, patre nullo, matre serva, ingenio virtute regnum tenuisse.*

kings, described as follows: "Servius Tullius became king between Tarquinius Priscus and his son or grandson (our authorities differ in this point). If we listen to our own writers, he was the son of Ocresia, a prisoner-of-war; if we give credit to the Etruscans, he was once the most faithful companion of Caelius Vivenna, and shared with him everything his fate involved. When good fortune deserted him, he withdrew from Etruria with all the remnants of the army of Caelius. He occupied the Caelian Hill [in Rome], giving to it the name of his former commander. Henceforth he changed his own name to Servius Tullius, for his Etruscan name was Mastarna, and ascended the throne to the greatest benefit of our State."

The two traditions concerning the good old king, the irreconcilable differences of which are well pointed out by the statement of Emperor Claudius, can be verified rather well in the rest of our tradition. The old myth of the miraculous birth of the future king by a slave woman who conceived by a spark jumping forth from the royal hearth, which belonged to the Roman version, occurs many times in ancient literature; [1] the Etruscan version in which the king is an alien also left behind all kinds of traces, surveyed below.

No one doubts that the equation of the venerable old king of the Roman legend with the Etruscan intruder is an arbitrary contamination. The question is only who created this confusion and for what purpose? Modern scholars attribute the mischief generally to wilfulness on the part of Claudius who, as some thought, wished to flatter the Etruscan pride of one of his wives.[2] This assumption is easily shown to be mistaken. The seriousness and honesty of this monarch, who unquestionably collected a treasure of priceless information in the twenty books of his Etruscan history,[3] should have deterred anyone from imputing such falsifications to him.

[1] Cic., *De re p.* II 21, 37. DH IV 1, 2 sqq. Liv. I 39, 1 sqq. Ovid., *Fast.* 6, 627 sqq. Fest., pp. 182. 460. 467 L. (Cf. Justin., *Epit.* XXXVIII 6, 7). Plin., *N.h.* XXXVI 27, 204. *Oratio Claudii, l.c.* (above, p. 212 n. 2). Plut., *De fort. Rom.* 10. *Id., Quaest. Rom.* 100. Serv., *Aen.* 2, 683. *Vir. ill.* 7, 1. Zon. 7, 9.

[2] Cf. e.g.: A. Schwegler, RG 1, 720. Mommsen, RG 1⁸, 122. G. De Sanctis, Klio 2, 1902, 100 sqq. Pl. Fraccaro, La storia romana arcaica, Milano 1952, 22. A. Momigliano, Secondo contributo alla storia degli studi classici, Roma 1960, 86 sq. (with additional bibliography). *Idem*, Riv. stor. Ital. 73, 1961, 803, etc.

[3] Suet., *Claud.* 42. Cf. B. G. Niebuhr, RG I², Berlin 1827, 13 sqq. A. Schwegler, RG 1, 719 sqq. J. Heurgon, CRAI 1953, 92 sqq. Cp. A. Momigliano, Claudius, the Emperor and his Achievement, New York 1961, 12 sqq.

ETRUSCAN RULE IN LATIUM AND ROME

There is no lack of other gratuitous hypotheses. One of them was made by a prudent and sober scholar of whom nobody would expect lighthearted guesses; his authority induced many others to follow his lead. His imputation is that Mastarna of Vulci is no one else but Porsenna of Clusium! [1] The evidence set out below suffices in itself to refute this absurd whim without further discussion. The other attempt to explain away the identification of Servius Tullius with Mastarna is at least founded on an ingenious linguistic combination. G. Herbig and P. Cortsen [2] conjectured, and they were followed by illustrious scholars, that the word *Macstarna* contained the root of the Latin word *magister* with the Etruscan suffix *-ar]na*. Consequently *Macstarna* would not be a personal name at all but the technical designation of a supposedly new, temperate and democratic form of the kingship—it would be nothing other than the *magister populi*, as the dictator was termed under the early Republic. But the person in question appears identified by the appended inscription as *Macstrna* on a wall painting from about 300 B.C. (pl. VIII) in Vulci, as a Vulcentane hero, not as a Roman king; as an individual with his proper name, and not as a magistrate without his personal name. Like the names of his comrades and enemies, enumerated below, *Macstrna* is unmistakably a proper name. This onomatic type belongs to an abundantly represented class of Etruscan names, ending in *-arna* or *-erna*, as *Perperna*, *Saserna*, etc.; [3] the very name *Masterna* occurs among them. [4]

On the other hand, the Roman king of the Etruscan period was not termed *magister* but *rex*, as the archaic inscription of the "black stone" (*Lapis niger*) in the Forum Romanum attests; and the religious duties of the king were not continued after 504 B.C. by the *magister* but by the *rex sacrificulus*. The supposed democratization of the kingship was based on the assumption that there was an uninterrupted constitutional development, making possible a gradual loosening

[1] G. De Sanctis, *op. cit.* 102. *Idem*, St. d. R. 1², 387, 434 sqq. P. Ducati, Etruria antica 2, Torino 1925, 7. L. Pareti, St. Etr. 5, 1931, 154 sqq. G. Giannelli, La repubblica romana², 1955, 101.

[2] G. Herbig, Indog. Forsch. 37, 1917, 185 n. 2. P. Cortsen, Etruskische Standes- und Beamtentitel, Copenhagen 1925, 131. F. Messerschmidt, Nekropolen von Vulci (JdI, Ergänzungsheft 12) 1931, 149 sq. S. Mazzarino, Dalla mon., *l.c.* M. Pallottino, Etruscologia³, 187 sqq. J. Heurgon, La vie quotid. 67.

[3] Cf. A. Ernout, Philologica (Études et commentaires 1) Paris 1946, 29 sqq.

[4] CIL XIII 5197, 11501. = Dessau, ILS 9272, 9272 a—the same person. Cf. W. Schulze, ZGLEN 85 sq., 94.

of the autocracy and its transformation into a moderate regime. But
the stability and security needed for such an evolution did not exist.
As we have seen, every generation brought a violent change to
Etruscan Rome, a new foreign intervention, releasing on every such
occasion by physical necessity a new wave of bloodshed and terror.
Our man was not the "Master of the people," but Mastarna.

All the scholars who saddled Claudius with the contamination of
the Roman and the Etruscan tradition referring to Servius Tullius
and Mastarna, respectively, overlooked a short passage in Dionysius
of Halicarnassus—the missing link at which we hinted. It runs:
Λατίνων δὲ καὶ τῶν ἄλλων συμμάχων ἔταξεν ἄρχειν ἄνδρα γενναῖον
μὲν τὰ πολέμια καὶ φρονεῖν τὰ δέοντα ἱκανώτατον, ξένον δὲ καὶ ἄπολιν
(referring to Tarquinius Priscus' dispositions)[1]. "Over the Latins and
the other allies he placed a man who was valiant in warfare and of
most competent judgment, *but a foreigner who had lost his nationality.*"
The ξένος καὶ ἄπολις of Dionysius is, of course, Mastarna, driven
out from Etruria, as Emperor Claudius reported; but his name is
already that of Servius Tullius, whose miraculous birth in Rome is a
vernacular myth. Generations before Claudius, the Etruscan intruder
and the legendary Roman king were identified with each other. Naturally, it was not the rhetor of Halicarnassus who mixed up the two: we
can safely trace back this irresponsible amalgamation to Fabius Pictor.

Let us first review the entire tradition concerning Mastarna, his
captain Caeles Vibenna, and also the latter's brother, Aulus Vibenna.
The arrival of Caeles—Caelius in Rome is related in the annalist
tradition under two different headings: either he is said to have come
to help Romulus against Titus Tatius,[2] or to Tarquinius Priscus. A

---

[1] DH III 65, 6. In IV 1, 2 sq., where he is returning to the origin of King
Servius, he recounts the Roman version of his birth.

[2] Varro, *LL* 5, 46 : *In Suburanae regionis parte princeps est Caelius mons a Caele
Vibenna, Tusco duce nobili, qui cum sua manu dicitur Romulo venisse auxilio contra
Tatium regem. Hinc post Caelis obitum . . . deducti dicuntur in planum. Ab eis dictus
vicus Tuscus,* etc. Cic., *De re p.* II 8, 14 : *et Lucumonis, qui Romuli socius in Sabino
bello occiderat.* (Cf. DH II 37, 2.) DH II 36, 2 (on Romulus) διαγγελλούσης δὲ
τῆς φήμης πολλαῖς πόλεσι τήν τε κατὰ πολέμους γενναιότητα τοῦ ἡγεμόνος καὶ
πρὸς τοὺς κρατηθέντας ἐπιείκειαν ἄνδρες τε αὐτῷ προσετίθεντο πολλοὶ καὶ ἀγαθοὶ
δυνάμεις ἀξιοχρέους πανοικίᾳ μετανισταμένας ἐπαγόμενοι, ὧν ἐφ'ἑνὸς ἡγεμόνος
ἐκ Τυρρηνίας ἐλθόντος, ᾧ Καίλιος ὄνομα ἦν, τῶν λόφων τις, ἐν ᾧ καθιδρύθη, Καίλιος
εἰς τόδε χρόνου καλεῖται. Cf. also II 42, 2 ; 43, 2. Propert. IV 1, 29 sqq. 2, 51
sq. Paul. Fest., p. 38 L. : *Caelius mons dictus est a Caele quodam ex Etruria, qui
Romulo auxilium adversum Sabinos praebuit, eo quod in eo domicilium habuit.* Serv.,
Aen. 5, 560.

ETRUSCAN RULE IN LATIUM AND ROME

mutilated passage of Festus, felicitously restored by R. Garrucci whose complements are supported by the texts and monuments presently to be discussed, mentions along with Mastarna and Caeles also his brother (*Volcientes fratres*).[1]

This brother, Aulus Vibenna, played an important role in Rome along with the other two, as is attested by a fragment of Fabius Pictor—unfortunately obscured by the pompous rhetoric of Arnobius, who applied its contents in his attack on the pagan religions.[2]

---

[1] Tac., *Ann.* IV 65, 1-2 : *Haud fuerit absurdum tradere montem eum antiquitus Querquetulanum cognomento fuisse, quod talis silvae frequens fecundusque erat. Mox Caelium appellitatum a Caele Vibenna, qui dux gentis Etruscae cum auxilium portavisset, sedem eam acceperat a Tarquinio Prisco, seu quis alius regum dedit ; nam scriptores in eo dissentiunt. Cetera non ambigua sunt, magnas eas copias per plana etiam ac foro propinqua habitavisse, unde Tuscum vicum e vocabulo advenarum dictum. Orat. Claud., l.c.* Fest., p. 486, 12 with the supplements of R. Garrucci and C. O. Mueller : *Tuscum vicum con(plures scrip) tores dictum aiunt ab (iis, qui Porsenna rege) decedente ab obsi(dione e Tuscis remanserint) Romae, locoque his dato (habitaverint, aut quod Volci)entes fratres Caeles et(A.) Vibenn(ae, quos dicunt ad regem) Tarquinium Romam se cum Max(tarna contulisse colue)rint. M. Varro quod ex Cael(io in eum locum deducti) sint.*

[2] Fab. Pict. fr. 12 (H. R. Rel. 1², p. 23 sq. Peter = F. Gr. Hist. 809 F 11 = Arnob. 6, 7): *Regnatoris in populi Capitolio qui est hominum qui ignoret Oli esse sepulchrum Vulcentani? quis est, inquam, qui non sciat ex fundaminum sedibus caput hominis evolutum non ante plurimum temporis aut solum sine partibus ceteris (hoc enim quidam ferunt) aut cum membris omnibus humationis officia sortitum? quod si planum fieri testimoniis postulatis auctorum, Sammonicus, Granius, Valerius Antias et Fabius indicabunt, cuius Aulus fuerit filius, gentis et nationis cuius, cur manu servuli vita fuerit spoliatus et lumine, quid de suis commeruerit civibus, ut ei sit abnegata telluris paternae sepultura. condiscetis etiam, quamvis nolle istud publicare se fingant, quid sit capite retecto factum, vel in parte qua areae curiosa fuerit obscuritate conclusum, ut immobilis videlicet atque fixa obsignati ominis perpetuitas staret. quod cum opprimi par esset et vetustatis oblitteratione celari, conpositio nominis iecit in medium ; et cum suis causis per data sibi tempora inextinguibili fecit testificatione procedere, nec erubuit civitas maxima et numinum cunctorum cultrix cum vocabulum templo daret, ex Oli capite Capitolium quam ex nomine Iovis nuncupare.* Aulus is mentioned again in the same context in some other works, namely : Serv., *Aen.* 8, 345 : *Quidam dicunt, cum Capitolii ubi nunc est, fundamenta iacerentur, caput humanum, quod Oli diceretur, inventum.* Chron. Vindob. (Chron. min., ed. Mommsen 1, 144) : *invenit caput humanum, litteris Tuscis scriptum 'caput Oli regis.'* Isid., *Orig.* XV 2, 31 : *. . . alii aiunt, cum Tarquinius Priscus Capitolii fundamenta Romae aperiret, in loco fundamenti caput hominis litteris Tuscis notatum invenit, et proinde Capitolium appellavit.* The rest of the tradition, based on Varro, mentions the prodigy of the head, but without *Olus* Vibenna. Cass. Dio ed. Boiss. 1, p. 29 sq. = Zon. VII 11, 5-8: Τὸν δὲ νεὼν τὸν ἐν τῷ Ταρπείῳ ὄρει κατὰ τὴν τοῦ πατρὸς εὐχὴν ᾠκοδόμει. τῆς δὲ γῆς εἰς τὴν τῶν θεμελίων καταβολὴν ἀναρρηγνυμένης, ἀνδρὸς νεοθνῆτος κεφαλὴ ἀνεφάνη ἔναιμος ἔτι. . . . . . ἐλπὶς οὖν κἀκ τούτου αὐτοῖς προσεγένετο. κἀντεῦθεν τὸ ὄρος μετωνομάσθη παρ᾽ αὐτῶν Καπιτώλιον, καπίτα γὰρ τῇ ῾Ρωμαίων διαλέκτῳ ἡ κεφαλὴ ὀνομάζεται. DH IV 61, 2 : ἐξ ἐκείνου καλεῖται τοῦ χρόνου Καπιτωλῖνος ὁ λόφος ἐπὶ τῆς

The kernel of this tale, the popular etymology of the word *Capito-lium*, explained as *caput Oli*, the head of *Olus* (Aulus), must be a Roman invention. The memory of this ruler of the city could well have been preserved in the oral tradition, as well as the obvious fact that he resided on the Capitol: the statement of a late chronicle, calling him *rex*, derived from old roots.

The extract of Pictor clearly implies also the use of the Vulcentane version of the story, i.e., the "Etruscan" source quoted by Claudius. The origin of *Olus* is specified as *Vulcentanus*. In the same way as his brother Caeles is said to be an immigrant and as Mastarna is reported by Claudius to have been driven out of Etruria, and as Mastarna is called again "a stranger and a stateless person" in Dionysius' account, so in Arnobius' extracts from Pictor Olus Vibenna was not allowed to rest in the soil of his native country.

We have already found in Festus the Vibenna brothers closely linked with Mastarna, and we shall meet the same group of three in the traditions of their place of origin. These threads reveal to us that Pictor was in fact acquainted with the "Etruscan" source of Claudius. This fact has momentous consequences. The Vulcentane wall paintings discussed below include the representation of the killing of a Roman king of the dynasty of the Tarquins by the companions of the Vibennae. This tradition made Pictor aware of the existence of another Tarquin, besides the last king, whose exploits were contained in all probability in the preamble to the consular lists, made public by Cn. Flavius. We have already recorded [1] the well-established fact that Pictor duplicated the deeds of the last king, partly transferring their features to the earlier one, located before Mastarna, partly distributing them between the two. And because the Vulcentane records also contained the information that Mastarna outlived the Vibenna brothers, Pictor inserted his reign between his two Tarquins, identifying him with one of the seven legendary

εὑρεθείσης ἐν αὐτῷ κεφαλῆς, κάπιτα γὰρ οἱ ῾Ρωμαῖοι καλοῦσι τὰς κεφαλάς. Varro, *LL* 5, 41 : *e quis Capitolinum (sc. montem) dictum, quod hic, cum fundamenta foderentur aedis Iovis, caput humanum dicitur inventum.* Liv. I 55, 5. V 54, 7 : *hic Capitolium est, ubi quondam capite humano invento responsum est eo loco caput rerum summamque imperii fore.* (Livy inspected also Pictor : I 55, 8). Plin., *N.h.* XXVIII 2, 15. Flor. I 1, 9. Plut., *Camill.* 31, 4. *Vir. ill.* 8, 4. Lact., *Instit.*, I 11, 49. Isid., *Orig.* XV 2, 31. Mart. Cap. 3, 223. Suda, s.v. Καπιτώλιον. These quotations were already collected by A. Schwegler, RG 1, 771 n. 3. 5 ; 722, n. 3.

[1] Cf. above, p. 133 sqq.

kings of Rome, with Servius Tullius, for whom he found no other place;[1] after that he decided to stick to the number of seven rulers in his work.

To sum up: the rather confused literary evidence preserved the following basic facts concerning the dynasts of Vulci, who captured Rome. According to Claudius, Mastarna, brother-at-arms and lieutenant of Caeles Vibenna, withdrew to Rome with the remnants of the army of Caeles. But the other version, according to which Caeles himself arrived and settled down in the city, seems to me to come nearer to the truth. To Festus we owe the information that his brother Aulus also came to Rome, and local legend remembered him as a king. The "slave" who killed him recalls Servius, son of a slave woman, who was confused with Mastarna: if he is meant, this could hardly be taken from Pictor, who left Aulus out of his history of the kings. This is certainly meager evidence, but nevertheless of high importance; by good fortune it can be complemented by archaeological data to which we will now turn our attention.

The indigenous legend of the *Caput Oli*, which was used by Fabius Pictor, and which was possibly already drawn upon in his source in regard to the history of the last Roman king, told that the head of Olus Vibenna was found intact when the foundations of the Capitoline temple were excavated, and that the best Etruscan expert on such portents disclosed, though reluctantly, the true meaning of this presage—that Rome would be the capital city of the whole of Italy.[2] A pre-annalistic representation of this tale has come down to us on engraved Italic gems in Etruscizing style, which succeeded the Etruscan scarabs in the line of evolution from the early decades of the third century on. The surprisingly great number of specimens preserved for us mirrors the predilection of the Romans for the theme illustrated (pl. XIII, 1-14 XIV 2).

---

[1] It has been supposed that Timaeus already wrote the history of the Roman kings ; cf. the notes of F. Jacoby to F. Gr. Hist. 566 F 58-61 (p. 565 in his commentary). But this assumption proved to be erroneous, as I have shown in RM 68, 1961, 64 sqq. The myth of the miraculous birth of Servius Tullius will be discussed in my volume on the oldest structure of the Roman state. The rationalization of this mythical figure by Pictor who attributed to him the fundamental institutions of the Republic was illustrated in our third and fourth chapters.

[2] The references to the ancient sources and to their modern discussions are to be found along with a learned commentary in an article by St. Weinstock, RE 17, 2445 sqq. He did not, however, realize the identity of King Olus with Aulus Vibenna.

Winckelmann has already established the correct interpretation of the scene engraved on these ring stones. If Ad. Furtwängler, in his epoch-making work on ancient gems,[1] followed him only conditionally and with reservations, it was he who was at fault: he connected them with some apparently similar but in fact unrelated types. First and foremost, the prophesying head of Orpheus with an adept of Orphic mysticism writing down his revelations on a tablet (as Furtwängler brilliantly explained) [2] has nothing to do with our subject. On the gems we have in mind, a man in the pallium of a Greek philosopher appears, with his chest uncovered, pointing with a rod [3] toward a human head lying on the ground (pl. XIII, 13-14).[4] There is no doubt that the Etruscan seer is meant, interpreting the prodigy. This is he who is speaking, not the head, as in the case of the Orphic head-oracle. The presage of the future greatness of Rome is, in accordance with the literary evidence, by no means foretold by the head but by the miracle of its intact preservation and its emergence, announcing by the will of the gods the vocation of the citadel, to become the *caput*, the "head" of Italy. There also exist more elaborate variations of this theme on the Etruscizing ring stones (pl. XIII, 1-10 and XIV, 2) [5] in which two Romans in the solemn attire of the *toga* are listening to the soothsayer's words. The finding of the head and the Roman envoys consulting the famous expert in his Etruscan home-city are here contracted in one scene, the tiny surface of the seal constraining the artist to express his theme in such an abbreviated form. Here, too, the head is silent, unmistakably so, and only the sage, disclosing the secret of the high destiny of Rome, speaks. The two Romans in their solemn garb are the witnesses of the event, giving a sort of legal authority to it, just as on another type of contemporary ring stones, where they also appear, to authenticate the dream of

---

[1] Ad. Furtwängler, Die antiken Gemmen, Leipzig-Berlin 1900, 246 sqq., 451 sq. On the style of these intaglios cf. *ibid.* 216 sqq. and 223. Cf. also St. Weinstock, *op. cit.* 2447 sq.

[2] Cf. the Attic vase reproduced by Furtwängler, *op. cit.* 3, 248, fig. 139.

[3] The pallium of the prophet implies that also the rod belongs to the paraphernalia of the Greek philosopher, taken from the same inventory of art-motifs. Cf., e.g., O. Brendel, RM 51, 1936, 1 sqq. with figs. 1-5 and pls. 1 and 10.

[4] Ad. Furtwängler, Beschreibung der geschnittenen Steine im Antiquarium der k. Museen zu Berlin, 1896, No. 403 = *Id.*, Antike Gemmen, pl. 22, 7.

[5] Ad. Furtwängler, Beschreibung no. 405 sqq. *Idem*, Antike Gemmen, pl. 22, 8-9. H. B. Walters, BMC Engraved Gems[2], London 1926, pl. 15, nos 995-97.

ETRUSCAN RULE IN LATIUM AND ROME

Rea Silvia announcing the great future of her offspring,[1] or, again, as Julius Proculus, testifies officially the ascent of Romulus to heaven. The fullest rendering of this story is to be found on a miniature intaglio in the Cabinet des Médailles in Paris (pl. XIII, 12 a-b) and on the whole rightly explained by E. Babelon.[2] Here, the Etruscan clairvoyant stands in the middle, pointing downward with his wand toward the head lying on a heap of excavated earth before him. Left of him, the herm of *Juppiter Terminus*[3] is exhibited, the divinity which would not allow himself to be dislodged or exaugurated when the area of the Capitoline temple was cleared, warranting permanence and unbroken vigor to the Roman state. Right and left of the soothsayer and the herm two naked workers are standing. On the extreme right, King Tarquinius sits, listening to the revelation of the seer. As has been already stressed,[4] Furtwängler would never have questioned the bearing of the prodigy of the head to the rise of Rome to supremacy could he have known in time of E. Babelon's publication of this intaglio.

Through the testimony of these little ring-stones we are aware that the legend of the *Caput Oli* was alive in Rome when Fabius Pictor wrote his Annals. After the collapses of the Roman army at Lake Trasimenus and Cannae, when he conceived the plan of his work, he used those prodigies as a statement of faith in final victory and as a propagandist illustration for the Greek world of the greatness of his fatherland.

The memory of the Roman King Olus from Vulci and of his associates was preserved, however, not only in Rome but also in his native city; an exceptional piece of luck saved it from oblivion there,

[1] Cf. the article of present writer in Mus. Helv. 7, 1950, 1 sqq. The two rustic figures meditating on the fate of a head they found (A. Furtwängler, Beschreibung, no. 410. H. B. Walters, *op. cit.* no. 998) do not belong to the group with which we are concerned ; nor does the old peasant contemplating a skull, on which the butterfly of Psyche is sitting (Ad. Furtwängler, Die antiken Gemmen, pl. 22, 12).

[2] E. Babelon, Collection Pauvert de la Chapelle. Intailles et Camées. Catalogue . . ., Paris 1899, 44 sq, no. 111 with drawing and collotype reproduction on pl. 7. Our interpretation differs from his in details.

[3] Neither of the two naked young men can be *Iuventas* who was always represented as a female figure. Augustine, *De civ. Dei* 4, 23 and 29 mentions also Mars with *Terminus* and *Iuventas*, but this seems to be a later addition, as was already Iuventas. Cf. G. Wissowa, in Roscher's Lex. II 1, 764 sqq. W. Kroll, RE 10, 1360 sqq. K. Latte, Röm. Religionsgeschichte, 256 n.l.

[4] S. Weinstock, RE 17, 2448.

to our benefit. More than a hundred years ago, wall-paintings of an Etruscan tomb were unearthed in Vulci which illustrate, along with subjects taken from Greek mythology, the gallantry of the two Vibennae, Caeles and Aulus, and the inseparable companion of the former, Mastarna. These frescoes of the so-called "tomba Francois," [1] detached from the walls of the tomb and transferred to Rome by the Torlonia princes, refer to one event illustrated by the single actions of five pairs of heroes whose names are written beside each of them. As was recognized long ago by the scholars who studied these inscriptions, these names fall in two categories: for those warriors who were at home in Vulci, only their personal names are given, whereas those coming from other Etruscan states were given the designation of their home-cities written after their own names. These five pairs of champions—the first couple being inseparable comrades, the other four pairs mortal enemies—are as follows:

1. Two naked, bearded men, mature warriors, stand turned toward each other (pl. VIII). The one on the left side, whose wrists are bound by a rope, is *Caile Vipinas*, our Caeles Vibenna. Opposite him, his friend *Macstrna*—our Mastarna—just arrived, cuts the cords with his sword, the sheath of which hangs from his neck; he brings another sword for his friend, freed from his fetters.

2. A warrior, called *Larth Ulthes*, clad in a girdled shirt, though without helmet and defensive armor and equipped only with a naked sword without its sheath, stabs in the ribs *Laris Papathnas*, from *Velznach*, i.e., Volsinii (pl. IX). The latter is caught unaware, certainly in his sleep, as all scholars agree. His mantle, in which his naked body was wrapped for the night, falls down from his shoulders by the sudden convulsion of his body. He is a beardless youth; his aggressor is bearded. Three more scenes of this kind are added:

3. *Rasce* from Vulci, painted in the same way as Caeles Vibenna and Mastarna, naked and bearded, with his sword sheath hanging from his neck, grasps with his left hand the hair of the young and beardless *Pesna Arcmsnas* from *Svetimach*, i.e., Sovana, and with his right hand thrusts his sword into the breast of his victim. The latter falls back-

---

[1] The most detailed publication of them is that of F. Messerschmidt, Nekropolen von Vulci (12. Ergänzungsheft of the JdI) Berlin 1930, 62 sqq. (architectural analysis by A. v. Gerkan), 92 sqq. (finds and paintings). The foundations of the historical interpretation have been laid by G. Körte, JdI 12, 1897 (1898), 74 sqq. Besides the studies quoted above cf. also E. Petersen, JdI 14, 1899 (1900) 46. J. Heurgon, Rech. 69.

ward—perhaps onto his bed—by the unexpected shock of the attack; his mantle, drawn up to his head, slips down behind him, uncovering his nude body except for his right leg (pl. X).

4. *Avle Vipinas*—Aulus Vibenna of Vulci (pl. XI), again naked and bearded and armed only with a sword, the sheath of which is suspended from his neck, like his comrades, runs his blade into the armpit of his victim, *Venthi Cau[le?]ş* from the city of .]*plsachs*, which place-name has not been identified with certainty.[1] This time the opponent of Aulus is alarmed in time, but only to put up his corslet and take his shield in hand but unable to reach a sword. The shield falls again from his hand and he collapses on it in death, while the assailant pulls his head back by the hair, to find the right spot for his mortal blow.

5. *Marce Camitlnas*[2] from Vulci (pl. XII), a naked and bearded tall man, is drawing his sword from its sheath suspended from his neck, and leaping at *Cneve Tarchu[nies]*, *Rumach*,[3] Cnaeus Tarquinius from Rome, the only bearded man among the victims. Tarquin is also undressed, stirred from sleep. He, too, is wrapped in a white mantle for the night, which slips down from his shoulders to the floor as he is overwhelmed and tries to catch the sword of the intruder, but grasping only the sheath.[4]

The interpretation of these paintings, the importance of which is unique, can gain some precision from a few observations on the clothing of the victims and their killers. We must never forget that clothes and shoes denoted rank and dignity with the Etruscans. Furthermore, the meaning of the single items of their distinctive apparel by which rank was represented is intelligible for us because the Romans took them over for their own use, retaining the original significance of the distinguishing marks for the leading class of their

---

[1] J. Heurgon, La vie quotid. 66, thought of Falerii ; S. Accame, in his university lectures on the Roman kings, of Salpinum.

[2] The Italic praenomen *Marce*, *Mamerce* (Marcus, Mamercus) occurs rather often in Etruria, cf. M. Pallottino, *Testimonia linguae Etruscae*; Firenze 1954, *index, s.v.*

[3] The name of Rome is written with *u* again as *Ruma* on an archaic milestone from Vulci ; cf. A. Degrassi, Hommages à A. Grenier (Coll. Latomus 58) 1962, 509.

[4] F. Messerschmidt, *op. cit.* 138 sq., wished to separate this scene from the foregoing ones, but this attempt was rejected by the research following his work.

society and for their magistrates.[1] The white cloak, corresponding to the Roman *trabea*, on *Laris Papathnas* and *Pesna Arcmsnas* has a red trimming—*praetexta* in Latin. Under the corslet of *Venthi Cau*[. . .]*s* the red braid on the neck of his shirt shows. Consequently this last mentioned man is not someone of low standing, as has been suggested,[2] but an important person, as are the two men in the *praetexta*. In the case of *Cneve Tarchunies* the red border stripe is not discernible, though I should think that it was once there. The Romans know that the *praetexta* belonged originally to the king, and from him it was inherited by the magistrates of the Republic; the same must have been true in Etruria. So we conclude that those men owning the shirt and mantle with red trimming were kings or dynasts.

The same is true of their aggressors. *Larth Ulthes*, the only one of them who is dressed, wears a shirt with a broad red trim around the neck and with narrower red stripes seaming the short sleeves and also connecting the braid around the neck with that which trims the sleeves. This is the same thing as the *tunica laticlavia* in Rome, which belonged to the privileged class, and certainly before them to the kings; its significance in the hierarchy of Etruria could hardly be different. Therefore, the aggressors came from the same leading class as the men attacked. If *Macstrna, Caile* and *Avle Vipinas*, as well as *Marce Camitlnas* are naked, this is because of a very special circumstance.

It has been maintained hitherto that the subject displayed by these murderous scenes is the liberation of Caeles Vibenna by Mastarna. But the nudity of Mastarna, of Aulus Vibenna, and of Marcus Camitlnas must have the same reason as the nakedness of Caeles Vibenna: they were certainly stripped of their costumes and weapons on the same occasion as Caeles; in other words, they were captured with him. This observation can be checked by the representation of the Trojans, victims of the wrath of Achilles, balancing the killings of Etruscan heroes in the "tomba François," where even mythical figures wear armor or are fully dressed, but where the prisoners to be executed

[1] Cf. A. Alföldi, Der frührömische Reiteradel, Baden-Baden, 1952. There is, as far as I know, one case which seems to contradict our statement. The clerk of King Porsenna in Liv. II 12, 7 *scriba cum rege sedens pari fere ornatu*. But the privilege to *sit* along with the monarch—the *consessus* in Rome—proves that the clerk was either an offspring of the nobility or a high official, like the Roman *quaestor* in later times.

[2] F. Messerschmidt, *op. cit.* 151, referring to the opinion of O. Danielsson.

are, again, naked. It becomes evident, therefore, that not only Caeles, whose shackles are still on his wrists, fell into captivity, but also all his friends who are still naked but armed with sword, and are forcing their way to liberty along with him. It may be that their beards grew long only after they were taken prisoner. Somebody brought them the swords with which they are butchering their enemies, who had captured them; their execution was delayed in all likelihood so as to put them first on show for the triumphal return of their captors, as was the custom also in Rome. The allies who got the upper hand over them before the event illustrated in our paintings were still together, therefore, either in their camp or in a place taken by them. *Larth Ulthes*, the only one of the Vulcentane group who is clad —though without being protected by armor—must be the man who brought the swords, stealing in darkness to the hostile camp.

This interpretation also broadens the meaning of the juxtaposition of the murderous scenes just reviewed with the sacrifice of the Trojan prisoners on the walls of the *tablinum* of the Vulcentane tomb. The comparison of the two subjects had a special meaning for the people of Vulci because they believed in their own Trojan origin.[1] On these paintings the inevitable end of the original Trojans after their capture is confronted with the miraculous escape of the Trojan offspring from the same hopeless situation: an allusion with symbolic meaning. The detailed display of bestial murder, four times repeated, in addition to the massacre of Achilles, may arouse our anger and disgust but we must not forget that vengeance and retaliation were the only forms of rendering justice in a time when no police force or federal court existed in Etruria.

The conscious confrontation of old and new Trojan war prisoners seems to suggest one more consequence: should we not infer from it that the Vulcentane descendants of the Trojans were also besieged as were the old Trojans: their capture could have happened not only on a battlefield but when their home city was taken. Furthermore, we know that the Vulcentane heroes were unable to return from Rome to their city of origin: Aulus Vibenna could not repose in the place of his birth; his brother Caeles died, too, if not on the battlefield, so in Rome; Mastarna was a stranger in the same city and had lost his original citizenship. This shows that Vulci remained in the hands

---

[1] Cf. my study, Die trojanischen Urahnen der Römer (Rektoratsprogramm Basel 1956) 1957, and below, p. 278 sqq.

of their enemies, most likely occupied by the victorious coalition whose leaders were killed in a night by their prisoners, who then escaped.

Since the paper of G. Körte, published in 1898, the correlation of the historical narrative of the paintings of the "tomba François" has often been confronted with the respective statements in the Roman literature. Their interdependence has been well established by Inez Scott Ryberg.[1] She has stressed that though the agreement between the written tradition and the tomb paintings is striking, and though the same characters and the same relationships between them appear in both cases, the actual happenings are not the same: they reproduce two different episodes of the same Etruscan account. "The Volcentian incident," she writes, "may be an earlier chapter of the same story with no implications as to the sequel; the Roman tradition a later chapter with no reference to the previous events. The painting records an episode from the history of Volci . . . There is no indication that the death of Tarquin of Rome is particularly important, nor that it will lead to any singular consequences for any of the victors . . . The sequel, Mastarna's [and we add: also Aulus Vibenna's] succession to the royal power held by Tarquinius of Rome, is [2] . . . not important to the painter who records the Volcentian tradition . . . The version presented by Claudius, on the other hand, deals with the same characters in a later stage of the same story . . ., in connection with events which did not come at all within the scope of the Volci tradition."

What could be the peculiar nature and original type of this Etruscan tale concerning the exploits of the Vibenna brothers and Mastarna? In order to draw nearer to the solution of this problem, we have first to cast a glance at the date and peculiar structure of the paintings. Scholars used to put their date in the fourth century B.C.,[3] but it seems to me that the arguments for a date of about 300 B.C. are of decisive weight; [4] the attempt of some distinguished scholars to go

[1] I. Scott Ryberg, Mem. Am. Ac. 7, 1929, 75 sq., 77 sqq.

[2] Mrs. Ryberg ponders the possibility that the accession of the Vulcentane leaders to the throne in Rome was unknown to the painter ; we exclude this eventuality.

[3] G. Körte, JdI 12, 1897 (1898) 64 sq. More recently : L. Pareti, St. R. 1, 1952, 310 sqq.

[4] R. A. L. Fell, Etruria and Rome, Cambridge 1924, 45. I. Scott, Mem. Am. Ac. 7, 1929, 74. L. Pareti, Rend. Pont. Acc. 3. ser. 7, 1929-31, 96. *Idem*, Atene e Roma n.s. 12, 1931, 215 n. 3. F. Messerschmidt, Nekropolen von Vulci,

down to the years near 100 B.C. cannot be maintained.[1] The peremptory proofs for this chronological assessment are furnished by the decorative elements accompanying the composition. The close relationship between the female heads emerging on top of scrolls, which are enlivened with trumpet-like flowers both on these paintings and on Apulian vases of about 300 B.C.; the same close correspondence between the painted decoration of the same two groups in the peculiar, pseudo-perspective treatment of the maeanders, painted at upright ribbons, as well as of the fish-scale pattern and the egg-shaped decorative chains, giving the illusion of plasticity by the effect of shade and light, must be features of contemporary art both in Apulia and in Etruria.[2] A further corroboration of this dating was made possible by the examination of the friezes with lions, griffons, and other animals.[3] Moreover, there is also the additional category of Etruscan art documents with analogous representations, making it easier for us to establish the chronology. We mean a series of engraved gems, with the same representation of the slaying of a collapsing unarmed human victim by a man drawing his sword. The motif occurs already on a forcefully modeled scarab (pl. XIV 3)[4] in the severe style of the fifth century B.C., this time applied awkwardly to the theme of the killing of Medusa by Perseus. Then we have the Etruscan ring-stones, engraved still in the severe style of the scarabs, as pl. XIV, 4, with a crouching youth, to be put to the sword by a warrior,[5] and several other such killings as, e.g., pl. XIV, 6[6] and

Berlin 1930, 118 sq. Further bibliography is given by H. and I. Jucker, Kunst und Leben der Etrusker, Ausstellungskatalog Köln 1956, 179. Cf. also F. Schachermeyr, RE 4A, 2362 sqq.

[1] A. v. Gerkan, RM 47, 1942, 146 sqq. M. Pallottino, La peinture étrusque, Genève 1952, 153 sq. *Idem*, Etruscologia[3], Milano 1955, 115 sqq. Undecided: R. Herbig, Gnomon 26, 1954, 324. *Contra*: C. C. van Essen, Bibliotheca Orientalis 12, 1955, 215 sq.

[2] F. Messerschmidt, *op. cit.* 112 sqq., 118 sq., and figs. 66, 67, 90, 93. A. Rumpf, Handbuch der Archäologie (6. Lieferung) 4, München 1953, 136 sqq. H. u. I. Jucker, *op. cit.* 178 suggest plausibly that, the prosperity of Vulci having been broken forever at the beginning of the third century B.C., a date beyond this time is unlikely.

[3] F. Messerschmidt, *op. cit.* 120 sqq. W. L. Brown, The Etruscan Lion, Oxford 1960, 158 sq., 160 n. 1.

[4] H. B. Walters, BMC Engraved Gems[2] 1926, no. 623.

[5] Ad. Furtwängler, Beschreibung der geschnittenen Steine im Antiquarium, Berlin 1896, 42 no. 483. *Idem*, Antike Gemmen pl. 21, 49. A. Sambon, Corolla B. V. Head, London 1906, 283 and pl. 14, 23.

[6] Ad. Furtwängler, Beschreibung no. 484.

immolations of men and women in the same manner, pl. XIV, 7-11. [1]
Like the paintings of our Vulcentane tomb, the themes of these
slayings are partly taken from the Greek mythological inventory,
but others may well illustrate the deeds of national heroes, such as
the bloody revenge of the Vibennae and their comrades (pl. XIV,
5-6). These Vulcentane champions were celebrated, indeed, throughout the whole of Etruria, a point to which we shall return later.

The testimony of the style of the tomb paintings of Vulci deserves,
likewise, to be adduced. The general concept which animates these
ferocious acts of murder, as well as the scene of the liberation of
Avile Vipienas, is not the baroque agitation and pathos of Hellenism,
nor the keen Alexandrine interest in petty details of everyday life
of common men, but the solemn atmosphere of the late classical
epoch. The figures of the Vibennae and of Mastarna resemble the
fourth-century statues of Zeus and Poseidon. The dying *Laris Papathnas* recalls the collapsing Niobides of the great classical sculptors.
The crossed legs of *Marce Camitlnas*, expressing haste and excitement,
derive from the same artistic environment and epoch.

Whereas the massacre of the Trojans, a popular theme in Etruscan
art,[2] is based on a well-conceived, unified Greek composition, the
exploits of the Vulcentane heroes are broken up into isolated single
scenes, each of them being reduced to two figures. This fundamental
divergence between the two complementary cycles must have a very
special reason. The pattern of the representation of the national one
is not only more archaic but also un-Greek: the simplified manner
of their narrative, parceling out a continuous chain of events in a
series of killings, is more akin to mediaeval book illumination than
to the metopes of a Greek temple.

The exaggerated proportions of the limbs and chests of the Vibennae and their helpers, the majestic outline of their profiles, accentuate
the fact that they are not just common folk but famous heroes. The
reduction of the narrative to separate actions of outstanding participants is a procedure well known also in other fields of ancient art
and fiction. Niebuhr observed long ago [3] that the description of the
battle at Lake Regillus in Livy does not give the clash of two armies

---

[1] Ad. Furtwängler, Beschreibung no. 488-489 ; *idem*, Antike Gemmen,
pl. 21, 51.
[2] G. Körte, *op. cit.* 67 sq. F. Messerschmidt, JdI 45, 1930, 64 sqq.
[3] B. G. Niebuhr, RG I², 1827, 582.

228

but a series of heroic duels, as in the *Iliad* of Homer. The commanders-in-chief try their strength and decide the victory, whereas the bulk of their armies have no share in their actions. This epic mechanism was, of course, dying hard and late;[1] but its exclusive prevalence, displayed on the cycle of the Vibennae in the "tomba François," is still witness to the epoch of its real flourishing. Of course the theme of mortal duels did not belong only to the epic style in poetry but also in life. It was still in the time of Polybius[2] an obligation of honor for a Roman nobleman to fight in single combat, when provoked to do so, before the eyes and between the battle-arrays of hostile armies; the clans of the aristocracy were boasting of such victorious duels of their ancestors even later.[3]

The epic style of the original account glorifying the deeds of the Vulcentane champions, which is reflected in the paintings of the "tomba François," explains why the artist did not force the representation of their acts of bravery into the unified pattern of a Greek scheme of composition, but rather reproduced their terrible revenge in the same way as the oral tradition narrated the heroic feats they accomplished: in isolated actions of each and every one of them. We must suppose this the more confidently because Etruscan epics celebrated other deeds by them, transferring their figures from the context of history into the nebulous sphere of myth.

We recall the adventure of the Vibenna brothers with Cacus, who, in the Etruscan legend, is not the monster he is in the Roman tale, though he is killed in both by Hercules, but a prophetic seer and enchanting singer, like Orpheus, a youth of Apollo-like beauty. The Etruscan account of his miraculous life left its traces again in the Roman Annals as well as in Etruscan art representations. And the two different sources again concern two different phases of the same epic recital; as G. de Sanctis observed, it was wrong to try to identify them. In any case, both these episodes are put in the epoch of mythical prehistory and the Vibenna brothers become superhuman characters being cast with Marsyas, Tarchon and Hercules.

---

[1] The way in which Appian (Lib. 195 sq., cf. 184, 187 sq.) tries to represent the final struggles of the second Punic war by the intended personal fight between Massinissa and Hannibal is a good example of the late repercussions of the old epic style along with many other similar cases.

[2] Polyb. VI 54, 4.

[3] Cf. the coin-types of C. Serveilius, M. Serveilius, Man. Fonteius, Q. Minucius Thermus, BMC Rep. pl. 30, 5 ; 32, 4 ; 48, 6 ; 95, 14.

Etruscan Domination over Rome

The fragment of the annalist Cn. Gellius [1] speaks only of Cacus, who came from Asia Minor to Tarchon, the founder-hero of the Etruscan nation. Being imprisoned by the latter, Cacus is able to escape and, returning again from his home-country to Italy, with his army invades Campania, but Hercules puts him to death in the defense of the Greek settlers. On the drawing of a bronze mirror from Volsinii [2] and on reliefs of ash-urns from the neighborhood of Clusium [3] the two Vibennae succeed in surprising the youthful seer, prophesying in a sacred grove, and constrain him to reveal their destiny. Cacus is represented in some cases in the effeminate pose of Paris, with an elaborate necklace: [4] this characterizes his Phrygian origin, and makes it plain that he is the same person as the Cacus in the account of Cn. Gellius. The general acquaintance of the Etruscans with this legendary account is illustrated by the fact that the sculptors who made those cinerary urns did not find it necessary to write the names of the Vibennae and of Cacus beside their figures: everybody knew them. [5]

[1] Cn. Gellius, *Ann.* fr. 7 (H. R. Rel. 1², p. 149 sq. = Solin. 1, 8): *hic* (sc. Cacus), *ut Gellius tradidit, cum a Tarchone Tyrrheno, ad quem legatus venerat missu Marsyae regis, socio Megale Phryge, custodiae foret datus, frustratus vincula et unde venerat redux, praesidiis amplioribus occupato circa Vulturnum et Campaniam regno, dum adtrectare etiam ea audet, quae concesserant in Arcadum iura, duce Hercule qui tunc forte aderat, oppressus est.* For the interpretation of this passage as well as of the art monuments quoted in the next note cf. E. Petersen, JdI 14, 1899 (1900) 43 sqq. G. De Sanctis, Klio 2, 1902, 104. J. Bayet, cf. above p. 201 n. 8. P. Ducati, Etruria antica 1, 1925, 115. F. Messerschmidt, JdI 45, 1930, 76 sq. J. Heurgon, La vie quotid. 64, 283, and others.

[2] G. Körte, in : E. Gerhard, Etruskische Spiegel 5, Berlin 1897, 166 sqq. and pl. 127. H. B. Walters, BMC Bronzes, Greek, Roman and Etruscan, 1899, 99 sq., n. 633. F. Messerschmidt, *op. cit.*, fig. 12. *Artile* is not reading the revelation of Cacus, but is writing it down, as is Cacus himself on the other mirror in Paris, F. Messerschmidt, *ibid.* fig. 3, where the head of Orpheus is speaking. Cf. above p. 219 n. 2.

[3] G. Körte, Rilievi delle urne etrusche 2, Rom-Berlin, 1890, 254 sqq. with pl. 119. E. Petersen, *l.c.* F. Messerschmidt, *op. cit.* fig. 14-20. G. Q. Giglioli, Arte Etrusca, Milano 1935, pl. 398, 1 ; 404, 3. J. Heurgon, *l.c.*

[4] On the urn from Città della Pieve in Firenze F. Messerschmidt, *op. cit.* fig. 15. The figure lying on the ground with portrait-like features and in a peacetime attire has a girdle high up under the breasts. Is this Phrygian *effeminatio*, too? *Alte cinctus* was a mode of dressing scorned in Rome for similar reasons. Is he the *Tarchon* Tyrrhenus of Cn. Gellius?

[5] It is not even impossible that the two Vibennae were worshipped as heroes in Etruria, as was Aeneas (cf. below, p. 250 sqq.). J. Heurgon, La vie quotid. 64 has called our attention to an Etruscan red-figured cup of unknown provenience, made in all probability in Vulci around 450 B.C., now in the Musée

ETRUSCAN RULE IN LATIUM AND ROME

On the other hand, the historicity of the Vibennae, and the epoch in which they captured Rome, cannot be doubted. M. Pallottino found the foot of a *bucchero* cup, made around the middle of the sixth century in Veii, with the dedication of a man called *Avile Vipiienas*, Aulus Vibenna in archaic Etruscan—in all likelihood our Aulus Vibenna himself.[1] This identification, if it is correct, as it seems to me, would be of great consequence. The dedication in Veii, offered by the king of Rome, would prove the friendly relations between the usurper and his nearest neighbor, north of his realm. In other words, just as his enemies were the forces of the Tarquins of Rome allied with Volsinii, Sovana, and a fourth Etruscan state, so he was able to rely on Veii, and perhaps on other cities. It would be important to know whether Caere agreed with his rule or not; but: *ignoramus*.

The evidence just surveyed is interwoven with the treacherous threads of myth, legend, and fiction, but free of political tendency and containing authentic reminiscences of an age in which events were not recorded in writing. The oral tradition which preserved the memories of events concerning Vulci and Rome was kept alive exactly in these two cities, where they were enacted. It is older by far than the beginning of the Roman Annals. The most relevant facts, which emerge from it, are the following:

(a) Not long after the middle of the sixth century, a Vulcentane army, vanquished by a coalition of Etruscan powers, was nevertheless able to capture Rome whose king, Cnaeus Tarquinius, fell in the war against Vulci. Our impression is that in these decades no Etruscan state any longer had overwhelming power, sufficient to crush discord, and that such violent changes must have been the order of the day. This dangerous insecurity might have brought one good thing for the future of Rome: the city was driven in on itself, the sense of

Rodin in Paris (CVA France 16, pl. 28-30. J. D. Beazley, Etruscan Vase Painting, Oxford 1947, 3 and 26. E. Fiesel, JHS 50, 1930, 24), with the inscription *Avles V(i)pinas*, on which the genitive could signify a dedication to him, as J. Heurgon supposes.

[1] M. Pallottino, St. Etr. 13, 1939, 455 sqq. *Idem*, Etruscologia[3], Milano 1955, 116 sqq. J. Heurgon, *l.c.* A fragment of the praetexta *Lupus* (*i.e.* : *lupus femina*, the she-wolf who nourished the twins) of Naevius (Fest., p. 334, 9 L. Cf. K. Meister, Lateinisch-griechische Eigennamen, Leipzig 1916, 76 sqq. O. Skutsch, Cl. Rev. n.s. 1, 1951, 176) contains the name of *Vel Vibe*, King of Veii, who visits King Amulius in Alba Longa. *Vel Vibe* sounds like an abridged form of *Avile Vibenna* (cf. CIL XI 1994), though both names are abundantly attested in the Etruscan nomenclature.

responsibility of the leading class was certainly awakened, and its political insight and experience strengthened.

(b) Aulus (possibly also Caeles) Vibenna ruled in Rome. It seems that the reign of Mastarna followed his death.

(c) The great Etruscan expedition against Cyme in 524 B.C. is the most likely date for the reestablishment of the dynasty of the Tarquins in Rome. A large army marching across a country is always liable to cause a rearrangement of allegiances and to establish new regimes in small states in the past as well as today. *Experto crede*!

Veii

Veii lay almost within sight of Rome, less than twenty Roman miles away to the north: *intra vicesimum lapidem, in conspectu prope urbis nostrae*.[1] And the territory of Veii was even nearer. Fidenae, a Veientan outpost on the Tiber, was only five miles from the city, Rome's rural possessions reaching only to the Anio—even quite a while after the downfall of the kings.[2] Closer still, immediately bordering on the city, was the Veientan territory which stretched along the right bank of the Tiber, down to the sea and remained Veientan, until the middle of the fifth century B.C. as will be shown in Chapter VII of this book. The immediate neighborhood of this powerful state, of a far bigger area and population than Rome, controlling the approaches to her, crippled her capacity for action like a hand on her throat.

Veii[3] did not belong to the twelve original member-states of the Etruscan League. Her prosperity began, as the topographical survey of J. B. Ward Perkins and his staff now in progress has revealed, only about 600 B.C.—Veii was probably a foundation of Tarquinii or Caere, the purpose of which can be read from the geographical map.

We see along the Tyrrhenian coast a series of Etruscan states, prospering through transmarine commerce and piracy. These states,

---

[1] Liv. V 4, 12.

[2] The sources are collected in A. Bormann, Altlatinische Chorographie und Städtegeschichte, Halle 1852, 239 sqq. Cf. O. Richter, Hermes 17, 1882, 437 sqq. L. A. Holland, TAPA 80, 1949, 289 sqq.

[3] The source material has been made available by K. O. Müller-W. Deecke, 1, 106 sqq. G. Dennis, The Cities and Cemeteries cf. Etruria³, London 1888, 1 sq. H. Nissen, It. Lk. II 2, Berlin 1902, 490 sqq. J. B. Ward Perkins, Veii, The Historical Geography of the Ancient City (PBSR 29) 1961. Cf. below, p. 338 sq.

however, are not placed on the shore: their sites are withdrawn to strongpoints in the immediate hinterland of the harbors. This precaution is due to their own experience as corsairs. They knew only too well how vulnerable is a settlement exposed to attacks from the sea.[1] The site of Veii, however, was apparently chosen with a different idea. She had no access to the sea, turning away intentionally from it, and looking toward the Tiber. Through the valley of the rivulet Cremera, Veii had a direct channel of communication with the "Etruscan river." At the mouth of the Cremera, on the opposite bank of the Tiber, her bridgehead Fidenae watched over the river traffic. Veii, therefore it seems, was founded for the economic exploitation of the shipping on the Tiber; her wealth and might had this same ultimate source. Yet this also means that she was able wholly to control the lowest section of the Tiber valley: though the goods arriving from the north passed through Fidenae on the Anio toward Praeneste and Campania, Veii needed also the coastal route running across Rome and Lavinium to the south for her commerce. Therefore, if Rome had possessed the power and reached the extension attributed to her by Fabius Pictor, Veii never could have risen to the importance and might which in reality was hers. The best illustration for this is the exploitation of the salt marshes north of the mouth of the Tiber by Veii, discussed below.[2] The first station of the "salt-road" passing through Rome into the Sabine region, after it crossed the stream on the bridge of the island at Rome, was Fidenae;[3] this means that Veii had her finger on the pulse of this artery, too.

The extensive road system developed by Veii in the zone east of Rome in the sixth century B.C. emerges now from the topographical researches of the British School at Rome with all desirable clarity. As L. A. Holland, a born topographer, has established,[4] only one-way traffic down the Tiber was practicable, and indeed easy—upstream navigation was even more arduous than crossing the country on foot, owing to the serpentine course and the strong current of the river. This elucidates the need for and the origin of the *Via Salaria*, and also the importance of Rome as a place of transshipment and crossing.

---

[1] Strab. V 2, 6 (p. 223 C.) already observed this.
[2] Cf. below, p. 289 sqq., with all the proofs of this fact in detail.
[3] Cf. the *tabula Peutingeriana* and L. A. Holland, *op. cit.* 308 sqq. J. B. Ward Perkins, PBSR 23, 1955, 45 sqq.
[4] L. A. Holland, *op. cit.* 283, 287.

We shall see later [1] that Veii made a direct perpendicular shortcut from her site to the salt marshes.

Besides her road-system, Veii also created a ring of bulwarks around her possessions. The Etruscan city of Solonium, situated south of the Tiber between Rome and Ostia,[2] seems to have belonged to these Veientan outposts, as did the ferry-place of Fidenae,[3] dominating the river immediately north of Rome. *Crustumerium*, a Sabine settlement to the northeast of Fidenae, seems to have been equally subject to Veii in the sixth century.[4] To the north the chain of these strongholds was completed by other bastions, protecting her against her fellow Etruscan enemies. These were: the rich Faliscan center of Falerii, depending on Veii;[5] Capena [6] near Mount Socrate; and finally Sutrium and Nepet, two citadels blocking the two arteries of communication across the otherwise almost impenetrable Ciminian forest, *velut claustra portaeque Etruriae*, as Livy calls them [7]—they were like doors to Etruria, which could be bolted and barred. Other fortified points on the outskirts of the Veientan territory could not be lacking.

This chain of peripheral military bases reflects the same defensive and expansive concepts as the steadily increased belt of Latin colonies planted around the federal territory by the Latin League in the fifth and early fourth centuries B.C., continued and developed systematically by Rome after 338 B.C.[8] Varro states that the Romans learned their policy of colonization from the Etruscans: no Etruscan prototype was closer at hand for observation and imitation than the zone of fortified Veientan places. Rome herself belonged in the last decades of the sixth century in some way or other to those Veientan bulwarks, as a dependent ally. The visit of the Veientan King *Vel Vibe* [9] in Alba Longa in the *Lupus* of Naevius is a mythical paraphrase of the en-

---

[1] *Ibid.* 303 sq. and p. 294 sq. below.

[2] M. Fluss, RE 3A, 981 sq. and below, p. 302 n. 3.

[3] Liv. I 14, 2 ; 15, 1. IV 17, 1. DH II 54, 3. Plut., *Rom.* 25, 2. Strab. V 2, 9 (226 C.).

[4] Plin., *N.h.* III 5, 52. Paul. Fest. p. 48, 12 L.

[5] Strab., *l.c.* Plin., *N.h.* III 5,51. Serv., *Aen.* 7, 607. Falerii was holding out on the side of the Veientanes until the last ; evidence given, e.g., by Chr. Huelsen, RE 6, 1969 sq.

[6] Cato, *Orig.* fr. 48 (H. R. Rel. 1², p. 68 = F. Gr. Hist. 706 F 9 = Serv. auct., *Aen.* 7, 697, and the note of H. Peter to his fr. 30. Liv. V 8, 4 sqq.

[7] Liv. VI 9, 4. IX 32, 1.

[8] Cf. below, p. 238 sqq.

[9] Cf. above, p. 230 n. 1.

ETRUSCAN RULE IN LATIUM AND ROME

croachment of Veii on Latium in the late sixth century. As we must return to this fact again in our last two chapters, it will suffice here to stress once more the point that the elaborate network of the Veientan communication system never could have been workable with a switch in the hand of a power independent of Veii—just as your neighbor cannot have a switch on your electric current, cutting it off or turning it on at his will.

In the same way as many other signs of Etruscan influence in Latium, the role of Veientan artists and craftsmen in the construction and decoration of the Capitoline temple—attested now not only by the written tradition [1] but illustrated also by the magnificent monuments excavated in Veii [2]—is far easier to understand when we realize that the connection between the two cities was not simply commercial, but was political dependence of Rome on Veii. Another hint to this fact is the Veientan grotta-oscura-tuff, used as material for a written official document from the end of the monarchy in the forum Romanum.[3] A hundred years later this stone would have been brought from the Veientan quarries to Rome because Veii was vanquished and Rome disposed of her resources. In the late sixth century, however, the Veientan artists and materials were granted to her subjectally as a favor of the stronger power.

Clusium

Twenty years after the crisis of 524 B.C., putting an end to Vulcentane domination in Rome, as we believe, and reinstating the dynasty of the Tarquins, another storm swept down on Rome from the north, dislodging this time along with the Tarquins the monarchy as a governmental institution in Rome. Our second chapter gave all the information available on this event, the subjugation of Rome by Porsenna, king of Clusium, about 505 B.C.[4] The Romans of later times still remembered the garrison of Porsenna, remaining permanently in the city, even if they gave to its presence a euphemistic interpretation.[5]

[1] A. Rumpf, RE 9A, 1223 sq.
[2] M. Pallottino, La scuola di Vulca², Roma 1948.
[3] Cf. G. Marchetti-Longhi, Arch. cl. 11, 1959, 50 sqq.
[4] We remind the reader of Plin., N.h. XXXIV 14, 139 : *in foedere, quod expulsis regibus populo Romano dedit Porsina, nominatim comprehensum invenimus, ne ferro nisi in agri cultu uteretur,* and of Tac., *Hist.* 3, 72 : *dedita urbe.* Cf. also L. Pareti, St. Etr. 5, 1931, 147 sqq.
[5] Liv. II 14, 9. DH V 36, 3.

Etruscan Domination over Rome

After the catastrophic defeat of his army at Aricia, Porsenna was constrained to concede to the Romans more freedom and to lend them his support against the Latins, backed by Cyme. This, at any rate, is how I interpret the evidence and this aid, I think, must have been of a decisive value for Rome.

Yet the ambitious plans of Clusium and its ruler in Latium were upset by the Latin states, who emerge after the great victory at Aricia as an autonomous political coalition, driving a wedge between Etruria proper and her colonial empire in the south of Latium. Now, after a long period of foreign domination, the ascent of Rome to the leadership of Latium begins. We shall try to describe this slow and unspectacular, but nevertheless grandiose, process, which was of enormous significance in its effects for the future of Italy. But, we must first make the acquaintance of two other centers, which were the leading powers of the Latin tribe long before Rome's ascent began.

Chapter VI

ALBA LONGA AND LAVINIUM:
THE OLD CAPITALS OF THE LATIN TRIBE

1. ALBA LONGA

Plato describes [1] how the civilized human community of the Greek city arose from the anarchy of savage beginnings: first, men establish-ed with their families on mountain heights came together and proceed-ed to form a patriarchal kingdom. Then they descended to the hill-sides, turned to farming and developed an aristocratic government. Finally, from the highland slopes they moved downward to the plain, building cities on suitable hills and discovering the advantages of democracy. In some parts of Greece and Sicily, where there was a lag in the general refinement of cultural life, Plato certainly could have observed such developments; in any case, the stages of evolution he describes were those of the Latins in Latium. Their first center after their immigration, no doubt the seat of their tribal kings, was Alba Longa on the Alban Mountain, a strategic base dominating all

[1] Platon, *Leg.* 3, 680 B sqq.

236

Latium,[1] well suited for the control and direction of the subdivisions and outposts of the tribe which surrounded it.[2] At the same time the summit of Monte Cavo above Alba, was a fit seat for the Father of Heaven —as was the "White" or "Golden" Mountain of the nomadic shepherd tribes of Eurasia. Such a natural fortress, which is both the original dwelling place of the kings and the cradle of the nation and at the same time also the White or Golden Mountain, the holy seat of the Heavenly Father, is a common phenomenon throughout Eurasia.[3] It is a typical feature of that archaic culture that things required for military and economic reasons in the bitter struggle for survival were embellished by superstitious imagination, and invested with supernatural significance. The myth of common origin, and the glorification of the institution of kingship served to tighten the bonds of social organization. And just as the nomads of northern Asia descended from their Holy Mountain to make raids and conquests, so too the Sabines descended from the heights of the Abruzzi around Amiternum and the Latins as well; after them—pressing the Latins hard—the Volscians and Aequians also came down from their heights. In the geographical area throughout which these cattle-rearing warrior peoples were at home, the royal residence was often called, even in later times, the "White-City" like Alba; the Sar-Kel of the

[1] B. G. Niebuhr, RG², Berlin 1827, 205, painted a charming picture of its site : ". . . auf den Abhang des Monte Cavo, von dessen Gipfel der Blick weiter reicht, als Roms Herrschaft vor den Samniterkriegen,—in der letzten Erleuchtung der Sonne Corsica und Sardinia erreichen kann—, und den Berg welchen Circes Name noch verherrlicht, in den ersten Strahlen ihres göttlichen Vaters als Insel sieht."

[2] Rightly pointed out by L. Homo, L'Italie primitive, Paris 1925, 90. For the topography cf. G. Tomasetti, La campagna romana 2, 1910, 101 sqq. Th. Ashby, Journ. of Philol. 27, 1901, 37 sqq., 42. H. Nissen, It. Lk. 2, 583. G. De Sanctis, St. d. R. 1², 178. A new attempt to localize the old capital is made by Fr. Dionisi, La scoperta topografica di Alba Longa (Quaderni dell' Alma Roma 3), Roma 1961. For the historical tradition see M. Gelzer, RE 12, 949.

[3] Cf., e.g., Menand., *Exc. de leg.*, ed. De Boor, pp. 193 and 207. Theophyl. Simm. VII 8, 11-12. Ed. Chavannes, Documents sur les T'ou-Kioue occidentaux, Paris 1900, 236 sq., 248 n. 1. J. Marquart, Über das Volkstum der Komanen, Abh. Gött. ph.-h. Kl., n. F. 13, 1914 no. 1, 63, 69, 84. V. Thomsen, Zeitschr. d. Deutschen Morgenländischen Gesellschaft 77, 1924, 131, 141. J. J. M. De Groot, Die asiatischen Hunnen der vorchristlichen Zeit, Berlin-Leipzig 1, 1921, 59. R. Hennig, Rh. Mus. n. F. 79, 1930, 388 sqq. P. Pelliot, T'oung pao 26, 1929, 212 sqq. B. Munkácsi, Vogul népköltési gyüjtemény 1, Budapest 1892, pp. CXLV, CCXLII sq. W. Radloff, Aus Sibirien 1, Leipzig 1884, 529. G. M. Potanin, Ethnographia 11, Budapest 1900, 260 sqq. F. v. Andrian, Höhenkultus asiatischer und europäischer Völker, Wien 1891 etc.

Volga-Bulgars, the Beograd of the southern Slavs, the Székes-Fehérvár of the Hungarians testify to this.[1]

The one-time predominant position of Alba is clearly mirrored in the ambition of the Romans to connect their origins with her. Their twin founders are said to be the descendants of the Alban kings; their mother is named *Alba* in versions as old as the fourth century B.C.,[2] or also Silvia [3] after the mythical first king of Alba. Important clans of the old Roman aristocracy wished to trace their descent to Alba [4] and make it believed that even their costume was Alban.[5] Yet Rome was not alone in this ambition. Lavinium strove in rivalry with Alba to demonstrate the priority of her aspirations to primacy, as we shall see. But the traces of the Alban preeminence are more concrete than these claims. We have already discussed the survival of the political and social organization which once was the basis of the power of the Alban kings. This is the confraternity of the thirty *populi Albenses*, the original tribal confederation of all the Latins, which in historical times was still permitted to assemble for their old tribal festival every year under Roman supervision.[6]

The first literary allusion to Alba Longa, though indirect, occurs as far back as the early sixth century B.C. This is the often quoted passage of the Theogony of Hesiod [7] where it is stated that Agrios and Latinos are ruling over the Etruscans north of the Cape of Circeii. Though the *combination* of the facts is entirely wrong—the very confusion of the nebulous information proves it to be of an early date—the single elements of this statement are highly significant. First, the two kings mentioned are the legendary first kings of Alba Longa and Lavinium: Latinus is connected throughout the tradition with the latter city, whereas Agrios can be no other than the mythical persona-

---

[1] Walde-Hoffmann, Etym. Wörterbuch 1, 27, explains the name as "Bergstadt."

[2] Alcimus, F. Gr. Hist. 560 F 4 (= Fest., p. 326, 35 L.) Cf. DH I 72,6. Euseb., *Chron.* I 45, 3. Syncell. p. 363 Bonn. A. Schwegler, RG 1, 400 n. 1.

[3] Cf. A. Schwegler, RG 1, 426 sqq. G. De Sanctis, St. d. R. 1², 202. A. Rosenberg, RE 1 A, 343.

[4] A. Schwegler, RG 1, 457, however, states correctly : "Es lst eine Grundvorstellung der römischen Sage, dass die ursprüngliche Bewohnerschaft des Palatin Hirtenvolk war, nicht troischer Adel, nicht ausgewandertes albanisches Patriziat."

[5] Fest., p. 128, 5 L., etc.

[6] These thirty *populi* are discussed above, p. 10 sqq.

[7] Hesiod, *Theog.* 1011-6 = F. Gr. Hist. 706 F 15; cf. Jacoby, *ibid.* Kommentar 3 B, 1955, 520 (concerning 560 F 4).

lity, Silvius,[1] the founder of Alba, whose name was the sole basis for Fabius Pictor's construction of the fictitious dynasty of the Silvii.[2] I would like to infer from this coincidence that both cities were present in the minds of the local people whose information reached Greece in the form of this shadowy picture. Second, as the Etruscans are

[1] This identification proposed by me in my study "Die trojanischen Urahnen der Römer" (Rektoratsprogramm der Universität Basel 1956) 1957, 24 sqq., was opposed by S. Weinstock, JRS 49, 1959, 170 sq., whose arguments, however, are not convincing. I know, of course, that *Silvius* in DH I 70, 2 (cf. Lyd., *De mag.* 21) is rendered *verbatim* as ῾Υλαῖος. Yet it is evident that at the time of the late Republic when this translation was made, the knowledge of the original character of the myth of origin already vanished. This myth of origin will be discussed in all details in my book on the Roman festival of the *Lupercalia*. ῎Αγριος, "living in the fields," "living wild" is an exact circumscription of the mythical type of the shepherd peoples in view. *Silvius .. regnat, .. casu quodam in silvis natus*, writes Liv. I 3, 6. Cf. DH I 70, 2: καὶ τὸ παιδίον ... Σιλούιον ὀνομάσας ἀπὸ τῆς ὕλης (where he came to world). Cato, *Orig.* fr. 11 Peter (= Serv., *Aen.* 6, 760) : *Lavinia timens insidias gravida confugit ad silvas et latuit in casa pastoris Tyrrhi . . . . . et illic enixa est Silvium . . . . . . qui (Ascanius) quoniam sine liberis periit, Silvio . . . . . suum reliquit imperium*. Verg., *Aen.* 6, 760 sq. Gell. II 16, 3. Ovid., *Fast.* 4, 41. Origo gent. R. 16, 1-5. Weinstock denies that on the unique *denarius* of Cornelius Cethegus (pl. VII, 5) the head represents the Trojan mother of the Latins and that the child with the Phrygian cap riding a goat on the reverse is Silvius, as I suggested *(ibid.)*. The "Trojan" headgear of both, mother and son, which accentuates their common origin, is decisive in favor of my view, I am sure (more on this point in my forthcoming study on regal attributes and agonistic symbolism). "And why should Silvius be represented as a child?" asked Weinstock. The answer is very simple : in the myths of origin of the type in question the childhood and youth of the hero are only and alone relevant. I have shown that even the investiture of the Persian kings contained a "mystical" initiation, in which the ruler was playing the role of the first king Cyrus who also *natus in silvis* (Schweiz. Archiv für Volkskunde 47, 1951, 11 sqq.). Cf. I. Widengren, Iranisch-semitische Kulturbegegnung in parthischer Zeit, Köln-Opladen 1960, 77 sqq. This also is the authentic atmosphere of the genuine legend of Roman origins, in Fabius Pictor's description of the growth of the twins : βίος δ'αὐτοῖς ἦν βουκολικὸς καὶ δίαιτα αὐτουργὸς ἐν ὄρεσι τὰ πολλὰ πηξαμένοις διὰ ξύλων καὶ καλάμων σκηνὰς αὐτορόφους (DH I 79, 11). *Adultis inter pastores de virtute cotidiana certamina et vires et pernicitatem auxere* (Justin. XLIII 2, 8 sqq.). Cf. also Cic., *Cael.* 26 : *quorum* (sc. germanorum Lupercorum) *coitio illa silvestris ante est instituta quam humanitas atque leges*. But Weinstock correctly reminds us of the fact that already M. Durante, La parola del passato 5, 1950, 216 sq., made the equation ῎Αγριος—*Silvius*, though for other reasons. This view is maintained also by O. Gigon, in : Sprachgeschichte und Wortdeutung. Festschrift für A. Debrunner, Bern 1954, 155. This escaped the notice of Weinstock as well as my own. Quite different is the origin of the *silvicolae homines bellique inertes* of Naevius, *Bell. Poenicum* fr. 15 Marm. : S. Mariotti, Il Bellum Poenicum e l'arte di Naevio, Roma 1955, 34 sqq., has convincingly proved that these are the innocent men of the Golden Age who lived in Nature without sweat and toil.

[2] This was realized already by B. G. Niebuhr, RG 1², Berlin 1927, 209, and

mentioned in those parts of Italy, the *terminus post quem* seems to be the decades around 650, when they occupied Latium. Later on such vague geographical definitions as the μυχῷ νήσων ἱεράων would no longer satisfy the Greeks. Third, the Latin territory in the south still reached the very limits of Campania: this means that the Volscians had not yet intruded in this area. The great importance of the Etruscan commerce across the plain of Latium could explain the rise of Lavinium as a new tribal center instead of Alba, which was situated off the route of the new transit-commerce. Not too far and not too near the seashore, Lavinium controlled the main line of communications between southern Etruria and the Campanian border. Fourth, in Hesiod the ancestors of the Latins are Odysseus and Circe. Aeneas, whose prevalence over the Greek heroes came with the Etruscan occupation—we shall discuss this later—is still absent. This picture of the early sixth century would, of course, have been very different if Rome had already conquered Alba, as is stated in the Roman Annals.

In the early imperial times, when inscriptions abound, the continuation of the Alban priesthoods by Rome becomes evident.[1] They are, however, linked with three different parts of the Alban Mountain. On the peak of the Monte Cavo where, as Mommsen has shown, the village of Cabum once was situated, the *Cabenses sacerdotes feriarum Latinarum montis Albani*[2] performed their duties

has been repeated often since, e.g., by G. De Sanctis, St. d. R. 1[1], 205 : 1[2], 201. Cf. also O. Leuze, Die römische Jahrzählung, Tübingen 1909, 88 sqq. W. Schnur, RE 12, 1004 sqq.

[1] The lists of these priests are compiled by G. Howe, *Fasti sacerdotum populi Romani publicorum aetatis imperatoriae* (Diss. Leipzig 1904) 75; for additions see G. Wissowa, in : Hermes 50, 1915, 2 sqq., and K. Latte, Römische Religionsgeschichte, München 1960, 404 sqq. The Annals date back the Roman management of the Alban cults to King Tullus (Liv. I 29, 6 ; 31, 1. V 52,8. DH III 29,5. Cic., *Pro Mil.* 31,85 *Albanorum . . . arae, sacrorum populi Romani sociae et aequales*. Tibull. I 7, 58. Strab. V 3,4 (C. 231). Fest., p. 186, 11 L.

[2] CIL XIV 2228, cf. VI 2174 sqq. G. Wissowa, in Hermes 50, 1915, 3. The *sacerdotes Caeninenses* were not created for the *feriae Latinae* as K. Latte, *l.c.*, believes it, but for the care of Caenina's cult ; the sacrifice of the youthful Romulus in Caenina, described by Fabius Pictor fr. 5 *b* Peter (H. R. Rel. 1[2], p. 12) : Ῥωμύλος μὲν οὖν . . ἐτύγχανεν ἅμα τοῖς ἐπιφανεστάτοις τῶν κομητῶν πεπορευμένος εἴς τι χωρίον Καίνιναν ὀνομαζόμενον ἱερὰ ποιήσων ὑπὲρ τοῦ κοινοῦ πάτρια, was of course featured on the basis of this existing practice. But K. Latte is right in supposing that these functionaries also were representing the decayed Caenina at the *Latiar*. G. Wissowa, *l.c.* translated the ὕπατος Καινείνηνσις

on the last day of the Latin Festival. On the site of Alba Longa itself was the temple of Vesta, where the *virgines Vestales arcis Albanae* [1] with their *Vestalis maxima* performed their duties. If they only made their appearance here twice a year, the *salii arcis Albanae* must have exhibited their solemn dance on the same spot; and here too must have been the place where the *pontifices Albani* officiated. Wissowa has shown in his brilliant paper that all these priesthoods were *sacerdotia publica populi Romani*, though not having the high rank of the corresponding urban priesthoods. [2]

However, the venerable heritage of Alba Longa was also fostered by the Romans in a third city of her surroundings. Imperial inscriptions mention the *Albani Longani Bovillenses*, [3] i.e., the people from Alba in Bovillae—a juridical fiction reminding us of the contemporary organization of the *Laurentes Lavinates* constituted for a similar purpose. Beloch is certainly wrong in his guess that Sulla attributed Alba to Bovillae owing to the depopulation of that region: the altar of the *gens Julia* of late Republican date in Bovillae is evidence that this Alban clan already had, before the reforms of Sulla its own sanctuary in Bovillae, [4] used the Alban ritual for its votive offerings (*lege Albana*), and certainly not only for occasional sacrifices but also for the entire ritual of Veiovis. It was not the administrative reforms of Sulla but

ἱερῶν δήμου 'Ρωμαίων IG III 623, 7 = 624,4 as *sacerdos Caeninensis maximus*. I think that he was rather a quasi-magistrate, *consul Caeninensis*, created *ad sacra*, just as the duties of the *dictator Albanus* were exclusively religious in historical times.

[1] Liv. I 20, 3 : *Virgines ... Vestales legit* (Numa), *Alba oriundum sacerdotium.* The same in DH II 65, 1. Further details in G. Wissowa, *op. cit.* This temple was not in Bovillae as was supposed, e.g., by Beloch, RG 162. Cf. Iuven. 4, 60 sqq. : *Utque lacus suberat, ubi quamquam diruta servat/Ignem Troianum et Vestam colit Alba minorem* and G. Lugli, I sanctuarii celebri del Lazio antico, Roma 1932, 26. This temple appears in the legendary tale of the beginnings in DH I 76, 4. II 65, 1. Liv. I 20, 3, etc.

[2] G. Wissowa, *op. cit.* 4, observed that the *pontifex Albanus minor* CIL IX 1595 is "minor" in relation to the *pontifices* of the city of Rome ; but the *Vesta minor* of Alba in Iuven. 4, 60 sqq., has the same relation to the Roman Vesta.

[3] H. Nissen, It. Lk. II 2, 585 sqq. K. J. Beloch, RG 152 and 162 sqq. H. Dessau, CIL XIV p. 231 and *ibid.* 2405, 2406, 2409, 2411.

[4] CIL XIV 2387=Dess. 2988=A. Degrassi, *Inscr. lib. rei publ.* 270. Liv. I 30, 2. Tac., *Ann.* 2, 41. 15, 23. On the *ritus Albanus* : Liv. I 7, 3 ; 31, 1 sq. Cf. G. De Sanctis, St. d. R. I¹, 386=I², 375. A. Rosenberg, Hermes 54, 1919, 151. For further details see P. De Francisci, Primordia civitatis, Roma 1960, 166. I do not think that the Iulii, prominent in Rome at the beginning of the Republic, came from Bovillae. It is much more likely that they erected their family shrine in that city to stress the Alban origin of their family—some time after they regained their political prominence.

242

the care for the *sacra Albana* which must therefore have been decisive in the role of Bovillae. This state of things involves some serious historical consequences. If the care of the Alban cults in Bovillae goes back to an old tradition, we must suppose with G. De Sanctis [1] that Bovillae had charge of them before the Romans took over. As G. Wissowa has stressed, the religious obligations of a Latin community did not end with its political autonomy or with its destruction: they were to be provided by the power which inherited its soil. And if Bovillae did this before Rome, then the Alban soil was subject to Bovillae before it belonged to Rome. This conclusion fits well into the general picture emerging from our inquiry.

The distribution of the rituals and cults of Alba between three neighboring communities cannot be a purely religious development, a simple continuation of the cult institutions of the old Latin capital city, but involves political complications of remote times resulting from the ambition of the neighbors and the aspirations and prestige of the ruling power.[2] The names of the Alban priesthoods contain a chronological implication for the early history, which was recognized long ago,[3] namely, that Bovillae had a *rex sacrorum*,[4] successor of its ancient kings, whereas the title of the supervisor of the cult organization of Alba Longa was *dictator Albanus*.[5] The Annals take it for granted that this dictatorship is a genuine Alban institution; the archaic regal costume worn by the Alban dictators [6] pleads strongly for this assumption.

[1] G. De Sanctis, *l.c.* We must correct his statement in one regard : neither Alba nor Bovillae were incorporated into the Roman state in the archaic epoch ; cf. below, p. 303 sqq.

[2] The mentioning of the ἱερὰ κοινὰ τὰ ἐν Ἄλβᾳ καὶ ἄλλα δίκαια πολιτικὰ in Strabo V 3,4 (C. 231), has projected back into the oldest history the *communio sacrorum* of the Latin confederation.

[3] Cf. Th. Mommsen, St. R. 2³, 1887, 171 n. 1 and 3. K. J. Beloch, RG 230 sqq. A. Rosenberg, Der Staat der alten Italiker, Berlin 1913, 75 and Hermes 54, 1919, 153. H. Rudolph, Stadt und Staat im römischen Italien, Leipzig 1935, 9 sqq. M. Gelzer, RE 12, 949 sqq. with literature.

[4] CIL XIV 2413 with a note by H. Dessau against Th. Mommsen (ad CIL VI 2125). G. Wissowa, RuK², 520 n. 6.

[5] CIL VI 2161=ILS 4955. Cato, *Orig.* 1. fr. 22 Peter has *Cloelius praetor Albanus*. Licinius Macer fr. 10 Peter *dictator* ; cf. DH III 2, 1 of Cloelius : τῆς μεγίστης ἀρχῆς ἀξιωθείς. Mettius Fufetius is στρατηγὸς αὐτοκράτωρ in DH III 5, 3 ; cf. 28, 6. Livy I 23, 4 ; 27, 1 styles him as *dictator*, but Cluilius as *rex* (I 23,4). Cf. Plut., *Romul.* 27, 1 : the Alban dictatorship instituted by Romulus.

[6] Cf. my remarks in : Studien über Caesars Monarchie 1, Lund 1953, 21 sq., and also in Mus. Helv. 8, 1951, 210.

As A. Rosenberg pointed out, the change from kingship to the annual magistracy could not have happened before the sixth century B.C. I believe we must go even further down in time: the overthrow of outdated political institutions normally takes place during a short period within the same area; and the fall of the monarchy in Alba could not have happened much earlier than in Rome. Alba Longa, therefore, still existed in the second half of the sixth century, when her king was superseded by the *dictator*. We arrive at the same result in another way. As we have seen above (p. 42 sq.), the dictatorship of the individual Latin states imitated the tribal dictator, who officiated at the annual festival of the Latins in Lavinium. As the Etruscan rule seems to have been intimately connected with the local dynasties, the city-dictators could hardly have emerged before the end of the Etruscan domination, or at least not long before the last decade of the sixth century B.C. We shall explore now how much longer Alba was in existence after the introduction of the new form of government.

When the late-born Roman historiography started, the tribal kingship belonged to an ancient past, and the generations after Fabius Pictor could comprehend the role of Alba Longa only as that of a leading city-state.[1] We know, however, that Alba did not become an important urban center. Her preeminent role belonged to the pre-urban period. An inventory of the tombs of the Iron Age population reveals, rather, an extensive shepherd settlement.[2] The archaeological survey of the site has shown that the necropolis so far explored was abandoned around the middle of the seventh century,[3] and this date would correspond to the pretended Roman destruction of the city[4]— an event which was certainly already described in Fabius Pictor.[5] But we have noticed that this statement is not reliable. Though Pliny the Elder has been censored for absent-mindedness when enumerating

---

[1] Cf., e.g., Cato in : *Orig. g. Rom.* 12, 5. DH III 31, 4 ; 34, 1. Liv. I 52, 2. Fest., p. 276, 18 L. Verg., *Aen.* 1, 270 ; 8, 48, etc.

[2] A. Pinza, Bull. Com. 28, 1900, 219. Cf. also Th. Ashby, in : Journal of Philology 27, 1901, 37 sqq. Papers of the Brit. School at Rome 5, 1910, 278 sqq.

[3] M. Pallottino, Archeol. 12, 1960, 27 and 34.

[4] Details given by A. Schwegler, RG 1, 1857, 583, 587 sq. M. Gelzer, RE 12, 949. F. Schachermeyr, RE 4 A, 2364, and elsewhere.

[5] Ennius had it (Ann. fr. 140 Vahlen[2]=143 Warm.), I think, from him. DH III 31, 4 : καθαιρεθεῖσα ἔρημος εἰς τόδε χρόνου διαμένει. Cf. *ibid.* VI 20, 3. Liv. I 29, 6. Serv., *Aen.* 1, 282. Cincius (the antiquarian) in Fest., p. 276 L. Cf. Diod. VIII 25, 1 sqq.

Alba among the existing *oppida* in the neighborhood of Rome,[1] we have some additional signs of her survival in historical times. The purpose of the amazing hydrotechnical achievement of the tunnel cut through the rock, thereby reducing the level of the Alban Lake to its present height, was made to enlarge the surface of the slope for agriculture and to prevent the inundation of a densely populated area. This immense effort extending over many years was certainly not expended to a deserted field of ruins, nor as the Roman Annals pretend, was its purpose to expiate a *prodigium*. The mural technique of the tunnel entrance corresponds to the date of the Annals (ca. 400 B.C.), as F. Castagnoli kindly informs me; but this seems to me to be only a repair or an improvement of an already existing structure. The style reminds us of the famous tunnel of the aqueduct of Eupalinus, constructed for Polycrates at Samos,[2] and fits into the framework of the imposing hydrotechnical enterprises of the Etruscans in the sixth century B.C. This means that Alba in that century was still a settlement of considerable size. The ancients knew her time-reckoning,[3] which could scarcely have been set down in writing before the fifth century B.C.[4] and could not have been known to later generations if Alba had disappeared in the seventh century B.C. Also we know that the border between Alba and Rome still ran across the *Fossae Cluiliae* in the fifth century,[5] and that the *ager Albanus* lay outside of the boundaries of the *ager Romanus antiquus*. This proves that the juridical personality of that community did not disappear. Rome annexed every bit of territory occupied up to the end of the fifth century, and only with Tusculum in 387 B.C. began expansion without direct incorporation (cf. our map, p. 297). The *ager Albanus* was included in the Roman tribes only in 338 B.C. In the same

---

[1] Plin., *N.h.* III 5, 63.

[2] Cf. E. Fabricius, Athen. Mitt. 9, 1884, 165 sqq., esp. 170 sqq. This comparison was suggested to me by H. Nesselhauf.

[3] Censorin., *De die nat.* 22, 5-6 (p. 66 Jahn). *At civitatium menses vel magis numero dierum inter se discrepant, sed dies ubique habent totos. Apud Albanos Martius est sex et triginta, Maius viginti et duum, Sextilis duodeviginti, September sedecim. Tusculanorum Quintilis dies habet XXXVI, October XXXII, idem October apud Aricinos XXXVIII.* Verrius Flaccus in the *Fasti Praenestini* (CIL I² p. 233) writes *Martius ab Latinorum (Marte appel)landi. itaque apud Albanos et plerosque (po)pulos Lat(in)os fuit ante conditam Romam, ut a(u)tem alii cre(du)nt quod et sacra* (sc. Martis) *fiunt hoc mense.* Ov., *Fast.* 3, 89. Cf. Fest., p. 306, 2 L.

[4] For Rome cf. A. Kirsopp-Lake Michels, TAPA 80, 1949, 320 sqq.

[5] K. J. Beloch, RG 169. Mommsen, RG 1¹, 45. H. Nissen, It. Lk. II 2, Berlin 1902, 498, 585. Cf. below, p. 300 sq.

way the meadows at the *caput aquae Ferentinae* where the annual gatherings of the Latins were held *sub monte Albano* until 340 B.C. were not included in the old Roman territory but belonged to Aricia or Tusculum.[1] This again means that the *ager Albanus* was not yet in Rome's possession.[2]

But about the middle of the fifth century, just when Ardea and Aricia were overpowered by Rome,[3] the list of the Roman officials presiding over the *feriae Latinae* also began.[4] If the date were a mere invention of later generations, the obvious starting point would have been the alleged organization of King Superbus, or at least not later than the beginning of the *Fasti*. We can assume with confidence that the Roman supervision of the *feriae Latinae* started in fact in the years of the *decemviri*.

The coincidence of the commencement of the Roman supervision of the Latin festival with Roman expansion in the region of Alba can hardly be due to mere chance. Though we have information about investments of the Roman state in Alban territory only at the end of the fifth century, we shall see later that neighboring cities were already dependent on Rome fifty years earlier.[5] The incorporation of Alba Longa in the Roman voting districts occurred, however, only in 338 B.C.[6]

The decay of Alba was not the consequence of the alleged Roman conquest but of a general development, through which the tribal kingship of the old eagle's nest was replaced by individual cities, subject first to new Etruscan overlords. But already before the Etrus-

---

[1] K. J. Beloch, RG 183 and above, p. 34 sqq.

[2] This has already been pointed out by B. G. Niebuhr, RG 1², Berlin 1827, who drew all the consequences from this observation : "aber . . . um zu bezweifeln, dass Alba von den Römern zerstört ward, scheinen sehr erhebliche Gründe obzuwalten. Nach dem Völkerrecht Italiens, welches in diesem Fall einer gänzlichen Zerstörung auch Naturrecht gewesen sein würde, müsste das Eigentum der albanischen Feldmark an Rom übergegangen sein. Allein nicht Rom, sondern die Latiner waren in ihrem Besitz ; hier, am Quell der Ferentina . . . hielten sie ihre Landesgemeinden. Danach dürfte eine ganz andere historische Wahrheit im Grund der Erzählung liegen : Alba von den Latinern und nicht von Rom zerstört sein." The opposite view is held by Beloch, RG 172, but cf. *ibid.* 183.

[3] Cf. below, p. 381 and 394.

[4] Cf. above, p. 31.

[5] Liv. V 15, 4 sqq.

[6] L. R. Taylor, Vot. Distr. (Papers and Monogr. Am. Ac. in Rome 20) 1960, 43 and below, p. 312. 318 sqq.

can conquest another Latin center emerged. Its central position on the coastal artery of communications between north and south gave it a religious significance even under foreign rule comparable to that of Volsinii among the Etruscan states. We turn our attention now to this new metropolis.

∾

2. LAVINIUM

Besides Alba Longa, the primeval seat of the tribal kings, another Latin state was also regarded as the mother city of Rome. As in the case of Alba where the ritual performances just reviewed preserved the memory of a political dependency on the part of Rome in centuries long past, there were also other religious obligations attesting Rome's dependency on Lavinium in a remote epoch: *maiores . . . sacra quaedam in monte Albano Laviniique nobis facienda tradiderunt*.[1]

The Romans of later times, of course, would never admit that they were once inferior in strength to any other Latin city. Consequently they did not trace the fulfillment of all these religious duties to a status inferior to that of Alba, respectively Lavinium in olden times, but explained them as spontaneous manifestations of their piety toward two mother cities.[2] And at least in this way they did not deny the truth that two such centers, one-time leaders of Latium, existed. Their leading role is reflected in the tradition in many ways.[3]

---

[1] Liv. V 52, 8 (speech of Camillus).

[2] The literary references are collected by A. Schwegler, RG 1, 283 sqq., 305, 317 sqq., 324 sqq. The foundation legends of Alba and Lavinium have been discussed anew by W. Ehlers in Mus. Helv. 6, 1949, 166 sqq., where all the source material is carefully assembled and analyzed. But Ehlers is interested only in the literary type of these narratives, not in their historical evaluation at which the present research is aimed.

[3] The general reader may be puzzled by the fact that sometimes in the sources the city of Lavinium is also called *Laurentum* and expressions such as *terra Laurens, ager Laurens, populus Laurens* occur rather frequently. The twofold denomination has been explained either by the assumption that the people themselves had the name of *Laurentes*, whereas *Lavinium* was the name of the urban center of this people (e.g., K. J. Beloch, RG 148, 153, 158. R. Lanciani, Mon. ant. 13, 1903, 142 sqq. J. Carcopino, Virgile et les origines d'Ostie 1919, 171 sqq. G. Bendz, Sur la question de la ville de Laurentum, (Opuscula archeol. [Skrifter Inst. R. Regni Suec. 4°] 1935, 47 sqq.), or by interpreting both Laurentum and Lavinium as cities (A. Boëthius in the periodical *Roma* 9, 1931, 55 sqq. B. Tilly, Vergil's Latium, Oxford 1947, 83 sqq. Cf. also H. Boas,

Lavinium

Lavinium was the *sedes regni* for Vergil as well as Alba.[1] Lucan[2] calls both these initial centers the homes of the ancestral gods of Rome, the *Penates*. If Romulus is considered in one case as the grandchild of Aeneas, this implies that his ancestry goes back to Lavinium;[3] if, at another time, he is regarded as the grandson of Numitor, this is to stress his Alban descent. The two names of the mother of the Roman twins reflect the same duplication: *Ilia* is the Lavinian offspring of the Trojan hero, *Silvia* is that of the mythical first king of Alba.[4] The original home of *Vesta* and of the *Penates* is located in one instance in Alba Longa,[5] in the other in Lavinium.[6] The prodigious sow, messenger of the divinity, guides the ancestor of the Latins sometimes to Lavinium, sometimes to Alba.[7] To harmonize the tradition of two such cradles of their race, the Romans put the sequence of events into chronological order, adapting the legend to suit their purposes. We can disregard this idle play of imagination. More relevant for us is the highly official recognition by the Romans of both centers as the roots of their existence. This was manifested by ritual acts, performed by the organs of the Roman state since time immemorial. They attest that if Alba was the seat of the primeval kings of the Latin tribe, Lavinium replaced her at the dawn of history as the metropolis of the Latins.[8]

Aeneas' Arrival in Latium, Amsterdam 1938, 123 sqq.). We hope to show in a forthcoming study on the *Lupercalia* that the pattern of such a twofold organization existed in Latium and that the combination of the two villages on the Palatine and the Quirinal as a double political unit was not the outcome of a mechanical growth, but came into existence on such a structural basis. *Laurentum—Lavinium* could be therefore eventually such a double organization.

[1] Verg., *Aen.* 1, 270 sqq.

[2] Lucan. 7, 394.

[3] Th. Mommsen, RF 2, 1879, 268 n. 62 and below, p. 257 sqq.

[4] Cf. Perizonius (*ad* Aelian., Var. hist. 7 p. 510 sqq.), quoted by B. G. Niebuhr, RG 1², Berlin 1827, 214 n. 536.

[5] DH II 65, 1. Ovid., *Fast.* 3, 11. Lucan. 5, 400 and above, p. 241.

[6] DH II 52, 3. V 12, 3 (cf. Liv. II 2, 10). DH II 52, 3. VIII 49, 6. Varro, *LL* 5, 144. Plut., *Coriol.* 29, 2. Val. Max. I 8, 8. Serv., *Aen.* 7, 661. *Orig. g. R.* 13, 7, etc. G. Wissowa, in: Roscher's Lex. 3, 1894. *Idem*, Hermes 50, 1915, 29 sqq.

[7] Details given most recently by W. Ehlers, Mus. Helv. 6, 1949, 166 sqq. and below, p. 271 sqq.

[8] Cf. F. Bömer, Rom und Troja, Baden-Baden 1951, 93 sqq. I repeat on the following pages some statements from my "Rektoratsprogramm" of Basle University 1956 (Basel 1957) in a more elaborate form; since that time my results have been corroborated by the highly important excavations of Prof. F. Castagnoli and Dr. L. Cozza in Lavinium. I wish to express my sincere

Yet even the intricate web of legendary tales was spun in a pattern containing historical threads, part of which is still traceable. One of these threads is the trace of the competition for primacy between the two leading cities of ancient Latium. The pretensions of Lavinium are based on the saga of the landing of Aeneas at the nearby seashore and on its claim to be the first Trojan settlement in Latium. The historian Timaeus, who visited Lavinium or met Lavinates in all likelihood about 315 B.C.,[1] already wrote down this story. It is significant that the first annalist, who as a member of the Roman aristocracy certainly imbibed at home in his youth the traditions of the origin of his people long before becoming acquainted with the work of Timeaus, confirmed this legendary priority of Lavinium. He modified the version of Timaeus only [2] in one respect—we shall come back to this—which does not affect the challenge of the Laurentes. Pictor was followed by Cato,[3] Varro,[4] and by most of the Roman writers on history.[5] Timaeus [6] heard in Lavinium or from men from Lavinium an additional story illustrating the superiority of that city over Alba Longa.[7] By the removal of the Lavinian colony to the new capital in the Alban Hills—so runs the story—the statues of

gratitude to both of these scholars for informing me about some decisive facts concerning the new evidence brought to light by them ; Prof. Castagnoli kindly allowed me to publish here his drawing reproduced on pl. XVI.

[1] F. Gr. Hist. 566 F 59-61. Lycophron v. 1253-56 has transcribed his narrative. Cf. below, p. 285 sq. Also Eratosthenes F. Gr. Hist. 24 F 45 identified the founder of Rome as the grandson of Aeneas ; yet it is not clear whether the first Trojan foundation in Latium was—in his view—Lavinium or Alba ; however, the former eventuality is more likely.

[2] F. Gr. Hist. 809 F 2.

[3] Cato, *Orig.* fr. 4 sqq. Peter : *Orig. g. R.* 12, 5 ; cf. W. Ehlers, Mus. Helv. 6, 1949, 170 sqq.

[4] Varro, *R R* II 4, 17-18 ; *id., LL* 5, 144.

[5] Liv. I 2, 4; 3, 3-4; 23, 1 (on the war between Rome and Alba) *civili simillimum bello, prope inter parentes natosque, Troianam utramque prolem, cum Lavinium ab Troia, ab Lavinio Alba, ab Albanorum stirpe regum oriundi Romani essent.* DH I 45, 2 ; 56, 2 sqq.; 63, 3; 66, 1; 73, 3. III 11, 2-3. VI 80, 1. Justin. XLIII 1, 12 sqq. Strabo V 3, 2 (C. 229). Verg., *Aen.* 1, 254 sqq. 258 sq. 267 sq. Vell. I 8, 5. Val. Max. I 8, 7 sqq. Cass. Dio 1, p. 2 sqq. Boiss. Tzetzes *ad* Lycophr. v. 1232. Serv., *Aen.* 1, 270 ; 3, 12. Aug., *Civ. Dei* 10, 16. Plut. *Rom.* 3, 2. Solin. 2, 16. Isid. XV 1, 52. sqq.

[6] F. Jacoby, F. Gr. Hist. 3 B Noten zum Komm., 1955, 332 n. 319, remarked that the story was shaped on the pattern of the statue of Diomedes (Timaeus F 53). Yet Timaeus certainly did not invent it ; he only recorded what he was told.

[7] Cf. J. Rubino, Beiträge zur Vorgeschichte Italiens, Leipzig 1868, 128 sqq.

the guardian gods of the state, the *Penates*, which had been carried away, also twice returned in the night from Alba to their old sanctuary. The miracle manifesting the will of the divinity constrained Ascanius to keep that ancestral cult in Lavinium and to take charge of its maintenance.[1] This story makes sense only if it was invented when Alba still existed and her claims were maintained. And it is a fact of great consequence that the tradition of the old preeminence of Lavinium was found intact by Timaeus, even after the complete subjugation of Latium by Rome; and also that Rome herself acknowledged this officially.

Yet another branch of the tradition, often contaminated or coordinated with the former, pleads for the cause of the primacy of Alba. The Sicilian Alcimus, contemporary of Dionysius II, who seems to have derived his information from the Romans,[2] did not include Lavinium in the genealogy of Rome,[3] whose Alban ancestry is traced directly to Etruscans and Trojans.[4] It appears[5] that also in the *Annales* of Ennius Aeneas came in contact with the king of Alba and married his daughter—not the daughter of the Lavinian ruler. Ennius presumably followed Naevius in this respect. In a version recorded by Conon[6] Aeneas settled down not in Lavinium but on the site of Alba. It is still more important that Fabius Pictor,[7] who must have

---

[1] From Timaeus derived, according to F. Jacoby, F. Gr. Hist., Notenband zum Komm. 3 B, 332 n. 319. Cf. DH I 67, 1-3. Cato, *Orig.* fr. 11 (cf. H. Peter, H. R. Rel. 1², 58). Serv., *Aen.* 1, 270. Val. Max., Cass. Dio, Augustin, Tzetzes *llcc* (cf. above p. 248 n. 5). Serv., *Aen.* 3, 12 (supplanting Alba by Rome). *Orig.g. R.* 17,2.

[2] He is the first writer mentioning the name of Romulus, F. Gr. Hist. 560 F 4 (=Fest. 326, 35 L.): *Alcimus ait Tyrrhenia Aeneae natum filium Romulum fuisse atque eo ortam Albam Aeneae neptem, cuius filius nomine Rhomus condiderit urbem Romam.* Cf. W. Hoffmann, Rom und die griechische Welt im IV. Jahrhundert v. Ch . Philol. Suppl. XXVII 1, 1934, 113 sq. F. Jacoby, F. Gr. Hist. 3 B 305, with further details and literature.

[3] *Contra* : W. Ehlers, *op. cit.* 169 n. 16.

[4] Leukaria (Alba) as mother of Rhomus (DH I 72, 6) or of Rhome (Plut., *Rom.* 2, 1) brings other playful combinations of the origin of the personified Alba Longa.

[5] As was assumed by Fr. Leo, Geschichte der römischen Literatur 1, Leipzig 1913, 166 sqq. Enn., *Ann.* fr. 33 Vahlen³=31 Warm.: *Olli respondit rex Albai Longai* could refer to other interlocutors ; cf. the quotation from the *Lupus* of Naevius in Fest., p. 334, 9 L., where the kings of Veii and of Alba are greeting each other. I would prefer this eventuality to the guess of E. M. Stewart who thinks of Ilia, quoting Porphyrio *ad* Hor., *Carm.* I 2, 17.

[6] F. Gr. Hist. 26 F 1 (XLVI 5).   [p. 271 sqq.

[7] Frg. 4 Peter=F. Gr. Hist. 809 F 2 Cf. K. J. Beloch, RG 180, and below,

seen the statue of the sow with the thirty pigs in Lavinium and who was also acquainted with Timaeus, who relates the story of the sow as taking place in Lavinium, connects this prodigy with Alba. Equally relevant is the notion [1] *cum omnes Latini ab Alba oriundi sint*, whereby the *omnes Latini* are the same as the *triginta populi Albenses*.[2] This tradition, kept alive in the annual gatherings of the Latins at the Alban Mountain, was without doubt the primary one, combined only subsequently with the Lavinian alternative. This is the ultimate reason for the fact that the Roman myth of origin connects the founders of the city with Alba and not with Lavinium; and also that there is no trace of prominent *familiae Lavinates* in Rome, but only of *Albanae*.[3] Among the Roman aristocracy the Alban origin possessed more prestige. Not only was the first king of Rome connected with Alba but also the origin of such institutions as the Roman dictatorship and the Vestal virgins.[4] The leadership of Lavinium was suppressed by Roman historiography to permit the rule of Rome to follow immediately after the rule of Alba.[5] We must therefore pursue the traces of the preeminence of Lavinium in by-ways where they were not deliberately wiped out.

୧

THE BELIEF IN TROJAN DESCENT, AND THE RITUAL OF THE "TROJAN" DIVINITIES IN LAVINIUM

"Which historian would like," argues Niebuhr,[6] in regard to the Latin legends of origin, "to trace the ever-changing shapes assumed by the clouds of mythology, the plaything of arbitrary story-tellers? . . . Who would dwell on them," he continues, "when more rewarding

---

[1] Liv. I 52, 2. Cf. DH III 31, 4.

[2] Concerning their list in Pliny cf. H. Nissen, It. Lk. II 2, 557. F. Ribezzo, Onomastica 2, 1948, 29 sqq., 34 sqq., and above, p. 10 sqq.

[3] But these ties of Rome with Alba do not reflect the pride of the *gentes Albanae*, they are religious survivals of a once real political dependence, as we have to stress again and again. Cf., e.g., G. De Sanctis, St. d. R. 1¹ 194 sqq., 202 sqq. G. Wissowa, RuK², 164 sqq. F. Münzer, Adelsparteien und Adelsfamilien, Stuttgart 1921, 133 n.i. P. De Francisci, Primordia civitatis, Roma 1960, 182 sq., etc.

[4] Licin.Macer fr. 10 Peter (= DH V 74, 4). Liv. I 20, 3.

[5] Liv. I 29, 6. DH I 65, 1. Serv., *Aen.* 1, 259. 268. 282. Cf. also Cincius in Fest., p. 276, 17 L.

[6] B. G. Niebuhr, RG 1², Berlin 1827, 84.

subjects wait to be analyzed?" But even the fantastic display of clouds can easily be explained by the scientist who understands the few factors giving rise to their display; and a few simple facts are also the basis of the capricious variability of the accounts in view.

We have seen already that the name of King Latinus, constructed from the name of his people, is also linked with Lavinium; we can extended this connection from Callias, the historian of Agathocles,[1] back to the Theogony of Hesiod. Still more transparent is the reference in the name of Lavinia to this city, whether or not she is purported to be the daughter of Latinus.[2] But Lavinium's principal claim to legendary glory was to be the landing-place of the Trojans, fleeing to Italy from their ransacked homes; sometimes Trojan women arrived there, dragged away by the returning Achaeans,[3] but chiefly it was Aeneas himself.[4] I have tried to show elsewhere [5] that this tradition existed in Lavinium from at least the sixth century B.C. The divinity indicated to Aeneas that he should settle down on the spot where he would consume along with the sacrificial meat the tables on which it was served. Timaeus was familiar with this story

[1] F. Gr. Hist. 564 F 5. Cf. below, p. 257 and 260.

[2] Cf. B. G. Niebuhr, RG 1², 201. R. H. Klausen, Aeneas und die Penaten 2, 1840, 572. More in H. Boas, *op. cit.* 79 sqq. W. Ehlers, *op. cit.*, 173 sqq. F. Gr. Hist. 840 F 38.

[3] Aristotle has this story. We must certainly emendate the Λατίνιον in DH I 72, 3 with Kiessling to Λαουίνιον.

[4] Details and references in R. H. Klausen, *op. cit.* 2, 1840, 620 sqq. A. Schwegler, RG 1, 279 sqq. Friedr. Cauer, *De fabulis Graecis ad Romam conditam pertinentibus*, Diss., Berlin 1884, 26 sqq. G. De Sanctis, St. d. R. 1², 196 sqq. J. Carcopino, Virgile et les origines d'Ostie (BEFAR 116) 1919, 171 sqq. E. Pais, St. d. R. 1³, 212 sqq., 259 sqq. H. Boas, Aeneas' Arrival in Latium (Allard Pierson Stichting, Arch.-hist. Bijdr. 6) Amsterdam 1938, 53 sqq., 221 sqq. J. Perret, Les origines de la légende troyenne à Rome, Thesis, Paris 1945; cf. against his views Momigliano, JRS 35, 1945, 101 sqq. B. Tilly, Vergil's Latium, Oxford 1947, 54 sqq. F. Bömer, Rom und Troja, Baden-Baden 1951, 57 sqq. 93 n. 13. A. Boethius, Gnomon 28, 1956, 256. S. Mazzarino, Stud. Rom. 8, 1960, 385 sqq.

[5] A. Alföldi, Die trojanischen Urahnen der Römer (Rektoratsprogramm der Univ. Basel 1956) 1957. Cf. A. Momigliano, Riv. Stor. Ital. 70, 1958, 129 sqq. A. Brelich, SMSR 29, 1958, 255 sqq. C. Vermeule, Schweizer Münzblätter 1958, 87 sqq. H. Mattingly, N. Chron. 17, 1957, 286 sqq. J. Perret, R. Et. Lat. 36, 1958, 375 sq. would postpone the decision until new archaeological evidence comes to light. Since he wrote, it has been produced. M. van den Bruwaene, Ant. cl. 27, 1958, 513 sqq., misunderstood my argument in supposing that I advocated the really Trojan origin of the Latins and that I denied their immigration from the North. The objections of S. Weinstock, JRS 49, 1959, 170 sqq., can be disregarded; cf. above, p. 239 n. 1.

already.[1] It has been proved [2] that this oracle is based on a special feature of the Lavinian cult of the *Penates*, in which *mensae paniciae* were used—flat cakes on which the victim's meat was served.

These legendary accounts are not of literary origin, even though antiquarians and poets subsequently included them in their works. They were first conceived to explain and justify a cult. This cult is that of Aeneas in Lavinium. It is an intricate and complex phenomenon, as revealed by the puzzling variety of the names of this divinity. They are: *Aeneas Indiges*,[3] (*deus*) *Indiges*,[4] *pater Indiges*,[5] πατὴρ θεὸς χθόνιος, ὃς ποταμοῦ Νομικίου ῥεῦμα διέπει,[6] and *Juppiter Indiges*.[7] All these names mean the same god worshipped in the same sanctuary.[8] This sacred grove in Lavinium is also termed, however, *lucus Solis Indigetis*.[9] The fresh water near the coast, where the arriving Trojans quenched their thirst, was sacred to this solar divinity: λεγόμενον ὑπὸ τῶν ἐπιχωρίων ἱερὸν Ἡλίου.[10] To this Sun-God Aeneas offered up his first sacrifice in gratitude for the water. But in fact there were two altars there: Καὶ βωμοὶ δύο παρ' αὐτῷ δείκνυνται ... Τρωϊκὰ ἱδρύματα, ἐφ' ὧν τὸν Αἰνείαν μυθολογοῦσι πρώτην θυσίαν ποιήσασθαι τῷ θεῷ χαριστήριον τῶν ὑδάτων.. They are reproduced on bronze medaillons of Hadrian and Antonius Pius. We see on them a higher and a lower altar (pl. VI, 1-2). By chance we know that the Olympians were honored with high altars and the divinities of the underworld with lower altars. Here we have both of them side by side: one more reference to the complex nature of the god venerated here. C. Koch connected this *Sol Indiges* of Lavinium with the references to the same cult in Rome.[11] The Roman stone calendars

[1] Lycophr. v. 1250 sqq.

[2] P. Kretschmer, Glotta 20, 1932, 189 sqq. W. Ehlers, Mus. Helv. 6, 1949, 167 sqq., 171 sq., with all the details.

[3] Verg., *Aen.* 12, 794, with the *scholia*. Serv. auct. 1, 260 ; Ovid., *Metam.* 14, 581 sqq. Cf. CIL I² p. 189 n. 1. Festus, p. 94, 19 L.

[4] Tibull. II 5, 39 sqq.

[5] Cass. Hemina fr. 7 Peter (= Solin. 2, 14). *Orig. g. R.* 14, 2.

[6] F. Gr. Hist. 840 F 39a = DH I 64, 5. Cf. C. Koch, Gestirnverehrung im alten Italien (Frankfurter Studien zur Altertumswissenschaft 3) 1933, 74.

[7] F. Gr. Hist. 840 F 39 b = Liv. I 2, 6. Serv., *Aen.* 1, 259.

[8] C. Koch, *op. cit.* 107 sqq. K. Latte, Röm. Religionsgeschichte, München 1960, 44 n. 1.

[9] Plin., *N.h.* III 5, 56 ; cf. C. Koch, *op. cit.* 105 and DH I 64, 5 : ἔστι δὲ χωμάτιον οὐ μέγα καὶ περὶ αὐτὸ δένδρα στοιχηδὸν πεφυκότα θέας ἄξια on Aeneas' tomb.

[10] DH I 55, 2 = F. Gr. Hist. 840 F 34.

[11] C. Koch, *op. cit.* 107 sqq.

have the annotation to the eighth of August: *Sol(is) Indigetis in colle Quirinale sacrificium publicum*; [1] the sacrifice was performed *in pulvinari Solis . . . iuxta aedem Quirini*, as attested by Quintilian.[2] The *Ag(onalia)* of the eleventh of December [3] are mentioned in the new Fasti of Ostia [4] [*Ag*]*on(ium) Ind(igeti)* and Lydus, *De mensibus* [5] announce the same day the ᾿Αγωνάλια δαφνηφόρῳ γενάρχῃ ῾Ηλίῳ. This Greek translation of *Sol Indiges*, which cannot reasonably be doubted, occurs also in the so-called oath of Drusus.[6]

This very complex divinity also had a tomb on the river Numicus (or Numicius): the reason given for this was that Aeneas had been drowned in the river after a victorious battle.[7] This apotheosis by means of strangulation (it may be the background of a primitive ritual) returns in Latium also in the mythical tales of Romulus and Rhea.[8] It belongs in the broad frame of a prehistoric religious concept, which existed among many peoples.[9] Such an antiquated concept of divinity as this *Indiges* was incomprehensible until scholars tried to explain it in terms of the classical Greek or even of the historical Roman religiosity.[10] It was only recently that an expert on Roman[11]

---

[1] *Fasti Vallenses*, Inscr. It. XIII 1, 1947, p. 318. *Fasti Amit.*, CIL I[2] p. 244.

[2] Quintil. I 7, 12.

[3] *Fasti Antiat. ministr. dom. Aug.* (Inscr. It. XIII 1, 1947, p. 330).

[4] CIL XIV 4547.

[5] Lyd., *De mens.* 4, 155, quoted by C. Koch, *op. cit.* 65 sq., 71.

[6] Diod. 37, 11. Cf. C. Koch, *loc. cit.* H. J. Rose, Herv. Theol. Rev. 30, 1937, 165 sqq., established that the stylistic formula of this oath is Greek ; but this result does not invalidate the equation *Sol Indiges* = Γενάρχης ῞Ηλιος, belittled by him, p. 178 sqq.

[7] F. Gr. Hist. 840 F 39 a (= DH I 64, 4-5), b (= Liv. I 2, 6), c (= Serv. *Aen.* 4, 620). Cato *,Orig.* fr. 10 Peter. Diod. VII 5, 2. Serv., *Aen.* 1, 259 ; 7, 150. Tibull. II 5, 43. Fest., p. 94, 19 L. Ovid., *Metam.* 14, 597 sqq. Arnob. 1, 36. We only wish to remind the reader that the river-gods of the Italic people were comprehensive divinities ; such a bull-shaped god was, I think, also *Liber pater*. Cf. L. Malten, JdI 1928, 90 sqq. F. Altheim, Römische Religions-geschichte, Frankfurt 1951, 22 sq.

[8] Cf. also DH I 71, 2. Liv. I 16, 1. Enn., *Ann.* 1, 54 Vahlen. Serv., *Aen.* 1 273 ; 6, 788, etc.

[9] R. H. Klausen, *op. cit.* 2, 1840, 595 n. 1088. E. Pais, St. d. R. 1[3], Roma 1926, 214 n. 1 ; 262 sqq. C. Koch, *op. cit.* 112 sq. St. Borzsák, Hermes 78, 1943 (1944), 248 sqq. *Idem*, Acta antiqua 1, Budapest 1951-52, 201 sqq., 209 sqq.

[10] Cf. R. H. Klausen, *op. cit.* 2, 901 sqq. A. Schwegler, RG 1, 327 sqq. G. Wissowa, *De dis Romanorum indigetibus et novensidibus* (Ind. lect. Marburg. 1892), 3 sqq. B. Tilly, *op. cit.* 78 sqq.

[11] C. Koch, *op. cit.* 11, 39, 54, 63 sqq., 74 sqq., 84 sqq., 98 sqq., 101, 105 sqq., 111. *Idem*, Der römische Iuppiter (Frankfurter Studien zur Alterumswissen-schaft 14), 1937, 39 sqq. Essential also, though mostly overlooked, is H.

ALBA LONGA AND LAVINIUM

religion was able to demonstrate the survival of analogous obsolete divine beings in the Graeco-Roman world. In the same geographical area there are other traces of a [1] divine ancestor of a people, who is at the same time its first mythical king, also the Sun [2] and the Lord of Waters. An even more tangible mythical pattern equivalent to this, however, is the primeval giant and first king of the Iranians, of a solar substance but also with chthonian aspects in his myth. His half-human, half-zoomorphoric appearance, surviving in the costume and headgear of the great king,[3] saved its oldest form from oblivion. The inauguration-ritual of the Persian king, displaying the same dramatic revival of the life and deeds of the founder of the state as the *Lupercalia* of the Romans [4] and also connected with the Indo-Arian concept of the "First Man" and the "First King," was a manifestation of the culture of the Eurasian shepherds, like the *Indiges* of the Latins.

The high antiquity of this mythical notion has an essential historical consequence. The rise of Aeneas as the ancestor of the Latins cannot be earlier than the late seventh century B.C. It was the consequence of the overwhelming Etruscan influence encroaching upon the life

Wagenvoort, Roman Dynamism, Oxford 1947, 83 sqq. L. Deubner, Archiv f. Rel.-Wiss. 33, 1936, 112 sq. The results of C. Koch are now fully accepted by St. Weinstock, JRS 50, 1960, 117 sq. *Contra* : H. J. Rose, *op. cit.* 165 sqq. F. Bömer, Ahnenkult und Ahnenglaube bei den Römern, Leipzig 1943, 53 sqq. Cf. Gnomon 21, 1949, 355.

[1] An interesting variant is given in the fragment of Cornificius by Fest., p. 212, 16 L. : . . . *Latinus rex, qui proelio, quod ei fuit adversus Mezentium, Caeritum regem, nusquam apparuerit, iudicatusque sit Juppiter factus Latiaris.* J. Carcopino, *op. cit.*, 597 sq., perceived behind Tiberis-Vulcanus such a complex divinity. *Semo Sancus Dius Fidius* (divided in two divinities by K. Latte, *op. cit.*, 126 sqq.; but cf. Ael. Stilo and Varro, *LL* 5, 66. Ovid., *Fast.* 6, 213-16. Fest. 276, 11 L.) was worshipped in Reate as the First King and as the god of the Sky. Cf. Cato, *Orig.* fr. 50 Peter. Augustin., *Civ. Dei* 18, 19. A. Schwegler, RG 1, 365 n. 5-7. G. Wissowa, RuK² 130 sqq. Ed. Norden, Aus altrömischen Priesterbüchern, Lund 1939, 177 sqq., 203 sqq., 209 sqq. The *Semones* of the *carmen Arvale* could well be *Semo Sancus* and *Salus Semonia*. L. Preller, Röm. Mythologie 1³, 1881, 95 sqq. Important is Pallottino's information, St. Etr. 2. ser. 26, 1958, 49 sqq., esp. 60 sqq., that the cult of the ancestors was connected also in Etruria with that of *Tinia-Juppiter*.

[2] The mythical genealogy, connecting Helios and Kirke with the Latins is, at least in my opinion, a secondary interpretation, even if occurring already in the Theogony of Hesiod. The opposite view is advocated by S. Weinstock, *loc. cit.*

[3] Cf. my study in : Jahrbuch d. Schweizerischen Gesellschaft für Urgeschichte 40, 1949-50, 17 sqq.

[4] Cf. my note in : Schweizer Archiv f. Volkskunde 47, 1951, 11 sqq., and Arch. Anz., 1931, 393 sqq. I hope to return to these problems soon.

of this people. The identification of the imported Aeneas with the vernacular *Pater Indiges* in Lavinium is, consequently, a secondary evolution. The preliminary condition for the localization of this tribal cult and ritual in Lavinium and its amalgamation with Aeneas is that *Indiges*, the ancestor of the Latin tribe, was already firmly established in Lavinium when the legend of the Trojan hero fascinated and captived the Latins. In other words: Lavinium must already have been their metropolis before 600 B.C.

The political and historical implications of this fact will be more obvious when we turn our attention, in a moment, to the connections of *Indiges* with *Vesta*[1] and the *Penates*. Before this, however, a few more words remain to be said on the character of the cult of Aeneas concerning which a new, highly important document has recently come to light.[2] This is a small *cippus*, once erected in a sanctuary at Tor Tignosa, 8 kilometers inland from Lavinium, with the inscription *Lare Aineia d(onom)*. M. Guarducci, who published it, dates it in the fourth century B.C.; in any case, it seems to be not later than the third century. Miss Guarducci rightly connected *Lar Aineias* with *Aeneas Indiges*. On the basis of this new evidence, S. Weinstock established the correctness of the interpretation of the *Lares* as deified ancestors, proposed long ago by A. Samter;[3] and demonstrated also that *Lar* and *Indiges* must have been identical, or at least related terms.[4] The dedication to *Lar Aineias* proves that the Trojan hero, as the ancestor of the Latin tribe, was a popular divinity at the place of his legendary arrival. It was set up at a date when Aeneas was previously supposed to have been smuggled in via Lavinium through literary fiction by the Romans as their ancestor.[5]

It has been thought[6] that the cult of Aeneas never reached Rome and that his cause was kept alive there only by the ambition of the *familiae Troianae*. This could be admitted if we possessed only vague,

---

[1] Serv., *Aen.* 7, 150. C. Koch, Gestirnverehrung 101 sqq.

[2] Published by M. Guarducci, Bull. del Museo della Civiltà Rom. 19 (in : Bull. Com. 76, 1956-58) 1959, 3 sqq., and discussed in details by S. Weinstock, JRS 50, 1960, 114 sqq.

[3] S. Weinstock, *op. cit.* 116.

[4] To the question whether the Roman *Lar* and the Etruscan *Lars* should be connected (as W. Schulze, ZGLEN 84 supposed) or not (cf. S. Weinstock, *l.c.*), the important evidence adduced by M. Pallottino, St. Etr. 2. ser. 26, 1958, 49 sqq., 58 sqq., on the cult of the ancestors in Etruria must be considered.

[5] Cf. my sketch in : Die trojanische Urahnen der Römer, 1957.

[6] S. Weinstock, JRS 50, 1960, 118.

ALBA LONGA AND LAVINIUM

general pronouncements concerning his divinization.[1] But we know that he belonged to the Roman pantheon.[2] Ovid [3] calls him *deum, quem turba Quirini nuncupat Indigetem, temploque arisque recepit.* Dionysius also attests to his official worship by the Romans,[4] and we have reliable information on this cult.[5] However the Roman cult of Aeneas was regularly performed in Lavinium [6] and not in Rome: special circumstances, upon which we shall enlarge, prohibited the transfer of this cult to the city of Rome.[7] We cannot dwell at this time

[1] E.g., Ennius in : Cic., *De divinatione* I 20, 40. Diod. VII 5, 2 : Αἰνείας . . . ἐξ ἀνθρώπων ἠφανίσθη καὶ τιμῶν ἔτυχεν ἀθανάτων. Gell. II 16, 9 : *Anchises enim, qui haec ad filium dicit, sciebat eum, cum hominum vita discessisset immortalem atque indigetem futurum.* Verg., *Aen.* 1, 259 sq. : *sublimem . . feres ad sidera coeli magnanimum Aenean.*

[2] Cf. also Serv., *Aen.* 6, 777 : *Secundum Ennium* (Romulus) *referetur inter deos cum Aenea.*

[3] Ovid., *Met.* 14, 607 sqq.

[4] DH I 49, 3 : Τῆς δ᾽ εἰς Ἰταλίαν Αἰνείου καὶ Τρώων ἀφίξεως Ῥωμαῖοί τε πάντες βεβαιωνταί καὶ τὰ δρώμενα ὑπ᾽ αὐτῶν ἔν τε θυσίαις καὶ ἑορταῖς μηνύματα Σιβύλλης τε λόγια καὶ χρησμοὶ Πυθικοὶ καὶ ἄλλα πολλά, ὧν οὐκ ἄν τις ὡς εὐπρεπείας ἕνεκα συγκειμένων ὑπερίδοι. Livy I 2, 6 writes of him as *quemcumque eum dici ius fasque est.* Though he adds the remark *Iovem Indigetem appellant,* the description reminds us of the *Indigetes di, quorum nomina vulgari non licet* (Fest., exc. Paul. p. 94, 13 L. Cf. also Strab. 5, 3, 5 (p. 232 C.) and R. Schilling, La religion romaine de Vénus, BEFAR 178, 1954, 67 sqq.

[5] Cf. below, p. 260 sqq.

[6] Serv. auct., *Aen.* 1, 260 : *Ascanius hostibus devictis in loco quo pater apparuerat, Aeneae Indigiti templum dicavit, ad quod pontifices quotannis cum consulibus veniunt sacrificaturi.*

[7] The worship of Venus, the *Aeneadum genetrix* in Lavinium (cf. S. Weinstock, RE 19, 434. R. Schilling, *op. cit.* 83 sqq.) is also older than the influence of the Trojan families of Rome in Latium, who could have fostered it. Her name *Frutis* (Cass. Hemina fr. 7 Peter), an Etruscan deformation of Aphrodite suffices to demonstrate the antiquity of her worship (S. Ferri, Studi or. e class. 9, 1960, 167 sqq. explains it as a Latin word meaning 'the Phrygian Lady' ; cf. also S. Mazzarino, Stud. Rom. 8, 1960, 386 sqq.) ; but it is not clear, at least to me, when she became a federal divinity of the Latins, since she does not belong to the original group *Indiges-Vesta-Penates.* Strabo V 3, 5 (C. 232) speaks of *two* federal sanctuaries of Venus in Latium, of one in Lavinium for the cult of which the city of Ardea was taking care from olden times (ἐπιμελοῦνται δ᾽ αὐτοῦ διὰ προπόλων Ἀρδεᾶται) and of another in the outskirts of Ardea (ἔστι δὲ καὶ ταύτης πλησίον Ἀφροδίσιον, ὅπου πανηγυρίζουσι Λατῖνοι). As the co-existence of two such shrines is unlikely, especially as Ardea is said to be in charge of both cults, I think that Strabo erroneously duplicated the temple of *Frutis,* using the extracts of two literary sources. Pliny, *N.h.* III 5, 56 and Mela, II 4, 71, mention correctly one Aphrodisium, placing it between Antium and Ardea. The latter city competed with Lavinium as a landing-place of Aeneas. The Trojan glories of both were later much contaminated; cf. Sil. Ital., *Pun.* 1, 658 sqq. ; 8, 357 sqq., etc. Cf. K. J. Beloch, RG 176. J. Carcopino, *op. cit.* 402 sqq. A. Boethius, "Roma" 12, 1934, 297 sqq., 305.

on the fact that apparently in some Latin cities King Latinus, not Aeneas, was identified with *Juppiter Indiges*.[1] On a bronze cista from Praeneste [2] (pl. XVII) the huge figure of Latinus, standing on a pile of arms [3] in the garb of the supreme god, overshadows the rest of the scene with Aeneas, victorious over Turnus on one side, Lavinia with Amata on the other, and the river Numicius with a fluvial divinity lying before them in the foreground. Latinus points with his finger to heaven,[4] presumably announcing the future deification of the Trojan hero.

The cult of Indiges was intimately connected in Lavinium with that of *Vesta* and of *Penates*, as already mentioned. The water of the river Numicius—in the waves of which was hidden the divine ancestor—was used exclusively for the ritual libations to *Vesta*.[5]

[1] We already quoted Festus, p. 212, 18 L., where a popular tradition is reported which made *Iuppiter Latiaris* of him.

[2] Published with an excellent commentary by H. Brunn, Annali dell' Ist. di corr. arch. 1864, 356 sqq. Monumenti inediti 8, pl. 7-8. The authenticity of this cista has been denied by such an expert as C. Robert, Archaeologische Hermeneutik, Berlin 1919, 327 sq., for reasons which lost their validity since his days. First of all, the ancient roots of the Trojan legend in Latium were not yet recognized. Second, the late Republican date of an important group of Praenestine cistae has only recently been established by R. Herbig, St. Etr. 24, 1955-56, 205 ; for further details see a paper to be published by L. Bonfante Warren in AJA 68, 1964. The drawing we reproduce on pl. XVII shows that the cista Pasinati clearly belongs to that Late Hellenistic group and the possibility of Ennius' influence could well be reflected on this composition. I can subsequently insert with thanks the important statement of R. A. Higgins, British Museum, in a letter of April 25, 1963 : "I have looked at the Pasinati cista. Of course, as Walters saw, the upper part of the body is missing; and the handle is probably alien, but to my untutored eye it looks absolutely all right." Hellenistic details such as the royal wreath fallen from the helmet of Turnus and brought to Aeneas, and the pile of arms, etc., would hardly be conceived by a forger. The ivy wreath of *Liber pater* in the neck of the central figure could well be an additional feature of the Lavinian cult. Cf. Augustin., *Civ. Dei* 7, 21.

[3] Cf. the personification of Aitolia sitting on a pile of arms, BMC Thessaly to Aetolia, London 1883, pl. 30, 3-5. 7 and Caligula standing on a similar pile of weapons on the phalera of Neuwied, Germania Romana[2], Bamberg *s.d.*, pl. 36, 5. This motif has nothing to do with the act of *devotio*, as H. Brunn supposed, p. 361.

[4] H. Brunn, *op. cit.*, interpreted the gesture as that of an oath. Cf. Verg., *Aen.* 8, 12, 196.

[5] Serv., *Aen.* 7, 150 : *Vestae enim libari non nisi de hoc fluvio (sc. Numici) licebat.* Cf. S. Weinstock, RE 19, 440. C. Koch, RE 8 A, 1720 sq. *Idem*, Studies D. M. Robinson 2, 1953, 1077 sqq. P. Lambrechts, Latomus 5, 1946, 321 sqq. A. Brelich, Vesta (Albae Vigiliae n.s. 7) 1949. F. Bömer, Rom und Troja, Baden-Baden 1951, 50 sqq., etc.

258

As everyone knows, Rome had two different cults of the *Penates*:
a cryptic one in the *penus Vestae*, and a small chapel on the *Velia*
visible to everybody, where they are represented as two sitting youths
with spears like the Dioscuri.[1] These two cults were said to be equally
the *sacra* of Troy.[2] They are, however, manifestly of a different origin.
The first one, with the gods in the *penus Vestae*, *qui sunt*, to quote
Varro, *introrsus atque in imis penetralibus*,[3] being the primary phenomenon. The *Penates*, in any case, as well as *Vesta*, are far older in
Latium than the arrival of the legend of Aeneas. In Rome the eternal
fire of Vesta is closely linked[4] with the *regia*. Recent research has
established that her sanctuary was in the Forum Valley as early as
the seventh century B.C.[5] and we can be sure that it was then already
connected with the house of the king. This correlation is a primeval
concept: the big round royal hearth beside the *megaron* of the king[6]
—round as the temple of Vesta—in the Mycenaean Palace in Pylos
and those in other Mycenaean palaces illustrate it as well as, e.g.,
the connection between the goddess of the hearth and the kingship
by the Iranians. The continuity of the cult of *Vesta* on the Alban
Mountain[7] makes it certain that a similar link also existed between
it and the tribal kingship of the Latins.

What is essential for our present problem is that all the elements
and combinations of these once regal cults appear also in Lavinium.
We shall find Lavinian elements in the Roman cults of the *regia*; and
the Romans themselves most solemnly declared that the Lavinian
Vesta and *Penates* are their own.[8] The priority belongs, therefore,

[1] Details : S. Weinstock, RE 19, 427.

[2] Cf. G. Wissowa, Gesammelte Abhandlungen, München 1904, 111 sqq.
Idem, Roscher's Lex. 3, 1888 sqq. S. Weinstock, RE 19, 436 sq. F. Bömer,
op. cit., 53 sq. C. Koch, RE 8 A, 1772 sqq., 1729 sqq. A different view in A.
Brelich, *op. cit.* 75 sqq.

[3] Cf. G. Wissowa, Ges. Abhandlungen 95 sqq. F. Bömer and S. Weinstock
ll.cc. P. Kretschmer, Glotta 8, 1917, 79 sqq. W. Ehlers, Mus. Helv. 6, 1949,
167 n. 10. K. Latte, Röm. Religionsgesch. 89 sqq., 108.

[4] C. Koch, RE 8 A, 1729, 1741, 1772 sqq. S. Weinstock, RE 19, 441.

[5] A. Bartoli, Mon. ant. 45, 1961, 19 sqq.

[6] AJA 63, 1959, pl. 33, fig. 12.

[7] Cf. above, p. 241.

[8] Serv., *Aen.* 2, 296. Macrob. III 4, 11. CIL X 797 quoted below. B. Tilly,
op. cit. 64, quotes the *Liber coloniarum* s.v. *Lavinium* (Lachmann-Rudorff, Die
römischen Feldmesser, I, Berlin 1848, 234) on the privileges of the Lavinian
cults granted them by the Roman state, cf. CIL XIV 2065, 2070. Cod. Theod.
VIII 5, 46. The domains of the Vestals are in the *lib. col.* in Lanuvium, not in
Lavinium.

clearly to Lavinium. Looking at the matter of this dependence, it would seem ultimately to be connected with a more comprehensive evolution. In other words, we can confidently conjecture that the cults of the patriarchal kingship of the tribe were copied by the rulers of the single cities when the central power declined and the tribal subdivisions of the Latin people became autonomous political units: one of them was Rome.

The religious concept of the *Penates* is inseparably associated with the idea of "home" and of "fatherland." [1] Therefore it is the more significant that in the mind of the Romans the home of their own *Penates* was Lavinium. *Nam ibi di Penates nostri* [2] says Varro of Lavinium. Asconius (p. 21, 8 Cl.), a serious and reliable scholar, mentions *sacra populi Romani Romani deum Penatium quae Lavini fierent*; similar usages have been noted in Plutarch and elsewhere,[3] and an official statement of the same fact from the time of the Emperor Claudius runs: *sacra principiorum populi Romani nominisque Latini, quae apud Laurentes coluntur*.[4] A pictorial illustration of this is displayed on the *denarius* of C. Sulpicius about 100 B.C. which shows the two youthful guardian gods with the sow and her thirty pigs. The birth of the piglets occurred in the version of the myth which prevailed in that epoch, in Lavinium. The heads of the same divine youths are nevertheless accompanied by the inscription *D(ei) P(enates) P(ublici)* (pl. IV, 1-2). This means on a Roman coin the divine guardians of the Roman state. The representation of the sow with the *Penates* watching over her is seen again on a fragment of a marble relief in Rome (pl. IV, 5) which can easily be restored with the help of this coin-type. It refers to the same divine patrons of the Roman state, whose cult was celebrated in Lavinium.[5] The ostentatious piety of the Roman state toward the common *Penates* of all the Latins was naturally also a courting of the emotional attachment of their allied fellow nationals. The *Penates-Dioscuri* were therefore often represented on the Roman

---

[1] G. Wissowa, in Roscher's Lex. 3, 1891.

[2] Varro, *LL* 5, 144.

[3] Plut., *Coriol.* 29, 2: ὅπου καὶ θεῶν ἱερὰ ʿΡωμαίοις πατρῴων ἀπέκειτο. Serv., *Aen.* 3, 12: ... *magnis diis potest tamen hoc pro honore dici ; nam dii magni sunt Iuppiter Juno Minerva Mercurius. qui Romae colebantur, Penates vero apud Laurolavinium.*

[4] CIL X 797, discussed below.

[5] For the role of the *Penates*, cf. their appearance to Aeneas in his dream, discussed by W. Ehlers, Mus. Helv. 6, 1949, 170 sqq.

coinage of the Punic Wars, which was the most obvious vehicle of propaganda in those crucial decades. The two youthful heads with laurel wreaths, united in the form of a herm (misinterpreted hitherto as *Fontus*), are nothing other than the *Penates publici* of Rome and of all the Latin peoples. They occur first on the heavy *asses* after the First Punic War (pl. III, 7),[1] then in the same time on the *quadrigati* of silver (pl. III, 1.3), and on the gold coins struck along with them, where their heads are coupled with the representation of the alliance between Aeneas, ancestor of the Romans, and King Latinus, the forefather of all the Latins (pl. III, 5-6).[2]

The conviction that the ancestral gods of Lavinium, like those of Alba, are the gods of the Romans themselves and not those of a decaying township separates their official cult completely from the *communio sacrorum* of Rome with Lanuvium, agreed upon in 338 B.C.: the latter is *expressis verbis* the official care of Rome for the municipal cult of an important Latin divinity,[3] not of a Roman one, maintained outside the city. The cults of Alba and Lavinium are still less comparable with the provisions of the Roman state for the divine services of annihilated or decayed cities of the neighborhood.[4] On the other hand, the cults of Alba and Lavinium were placed by the Romans in the same special category: *maiores . . . sacra quaedam in monte Albano Laviniique nobis facienda tradiderunt*, as Livy has Camillus say.[5]

The Lavinian cults in question were offered, in addition to the divine ancestor of the Latins to the *patrii Penates . . . qui huic urbi et rei*

---

[1] E. J. Haeberlin, Aes grave, Frankfurt 1910, pl. 31, 1-4 ; 38, 1-6. The same herm on the heavy asses of Volterrae (*ibid.* pl. 82 sqq.) represents, of course, the Dioscuri and not the Roman *Penates* ; similarly, the terra-cotta double head from Tarquinia, pl. III, 2 (after San Giovenale, Stockholm 1959, fig. 240), or that on the bronze coins of Capua revolting against Rome, pl. III, 4 (A. Sambon, Les monnaies antiques de l'Italie, Paris 1906, 395 n. 1023). The same double head represents, of course, the *Penates* again on some asses of L. Piso and C. Vibius Pansa, partisans of Marius (BMC Rep. pl. 36, 19, etc.) and on the denarii of two Fontei (*ibid.* pl. 114, 12-13 ; cf. pl. 30, 16-18) who came from Tusculum where the Dioscuri played a great role. Cf. also R. Thomsen, Early Roman Coinage 1, Copenhague 1957, 158 sqq. K. Latte, *op. cit.* fig. 15.

[2] Cf. AJA 63, 1959, 20 sqq.

[3] Cic., *Pro L. Murena* 41, 90 : *date hoc . . . etiam Lanuvio municipio honestissimo . . . nolite a sacris patriis Iunonis Sospitae cui omnes consules facere necesse est, domesticum et suum consulem potissimum avellere.* Cf. Liv. VIII 14, 2.

[4] As G. Wissowa, Hermes 50, 1915, 1 sqq., 21 sqq., supposed, and Latte, *op. cit.* 295 n. 5, followed him.

[5] Liv. V 52, 8.

publicae praesidetis,[1] to the patrons of the Roman state, and the strict observance of their ritual in Lavinium was the duty of the Roman magistrates and state priests themselves. Extracts from Varro [2] attest the obligation of all the Roman governing officials to offer propitiatory sacrifices year by year in Lavinium,[3] accompanied by the pontiffs and the *flamines*.[4] The neglect of this ritual or the disregard of the gods' dissatisfaction, manifested during its performance, was considered to be an offense against the welfare of the Roman state, like the commission of faults in the care of the *sacra Albana*.[5] Such shortcomings could still in the second century B.C. cause great harm to important personalities: we know the case of C. Hostilius Mancinus, consul in 137 B.C.,[6] and the lawsuit against Aemilius Scaurus by the tribune Cn. Domitius Ahenobarbus in 104 B.C.[7] But the oldest

[1] Cic., *De domo sua* 57, 144.

[2] G. Wissowa, Ges. Abh. 102 sqq.

[3] Serv. auct., *Aen.* 3, 12 : *quos* (sc. Penates) *inter cetera ideo magnos appellant, quod de Lavinio translati Romam bis in locum suum redierint: quod imperatores in provincias ituri apud eos primum immolarint.* Macrob. III 4, 11 : *eodem nomine appellavit* (sc. Vergilius) *et Vestam, quam de numero Penatium certe comitem eorum esse manifestum est adeo, ut et consules et praetores seu dictatores, cum adeunt magistratum, Lavini rem divinam faciant Penatibus pariter et Vestae.* Serv., *Aen.* 2, 296 : *hic ergo quaeritur, utrum Vesta etiam de numero Penatium sit, an comes eorum accipiatur, quod cum consules et praetores sive dictator adeunt magistratum, Lavini sacra Penatibus simul et Vestae faciunt.* The close connection of this text with the former ones makes it certain that *abeunt magistratu* in the mss. is an error of an excerptor or copyist for *adeunt magistratum*, as Th. Mommsen, St. R. I[3], 619 n. 3, H. Dessau, CIL XIV p. 187 n. 2, and others already concluded. The proposal of K. Latte, *op. cit.* 295 n. 5 to reverse this emendation and to read *abeunt* instead in the former passages as well does not work, as we shall see in the case of C. Hostilius Mancinus. There is no trustworthy reference to sacrifices of magistrates in Lavinium at the end of their term of office ; *vita Marci* 27, 4, quoted by S. Weinstock, RE 19, 428 is not clear and not reliable enough.

[4] Schol. Veron., *Aen.* 1, 239 : *Aeneae Indigeti templum dicavit, ad quos pontifices quotannis cum consulibus (ire solent sacrificaturi).* Serv., *Aen.* 8, 664 : *flamines in capite habebant pilleum, in quo erat brevis virga . . alii dicunt . . . hoc factum, . . . quia cum sacrificarent apud Laurolavinium et eis exta frequenter aves de vicinis venientes lucis abriperent, eminentia virgarum eas terrere voluerunt.*

[5] Th. Mommsen, St. R. I[3], 1887, 619 n. 1 ; cf. 618 sq.

[6] Val. Max. I 6, 7 : . . . . *C. Hostilius Mancinus . . . cui consuli in Hispaniam ituro haec prodigia acciderunt : cum Lavinii sacrificium facere vellet, pulli cavea emissi in proximam silvam fugerunt summaque diligentia quaesiti reperiri nequiverunt.* Cf. Obsequens (24) 73. Augustin., *Civ. Dei* 3, 21.

[7] Ascon., *In Scaurianam* 18-19 (p. 21 Cl.) : *"Subiit etiam populi iudicium (sc. pater Scauri) inquirente Cn. Domitio tribuno plebis".* Cn. Domitius qui consul fuit cum C. Cassio cum esset tribunus plebis, iratus Scauro quod eum in augurum collegium non cooptaverat, diem ei dixit apud populum et multam irrogavit, quod eius opera sacra populi Romani deminuta esse diceret. Crimini dabat sacra publica populi Romani deum*

ALBA LONGA AND LAVINIUM

observation of a *prodigium* occurring at the public sacrifices in Lavinium is one reported by Cato the Elder,[1] which has been overlooked until now.

The scholars studying the religious institutions of Rome correctly recognized that the ritual obligations of the Roman state in Lavinium unmistakably bear the imprint of her political dependence on this old Latin metropolis [2] in an ancient past. They also perceived the federal character of these cults as well as the fact of their reorganization in 338 B.C. But no attempt was made to exploit these highly relevant data for the history of early Rome or to define the epoch of the predominance of Lavinium. We hope that its role has already emerged clearly enough by our general reconsideration of the history of early Latium; but relevant facts are also preserved in the details of the organization of the state sacrifices in question.

It cannot be doubted that all the Latin cities together performed the sacrifices in Lavinium in olden times. The definition of these ritual duties was originally, I think, *sacra principiorum nominis Latini*, and only after 338 B.C. did they assume, in addition to their tribal quality,

---

Penatium quae Lavini fierent opera eius minus recte casteque fieri. Quo crimine absolutus est Scaurus quidem, etc. Cf. T. R. S. Broughton, MRR 1, 1951, 562 n. 7.

[1] Cato, *Orig.* fr. 55 Peter (= Serv. auct., *Aen.* 10, 541): *Immolari proprie dicuntur hostiae non cum caeduntur, sed cum accipiunt molam salsam : Cato in Originibus ita ait : Lavini boves immolatos, prius quam caederentur, profugisse in silvam.*

[2] Cf., e.g., R. H. Klausen, Aeneas und die Penaten 2, Hamburg 1840, 620 sqq. J. Marquardt, St. V. 3² Leipzig 1885, 252, 478. Th. Mommsen, St. R. *l.c.* G. Wissowa, Hermes 50, 1915, 28 sqq. *Idem*, RuK² 164 n. 6, 520 n. 2. E. Pais, St. d. R. I³, Roma 1926, 277 sqq. C. Koch, Gestirnverehrung im alten Italien, Frankfurt 1937, 100. S. Weinstock, RE 19, 429 sqq. The attempt of K. Latte, *op. cit.* 295 to invalidate the source evidence is untenable : 1) We cannot lightly reject Liv. VIII 11, 15, giving the date of the *annual* renewal of the *foedus* between Rome and Lavinium as 338 B.C. 2) The supposition that Emperor Claudius initiated this, is excluded by Livy *l.c.* who lived before the age of Claudius and by DH I 67, 2 (on the ancient μελεδωνοὶ τῶν ἱερῶν in Lavinium) which precludes as well the possibility of an Augustan reform. 3) The evidence for the solemnities in Lavinium comes not merely from the last century of the Republic, but, as we have seen, one passage is earlier than 150 B.C. (Cato, *Orig.* fr. 55 P.), the others concern the years 137 and 104 B.C. 4) Hostilius Mancinus provides a proof not only for the *augurium pullarium*, but he offers a sacrifice as well : *cum Lavini sacrificium facere vellet.* 5) These *sacra* are not performed by the Romans for a decayed Latin community ; cf. above. 6) The rites of Vesta and the Penates are not based primarily on the legend of Aeneas ; yet the influence of this legend on public rites does not begin only at the end of the third century B.C., but in the sixth century (cf. my study "Die trojanischen Urahnen der Römer," *passim*).

that of *sacra principiorum populi Romani Quiritium*: [1] the general co-ordination of all the Latin cities under Roman direction is, as we set forth at length, the final result of the struggle ending with that date. The same fictitious projection of this final balance of power back to a remote antiquity, which is demonstrated in the Annals, was applied also to the mythical explanation of the Roman sacrifices in Lavinium. Aeneas, ancestor of the Romans, and Latinus, king of all the Latins, made a solemn pact in Lavinium,[2] which was to be valid forever. Violated by the crime of Titus Tatius and disturbed once more by the bloody vengeance of the Lavinians, this *foedus* was renewed by Romulus.[3] Other traditions attributed the Roman celebrations in Lavinium to Ascanius [4] or to Numa, the originator of all religious institutions of Rome.[5] But it goes without saying that before 340 B.C. no such treaty as that attributed to Romulus was needed for a Latin city to be admitted to ancestral worship in the old metropolis of the nation. No doubt every Latin state sent its envoys in those olden days to Lavinium each year, to carry out the same rites for the welfare of their communities as were performed, after their subjugation, by the ruling city alone.[6] In 338 B.C. they were excluded for an obvious reason: Rome after her final victory prohibited the Latin cities from having free political, juridical, and economic interrelations.[7] Their homage to their ancestral gods was henceforward paid by Rome, who substituted for them on grounds of a curious and special juridical fiction. This was the *foedus* sometimes ascribed to Romulus, which was renewed annually between the magistrates having charge of Rome and of Lavinium.[8] Because of this political precaution taken by the conqueror none of the Latin communities thereafter partici-

---

[1] CIL X 797 ; cf. below, p. 264.

[2] DH I 59, 1-2. Verg., *Aen.* 12, 161 sqq. W. Schur, RE 12, 928 sqq. This is also represented on the *aureus* shown on pl. III 5-6. Cf. AJA 63, 1959, 21 sqq. Cf. also G. Wissowa, Hermes 50, 1915, 29.

[3] Varro, *LL* 5, 152. Liv. I 14, 3. DH I 51, 1-52, 5. Strab. V 3, 2 (C. 230). Plut., *Rom.* 23, 3.

[4] Schol. Veron., *Aen.* 1, 239.

[5] Lucan. 7, 395 sqq.

[6] DH II 52, 3 : ... παραγενόμενος εἰς τὸ Λαουίνιον ἕνεκα θυσίας, ἣν ἔδει τοῖς πατρῴοις θεοῖς ὑπὲρ τῆς πόλεως θῦσαι τοὺς βασιλεῖς, κτλ.

[7] Liv. VIII 14, 10 : *Ceteris Latinis populis conubia commerciaque et concilia inter se ademerunt.*

[8] Liv. VIII 11, 15 (after the Roman victory) *extra poenam fuere Latinorum Laurentes ... quia non desciverant ; cum Laurentibus renovari foedus iussum renova-turque ex eo quotannis post diem decimum Latinarum* (sc. feriarum).

pated in the tribal worship except Rome and Lavinium.[1] The Roman Annals claim that Lavinium was honored with this *foedus* only because she did not participate in the upheaval against Rome; but this is not entirely correct [2] and moreover it is incompatible with the fact that a similar favor [3] was granted to the mutinous Lanuvium.[4] So the shrewd device of the annually renewed pact—it was said to have been ordered by the Sibylline oracles [5]—had the purpose of adapting the tribal cult in Lavinium to the new situation in 338 B.C. The annual *foedus* and the sacrifices continued to be celebrated during the Empire.[6] To create a more dignified Lavinian partnership for the flower of Roman society officiating in Lavinium, a corporation of Roman knights called *Laurentes Lavinates* was created at the beginning of imperial times.[7] These men took the place of real citizens of Lavinium as *patres patrati* and priests of her cults on the day of the celebrations.[8] The official name of these cults was *sacra principiorum p. R. Quiritium nominisque Latini, quae apud Laurentes coluntur.*[9] We do not know how

[1] As H. Dessau, CIL XIV p. 187 n. 3, already observed.

[2] *Liv., l.c.* The emendations of the text, aiming at eliminating the inconsistency of these statements with the data of the Fasti (e.g., those of S. Weinstock, RE 19, 429 sq., and R. Schilling, La religion romaine de Vénus [BEFAR 178] 1954, 81 sqq. H. Dessau, CIL XIV p. 187) are, I think, inadmissible. *Fasti triumph.* p. 69 Degrassi: *C. Maenius P.f.P. n.cos. de Antiatibus Lavinieis, Veliterneis pridie K.Oct. an. CD XV.* Cf. also G. Bendz, *Opusc. arch.* 1, 1935, 47 sqq. This triumph over Lavinium is well founded ; cf. Liv. VIII 11, 3-4 : *Latinis quoque ab Lavinio auxilium, dum deliberando terunt tempus, victis demum ferri coeptum. Et cum iam portis prima signa et pars agminis esset egressa, nuntio allato de clade Latinorum cum conversis signis retro in urbem rediretur, praetorem eorum nomine Milionium dixisse ferunt pro paulula via magnam mercedem esse Romanis solvendam.*

[3] Liv. VIII 14, 2 : *Lanuvinis civitas data sacraque sua reddita, cum eo ut aedes locusque Sospitae Iunonis communis Lanuvinis municipibus cum populo Romano esset.* Cf. G. Wissowa, Hermes 50, 1915, 21 (on Tusculum).

[4] Liv. *l.c. Fasti triumph. l.c.* H. Dessau, *l.c.* G. Wissowa, *l.c.* 29.

[5] CIL X 797, cited below. G. Wissowa, *op. cit.* 31. *Idem*, RuK², 520.

[6] H. Dessau, CIL XIV p. 187, overlooked Lucan. 7, 393 sqq., who (deploring the desolation of Latium) writes : *pulvere vix tectae poterunt monstrare ruinae Albanosque Lares Laurentinosque Penates rus vacuum ; quod non habitet nisi nocte coacta, invitus questusque Numam iussisse, senator.* What Numa ordered, was, of course, the performance of the rites in question.

[7] H. Dessau, *l.c.* G. Wissowa, Hermes 50, 1915, 28 sqq. A. Rosenberg, *ibid.* 416 sqq. K. Latte, *op. cit.* 295 n. 5, 407.

[8] The idea that in Lavinium μελεδωνοὶ τῶν ἱερῶν were necessary (DH I 67, 1-2) may have been conceived in connection with this reorganization.

[9] I gave the reasons for reading *sacra principiorum* and not *sacra principia* in : Die trojanischen Urahnen der Römer 46 n. 124-125. *Sacer* as referring to the State and the Emperor is used but very scarcely in the first century A.D. (e.g., Prop. IV 1, 3 *sacra palatia*) and becomes a regular attribute of everything con-

old is the calendar date of these vows and sacrifices for the welfare of the Latins and of Rome. The annual pact is mentioned by Livy as taking place *post diem decimum* (*feriarum*) *Latinarum* (VIII 11, 15). This date is set, however, in accordance with the vows of the magistrates on the Capitol and the *arx Albana*, and therefore must have been established with the hegemony over Latium. But there is a fact which reveals once more the central role of Lavinium in the early history of the Latins. The festival of *Sol Indiges* in Rome, along with that of *Vesta* (and the *Penates* in her inaccessible *penus*) was already part of the ritual celebrations of the Roman state when the oldest calendar was fixed,[1] i.e., in the fifth century B.C. In spite of this, the same divinities, regarded as vital to the existence of the state, were also honored in their original homes in Alba and in Lavinium by the Roman state, which acknowledged their primeval political primacy by caring for these cults down to the end of its pagan existence.

❦

THE NEW ARCHAEOLOGICAL EVIDENCE OF THE FEDERAL SANCTUARY IN LAVINIUM

The results so far presented to the reader were gathered from evidence already well known in 1956.[2] Three years later the sacred precinct of the Latins, where the cult acts just discussed were performed, was discovered by Professor F. Castagnoli and Dr. L. Cozza.[3] The site

nected with the ruler only in the third century A.D. (O. Hirschfeld, Die kaiserlichen Verwaltungsbeamten[2], Berlin 1905, 284 n. 3). The *sacra principiorum* in Lavinium are identical with their description in Plutarch, *Coriol.* 29, 2 : Λαουί-νιον, . . ὅπου καὶ θεῶν ἱερὰ ʽΡωμαίοις πατρῴων ἀπέκειτο καὶ τοῦ γένους ἦσαν αὐτοῖς ἀρχαὶ διὰ τὸ πρώτην πόλιν ἐκείνην κτίσαι τὸν Αἰνείαν. Cf. also DH VIII 21, 1. The inscription quoted runs as follows : *Sp. Turranius L.f. Sp. n.L. pron. Fab. Proculus Gellianus . . . praif. pro pr. i.d. in urbe Lavinio pater patratus populi Laurentis foederis ex libris Sibullinis percutiendi cum p. R., sacrorum principiorum p. R. Quirit. nominisque Latini, quai apud Laurentis coluntur, flam. Dialis, flam. Martial., salius praisul, augur, pont.,* etc. (ILS 5004). Cf. also Sil. Ital. 1, 658 sqq. : *per vos culta diu Rutulae primordia gentis Laurentemque larem et genetricis pignora Troiae.*

[1] A. Kirsopp Michels, TAPA 80, 1949, 320 sqq.

[2] Cf. my study, Die trojanischen Urahnen der Römer.

[3] The first reports with some illustrations were promptly made available to the newspapers ; cf. *New York Times* May 13, 1959 and *New York Herald Tribune* May 17, 1959. The discoverers reported their findings to the Pont. Accademia Rom. di Archeologia on April 2, 1959. The archaic dedication to the Dioscuri mentioned below was published by Prof. F. Castagnoli, with an

of the discovery is the area called Madonella, about 200 or 300 meters *outside* the city walls of Lavinium, where a row of 13 huge archaic altars (pl. XVI) was found *in situ*. I owe to Professor Castagnoli the precious information, that in 1963 some more such fragments came to light. They are made of the soft local stone and are of a rather coarse workmanship, reaching sometimes almost four meters in length, with profiles of changing outlines and other traces of differing epochs.[1] But their occasional replacement by new ones can be due only to erosion and all of them seem to me to have been used at the same time. On the stone platform of the oldest one, number 13 of the excavation records, a still unpublished Attic vase-fragment with a sphinx and a siren was found, which may be dated in the years 570-50 B.C., as Professor Castagnoli kindly informs me. It can be assumed confidently that this vase was a votive offering, brought to the sacred precinct shortly after its fabrication. Consequently, at least the altar on the stone pavement where this potsherd was found was already standing about 550 B.C. Another precious chronological indication is gained from the bronze inscription once fixed to the tufa base of a votive gift beside the eighth altar offered to the Dioscuri (p. XVIII, 5)[2]: its archaic letters are the same as those of the *lapis niger* in the Forum Romanum.

The simultaneous use of so many and such big altars can be explained by a few literary data concerning the federal cult in Lavinium. Dionysius, who was personally acquainted with the Lavinian precinct,[3] gives the following account: Romulus had gone with his co-regent, Titus Tatius, to Lavinium [4] to offer the annual sacrifice to the

excellent commentary ; cf. below, n. 2. I owe to both scholars important informations and invaluable help. I wish to express also here my very sincere thanks to them. Their publication is due very soon. B. Tilly (*op. cit.* 100 sqq.) suspected already in 1947 that "the scene of the rites of the Indiges" must be sought there.

[1] A detailed analysis by F. Castagnoli of their shapes appeared already in the Bull. Com. 77, 1959-60 (1961) 3 sqq. Cf. L. Shoe, Year Book of the Amer. Philosophical Soc., Philadelphia 1962, 624 sqq., on the architectural moldings in Central Italy. She has kindly permitted me to quote her as saying that the profiles of these altars are not Greek, but Etruscan.

[2] F. Castagnoli, SMSR 30, 1959, 109 sqq.

[3] DH I 55, 1-2.

[4] *Idem*, II 52, 3. Cf. also Varro, *LL* 5, 152. Liv. I 14, 3. Plut., *Rom.* 23, 1-4. Solin. 1, 21. Zon. 7, 4 (2, p. 95 Dind.). A. Schwegler, RG 1, 516 n. 2, connected the verse of Enn., *Ann.* 1, 109 V.[2] *o Tite tute Tati, tibi tanta tyranne tulisti* with this account.

ancestral gods for the prosperity of Rome, just after Tatius had some envoys of Lavinium assassinated. The companions and relatives of the assassinated men conspired against him and slew him at the altars with knives and spits used in cutting up the oxen for roasting (ἐπὶ τῶν βωμῶν ταῖς μαγειρικαῖς σφαγίσι καὶ τοῖς βουπόροις ὀβελοῖς παιόμενος). The *prodigium* reported by Cato [1] also attests that several oxen were slain at the same time for the sacrifice in question: *Lavini boves immolatos, priusquam caederentur, profugisse in silvam.* The same sort of ritual was in Vergil's mind when he described the *foedus* between Latinus and Aeneas as concluded not by the habitual pig-sacrifice but with the offering of cattle (12, 213 sq.): *Tum rite sacratas | in flammam iugulant pecudes et viscera vivis | eripiunt cumulantque oneratis lancibus aras.* This sort of collective sacrifice under the open sky seems to have been one of the oldest Latin ritual habits.[2] If as many oxen were killed as there were altars, this means that a great crowd shared in the meat of the victims: modern army rationing provides one ox for a battalion of a thousand soldiers.[3] Therefore, the row of a dozen or more altars served the representatives and citizens of all the Latin cities, including Rome, performing their sacrifice to *Indiges*, *Vesta*, and the *Penates* in the holy area where Aeneas was supposed to have made his initial sacrifice to his ancestral gods. An essential feature of the federal sanctuaries of Latium was that they were outside the boundaries of the cities which were in charge of their ritual: we have seen this juridically relevant exterritoriality in the case of the Aventine precinct of Diana,[4] and other examples [5] are not lacking. No local municipal cult of such dimensions could exist outside a city in the archaic epoch or have any reason to be placed *extra pomerium*: such a location would be more obvious for the tribal rites and the original gatherings connected with them.

After 340 B.C., when the Latin cities were excluded from the actual performance of the federal cult by Rome and the political importance

---

[1] Cato, *Orig.* fr. 55 Peter, quoted above. Cf. also F. Bömer, Gymnasium 68, 1961, 190 sq.

[2] Liv. XXII 1, 19 (217 B.C.) : *decemviri Ardeae in foro maioribus hostiis sacrificarunt.* It is likely that the sacrifice was offered to the ancestral divinity of *Venus-Frutis*, with the federal cult of which the *Ardeates* were entrusted διὰ προπόλων (Strabo V 3, 5. C 232).

[3] As my dear friend K. Meuli, Basel, reminds me.

[4] Cf. above, p. 89 and 99 sq.

[5] Cf. my note in : Gymnasium 67, 1960, 193 sqq.

of the sacred district of Lavinium was restricted to one day a year, a wave of private religiosity swept over this holy area. The dedications [1] to Ceres and Vesperna from a little temple excavated by the discoverers of the federal precinct not far from it, bear witness to this phenomenon; and it is illustrated still more concretely by the votive terra-cottas often found here before and now brought to light in enormous quantities by F. Castagnoli and L. Cozza. These terra-cottas mirror the same phase of religious evolution in southern Etruria and Latium which was recently illuminated by Q. F. Maule and H. R. W. Smith: [2] "By the fourth century the flood of anatomical parts has begun—as E. Hill Richardson sums up their results.[3] To judge from the ex-votos, all the great goddesses of Southern Etruria and Latium are concerned with childbirth and healing, but the frequency of male parts among the ex-votos is the only indication that this religion was not entirely in the hands of women." The terra-cotta offerings of Lavinium broaden this aspect still more: heads of men and other parts of the male body occur as frequently as the female, and there are just as many figurines representing domestic animals or parts of them. The general healing and blessing capacity of the divinity is invoked by the agricultural folk in a way which is essentially a sort of imitative magic. In the flood of these magic conceptions the individuality of the gods is submerged.

૪

THE *PENATES* AS DIOSCURI IN LAVINIUM AND ROME

As already noted,[4] the cult of the *Penates* [5] in Rome had two distinctly

---

[1] M. Guarducci, Arch. cl. 3, 1951, 99 sqq., and *ibid.* 11, 1959, 206 sqq. S. Weinstock, JRS 42, 1952, 34 sqq. R. Bloch, CRAI 1954, 203 sqq. Le Bonniec, Le culte de Cérès à Rome, Paris 1958, 463 sqq. H. Wagenvoort, Mnemosyne 4. ser. 14, 1961, 217 sqq.

[2] Q. F. Maule - H. R. W. Smith, Votive Religion at Caere (Univ. of Calif. Publ. in Class. Arch. 4, 1) Berkeley-Los Angeles 1959.

[3] AJA 64, 1960, 294.

[4] Cf. above, p. 258.

[5] M. Albert, Le culte de Castor et Pollux en Italie, Thèse, Paris 1883. E. Petersen, RM 15, 1900, 309 sqq. W. Helbig, Hermes 40, 1905, 101 sqq. K. Meister, Lateinisch-griechische Eigennamen, Leipzig 1916, 113. F. Altheim, Griechische Götter im alten Rom, Giessen 1930, 4 sqq. Ch. Picard, R. Ét. Lat. 17, 1939, 367 sq. S. Weinstock, RE 19, 451 sqq., and the studies quoted in the subsequent notes.

diverging forms. One was the cult of small aniconic objects or primitive figurines,[1] inaccessible to everyone except its guardians; the other was a chapel on the Velia, where are publicly exhibited the statues of two sitting youths with their spears, with the dedication *Magnis Diis*.[2] Every attempt to explain this double aspect, or to reconcile the two with each other, is condemned to failure in advance. But if we simply acknowledge the discrepancy the reason for it becomes evident: the secret *Penates* hidden with the fire of *Vesta* belong to the oldest group of Latin divinities, whereas the Greek concept of the Dioscuri was introduced as a sort of modernized interpretation of the *Penates*, which, though becoming rooted in the open worship, could not replace them in the cryptic state ritual. A similar chapel with the sitting youths existed in Lavinium: it was represented with Aeneas making a sacrifice to them, on a relief of the *ara Pacis*.[3] The archaic bronze inscription of an ex-voto in the federal sanctuary of Lavinium, found by the two Italian scholars and published by F. Castagnoli,[4] now attests the presence of Castor and Pollux in Lavinium at the end of the sixth century B.C. Since it was found beside the great altars, it seems certain that the *Penates* of the Latins[5] are meant with this dedication to the *Dioscuri*.

The inscription runs: CASTOREI PODLOVQEIQVE QVROIS. It is evident that *Polydeukes* was called in Latin *Poldoukes* before the curious metathesis DL instead of LD in the middle of the word distorted the original form of the name. *Poldoukes* corresponds to the Etruscan *Pultuke*,[6] demonstrating the contemporary transmission of the cult to the

[1] The view of F. Bömer, Rom und Troja, Baden-Baden 1951, 95 ff., that the clay figurines accompanying the hut-urns of the Alban territory are the antecedents of the cult-objects of the *penus Vestae* deserves serious consideration. Cf. A. Andrén, Rend. Pont. Acc. 32, 1960, 48 fig. 17 and n. 67 (lit.). G. Pugliese Carratelli, La parola del passato, fasc. 82, 1962, 15 sqq.

[2] Details given, e.g., by S. Weinstock, RE 19, 449 sqq. Cf. *idem*, JRS 50, 1960, 56 sqq.

[3] S. Weinstock, JRS 50, 1960, 113. Kr. Hanell, Opusc. Rom. 2 (Skrifter Svensk. Inst. i Rom 4°, 20) 1960, 91 sq., reminds us (with G. Wissowa, RuK², 165 n. 3) of the fact that the two sitting youths are bearded in this case—a feature unknown elsewhere in Latium.

[4] F. Castagnoli, SMSR 30, 1959, 109 sqq. Cf. S. Weinstock, JRS 50, 1960, 112 sqq. R. Bloch, Revue de philol. 3. sér. 34, 1960, 182 sqq. R. Schilling, Hommages à G. Dumézil (Coll. Latomus 45) 1960, 177 sqq.

[5] This possibility was considered already by F. Castagnoli, *l.c.*, and accepted by S. Weinstock, *op. cit.* 114.

[6] E. Fiesel, Namen des griechischen Mythos im Etruskischen, Göttingen 1928, 83 and 288. S. Weinstock, *l.c.* R. Enking, RE 23, 1975.

Etruscans along with the Latins. *Poloukes* occurs in Praeneste,[1] emerging from the same current of religiosity; we know of the existence of an equally old cult of the Dioscuri in Ardea,[2] and also of the great importance of the same cult in Tusculum. The statues of these divine youths found at the *lacus Iuturnae* in Rome (Frontispiece and pl. II) are of Greek workmanship of the early fifth century B.C.[3] The fact that their temple, built in the same epoch, was erected *intra pomerium*, proves unmistakably that their cult was then taken as an indigenous one; its reception, therefore, must be anterior to the battle at Lake Regillus.[4] They are called *quroi* on the new inscription and everybody agrees therefore with F. Castagnoli that they arrived in Latium directly from the Greek South. R. Bloch[5] thinks they came from Locri, H. Wagenvoort[6] argues, reasonably, for Tarentum. *Kuroi* characterizes the divine brothers in Sparta as horsemen[7] and their great popularity in archaic Latium coincided with the emergence of the overwhelming military and political importance of the cavalry.[8]

The once leading role of Lavinium would make obvious the supposition that the Dioscuri in Rome were taken over from Lavinium, even if the new dedication had not brought welcome support for this view.[9] Moreover, the source-goddess Iuturna who was associated with the Dioscuri in Rome was also indigenous to Lavinium,[10] no doubt having come with them from Lavinium.[11] Her salutary water was also used

---

[1] CIL XIV 4094 and 4095. Cf. Serv., *Aen.* 7, 678 on Praeneste, where *duo fratres qui divi appellabantur* had a cult of their own. Cf. Solin. 2 , 9.

[2] Serv., *Aen.* 1, 44.

[3] A thorough publication of them would be welcome and is expected from E. Paribeni. The palm-trunks under the horses are a late addition made from a different stone.

[4] As R. Schilling, *op. cit.* 182, stressed it.

[5] R. Bloch, *op. cit.* 186 sqq.

[6] H. Wagenvoort, Mnemosyne 44, ser. 13, 1960, 121 sqq. S. Weinstock, *op. cit.*, 114.

[7] As R. Schilling, *op. cit.* 178, has pointed out. The two sitting youths with their spears are, I think, the same horsemen gods. *Contra* : S. Weinstock, *op. cit.* 114.

[8] W. Helbig, *op. cit.*, and my study, Der frührömische Reiteradel, Baden-Baden 1952.

[9] S. Weinstock, op. cit. 112.

[10] Serv., *Aen.* 12, 139. E. Petersen, RM 15, 1900, 338 sqq. F. Altheim, *op. cit.* 14 sq., 29 sqq. R. Schilling, *op. cit.* 185 sqq. and our pl. XVII.

[11] K. Latte, RE 10, 1348, takes an opposing view in his Röm. Religionsgeschichte 78, n. 1.

for the ritual of Vesta,[1] and so the transfer of secondary divinities of a cult-complex from Lavinium, along with the great gods, becomes even more apparent. In the same way the mythical attendants of the Arician Diana accompanied her to Rome.[2]

ℰ

THE MYTH OF THE SOW WITH THE THIRTY PIGLETS AND ITS TRANSFORMATIONS

The claim of Lavinium to preeminence in times past was displayed in an art monument in the marketplace of this city, mentioned for the first time by the historian Timaeus who got his information in the decades around 300 B.C.[3] This monument was the bronze image of a sow with thirty newly born piglets, symbolizing the mother-city of all the Latins and the thirty Latin strongholds founded by her.[4] This tangible memorial of the hegemonial aspirations of Lavinium in a distant past [5] was still there in the time of Varro.[6] It could have

[1] Serv., *Aen.* 12, 139 : *de hoc autem fonte Romam ad omnia sacrificia aqua adferri consueverat.* Cf. G. Boni, Not. Scav. 1900, 591. Other sources used for the purpose of the Vesta cult : E. Petersen, *op. cit.* 341 n. 3. K. Latte, *op. cit.* 77.

[2] Cf. above, p. 87 sq. On the *Penates-Dioscuri* in Rome and Middle Italy cf. above, p. 268 sq.

[3] F. Jacoby, F. Gr. Hist. III b Kommentar 532 sq., thinks that Timaeus dealt with this problem "in den Pyrrhosbüchern" toward the end of his long life. But, if we assume that his excerptor, Lycophron, was living in the court of the second Ptolemy (cf. A. Momigliano, Riv. Stor. Ital. 71, 1959, 551 sqq., with the literary data), it becomes clear that he wrote on Lavinium earlier in his general work. I see no reason to deny with F. Jacoby (*ibid.* 566) that Timaeus came in touch with the ἐπιχώριοι of Lavinium itself : this was much easier than to provide information on Liguria and on the Celts in Northern Italy (Polyb. XII 28 a 3).

[4] We do not have the original text of Timaeus, only a deliberately enigmatic poetic transcription in Lycophr., *Alex.* 1253 sqq. (on Aeneas) : κτίσει δὲ χώραν ἐν τόποις Βορειγόνων ὑπὲρ Λακίου Δαυνίου τ' ᾠκισμένην, πύργους τριάκοντ' ἐξαριθμήσας γονὰς συὸς κελαινῆς, ἣν ἀπ' Ἰδαίων λόφων καὶ Δαρδανείων ἐκ τόπων ναυσθλώσεται, ἰσηρίθμων θρέπτειραν ἐν τόκοις κάπρων. ἧς καὶ πόλει δείκηλον ἀνθήσει μιᾷ χαλκῷ τυπώσας καὶ τέκνων γλαγοτρόφων. The provenience from Timaeus is certain ; cf. even F. Jacoby, F. Gr. Hist. 3 B, Notenband zum Kommentare 332 n. 318.

[5] U. v. Wilamowitz, Kleine Schriften 2, Berlin 1883, 23 (quoted by W. Ehlers, Mus. Helv. 6, 1949, 167) : *perspexit (Timaeus) melius quam Romani ad unum omnes scriptores triginta porcellis dici triginta foederis Latini urbes.* The foundation of the 30 cities is not connected with the *prodigium* of the tables, as W. Ehlers, *op. cit.*, thinks, but with the sow, and is not to be separated from the *populi Albenses* of Pictor (*ibid.* 169).

272

ALBA LONGA AND LAVINIUM

been a very old monument in the age of Timaeus, possibly as old
as the sixth century B.C.; but it could also have been a quite recent one,
erected not long before 340 B.C. However, this city-state's ambitions
for the leadership embodied in this statuary group could not have
existed prior to the seventh century B.C.

We are also acquainted with other representations of the sow as a
badge of the Latins. After the victory over Pyrrhus, the Romans had
it reproduced on their new ingot money (pl. XVIII 4) along with the
elephant of the invading power: everyone using the bronze bars must
have known that the indigenous animal meant the Latins,[1] contrasted
with the strange beast which was the pictorial symbol of the vanquished foreign intruder. It even seems that the statue of the sow with her
piglets was erected in all the forums of the new colonies of Rome
which had a Latin status. The earliest trace of this is the sow found
on bronze coins of the Umbrian town of Tuder (pl. IV, 3)[2] from the
late third century B.C. On these coins the sow has only three piglets;
but *aurei* and *denarii* of Vespasian, representing the same archaic
statuary type as the Latin sow (pl. IV, 4), prove that the three stand
for thirty. Though we know that Tuder obtained Roman citizenship
only in the Social War,[3] we must assume by reason of this representation that the Romans moved a Latin colony to this key position
on the road to the south as early at in the third century B.C. Another
case [4] is the statue of the *scrofa cum porcis triginta* erected by C. Cornelius Caeso, the mayor of the city of Obulco south of Corduba, and

---

[6] Varro, *R R* II 4, 17 sqq. : (scrofa) *si plures* (quam quot mammas habeat)
*pariat, portentum. in quo illud antiquissimum fuisse scribitur, quod sus Aeneae Lavini
triginta porcos peperit albos. Itaque quod portenderit factum, <post> tricesimum ut
Lavinienses condiderint oppidum Albam. huius suis ac porcorum etiam nunc vestigia
apparent, quod et simulacrum eorum ahenea etiam nunc in publico posita, et corpus matris
ab sacerdotibus, quod in salsura fuerit, demonstratur.*

[1] Cf. RM 68, 1961, 71 sqq.

[2] A. Sambon, Les monnaies antiques de l'Italie, Paris 1903, 89 no. 156.

[3] Th. Mommsen, Römisches Münzwesen[2], Berlin 1860, 329 (on the basis of
L. Cornel. Sisenna fr. 119 Peter). L. R. Taylor, Vot. Distr. 83 n. 13 ; 85 ; 107 ;
113 n. 31 ; 114.

[4] It has been assumed by several scholars that a statue of the sow also stood
in Milan. But the passages, on which this assumption was based, display only
a childish etymology of the name of Mediolanum : Isid. XV 1, 57 : *Vocatum
autem Mediolanum ab eo quod ibi sus medio lanea perhibetur inventa.* Claud. Claudian.,
Epithal. de nupt. Honorii Aug. 182 sqq. : . . . *ad moenia Gallis condita lanigeri suis
ostentantia pellem pervenit.* Sidon., *Epist.* VII 17, 2 v. 20 : *et quae lanigero de sue
nomen habet.* There is no reference to a statue.

his son; Ad. Schulten has recognized that this proves the *ius Latinum* of this community.[1]

We do not know the original destination of the life-size marble group of the sow with her piglets found in the Valle S. Vitale between the Quirinal and the Viminal (pl. V).[2] This amusing creation of the second century A.D., in a naturalistic style with a slightly comical touch, could have nevertheless been an official monument because the same composition appears in the same style on the coins of Antoninus Pius (pl. VII, 1-4), who was born in the Latin countryside[3] and could have revived the myth.

The principal feature of the Lavinian version of this Latin myth is its "Trojanization." Already in Timaeus it is Aeneas who finds the sow and founds Lavinium under her guidance, and the reference to the Trojan hero, founder of Lavinium, from that time on becomes a constant feature of every account we possess[4] as well as in art representations.[5] On some bronze medallions struck under Hadrian and again under Antoninus Pius[6] with the representation of the sow (pl. VI, 1), Aeneas appears on the high ground with Anchises on his shoulder, between a higher and a lower altar for the heavenly

[1] CIL II 2126. Cf. Ad. Schulten, RE 17, 1750 sq. I overlooked this important document to which T. R. S. Broughton drew my attention.

[2] W. Amelung, Die Skulpturen des Vatikanischen Museums 2, Berlin 1908, 373 no. 194, and pl. 40 (with previous literature).

[3] *Script. hist. Aug., v. Pii* 1, 8 : *natus est . . . in villa Lanuvina.* Vict., *Caes.* 15, 2 : *vir veterrimae familiae, e Lanuvino municipio.* But the codex Oxoniensis has *Lavinio* instead of Lanuvino. As the two cities were often confounded by the ancients (and even by F. Jacoby, in the F. Gr. Hist.), the latter reading is possible. On the estate of his parents in Lorium at the *via Aurelia,* cf. H. Philipp, RE, *s.v.*

[4] Cf., e.g., J. Rubino, Beiträge zur Vorgeschichte Italiens, Leipzig 1868, 150 sqq. Fr. Cauer, Jahrb. f. Philol., Suppl. 15, 1887, 107. Joh. Geffcken, Timaios' Geographie des Westens, Berlin 1892, 45 sq. W. Schur, Klio 17, 1921, 140. B. Rehm, Das geographische Bild des alten Italien in Vergils Aeneis, Philol. Suppl. 24/2, 1932, 47 sqq. W. Hoffmann, Rom und die griechische Welt, Leipzig 1934, 115 sqq. J. Carcopino, Virgile, etc. 438 sqq. W. Ehlers, Mus. Helv. 6, 1949, 166 sqq. F. Bömer, Rom und Troja, Baden-Baden 1951, 20 sqq. Cf. also my study "Die trojanischen Urahnen der Römer." E. Bickel, Rh. Mus. n.F. 100, 1957, 225 sqq.

[5] E. Studniczka, Jahreshefte d. Österr. Arch. Inst. 6, 1903, pl. 5, 9. E. Rizzo, RM 21, 1906, 289 sqq. C. Robert, Antike Sarkophagenreliefs III 3, Berlin 1919, 564 sqq. G. Q. Giglioli, Bull. Com. 67, 1939, 109 sqq. J. Le Gall, Recherches sur le culte du Tibre, Paris 1953, 7 sqq.

[6] F. Gnecchi, I medaglioni romani, Milano 1912, pl. 54, 9 ; 55, 8. J. M. C. Toynbee, Roman Medaillons, New York 1944, pl. 25, 4. J. Carcopino, Virgile, etc. 719 sqq. I. Scott Ryberg, Mem. Am. Ac. 19, 1949, 81. J. M. C. Toynbee, Proceed. Br. Ac. 39, 1953, 67 sqq. S. Weinstock, JRS 1960, 56 sqq.

and the chthonic divinities.[1] On the left appears a round hut, the καλίας described by Dionysius,[2] where Aeneas sacrificed the sow with her young to his ancestral gods. It may once have been situated at the place of the little round church of the Madonella, in the neighborhood of the great altars. The same scenery with the two altars and the hut appears again on another medallion of Pius (pl. VI, 2) showing the landing of the hero and the discovery of the sow. This sacred hut, kept inaccessible to the public, reminds us of the hut urns and the *casa Romuli* in Rome.[3] It originated certainly in highly archaic concepts of the cult of the tribal ancestor.

But the Lavinian version of the myth of the sow was not the original one, even if we disregard its secondary connection with Aeneas. The competition between Lavinium and Alba Longa, some aspects of which we followed above, is reflected also in certain versions of the myth in question.[4] Fabius Pictor, who must have known from living tradition the story of the prodigious sow, orally transmitted from generation to generation, still related in his Annals, that Alba Longa, not Lavinium, was the original place to which the sow, messenger of the divinity, guided the ancestor of the nation.[5] Nobody doubts that this was the primary version. Nor is it likely that Pictor simply invented the notion of the white sow, the *sus alba*, from whose color the name of the first Latin city was supposed to have been taken.[6] Pictor contaminated this oral tradition with the Lavinian account of Timaeus, reinterpreting freely the thirty piglets as thirty years after which Aeneas was ordered by the ancestral gods to found Alba. But such secondary combinations cannot obscure the fact that the sow did not

---

[1] F. Gr. Hist. 840 F 34 = DH I 55, 2. Cf. S. Weinstock, JRS 50, 1960, 117. Verg., *Aen.* 7, 136 sqq. Vitruv. 4, 9. P. Lambrechts, Med. Vlaam. Akad. Lett. XII 7, 1950, 10 sqq.

[2] DH I 57, i.

[3] A. Schwegler, RG 1, 394. B. Tilly, Vergil's Latium, Oxford 1947, 58 sq. S. Weinstock, RE 19, 441 (on the oldest temples of Vesta).

[4] We do not need to enlarge upon the clumsy attempts to coordinate the role of the two capitals ; cf., e.g., the quotations by W. Ehlers, *op. cit.* 168 sqq.

[5] F. Gr. Hist. 809 F 2 (= fr. 4 Peter). μέλλοντος δ' αὐτοῦ θύειν ὗν ἔγκυον τῷ χρώματι λευκὴν ἐκφυγεῖν ἐκ τῶν χειρῶν καὶ διωχθῆναι πρός τινα λόφον, πρὸς ᾧ κομισθεῖσαν τεκεῖν λ' χοίρους.

[6] Pictor, *l.c.* (quoted in the foregoing note). Varro, *LL* 5, 144. *Idem, RR* II 4, 18. Verg., *Aen.* 8, 42 sqq. Serv., *Aen.* 1, 270. *Aen.* 3, 392. Propert. IV 1, 35. Iuven. 12, 70 sqq. *Origo gent. Rom.* 17, 1. Isid. XV 1, 53. Cass. Dio 1, p. 2 Boiss. (= Zon. 7, 1). Tzetz., ad Lycophr. 1232.

arrive with Aeneas on shipboard, but that in the myth she led the Latins originally to Alba.

The mythology of the Indo-European hunters and shepherds abounds with powerful animals, of this sort, who are sent by heaven to lead the migrating tribes to the region where they were to found their new fatherland.[1] The typical combination of these myths, in which the name of the people, the headgear of its warriors, the standards carried before them in battle, all emblematic of a theriomorphic ancestor revealing the way to a promising new homeland, is not lacking in Italy. As the *picus* led the Picentes, the *hirpus* the Hirpini, the bull the Samnites to their respective countries, so the sow led the Latins. The concept of a sow as prospective food arriving on board ship with the new settlers transformed the myth of migrating cattle-rearers arriving by land into a saga of sailors and pirates landing on a seashore.

The original form of this animal was certainly not a domesticated pig but a female wild boar. The dark swine of Timaeus [2] is a κάπρος, and the learned Vergil also depicts her as a wild boar:

> *cum tibi sollicito secreti ad fluminis undam*
> *litoreis ingens inventa sub ilicibus sus*
> *triginta capitum fetus enixa iacebit*
> *alba solo recubans, albi circum ubera nati,*
> *is locus urbis erit, requies ea certa laborum.*[3]

The furious boar was a favorite mythical prototype of the maniacal warrior-ideal of the Indo-Europeans: the enraged Indra, the frantic Rudra, the irresistible Verethragna were conceived as such; [4] it was the totemic-ancestor of the Kirghis-Turks in northern Asia [5] and the name of princes and warriors in the same region,[6] where we also

[1] E. Pais, St. d. R. 1³, 1926, 263. A. Alföldi, Arch. Anz. 1931, 393 sqq.

[2] Lycophr. 1255 sq. : γονὰς / συὸς κελαινῆς with the commentary of Tzetzes : ταύτην οὗτος μέλαιναν λέγει. Lycophr. 1258 : ἐν τόκοις κάπρων.

[3] Verg., *Aen.* 3, 389 sqq. ; cf. 8, 4 sq. *Sus* meant also "boar" ; cf. Enn., *Ann.* fr. 105 Vahlen³. The same word was also used for the female animals, like the *lupus femina* in Enn., *Ann.* fr. 68 Vahlen³. A similar ambivalence existed also for *porca* : cf. Varro, *LL* 5, 97 : *porcus, quod Sabini dicunt aprunu(m) porcu(m).*

[4] Cf., e.g., A. Bergaigne, La religion védique 2, Paris 1883, 159 sqq. H. S. Nyberg, Die Religionen des alten Iran, Uppsala 1938, 69 sq. G. Dumézil, Mél. Grégoire 1, Bruxelles 1949, 223 sqq.

[5] U. Holmberg, The Shaman Costume, Helsinki 1922, 27.

[6] J. J. Mikkola, Journ. de la Soc. Finno-Ougrienne 30, 1933, 12.

276

find the boarhead as the headgear of mythical warriors.[1] We find in the same way the heroic ideal of the raving boar and the image of the battling boar on early mediaeval helmets in Scandinavia;[2] and Celtic analogies are not lacking.[3] Among the Greeks we find a boar guiding the Ephesians to a site where a sanctuary was to be built;[4] and Heracles with the boarhead instead of the lion's skin is found among the Greeks of Magna Graecia.[5] Because of these manifold antecedents and possibilities, and the lack of information, we cannot decide whether a powerful boar on an early Etruscan coin (pl. XVIII, 3),[6] the head of a divinity on cast bronze coins of the third century B.C.,[7] or a male figurine in Perugia with the same sort of headgear,[8] are influenced by the myth of Greek hero's or are autochthonous conceptions.

We have more solid ground under our feet in Latium where the myth of the sow is a genuine Latin carry-over from a prehistoric religious pattern. The furious boar was a common occurrence around Lavinium:

> *Sicut aper longe silvis Laurentibus actus*
> *Fulmineo celeres dissipat ore canes,*

as Ovid describes it.[9] There were indeed so many of them in the forests around that city that the *Laurens aper* was a common article in the meatmarkets of the capital.[10] In the archaic societies of hunting

---

[1] A. Salmony, Sammlung J. F. H. Menten, Chinesische Grabfunde und Bronzen. Hrsg. vom Kunstgewerbemuseum der Stadt Zürich, Zürich 1948.

[2] Beowulf 303 sq. 1111. 1285 sq. 1448 sq. Cf. also the saga of Hrolf Kraki (Thule 21, 1926, 221 sqq.) in Snorri, Skaldsk c. 41 (Thule 20, 1925, 197 sqq.). Saxo gramm., 52 sqq. ed. Holder. More details in O. Höfler, in : Brauch und Sinnbild E. Fehrle gew. 1940, 124. M. Ninck, Wodan und germanischer Schicksalsglaube, Jena 1935, 46 sqq. K. Meuli, Handwörterbuch des deutschen Aberglaubens 5, 1932-33, 1847. Cf. the early medieval helmet from Benty Grange in the City Museum in Sheffield, Yorkshire.

[3] E.g., Dorothy Hill, Catalogue of the Class. Bronze Sculptures in the Walters Art Gallery, Baltimore 1949, no. 90, 94, 95.

[4] Creophylus in Athen. 8, 62 (361 sqq. C.), quoted already by W. Ehlers, *op. cit.* 172.

[5] J. Bayet, Les origines de l'Hercule romain, Paris 1926, 42, 63. Joh. Geffcken, *op. cit.* 9 n. 1 (Diomedes).

[6] A. Sambon, *op. cit.* no. 19.

[7] E. J. Haeberlin, Aes grave, Berlin 1910, pl. 56, 11-12, 14, 24-30 ; pl. 94, 12.

[8] A. Stenico, Athen, n.s. 25, 1947, 55 sqq. with pl. 2, 8.

[9] Ovid., *Fast.* 2, 231 sq. Cf. Verg., *Aen.* 10, 707 sqq.

[10] Hor., *Sat.* II 4, 40 sqq. Mart. IX 48, 5 sqq. X 45, 3 sqq. Verg., *loc. cit.*

peoples such an important beast of prey usually assumed the role of a totem; survivals of such concepts occur everywhere, even on the threshold of high cultures: this is the case with the Latin *scrofa*.[1]

The primeval stage of this myth fortunately left traces in Rome, where a cult, the *Lares Grundules*,[2] was made of the sow and her thirty piglets. Nothing could illuminate more concretely the tribal roots and the tribal ties of the Roman community in its primordial stage than this theriomorphic cult. The same cult also must have been present in the other member-states of the League of the Thirty Peoples. The statuary groups of the *scrofa* in their marketplaces were originally cult-images.

Though Lavinium was acknowledged by the Latins after the decline of Alba Longa as the place where the sow led their common ancestor, the proper theriomorphic patrons of this city-state were not forgotten, as proved by a saga narrated by Dionysius.[3] "In the time when the city of Lavinium was under construction," so runs the tale, "a fire rose spontaneously in the forest covering the site [manifestly the simplest way to clear the area for future buildings]. A wolf brought dry wood in his mouth and threw it upon the fire; and an eagle flying thither fanned the flame with the motion of his wings. But working in opposition to these animals, a fox after wetting his tail in the river endeavored to beat out the flames. Now those that were kindling the fire would prevail, then the fox who was trying to put it out would prevail. But at last the eagle and the wolf got the upper hand and the fox went away, unable to do anything further." This contest was also portrayed [4] in the forum of Lavinium by an old group of bronze

---

[1] I hope to demonstrate elsewhere that the theriomorphic predecessor of Quirinus in Rome was the boar, in the same way as Mars was a wolf in an early epoch. Cf. my note in Germania 30, 1952, 188 n. 11.

[2] Cass. Hemina fr. 11 (H. R. Rel. 1², 101 sqq.) reported after the election of Romulus and Remus to their leaders by the shepherds : *monstrum fit : sus parit porcos triginta, cuius rei fanum fecerunt Laribus Grundulibus.* Cf. Non. s.v. (p. 114 K) : *Grundules Lares dicuntur Romae constituti ob honorem porcae, quae triginta pepererat.* Cf. also A. Schwegler, RG 1, 323. H. Peter, *loc. cit.* J. Rubino, Beiträge zur Vorgeschichte Italiens, Leipzig 1868, 222 sqq. J. Carcopino, Virgile, etc. 102 sqq. W. Ehlers, *op. cit.* 169 n. 22, erroneously considers this a literary fiction. The dogs and the dogskin clothes of the *Lares Praestites* demonstrate sufficiently that such prehistoric remnants existed in the cult of the *Lares*.

[3] DH I 59, 2 sqq.

[4] DH I 59, 5 : ἔστιν αὐτῶν μνημεῖα ἐν τῇ Λαουινιατῶν ἀγορᾷ χαλκᾶ εἴδωλα τῶν ζῴων ἐκ πολλοῦ πάνυ χρόνου διατηρούμενα.

images of these animals. The opponent of the helpful wolf and eagle was the fox whose reddish color clearly alluded to the name of the *Rutuli*, the hostile neighbors of the Lavinians; the other two are the once totemistic beasts of their ancestors. They are also reproduced, kindling the fire, on the denarii of L. Papius Celsus, struck in the last years of Caesar (pl. XIII, 15-18). They reveal beyond question an important detail, hitherto unnoticed, namely, that the wolf is female. The she-wolf with her bird-helper, the eagle, is strongly reminiscent of the Roman *lupa* with her helpful bird, the woodpecker. Furthermore, on a Roman bronze quadrans from the end of the Second Punic War, the Roman she-wolf is accompanied by an eagle bringing grapes for the twins (pl. XVIII, 1); the eagle, with Hercules, also watches over the doe nursing young Telephus on a medallion of Antoninus Pius (pl. VI, 3). This parallelism suggests that Lavinium's authentic myth of origin had the same pattern as the Roman one.[1]

TROJAN LEGEND AND ETRUSCAN DOMINATION IN LATIUM

The present writer believes that he established, in an earlier study, the fact that the role of Aeneas as ancestor of the Latins is a direct consequence of the Etruscan rule in Latium. Subsequent archaeological discoveries and other research have corroborated his results. The main points of the evidence can be recapitulated as follows.[2]

[1] In the version of the Roman myth of foundation in DH I 84, 4 the wife of Faustulus is called *Laurentia* instead of *Larentia*.

[2] A. Alföldi, Die trojanischen Urahnen der Römer, 14 sqq. with details. For an introduction to the problems in question cf. B. G. Niebuhr, RG 1², Berlin 1827, 191 sqq. R. H. Klausen, Aeneas und die Penaten : Die italischen Volksreligionen unter dem Einfluss der griechischen 2, Hamburg-Gotha 1840, 566 sqq. Fr. Cauer, De fabulis Graecis ad Romam conditam pertinentibus, Diss. Berlin 1882. E. Pais, Storia della Sicilia e della Magna Graecia 1, Torino 1894, 451 sqq., 470. Fr. Kampf, Die Quellen der römischen Gründungssage, Diss. Leipzig 1913. W. Schur, Klio 17, 1921, 139, 141. L. Malten, Archiv f. Religionswissenschaft 29, 1931, 48 sqq. E. Wikén, Die Kunde der Hellenen von dem Lande und den Völkern der Appenninenhalbinsel bis 300 v. Chr., Diss. Lund 1937. E. D. Phillips, JHS 73, 1953, 53 sqq. F. Altheim, A History of Roman Religion, London 1938, 297 sqq. J. Bérard, R. Et. Gr. 57, 1944, 71 sqq. J. Perret, Les origines de la légende troyenne à Rome, Paris 1942. A. Enking, RE 9 A, 1189 sqq. Rhys Carpenter, Folk Tale, Fiction and Saga in

Trojan Legend and Etruscan Domination

About 500 B.C.[1] in Stesichoros the Etruscans are already Trojans, which mirrors a much older concept. In Timaeus the Trojan hero Aeneas arrived at Etruria by land, coming from Thrace and proceeding across Pisa and Agylla-Caere to Latium and Campania.[2] In Etruria, he meets Nanos-Nanas, the founder-hero of Cortona, identified with Odysseus. Tarchon and Tyrsenos, the sons of the Mysian hero Telephus—some of the Etruscans traced their origin in Asia Minor to Mysia and not to Troy—join the alliance of the former two. Vergil combined this Etruscan tradition with the landing of Aeneas in Lavinium:[3] Aeneas makes a trip to Caere to secure the help of Tarchon and obtains new armor made by Vulcanus from his divine mother in a grove nearby.

Another expression of this Etrusco-Trojan origin of the Latins is the version to be found in Alcimus, a Sicilian contemporary of Dionysius II,[4] in which the ancestors of the Romans were Aeneas and Tyrrhenia,[5] their family tree being traced to the kings of Alba and not to Lavinium. The same idea, based on a secondary connection of the Trojans with the Etruscans, returns in a anonymous version,[6] in which Telephus' daughter, ancestress of the Etruscans, is the wife of Aeneas. The Etruscan roots of this tradition become manifest in the Etruscan Capua, where coins from the end of the third century

the Homeric Epics (Sather Lectures 20) 1946, 63 sqq. F. Bömer, Rom und Troja, Baden-Baden 1951, 23 sqq. M. Guarducci, Bull. Mus. Civ. Rom. 19, 1959, 10 sqq. M. Pallottino, St. Etr. 26, 1958, 336 sqq. S. Mazzarino, Stud. Rom. 8, 1960, 387. K. Schauenburg, Gymnasium 67, 1960, 176 sqq. S. Ferri, Hommages à L. Herrmann (Coll. Latomus 44) 1960, 352. *Idem*, Studi in onore di L. Castiglioni, Firenze 1960, 293 sqq. J. Gagé, Mél. 1961, 69 sqq. A. Momigliano, Riv. stor. Ital. 70, 1958, 129 sqq., and the studies quoted in the following notes. G. Pugliese Carratelli, La parola del passato fasc. 82, 1962, 22.

[1] W. Christ, Griechische Nachrichten über Italien (SBBayr. Ak. 1905, I) 106 sq. W. Hoffmann, Rom und die griechische Welt im IV. Jh. v. Chr. (Philol., Suppl. 27, 1) 1934, 111. *Contra*: J. Perret, *op. cit.* 111, 307.

[2] Lycophr. 1238 sqq. J. Geffcken, Timaios' Geographie des Westens (Philol. Unters. 13) 1892, 39 sqq. C. von Holzinger, Lykophrons Alexandra, Leipzig 1895, 339. L. Malten, *op. cit.* 48 sqq. J. Perret, *op. cit.* 408 sq. F. Jacoby, F. Gr. Hist. 3 B Komm. 566 sq. (ad 566 F 62).

[3] Verg., *Aen.* 8, 475 sqq. Cf. J. Gagé, Mél. 1961, 76 sqq. R. Enking, RM 66, 1959, 65 sqq. E. D. Phillips, *op. cit.* 61.

[4] F. Jacoby, F. Gr. Hist. 3 B, Komm. 1955, 517 sq.

[5] F. Gr. Hist. 560 F 4 (= Fest., p. 326, 35 L.). Cf. *ibid.*, Komm. 520 sqq.

[6] Plut., *Rom.* 2, 1. Cf. DH I 28, 1. F. Schachermeyr, Wiener Studien 47, 1929, 154 sqq. A Rosenberg, RE 1 A, 1082. J. Bayet, Mél. 38, 1920, 75 sqq.

B.C. (pl. XVIII, 2) [1] illustrate the myth of Telephus as the ancestor of the Trojan Capys, the founder of this city.

There are additional traces of the Etruscan roots of the Latin legends of origin. A mythical king of Alba Longa is called *Tarchetios* in a fragment of Promathion[2] (an Etruscan name which corresponds to *Tarquitius* in Latin, a variety of *Tarquinius*); this king consults the oracle of Thetis in Etruria. The royal shepherd in the myth of Silvia, corresponding to the Faustulus of the Roman version of the same saga, has the name of *Tyrrhus*,[3] identical with *Tyrrhenus*. Nor is it without significance that the mother of Aeneas was venerated in Lavinium as *Frutis*,[4] i.e., Aphrodite in the Etruscan tongue.

These literary traces are complemented by a considerable amount of archaeological data. First, the Etruscan origin of the "Trojan game," an exhibition of horsemanship by the noble youths in Rome, is attested by the famous earthenware jug of Tragliatella from the outskirts of Caere, which dates back to the end of the seventh century B.C. (pl. XIX-XXII).[5] The drawings which decorate this jug, though scratched in an awkward manner on the surface, derive from well-known iconographical schemes—mostly defying a reliable explanation. The naked man of imposing stature, taming a wild goat (pl. XIX, 1), may be Heracles, as also may be the other naked giant with a long cudgel, who marches behind the warriors of a boar-clan (pl. XIX, 3). Another male figure with a loincloth also seems to occur twice: first as arriving by boat, being greeted by a woman or, in reverse, embarking and taking the woman with him, like Theseus and Ariadne[6] (pl. XIX, 1); and again named *amnu arce*, with a little girl *velelia*, and receiving a round object from a woman called *thes athei*.[7] There is no clue as to the identity of the woman standing beside two empty chairs (pl. XIX, 2), and we mention the very Etruscan erotic *sympleg-*

---

[1] A. Sambon, Les monnaies antiques de l'Italie 1, Paris 1903, 403 no. 1046 ; cf. no. 1049.
[2] Plut., *Rom.* 2, 4 sqq. The age of this author is uncertain ; cf. S. Mazzarino, Stud. Rom. 8, 1960, 387.
[3] Cato, *Orig.* fr. 11 Peter. DH I 70, 2.
[4] R. Schilling, La religion de Vénus, 75 sqq.
[5] G. Q. Giglioli, St. Etr. 3, 1929, 111 sqq. *Id.*, Bull. Mus. Imp. Rom. 12, 1941, 4 sqq.
[6] Cf. M. Cagiano de Azevedo, Saggio sul labirinto, Milano 1958, pl. 1.
[7] E. Fiesel, in : Roscher's Lex. 6, 177 sqq. M. Buffa, Nuova raccolta di iscrizioni etrusche, Firenze 1935, no. 892. M. Pallottino, *Testimonia linguae Etruscae*, Firenze 1954, no. 74 ; cf. 104, 150, 169, 170, 329, 768, etc.

mata only for the sake of completeness. In addition to these subjects there is one scene of great interest for our present concern (pl. XX, 1 and XXII).

Two young horsemen with round shields, one of them also carrying a spear, perform the *lusus Troiae*, the "Trojan game": beside them there is a labyrinth-pattern with the Etruscan word *truia* inscribed in it. Scholars of the nineteenth century already realized that this word in Etruscan can mean only "Trojan," [1] in the same way that a Trojan prisoner-of-war on the wall painting of the "tomba François" in Vulci is called *Truials*. Later an excellent archaeologist tried to refute this fact by interpreting *truia* as belonging to an old Indo-European expression for "keep moving," *truare*. The verb *amb(p)-truare*, "hop around," was the *terminus technicus* for the dance of the Salii. It indeed reaches back to the archaic epoch; and the consonance of the Latin *trua-re* with *truia*, the designation of Troy in the Etruscan tongue, could eventually have been the basis of the Trojan interpretation of this game in Latium. But even this is unlikely: *truare* seems to be an Etruscan loan-word in the Latin language.[2] Quite apart from this inconsistency, it is a methodical impossibility to explain an Etruscan word on an Etruscan jug by a Latin verbal root in Latin usage. The establishment of the cavalry in the Roman army was accomplished by Etruscan kings, thereby introducing an Etruscan institution: [3] the Etruscan origin of the "Trojan game" fits very well into this pattern.

The "Trojan game" in Rome in the Augustan age still reflects its original connection with the organization of the most ancient cavalry; the display exhibited the highly skilled horsemanship and military preparedness of the noble youths. But at the same time the *lusus Troiae* was the performance of a magic ritual.[4] This last aspect is proved by the representation of the labyrinth, a complicated pattern for group dances, as well as the two young horsemen on the oinochoë

---

[1] Cf. W. Helbig, Bull. dell' Instituto 1881, 65 sqq. *Idem*, Annali dell' Instituto 1881, 160 sqq. *Idem*, Abh. Bayr. Ak. XXIII 2, 1905, 300 sqq. O. Benndorf, in: Reichel, Über homerische Waffen, Wien 1894, 133 sqq., etc. *Contra*: G. Q. Giglioli, St. Etr. 8, 1929, 124 sqq. J. L. Heller, Class. Journ. 42, 1946-47, 123 sqq., 137.

[2] J. Heurgon, La vie quotid., 249.

[3] Cf. my study, Der frührömische Reiteradel, Baden-Baden 1952.

[4] A. v. Premerstein, Festschrift für O. Benndorf, Wien 1898, 261 sqq.

ALBA LONGA AND LAVINIUM

of Tragliatella.[1] Everyone agrees with G. Q. Giglioli [2] that the juxtaposition of the labyrinth-pattern with the two young horsemen is no mere chance. The dancing floor called *truia* in this case and the display of the youngsters on horseback are coupled in the same sense —we are not the first to notice this—as in Vergil:[3]

> *ut quondam Creta fertur labyrinthus in alta*
> *parietibus textum caecis iter ancipitemque*
> *mille viis habuisse dolum, qua signa sequendi*
> *falleret indeprensus et inremeabilis error:*
> *haud alio Teucrum nati vestigia cursu*
> *inpediunt texuntque fugas et proelia ludo.*

The drawings of the oinochoë and these verses written six hundred years later reflect the same legendary account based on a belief in the Trojan descent of the Etruscans.

There is a small iconographical detail in the *lusus Troiae* of the Tragliatella jug which deserves our attention. Behind the first horseman (pl. XX, 1 and XXII) a crouching animal is seated, apparently touching the shoulder of the boy with its left foreleg; no doubt it is a monkey, a favorite motif in Etruscan art [4] occurring from the archaic phase onward (pl. XX 7). We are concerned this time only with instances in which the pet animal is squatting behind a mounted man. On a wall painting in Veii [5] (pl. XX, 2) the pet is rendered by the artist as a leopard but was rather meant to be a monkey, as were also the clumsy animals behind mounted men on a series of bronze fibulae. We reproduce such pins from the Bocchoris grave in Tarquinia (pl. XX, 4), one from Marzabotto (pl. XX, 3), and one from Bologna (pl. XX, 5).[6] A more elaborate specimen from Este (pl. XX, 6) [7] has three young riders with round shields like the

[1] The whole range of the abounding special studies on the labyrinth and on the Trojan game is surveyed in the following works : H. Jeanmaire, Couroï et Courètes, Lille 1939. C. Sachs, Weltgeschichte des Tanzes, Berlin 1933, 107 sqq. K. Kerényi, Labyrinth-Studien[2], Zürich 1950. A. Brelich, Gli eroi greci, Roma 1958, 170. A. B. Cook, Zeus 1, Cambridge 1914, 467 sqq. E. Mehl, RE Suppl. 8, 888 sq., 904 sq. H. v. Petrikovits, Festschr. f. R. Egger, Klagenfurt 1952, 126 sqq. M. Cagiano de Azevedo, Saggio sul labirinto, Milano 1958.

[2] G. Q. Giglioli, *loc. cit.*

[3] Verg., *Aen.* 5, 588 sqq.

[4] Cf. J. Heurgon, La vie quotid. 147 sqq. M. Pallottino, *Testimonia linguae Etruscae* no. 811.

[5] G. Dennis, The Cities and Cemeteries of Etruria 1[3], London 1883, 34.

[6] Joh. Sundwall, Die älteren italischen Fibeln, Berlin 1943, 256.

[7] Piccola guida della preistoria italiana, Firenze 1962, pl. 43, 12.

two on the Tragliatella jug, with a monkey seated behind each of them. The Atestine civilization, at the gateway of Italy and strongly influenced by the Etruscan culture, transmitted Etruscan influences toward the north, among which could have been the Etruscan version of the Trojan legend, flourishing later in the Teutonic world.[1] The little monkeys behind the rider seem at least to indicate this: the horsemen of the *lusus* did not migrate as simple ornaments, but presumably along with their spiritual background.

The extraordinary popularity of Aeneas in Etruria becomes evident in a recent survey by K. Schauenburg [2] of the representations of Aeneas on vase paintings. He collected 57 examples of the scene of the flight of the hero with his family on Attic vases. Most of these (52 specimens) date from the last quarter of the sixth century B.C., and only five items from the first decades of the fifth century. Ten of them were found in Vulci, three in Caere, one in Tarquinia, three from Etruscan Nola, and one from South Italy. Five came from Sicily, where the Elymes were aware of their immigration from Asia Minor.[3] Many of these vases, which have no exact provenience, are known to have been found in Etruria, as well as other Attic vases with Aeneas represented fighting with the Greeks, not yet fleeing. As Schauenburg pointed out,[4] the theme of the flight of Aeneas was chosen by the Attic potters and painters for exportation to Etruscan customers. We must add that if the huge quantity of Attic imports to the new Etruscan cities of the Po Valley contained so few examples of the migration of the hero to the West, this must be because the Etruscans of Spina, Melpum, etc., were not as much attracted by it as was Southern Etruria, the cities of which had previously bought so many of the vase paintings depicting the arrival of Aeneas. It has escaped notice that one of the few red-figure representations of this subject found in Italy, the splendid Iliupersis of the "Altamura" painter in Boston (pl. XXIII),[5] represents Antenor, the founder of the Etruscan cities in the Po Valley, as marching ahead of Aeneas.

---

[1] O. Höfler, Siegfried, Arminius und die Symbolik, Heidelberg 1961, 11 sq. On Mycenean contacts with the Teutonic tribes cf. E. Sprockhoff, Germania 39, 1961, 11 sqq.

[2] K. Schauenburg, Gymnasium 67, 1960, 177 sqq.

[3] Cf. Die trojanischen Urahnen der Römer, 28.

[4] K. Schauenburg, *op. cit.* 186 sqq.

[5] I am grateful to C. C. Vermeule for his kind permission to reproduce it. Cf. his publication in the *Ill. London News*, Oct. 10, 1959, 398.

284

His presence on late black-figure paintings, such as on a vase in Hamburg where he accompanies Aeneas in Phrygian attire (pl. XXIV),[1] hints at Attic imports in the new Padane Etruria.

The extraordinary popularity of Aeneas in Etruria, as revealed in the survey by K. Schauenburg, reflects of the immense respect with which a founder-hero was regarded. At this juncture I must clear up a misunderstanding. A scholar of the highest merit thought that I try to make of Aeneas the ancestor of the *whole* Etruscan people.[2] What I really mean is, however, that Aeneas was celebrated in some cities of Southern Etruria as their founder-hero: precisely in the cities which were in turn the overlords of Rome.

The migration of Aeneas to the west was certainly not only "one of the numerous epic motifs" borrowed by the Etruscans from the Greeks.[3] This can be demonstrated by the role of the holy Trojan relics, the *sacra Troiana*, on Etruscan representations of the pilgrimage of Aeneas. As I have stressed before, the Greeks had no interest in the resurrection of Troy; for them Aeneas was simply a legendary antagonist of their ancestors. Therefore, they never illustrated the salvation of the sacred objects in question, which were meaningless for them.[4] More profound was the significance of those relics for new "Trojan" foundations where they were regarded as warrants of the welfare and might of the community, as *pignora imperii*.

Such a representation of the sacred relics of Troy was found by the present writer on a local vase painting from Vulci, dating from the first half of the fifth century B.C.[5] The rigid and uncanny composition (pl. XXV) bears no relation to the brilliant Greek achievements of the same years; but the artist succeeded, nevertheless, in expressing the awe and solemnity of this procession. Aeneas, to ease the burden he carries on his shoulder, leans on his spear, as on the scarab (pl. XIV, 1), discussed below. The object which his wife carries

[1] B. Segall, who sent me the picture and allowed me to reproduce it, must be gratefully remembered.

[2] M. Pallottino, St. Etr. 26, 1958, 338. Cf. Die trojanischen Urahnen der Römer 18.   [3] St. Etr. 26, 1958, 337.

[4] C. Praschniker, Parthenonstudien, Wien 1928, 107 sqq. (Cf. F. Studniczka, Neue Jahrbücher 5, 1929, 645) assumed their presence in his reconstruction (108 fig. 78) of a metope of the Parthenon ; but the actual remains (21 fig. 13) clearly show that there is no space left for such objects on the relief in question. The following metope (*ibid.* 109, fig. 79) exhibits the flight of Aeneas with his father, wife, and son, but without the Trojan *sacra*.

[5] For details cf. Die trojanischen Urahnen der Römer, 16 sqq.

on her head is an indigenous feature. It has been described before as a pillow but it has no folds or wrinkles; it is not bent as a pillow would be, but has a straight, even surface, ending in the shape of a bottle-neck held by Creusa-Eurydice. No doubt it is a little terra-cotta barrel.[1]

We are acquainted by a lucky chance with the fact that such a container of the sacred objects of Troy was known to the ancients. The information comes from Timaeus,[2] transmitted to us by Dionysius: "Concerning their shape and appearance, Timaeus the historian makes the statement that the holy objects preserved in the sanctuary at Lavinium are iron and bronze heralds' wands (κηρυκία σιδηρᾶ καὶ χαλκᾶ)[3] and a Trojan earthenware vessel (κέραμος Τρωϊκός); this, he says, he himself learned from the inhabitants."

We also know that this "Trojan earthenware" appeared in the Roman popular legend.[4] The sacred objects brought by Aeneas from Troy were preserved by the Vestal Virgins in Rome—so runs the oldest version of the tale—in a little earthenware barrel (*doliolum*). After the Gauls defeated the Roman army at the Allia but before they entered the city the Vestals hid this *doliolum* in the earth, with a second one which was empty and served only as a camouflage for the other.[5] The spot on the Forum Romanum underneath which

---

[1] Even if it were a textile, it could only be the wrapping for the sacred objects (cf. Lycophr. 1266 πατρῷα ἀγάλματα πέπλοις περισχών; more in the article by S. Weinstock, RE 19, 435). My interpretation is accepted by K. Schauenburg, *op. cit.* 191, and others.

[2] F. Gr. Hist. 566 F 59 (= DH I 67, 4).

[3] S. Weinstock, RE 19, 438, interprets these *caducei* as an "Abbild des Szepters (bzw. der Lanze), das in der Hand des Herrschers Symbol der Macht ist." But such an absurd contamination of insignia and divine symbols did not exist. The *caducei* belonged in the religious symbolism exclusively to Mercury. Miniature *caducei* occur on the votive terra-cotta discs in Tarentum (P. Wuilleumier, Rev. arch. 5, sér. 35, 1932, 26 sqq. K. Kerényi, Archiv f. Religionswiss. 30, 1933, 271 sqq. S. Weinstock, JRS 50, 1960, pl. 13, 3), but also on coins of Populonia (A. Sambon, *op. cit.* no. 52, 115, and 118) where two of them are coupled with the head of Mercury. This god is, indeed, intimately connected with the arrival of Aeneas in Italy in the legend: he accompanies Aeneas on the *tabula Iliaca*; he builds a ship for Aeneas in the *bellum Punicum* of Naevius (Serv., Dan., *Aen.* 1, 170); cf. K. Büchner, Humanitas Romana, Heidelberg 1957, 13 sqq., 26 sqq. Further on, the coupling of his head on the heavy asses (pl. III, 7) with the double head of the Penates seems to me a hint on the Lavinian legend of Aeneas. Of course, these herald's wands (seemingly offerings of Aeneas for his safe arrival in the promised homeland) were not objects brought from Troy: it is not clear how they were confused with them.

[4] Details are to be found in: A. Schwegler, RG 3, 1858, 250 n. 2. S. Weinstock, RE 19, 439 and in my study quoted above, 16.

[5] S. Weinstock, JRS 50, 1960, 113 sq., compares the *doliolum* containing the

these objects were once sheltered was called *doliola* and the people refrained from spitting there so as not to desecrate the earth which harbored the numinous relics.[1] We have, consequently, three successive chronological layers of this peculiar tradition: one from Vulci, where Aeneas as an ancestor was already venerated in the sixth century B.C., as his popularity, evident by the imported Attic vase paintings attests; one in Lavinium, which certainly does not have a priority over Vulci; and the Roman one, in all likelihood imitating Lavinium.

The *sacra* of Troy are brought by Anchises in a basket (*cista*) on the Etruscan scarab of the collection of the Duc de Luynes (pl. XIV, 1)[2] an outstanding achievement of the archaic period of Etruscan art. Anchises exhibits the basket in his raised right hand, as a priest would do in a sacred procession. This was meant to represent not the rescue of the *sacra* but the arrival of the founder-hero with his family. M. Pallottino[3] wishes to lower the date I had in mind (late sixth century B.C.) by some decades. If his date should be correct, it

Trojan relics and its empty companion-vessel with the two *amphorae* on Spartan coins. But these latter are sacred vessels of the Dioscuri, sometimes marked by the star of the divine youths above each of them (Cf. J. Babelon, Catalogue de la coll. du Duc de Luynes 1, Paris 1924, pl. 12 no. 243 ; cf. also M. Albert, Dict. d. ant. 2, 255) : both containers are of full religious and symbolic value, unlike the *doliola* of which only one counts. The *ollae* of the *Mater Larum* with food (ILS 9522, 22) are not comparable either with our *doliolum* (S. Weinstock, *op. cit.* 114 n. 33).

[1] Plut., *Camill.* 20, 3 sqq. : ἐν πρώτοις δὲ τῶν ἱερῶν ἃ μὲν εἰς τὸ Καπιτώλιον ἀνεσκευάσαντο, τὰ δὲ τῆς Ἑστίας αἱ παρθένοι μετὰ τῶν ἱερέων ἔφευγον ἁρπασάμεναι ... καὶ πλεῖστος μὲν λόγος κατέχει τὸ Τρωικὸν ἐκεῖ Παλλάδιον ἀποκεῖσθαι δι' Αἰνείου κομισθὲν εἰς Ἰταλίαν ... οἱ δὲ ... δύο φασὶν οὐ μεγάλους ἀποκεῖσθαι πίθους, τὸν μὲν ἀνεωγότα καὶ κενόν, τὸν δὲ πλήρη καὶ κατασεσημασμένον, ἀμφοτέρους δὲ ταῖς παναγέσι μόναις παρθένοις ὁρατούς. ἄλλοι δὲ τούτους διεψεῦσθαι νομίζουσι τῷ τὰ πλεῖστα τῶν ἱερῶν τότε τὰς κόρας ἐμβαλούσας εἰς πίθους δύο κρύψαι κατὰ γῆς ὑπὸ τὸν νεὼν τοῦ Κυρίνου, καὶ τὸν τόπον ἐκεῖνον ἔτι καὶ νῦν τῶν Πιθίσκων φέρεσθαι τὴν ἐπωνυμίαν. Paul. Fest. p. 60, 26 L. : *Doliola locus in urbe sic vocatus, quia invadentibus Gallis Senonibus Urbem sacra in eodem loco doliolis reposita fuerunt. Qua de causa in eodem loco ne despuere alicui licebat.* Liv. V 40, 7-8 : *flamen interim Quirinalis virginesque Vestales omissa rerum suarum cura, quae sacrorum secum ferenda, quae quia vires ad omnia ferenda deerant, relinquenda essent, consultantes, quisve ea locus fideli adservaturus custodia esset, optimum ducunt condita in doliolis sacello proximo aedibus flaminis Quirinalis, ubi nunc despui religio est, defodere ; cetera inter se onere partito ferunt via quae sublicio ponte ducit ad Ianiculum.* Val. Max. I 1, 10. Flor. I 7, 11-12. Varro, *LL* 5, 157 : *locus qui vocatur doliola ad cluacam maxumam, ubi non licet despuere, a doliolis sub terra. eorum duae traditae historiae, quod alii inesse aiunt ossa cadaverum, alii Numae Pompilii religiosa quaedam post mortem eius infossa.*

[2] Details in : Die trojanischen Urahnen der Römer 16.

[3] M. Pallottino, *op. cit.* 337.

would not mean that the role of Aeneas as an Etruscan city-founder started just at that time: even the great mass of Attic black-figure vase paintings imported to Etruria in the last quarter of the sixth century do not mark the beginning of his role but only reflects its importance.[1]

Veii is another Etruscan city where Aeneas was honored with cult. I must maintain with the late H. Fuhrman, S. Ferri, K. Schauen-burg, and other scholars that the splendid great figure of a mother holding her child on her shoulder and moving forward with vigorous steps is Creusa-Eurydice.[2] All the more so as we now know part, at least, of another statue of the same time, size, and environment representing Aeneas carrying Anchises on his shoulder. This is a fragment in a private collection, published by H. and I. Jucker, which K. Schauenburg has already called to the attention of scholars.[3] The Creusa of Veii certainly followed Aeneas with his father, i.e., a statue of the same sort as the fragment just mentioned was the companion piece to the figure of Creusa. It is true that these statues were not cult-images but, as M. Pallottino clearly demonstrated, they were erected on the *columen* of the roof of a sanctuary as a decoration. Yet, we also have representations of Aeneas from Veii, which were doubtlessly cult-offerings. These are the terra-cotta statuettes of Aeneas carrying Anchises.[4] Numerous specimens were found in different sanctuaries of Veii as votive gifts. Their dating is still debated; but no one can reasonably doubt that they were offered to the different Veientan divinities before the capture of this city. They bear witness to the role of Aeneas as founder—whether they are nearer in time to 500 B.C. or to 400 B.C.[5] Aeneas had a cult in Lavinium and also in Sicily among the Elymians. What we have just explained proves that he also had a cult in the Etruscan cities—certainly before he had in Latium.

---

[1] For details : Die trojanischen Urahnen, 17 sqq. *Contra* : M. Pallottino, *op. cit.* 337. I can now add the reference to the study by D. Rebuffat-Emmanuel, Latomus 20, 1961, 469 sqq.

[2] The splendid publication of M. Pallottino, Arch. cl. 2, 1950, 122 sqq. with pl. 30 sqq., offers a solid basis for all future observations on style and execution.

[3] H. und I. Jucker, Kunst und Leben der Etrusker (Ausstellungskatalog) Köln 1956, 139, no. 359. K. Schauenburg, Gymnasium 67, 1960, 177.

[4] Cf. Die trojanischen Urahnen . . . 17. An importation of the mold of these figurines from a Faliscan or Latin site is considered by M. Pallottino, *op. cit.* 338 ; this appears to me to be impossible.

[5] J. Gagé, Mél. 1961, 71 sqq. K. Schauenburg, *loc. cit.*

Chapter VII

TOPOGRAPHICAL AND ARCHAEOLOGICAL
REALITIES VERSUS LITERARY INVENTION

The emergence of the autonomous Roman power in Latium after
the end of the Etruscan domination can be well documented, not
only by the literary tradition which from 500 B.C. on contains a
solid kernel of historical truth, but also by the reexamination of the
geographical data at our disposal, with which we start this chapter
of our investigations.

THE ETRUSCANS AT THE MOUTH OF THE TIBER

Veii's alleged humiliation by Rome's founder and the tale of its conquests by the fourth king furnish a valuable clue for the history of
the maritime tract nearest to Rome. We learn from these stories that
the saltworks to the north of the mouth of the Tiber and the forest
called *Maesia* [1] adjacent to it, further on the so-called *Septem pagi*

---

[1] Liv. I 33, 9 (under King Ancus) *silva Mesia Veientibus adempta usque ad mare
imperium prolatum*. Schwegler 1, 601 n. 5, has connected this passage with

288

The Etruscans at the Mouth of the Tiber

on and around the Vatican territory,[1] were originally in the possession of the Veientans. They lost these *salinae*—I am sure—in the fifth century B.C. and not before. In order to prove this, we must go into details.

After his victory, Romulus imposes penalties on the Veientans, as is stated in our sources.[2] They have to deliver up to him the *Septem pagi*—Livy calls them expressly part of their territory (*agri* [*Veientis*] *pars*)— and the saltworks: this seems to mean the right bank of the Tiber opposite Rome down to the sea. The Veientans are said to have tried to reconquer those possessions under King Ancus.[3] Afterwards we hear again that Porsenna forced the Romans to give back the *Septem pagi* to Veii, but this noble king of Clusium is said to have donated this district to the Romans again when they became his allies.[4] All these assertions are arbitrary inventions; they betray a well-known pattern of the Annals, repeating events of the early Republic as happening under the kings, so as to make the glory of Rome older than it was in reality. In truth, the Romans captured those possessions much later. As late as in 390 B.C., after the capture of Veii, other Etruscan cities were still trying to seize the salt-beds,[5] even if without success. In fact, in 356 another attempt was made by

statements by Cicero, *De re p.* II 18, 33 (Ancus) *silvas maritumas omnes publicavit quas ceperat*, and in the *Vir. ill.* 5, 2 : *silvas ad usum navium publicavit*. It seems to me that these assertions were written in the knowledge of works by Greek authors who stated that the Etruscans, and not the Romans, exploited the timber of Latium for the building of ships. Cf. Theophrast., *Hist. plant.* V 8, 3 : Ἡ δὲ τῶν Λατίνων ἔφυδρος πᾶσα. καὶ ἡ μὲν πεδεινὴ δάφνην ἔχει καὶ μυρρίνους καὶ ὀξύην θαυμαστήν. τηλικαῦτα γὰρ τὰ μήκη τέμνουσι ὥστ' εἶναι διανεκῶς τῶν Τυρρηνίδων ὑπὸ τὴν τρόπιν. The *silva Maesia* may eventually be the same as the Μαίκιον ὄρος mentioned in 389 B.C. in Plut., *Camill.* 33, 2 and 34, 2, corresponding to the *ad Mecium is locus dicitur* in Liv. VI 2, 8, *nec procul a Lanuvio*. The Lanuvian territory should have reached the Tiber, because Solonium also belonged to it; but a confusion with Lavinium is probable.

[1] One of the conditions under which Romulus is said to have conceded the peace to the Veientans was χώραν τε παραδοῦναι Ῥωμαίοις τὴν προσεχῆ τῷ Τεβέρει, τοὺς καλουμένους Ἑπτὰ πάγους in DH II 55, 5 ; χώραν τε πολλὴν . . .ἣν Σεπτεμπάγιον καλοῦσιν in Plutarch, *Rom.* 25, 5 sq. De Sanctis 2², 118 connected rightly these data with Paul. Fest. p. 331, 1 L. : *Romulia tribus dicta, quod ex eo agro censebantur, quem Romulus ceperat ex Veientibus.* We shall see below (p. 310 sqq.) that the *Romilia* tribe was situated in the Vatican area to *Magliana* in the south. This fact enables us to define more precisely the site of the "Seven districts."

[2] Liv. I 15, 5. DH II 55, 5-6. Cf. Liv. II 13, 4. Plut., *Rom.* 25, 5.

[3] DH III 41, 1-3. Another version is that Ancus started the exploitation of the *salinae* after the foundation of Ostia : Liv. I 33, 9. Plin., *N.h.* XXXI 7, 89.

[4] Liv. II 6, 3-4 ; 13, 4 ; 15, 6. DH V 31, 4 ; 32, 1-2 ; 36, 4 ; 65, 3.

[5] Liv. V 45, 8.

TOPOGRAPHICAL AND ARCHAEOLOGICAL REALITIES

Tarquinii and the Faliscans to snatch them away from the Romans.[1] Modern scholars realized, of course, that the exploitation of the salt beds at the mouth of the Tiber was initiated and monopolized by Veii, but they preferred to accept as a historical fact the occupation of this spot under the kings [2] as well as the capture of Ficana, situated on a height dominating the river halfway between Rome and the sea;[3] some experts are inclined to give credit to an early foundation of Ostia, attributed by the annalists—first, I think, by Pictor—to King Ancus Marcius.[4] But we know by now the fictitious picture in which this pretended capture of the mouth of the Tiber from the Veientans belongs. Its assumption became necessary for the author of this concept as a preliminary fact for the antedating of the first treaty with Carthage. The course of events, however, involved Rome—we shall see it shortly—only in the fourth century B.C. in the maritime

---

[1] Liv. VII 17, 6-9 : *concitatur deinde omne nomen Etruscum, et Tarquiniensibus Faliscisque ducibus ad salinas perveniunt. adversus eum terrorem dictator C. Marcius Rutilus primus de plebe dictus ... profectus ab urbe utraque parte Tiberis ratibus exercitu quocumque fama hostium ducebat, traiecto multos populatores agrorum vagos palantes oppressit ; castra quoque necopinato adgressus cepit et octo milibus hostium captis ceteris aut caesis aut ex agro Romano fugatis sine auctoritate patrum populi iussu triumphavit.* Diod. XVI 36, 4.

[2] H. Nissen, It. Lk. II 2, 490 sq. G. De Sanctis, St. d. R. 2, 1907, 125 sq. Th. Ashby, JRS 2, 1912, 153 sq. *Idem*, The Campagna in Classical Times, London, 1927, 29. K. J. Beloch, RG 146. J. Carcopino, Virgile et les origines d'Ostie, Paris, 1919, 18 sq. T. Frank, Cl. Phil. 14, 1919, 317 sq. R. Meiggs, Roman Ostia, Oxford 1960, 16 sq., 479 sq., etc.

[3] Liv. I 33, 2. DH III 38, 3-4. It is not impossible that Pictor mentioned the *Puilia saxa* in this context. Cf. Fest., p. 298, 6 L. : *Puilia saxa esse ad portum, qui sit secundum Tiberim, ait Fabius Pictor* ; *quem locum putat Labeo dici, ubi fuerit Ficana via Ostiensi ad lapidem undecimum.*

[4] Enn., *Ann.* 2, 22 v. 144 sq. Vahlen. Cic., *De re p.* II 3, 5 ; 18, 33. Liv. I 33, 9. DH III 44, 4. Strab. V 3, 5 (C. 232). Fest., p. 214, 20 sq ; 304, 18 L. Plin., *N.h.*, III 5, 56 (cf. XXXI 7, 89). Flor. I 4, 2. *Vir. ill.* 5, 3. Eutr. 1, 5. Serv., *Aen.* 6, 815. Isid. XV 1, 56. CIL XIV 4338. Additional evidence for the alleged foundation of Ostia by King Ancus, hitherto overlooked, is preserved by two reverse-types of the *asses* of C. Marcius Censorinus, the partisan of Marius, Sydenham, R. Rep. Coinage, 1952, nos. 715-16. These representations were misunderstood. One of them shows two arches ; under one of these passes a warship, whereas under the second one a column surmounted by the statue of Victory is standing. It is incomprehensible to me how this scene could be defined as an aqueduct. It is evidently the representation of a harbor ; and the head of Ancus Marcius (coupled with that of Numa, cf. Polyb. VI 11 a, 6) on the obverse proves that the harbor in question is Ostia. Since the column with Victory returns on the accompanying type along with two warships beside it, the identification of the scenery with the same harbor becomes once more manifest. The monument may refer to the victory of the Marian party at Ostia.

politics of the great sailing nations of the Mediterranean. Over and above this, the irrefutable evidence of the excavations [1] shows that the Annals are wrong. The archaeological investigations have definitely demonstrated that the beginnings of Ostia were about the middle of the fourth century B.C.[2] This belated inception is due to the fact that the site of Ostia "did not offer a safe or convenient natural harbour: it was only under the Empire that by elaborate works the Romans partially remedied for the time being the defects of the natural situation." [3]

The Romans of historical times were well aware of the fact that the right bank of the Tiber down to the sea once belonged to the Etruscans. As evidence for this are the explicit statements of the writers,[4] and even more revealing are official inscriptions of the years 73, 74, and 198 A.D., which designate the riverbank opposite

[1] K. J. Beloch, RG 158, believes in the early foundation, as does R. Meiggs, *l.c.*, who suspects that Ostia of the kings must be sought on a neighboring site and tries to discard the testimony of the archaeological evidence. But this place-name is bound to the site of the later Ostia ; there is no reason whatsoever to suppose such a transfer, except a desperate attempt to save the allegations of a forged tale. On the other hand, the Veientans must have had a smaller settlement somewhere nearby for the safeguard and control of the saltworks.

[2] G. De Sanctis, St. d. R. 1, 1907, 370 and 2, 1907, 126. T. Frank, Cl. Philol. 14, 1919, 316, 317. J. Carcopino, *l.c.* E. Pais, St. crit. 1, 1918, 470 and *idem*, Mem. Lincei, ser. 5, 17, 1924, 314 sq. G. Calza, RE 18, 1655, 61 and 1657, 29 sq. (the statement 1656, 63 sq., is due to an erroneous translation). L. Pareti, Atene e Roma, n.s. 12, 1931, 213 sq. G. Becatti, JRS 51, 1961, 199 sq. Cf. below p. 317. sq.

[3] L. A. Holland, TAPA 80, 1949, 302. Cf. also Strab. V 3, 5 (p. 231 C.). Plut., *Caes.* 58, 10. Iustin. XLIII 3, 4 is not historical. Mrs. Holland rightly points out (*ibid*. 316 sq.) that "there seems no evidence for an early road to Ostia. There would indeed be little use for it before the fourth century B.C., when Rome's military outpost at the Tiber mouth had to be kept in close touch with the city" ; and further that "the maritime trade at Rome was even in the fourth century B.C. negligible" (*ibid*. 301).

[4] Liv. I 3, 5 : *pax ita convenerat, ut Etruscis Latinisque fluvius Albula, quem nunc Tiberim vocant, finis esset*. Isid. XIV 4, 22. Hor., *Carm*. I 2, 13 sq., calls the quais opposite the city *litus Etruscum* ; cf. Chr. Hülsen, RM 4, 1889, 287 n. 2 and H. Nissen, It. Lk. II 2, 490 sq. L. A. Holland, Ianus and the Bridge, Roma 1961, 141 sqq. Fest., p. 232, 23 L. : *Pectuscum Palati dicta est ea regio urbis quam Romulus obversam posuit ea parte, in qua plurimum erat agri Romani ad mare versus . . , cum Etruscorum agrum a Romano Tiberis discluderet*. Vell. I 8, 5, thinks of the dangers menacing Romulus *tam vicinis Veientibus*. Cf. also Liv. III 13, 8-10. DH III 45, 1. X 8, 4. Iuven. 8, 264. Serv., *Aen*. 11, 598. Stat., *Silv*. IV 4, 4. The notion in Livy III 25, 8 and Plin., *N.h*. XVIII 3, 20, that Cincinnatus possessed a small estate in the Vatican territory in 458 B.C. is a fiction spun out of the name of the *Quinctia prata* ; cf. G. De Sanctis, St. d. R. 2², 111.

TOPOGRAPHICAL AND ARCHAEOLOGICAL REALITIES

the city as the *ripa Veiens*.[1] Before the removal of the Veientans from
the mouth of the Tiber, Rome would have had to remove them from
their position on the *collis Vaticanus* and the Janiculum,[2] their all-
important bridgehead toward the north.[3] Beloch thought [4] that the
frontier between Veii and Rome in the fifth century B.C. reached the
coast somewhere between Portus and Fregenae, thus including the
surroundings of the former site. But the military situation of the
Fabian armed forces, wiped out at the Cremera, as described by Livy
(II 49, 8-9)—on which description this assertion is based—does not
involve any stable Roman arrangements in this environment; the
crushing defeat of the Romans rather implies the assumption that
after the battle the Veientans continued to hold the right bank.[5]

For a full understanding of this situation we have to realize that a
lasting peaceful coexistence between the two rival cities on the Tiber
was simply impossible without the subordination of one of them to
the other. The natural lines of communication connecting Veii
with the sea and her salt beds were crossing the territory facing Rome
on the right bank. It was vital for Veii to hold in her hands this whole
area. The outstanding importance of the salt trade in the epoch with
which we are concerned is well known, as is the fact that the Etruscans
were extracting this invaluable merchandise from the sea only. We also
must be aware that the technical facilities available in that age allowed
the installation of salt works only in a few places along the long shore-

---

[1] CIL VI 31547 (ILS 5928). 31548 a-c. 31555 (ILS 5943). Cf. Chr. Hülsen, RM
4, 1889, 287 n. 1. J. Le Gall, Le Tibre, Paris 1953, 157 sq. 163. 165.
[2] Plin., *N.h.* III 5, 53, says that the Tiber separates *Latinum (sc. agrum) a
Vaticano*. Paul. Fest., p. 519, 24 sq. L.: *Vaticanus collis appellatus est, quod eo
potitus sit populus Romanus vatum responso, expulsis Etruscis*. Cf. Gell. XVI 17, 1.
Plin., *N.h.* XVI 44, 237 : *Vetustior autem urbe in Vaticano ilex, in qua titulus aereis
litteris Etruscis religione arborem iam tum dignam fuisse significat*. Paul. Fest. p. 93,
1. L.: *Ianiculum dictum, quod per eum Romanus populus primitus transierit in agrum
Etruscum*.
[3] Paul. Fest., p. 331, 1 L. : *Romulia tribus dicta quod ex eo agro censebantur, quem
Romulus ceperat ex Veientibus*. J. Beloch has proved that this *tribus* comprised
the *ager Vaticanus* (J. Beloch, Der italische Bund, 29). Cf. L. R. Taylor, Vot.
Distr. (Mem. Am. Ac. Rome 20), 1960, 38, 41, 70, and below, p. 302 n. 3 on
the *ager Solonius*.
[4] K. J. Beloch, RG 173.
[5] Liv. II 51, 2 (476 B.C.) : *tum quoque male pugnatum est et Ianiculum hostes
occupavere obsessaque urbs foret . . . . .—transierant enim Etrusci Tiberim—ni Horatius
consul ex Volscis esset revocatus, adeoque id bellum ipsis institit moenibus, ut primo
pugnatum ad Spei sit aequo Marte, iterum ad portam Collinam. ibi quamquam parvo
momento superior Romana res fuit, etc.*, DH IX 25 sq.

lines of the peninsula. Best known among these were the shallow pools near the mouth of the Tiber, in which the sea water evaporated and left behind its content of salt.[1]

As we saw, the Roman Annals do not deny that these salt beds were originally operated by the Veientans, yet they pretend that their site was captured from them as early as by Romulus,[2] or by Ancus Marcius.[3] The Veientan salt pans were evidently on the Etruscan bank of the Tiber: in fact, only those were exploited originally, and alone remained important for the Tiber trade.[4] The salt marshes of the right bank were—as Mrs. Holland has observed [5]—preferable to those on the left not only for the nearby favorable landing place on the river, but by the accident that the easiest land route along the Tiber valley happened also to be on the right bank. On the other hand, the *via Salaria*, carrying the salt to the Sabines [6] also crossed the river at the Tiber-isle for the right bank,[7] continuing in the *via Campana*, leading—as revealed by its name—to the *campus calinarum*, the salt beds. Consequently, the Veientan saltworks and not the Roman ones were producing the salt which went to the Sabines across the city of Rome: the Veientan factory could have helped the Romans to enrich themselves by this transit-traffic, but their sovereignty over the region of Ostia does not follow from this prosperous commercial circulation.

Recent researches have revealed that the cities of Southern Etruria created at the height of their power a highly developed road system. From Veii roads capable of carrying heavy wheeled traffic radiated in every direction.[8] Besides the road on the right bank there was another direct communication between Veii and the salt banks,

[1] V. Hehn-O. Schrader, Das Salz, eine kulturhistorische Studie[2], Berlin 1901. M. Besnier, D.-S. 4, 1009 sqq. H. Blümner, RE 1 A, 2075 sq. Müller-Deecke, 1, 231. H. Nissen, It. Lk. 1, 107 sqq. L. Pareti, La tomba Regolini-Galassi, Città Vaticano 1947, 56. Th. Ashby, The Roman Campagna in Classical Times, New York 1927, 31. L. A. Holland, TAPA 80, 1949, 281 sqq. Meiggs, Roman Ostia, Oxford 1960, 19 sq. 294.

[2] DH II 55, 5. Plut., *Rom.* 25, 5. Cf. Liv. I 15, 5.

[3] Liv. I 33, 9. DH III 41, 3. Plin., *N.h.* XXXI 7, 89. *Vir. ill.* 5, 2.

[4] L. A. Holland, TAPA 80, 1949, 284 sq.

[5] *Ibid.* 285.

[6] Plin., *N.h.* XXXI 7, 89. Fest., p. 436, 8 L. Paul. Fest., p. 437, 4 L.

[7] Th. Ashby, The Roman Campagna in Classical Times, New York 1927, 30 sq., 227. L. A. Holland, *op. cit.* 313.

[8] J. B. Ward Perkins, PBSR 23, 1955, 44 sqq. *Idem*, JRS 47, 1957, 140. Cf. his recent survey : PBSR 29, 1961.

reaching the Tiber a short distance beyond the outlet of the rivulet, called today *Fosso Galeria*. The valley of this small river, whose sources are on the watershed just west of Veii, offers an obvious shortcut between that Etruscan stronghold and her salt-producing establishment, as Mrs. Holland recently observed.[1] Since then the British School at Rome has obtained important results in exploring this line of communication. Dr. J. B. Ward Perkins most kindly allowed me to reproduce a passage of his letter, written September 20, 1961, to me, recounting these results as follows:

"Our survey has not yet extended to the lower Tiber valley in any detail; but we have explored the area immediately to the south and west of Veii, and this indicates two rather different stages in the development of the road system. During the first of these (Villanovan—early Orientalizing) there is no trace of any road leading in this direction other than the track which crosses the valley just below Isola Farnese and climbs up to join the line of the later Via Cassia south of La Storta, whence it presumably continued on into Rome itself down the line of the via Triumphalis.

"The second (I cannot date it precisely but it was probably functioning by about 600, to judge from the development of the cemeteries) crossed the valley just above the falls, climbed up to the Via Cassia just where there is now the turning to Isola Farnese, and then continued along the ridge followed by the present-day (and Roman) road from La Storta towards Ponte Galera. This latter road is indicated by finds of pottery, and by some quite substantial road-cuttings. It remained in use under the Republic when it was the site of much farming settlement. I have not yet followed it right along.

"The overall impression which I have received from the study of the road-system and from finds at Veii itself are that prior to the 6th century Veii was not a major power either territorially or politically and was frequently at any rate on excellent terms with Rome. The expansion into the Western Ager Faliscus (Sutri and Nepi) may even be as late as the 5th century. I would expect therefore that the development of an independent route to the Tiber mouth might be a similarly late development. This is a guess, but I offer it for what it is worth."

The Tiber itself was not a real boundary in a military sense, separating Veientan and Roman territory, but was a highway toward the south, controlled either by Veii, or by Rome. Its ever winding meander between Rome and the sea offered no real demarcation line, isolating the two opponents from each other, since the shallow riverbed was no obstacle. All these considerations inevitably suggest the dependence of Rome on Veii when the latter city was at the height of her power. This will become even more evident when we turn to the date of origin of the *tribus Galeria*, named from the valley of the

[1] L. A. Holland, *op. cit.* 282 and 291.

Fosso Galeria. By the occupation of this river-valley, the Romans cut the vital artery of Veii between her and the saltworks.

In the Twelve Tables we find the notion that the other side of the river opposite Rome is an *ager hosticus*: the insolvent debtors, if not executed, were sold *trans Tiberim*.[1] This means that until the middle of the fifth century the right bank was Etruscan, since the evidence of the Twelve Tables cannot be questioned. But a new turn of events was then approaching. Since before and after *T. Romilius Rocus Vaticanus*, consul 455 B.C., no prominent member of his clan emerged, he or one of his descendants seem to be the only possible candidates —as we shall see—for lending the name of the *tribus Romilia* to the district installed around the *ager Vaticanus*,[2] the constitution of which tribe must be the direct consequence of the capture of *ripa Veiens*. This therefore must have happened not much later than the decemvirate, but in any way prior to the capture of Fidenae about 426 B.C.

In the epoch of the kings not only Veii hindered Rome's expansion toward the sea. The territory of *Lavinium* then certainly reached from the south the mouth of the river: even in imperial times, the area of Ostia ended with the outlet of the Eastern lagoon, only two miles away;[3] there was no real barrier, valley or water there. In those early days, the mouth of the river did not mean a potential harbor for Rome, even if its possession was coveted for the exploitation of the highly rewarding saltworks.[4] Her whole struggle for existence and prosperity was not directed toward the sea—this point we must stress again and again—until the middle of the fourth century; her aims were territorial. The whole social structure of her cattle-rearing shepherd people as well as the geographical environment pointed to this: "a glimpse from the seven hills is sufficient to realize why the national character (of the Romans) was so earthbound and not sailor-

---

[1] Gell. XX 1, 47. Cf. Mommsen, Gesammelte Schriften 3, 4. Something quite different is the deportation of turbulent or suspect elements *trans Tiberim* in 338 and 329 B.C. or even later, mentioned by J. Le Gall, Le Tibre, Paris 1953, 47.

[2] L. R. Taylor, Vot. Distr. (Mem. Am. Ac. Rome 20) 1960, 38, 75, 250, 283, and below, p. 310.

[3] Verg., *Aen.* 8, 31. Serv., *Aen.* 7, 661. H. Nissen, *op. cit.*, 571. K. J. Beloch, RG 1, 158.

[4] Plin., *N.h.* XXXI 7, 89 : . . . *nomine Salariae viae, quoniam illa salem in Sabinos portare convenerat*. Paul. Fest., p. 437, 4 : *Salaria via Romae est appellata, quia per eam Sabini sal a mari deferebant.* Cf. J. Le Gall, Le Tibre, Paris 1953, 48 sq. L. A. Holland, TAPA 80, 1949, 281 sqq., and above, p. 292.

TOPOGRAPHICAL AND ARCHAEOLOGICAL REALITIES

like at all." [1] Livy thought of this when he [2] described the mission of Tarquinius Superbus' sons to Delphi as a voyage *per ignotas ea tempestate terras, ignotiora maria*, "across countries, unknown in those times, and across seas, even more unknown."

The fact that Rome encroached on the right bank of the Tiber only in the fifth century gives us the opportunity to reconsider the date of a series of religious landmarks illustrating the extent of the Roman territory at a definite moment of its existence—a problem discussed several times since Mommsen. [3]

❧

THE SACRED BOUNDARY OF THE *AGER ROMANUS*

The boundary-line of the Rome of the Etruscan kings and its additional expansion in the fifth century B.C. can be pinned down by the location of magical rites performed at points where transversal roads crossed it. These points were as follows:

a) The annual solemnites of the *Ambarvalia* belonging to the *feriae conceptivae*, i.e., festivals the precise day of which was fixed year by year, in the month of May. [4] Many scholars thought [5] that these ritual performances were supplanted under Augustus by the festival of the Arval brethren, but this hypothesis must be abandoned, for the following reasons: 1) Strabo [6] narrates that the rites of the Ambarvalia

---

[1] H. Nissen, *op. cit.*, II 482.

[2] Liv. I 56, 5-6.

[3] K. J. Beloch, RG 169, to whom we owe highly important remarks on this problem, speaks of the "älteste Gebietsgrenze" which would have been "ursprünglich." This is meaningless. He rightly points out however, that the size of territory included surpasses that of the other Latin cities of the early times. Th. Ashby, The Roman Campagna in Classical Times, 29, thought that the territory of Rome indicated by a circle of the *ager Romanus* with a radius of 4-6 *m.p.* around her, included all 16 *tribus rusticae*. But this is impossible for geographical and chronological reasons. Cf. below, p. 304 sqq. L. R. Taylor, Rend. Pont. Acc. 27, 1952-54, 236, maintained the view that this boundary was that of the oldest rural tribes, as we hope to prove ; but she withdrew her statement in her latest book (see above p. 295 n. 2), 75.

[4] G. Wissowa, Religion und Kultus der Römer², München 1912, 142 sq., 561 sq.

[5] *Ibid.* 562 n. 4 ; in the same sense K. Latte, Römische Religionsgeschichte, München 1960, 165, and others.

[6] Strabo V 3, 2 (C. 230) in the tale of the foundation-myth : μεταξὺ γοῦν τοῦ πέμπτου καὶ τοῦ ἕκτου λίθου τῶν τὰ μίλια διασημαινόντων τῆς Ῥώμης καλεῖται τόπος Φῆστοι. τοῦτον δ'ὅριον ἀποφαίνουσι τῆς τότε Ῥωμαίων γῆς, οἵ δ'ἱερομνήμονες

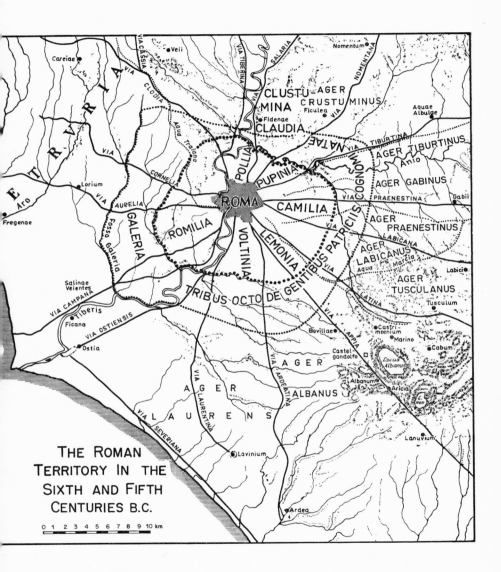

THE ROMAN
TERRITORY IN THE
SIXTH AND FIFTH
CENTURIES B.C.

0 1 2 3 4 5 6 7 8 9 10 km

were performed in his time—i.e., in the time of Augustus—by the *pontifices*, and Lucan [1] corroborates this. This attests that the *Fratres Arvales*—a different time-honored priest-corporation—had not taken over these sacred duties. 2) Strabo states that the Ambarvalia are performed at a place called Φῆστοι unknown otherwise [2]—on a point of the ancient Roman frontier, between the fifth and sixth milestones from the city on some transversal road; but he adds that on the same day, the pontiffs perform the same sacrifices at a series of other points of the old boundary under discussion: ἐν ἄλλοις τόποις πλείοσιν; the ritual in question is, therefore, not tied down to the time-honored grove of *Dea Dia*, but was spread over a number of crossroads, on the threshold of the *ager hosticus*. This repetition of the ceremonies, made all around the old boundary, the salient points of which were preserved by this ritual and by other analogous ones in the memory of the Romans, seems to me to be the reasonable substitute for the original pilgrimage all around the boundary, which became an impossible enterprise even for a boundary zone with a radius of 8-10 km. [3] 3) The identification of the locality Φῆστοι of Strabo with the grove of the Arval Brethren, suggested by G. B. De Rossi [4] and accepted by all the subsequent scholars dealing with this subject, is to be rejected in the face of the arguments adduced. The sacred *lucus* in which the twelve Arvals met had doubtlessly for centuries been in the same place where Augustus revived the rites, the uninterrupted existence of which is proved by the preservation of the *carmen Arvale*. Though situated at about the same distance from the city as the unknown *Festi*, that grove clearly did not belong to the stations of the *Ambarvalia* even if eventually the ritual performances of the Arvals would be coordinated in time with those of the pontiffs officiating around the

θυσίαν ἐπιτελοῦσιν ἐνταῦθά τε καὶ ἐν ἄλλοις τόποις πλείοσιν ὡς ὁρίοις αὐθημερόν, ἢν καλοῦσιν ᾿Αμβαρουίαν. Vgl. G. Wissowa, RE 1, 1796.

[1] Lucan. 1, 592 ff. : (the *haruspex* consulted) *mox iubet et totam pavidis a civibus urbem ambiri et festo purgantes moenia lustro longa per extremos pomeria cingere fines pontifices, sacri quibus est permissa potestas*. Though this is not the annual celebration mentioned here, it is an identical *lustratio urbis et agrorum* as that of the *amburbium* and of the *ambarvalia* and these were implemented, no doubt, by the same corporation of priests.

[2] Great scholars risked idle guesses on its meaning : F. Münzer, RE 4, 1832. W. Schulze, ZGLEN 564 n. 3. Ed. Norden, Aus altrömischen Priesterbüchern, Lund 1939, 175 sq.

[3] As K. Latte, *l.c.*, rightly observed.

[4] G. B. Rossi, Annali dell' Ist. 1858, 62 sqq. Before him the opposite view prevailed ; cf. A. Schwegler, RG 1, 434 n. 2.

same circumference of that old rural district of Rome on the day of the *Ambarvalia*. 4) The sources mention the *Ambarvalia* as an existing institution in the imperial age,[1] which could not be the case if it had become obsolete and had been supplanted by the Arval rites.

As Wissowa brilliantly observed,[2] the old magic procession around the Roman territory was propitiating Mars: not a meager harvest, but war was the real menace in those days, when looting bands and attacking armies were sweeping over the country again and again.

b) The annual rites of the Arval Brethren.

The topographical definition of the grove, where these rites were celebrated every May on three continuous days, is given in the protocol of the year 224 A.D.: [3] *in luco Deae Diae via Campana apud lap(idem) V*. As we just saw, we have no reason whatsoever for the assumption[4] that this *lucus* was established by Augustus on a new site: the name of the archaic brotherhood as well as its rites and the time-honored *carmen* so fortunately preserved refer to a celebration performed since time immemorial on the very frontier of the Roman *ager* toward the *Campus salinarum*, the saltworks from which the *via Campana* got its name.

The *lustratio agri* by the *fratres Atiedii* in Iguvium offers a close

---

[1] Serv., *Buc.* 3, 77 : *dicitur autem hoc sacrificium ambarvale, quod arva ambiat victima: hinc ipse (sc.* Vergilius) *in Georgicis* (1, 345) '*terque novas circum felix eat hostia fruges.*' Cf. also *ibid.* 5, 75. Strabo, *l.c.* (above p. 296. n. 6). Lucan., *l.c.* Paul. Fest., p. 5, 1 L. : *Ambarvales hostiae appellabantur, quae pro arvis a duobus fratribus sacrificabantur.* Most scholars adapted the emendation of the edition of Augustinus (of 1559) who wrote *duodecim* instead of *duobus.* But the *duo fratres* are clearly Romulus and Remus : also Strabo describes the *Ambarvalia* in connection with the activities of the founder, and the extract of Paulus Diaconus must come from the same context. This arbitrary alteration contributed much to the belief that the twelve *fratres Arvales* were acting at the rites in question. Macrob., *Sat.* III 5, 7 : *ambarvalis hostia est, ut ait Pompeius Festus, quae rei divinae causa circum arva ducitur ab his, qui pro frugibus faciunt.*

[2] G. Wissowa, *op. cit.* 143.

[3] Guil. Henzen, *Acta Fratrum Arvalium*, Berlin 1874, p. CCVIII sq. Cf. A. Pasoli, *Acta Fratrum Arvalium* (Studi e richerche, Univ. di Bologna, Fac. Lett. 7), Bologna 1950, 57 sq.

[4] The contrary view is maintained by K. Latte, *op. cit.* 65. Varro, *LL* 5, 85 : *Fratres Arvales dicti, qui sacra publica faciunt* (this means that there was no interruption at the end of the Republic!) *propterea ut fruges ferant arva.* Masurius Sabinus in Gell. VII 7, 8. Plin., *N.h.* XVIII 2, 6. The opinion of Wissowa (*op. cit.* 561 n. 7) that the Romulean origin and the mythical connection of the Arvales with Acca Larentia was invented by Masurius in order to give more prestige to the Augustan *Arvales* is strange, at least for me. This priesthood of great antiquity did not need a newly made halo.

TOPOGRAPHICAL AND ARCHAEOLOGICAL REALITIES

parallel, invoked already by Wissowa, illustrating the common roots and prehistoric antecedents of those brotherhoods. The location of the grove of Dea Dia on the right bank, on a hill beside the road leading toward the saltworks,[1] has its *terminus post quem* in the expansion of Rome's sovereignty to the nearby *ripa Etrusca*, about the middle of the fifth century B.C., as we have seen. The protection of the young crops by prayer and sacrifices was originally offered also here to the *Lares*, patrons of the land, and to Mars, "the wild spirit of the outland," "where wolves and human enemies might be met with,"[2] a concept appropriate for the boundary zone of a still small, constantly threatened city-state, and no longer fit for later times, when peace was ruling in the Latin fields.

c) The festive act of the *Terminalia*.

This was performed at the sixth milestone of the *via Laurentina*[3] on February 23. The distance shows that the spot selected for the state sacrifice was situated again on the old boundary line now under consideration; the choice of the place seems to have been made in view of a wholesale distribution of the different rites and sacrifices all around the frontier. We shall return later to the date when the demarcation line was drawn.

d) The sanctuary and festival of *Fortuna muliebris*.

This was on the *via Latina*, four miles from the city, behind the *fossa Cluilia*, one more mile ahead, which distance corresponds to the course of the same ancient circuit.[4] The legend connected with it is based

---

[1] Chr. Hülsen, RE 3, 1434.

[2] W. Warde Fowler, The Religious Experience of the Roman People, Oxford 1933, 131, quoted by Ed. Norden, Aus altrömischen Priesterbüchern, Lund 1939, 140. Cf. G. Wissowa, 143, 561 sq., and Ed. Norden, *op. cit.* 114 sqq., 120 sqq.

[3] Ovid., *Fast.* 2, 679-82 : *Est via, quae populum Laurentes ducit in agros,* . . . *illa lanigeri pecoris, tibi, Termine, fibris, sacra videt fieri sextus ab urbe lapis.* Cf. G. Wissowa, *op. cit.* 137 and E. Marbach, RE 5A, 782, for further information.

[4] DH VIII 36, 3 (Coriolanus) σταδίους ἀποσχὼν τῆς πόλεως ὀλίγῳ πλείους τῶν τριάκοντα παρὰ τὴν ἐπὶ Τυσκλανοὺς φέρουσαν ὁδὸν κατεστρατοπέδευσεν. *Ibid.* 55, 3 (in the sanctuary of Fortuna built on the spot where the women appeased Coriolan) ἐν ᾧ τὰς περὶ τῆς πόλεως ἐποιήσαντο λιτὰς χωρίῳ, θυσίας τε καθ' ἕκαστον ἔτος αὐτῇ συνιούσας ἐπιτελεῖν ἐν ᾗ τὸν πόλεμον ἔλυσαν ἡμέρᾳ. (Cf. *ibid.* 55, 4-5). Fest., p. 282, 18 : *Pudicitiae signum in Foro Boario est,* . . . *eam quidam Fortunae esse existimant. Item via Latina ad milliarium IIII Fortunae Muliebris, nefas est attingi, nisi ab ea, quae semel nupsit.* Val. Max. I 8, 4 : *Fortunae etiam Muliebris simulacrum, quod est Latina via ad quartum miliarium, eo tempore cum aede sua consecratum, quo Coriolanum ab excidio urbis maternae preces reppulerunt, non semel sed bis locutum constitit etc.* Cf. *ibid.* V 2, 1. Plut., *Coriol.* 37, 4. *Idem, De fortuna Rom.* 5. On the

upon the supposed fact of how a deadly danger was averted at the crossing of the ancient boundary by the Latin highway—a legend in all appearance spun out of rites aimed at keeping off the enemy by magic.

e) The *Robigalia*.

One additional point of that obsolete delimitation of the Roman landmark is revealed by the place, where on April 25 the sacrifices to *Mars* and *Robigus* were made on the *via Claudia ad milliarium V.* by the *flamen of Quirinus*, the second war-god of early Rome.[1] Here, too, the ceremony is manifestly concerned with warding off war rather than ensuring the success of the crops. Mommsen already observed that the games consecrated to Mars with Robigus imply the relationship of this latter rural divinity with the war menace around early Rome. This cult offers some positive data revealing the origin of its territorial fixation. First, the *Robigalia* are already contained in the oldest list of Roman *feriae*. Besides this, the geographical position of the site, where the ritual offerings to Mars and Robigus were accomplished, gives us a clue for the chronology. In the same way as the grove of the Arval Brethren defines the point where this old boundary crossed over to the right bank in the south,

Fossa Cluilia Liv. I 23, 3 and II 40, 5 *(quinque ab urbe milia passuum)*, *etc.* All the source material collected by A. Schwegler, RG 1, 584 sqq. ; 2, 362 sqq., 382 sqq. Cf. Mommsen, RG 1, 45. K. J. Beloch, RG 169 sq. W. F. Otto, Philol., n. F. 18, 1905, 192 sqq. G. Wissowa, *op. cit.* 257 f., and Gesammelte Abh. 1904, 272.

[1] Verr. Flacc. in the *Fasti Praenestini* (CIL I² p. 316 Mommsen) : *Feriae Robigo via Claudia ad milliarium V, ne robigo frumentis noceat. Sacrificium et ludi cursoribus maioribus minoribusque fiunt.* Varro, *LL* 6, 16 : *Robigalia dicta ab Robigo ; secundum segetes huic deo sacrificatur, ne robigo occupet segetes.* Paul. Fest., p. 325, 7 L. : *Robigalia dies festus septimo Kalendas Maias, quo Robigo deo suo, quem putabant robiginem avertere, sacrificabant.* Serv. auct., *Georg.* 1, 151 : *inde et Robigus deus et sacra eius decimo Kal. Maias Robiginalia appellantur.* Plin., *N.h.* XVIII 29, 285 : *Robigalia Numa constituit anno regni sui XI, quae nunc aguntur a.d. VII Kal. Mai., quoniam tunc fere segetes robigo occupat.* Gell. V 12, 14. Tertull., *De spect.* 5 : *post hunc Numa Pompilius Marti et Robigini (sc. ludos) fecit (nam et Robiginis deam finxerunt).* Ovid., *Fast.* 4, 901 sqq. : *Sex ubi, quae restant, luces Aprilis habebit, /in medio cursu tempora veris erunt, /et frustra pecudem quaeres Athamantidos Helles,/ signaque dant imbres, exoriturque canis./ Hac mihi Nomento Romam cum luce redirem,/ obstitit in media candida turba via./ flamen in antiquae lucum Robiginis ibat,/ exta canis flammis, exta daturus ovis./ protinus accessi, ritus ne nescius essem: edidit haec flamen verba, Quirine tuus, etc.* The topographical indication of Ovid, differing from that of Verrius, is not to be taken seriously. Cf. Mommsen, CIL I² p. 316. H. Usener, Das Weihnachtsfest², Bonn 1911, 306 sqq. G. Wissowa, RuK², 196. Sir James Frazer, *P. Ovid. Fastorum libri VI*, vol. 3, 1929, 408 sq. K. Latte, *op. cit.* 67.

so the sanctuary of *Robigus* reveals its course in the northwest. It is so near to the valley of the Cremera, connecting *Veii* with *Fidenae*, her bridgehead on the left bank, that the utter defeat of the Fabian army at that small river must have belonged to the past at the moment when the power of Rome had reached this distance here. Fidenae was five miles north from Rome, according to Dionysius,[1] but six miles according to Eutropius (1, 4). The establishment of the demarcation marked out by the sacrificial area of the *Robigalia* five or six miles from Rome on the right bank was a mortal blow for Fidenae and could therefore have happened only sometime in the two decades before the capture of this city in 426 B.C. The Anio, the old boundary of Rome facing this city,[2] was already outflanked by this Roman advance.[3]

f) The old boundary facing Gabii.

One more section of this old boundary line can be traced by the rules of augural practice, that is, the segment of that frontier in the east, on the *via Praenestina*—presumably running along one of the parallel hill-crests crossing that road—where the *ager Gabinus* met the *ager Romanus*.[4]

g) The statue of Mars on the *via Appia*.

We learn from Livy that there was a statue of Mars accompanied by several wolves on the *via Appia*. This group must be connected with the shrine of Mars on the same highway. We know that this highway was paved in two stages up to *Bovillae*, 10 or 11 Roman miles from the city, and that the first of these two stages extended to this sanctuary, as the second began from it: so this Mars with the wolves stood just as the distance from Rome, where we must look for

---

[1] DH II 53, 2: τὴν Φιδηναίων . . . πόλιν, ἀπὸ τετταράκοντα σταδίων τῆς ʽΡώμης κειμένην. The same statement : III 27, 1 and X 22, 3.

[2] Cf. DH V 37, 4. Plin., *N.h.* III 5, 54. O. Richter, Hermes 17, 1882, 431 sqq.

[3] Outside this landmark in the southwest, somewhat beyond the 12th milestone toward Ostia another agrarian sanctuary of the Roman state existed, Fest., p. 296, 15 L. : *Pomonal est in agro Solonio, via Ostiensi ad duodecimum lapidem, diverticulo a miliario octavo.* No doubt, the *flamen Pomonalis* (Varro, *LL* 7, 45. Fest., p. 144, 13 L. CIL III 12732. G. Wissowa RuK² 189 sq. W. Ehlers, RE 21, 1876 ff.) fulfilled there his devotional duties.

[4] Varro, *LL* 5, 33: *Ut nostri augures publici disserunt, agrorum sunt genera quinque : Romanus, Gabinus, peregrinus, hosticus, incertus. Romanus dictus unde Roma ab Romo ; Gabinus ab oppido Gabi[i]s ; peregrinus ager pacatus, qui extra Romanum et Gabinum, quod uno modo in his servantur auspicia,* etc.

our old demarcation line.[1] Here also Mars was watching over the rural frontiers of early Rome.

If we connect these seven points of the demarcation line with which we are presently concerned, we obtain a circular area with a diameter of 16 kilometers and a surface of roughly 250 square kilometers. It is likely that already before the circle was completed on the right bank of the Tiber in the fifth century B.C., incorporating in itself the surroundings of the *Ianiculum* and the *ager Vaticanus*, the bulk of the Roman territory on the left bank had reached this extent. This is, consequently, the domain of Rome under the Etruscan kings. Altogether, the size of the area thus defined is very modest, but it can stupefy only the believers in a huge Rome under the Tarquins: we must not forget that *"this is a considerable size for archaic Latin conditions,—larger than the size of any other city in Latium before the great Latin war"* (in 340 B.C.), to quote the words of Beloch.[2] On the other hand, we have every reason to believe Livy,[3] that the agrarian territory of Veii was greater than that of Rome, even about 400 B.C., after the Roman expansion throughout the fifth century B.C., which cut away from her the "Seven Districts" on the right bank of the Tiber. The extent of the Veientan territory mentioned by Livy is exactly circumscribed by the area of the four Roman *tribus* established in 386 B.C. on it.[4] The comparison between the Veientan and the Roman territory in Livy[5] means, consequently, that the size of these four tribes constituted from the Veientan state land was bigger in itself than the seventeen rural tribes[6] included in the territory of Rome before the capture of Veii. As we shall see below, out of these seventeen tribes only six were situated inside the sacred boundary just discussed. The remaining eleven *tribus* must therefore represent the conquest of the

---

[1] Liv. XXII 1, 12: *Romae signum Martis Appia via ac simulacra luporum sudasse.* Cf. *idem* X 23, 12; 47, 4; XXXVIII 28. 3. Cf. also Dessau, CIL XIV p. 230, about the distance to *Bovillae.* The circular shape of the Roman territory comprised by that old landmark also calls for attention.

[2] K. J. Beloch, RG 170.

[3] Liv. V 24, 5: *cum . . . ager . . . . Veientanus in conspectu sit, uberior ampliorque Romano agro.*

[4] Liv. VI 5, 8: *eo anno . . . tribus quattuor ex novis civibus additae: Stellatina, Tromentina, Sabatina, Arniensis; eaeque viginti quinque tribuum numerum explevere.*

[5] Liv. V 24, 5, and VI 5, 8.

[6] This figure emerges if we deduct—in addition to the four Veientan tribes —the four urban tribes comprised in the 25 by Liv. VI 5, 8.

second half of the fifth century. This dating will be reconfirmed soon by other considerations.

As to the date of origin of the solemn rites protecting the boundary line encircling the city with a radius of 5 to 6 Roman miles, this is defined by the fact that they are coordinated in the old cycle of festivals in the Roman calendar. The men who made its redaction were fitting into it this series of ceremonial duties aiming at the defense of the frontier line of the state which was then valid. This calendar was dated until recently to the sixth century B.C. But A. Kirsopp Michels contends that in truth its date is decemviral. Even if we do not accept all her arguments, it is enough to prove that the cycle of calendar feats included in it cannot be earlier than 450. We must descend even more with the dating in the second half of the fifth century: the ritual performed in the grove of the Arvals began after the constitution of the *Romilia* and the ritual of the temple of Ceres is still later.[1] Of course, the sea had not yet been reached at that time. The Latin cities in the Alban Hills and on the seashore were not yet incorporated. No Roman fleet existed. No treaty with Carthage could have been concluded, no large-scale international politics contemplated.

THE RURAL DISTRICTS WITHIN AND BEYOND THE SACRED BOUNDARY OF THE *AGER ROMANUS*

The ancient boundary of Rome still living in the religious manifestations just discussed also continued to have some juridical function and administrative significance in historical times, as the *ager Romanus* proper, or the *ager Romanus antiquus*.[2] Its existence reflects the limits of the Roman conquest under the kings, complemented with the bridgehead on the right bank of the river around the middle of the fifth century. No further territory was incorporated around it: the *ager Solonius* toward the south,[3] the *ager Albanus* and the *ager Gabinus* [4] toward the east, the *ager Crustuminus* in the north of the city [5] were

[1] A. Kirsopp Lake Michels, TAPA 80, 1949, 320 sqq. Cf. A. Alföldi, Studi e Materiali 32, 1961, 21 sqq.

[2] This was realized, e.g., by Mommsen, St. d. R. 3, 824 sq. W. Kubitschek, RE 1, 780 sq. K. J. Beloch, Der italische Bund, Leipzig 1880, 43 sqq., *etc.*

[3] Details are given by M. Fluss, RE 3A, 981 sqq. Cf. above, p. 190 and 233.

[4] Cic., *De lege agr.* 2, 66. Liv. I 23, 4. VII 11, 3, etc.

[5] Cic., *Pro Flacco* 71. Liv. XLI 9, 4, *etc.*

preserved correspondingly as territorial definitions used even long after their conquest, as was the *ager Veiens*.[1]

This restraint was dictated first of all by necessity. Rome did not swallow Latium at once, as the Annals would make us believe, but was striving first for a hegemonial position, leaving the territories of the adjacent Latin communities untouched. The Latin cities stood as equal partners along with Rome in the fifth century, when the Volscian and Aequian danger constrained them to collaborate with the Romans; even the gradual emergence of Rome as the leading power of the League and her final victory over her Latin allies could not abolish the individuality and persistence of their communities. The restricted territory of the *ager Romanus* was therefore an entity of the same kind as the adjacent ones of the *ager Bolanus, Gabinus, Tusculanus, Labicanus, Praenestinus, Laurens, Ardeas, Antias, Lanuvinus*, etc. The significance of these demarcations was, of course, quite different in the fifth century from what it was later, when they became parts of the Roman recruiting and voting districts. *Ager* as the political and juridical definition of the rural area of a Latin state originally meant a sovereign territory,[2] but even after these communities lost their independence, their local autonomy continued under the Roman supremacy, and thus *ager* remained the technical term for their territory. This term reflects, therefore, exactly the political geography of Latium in the fifth century as well as the size of the part of it possessed by the Romans before 450 B.C.[3] The great importance

---

[1] Cic., *Pro Sex. Rosc.* 47. Liv. IV 19, 6 ; 21, 1. V 24, 5 ; 30, 8 ; 45, 4. XLI 21, 12. XLIV 18, 6 ; *etc.*

[2] Cf. Mommsen, St. R. 3, 824 sq. K. J. Beloch, Der ital. Bund 43. W. Kubitschek, RE 1, 780 sq. P. Catalano, Atti Accad. Torino 96, 1961-62, 1 sqq.

[3] For the use of *ager* in this sense see : *A. Albanus* : Cic., *De lege agr.* II 25, 66. Liv. I 23, 4. VI 42, 6. VII 11, 3. *A. Antias* : Liv. V 45, 3. VIII 12, 3. *A. Ardeas* : Liv. VIII 12, 2. *A. Bolanus* : Liv. IV 49, 11. *A. Coranus* : Liv. VIII 19, 5. *A. Castrimoeni* : Gromat. 1, 233. *A. Circeiensis* : Plin., *N.h.* XIX 8, 134. *A. Crustuminus* : Cic., *Flacc.* 29, 71. *A. Gabinus* : Varro, *LL* 5, 33. Liv. III 8, 6. VI 27, 10. *A. Labicanus* : Liv. III 7, 3 ; 25, 6. IV 47, 6 ; 49, 4. VII 11, 3. XXVI 9, 11. *A. Lanuvinus* : Cic., *De div.* I 36, 79. *A. Latiniensis* : Cic., *De harusp. resp.* 10, 20. *A. Laurens* : Varro, *RR* III 13, 2. Liv. I 1, 4. 7. Cf. Verg., *Aen.*, 11, 431. *A. Norbanus* : Liv. VIII 19, 5. *A. Ostiensis* : Liv. VIII 12, 2. *A. Praenestinus* : Cic., *De lege agr.* II 28, 78. Liv. III 8, 6. *A. Romanus* : Varro, *RR* I 10, 1. *LL* 5, 55. Liv. I 10, 3 ; 23, 3. II 6, 5 ; 11, 3 ; 13, 4 ; 39, 5 ; 40, 10. 12 ; 43, 1 ; 49, 9 ; 51, 4. III 5, 2. 10 ; 6, 7 ; 30, 4. 38, 3. IV 17, 11 ; 21, 7-8 ; 30, 5. V 24, 5 ; 31, 5 ; 45, 4. VI 31, 3. VII 17, 9. XXVIII 11, 4. XLI 9, 5. XLIV 18, 6. A. *Setinus* : Liv. XXXII 26, 7. *A. Tusculanus* : Varro, *RR* I 14, 4. Cic. *De off.* I 7, 21. Liv.

of this picture of the *status quo* of Latium before the Decemvirate is obvious. We cannot analyze it any further at the moment; but the fact of the subsistence of the *ager Solonius*, the *ager Gabinus*, the *ager Albanus*, attesting that these cities were not conquered by Rome in the regal age, can illustrate the weight of its testimony. How and when these areas of Latium were included in the Roman tribes is scarcely registered in our sources. The meager evidence has been recently reexamined in a stimulating and valuable book of L. R. Taylor, to which we owe much; even if we must contradict her in details, her gallant attempt to illuminate the earliest history of the tribes was a great help for us.[1]

There is no difference of opinion about the basic fact that the first four regional *tribus*, those of the city-territory, are the districts established in the new, urbanized city of Rome by one of the Etruscan kings. The next step, the organization of the earliest *tribus* in the agrarian territory of the city, is dated by the annalist tradition to 495 B.C. Livy has the notice in that year: *Romae tribus una et viginti factae* (II 21, 7),[2] and a few years later Dionysius inserts the remark: μιᾶς γὰρ καὶ εἴκοσι τότε φυλῶν οὐσῶν (VII 64, 6) from the same ultimate source. This date was long ago challenged. Mommsen,[3] e.g., considered it not impossible, yet problematical; G. De Sanctis [4] points to the first half of the fifth century B.C. as the date of origin of the rural tribes. Then, K. J. Beloch [5] adduced weighty arguments for their assignment to the second half of the same century. L. R. Taylor [6] tried again to save the traditional date, but she was not able to invalidate the arguments of Beloch. Since the date of 495 is inseparably connected with the forged date [7] of immigration of the *gens Claudia*, it will have to be discarded.

II 19, 3. III 7, 3 ; 25, 6 ; 31, 3 ; 38, 5. IV 45, 6. VII 11, 3. *A. Veiens* : Cic., *S. Rosc.* 47. Liv. IV 19, 6 ; 21, 1. V 24, 5 ; 30, 8 ; 45, 4. XLI 21, 12. XLIV 18, 6.

[1] L. R. Taylor, Vot. Distr. (Papers and Monographs of the Am. Acad. Rome 20) 1960.

[2] The manuscripts mention *una et triginta*, but the *periochae* give *una et viginti*. Cf. Mommsen, St. R. 3, 166 n. 3. W. Kubitschek, *De Romanarum tribuum origine et propagatione*. Wien 1882, 17. *Idem* RE 6 A 2496 sqq. A. Bernardi, Athen. 1952, 20, n. 2. L. R. Taylor, Vot. Distr. 6 and 36.

[3] Mommsen, St. R. 3, 153, 166, 170 sqq.

[4] De Sanctis, St. d. R. 2, 1907, 18 sqq.

[5] K. J. Beloch, RG 264 sqq., 271 sq.

[6] L. R. Taylor, Vot. Distr. 6. *Contra* : E. Meyer, Gnomon 33, 1961, 603.

[7] Cf. above, p. 159 sq.

A new starting point for the checking of the scanty evidence just quoted is emerging from the following observation. It has been generally taken for granted that the names of the seventeen oldest rural tribes are *gentilicia* of patrician clans, with one exception only, the *Clustumina*, which was on the territory of *Crustumerium*.[1] Of course it has never escaped the attention of historians that these supposed gentile names fall into two distinct groups: one bearing the *nomina* of the most prominent aristocratic clans of the fifth century—we shall come back to this group shortly—and the other with totally unknown names, taken therefore as once powerful *gentes*, extinct already in the regal age. This assumption is in part flatly contradicted by our sources, in part not reasonable at all.[2] The group of unknown names comprises the following *tribus*:

a) *Lemonia*. In the excerpts of Festus[3] there stands a clear statement on the geographical character of the name of this district: *Lemonia tribus a pago Lemonio appellata, qui est a porta Capena via Latina.* The great importance of this information lies in the evidence that the Lemonia joined immediately the *pomerium* of the city. No doubt, its outside perimeter reached exactly the eastern boundary of the *ager Romanus*. The nucleus of the Roman territory within the sacred boundary line starts with a tribe having a *geographical* designation and so we can guess that other small tribes with names of the same kind continued to surround the city, between the *pomerium* and the boundary line of the *ager Romanus*.

b) *Pollia*. The key for the location of this tribe is given by an important observation of L. R. Taylor: "The *Pollia* tribe possessed a common tomb, from which ten imperial inscriptions have come to light between the *Via Salaria* and the *Via Po*.[4] The tomb may well have been placed on the territory of the old tribe, which, I would suggest, extended from the Tiber to the Via Salaria, . . ."[5] The collective tomb corresponds to the collective landed property of the tribes, which is attested; on such a collectively owned piece of the district

[1] Mommsen, RG 1[7], 1881, 35 took the lead.

[2] E. Meyer, *op. cit.* 603, is looking for a solution similar to ours, but independently from us.

[3] Paulus Fest., p. 102, 20 L.—L. R. Taylor, *op. cit.* 38.

[4] CIL VI 33992-6 ; cf. 37846 a. 37945. 38125. 38460.

[5] L. R. Taylor, Vot. Distr. 39. We do not agree with her concerning the expansion of the *Pollia* to the north and its geographical interrelation with the *Claudia* and the *Sergia*. Cf. below, p. 311.

must have been the common burial ground. This small *tribus*, extending from the northern part of the *pomerium* as far as the fifth milestone, where the *ager Romanus* ended, shows in her name no more connection either with the great princely houses than does the Lemonia. The name seems to me to have been taken from the name of a site included in it.

c) *Pupinia*. This tribe again has a geographical name. A mutilated passage of Festus reads with the supplements of Scaliger: [1] <*Pupinia tribus*> *ab agri nomine* <*dicta, qui Pupinius dicitur, inter*> *Tusculum urbem*<*que situs, cuius Lucilius me*> *minit*: '*invictum* <*Pupinia fert, quoi pauper agellu' est.*> This means: "The *Pupinia* district bears the name of a rural area, called *ager Pupinius*, situated between Tusculum and the city of Rome. Lucilius mentions this with the words 'The invincible commander was brought up in the territory of the Pupinia tribe, which has a poor soil . . .'" The definition "between Tusculum and Rome" implies that the territory of the tribe reached the *pomerium* of the city. The same is apparent also in other texts referring in some way to the site of this *tribus*. When in the account of Livy [2] Hannibal, arriving from the direction of *Gabii* at the outskirts of Rome, launches an attack on the area of the *Pupinia* and then pitches camp eight Roman miles from the city, the two moments, the incursion into the suburban region and the choice of the site of this encampment, are to be dissociated. It is not correct, at least in the mind of the present writer, to refer the given distance of Hannibal's camp to that of the location of the *Pupinia* tribe. We must assume that such a military genius did not simply settle down without preliminary precautions on the most advanced spot in the face of the enemy reached by his raiding forces, but that he terrified the Romans first by pushing forward toward the city, and then he withdrew to a well-chosen position.[3] The immediate neighborhood of the *Pupinia* to Rome is also manifest in a passage of Cicero, where he puts her on par with

[1] Fest., p. 264, 9. L. W. Kubitschek, *De Rom. trib. orig.* 12. Cf. Paul. Fest., p. 265, 1 L.: *Pupinia tribus ab agro Popinio.* For further details see L. R. Taylor, *op. cit.* 38 sq.

[2] Liv. XXVI 9, 12: *inde* (sc. a Labicano agro) *Algido Tusculum petiit, nec receptus moenibus infra Tusculum dextrorsus Gabios descendit. inde ad Pupiniam exercitu demisso octo milia passuum ab Roma posuit castra.*

[3] His next move was to push forward with his camp to within three miles of Rome. Liv. XXVI 10, 3; cf. 13, 11 and Polyb. IX 5, 9.

the meager fields of the Vatican,[1] so that their relative distances from the center of Rome must be about the same. The site of the *Pupinia* seems to have been next to the *Pollia* inside of the northern perimeter of the *ager Romanus*, because a consul draws up his troops on her soil in expectation of an Umbrian attack.[2]

There are two more rural *tribus* with names not connected with the leading clans of the early Republican aristocracy, which seem to me to belong to the same series of small agrarian tribes inside the *ager Romanus*. They are:

d) *Voltinia*. Her localization has been lately discussed by L. R. Taylor.[3] She observed that there was an established order of the tribes which was followed in the *census* and that after the urban tribes, the *Romilia* was the first in rank and that the others followed in a circle counterclockwise, the second being the *Voltinia*. This was made plausible enough by her; but an inner circle must be postulated for the oldest *tribus* within the perimeter of the *ager Romanus*, to which the *Voltinia* belonged; only after this was counted through could the ring of later districts follow.

e) *Camilia*. Though family names such as *Camelius*, *Camellius*, *Camellianus*, *Camilius* are, even if rarely, to be found,[4] there is nothing to prove either that they are old or that they belonged to the oldest aristocracy. It is more likely that the tribe got this name from a *pagus* or *ager*. The location again is not explicitly pointed out in our sources,[5] but there is a great probability that the *Camilia* was one of the oldest rural tribes inside of the circuit surrounding Rome in the distance

---

[1] Cic., *De lege agr.* II 35, 96 (on the prospects of a colony to be deduced in Capua): *quos illorum animos, quos impetus, quam ferociam putatis? Romam in montibus positam et convallibus, cenaculis sublatam atque suspensam, non optimis viis, angustissimis semitis, prae sua Capua planissimo in loco explicata ac praeclarissimis viis irrid[d]ebunt atque contemnent. agros vero Vaticanum ac Pupiniam cum suis opimis atque uberibus campis conferendos scilicet non putabunt: oppidorum autem finitimorum illam copiam cum hac per risum et iocum contendent.* The vicinity of the Pupinia to the capital city is implied, even if without concrete references, in the idyllic illustrations of the simplicity of olden times, with the small farm cultivated by M. Atilius Regulus (consul of 267 B.C.) in the Pupinia district. Val. Max. IV 4, 6. Columella I 4, 2 sqq.

[2] Liv. IX 41, 10: *quod inceptum eorum ubi ad Decium consulem perlatum est, ad urbem ex Etruria magnis itineribus pergit et in agro Pupiniensi ad famam intentus hostium consedit.*

[3] L. R. Taylor, *op. cit.* 44 sq., 69. Cf. W. Kubitschek, RE 6A, 2500.

[4] W. Schulze, ZGLEN 140. *Th.l.L., Onom.* C, 116. 120.

[5] L. R. Taylor, *op. cit.* 43 sq., brings no conclusive arguments.

of 5 to 6 miles. There is a small terminal cippus of Republican date hewn from stone of Gabii and found somewhere in Rome herself, with the inscription *iter privatum tribus Camilliae*, attesting the property of the tribe in the immediate neighborhood,[1] in the same way as the sepulchral area of the *Pollia*. Her geographical position can be looked for only to the southeast from the city, either between the *Pupinia* and the *Lemonia*, or between the latter and the *Voltinia*.

Outside of this oldest circle of small rural districts followed a zone of tribes bearing the names of the patrician clans, prominent in the fifth century B.C. The new style of the nomenclature of these tribes, surrounding the bloc of the old rural tribes with geographical names, marks them out as a subsequent stage of the Roman expansion beyond the *ager Romanus*. The following short remarks are to give some comments on their sites, dates of origin, and their peculiar structure:

a) *Romilia*. We have good reasons for assuming that this tribe completed the circle of the *ager Romanus* with the *ager Vaticanus* on the right bank, reaching in the south only as far as the fifth milestone on the *Via Campana* and in the north to the same distance along the *Via Claudia*. Her boundary line in the west was the rivulet *Magliana*, behind which line in the same direction the *tribus Galeria* was situated. The antiquarians of the first century B.C. still knew that it had been conquered from the Veientans—just after the middle of the fifth century, as we saw. Among the modern historians it was K. J. Beloch who realized that its name comes from the person or offspring of *T. Romilius Rocus Vaticanus*, consul in 455 B.C. and *decemvir legibus scribundis* in 451.[2] The immediate connection with the small tribes of the *ager Romanus*, older than herself, gives a priority to the *Romilia* among the rural tribes with gentile names. As L. R. Taylor stressed, she was the first among the *tribus rusticae* in casting

---

[1] C. Pietrangeli, Bull. Com. 69, 1941, 168. A. Degrassi, ILLRP 488. L. R. Taylor, *op. cit.* 14.

[2] Paul. Fest., p. 331, 1 L.: *Romulia tribus dicta quod ex eo agro censebant, quem Romulus ceperat ex Veientibus. Ibid.* 519, 24 L.: *Vaticanus collis appellatus est, quod eo potitus sit populus Romanus vatum responso expulsis Etruscis.* Plin., *N.h.* III 5, 53: *Tiberis ... Etruriam ab Umbris ac Sabinis, mox citra XVI p. urbis Veientem agrum a Crustumino, dein Fidenatem Latinumque a Vaticano dirimens.* Varro, *LL* 5, 56: *quinta (sc. tribus), quod sub Roma, Romilia.* W. Kubitschek, *De Rom. trib. orig.* 10. K. J. Beloch, RG 169. L. R. Taylor, *op. cit.* 38. The *Ponte Galeria* on the Tiber at the south end of the *Fosso Galeria* demonstrates that the *tribus Galeria* (cf. below) was situated on the west side of the *Romilia*.

her vote in the tribal assembly—perhaps because Romulus was supposed to have been her founder.

b) *Claudia*. The immigration of the ancestor of the *Appii Claudii* from his Sabine home was dated by Fabius in the year 495 B.C., a fictitious date, belonging to the campaign of denigration of these opponents of the Fabian house, as we hope to have demonstrated.[1] Though we must reject the date,[2] the localization of the tribe, mentioned in that story, is well established. Dionysius narrates that the Roman state gave to the first Claudius besides a portion of the city-area for himself and his ꜟretinue χώραν . . τὴν μεταξὺ Φιδήνης καὶ Πικετίας, . . ἀφ' ὧν καὶ φυλή τις ἐγένετο σὺν χρόνῳ Κλαυδία καλουμένη,[3] i.e., the region between Fidenae and the unknown *Picetia*. Livy[4] gives another geographical indication for the same event: *namque Attius Clausus, cui postea Appio Claudio fuit Romae nomen, . . . magna clientium comitatus manu, Romam transfugit. his civitas data agerque trans Anienem: vetus Claudia tribus . . . appellata.* Fidenae belonged, no doubt,[5] from the beginning to this tribe north of the Anio, and this particular fact gives us a clue to the date of origin of the *tribus Claudia*. Fidenae was the key position controlling the traffic on the Tiber for Veii, as well as an obstacle along the *Via Salaria* for Rome. The ruin of Fidenae in 426 B.C. foreshadowed the fall of Veii a generation later. At the fictitious date of the foundation of the gentile *tribus*, in 495 B.C., Rome had just survived a heavy war against the Latins, and could not have risked turning northward. In the first half of the century, Veii was still superior to her: a lasting Roman establishment around Fidenae and east of her before the final conquest of this city is, as Beloch already stressed, impossible. Nor has the *Sergia* room near Fidenae for the same reason before 426; and after this date, there is no room there for the *Sergia* besides the *Claudia*.

[1] Cf. my note in the *Festschrift für E. Salin*, Tübingen 1961, and above, p. 159.

[2] L. R. Taylor, *op. cit.* 35 sq., gives the details. She retains the date as authentic in agreement with A. Bernardi, Athen., n.s. 30, 1952, 20 n. 2., and other scholars.

[3] DH V 40, 5. A. Bormann, Altlatinische Chorographie, Halle 1852, 251 n. 508, read (Φ)ικ(ολνέ)ας instead of Πικετίας with the approbation of W. Kubitschek, *De Rom. trib. orig.* 14, and RE 6 A 2501, L. R. Taylor, *l.c.*, and others. But C. Jacoby did not accept this hazardous emendation. Nor can we justify it palaeographically.

[4] Liv. II 16, 4-5. Plut., *Poplic.* 21, 10, has χώραν . . . περὶ τὸν Ἀνίωνα ποταμόν.

[5] *Contra*: L. R. Taylor, *loc. cit.*, who noticed that a *dictator Fidenas* belonged to the *Claudia*, but she thought that this territory was added to that tribe only later.

TOPOGRAPHICAL AND ARCHAEOLOGICAL REALITIES

We have only some slight indications for the localization of the following gentile tribes:

c) *Fabia*. The guess of W. Kubitschek,[1] that Veientan attacks on the property of the *gens Fabia* in the region of the Cremera-brook would explain why that clan made war against Veii, supposes a previous expansion of Rome on the right bank, which we cannot admit. On the other hand, later on, after the bridgehead of the *ager Vaticanus* had been conquered in the second half of the fifth century a further Roman expansion north of the *Romilia* was achieved, by which the *Fabii* could eventually acquire great estates along the right bank of the Tiber and give the name there to a new tribe.

d) *Horatia*. The legendary role of the *Horatii* in the alleged conquest of Alba Longa by Rome was supposed to be based on the existence of estates of that family around her site; for this reason, the *tribus Horatia* was thought to have been established there.[2] But even at a date comparatively so late as the fifth century, when the Romans in fact expanded in these regions, they could not incorporate the territory of the decayed Alba *en bloc* in one tribe, nor were they able to do this with the rural surroundings of the other Latin cities. This fact is clearly demonstrated by the attribution of the neighboring Latin communities to a series of different Roman *tribus*, as shown by L. R. Taylor:

> *Lanuvium* was inscribed in the *Maecia* (*op. cit.* 66 and 96),
> *Aricia* in the *Horatia* (*ibid.* 96),
> *Tusculum* belonged to the *Papiria* (*ibid.* 160),
> *Castrimoenium* to the *Falerna* (?), (*ibid.*),
> *Bovillae* to the *Pomptina* (?), (*ibid.*), etc.

The reason of this haphazard distribution cannot be doubtful. After the subjugation of the Latins in 338 B.C., when the right of political gatherings, commercial activities, lawful marriages between the citizens of their cities, was denied to them by Rome, their enrollment in so many different voting districts made it impossible for them to conspire against the victorious power under the cover of the Roman organization. But on the other hand, this arrangement was possible only when, before that turning point of Latin history, the region of the Alban hills was not yet included in the network of the Roman

---

[1] W. Kubitschek, *De Rom. trib. orig.* 12. L. R. Taylor, *op. cit.* 40 sqq.
[2] W. Kubitschek, *op. cit.* 13. L. R. Taylor, *op. cit.* 43.

rural tribes. Otherwise all these cities would have the same tribe. The checkered attribution of neighboring cities in different *tribus* also implies a date: such a provision became feasible only when the tribes ceased to be geographical units and the newly enrolled territories, assigned to them, could be situated anywhere, their attribution being merely a theoretical measure.[1]

e) *Papiria*. Her original site seems to have adjoined the *Pupinia* [2] toward the east and extended to *Tusculum* soon after 381 B.C., when this city was enfranchised. The prominence of the *Papirii* begins with their consulates in 444, 443, 441 B.C., obtained frequently afterward also; the creation of the tribe could be not earlier in any way.

f) *Aemilia* and *Menenia*. The city of Gabii belonged to one of these tribes.[3] But by the *foedus Gabinum*, concluded at some date after 468 B.C.,[4] this city maintained even much later still a quasi-independent existence [5] and therefore cannot have been incorporated in one of the Roman tribes just mentioned when they were organized.

g) *Voturia*. Pl. Fraccaro has drawn attention to a fragment of a speech of Cato the Elder,[6] where the shrine of the *gens Veturia*, fifteen miles away from the Anio, is mentioned. He cleverly pleaded for his view that this indication is not inconsistent with the location of the tribe on the left bank of the Tiber near the coast. But there is no need to presume that the original home of a clan with her gentile sanctuary should have coincided with the rural district designated with her name later on. And the preliminary condition for the assignment of this region to a tribe was the conquest of the *Septem pagi* from Veii which were attributed to the *Romilia* in the second half of the fifth century; only after this event and the capture of the Veientan saltworks could the further expansion toward the coast follow. We shall return to this question in connection with the *Galeria* once more.

The original location of the remaining territorial *tribus* with gentile names remains uncertain. They are the *Sergia*,[7] *Aemilia*,[8] *Cornelia*,[9] and

---

[1] L. R. Taylor, *op. cit.* 78 sq.

[2] Cf. above, p. 308, and L. R. Taylor, *op. cit.* 43.

[3] L. R. Taylor, *op. cit.* 44.

[4] Cf. above, p. 379.

[5] K. J. Beloch, RG 155 sq., 163, 320.

[6] *Or. Rom. Fr.* ed. H. Malcovati[2], 1955, 34 sq. no. 72 sqq. Pl. Fraccaro, Athen., n.s., 2, 1924, 54 sqq. (*Opusc.* 2, 1 sqq.). L. R. Taylor, *op. cit.* 42.

[7] L. R. Taylor, *op. cit.* 40, suggests that L. Sergius and Q. Servilius did not only obtain the *cognomen Fidenas* on account of their successful diplomacy after the raids of the Fidenates in 428 B.C., and that they did not—as Münzer thought

Menenia,[1] named after leading clans of the Roman state in the first century of the Republic.

In spite of all the precariousness of our information, the general scheme of geographic distribution of the gentile tribes is well illustrated by the map of L. R. Taylor:[2] they were included between the mains roads, radiating around Rome in all directions. Yet I hope to have demonstrated that they in no case joined the urban *pomerium*, but surrounded with their belt the old *ager Romanus* (see the map p. 297). Consequently, they represent a new stage of development. The general scheme of their sites was conceived globally, a priori, distributing their areas in the sense of a premeditated plan. This fact hints at a single governmental decision for their establishment, just as the tradition asserts, though with premature dating. All the chronological indications we registered speak for their having been organized at a certain date in the decades after the decemvirate.

The breadth of this new rural zone is generally indicated by the fact that beyond the tenth milestone of Rome the extraurban area of the *fora et conciliabula* began (Liv. XL 37, 4). This distance corresponds to the perimeter of the suburban region of imperial times, ultimately based on very old antecedents. Outside of the *regio suburbana* followed immediately the municipal territories of the Latin cities: as they were unable to expand at the expense of Rome after the great Latin war, the demarcation in question perpetuated a situation valid in 338 B.C. On the other hand, the date of origin of this belt of the gentile tribes, constituted globally, becomes apparent by the fact that one of them, the *tribus Claudia*, was established on the territory of Fidenae, captured in 426 B.C. This is the *terminus post quem* for the constitution of the gentile tribes.

To understand the role of the leading clans of the aristocracy in the framework of the territorial tribes in the fifth century, we must first recall the fact that, before the geographical areas became the

---

(RE 2 A, 1711 no. 25 and *ibid.* 1803 sqq. no. 75)—acquire estates in the Fidenate territory at that time, but that they owned them already when the inroads happened. This means that *Fidenae* belonged to the *Sergia tribus* before her conquest in 426 B.C. We cannot accept this suggestion; we have seen already that *Fidenae* was inscribed in the *Claudia*.

[8] L. R. Taylor, *ibid.* 44 sq.
[9] *Ibid.* 43 sqq., 80.
[1] *Ibid.* 43 sq.
[2] *Ibid.* facing p. 35.

organizatory basis of recruitment, tax-paying, and casting of votes, the *tribus* were the organisation of clans for the purpose of war and collective hunting and for the distribution of the pastureland. The geographical tribes also preserved some obsolete sociological features: their common property and common burial grounds mentioned above seem to be remnants of such archaic gentile ties.

After the monarchy was dissolved, the closed ring of the patriciate was ruling—at least in the first century of the Republic—over the rest of the population, not only by having sovereign rights in the years of magistrature, but also as a privileged class. The patricians possessed the exclusive claim to become state functionaries. The centuriate organization did not include them in the timocratic classes; they were above them. The care for certain state-cults was attributed to some of their families, as the *Lupercalia* to the *Fabii* and *Quinctii* (cooperating also in the consular elections), the cult of Hercules at the *ara maxima* to the *Valerii Potiti* [1] and the *Pinarii*, etc.

This sort of patrician preponderance must have been present over the tribes with gentile names, too. Some hints of it are not lacking even in the defective literary tradition.[2] The main source of wealth on the meager soil of Latium still being cattle-rearing, not corn, the *ager publicus* occupied by the aristocracy as pastureland had a far greater economic significance in the fifth century than later on.

In a state of a still archaic structure, where no police force existed and no protection of small people other than the *fides* of mighty patrons, able to retaliate for the mischief committed against their adherents, the *obsequium* of the common man must have been originally that of an armed retainer.[3] Even the mobilization of all the followers for a war by their protecting overlord was possible. The expedition of the *Fabii*, ending with their total defeat at the *Cremera*, is an example

---

[1] I hope to give the reasons for this elsewhere.

[2] Paul. Fest., p. 289, 1 L.: *Patres senatores ideo appellati sunt, quia agrorum partes adtribuerant tenuioribus ac si liberis propriis*. Ibid. p. 262, 22: *Patrocinia appellari coepta sunt, cum plebs distributa est inter patres, ut eorum opibus tuta esset*. Cic., *De re p.* II 9, 16 : (Romulus) *habuit plebem in clientelas principum discriptam*. Liv. V 32, 8 (on Camillus) : *cum accitis domum tribulibus clientibusque, quae magna pars plebis erat*, etc. DH XIII 5, 1, refers to οἱ πελάται τε καὶ συγγενεῖς αὐτοῦ in the same connection. The at least partial identity of *tribules* and *clientes* is well illustrated by the story of *Attius Clausus* : though the date of the immigration is a tendentious forgery, the social structure depicted in it is authentic : the princely clan is settled in a rural district with thousands of dependants.

[3] For the latest literature see P. De Francisci, Primordia civitatis, Roma 1959, 185 sq. Cf. also S. Mazzarino, in : Iura 12, 1961, 24 sqq.

of this. This is no doubt authentic as a structural feature,[1] the more so as Etruscan oligarchs also could raise such private armies.[2]

If the ruling position of the patrician clans in the fifth century is mirrored in the tribe names just discussed, the total absence [3] of such names among the new tribes founded after them cannot be ascribed to mere chance, but must coincide with the transformation of the social and political organization. This is the time when the admission of nonpatricians to the cavalry, the new importance of the armored infantry, the introduction of the soldier's pay in the hard struggle with Veii involved also other political concessions, undermining the exclusive rule of the patriciate. One of the social consequences of this evolution seems to be that no more gentile tribes, strongholds of feudal families, were created.

The new belt of tribes, bearing geographical names again, started with two tribes, which came into being even before the Veientan territory got its Roman organization. These are:

a) the *Galeria*. Though she was regarded as one of the tribes with gentile names, it has been recognized long since [4] that she got her name from a little stream, the *Rio Galera* of mediaeval documents, which starts its vertical course south of Veii and reaches the Tiber halfway between Rome and Ostia. This riverbed, adjusted by the Veientan engineers,[5] offered direct access from Veii to the salt marshes at the mouth of the Tiber as we saw earlier. This route, vitally important for the Veientans, was certainly threatened in the fight for the hotly contested *Septem pagi*. The occupation of the "Seven Districts" by the Romans around the bridgehead of the *ager Vaticanus*,

---

[1] In DH X 14, 1 Appius Herdonius συνήθροιζε τοὺς πελάτας καὶ τῶν θεραπόντων οὓς εἶχεν εὐτολμοτάτους. Livy III 15, 5, has *exules servique* in the same context.

[2] DH IX 5, 4 and the important elucidations of J. Heurgon, Latomus 18, 1959, 713 sqq.

[3] The *tribus Poblilia* does not seem to bear the name of the plebeian *Poblilii*, but is rather taken from a Volscian geographical name of the territory on which the Roman tribe had been established. This is the solution of the difficulties. Cf. W. Hoffmann, RE 23, 1908 sqq.

[4] A. Nibby, Analisi storico-topografico-antiquaria della carta de' dintorni di Roma, Roma 1837, 97 sq. W. Kubitschek, *De Rom. trib. orig.* 13. H. Nissen, It. Lk. II 2, 564 sqq. L. R. Taylor, *op. cit.* 39.

[5] L. A. Holland, TAPA 80, 1949, 290 sqq. Cf. B. J. Ward Perkins, PBSR 23, 1955, 68 sq., and his letter quoted above, p. 294. L. R. Taylor, *loc. cit.*, thinks that the spot where *S. M. di Galeria* is situated today was an extension of the *tribus Galeria* before the fall of Veii, but in my opinion it belonged to the original territory of the tribe. Cf. above, p. 310.

incorporated in the Roman territory as the *tribus Romilia,* was a hard blow for Veii. The occupation of the valley of the *Rio Galera* west of it cannot be earlier than the last decades of the fifth century. The open flank toward the Caeretan territory shows once more that Rome proceeded there in agreement with Caere, to whom the nearby *Fregenae* on the coast belonged. It has been already noticed that the foundation of the *Galeria* is previous to the establishment of the four tribes, formed from the Veientan territory, i.e., earlier than 387 B.C.[1]

b) *Clustumina.* This was the second—not the first as is believed— tribe with a geographical name, which was established after the zone of the gentile tribes around the *ager Romanus* was completed. It was situated north of Fidenae, belonging to the *Claudia,* on the *ager Crustuminus,* the territory of *Crustumerium.* We maintain with Beloch[2] that the way to *Crustumerium* was opened to the Romans only by the capture of Fidenae in 426, and that they conquered it still before the doom of Veii in 396 B.C.

To sum up: we distinguish the following phases in the formation of the Roman tribes. The four tribes of the city, constituted in the sixth century by the Etruscan kings, bear geographical names: *tribus dictae ab locis Suburana, Palatina, Esquilina, Collina.*[3] An organic continuation of these urban tribes are, as we hope to have shown, the small tribes inside of the *ager Romanus,* also with geographical names, the *Lemonia, Pollia, Pupinia, Camilia, Voltinia.* This is the stage of evolution, when the rural districts were simply the suburban fields: *initio, omnium tribuum . . . agri in propinquo erant urbis.*[4] The circle of these small districts was complemented soon after the middle of the fifth century on the right bank with the first tribe with a gentile name, the Romilia. Then followed soon after 426 B.C. the belt of the gentile tribes around the *ager Romanus,* mirroring the hegemony of the patriciate. But not much before 400 B.C. the new series of tribes

[1] Liv. VI 5, 8 : *tribus quattuor ex novis civibus additae : Stellatina, Tromentina, Sabatina Arniensis : eaeque viginti quinque tribuum numerum explevere.*

[2] K. J. Beloch, RG 159 (cf. 264 sqq., 270 sqq., 301, 317.). *Contra* : L. R. Taylor, *op. cit.* 36 sq. Cf. also H. Nissen, It. Lk. II 2, 561.

[3] Varro, *LL* 5, 56. Liv. I 43, 13 : *quadrifariam enim urbe divisa regionibus colli-busque, qui habitabantur, partes eas tribus appellavit, ut ego arbitror, ab tributo ; nam eius quoque aequaliter ex censu conferendi ab eodem* (sc. Servio Tullio) *inita ratio est ; neque eae tribus ad centuriarum distributionem numerumque quicquam pertinuere.* The last discussion of this passage seems to be that of J. J. Nichols, AJP 77, 1956, 225 sqq.

[4] Fest., p. 508, 27 L.

with place-names began. Unfortunately, the new method of adding
new territory to old rural tribes without a geographical coherence [1]
does not allow us to pursue (after 387) any further the march of
conquest; nevertheless, the important fact emerges that the incorporation of the main Latin cities in the Roman tribes did not follow
before the fourth century, for the majority of them not before 338 B.C.
The progress of the subjugation of the Latins, as mirrored in the
Annals, corroborates this picture and explains this late date of the
Roman expansion.

☙

THE DREAM OF THE "GRANDE ROMA DEI TARQUINII"

Since Niebuhr's days when the foundations for scientific analysis of
the literary sources were laid, great results have been obtained; every
generation of scholars has made its contribution to the advancement
of our knowledge of Early Rome. But the continuous progress also
brought about new dangers. Confidence in the reliability of our
written evidence was shaken and the general trend of research in this
field became, roughly speaking, more and more animated by the
desire to eliminate as much as possible of the scanty data we possess,
and to overbid in this way the preceding critics. There were exceptions, of course. The genius of Mommsen stood above the currents
of time. The "critica temperata" of G. de Sanctis saved him from
distorting exaggerations. Nor are some few other instances lacking
for a healthy self-restraint in this respect. But the voice of the moder-
ates was unheard. Since archaeological evidence for the Etruscan
domination in Rome was still lacking, a brilliant scholar pushed
distrust in the source evidence so far as to discard completely the tale
of the Annals and even to deny the existence of the City in the early
centuries. To him the history of Rome began with the Celtic invasion,
let us say with the fourth century B.C. He made a still greater mistake
by trying to replace the legendary tales by a willful, pseudo-rational-
istic interpretation. No wonder a sharp reaction arose against this
highly arbitrary and over-simplified procedure.

The new trend, emerging in opposition to the decried "hypercriti-
cal" method, betrays the endeavor to vindicate even the last bit of

---

[1] L. R. Taylor, *op. cit.* 75 sq.

the written tradition as authentic if the least chance for such an attempt exists. This effort has our full approval as far as the crumbs to be saved are really reliable. But only so far. Yet just as the protection of everything preserved in the Annals became a fashion in the last generation, it is now a kind of sport for its own sake, a sort of mannerism encouraging zealots and opportunists to decry the critical attitude so fundamental for the historian—in the same way as before the opposite current induced them to wipe out everything possible of the written record. As Vergil would say, the monster Scylla attacks us from the right and from the left the pitiless Charybdis: *dextrum Scylla latus, laevom inplacata Charybdis obsidet.*

In the meantime, finds from the sixth century B.C. came to light in the Eternal City and are increasing steadily. Owing to the influx of these new documents, research on Early Rome faced a new situation. An outstanding scholar, realizing the importance of this new source evidence, took the lead in celebrating the resurrection of what he called "la grande Roma dei Tarquinii." [1]

The existence of a flourishing urbanized Rome in the sixth century was firmly established indeed. But did the proof of her existence also mean that this flourishing city was already the leading power in Middle Italy in that remote epoch, as Fabius Pictor's propaganda pretends? Our previous chapters have shown, I hope, that the excavations and finds proving the prosperity of Etruscan Rome—a boom which was not lacking elsewhere in Latium—do not mean the sovereignty of Rome over the Latin nation.

[1] G. Pasquali, La nuova antologia 386, 1936, 405 sqq. G. Lugli, Eranos 41, 1943, 18 sqq. The consequences drawn by Pasquali from the emergence of the new archaeological evidence could seem the more obvious, as, the extreme views of Pais being refuted at the same time, the rest of the historians followed the Annals in taking the Roman hegemony over Latium under the kings for granted; cf., e.g., Ed. Meyer, Geschichte des Altertums 5, 1902, 136 sq. *Idem*, Kleine Schriften, Halle 1924, 297. M. Gelzer, RE 12, 950 sq. K. J. Beloch, RG 227. A. N. Sherwin-White, R. Citiz., Oxford 1939, 14 sqq., etc. L. Homo, L'Italie primitive, Paris 1925, 140 sq., 146 sq., realizes the distortions of the annalists, but he celebrates nevertheless Early Rome as the mistress of the Latins. He writes, *ibid.* 162: "Les Etrusques avaient fait de Rome la base de leur domination dans le Latium et la ville avait exercé à ce titre une véritable hégémonie au sein du pays latin" and in the same sense p. 141: "Rome, grâce à sa situation exceptionnelle, va devenir la clef de voûte de l'Empire étrusque tout entier et pour la première fois dans l'histoire, s'essayer à son glorieux rôle de capitale d'une Italie unifiée." The idea that the Etruscans would yield the fruits of their bloody efforts to Rome and would install her as the ruling power in Italy is queer and absurd.

TOPOGRAPHICAL AND ARCHAEOLOGICAL REALITIES

Misinterpretations of this kind are, of course, no novelty at all. No less an authority than B. G. Niebuhr [1] asserted that the technical achievements of sixth-century Rome, such as the *cloaca maxima*, the Servian wall, and the Capitoline temple "are an irrefutable proof for the fact that the Rome of the last kings was the capital of a great commonwealth." Niebuhr's statement has been repeated by others again and again, *ad nauseam*. It is no longer necessary to enlarge upon the date of the great sewer, which is in reality much later than the age of the Tarquins; but a few remarks must be made on the date of two other great architectural achievements of Early Rome.

The testimony of the so-called Servian wall to the political pre-eminence of the Rome of the Tarquins, [2] as postulated by Niebuhr, [3] was even more overrated by later scholars. Beloch [4] holds that the size of its perimeter makes it certain that the city it surrounded was not only the largest of Latium in the sixth century but one of the biggest in the whole of Italy. Ed. Meyer [5] speaks of regal Rome enclosed by the wall as one of the largest cities of the Mediterranean world.

Since the days of these great historians archaeological investigations of the so-called Servian wall [6] have revealed the real date of this great fortification: it is the wall built with regularly hewn stone

[1] B. G. Niebuhr, RG 1², Berlin 1827, 410.
[2] The data on the literary sources are collected in A. Schwegler, RG 1, 727 sq.
[3] B. G. Niebuhr, RG 1², 410, echoed in A. Schwegler, RG 1, 730.
[4] J. Beloch, Der italische Bund, Leipzig 1880, 92. *Idem*, RG 230.
[5] Ed. Meyer, GdA 5, 1902, 134 sqq. *Idem*, Kleine Schriften 2, Halle 1924, 298 sqq. Cf. also : I. G. Scott, Mem. Am. Acad. Rome 7, 1929, 81 sqq. L. Wickert, Klio 31, 1938, 350. B. Combet-Farnoux, Mél. 69, 1957 (1958), 11 sqq. But there were scholars who rejected the annalist fiction even before the archaeological research cleared up the real situation, as did G. De Sanctis, St. d. R. 1¹, 1907, 392 sqq.=1², 380 sqq. ; cf. 2², 161. J. Binder, Die Plebs 1909, 81. A. Piganiol, Essai sur les origines de Rome, Paris 1916, 303 sq.
[6] Fundamental is the work of G. Saeflund, Le mura di Roma repubblicana (Acta Inst. Rom. Regni Sueciae 1), Lund 1932. Cf. G. Lugli, Historia (Milano-Roma) 7, 1933, 3 sqq. *Idem*, Roma antica, il centro monumentale, Roma 1946, 11 sq. F. Castagnoli, Topografia e urbanistica (Storia di Roma, vol. 22) 1958, 66. P. Quoniam, Mél. 59, 1947, 41 sqq., observed on the Aventine that the lowest layers of the Servian wall consist of soft tufa called *cappellaccio* whereas the upper ones are of the more resistent sort of the same stone, called *grotta oscura*, brought from the quarries of Veii. He considered this as evidence for two consequent building periods and his view was followed by A. Piganiol, Journal des Savants 1960, 23. But the most competent specialists did not accept this. Cf. G. Lugli, La tecnica edilicia 1, Roma 1957, 22. 186 sqq., 191, 204, 230 sq., 248, 250, 252, 255 sq., 258 sq., 268, 274, 277, 297. A. Boëthius, Palladio

blocks [1] after the Celtic storming of Rome, as the Annals duly recorded. And the material used for this huge fortress came from the outskirts of Veii; the Greek letters carved on them [2] attest that Greek architects were employed for this undertaking.

The identity of the "Servian" wall with the fortification system created after the conflagration of the Celtic attack was also fore-shadowed by the results of our second chapter.[3] We have demonstrated that the Aventine hill was still excluded from the territory of the city proper, when the grove of Diana became the federal sanctuary of the Latins some time after the battle at Lake Regillus; after 456 B.C. when the Aventine became the stronghold of the *plebs*, it remained never-theless outside the sacred boundary line of the urban area, the *pome-rium*, preserving the freedom of association for the revolutionary organization of the plebeians, which could remain immune only outside the legal sphere of police control of the state. At the time of building the Servian wall, however, the Aventine, though left *extra pomerium*, was included in the new stronghold to protect the seat of

(Riv. Stor. Architett.) 1958, no. 1, 3. E. Gjerstad, Studies Robinson 1, 1951, 412 sqq. *Idem*, Bull. Com. 73, 1949-50, 29 sqq. *Idem*, Opuscula Romana 1 (Acta Inst. Rom. Regni Sueciae 18) 1954, 50 sqq. and 3, 1960, 69 sqq., would like to date the earthen rampart behind the wall into the fifth century B.C. on the basis of an Attic sherd found in it, and because of the stone masonry in the decades after the Celtic storm. Concerning the date of the sherd in question, I am permitted to quote the expert opinion of E. Paribeni : "The cup fragment from the *agger* is so tiny and the cup must have been so poor as to justify such an uncommon vague datation by Beazly as between 520 and 470 B.C. I must say I would be prepared to take the plunge and decide for 490 B.C. which is what J. D. Beazley himself thinks more probable. As far as I am able to see on the picture, the cup should have been an uncommonly bad specimen of that very large and very poor group of the 'Pithos painter' and his companions." As A. v. Gerkan, Rh. Mus. n. F. 100, 1957, 92 sqq., pointed out, this sherd was buried in the area of the wall, before the wall was built and it can offer only a vague *terminus post quem*. See also F. Castagnoli, Bull. Com. 77, 1959-60 (1961), 7 (of the reprint). E. Gjerstad, Early Rome 3, Lund 1960, 27 sqq. A. v. Gerkan, Rh. Mus. n. F. 104, 1961, 135 sqq.

[1] DH III 67, 4, characterizes the stone blocks of the wall he ascribes to Tarquinius Priscus as built of λίθοις ἁμαξιαίοις εἰργασμένοις πρὸς κανόνα ; but these regularly hewn blocks are just those of the fourth-century wall, con-structed with *saxo quadrato*, cf. Liv. VI 32, 1-2 ; VII 20, 9.

[2] G. Saeflund, *op. cit.* 105, fig. 41. G. Lugli, La tecn. edil. 204. The large size of the area included within the new wall may be partly due to the habitual wartime precaution to drive the herds of cattle into the city when looting hostile bands appeared ; cf. Liv. III 6, 2 : *terrore populationis pecora agrestesque in urbem accepti*.

[3] Cf. above, p. 90 sqq.

the *plebs* in the same way as all the other parts of the community. This inclusion of the hill in the stone rampart, involving heavy additional effort and cost in a time of distress, would have been superfluous for the annual conventions of the League, which did not meet in wartime at all. It was the more necessary after the establishment of the revolutionary center in that very area and the accommodation of the *plebs* with the ruling patrician group, i.e., since the decemvirate. But the Volscian and Aequian menace being already at low ebb in the second half of the fifth century, the great effort of the wall construction, which certainly included particular prehistoric fortifications at different points of Rome, became an urgent task only after the capture of Rome by the Celts—some hundred and fifty years after the date given to the rule of Servius Tullius in the Annals.

The Etruscan kings, residing on the Capitoline Hill, had a concept of defense very different from such an overall stone wall around the whole city. This older conception is still preserved in the Roman ritual language of later times. We mean the solemn formula "citadel and town," *arx et urbs*, corresponding to the expression *ocar* and *tota* of the Umbrian tablets from *Eugubium*-Gubbio.[1] The *arx* was the only fortified stronghold, where the population took refuge in times of war, as in Athens in the same epoch.[2] The old system of partial defense was still in existence at the time of the Celtic invasion. After the crushing defeat of the Roman army at the river Allia the city lay open to the mercy of the wild enemy.[3] It has been rightly stressed that the invaders did not have at the beginning of the fourth century the technical equipment and training to besiege a fortified city, and that the Romans would in no case have given up their homes if the city wall had been there already. There was no alternative, indeed, in the circumstances to abandoning the mass of the inhabitants —seeking refuge where they could—to their fate and admitting to the citadel only those men capable of defending it, and with them the governing circles. It was also due, no doubt, to a correct decision that the survivors of the Allia battle were ordered to assemble in the stronghold of Veii.[4]

---

[1] Paul. Fest., 102, 11 L.: *Lapidem silicem tenebant iuraturi per Iovem, haec verba dicentes*: "*Si sciens fallo, tum me Dispiter salva urbe arceque bonis eiciat, ut ego hunc lapidem.*" Cf. U. Coli, Il diritto pubblico di Umbri, Milano 1959, 81, 83 sqq.

[2] As A. v. Gerkan, *loc. cit.*, has already observed.

[3] Cf. J. B. Carter, Proc. Amer. Philos. Soc. 48, 1909, 130 sqq.

[4] Fr. Schachermeyr, Klio 23, 1930, 300 sqq. The Annals glorifying the

The "*Grande Roma dei Tarquinii*"

All this evidence combines to show that the mighty wall, *inter prima opus mirabile*,[1] had nothing to do with the kings. Its imposing perimeter reveals, accordingly, the extent of Rome after the substantial growth of the fifth century.

The grandiose temple of *Juppiter optimus maximus* is universally taken as evidence of considerable prosperity. Before we begin a close examination of the date of origin of this magnificence, a warning against the light-hearted acceptance of appearances seems to me necessary. If we knew nothing, for example, of the strength and extent of the power of Augustus, of Septimius Severus, and of Diocletian respectively, and knew only the exact measurements of their houses on the Palatine and elsewhere, we could conclude in the same way as is usually done with the Capitol that the greater the buildings of those rulers were, the mightier they were. The measurements would deceive us. Yet far more revealing than such theoretical considerations is the well-established fact that Veii, at the time of her capture by the Romans, i.e., about 400 B.C., still surpassed her oppressor in respect of the proportions and beauty of architecture. The common citizen wished to migrate to Veii, superior in this respect to Rome, as their spokesman states in Livy:[2] *cum pulcherrima urbs Veii agerque Veientanus in conspectu sit, uberior ampliorque Romano agro? Urbem quoque urbi Romae vel situ vel magnificentia publicorum privatorumque tectorum ac locorum praeponebant.*

But a closer look into the available source material shows again that we cannot take the account of the Annals at its face value.

The origins of the Capitoline sanctuary go back as far as the sixth century B.C.: no doubt can arise about this. The 204 annual nails driven in the wall of the *cella* of Jupiter, which were counted in 304 B.C., make it certain that it was consecrated in 509 B.C. The participation of Veientan artists who furnished its plastic decoration and cult statues is well established; archaeological remains from the archaic epoch corroborate this early date.[3] But is there conclusive

Etruscan kings for the great technical achievements of the wall construction could not admit that the city stood unprotected. But they disclose the truth when they pretend that the gates were left open in the chaos (Liv. V 38, 10 ; 41, 4. Plut., *Camill.* 22, 1. Flor. I 7, 14. Serv., *Aen.* 8, 652. Oros. 2, 19, 7. Zonar. 7, 23 (p. 154 Dind.) or that the Celts broke the gates open without being molested (Diod. XIV 115).

[1] Plin., *N.h.* III 5, 67, calls the wall *agger Tarquinii Superbi.*
[2] Liv. V 24, 6.
[3] R. Paribeni, N. Sc. 1921, 38 sqq. G. Lugli, Roma antica, il centro monu-

evidence for the fact that this first sanctuary of the regal age was as large as the temple burned in 83 B.C. and as its successors were? The Annals assert this,[1] and illustrate the splendor of regal Rome with its size; the moderns follow them. Yet we have good reason to be more cautious.

Fortunately enough our information on this topic is far superior to most other questions of early Roman history. In the first place, the literary tradition has preserved some basic facts concerning this principal sanctuary of the Eternal City. The first writer of the Annals knew a short account of the exploits of the last king.[2] Though we can give no credit to the alleged capture of Suessa Pometia from the Volscians by King Superbus,[3] who is said to have built the temple of *Juppiter optimus maximus* from the booty of that city, we cannot doubt the fact that he constructed the temple itself; nor can we doubt the participation in it of Veientan artists who furnished the terra-cotta cult statues and plastic decorations of the same kind for it.[4]

There are secondary modifications in this pre-annalistic tradition of the architectonic origins of the Capitoline temple, which are arbitrary. They are due in the first instance to Fabius Pictor. He knew that another Tarquin existed in Rome and, using one of his usual devices, he duplicated the tale of his source on the construction of the Capitoline shrine [5] by the last Tarquin, in transferring part of this building program to the elder ruler of the same Etruscan dynasty.[6] But no

mentale, 19 sq. M. Cagiano de Azevedo, in Mem. Pont. Acc. 5, 1940, 1 sqq. A. Boëthius, Gnomon 25, 1953, 407 sqq. A. Andrén, Rend. Pont. Acc. 32, 1959-60, 21 sqq., 45, 56. E. Gjerstad, Early Rome 3, 1960, 27 sq., 168 sqq., 177 sqq. (size).

[1] The source material is collected by A. Schwegler, RG 1, 674 n. 6 ; 771 sqq. n. 1 sqq.

[2] Cf. above, p. 78 sq. and p. 139 sq. The role of Pictor is revealed in Liv. I 55, 7-9.

[3] Cic., *De re publ.* II 20, 36 ; 24, 44. *Idem, Verr.* V 19, 48. DH III 69, 1-2 ; IV 50, 2-5 ; 59, 1-2 ; V 35, 3. Liv. I 53, 1-3 ; 55, 1. 7-9. Strab. V 3, 4 (C. 231). Plin., *N.h.* III 5, 70 ; VIII 42, 161. Tac., *Hist.* 3, 72. Plut., *Poplic.* 14, 1 sqq. Cass. Dio *fr.* 11, 5 Boiss. Serv., *Aen.* 9, 446.

[4] Plin., *N.h.* XXXV 12, 157 ; XXVIII 2, 16. Fest., p. 340, 31 L. Serv., *Aen.* 7, 188. Liv. I 56, 1. Plut., *Poplic.* 13, 1-3.

[5] I. Scott Ryberg, Mem. Am. Ac. 7, 1929, 14, has already called our attention to the systematical repetitions in the Annals which engendered double records on the erection of important temples.

[6] The Volscian city, from the booty of which the elder Tarquin is said to have drawn the sums for his building enterprise, is called *Apiola*, Plin., *N.h.* III 5, 70. Strab. *l.c.* E. Pais recognized in this name the translation of *Pometia*. The translation into Greek makes it certain that the author of this deceit wrote

one doubts today that in the original source there was only one king mentioned who accomplished the whole task. There are also some archaeological remnants which may belong to the original sanctuary of the last king: a frieze and terra-cotta fragments of an antefix. Over and above them, we know the exact date of the inauguration. The solemn practice in which the leading magistrate drove a nail into the right wall of the *cella Jovis* every year on the day of the dedication had produced in the year 304 B.C. two hundred and four of these "annual nails." [1] This figure attests the year 509 B.C. for the first performance of this rite. At the same time it becomes evident that in 304 B.C. at least the wall just indicated in the interior still existed.

But here we must ask whether this also means that the whole structure rose at once at the end of the sixth century in the mighty proportions known to later generations. In general the archaic temples in the Etruscan cities which ruled over Rome in that epoch are smaller; only in much later times do sanctuaries of comparable dimensions emerge, such as the late fourth century B.C. temple in Tarquinii called "Ara della Regina." [2] Rome hardly took the initiative in this magnificence; and we have some evidence for a partial reconstruction of the Capitoline temple after the Celtic siege.

Roman historians of later times admit that the Celts once penetrated as far as the peak of the Capitoline hill, but usually pretend that they were instantly rebuked and the temple remained intact with the whole citadel. [3] But it has been shown quite recently [4] that another old tradition has been overlooked, which attests heavy fighting on the

---

in Greek, and Pictor is the only serious possibility for this trick. Cf. above, p. 140.

[1] Liv. VII 3, 4-8 : *ea religione adductus senatus dictatorem clavi figendi causa dici iussit . . . . . lex vetusta est, priscis litteris verbisque dicta, ut qui praetor maximus sit, idibus Septembribus clavum pangat ; fixa fuit dextro lateri aedis Iovis optimi maximi, ex qua parte Minervae templum est. eum clavum, quia rarae per ea tempora litterae erant, notam numeri annorum fuisse ferunt eoque Minervae templo dicatam legem, quia numerus Minervae inventum sit. Volsiniis quoque clavos indices numeri annorum fixos in templo Nortiae, Etruscae deae, comparere diligens talium monumentorum auctor Cincius adfirmat. Horatius consul ea lege templum Iovis optimi maximi dedicavit*, etc. Cf. above, p. 78 sq.

[2] P. Romanelli, Bollettino d'Arte 33, 1948, 54 sqq. *Idem*, N. Sc. 1948, 193 sqq. A. Andrén, Rend. Pont. Acc. 321, 1960, 30 sqq.

[3] Cf., e.g., Claud. Quadrig. fr. 7 (vol. 1², 206 Peter). Liv. I 53, 9; VI 40, 17. Ovid., *Fasti* 1, 453 sqq. Tac., *Hist*. 3, 72. Aug., *Civ. Dei* 3, 29, etc.

[4] O. Skutsch, JRS 43, 1953, 76 sqq. His result was rejected by J. Wolski, Historia 5, 1956, 44 sqq., without due consideration.

Capitol or even its capture by the Celtic host.[1] The complete occupation of the citadel is out of question because in this case the Senate and the magistrates would have perished and the vigorous rise of Rome from her ruins and the quick recovery of her power would have been impossible. However, if it was not the actual capture of the citadel, as Ennius asserts, but only a bloody, desperate struggle on the hilltop, this can be taken for granted: the poet certainly did not invent such disgraceful developments. The cackling of the geese of Juno, a story confirmed by an old popular procession, rewarding their vigilance and punishing the silence of the watchdogs, reveals a break-through on the citadel, but the sanctuary, also involved in the battle,[2] is only a cockstride from there.

Everyone acquainted with the work of excavation knows that wholesale firebrands mark every such invasion. The Romans themselves report the combustion of the city,[3] and the shrines were not at all exempt from the ordeal.[4] Firebrands were a powerful weapon against a besieged garrison, and the wooden structure of the upper parts of a Tuscan temple like the Capitol became very easily the prey of flames.

In any case, something had happened here because some years later the area around the temple of the Capitoline triad received new substructures in squared stones—an imposing piece of work even in the eyes of the Augustan age.[5] It is evident that these supporting walls, part of the new post-Celtic defensive wall system, are the same

---

[1] Enn., *Ann.* fr. 164 Vahlen : *qua Galli furtim noctu summa arcis adorti | moenia concubia vigilesque repente cruentant.* Verg., *Aen.* 8, 657 : *Galli per dumos aderant arcemque tenebant.* Sil. Ital., *Pun.* 1, 625 sqq. : *Gallisque ex arce fugatis | arma reverentis pompa gestata Camilli.* 4, 150 sq. : *ipse tumens atavis Brenni se stirpe ferebat/Crixus et in titulos Capitolia capta trahebat.* 6, 555 sq. : *Allia et infandi Senones captaeque recursat | attonitis arcis facies.*

[2] Cf., e.g., DH XIII 7, 3. Plut., *De fort. Rom.* 12. The evidence for the popular procession was given by A. Schwegler, RG 3, 1858, 259 n. 3.

[3] The references to the sources were compiled by A. Schwegler, RG 3, 253.

[4] Plut., *Camill.* 31, 1 : χαλεπῶς μὲν οὖν καὶ μόλις αἱ τῶν ἱερῶν ἀνεκαλύπτοντο χῶραι φιλοτιμίᾳ τοῦ Καμίλλου καὶ πόνῳ πολλῷ τῶν ἱεροφαντῶν. Liv. V 50, 1-2 : *omnium primum . . . quae ad deos immortalis pertinebant, retulit et senatus consultum facit* (Camillus), *fana omnia, quoad ea hostis possedisset, restituerentur, terminarentur expiarenturque, expiatioque eorum in libris per duumviros quaereretur.* There is also archaeological evidence : E. Gjerstad, *op. cit.* 1, 75, 78 ; 3, 220, 294, 354.

[5] Liv. VI 4, 12 (388 B.C.) : *Eodem anno . . . Capitolium quoque saxo quadrato substructum est, opus vel in hac magnificentia urbis conspiciendum.* Plin., *N.h.* XXXVI 15, 104 : *sed tum senes . . . substructiones Capitolii mirabantur.* Cf. E. Gjerstad, *op. cit.* 3, 27 sqq.

"The Grande Roma dei Tarquinii"

as those attributed by Fabius Pictor to Tarquin the Elder.[1] The new
and certainly enlarged *area Capitolina* provided the idea and the possibility for the propitiatory games which were celebrated by the Romans
before the temple of the Supreme God in gratitude for the overcoming
of the Celtic danger.[2]

But the temple also was restored at the same time. Cn. Flavius, who
in 304 B.C. counted the 204 nails in the *cella* of Jupiter, and his
followers believed that the M. Horatius whose name they read on
the architrave of the temple was the magistrate who had dedicated
it in 509 B.C.[3] We know now that in that year either the last king was
still in power or Porsenna had chased him away, subjugating the
Romans with an iron fist: there is in neither case room for a Roman
republican magistrate. There was, however, another M. Horatius
who could again consecrate the sanctuary after its restoration in the
years following the Celtic disaster. This was the *tribunus militum consu-*

---

[1] DH III 69, 1-2 : Ἐνεχείρησε δὲ καὶ τὸν νεὼν κατασκευάζειν τοῦ τε Διὸς καὶ
τῆς Ἥρας καὶ τῆς Ἀθηνᾶς ὁ βασιλεὺς οὗτος ... τὸν μὲν ... λόφον, ἐφ' οὗ τὸ ἱερὸν
ἔμελλεν ἱδρύεσθαι, πολλῆς δεόμενον πραγματείας .... ἀναλήμμασιν ὑψηλοῖς
πολλαχόθεν περιλαβὼν καὶ πολὺν χοῦν εἰς τὸ μεταξὺ τῶν τε ἀναλημμάτων καὶ τῆς
κορυφῆς ἐμφορήσας, ὁμαλὸν γενέσθαι παρεσκεύασε καὶ πρὸς ἱερῶν ὑποδοχὴν ἐπι-
τηδειότατον. Cf. also Liv. I 38, 7 : *et aream ad aedem in Capitolio Iovis, quam voverat
bello Sabino, iam praesagiente animo futuram olim amplitudinem loci occupat funda-
mentis.* What Livy calls *saxo quadrato* corresponds to the λίθοις . . εἰργασμένοις
πρὸς κανόνα in DH III 67, 4, on the wall built by King Priscus, evidently the
same thing, as we saw it in connection with the date of the "Servian" wall.

[2] Liv. V 50, 4, mentions it too early, under 390 B.C. : (*rettulit Camillus et
senatus consultum facit, ut) ludi Capitolini fierent, quod Iuppiter optimus maximus suam
sedem atque arcem populi Romani in re trepida tutatus esset collegiumque ad eam rem
M. Furius dictator constitueret ex eis, qui in Capitolio atque arce habitarent.* 52, 11 :
*Capitolinos ludos sollemnibus aliis addidimus collegiumque ad id novum auctore senatu
condidimus.* Cf. Tert., *De spect.* 5, where these games are retroprojected in the
mythical age : *Romulus Iovi Feretrio ludos instituit in Tarpeio, quos Tarpeios dictos et
Capitolinos Piso tradidit.* The *collegium* constituted by the state for this purpose
became obsolete in the time of the late Republic ; but the state maintained it
as a religious obligation for the organization of the Capitoline games, and
appointed for its management a president in common with the analogous
associations of the *pagani Aventinenses, Mercuriales,* and the brotherhood of the
Luperci. Cic., *Ad Q. fr.* II 5, 2. CIL I² 1004 (with penetrating remarks by
Mommsen). XIV 2105. The chariot racing on the Capitol during the days of
the *Feriae Latinae* reported in Plin., *N.h.* XXVII 7, 45, was also held on the
area Capitolina, of course ; *pace* K. Latte, Röm. Religionsgesch. 146 n. 1.

[3] References given in : A. Schwegler, RG 2, 51. Fr. Münzer, RE 8, 2401 sqq.,
who is wrong in supposing that M. Horatius' name was taken from the original
fasti. O. Leuze, Die römische Jahreszählung, Tübingen 1909, 325 sqq. K. J.
Beloch, RG 35 sqq.

lari potestate of 378 B.C.[1] Though the authorities began the rebuilding of the city with reconstruction of the shrines [2] immediately after the agreement and the withdrawal of the Celtic host, the devastation was so great and the urgent need to protect the city in a more efficient way brought such a strain on all forces, that even the new city wall was finished only after several decades. It is a reasonable guess, however, that the citadel (including the new substructures of the Capitol) was reconstructed first, so as to give to the city the same sort of partial protection as she had before, and that only then the building of the wall began. This supposition is fully supported by a note of the Annals to the year 378 in Livy (VI 32, 1) that the allocation of the wall construction by the censors was made just at this time: *murum a censoribus locatum, saxo quadrato faciundum*. If our assumption is right, the Capitol was just finished and could be rededicated.

The Celtic storm did not hamper the ambitions of Rome to rule over Latium; now she was really struggling for hegemony. The drive for greatness and ambitious magnificence belong together, and if the temple finished in 509 was of a more modest size, a program of aggrandizement could have been at no moment more appropriate than in 378. The decision lies with the archaeologists. And as Frank Brown, an authority in this matter, is preparing a thorough survey of all the remnants and all the protocols of modern excavations, it is to be hoped that the great puzzle will soon be solved.

The might of the last Tarquin, as inferred from the measurements of the Capitol, engendered another illusion. The stone substructure on top of the *mons Albanus* gave the impression of a platform for a temple like that on the Capitoline hill. It has been suggested that on this presumed stone basement on the *Monte Cavo* a replica of the Roman sanctuary of Jupiter was built under King Superbus. A great scholar has gone even a step further: [3] he took the supposed con-

[1] Mommsen, RF 2, 28, followed by Fr. Münzer, RE 7, 928 and 8, 2327, 5, thought that the names of M. Horatius and L. Geganius must be spurious, because Diodor XV 57, 1, does not mention them in 378 with the four others registered also by Livy VI 31, 1. This is, however, inadmissible : no later Horatius occurs in the *fasti* and only one Geganius in 367. Consequently, there was nobody there in the third and second centuries who would have had an interest in smuggling additional names of his clan into the lists. Therefore we must retain their names as T. R. S. Broughton does , MRR 1, 107 ; cf. A. Degrassi, Inscr. It. XIII 1, 102.   [2] Cf. above, p. 326 n. 4

[3] H. Jordan, Topographie d. Stadt Rom I 2, 9. G. Wissowa, RuK², 39 sq., 124 sq. J. Vogt, Die römische Republik², Freiburg 1951, 29 sq., and others.

gruency and the equally supposed contemporaneity of the two temples of Jupiter in Rome and on the Alban Mountain as proof of the founding of the Latin Festival by the last Tarquin, as alleged by the Annals. But no one today believes that an archaic temple stood on the sacred mountain of the Latins.

It is obvious that the actual remains of the monumental architecture of that early period cannot be as numerous and as intact in the area of the Eternal City as on neighboring sites in Latium, which were already decayed in antiquity and have not been built over since then. We must fully recognize the fact that the continuous building activity of twenty-five hundred years in Rome destroyed innumerable terra-cotta revetments with other architectural decorations which were kept unharmed in fields of ruins, already abandoned in antiquity. But the immensely superior intensity of the research done in Rome over the exploration of the sites of famous Latin strongholds compensates the loss just indicated; and so a comparison between early Rome and her neighbors, as mirrored by the excavations and finds, is nevertheless justified.

Caution is, of course, needed. If the terra-cotta revetments found in Rome are neither inferior nor superior to those of other sites in Southern Etruria and Latium, this is due to the existence of common artistic and distribution centers. On the other hand, an essential part of these architectural terra-cottas do not testify to the superior power of the Tarquins in Rome, as was believed, but to its continuous flourishing in the fifth century B.C.,[1] a period the importance of which tends to be underestimated.

Taking into account these and other considerations, which forbid the direct equation of the testimony of actual remains with historical developments, the archaeological evidence offers in general a reliable picture of the cultural level and the specific character of the civilization of the Rome of the Etruscan kings, as compared with her environment.

"In the eighth, seventh and sixth centuries"—we quote the conclusions of Inez Scott Ryberg, whose invaluable survey has given us a real insight into these situations and evolutions[2] —"the finds

[1] R. Bloch, R. Et. Lat. 37, 1959, 121, 123 f. P. J. Riis-E. Gjerstad, Op. Rom. 3, 1960, 88 sq.

[2] I. Scott Ryberg, An Archaeological Record of Rome from the Seventh to the Second Century B.C. (Studies and Documents ed. by K. Lake and S. Lake XIII 1) London-Philadelphia 1940, 202 sqq. Besides this important synopsis

of pottery, bronzes and other objects show that Rome was part of a rather closely-knit cultural unit in the lower Tiber valley, including the southern neck of Etruria, Faliscan territory and the region of Latium between the Alban Hills and the Tiber. Within this cultural circle Rome was a peripheral point, an outpost rather than a center, affected by importation and local adaptation of wares and fashions from a few southern Etruscan centers and even more from Faliscan towns, but contributing little or nothing to their invention. Rome was largely a passive participant in the flourishing trade which was carried on among the towns within this area and she offered little market for the more expensive articles of luxury which Etruscan merchants were supplying in some abundance to the Faliscans."
"While the finds of pottery and bronze objects associate Rome particularly with Southern Etruria and Faliscan territory, the architectural terra-cottas are of types which occur commonly at Satricum, Praeneste, Velitrae and Lanuvium, as well as at Falerii and, less frequently, at Caere. Roman burials are poor in comparison with Etruscan and Faliscan tombs, but the surviving fragments of terracotta revetments are of considerable variety and equal in quality to those found at other sites . . . Fragments from various sites in Rome attest the construction in the sixth and early fifth centuries of some fifteen temples." [1]

"Rome was slower than Praeneste and Satricum to absorb the Etruscan culture which was spreading over all of central Italy in the seventh century B.C. and at no time shows evidence of the wealth displayed in the two rich chamber tombs of Praeneste, or of the flourishing trade in Greek and Italogeometric pottery attested by the votive deposit at Satricum." [2] Mrs. Ryberg tries to explain this,[3] as did T. Frank and others, with the Roman prejudice against luxury, censured in the Twelve Tables, with agrarian conservatism, preferring

cf. also a previous account in : Mem. Am. Ac. 7, 1929, 21 sqq., testing the literary accounts with the help of the archaeological discoveries. Since 1940, the archaeological material has been growing steadily, but the overall picture presented by Mrs. Ryberg remains valid. The most recent up-to-date registration and discussion of all finds in Rome is the voluminous work by E. Gjerstad now in progress : Early Rome 1, 1953 ; 2, 1956; 3, 1960.

[1] I. Scott Ryberg, An Archaeol. Record 203. The latest general survey of the architectural remains is presented by G. Lugli, La tecnica edilizia 1957, 245 sqq.

[2] I. Scott Ryberg, *ibid*. 5.

[3] *Ibid*. 49 sqq.

a frugal and simple standard of life to the Etruscan delight in gorgeous pomp and effeminating comfort, concentrating the attention of the community on valor and conquest—an ideal still glorified by later generations.

Yet the *prisca simplicitas*, the frugal way of life of Roman shepherds and husbandmen in those early days, does not tell us the whole story. The Etruscan rulers of Rome with their retinues and hangers-on living in the *vicus Tuscus*, the Etruscan quarters at the foot of the Capitol, as well as the Etruscan clans of the aristocracy shared, naturally, the Etruscan ideals of magnificence and exuberant pleasures. The Romans themselves realized that their civilization was lagging behind the times. This is manifest in their eager acceptance of urban life, religious concepts, and the state organization of their Etruscan overlords. Other Latin cities were quicker in their assimilation to the higher culture of their conquerors: even small Gabii east of Rome was in the early epoch superior in civilization—the Romans were still aware in later times that their noble youth were sent preferably to Gabii for higher education.[1]

The two ways of thinking, Etruscan and Roman, though markedly different, were also blended. The nobleman cavalry of the Tarquins, e.g., went into battle naked to the waist instead of covered with heavy armor like the Greeks. Yet the same highly conservative ruling class which resisted the introduction of coined money until the conflict with Carthage and based its fortune on its herds of cattle, accepted nonetheless the Etruscan array of pomp in triumphal processions, in the gala costume and attributes which distinguished magistrates and patricians alike from the rest of society. State organization, public life, and religious concepts of Rome were greatly influenced by the Etruscans; the whole technical civilization was Etruscan. The *mos maiorum*, "the way of life of the ancestors," was in reality in the early Republic something very different from what it seemed to the nostalgia of the elderly Cato for the Old Franconian simplicity of olden days.

The primitive features of early Roman life as compared with the greater cultural progress of her neighbors are not due, therefore, to a conscious reaction against foreign luxury—we will soon see striking proofs of this—but to the backward state of her evolution. The ar-

[1] DH I 84, 5. Plut., *Rom.* 6, 2. *Idem, De fort. Rom.* 8. *Origo gentis Rom.* 21, 3 Steph. Byz. *s.v.* Τάβιοι *(sic !)*.

chaeological evidence which reveals this corresponds to the historical picture we obtain by eliminating the ficticious grandeur of the Annals which obscured by their pyrotechnics the real beginnings of the ascent of Rome—not so spectacular as their picture, but more impressive in the enormous effort which brought forth fruit only after a protracted, tenacious struggle first for survival and then for power.

The overestimation of the flourishing of Etruscan Rome has a corollary in the undervaluation of the Early Republic, again under the spell of Fabius Pictor and his followers.

At the very moment when the real history of Rome starts with the consular lists and the meager notes added to them, the imaginary empire of the Tarquins vanishes instantly, and the reader of the Annals is dropped without any transition from that glorious castle in the air into the sober atmosphere of a Latin community of moderate size—like somebody awakening in a grey everyday morning after a night spent in carousal. Though our sources give no indication of such a reversal, and therefore no explanation of it can occur in them, modern historians interpret the sudden disappearance of the ruling position of Rome as a total collapse after 509 B.C.[1] In the picture painted by them, the city shrivels up to a tiny little point in the outskirts of the Mediterranean world.

The archaeological documentation seemed to justify this picture. A brilliant French savant, struck by the supposed lack of imported Greek vases in the fifth century, based on it a new theory, a theory much exploited by others: Rome, reduced to poverty and insignificance, resolutely renounced such foreign luxuries—so it was thought—and became absorbed in her struggle for existence and her new political structure. This view seemed to be supported by the survey of the archaeological evidence of this epoch. It is a fact that in the whole of Latium, and not only in Rome, new types of pottery are missing, archaic forms remain prevalent, and Greek imports decrease markedly everywhere.[2] This cannot surprise us. The situation of Latium in the sixth century under Etruscan rule was more stable and favorable

---

[1] It is sufficient to quote the opinion of a few distinguished scholars: A. Schwegler, RG 2, 203. M. Gelzer, RE 12, 952. G. Wissowa, RuK² 51. L. Homo, L'Italie primitive, Paris 1925, 163. G. Pasquali, La nuova antologia 386, 1936, 416, and others.

[2] A. Blakeway, JRS 25, 1935, 136 n. 26. I. Scott Ryberg, An Archaeol. Record, 51 sqq., 74 sqq., 79.

than after its dissolution, with ceaseless local wars under the great pressure of mountain tribes.

But the supposed lacuna of Greek imports is no longer there. E. Paribeni has unearthed in the magazines of the "Antiquario del Foro Romano" almost 250 Greek potsherds, excavated long ago and listed with his usual care and accuracy by the excellent Boni. These sherds range in time from the eighth century B.C. to the fourth, in a continuous chain; the products of no major Attic workshop of the fifth century are missing.[1] This is a dramatic turn in our appraisal of the historical evolution with which we are concerned. A second observation—already touched upon—helps to clear up the prospect. Part of the terra-cotta revetments, adduced usually for the illustration of the might of the Tarquins, was produced, as has recently been proved,[2] only after their fall. They were made for the decoration of sanctuaries built in the course of the fifth century. The uninterrupted building program of state temples, of which the Annals register the votive offering to the gods concerned as well as their consecration, is, generally speaking, verified by the fifth century date of these plastic terra-cotta fragments. There was no hiatus, no breakdown, in the first century of the Republic.

The overvaluation of the sixth century by Roman historiography and the underestimation of the fifth by the moderns has had another consequence. It is assumed, quite generally I think, that the expansion of Rome after the expulsion of the Tarquins was only the gradual recovery of her lost hegemony, the complete repetition of a process which had run its course already. This view is untenable.

The conquest of Latium by the Romans in the two centuries after the patricians took over the government was the result of a very slow and tenacious struggle, the phases and the progress of which can be, in the main, reliably grasped from the Annals, even if many details are lacking and others distorted. We have no reason whatsoever to assume that the tedious, prolonged process of the subjugation of the Latins was nothing but the *regaining* of possessions conquered by the kings, whose portentous realm should have vanished with them as by a stroke of the magican's wand. We know by now that the Rome of the Tarquins was a flourishing Latin community,

---

[1] E. Paribeni, Bull. Com. 76, 1959, 3 sqq. Attic red-figure sherds from the Palatine are inventorized by E. Gjerstad, Early Rome 3, fig. 88 and p. 130.
[2] Cf. R. Bloch, R. Et. Lat. 37, 1959, 121, 123 sqq.

dependent on Etruscan balance of power and on her Etruscan neighbors, but not yet an independent sovereign state. After the period of the kings there were certainly great crises to overcome, but the firm foundations of a great future had already been laid.

The reason why the Etruscans did not try again to recover Latium and allowed the land bridge from their mother country to Campania to be lost must be looked for in their new great adventure, the colonization of the Po Valley. This enormous, highly successful enterprise seems to have tied down all their forces. In this way the Latin cities, as well as their Volscian, Aequian, and Hernican neighbors, left to their fate by the Etruscans, could embark unimpeded on their bloody contest for supremacy in Latium.

The unceasing local wars in the Latin countryside appeared to be ridiculous little skirmishes to the Romans after they had conquered the whole civilized world. "Hitherto they had fought for their freedom," writes L. Annaeus Florus [1] in the heyday of the Empire concerning the beginning of the Republic. "Hereafter they became involved in an unremitting and ceaseless war with the same Latins, fighting to their boundaries. *Cora*—it sounds unbelievable—and *Alsium* were formidable. *Satricum* and *Corniculum* were attributed to our magistrates as the districts of their jurisdiction (*provinciae*)! Over *Verulae* and *Bovillae*—I am ashamed, but—we triumphed. On *Tibur*, now a suburban residence for us, and *Praeneste*, now our delightful summer resort, we marched after the solemn vows of the general in the Capitol were performed. *Faesulae* meant then the same to us, as *Carrhae* recently. The grove of *Aricia* was then as nowadays the Hercynian Forest in Germany, *Fregellae* was as *Gesoriacum* (Boulogne-sur-Mer) today; the Tiber corresponded for those generations to the Euphrates in the present day. It was so glorious an exploit—I am again ashamed—to earn a victory over *Corioli*, that Cnaeus Marcius added this city as a title of fame to his name, being called henceforward *Coriolanus*, as though he had conquered Numantia (in Spain), or Africa. Spoils won from Antium still exist, fixed upon the tribunal of the Forum, after the capture of the fleet of this enemy,—if it can be called a fleet, for it consisted of only six beaked ships; yet in those early days six ships were enough for a war at sea."

In the reality of the young Republic, however, this assiduous

[1] Flor. I 5, 5-10.

conduct of wars in the vicinity, which seems so comical to Florus, was a deadly serious fight for the very subsistence of the Latin communities. These unceasing wars were the ordeal in which the leadership of Rome over the rest of the Latins was established. She was growing under this concentric pressure, and when this pressure from outside was overcome, nothing could challenge her supremacy in Latium, nor her expansion from this new and broader platform.

Chapter VIII

THE ASCENT OF ROME DURING THE EARLY REPUBLIC

The simplest way to illustrate the gradual rise of the might of Rome in the one and a half centuries after the flight of the Tarquins is, it seems to me, to show the development of her relations with neighboring peoples and foreign countries. During the greater part of the fifth century the Latins were occupied with the struggle against the mountain tribes; at the same time Rome was accomplishing the first modest steps of expansion in her own surroundings. The increased pace of her growth after the Celtic storm, however, soon had its affect on the spheres of interest of the major powers in the Mediterranean world, arousing hostility in some states, and sympathy in their adversaries. The main actors on the stage of Latian history in that epoch therefore must be introduced one by one, if only briefly.

336

ੴ

SOUTHERN ETRURIA AND ROME AFTER THE KINGS

The conquest of Rome by Porsenna and the defeat of his host at Aricia [1] brought about a real change in the history of Latium. In the sixth century, as we have seen, the free interplay of forces among the cities of Southern Etruria competing for markets and for power decided the political situation of the flourishing new city of Rome. But now, after Aristodemus of Cyme had crushed the offensive power of Clusium, the Latins of the Alban Hills, and south of them the Volscians, sweeping down from their mountains to the Pomptine plain, blocked direct access by land for Etruscan commerce with Campania across Latium. Porsenna was constrained to make his peace with the Romans. Our sources are completely reticent on all the consequences of these great events, but it seems to me reasonable to assume that the lasting peace (*pax fida*) between Porsenna and the Romans enabled the latter to hold their own against the Latins at Lake Regillus, a few years after the shock of their subjugation.

There are in fact indications of a continuing alliance between Clusium and Rome. One of the versions explaining the origin of the *vicus Tuscus* situated under the Capitoline hill assumes that this Etruscan settlement consisted of the remnants of Porsenna's army which fled back to Rome after the disaster at Aricia. This cannot be historical: as soon as the Etruscan king established his seat on the top of the Capitoline hill, his retinue doubtless settled down next to him on the slope beneath. But it does prove the point that the annalist from whom this statement came was convinced of the long-term connection of the city with the king.

More important than this belief is a specific fact. After the three forged pairs of consuls at the beginning of the *fasti*, "the list of magistrates," the names of *Spurius Larcius* and *Titus Herminius* are given as consuls for the year 506 and *Titus Larcius* is stated to have been the first dictator in 501 B.C.[2] These three Etruscans are historical persons and they were in all probability confidants of Porsenna. It is likely, too, that in 499 or 496, when the Latin confederacy of Aricia, along with the Roman partisans of the last Tarquin, fought the battle

[1] DH V 36, 1 sqq. Liv. II 14, 5 sqq. Cf. above, p. 47 sqq.

[2] Quotations and modern literature are to be found in T. R. S. Broughton, MRR 1, 1951, 6 sq., 9. Cf. also W. Schulze, ZGLEN 75, 83, 89, 173, 278, 335 (*Herminius*) ; 83, 109 *(Larcius)*.

of Lake Regillus with the Romans near Tusculum, the latter still had the backing of the king of Clusium. Finally, in 492 B.C., when a great famine was crippling Rome, and no wheat could be imported from the south, provisions were obtained "from the Etruscans," [1] probably still as the fruit of the alliance with Clusium.

Not much later, in the decade of the continuous consulates of the clan of the Fabii (485-77 B.C.), Roman relations with Southern Etruria reflect a completely changed situation. The southernmost Etruscan city, Veii, crushed the attempt of the Fabian army to cut her off, by means of a stronghold blocking the valley of the rivulet Cremera near the Tiber,[2] from her bridgehead Fidenae on the right bank of the Tiber. By now Rome and Veii were fighting each other without the intervention of any other Etruscan power. In the 470's Veii was, as we have seen, still superior in this struggle, but around the middle of the century Rome encroached upon the right bank of the Tiber and in the last decades she seized the saltworks of Veii, captured Fidenae in 426, and destroyed Veii itself by a supreme effort in 396.[3]

When Fidenae fell, the fate of Veii was sealed. But it was in vain that she invoked, along with the neighboring Faliscans, the help of the Etruscan League.[4] Why did the cities of Etruria, expanding across Latium toward the south of Italy with irresistible force in the previous hundred years, remain idle spectators of the local wars in Latium throughout the first century of the Roman Republic? The fatal blow at Aricia was accompanied, no doubt, by a chain-reaction, released by it: in addition to the Latins the Volscians, Aequians, and Picentes were also shaking off their Etruscan overlords about the same time. On the other hand, the complete breakdown of Etruscan rule on the southern flank of their territory was balanced by an unheard-of prosperity in their newly conquered province in the north. The overall effort of the twelve Etruscan cities, which founded in common the new *dodekapolis* in the Po Valley, tied them down com-

---

[1] Liv. II 34, 5 : *ex Tuscis frumentum Tiberi venit, eo sustentata est plebs.*

[2] O. Richter, Hermes 17, 1882, 425 sqq. G. De Sanctis, St. d. R. 2², 1960, 121 sqq. A real reminiscence of the struggle of Rome against Veii and Fidenae in the fifth century B.C. is found in Macrob., Sat. III 9, 13 : *in antiquitatibus autem haec oppida inveni devota* : [*Hi*]*stonios Fregellas Gavios Veios Fidenas.*

[3] Cf. above, p. 289 sqq. A. Schwegler, RG 2, 1856, 735 sqq. G. De Sanctis, St. d. R. 2¹, 1907, 121 sq., 125 sqq. A. Klotz, Livius und seine Vorgänger, Berlin 1941, 250. A. Momigliano, Cl. Q 36, 1942, 111 sqq. R. M. Ogilvie, JRS 48, 1958, 41. M. Sordi, I rapporti Romano-Ceriti, Roma 1960, 1 sqq., etc.

[4] Liv. IV 24, 2 ; 25, 7-8.

pletely but also compensated them for what was lost in the south.[1] After about 400 B.C., when the Celtic tempest swept away their prosperous new cities on the fertile Lombard plain, the Etruscans lost forever their chances to interfere in Latium.

The Etruscan sea power,[2] the real foundation of their greatness, did not crumble, however, with the collapse of their empire on the soil of Latium. If in 504 B.C. it proved to be toilsome and dangerous for ships carrying the troops of Aristodemus from Cyme to the height of Aricia along the coast—τὸ μεταξὺ πέλαγος ἐπιπόνως καὶ κινδυνωδῶς διανύσας [3]—it was not, it seems to me, a stormy sea which brought the trouble but the Etruscan naval power. The victory of the same Cymean general at Aricia, though fatal for Etruscan territorial supremacy in Latium, did not break their rule of the waves. They lost control of the harbors of Antium, Tarracina, Circeii; but they could use them en route to the south and returning home as stations for food and water supply: the Volscians of Antium, much later still participated in their piratical expeditions [4] and consequently had some sort of agreement with them. In 474 B.C. the Etruscans suffered a major reverse in this region [5] when their fleet attacking Cyme was defeated by the combined forces of this Greek city and of Syracuse. Hieron, the victorious ruler of this latter city, also founded a naval base on the isle of Pithekusai (the present Ischia) but it was soon abandoned. Syracuse, now overshadowing all other Sicilian cities, continued to contest the command of the seas with Carthage and Etruria. We have only scattered evidence of their clashes. There is a notice, for instance, that in 453 B.C. two naval squadrons from Syracuse invaded the Etruscan establishments of Elba, smelting the precious iron ore; the raiders were also stirring up the coastal cities

---

[1] A useful and abundant bibliography on Northern Etruria is compiled by M. Bollini in : Mostra dell' Etruria Padana e della citta di Spina 2, Bologna 1960, 19-34. Cf. R. Chevalier, R. Et. Lat. 37, 1959 (1960), 132 sqq.

[2] Diod. V 13, 4 ; 20, 4 ; 40, 1 ; XI 51, 1. Cf. T. J. Dunbabin, The Western Greeks, Oxford 1948, 346 sqq. and 499 (index). Strab. V4, 9 (C. 248).

[3] DH VII 6, 1.

[4] Strab. V 3, 5 (C. 232) : (the Antiates) πρότερον δὲ ναῦς ἐκέκτηντο καὶ ἐκοινώνουν τῶν λῃστηρίων τοῖς Τυρρηνοῖς, καίπερ ἤδη ʻΡωμαίοις ὑπακούοντες.

[5] Pindar, *Pyth.* 1, 72 sqq. Diod. XI 51, 1-2. IGA 150 (Etruscan helmet dedicated to Zeus in Olympia from the booty of this battle). Ad. Holm, Geschichte Siciliens im Altertum 1, Leipzig 1870, 275 and 419 sqq. G. Busolt, Griechische Geschichte 2², Gotha 1895, 804.

of Etruria and ravaging the Etruscan settlements on Corsica.[1] When the main Etruscan center in Campania, Capua, was lost in 423 B.C.,[2] along with the rest of their settlements, their coastal traffic was certainly hampered and reduced. They fostered vain hopes in 415-13 for the fall of Syracuse, and Alcibiades counted on their help in making his plans. Some Etruscan cities supported the Athenian expedition against Syracuse with three men-of-war and troops who fought bravely.[3]

The bitter contest between Syracuse and the Etruscans to safeguard maritime commerce and for the command of the seas was prolonged after the collapse of the Athenian invasion.[4] To make intelligible the consequences for Latium of this conflict in the fourth century, we must draw the reader's attention to the close relationship of Rome with one of the important city-states of southern Etruria: Caere.

The conquest of Rome by Porsenna also entailed the subordination of Veii to his will. At the moment, however, when his power vanished, these two cities, each trying to monopolize the commercial opportunities offered by the same geographical environment, became mortal enemies. Caere, with its harbor Pyrgi, to whom the coastal strip north of Ostia belonged, must have taken the side of Rome at least from the middle of the fifth century onward. The Annals are silent concerning Caere's role, revealing only that no hostilities between her and Rome occurred in the fifth century. But it is obvious that

[1] Diod. XI 88, 4 sqq. Cf. K. F. Stroheker, Dionysios I., Wiesbaden 1958, 2 n. 6.

[2] Diod. XII 31, 1 (with an earlier date.) Liv. IV 37, 1-2. Serv., Aen. 10, 145. J. Heurgon, Rech. (BEFAR 154) 1942, 85 sqq., discusses all details.

[3] Thucyd. VI 88, 6 : καὶ ἔπεμψαν μὲν (οἱ ᾿Αθηναῖοι) ἐς Καρχηδόνα τριήρη περὶ φιλίας, εἰ δύναιντό τι ὠφελεῖσθαι ἔπεμψαν δὲ καὶ ἐς Τυρσηνίαν, ἔστιν ὧν πόλεων ἐπαγγελλομένων καὶ αὐτῶν ξυμπολεμεῖν. VI 103, 2 : ἦλθον δὲ καὶ τῶν Σικελῶν πολλοὶ ξύμμαχοι τοῖς ᾿Αθηναίοις, οἳ πρότερον περιεωρῶντο, καὶ ἐκ τῆς Τυρσηνίας νῆες πεντηκόντοροι τρεῖς. VII 53, 1-2. 54: ὁ δὲ Γύλιππος . . . παρεβοήθει ἐπὶ τὴν χηλὴν μέρος τι ἔχων τῆς στρατιᾶς καὶ αὐτοὺς οἱ Τυρσηνοί (οὗτοι γὰρ ἐφύλασσον τοῖς ᾿Αθηναίοις ταύτῃ) ὁρῶντες ἀτάκτως προσφερομένους, ἐπεκβοηθήσαντες καὶ προσπεσόντες τοῖς πρώτοις τρέπουσι καὶ ἐσβάλλουσιν ἐς τὴν λίμνην τὴν Λυσιμέλειαν καλουμένην . . . μετὰ δὲ τοῦτο Συρακόσιοι μὲν τῆς τε ναυμαχίας τροπαῖον ἔστησαν, . . . ᾿Αθηναῖοι δὲ ἧς τε οἱ Τυρσηνοὶ τροπῆς ἐποιήσαντο τῶν πεζῶν ἐς τὴν λίμνην καὶ ἧς αὐτοὶ τῷ ἄλλῳ στρατοπέδῳ. 57, 11 : ξυνεστράτευον . . . Τυρσηνῶν τέ τινες κατὰ διαφορὰν Συρακοσίων . . . . τοσάδε μὲν μετὰ ᾿Αθηναίων ἔθνη ἐστράτευον. R. A. L. Fell, Etruria and Rome, Cambridge 1924, 105 sqq. M. Treu, Historia 3, 1954-1955, 41 sqq. K. F. Stroheker, ibid. 163 sqq.

[4] R. A. L. Fell, l.c., gives the relevant passages. More information is given below, p. 341 sqq.

if Caere had combined her forces with Veii, the Romans could not have infringed on the Veientan bank of the Tiber at the time of the decemvirate, nor could they have seized the saltworks and destroyed Fidenae and Veii thereafter.

Caere was an important ally for Rome. Herodotus, who ignored Rome, knew what to report on Caere-Agylla, whose sailors did not sack the merchantmen of continental Greeks as did the rest of the Etruscans. It was not by mere chance that Roman votive offerings to the Apollo of Delphi were kept in the treasury of the Agyllaeans; nor can it be doubted that the continuous flow of Attic ceramics to Rome throughout the fifth and into the fourth century, as revealed to us by Enrico Paribeni, came via Caere.[1] If Veii furnished the colorful terra-cotta statues and revetments for the temples of Rome under the last Tarquin, the corresponding decorative elements of the early fifth century [2] must have come from Caere.

This alliance was of vital importance for Rome in the first half of the fourth century B.C., when she was humiliated by the Gauls and her subjects, allies, and enemies all alike combined against her; Caere alone continued to cooperate with her.[3] The Vestal virgins with many important people, fleeing before the Gauls, were sheltered there.[4] Over and above this, the Caeretanes fell upon a Celtic contingent returning from the south where they had been marauding after the sack of Rome, taking them by surprise and beating them.[5] A solemn

---

[1] Herod. 1, 167. Ed. Meyer, GdA 5, 1902, 123. Strab. V 2, 3 (C. 220). In Cic., *De re publ.* II 4, 9, I identify the *maritimi* who were sailing *mercandi causa* with the Etruscans and those who did it *latrocinandi causa* with the Carthaginians ; in truth, however, both were trading as well as marauding as were the Greeks of Homer.

[2] P. J. Riis-E. Gjerstad, *Opusc. Rom.* 3,1960, 88 sqq. R. Bloch, R. Et. Lat. 37, 1959, 118 sqq., 124 sqq., 130. Cf. also T. Frank, Mem. Am. Ac. in Rome 5, 1925, 79-102, on the temple of the Dioscuri.

[3] The last survey of these relations is that of Marta Sordi, I rapporti romano-ceriti Roma 1960, 22 sq., 32 sqq.

[4] All passages bearing on this topic are quoted by A. Schwegler, RG 3, 1858, 249 sqq.

[5] This Caeretane victory was certainly not such an overwhelming success as our sources depict it. Cf. Diod. XIV 117, 7 (after the Celtic catastrophe) : οἱ δ'εἰς τὴν Ἰαπυγίαν τῶν Κελτῶν ἐληλυθότες ἀνέστρεψαν διὰ τῆς τῶν Ῥωμαίων χώρας καὶ μετ' ὀλίγον ὑπὸ Κερίων ἐπιβουλευθέντες νυκτὸς ἅπαντες κατεκόπησαν ἐν τῷ Τραυσίῳ πεδίῳ. Strab. V 2, 3 (220 C.) : Περὶ μὲν τῆς ἐπιφανείας τῶν Τυρρηνῶν ταῦτα καὶ ἔτι τὰ τοῖς Καιρετανοῖς πραχθέντα ... καὶ γὰρ τοὺς ἑλόντας τὴν Ῥώμην Γαλάτας κατεπολέμησαν ἀπιοῦσιν ἐπιθέμενοι κατὰ Σαβίνους καὶ ἅ παρ' ἑκόντων ἔλαβον Ῥωμαίων ἐκεῖνοι λάφυρα ἄκοντας ἀφείλοντο.

treaty of friendship was now concluded between the two cities in order to consolidate their association: *ut . . . cum Caeritibus hospitium publice fieret* (Liv. V 30, 3). On the other hand, the events in and around Latium now lost their purely local character and assumed an increasingly international significance: Caere, going along with Rome, was struck by the powerful ruler of Syracuse, who used the Celtic invaders of Rome as mercenaries; the Latins in their attempt to shake off the rule of Rome also used Celtic auxiliaries. Later on, Syracuse invaded the Latian coast with her fleet, protecting the Volscians of Antium against the Romans, whereas Rome concluded two treaties, one soon after the other, with the old ally of Caere and the deadly enemy of Syracuse: Carthage. These conflicts and associations must be followed up here more carefully in detail.

The direction of foreign affairs in Syracuse was in the hands of Dionysius I from 406-5 until 367 B.C., and his policies were continued by his son in the two decades following his death, even if not so forcefully as under Dionysius I.[1] The main obstacle to the maritime commerce of Syracuse was the superior war fleet and coastal stations of Carthage, which controlled the trade in the western half of the Mediterranean. There were, however, possibilities of expansion for Sicilian commerce in the Adriatic sea, where Dionysius I, between 390 and 384 B.C., succeeded in reinforcing Greek influence; here his successor pushed his initiative still further. Dionysius I strove in this area to safeguard the passage of Syracusan ships to and from Greece and to join the reloading points of trade coming southward from continental Europe. The network he built up for these operations was founded on the cooperation of his allies in Epirus and on the Dalmatian isle of Pharos, his fleet station at Issa—also near the Dalmatian coast—as well as in Lissos-Alessio in southern Albania; he resettled the important emporium of Hatria at the mouth of the Po and founded the colony of Ankon (Ancona) where he had direct access to his new allies, the Celtic invaders of northern Italy.[2] These activities of Syracuse in the Adriatic were of consequence for the whole of Italy, but they could not be supported by the full strength of the Syracusan state, because of Carthage, its principal adversary,

---

[1] Cf. the remarks by E. Kornemann, RG 1[3], Stuttgart 1954, 103 sqq., and the lucid survey by K. F. Stroheker, Dionysios I., Wiesbaden 1958, 120 sqq., 126 sqq., 128 sqq., whom we follow in this short sketch.

[2] K. F. Stroheker, *op. cit.* 122 sq.

against which Dionysius was again waging war once more after 382, which required all his resources.

How was Latium affected by the Italian politics and aspirations of Dionysius I? Excellent scholars have thought that Rome became his ally.[1] The Roman Annals mentioned in fact, under the heading of the consuls of 492 B.C., that their envoys were sent to him demanding corn and that they indeed obtained the wheat they needed. But his name was used in this connection only by a chronological mistake of Roman historians for which Dionysius of Halicarnassus already censured them.[2] In actuality, the tyrant of Syracuse supported the enemies of Rome and fought her allies.

In the years when Dionysius was establishing his naval bases in the Adriatic area, he also proceeded to attack Caere.[3] Successfully surprising Pyrgi, the harbor of the Caeretanes, he won the ensuing battle and ravaged the region. His huge loot of gold enabled him to mobilize a new army against Carthage. Carrying his sea raid further, Dionysius struck at the Etruscan settlements on Corsica, where the harbor called "Syracusan" must have been his foundation.[4] It seems

---

[1] Ed. Meyer, GdA 5, 1902, 148 sq. A. Momigliano, SDHI 5, 1939, 393 sqq. *Contra* : K. F. Stroheker, *op. cit.* 230 sq., n. 141. M. Sordi, *op. cit.* 68 sqq.

[2] DH VII 1, 4-6.

[3] Diod. XV 14, 3-4: Διονύσιος δὲ χρημάτων ἀπορούμενος—this motivation reflects the hostile attitude of Timaeus, the source of Diodorus, toward the rulers of Syracuse, cf. K. F. Stroheker, *l.c.*—ἐστράτευσεν ἐπὶ Τυρρηνίαν, ἔχων τριήρεις ἑξήκοντα, πρόφασιν μὲν φέρων τὴν τῶν λῃστῶν κατάλυσιν, τῇ δ'ἀληθείᾳ συλήσων ἱερὸν ἅγιον, γέμον μὲν ἀναθημάτων πολλῶν, καθιδρυμένον δ'ἐν ἐπινείῳ πόλεως 'Αγύλλης Τυρρηνίδος. τὸ δ'ἐπίνειον ὠνομάζετο Πύργοι. Καταπλεύσας δὲ νυκτὸς καὶ τὴν δύναμιν ἐκβιβάσας, ἅμ'ἡμέρᾳ προσπεσὼν ἐκράτησε τῆς ἐπιβολῆς. ὀλίγων γὰρ ὄντων ἕν τῷ χωρίῳ φυλάκων βιασάμενος αὐτοὺς ἐσύλησε τὸ ἱερὸν καὶ συνήθροισεν οὐκ ἔλαττον ταλάντων χιλίων. τῶν δὲ 'Αγυλλαίων ἐκβοηθησάντων, μάχῃ τε ἐκράτησεν αὐτῶν καὶ πολλοὺς αἰχμαλώτους λαβὼν καὶ τὴν χώραν πορθήσας ἐπανῆλθεν εἰς τὰς Συρακούσας. ἀποδόμενος δὲ τὰ λάφυρα συνήγαγεν οὐκ ἐλάττω ταλάντων πεντακοσίων. εὐπορήσας δὲ χρημάτων ἐμισθοῦτο στρατιωτῶν παντοδαπῶν πλῆθος, καὶ δύναμιν ἀξιόλογον συστησάμενος φανερὸς ἦν πολεμήσων Καρχηδονίοις. Aelian., *Var. hist.* 1, 20, says that the temple which was looted in Pyrgi belonged to Apollon and Leukothea. Polyaen. V 2, 21, also speaks of the sanctuary of Leukothea. This author used the same source as Ps.-Arist., *Oecon.* 2, 1349 b-1350 a. Strab. V 2, 8 (C. 226) : ἔχει δὲ Εἰλειθυίας ἱερόν, Πελασγῶν ἵδρυμα, πλούσιόν ποτε γενόμενον. ἐσύλησε δ'αὐτὸ Διονύσιος ὁ τῶν Σικελιωτῶν τύραννος κατὰ τὸν πλοῦν τὸν ἐπὶ Κύρνον. Cf. K. O. Müller-W. Deecke, 1, 189 sq. 190 n. 33. Ad Holm, Geschichte Siciliens 2, Leipzig 1874, 135 sq., and R. A. L. Fell, *op. cit.* 105 sq. K. F. Stroheker, *op. cit.* 127 sq. M. Sordi, *op. cit.* 66 sq. On the new excavations of M.Pallottino at Pyrgi, cf. Arch. cl. 9, 1957, 206 sqq; 10, 1958, 315 sqq.

[4] Diod. V 13, 4 (concerning the two principal cities of Corsica) : τούτων δὲ τὴν μὲν Κάλαριν Φωκαεῖς ἔκτισαν, καὶ χρόνον τινὰ κατοικήσαντες ὑπὸ Τυρρηνῶν

certain that Dionysius also recaptured Elba, because large quantities of iron suddenly inundated the Syracuse market, which "must inevitably have come from Elba, the great center of the iron mining of Italy." [1] At the same time Syracusan aspirations were also extended to the island of Sardinia.[2] The power of Syracuse under Dionysius I was felt in Latium too; nor could this influence have been absent in the following two decades when Dionysius II succeeded him. Even when this ruler lost Syracuse by the *coup d'etat* of Dion, he sailed to Italy with a powerful fleet and army, intending to strengthen his position in the Adriatic; [3] in the following decade, though based on Rhegion and Lokroi, his eventual intervention on the coast up to Etruria was still a menace.

Livy under the year 349 records, in fact, the presence of a Greek naval force on the Latian coast.[4] Livy found no indication in his

ἐξεβλήθησαν ἐκ τῆς νήσου. τὴν δὲ Νίκαιαν ἔκτισαν Τυρρηνοὶ θαλαττοκρατοῦντες καὶ τὰς κατὰ τὴν Τυρρηνίαν κειμένας νήσους ἰδιοποιούμενοι. ἐπὶ δέ τινας χρόνους τῶν ἐν τῇ Κύρνῳ πόλεων κυριεύοντες ἐλάμβανον παρὰ τῶν ἐγχωρίων φόρους ῥητίνην καὶ κηρὸν καὶ μέλι, φυομένων τούτων δαψιλῶν ἐν τῇ νήσῳ. Cf. *ibid.* 13, 3 : ... νῆσός ἐστιν ... Κύρνος ... κάλλιστον ἔχει λιμένα τὸν ὀνομαζόμενον Συρακόσιον. Ptolem., *Geogr.* III 2, 4 : Συρακουσανὸς λιμήν. Cf. E. Pais, Studi Storici 2 (Pisa 1893) 315 sq. 348 n. G. De Sanctis, St. d. R. 2², 1960, 179.

    [1] Arist., *Pol.* I 11, 12 (p. 1259 a), evaluated by G. De Sanctis, St. d. R. 2², 1960, 179. R. A. L. Fell, *op. cit.* 105 sq.

    [2] E. Pais, Studi storici 2, 1893, 348 n. A. Momigliano, SDHI 5, 1939, 389 sq.

    [3] Diod. XVI 10, 2 : κατὰ δὲ τοῦτον τὸν καιρὸν ὁ μὲν τύραννος περὶ τὰς νεοκτίστους πόλεις κατὰ τὸν Ἀδρίαν διέτριβε μετὰ πολλῶν δυνάμεων. Plut., *Dion.* 26, 1 : Μάλιστα δ'αὐτοὺς ἐθάρρυνε τὸ συμβεβηκὸς αὐτομάτως περὶ τὴν ἀποδημίαν τοῦ Διονυσίου· νεωστὶ γὰρ ἐκπεπλευκὼς ἐτύγχανεν ὀγδοήκοντα ναυσὶν εἰς τὴν Ἰταλίαν. Cf. 26, 4. Corn. Nepos, *Dion* 5, 4 : *eo tempore aberat Dionysius et in Italia classem opperiebatur adversariorum, ratus neminem sine magnis copiis ad se venturum.*

    [4] Liv. VII 25, 3-4 : *Galli ex Albanis montibus, quia hiemis vim pati nequiverant, per campos maritumaque loca vagi populabantur ; mare infestum classibus Graecorum erat oraque litoris Antiatis Laurensque tractus et Tiberis ostia, ut praedones maritimi cum terrestribus congressi ancipiti semel proelio decertarint dubiique discesserint in castra Galli, Graeci retro ad naves, victos se an victores putarent.* 7-9 : *inter duo simul bella externa defectione etiam sociorum senatus anxius ... contendere omnes imperii vires consules dilectu habendo iussit ; ...decem legiones scriptae dicuntur quaternum milium et ducenorum peditum equitumque trecenorum quem nunc novum exercitum, si qua externa vis ingruat, hae vires populi Romani, quas vix terrarum capit orbis contractae in unum haud facile efficiant.* 12-13 : *consul duabus legionibus urbe praepositis, octo cum L. Pinario praetore divisis, ... Gallicum sibi bellum extra sortem sumit, praetorem maritimam oram tutari Graecosque arcere litoribus iussit.* 26, 10-11 (after Camillus defeated the Gauls) : *consul .... iussus ab senatu bellum maritimum curare cum praetore iunxit castra. ibi quia res trahi segnitia Graecorum non committentium se in aciem videbantur ..... 13-15 : cum Graecis a Camillo nulla memorabilis gesta res ; nec illi terra, nec Romanus mari bellator erat. postremo cum litoribus arcerentur, aqua etiam praeter cetera necessaria usui deficiente Italiam reliquere. cuius populi ea cuiusque*

sources as to what Greek state this fleet belonged; his guess was that it was that of the "tyrants of Sicily." We can only deduce from his vague narrative, first, that the Greek expeditionary force presumably relied on the help of the Volscian Antium, then hostile to Rome, because without such a base no prolonged sojourn in the coastal waters is imaginable under the technical conditions then prevailing; and second, that the pitched battle of these Greeks with the Celtic host, descending from the Alban mountains where its operational base was established, demonstrates that only one of these opponents could possibly belong to the armed forces or allies of Dionysius II. If the Varronian date of 349 were valid also for the Sicilian chronology, there would be no doubt that the Greek ships in question were those of the Syracusan tyrant, as Livy thought. But the year 349 corresponds in Greek time reckoning to ca. 343 B.C., when the Greeks of Sicily overcame Dionysius II, under the leadership of Timoleon. On the other hand, Timoleon and Archidamos had to concentrate their efforts on the great clash with Carthage,[1] which was decided about 340 at the Crimisos, where Timoleon won a great victory.[2]

Under such circumstances we cannot establish the exact provenience of the attacking fleet.[3] It is a mistake to belittle its role and to explain its appearance around the mouth of the Tiber and off the shore south of Ostia as a piratical adventure on the part of erratic Greek mercenaries coming from continental Greece. The clash of these Greeks with the Celtic invaders, mentioned above, is in itself evidence that their enterprise was of considerable size; even more impressive is the array of terrestrial forces, with which the Romans opposed them. First they sent four legions (16,800 infantrymen with 1200 horsemen) against them, and after their victory over the Gauls this number was doubled: it was the largest army mobilized by Rome up to that time.

---

gentis classis fuerit, nihil certi est. maxime Siciliae fuisse tyrannos crediderim ; nam ulterior Graecia ea tempestate intestino fessa bello iam Macedonum opes horrebat.

[1] Cf. E. Pais, Studi storici (Pisa) 2, 1893, 350 sqq., 429 sqq. G. De Sanctis, St. d. R. 2², 1960, 251.

[2] Cf. J. Beloch, Griechische Geschichte III 2², Berlin-Leipzig 1923, 380 sq. H. E. Stier, RE 6A, 1278. E. Sjöquist, Kokalos 4, 1958, 3 sqq.

[3] Fabius Pictor knew this, because the work by the contemporary Athanis (or Athanas) of Syracuse who wrote the history of those years (F. Jacoby, F. Gr. Hist. 3 B, Kommentar 1955, 522) was used by Pictor's source, Timaios. But it was hardly possible for him to admit that in the middle of the fourth century Rome was an enemy of the Sicilian Greeks and an ally of Carthage !

ROME DURING THE EARLY REPUBLIC

Though the supreme effort was made because of the fear of an imminent war with the Latins, they employed their full roster of eight legions against the Greeks—something they would never have done without serious military reasons.

The unquestionably large dimensions of this Greek naval expedition would justify the opinion that it was Syracusan—either sent out by Dionysius II starting from his bases in southern Italy (whose activities are synchronized with the developments in Latium in Livy), or by Timoleon, which would have more chronological likelihood but less historical probability. The crucial importance of this move was that in the next year the envoys of Syracuse's arch-enemies appeared in Rome and the first treaty of Rome with Carthage was concluded. It is not relevant whether the naval action of Syracuse was launched by Dionysius or by Timoleon: both were antagonists of Carthage. The new alliance was the only possible answer to the Syracusan aggression: Niebuhr perceived this long ago.

Diodorus reports [1] that Timoleon executed *Postumius*, an "Etruscan" pirate, who sailed with twelve ships into the harbor of Syracuse with friendly intentions. The man's name is a good Latin one, and though the story lost its real meaning with its original context which is unknown to us, it reflects again the tension between Syracuse on one hand, and the South-Etruscan and Roman sphere on the other. This antagonism is also revealed in another episode which occurred in the same epoch.[2] In the two wings of the *comitium*, the place where the meetings of the citizen-body were held, there once stood statues of *Pythagoras* and *Alcibiades*, erected at the time of the Sammite wars when a Delphic oracle commanded that the wisest and the most virtuous of the Greeks be honored. By the selection of Pythagoras, it was hoped that the sympathies of *Magnae Graecia* would be won. But the virtue of Alcibiades in the eyes of the Romans of the fourth century B.C. was merely that he was the champion of Athenian politics against Syracuse.

[1] Diod. XVI 82, 3. Cf. E. Pais, Studi storici 2, 1893, 441 sq., and often elsewhere.

[2] Plin., *N.h.* XXXIV 6, 26 : *Invenio et Pythagorae et Alcibiadi in cornibus comitii positas, cum bello Samniti Apollo Pythius iussisset fortissimo Graiae gentis et alteri sapientissimo simulacra celebri loco dicari. eae stetere, donec Sulla dictator ibi curiam faceret. mirumque est, illos patres Socrati cunctis ab eodem deo sapientia praelato Pythagoram praetulisse aut tot aliis virtute Alcibiaden et quemquam utroque Themistocli.* Plutarch, *Numa* 8, 20, reproduces the same story, though stripped of all the valuable special indications of Pliny. So far I see, the tendency of this ostentative honor offered to Alcibiades escaped notice hitherto.

℘

THE BEGINNINGS OF ROMAN SEA POWER

Before Rome could consider the possibility of developing sea-going trade and prepare for naval warfare, she first had to have access to the sea from her own territory. Even when she took possession of the mouth of the Tiber, her ambition was, as we have seen,[1] not to sail overseas but to capture the saltworks of Veii. In the same way, when she incorporated more and more of the Latian seashore in the following decades, she was concerned mainly with coastal defense, not with naval activity. Nevertheless by around 400 B.C., she had already established some long-distance contacts with maritime countries.[2] The story of the golden vessel, offered to Apollo after the capture of Veii, which was stolen en route by pirates of Lipara but was restored to the Romans and preserved in Delphi in the treasury of the Massaliotes,[3] shows that the corsairs of these small islands were then far superior to the Romans at sea. The friendly relations with Massilia (Marseille) must be historical, even if Rome's alliance with them after the Gallic catastrophe is not as authentic as was recently believed.[4]

Diodorus notes in the year 378-7 B.C.—this would correspond to 386 in the Varronian chronology of the Roman Annals—that Rome dispatched five hundred colonists to Sardinia. We agree with A. Sordi that this transmarine enterprise, which took place not long after the debacle at the Allia, can be historical only if it was accomplished in conjunction with Caere.[5] And the attempted foundation of a

[1] Cf. above, p. 289 sqq.

[2] For a detailed survey see J. H. Thiel, A History of the Roman Sea-Power before the Second Punic War, Amsterdam 1954, 3 sqq.

[3] Diod. XIV 93, 3-5. Liv. V 25, 10 ; 28, 2-5. Plut., *Camill.* 8, 3-8. App., *Ital.* 8, 1. Cf. G. De Sanctis, St. d. R. 2², 138. A. Klotz, Rh. Mus. n. F. 86, 1937, 213. H. Ormerod, Piracy in the Ancient World, Liverpool-London 1924, 157. J. H. Thiel, *op. cit.* 6 sqq. M. Sordi, I rapporti 92.

[4] Cf. A. Momigliano, SDHI 5, 1939, 394 sqq. G. Nenci, Rivista di Studi Liguri 24, 1958, 24 sqq., 80 sqq. M. Sordi, I rapporti 94 sqq. Justin. XLIII 5, 10, writes: *immunitas illis decreta et locus spectaculorum in senatu datus*; but the seats of the senators were separated from those of the other citizens at the games only by Scipio the Elder in the year of his consulate, and therefore such clauses cannot be included in official documents before 205 B.C. (A different view in G. Nenci, *op. cit.* 91 n. 220). In the same way, the financial assistance of Massalia to Rome could not have been given, at least in my opinion, as a ransom to the Celts for breaking up the siege ; if assistance was ever given, it was at a later date.

[5] Diod. XV 27, 4 (378-77 B.C.): ''Ἅμα δὲ τούτοις πραττομένοις ʹΡωμαῖοι μὲν ἐπὶ ἀτελείᾳ πεντακοσίους ἀποίκους εἰς Σαρδονίαν ἀπέστειλαν. The modern views concerning this topic are discussed in the book by M. Sordi, *op. cit.* 94 sqq. Cf.

348

Roman colony at Corsica, perhaps 357 to 354 B.C. (the mentioning of which we owe to a stray fragment of the Botanical History of Theophrastus), could not have been undertaken in a different way: the twenty-five ships of this expedition might well have been Caeretane craft.[1]

In 353 B.C. the uprise of Tarquinii and the Faliscans also induced the Caeretanes to cooperate with them in trying to stop Roman expansion. In consequence of their failure Caere became part of the Roman state, though preserving her local autonomy, deprived of the political privileges but also exempt from the financial and military burdens of the Roman citizen:[2] from then on their fleet could be employed for Roman purposes in one way or another, though we have no data in our scanty evidence to indicate that this possibility was realized. By chance, however, we do know of an instance in which the ships of Antium played a role under Roman rule,[3] and we shall see that Roman commercial activity at sea preceded their naval activities in war.

In the continuous warfare of the fourth century, the complete lack of a Roman navy becomes obvious. In 349 B.C. the Romans prevented,

also O. Meltzer, Geschichte der Karthager 1, Berlin 1879, 339 sqq. Ed. Meyer GdA 5, 820. 826.

[1] Fr. Gr. Hist. 840 Anhang 24 b (=Theophrast., Hist. plant. V 8, 2.). The tentative date is that of F. Jacoby. Cf. M. Sordi, *ibid.*, with the quotations of modern works dealing with this problem.

[2] Diod. XVI 36, 4. Liv. VII 19, 6-20, 8 : *In bellum Etruscum intentam civitatem, quia Caeritem populum misericordia consanguinitatis Tarquiniensibus adiunctum fama ferebatur, legati Latini ad Volscos convertere . . . . . inclinavit deinde pars maior curae in Etruscum bellum, postquam . . . cognitum est depopulatum agrum circa Romanas salinas praedaeque partem in Caeritum fines avectam et haud dubie iuventutem eius populi inter praedatores fuisse. . . is . . (T. Manlius L. f. dictator) Caeritibus bellum indixit. tum primum Caerites . . . verus belli terror invasit, et . . . pro se quisque legatos mitti iubebat ad petendam erroris veniam . . . . movit populum non tam causa praesens quam vetus meritum . . . itaque pax populo Caeriti data, indutiasque in centum annos factas in aes referri placuit.* The appraisal of the value of the sources by E. Ferenczy, Acta Antiqua 1, 1951-52, 154 sqq., seems to be too radical. Cf. G. De Sanctis, St. d. R. 2², 1960, 24 sqq. On the *civitas sine suffragio* of Caere see : Gell. XVI 13, 7. Strabo V 2, 3 (C. 220), and the passages discussed recently by A. Bernardi, Athen., n.s. 16, 1938, 239 sqq. A. N. Sherwin-White, R. Citiz., Oxford 1939, 37 sqq. J. Pinsent, Cl. Q. 48, 1954, 158 sqq., and 51, 1957, 89 sqq. F. De Visscher, Studi in onore di U. E. Paoli, Firenze 1955, 249. E. Badian, Foreign Clientelae, Oxford 1958, 16 sqq. M. Sordi, *op. cit.* 107 sqq., and the modifications of her conclusions suggested by A. Bernardi, Athen., n.s. 39, 1961, 178 sqq., and L. R. Taylor, A. J. Ph. 82, 1961, 449 sq.

[3] Strabo V 3, 5 (C. 232) ; cf. my study : Die trojanischen Urahnen der Römer, Basel 1957, 28, with n. 187.

a Greek invasion fleet from landing by their field army, beating off this attack from the sea only by a land blockade. In 338 B.C. the Volscian naval base of Antium seems to have been taken from the land without naval assistance, as happened at Naples in 327-26. The small squadron of the *duoviri navales* marks the beginning of the Roman war fleet after 311 B.C.[1] The maritime colonies of Rome, founded in the second half of the fourth century, served first as coastal defenses and were not originally naval bases.[2]

The first and second treaties of 348 and 343 B.C. with Carthage, both attesting to enormous tension in Latium, reflect on the one hand the lack of a Roman war fleet—more will be said about the general situation in those years in our next paragraphs—and on the other a considerable Roman commercial activity at sea, which cannot be imagined without the participation of Caere and Antium under the Roman flag, i.e., under the protection of their Roman citizenship. This participation explains why the allies of Rome were also explicitly mentioned in those documents, as we know from Polybius.[3] The Romans and their allies in these two treaties are supposed to enter the harbors of Carthage itself, as well as some others in Libya, and those of Carthaginian Sicily and Sardinia.

Before the Roman sea power arose, Rome became a coastal power of consequence, taking over the Latian littoral. With this as a springboard, she embarked in the third century on her battle for the rule of the sea. This is what Polybius proposed to describe: πῶς καὶ πότε καὶ δι' ἃς αἰτίας πρῶτον ἐνέβησαν εἰς θάλατταν Ῥωμαῖοι: "how, when and for what reasons did the Romans set sail the first time"[4] to conquer overseas. Nothing could illustrate their new ambitions more impressively than the representations of their new coinage, boasting —besides their victories over Pyrrhus and over the Gauls—their thalassocracy.[5] This explains also why just a little while before a Greek poet could flatter them as those who took over the rule on land and on sea, γῆς καὶ θαλάσσης σκῆπτρα καὶ μοναρχίαν λαβόντες.[6]

---

[1] These facts were stressed by J. H. Thiel, *op. cit.* 8 sq., 48.

[2] A. N. Sherwin-White, R. Citiz. 73. Ch. J. Starr, Am. J. Ph. 64, 1943, 56 sqq. J. H. Thiel, *op. cit.* 12. E. T. Salmon, Phoenix 9, 1955, 65 sq.

[3] Polyb. III 22, 5. 11 ; 24, 3. 9.

[4] Polyb. I 20, 8 ; cf. I 5, 1 sqq. ; 12, 5. V 104, 3.

[5] A. Alföldi, RM 68, 1961, 64 sqq.

[6] Lykophr., *Alex.* 1229. Cf. A. Momigliano, JRS 32, 1942, 53. P. Lévèque, R. Et. Anc. 57, 1957, 36.

℘

THE FIRST AND SECOND TREATIES BETWEEN CARTHAGE AND ROME

It was a long time before those Roman landlubbers became old sea dogs, as we have just seen. More puzzling is the fact that such a well-informed historian as Polybius dates their first treaty with Carthage in the first year of the Republic.[1] Mommsen came to the conclusion a hundred years ago that this date was spurious, but H. Nissen disagreed with him. Mommsen's authority prevailed for a time until, in our generation, the Polybian date again has been accepted, almost unanimously. Recently A. Aymard expressed the view that a final decision can be reached only by a general reconsideration of all the circumstances involved:[2] and this is what we have tried to do.

[1] Polyb. III 22, 1.

[2] We give only samples of this endless debate without any claim to completeness. a) The first year of the Republic as the date of the first treaty with Carthage accepted by the following scholars : A. Schwegler, RG 1, 1853, 791. H. Nissen, Fleckeisens Jahrb. f. Philol. 1867, 321 sqq. K. Neumann, Das Zeitalter der punischen Kriege, Breslau 1883, 33 sq. O. Meltzer, Geschichte der Karthager 1, Leipzig 1879, 173 sq. Ed. Meyer, GdA 2, 1902, 500. *Idem*, Kleine Schriften 2, 1924, 296. St. Gsell, Histoire ancienne de l'Afrique du Nord 3, 1918, 67 sqq. L. E. W. Adams, A Study in the Commerce of Latium, Northampton, Mass. 1921, 66. L. R. Taylor, Papers and Monogr. Am. Ac. Rome 2, 1923, 10. H. Last, CAH 7, 1928, 859 sqq. V. Ehrenberg, Karthago (Morgenland, Heft 14) 1927, 5. F. Altheim, Griechische Götter im alten Rom, Giessen 1930, 32. H. Horn, Foederati. Diss. Frankfurt 1930, 88 sq. M. Gelzer, RE 12, 951. E. Ciaceri, Atti Acc. di Archeol. Napoli n.s. 12, 1931-32, 295 sqq. G. Pasquali, La nuova antologia 386, 1936, 414. L. Wickert, Klio 31, 1938, 349 sqq. *Idem*, Rh. Mus. 100, 1958, 96. A. N. Sherwin-White, R. Citiz., Oxford 1939, 15 sqq. B. L. Beaumont, JRS 29, 1939, 74 sqq. A. Schulten, Tartessos, Hamburg 1950, 67. H. H. Scullard, A History of the Roman World from 753 to 146 B.C.[2], London 1951, 425. E. Ferenczy, Acta Ant. Acad. Sci. Hung. 1, 1951, 136 sqq. L. Pareti, St. d. R. 1, 1952, 330 sqq. E. Colozier, Mél. 65, 1953, 90 sqq. G. Devoto, Historia mundi 3, Bern 1954, 385 sq. Pl. Fraccaro, Rendiconti dell' Istituto Lombardo di Scienze e Lett. 85, 1952, 85 sq.=Opuscula 1, Pavia 1956, 8. G. Gianelli, Trattato di storia romana 1, 1953, 137 sqq. R. Paribeni, Storia di Roma 1, 1954, 133 sq. J. H. Thiel, A History of the Roman Sea-Power, Amsterdam 1954, 6 n. 10. J. Vogt, Die römische Republik[3], 1955, 32 sq. G. Picard, Le monde de Carthage, Paris 1956, 193. M. Hoffmann, RE Suppl. 8, 1956, 1147. F. W. Walbank, A Historical Commentary on Polybius 1, Oxford 1957, 338. F. Hampl, Rh. Mus. 101, 1958, 58 sqq. M. Sordi, I rapporti romano-ceriti, Roma 1960, 91, 100 sq. b) 348 B.C. as the date of the first treaty is advocated by : Mommsen, R. Chron.[2] Berlin 1859, 320 sq., 375. W. Ihne, RG 1, 1868, 58. G. F. Unger, Rh. Mus. 37, 1882, 153 sq. W. Soltau, Philol. 48, 1889, 131 sq., 276 sq. K. J. Neumann, Hermes 31, 1896, 519 sqq. A. Klotz, Berliner Philol. Wochenschrift 1908, 446 sqq. G. De Sanctis, St. d. R. 2[1] 1907, 251 sq.=2[2], 240. E.

The impossibility of that early date becomes obvious through the results of our survey, namely:

1. The year 509 B.C. (corresponding to a date some years later in the Cymean chronology of early Roman history evaluated in our second chapter) was fixed as the first year of the Republic when the aedile Cn. Flavius counted 204 annual nails in the wall of the *cella Iovis*. As there were fewer than 204 pairs of consuls in the list of the magistrates, which was kept by the *pontifices*, a gap became evident between the year of the consecration of the Capitoline temple and the first magistrates of the *fasti*. This gap was filled by fictitious consuls some time afterwards.

2. One of these was M. Horatius, whose name stood on the architrave of the temple front. Evidently the number of the annual nails revealing the year of the dedication of the sanctuary and the name of the magistrate, engraved above the entrance and visible to everybody in 304 B.C., suggested the dating of M. Horatius' office—a republican magistrature—to the year of the dedication. But 204 years before 304 B.C. either the last Tarquin was still ruling in Rome or Porsenna had just subjugated the city. Therefore no representative of the Republic was yet there and we have tried to prove that M. Horatius' name was inscribed over the entrance in 378 B.C., when he rededicated the sanctuary.

3. M. Junius Brutus had a nickname, *Brutus*, which originally was opprobrious; this nickname belonged exclusively to a prominent clan, which rose to great political power in the second half of the fourth century B.C. In 509 or 508 B.C. no plebeian magistrates yet existed. Brutus as an eponymous magistrate of the early Republic was a creation, as was M. Horatius, of the historical speculation

Täubler, Imp. R. 1, 1913, 254 sq., 268. T. Frank, Cl. Phil. 14, 1919, 318. M. Cary, JRS 9, 1919, 69. A. Rosenberg, Hermes 54, 1919, 164. U. Kahrstedt, Göttinger Gel. Nachr. 1923, 100. Joh. Hasebroek, Staat und Handel im alten Griechenland, Tübingen 1928, 126 sq., 136. F. Schachermeyr, Rh. Mus. n.f. 86, 1930, 350 sq. A. Stein, Römische Inschriften in der antiken Literatur, Prag 1930, 19 sq. W. Schur, RE Suppl. 5, 1931, 364. E. Kornemann, Hist. Zeitschr. 145, 1932, 298 n. 3. E. Pais, Storia di Roma durante le guerre Puniche 1² 1935, 77 sq. A. Piganiol, Histoire de Rome³ 1949, 60. J. Le Gall, Le Tibre, Paris 1953, 60 sq. A. Aymard, R. Et. Anc. 59, 1957, 292 sq. c) The first treaty is dated about 400 B.C. by : B. Niese-E. Hohl, Grundriss der römischen Geschichte⁵, München 1923, 102. V. Constanzi, Rivista di filol. n.s. 3, 1925, 381 sqq. K. J. Beloch, RG 298, 309. W. Hoffmann, Rom und die griechische Welt im IV Jahrhundert (Philol., Suppl. 27, 1) 1935, 14 n. 24.

of the *pontifices* and the annalists; these names could not have appeared at all in the original document published by Polybius.[1]

4. The names of this fictitious pair of consuls in what was supposed to be the first year of the Republic were connected with the first treaty with Carthage—consequently before Polybius and after 304 B.C. at the earliest. As the *annales maximi* inserted only the names but did not invent the stories told about them, the relation of these two names to the text of the first treaty was established by some of the early annalists. Since the concept of projecting Roman might back into the epoch of the kings was the creation of Fabius Pictor, he is the only possible author of this forgery.[2]

5. Polybius was deceived by Pictor, and in this was certainly influenced by his Roman friends (συνετώτατοι III 22, 3), who helped him in the interpretation of the documents in question. There is a second case which demonstrates how heavily he relied on his informants concerning the whole complex of the treaties with Carthage: he let himself be persuaded that the treaty mentioned by Philinus, being politically inopportune for Roman politics, could not have existed because it was not found in the archive of the *aediles* on the Capitol—though this archive was neither on the Capitoline hill nor did it contain treaties with foreign powers.[3]

6. It was realized long ago that Antium and Tarracina, mentioned in the first treaty by Polybius, were not yet conquered by Rome in 509-8 B.C.[4] But far more important is the general fact that Roman

---

[1] The *cognomen* was not used in official documents at the time of the early Republic. Cf. Mommsen, RF 1², 45 sqq. C. Cichorius, *De fastis consularibus antiquissimis* (Leipziger Studien 9) 188., 177 sqq. K. J. Neumann, Strassburger Festschrift zur 46. Versammlung deutscher Philologen 1901, 314 sqq. But the introduction of monetary values in the text of the Twelve Tables offers a good example for the literary re-elaboration of archaic texts, so that not the *tria nomina*, but the historical absurdity of the surreptitious consulate of Horatius and Brutus give us the certainty of falsification. Cf. also Mommsen, Röm. Chronol. ², 1859, 322.

[2] In this sense wrote K. Hanell, Histoire et historiens dans l'antiquité, Genève 1956, 166. For a possible relationship with the *Origines* of Cato, cf. G. Nenci, Historia 7, 1958, 263 sqq. (with detailed modern bibliography).

[3] Polyb. III 26, 1-5. Cf. M. Cary, JRS 9, 1919, 67 sqq. P. Bung, Quintus Fabius Pictor, Diss. Köln 1950, 143 sq. *Contra* : G. Nenci, *loc. cit.*

[4] Cf. Mommsen, CIL X p. 660, 663 sq. W. Soltau, Philol. 48, 1889, 282 sq. The very old name of Tarracina (cf. Schachermeyr, Rh. Mus. n. F. 86, 1930, 357 n. 2) subsisted, of course, besides the Volscian *Anxur* during the early

territory did not even extend to the sea in those years; we shall enlarge later on the process by which she annexed Latium, progressing step by step toward the south in the fifth and fourth centuries B.C.

7. Correspondingly, Roman sea power did not develop until the same period, as a result of new problems of conquest and the necessity of creating a new arm for new tasks. The achievements, both on land and on sea, took place simultaneously. There is no other logical place for the first treaty with Carthage than at the moment when Rome, already in possession of a considerable stretch of the coast and being attacked by a Greek naval expeditionary force from Sicily, took the side of the antagonists of Syracuse.

At this very moment Diodorus, one of our most important sources, records that Rome and Carthage concluded their first covenant.[1] Livy notes the same event under the same consuls. There is no doubt that he too meant this as the first treaty, and that not only Orosius, who used him exclusively as his source for early Roman history, was not the only one to understand him in this way. Livy several times stressed the point that the Romans of the early epoch ignored the sea and were no sailors [2]—though he was, of course, well aware of the

---

Republic. The believers in the letter of the Annals may also be embarrassed by the mentioning of Ardea in the first treaty, though in the story of the overthrow of the last Tarquin Ardea was *not* conquered by the tyrant.

[1] Diod. XVI 69, 1 : ... Ῥωμαῖοι κατέστησαν ὑπάτους Μάρκον Οὐαλέριον καὶ Μάρκον Ποπίλιον, .. ἐπὶ δὲ τούτων Ῥωμαίοις μὲν πρὸς Καρχηδονίους πρῶτον συνθῆκαι ἐγένοντο. His source is not Pictor, but a subsequent annalist ; cf. A. Klotz, Rh. Mus. n. F. 86, 1937, 206 sqq. The most recent discussions noted in G. Perl, Kritische Untersuchungen zu Diodors römischer Jahrzählung. Berlin 1957.

[2] Liv. VII 27, 2 : *et cum Carthaginiensibus legatis Romae foedus ictum, cum amicitiam ac societatem petentes venissent.* Cf. Oros. III 7, 1-2 : *numerandum etiam inter mala censeo primum illud ictum cum Carthaginiensibus foedus, quod isdem temporibus fuit. .. anno siquidem ab urbe condita CCCCII legati a Carthagine Romam missi sunt foedusque pepigerunt.* (On the date of Orosius cf. O. Leuze, Die römische Jahrzählung, Tübingen 1909, 94 sqq. Livius seems to have opposed the idea of an early treaty with Carthage in his following statements : (I 56, 5-6) (Tarquinius Superbus). . . . . *hoc velut domestico exterritus visu Delphos ad maxime inclitum in terris oraculum mittere statuit ; neque responsa sortium ulli alii committere ausus duos filios per ignotas ea tempestate terras, ignotiora maria in Graeciam misit.* IV 29, 8 (431 B.C.) : *insigni magnis rebus anno additur nihil tum ad rem Romanam pertinere visum, quod Carthaginienses, tanti hostes futuri, tum primum . . . in Siciliam exercitum traiecere.* VII 26, 13 (on the clash of the Greek fleet with the Roman army) : *nec illi terra, nec Romanus mari bellator erat.* Cf. G. De Sanctis, St. d. R. 2², 239 sq. A. Aymard, R. Et. Anc. 59, 1957, 292 sq., etc.

ROME DURING THE EARLY REPUBLIC

alleged early dating of the treaty in Polybius;[1] his assertions sound like an attack upon the unwise belief in the possibility of a treaty with Carthage in the first year of the Republic. He was entirely right.

Besides the first treaty, which was signed in fact in 348 B.C. and preserved by Polybius (III 22, 1-23, 6), a second one was also reproduced by him (III 24, 1-16). The close connection of the two was noticed long ago;[2] but the political and chronological consequences of this intimate correlation have been uncovered only recently.[3] Though the wording of the second treaty is completely changed, the substance, except for a few details, is unaltered, as though the terms of the first must have remained valid for the second: these are conclusions of A. Aymard which we accept; but we must rely on the fact that because both treaties mirror the same political and military situation, they cannot be separated by more than a very few years—a very few years after 348 B.C., the date we hope to have established finally for the first treaty. The state of affairs in Latium as reflected in the second treaty, in which there still existed cities not yet subject to Rome, makes it certain that the renewal of the first document took place before the subjugation of the Latins in 340 B.C.[4] The close collaboration of the two powers concerned is well attested in those years. Livy mentions that by the victorious end of the first Romano-Samnite war "the Carthaginians also sent envoys congratulating the Romans with the gift of a golden wreath, weighing twenty-five pounds, and deposited it in the *cella Iovis* on the Capitol."[5] An alliance is not mentioned, but we can reasonably assume that the revised form of their covenant was drawn up at that time, in 343 B.C.

The international entanglements in the background of this agreement have been noticed already, as well as the warlike suspense and chaotic conditions in Latium,[6] whose inhabitants were outlawed

[1] Liv. IX 19, 13 (on the chances of a possible clash between Alexander the Great and the Romans): *et forsitan, cum et foederibus vetustis iuncta res Punica Romanae esset et timor par adversus communem hostem duas potentissimas armis virisque urbes armaret, simul Punico Romanoque obrutus bello esset.*

[2] F. Schachermeyr, Rh. Mus. n. F. 86, 1930, 356 sqq. W. Hoffmann, *op. cit.* 14. G. De Sanctis, Rivista di filol. n.s. 13, 1935, 401. L. Wickert, Klio 31, 1938, 352 sqq., 361, etc.

[3] F. Hampl, Rh. Mus. n. F. 100, 1958, 58 sqq. A. Aymard, R. Et. Anc. 59, 1957, 277 sqq.

[4] Ed. Meyer, Kleine Schriften 2, Halle 1924, 296 sqq. K. J. Beloch, RG 309.

[5] Liv. VII 38, 2.

[6] Cf. above, p. 353. Ed. Meyer, *op. cit.* 259 sqq. E. Ferenczy, Acta Antiqua 1, 1951-52, 136 sqq.

by the second treaty if they failed to obey the Romans. The actual purpose of this renewed alliance for Rome at the moment was to deliver up the Latins, not yet incorporated in her empire, to the mercy of Carthage, or, better, to compel them to surrender by threatening them from the sea. The paragraphs on overseas trade may have been regarded as relevant for the future; for the present, the conquest of Latium was evidently in the foreground.

ॐ

THE CELTIC INVASIONS

The Roman Annals under the year 390 B.C. tell of the complete breakdown of the Roman army, attacked unexpectedly by the Gauls at the small river Allia, on the left bank of the Tiber—not much farther north from Rome than Veii on the right bank—and the capture of the city. Though the more exact Greek chronology assigns this catastrophe to 387,[1] we shall follow the Roman datings throughout the following discussion for practical reasons. Although the collapse of Rome aroused some interest and sympathy in the Greek world, our information on the Gallic inroads is very fragmentary. And what is preserved consists mainly of the inflated accounts of the later annalists, who obscured basic facts by freely applying literary embroidery and patriotic embellishments.

The origin and development of this corrupt historiographical tradition were recognized, however, by Mommsen.[2] He realized that the short and sober summary of the Celtic invasions in Polybius was drawn from the same source—Fabius Pictor, according to

[1] Polyb. I 6, 1 sq. Cf. W. F. Unger, SBBayr. Ak. 1876, 533 sqq. O. Leuze, *op. cit.* 115 sq. F. W. Walbank, A Historical Commentary on Polybios 1, Oxford 1957, 46 sq. K. F. Stroheker, Dionysios I., Wiesbaden 1958, 221 n. 52.

[2] Mommsen, Hermes 13, 1878, 515 sqq. (reprinted with complements in RF 2, 297 sqq.) The literary data are collected by A. Schwegler, RG 3, 1858, 234 sqq. O. Clason, RG 1, Berlin 1873, 265 sqq. Cf. also B. Niese, Hermes 13, 1878, 401 sqq. G. Thouret, in : Fleckeisen's Jahrb. f. class. Philol., Suppl. 11, 1880, 93 sqq. O. Leuze, Die römische Jahrzählung, Tübingen 1909, 120 sqq. J. Kromayer, AbhSächs Ak., ph.-h. Kl. 34 no. 5, 1921. K. J. Beloch, RG 132 sqq. Ed. Meyer, Kleine Schriften 2, Halle 1924, 307 sqq. F. Schachermeyr, Klio 23, 1930, 277 sqq. L. Homo, CAH 7, 554 sqq. G. De Sanctis, St. d. R. 2², 147 sqq., 245 sqq. J. Bayet, Tite-Live 5, Paris 1954, 156 sqq. J. Wolski, Historia 5, 1956, 24 sqq. References to other modern discussions may be found in these works.

Mommsen—who also provided the basis for the elaborate fictions of the later Annals. But I think we can advance a little further along two lines: first, by the reinterpretation of a passage of Polybius; and second, by retaining a few authentic features in the late Annals, which were disregarded in the short extract of Polybius, yet preserved in Latin historical accounts.

The fact that Rome survived was certainly not due to the small group of warriors and magistrates besieged on the Capitoline hill, nor to the women and children scattered throughout the neighboring countryside. The sources agree in relating that the immense impetus of the Celtic attack turned the clash at the Allia [1] into an instant rout. The chances of escaping unharmed in such a panic are far greater than in a pitched battle. An important aspect of this rout is that the Roman soldiers were not scattered in all directions but crossed the Tiber and occupied the strong natural fortress of the citadel of Veii.[2] This was certainly not an obvious solution for the terrified soldiers, and certainly not the easiest way of escape. Anyone who, after such a crushing defeat, has ever had to flee to save his life, as has the writer, knows all too well that on such occasions the common man is at the mercy of his instincts and that normally the result is a complete dispersal. Consequently there was someone at the battle of the Allia, a high officer who did not lose his head, who made the right decision. It was impossible to defend Rome since it had no walls: therefore the army had to be reorganized elsewhere. The same stubborn resolution saved the state when the small garrison and the magistrates on the Capitol defended themselves, whereas the city was abandoned to her fate and the civilians were left equally unprotected—another decision of immense consequence, made immediately after the debacle.[3]

Nor was the stay of the defeated army in Veii without effect. Polybius (II 18, 3) writes that after the capture of Rome the Gauls were struck by a counteraction (γενομένου δ'ἀντισπάσματος) and at the same time their own territory was invaded by the Veneti

[1] Diod. XIV 114, 4-7. Liv. V 38, 6. Plut., *Camill.* 18, 8, etc.

[2] Diod. XIV 115, 2 ; 116, 1-2. Liv. V 38, 5 ; 43, 4 ; 45, 4-8 ; 46, 4 sqq. 11 ; 48, 5 ; VII 13, 5. Plut., *Camill.* 18, 9 ; 29, 1 sq.

[3] Polyb. I 6, 2-3 ; II 18, 2. Diod. XIV 115, 3-4. Liv. V 38, 10 ; 39, 9-10. 12 ; 41, 1 ; 42, 3 ; 44, 5 ; 46, 2-3. 9-10 ; 47, 1 sqq. ; 48, 1 sq. ; 51, 9. Plut. *Camill.* 20, 3 ; 22, 5-7 ; 23, 1 ; 24, 1 sq. ; 27, 1 sq. 28, 2-3. App., *Celt.* 1. Cass. Dio fr. 25, 5-6 (1, p. 80 Boiss.). Eutr. 1, 20. *Vir. ill.* 23, 9 ; 24, 1. 3, etc.

(καὶ τῶν Οὐενέτων ἐμβαλόντων εἰς τὴν χώραν αὐτῶν); they therefore concluded a pact with the Romans, gave up the city, and returned home. As I see it, this passage has been misunderstood: hitherto the setback (ἀντίσπασμα) has been generally referred to as the invasion of the Veneti, the "and" (καί), which connects the mention of the two events being taken as an introduction to the specification of the unfavorable occurrence which was the attack of the northern neighbors. Polybius is apparently the first Greek historian to use the word ἀντίσπασμα which has been mistranslated as "distraction," "diversion in war" only on the basis of the preconception that the two events were identical.[1] Ἀντισπάω means "draw the contrary way, hold back," and in the passive "suffer a check," "to be drawn in the contrary direction." No other meaning can be suggested by the substantive, composed of this verb, especially as introduced for the first time in a historical narrative. The καὶ after it must therefore refer to another happening. The ἀντίσπασμα is, in my view, a Roman counterstroke, even if the expression is not specific.

We have, in fact, the certain evidence that a Roman success was then achieved. Long before the birth of the Annals, Aristotle (+322-21) mentioned in connection with the capture of Rome that the city was saved by a certain *Lucius*, whom we are unable to identify with any Roman personality of that epoch.[2] Plutarch, who preserved this invaluable statement, thought that the philosopher confused the names and that he really meant Camillus, whose *praenomen* was *Marcus*.

We can hardly impute to the reorganized Roman army in Veii more than efficient harassing actions against the formidable victors. The authentic kernel of the legend of Camillus, afterward blown up into resplendent victories by patriotic fiction,[3] was in truth a modest success, in all likelihood already inflated in Fabius Pictor—the source

---

[1] Liddel, Scott, and Jones give the meaning mentioned in the text. A. Mauersberger, Polybios-Lexikon 1, Berlin 1956, 140, has "anderseitige (militärische) Inanspruchnahme." G. Thouret, *op. cit.* 108 n. 45, uses the word with the same meaning : "als ihre Aufmerksamkeit abgelenkt wurde,—nämlich durch den Einfall der Veneter." W. R. Paton translates the passage with "being diverted by an invasion of their own country by the Veneti" and disregards the καί ; etc.

[2] Plut., *Cam.* 22, 4 : Ἀριστοτέλης δ' ὁ φιλόσοφος τὸ μὲν ἁλῶναι τὴν πόλιν ὑπὸ Κελτῶν ἀκριβῶς δῆλός ἐστιν ἀκηκοώς, τὸν δὲ σώσαντα Λεύκιον εἶναί φησιν. ἦν δὲ Μᾶρκος, οὐ Λεύκιος, ὁ Κάμιλλος.

[3] Cf. A. Momigliano, Secondo Contributo alla storia degli studi classici, Roma 1960, 89 sqq. J. Bayet, Tite-Live 5, Paris 1954, 140 sqq.

ROME DURING THE EARLY REPUBLIC

of Polybius—who, I think, consciously reduced its significance by the colorless technical word ἀντίσπασμα. It was in any case the first sign of the unsurpassed vitality of the Romans, who, "after making a truce on conditions satisfactory to the Gauls and being thus contrary to their expectation reinstated in their home, and as it were now started on the road of aggrandizement, continued in the following years to wage war on their neighbors." [1] In a generation they became again the leading power of Latium.[2]

Polybius [3] informs us that the Celts, after the sack of Rome, were forced to return to the north of Italy to deal with the Veneti who were raiding their homes. But the prospect of adventure and booty lured a group of them to push forward from Rome toward the south. The Celts then were living through the storm-and-stress period of their national life, displaying their indomitable energies in a manner similar to the Teutonic tribes many centuries later; soon afterwards the armies of the Hellenistic rulers around the Mediterranean sea were filled with Celtic mercenaries.[4]

The band which turned southward from Rome reached Apulia, where Dionysius I of Syracuse was trying hard to conquer the Greek cities. They offered Dionysius their help and in them the great tyrant won most valuable allies.[5] He "seems to have quickly realized the advantages of an association with this vigorous new element, which harassed Etruscans and Italic peoples from the opposite direction, but did not constitute a threat to Sicily. Besides Iberians and Campanians the Celtic mercenaries from now on became the best part of his army. In the following years, when the sea-power of Syracuse was

---

[1] Polyb. I 6, 3 : 'Ρωμαῖοι . . . γενόμενοι πάλιν ἀνελπίστως τῆς πατρίδος ἐγκρατεῖς, καὶ λαβόντες οἷον ἀρχὴν τῆς συναυξήσεως, ἐπολέμουν ἐν τοῖς ἑξῆς χρόνοις πρὸς τοὺς ἀστυγείτονας.

[2] Polyb. II 18, 5: ἐν ᾧ καιρῷ 'Ρωμαῖοι τήν τε σφετέραν δύναμιν ἀνέλαβον καὶ τὰ κατὰ τοὺς Λατίνους αὖθις πράγματα συνεστήσαντο.

[3] Polyb. II 18, 3. Cf. Mommsen, RF 2, 336 sq.

[4] Cf. A. Wienicke, Keltisches Söldnertum in der Mittelmeerwelt bis zur Herrschaft der Römer. Breslau 1927.

[5] Iustin., Epit. XX 5, 1-6 : Igitur Dionysius tyrannus, quem supra a Sicilia exercitum in Italiam traiecisse bellumque Graecis intulisse memoravimus, expugnatis Locris Crotonienses . . . adgreditur, qui fortius cum paucis tanto exercitui eius quam antea cum tot milibus Locrensium paucitati restiterunt . . . Sed Dionysium gerentem bellum legati Gallorum, qui ante menses Romam incenderant, societatem amicitiamque petentes adeunt, gentem suam inter hostes eius positam esse magnoque usui ei futuram vel in acie bellanti vel de tergo intentis in proelium hostibus adfirmant. Grata legatio Dionysio fuit. Itaque pacta societate et auxiliis Gallorum auctus bellum velut ex integro restaurat.

expanding successfully into the coastal regions of the Adriatic sea, its connections with the Gauls became even closer." [1] Ankon, the present Ancona, was his foundation "which can now be fitted into the system of the Adriatic strong-points of Dionysius. This city was enfilading the new Celtic territory on the Adriatic coast in the South, as did correspondingly Hadria (another foundation of the same ruler in this region) in the North of it. Ankon provided the shortest connection between Sicily and the Celtic tribes of Italy, with whom Dionysius became connected some years earlier—as we saw—and which furnished for him a most valuable supplement to his mercenary-armies." [2]

The Celtic host returning from Apulia again crossed Latium, and soon thereafter suffered a reverse at the hands of the Caeretanes— invested by local pride with the dimensions of a crushing defeat.[3] In view of the alliance of Syracuse with these same Celts, and the far-reaching implications of Dionysius' politics in Italy, it was legitimate to question [4] whether the naval attack on Pyrgi-Caere in 384-83 B.C. and the presence of his Celtic allies in the rear of the Caeretanes were not parts of a coordinated action. Yet the return of the Celtic host to the north seems to have taken place earlier than the naval raid on Pyrgi, and the alleged analogous combination of a Greek fleet action with a Celtic invasion in Latium a generation later simply did not occur.[5]

---

[1] K. F. Stroheker, Dionysios I. Wiesbaden 1958, 119.

[2] *Ibid.* 125 sqq.

[3] Diod. XIV 117, 7 : οἱ δ᾽εἰς τὴν Ἰαπυγίαν τῶν Κελτῶν ἐληλυθότες ἀνέστρεψαν διὰ τῆς τῶν Ῥωμαίων χώρας. καὶ μετ᾽ ὀλίγον ὑπὸ Κερίων ἐπιβουλευθέντες νυκτὸς ἅπαντες κατεκόπησαν ἐν τῷ Τραυσίῳ πεδίῳ. Strab. V 2, 3 (C. 220) : καὶ γὰρ τοὺς ἑλόντας τὴν Ῥώμην Γαλάτας κατεπολέμησαν ἀπιοῦσιν ἐπιθέμενοι κατὰ Σαβίνους, καὶ ἃ παρ᾽ ἑκόντων ἔλαβον Ῥωμαίων ἐκεῖνοι λάφυρα ἄκοντας ἀφείλοντο. Cf. also Frontin., Stratag. II 6, 1.

[4] As M. Sordi did, *op. cit.* 67 sqq.

[5] *Ibid.* 67 sq. : "Attacchi combinati greco-gallici dalla terra e dal mare si verificarono effettivamente negli anni successivi : nel 350 e nel 349, in particolare, i Galli che venivano dall' Apulia ma che avevano le loro basi alle porte stesse di Roma, sui colli Albani, agivano in corrispondenza con le forze navali greche che incrociavano tra Anzio e la foce del Tevere, e quando furono battuti dai Romani si rifiugarono in parte, come al solito, in Apulia (Liv. VII 26, 9), in parte sulle navi greche (Liv. VII 32, 9) . . . Nel 350 e 349 i Galli che attaccavano Roma erano dunque, con ogni probabilità, mercenari al servizio di Siracusa . . ." Miss Sordi has unfortunately overlooked Liv. VII 25, 3-4, which attests that the Gauls not only had no relations with the Greek fleet, but that they fought a great battle against each other : *Galli ex Albanis montibus*

ROME DURING THE EARLY REPUBLIC

There were more Gallic invasions after that first terrible tempest and before the conquest of Latium by Rome in 338 B.C. According to our earliest authority, Polybius, there were only two such inroads which, though not setting off a new conflagration, still produced more anxiety than real success for the Romans. In our literary evidence of a later date than Polybius, this picture changes to an ever-increasing series of resplendent Roman victories. However, it was recognized long ago that the glamour of the later Annals has no historical basis other than the short recapitulation in Polybius, extracted in all probability from Fabius Pictor.[1]

Polybius reports the following main facts:

1. After their return to their new settlements in the Po valley, the Celts were tied down there by domestic wars and by frequent attacks from the neighboring Alpine tribes (II 18, 4).

2. "Thirty years after the capture of Rome, the Celts again arrived in the Alban Hills. The Romans did not venture to oppose them with their army because they were caught unawares by the sudden invasion and unable to collect the forces of their allies" (II 18, 6).

3. "But when twelve years later the Celts again marched in with a great army they were informed in advance of it, and assembling their allies they marched out with great resoluteness against them, rushing to meet them in the field and take all risks for the common welfare. The Celts, perplexed by this challenge and at variance among themselves, withdrew by nightfall and set off for home, their retreat resembling a flight. After this, paralyzed with fear, they kept quiet for thirteen years . . ." (II 18, 6-9).

The thirty years between 390 and 360 B.C. (following the Varronian era) in which the Gauls did not make any serious expedition into Latium, allowed the Romans to recover their strength. The second invasion about 360, in Polybius, was replaced in the later Annals, as noticed already, by a series of attacks so as to provide an occasion

---

quia hiemis vim pati nequiverant, per campos maritimaque loca vagi populabantur ; mare infestum classibus Graecorum erat oraque litoris Antiatis Laurensque tractus et Tiberis ostia, ut praedones maritimi cum terrestribus congressi ancipiti semel proelio decertarint dubiique discesserint in castra Galli, Graeci retro ad naves, victos se an victores putarent. On the other hand, we agree with her (*op. cit.* 69 n. 2) concerning the general appraisal of the relations between Rome and Dionysius I, as against A. Momigliano, SDHI 5, 1939, 393 sq.

[1] B. Niese, Hermes 13, 1878, 401 sqq., 411 sq. Mommsen, Hermes 13, 1878, 551 sqq.: RF 2, 362 sq. G. De Sanctis, St. d. R. 2², 245 sq., etc.

for many invented Roman victories, and to compensate the reader for the shameful collapse at the Allia and the sack of the city with more and more manufactured titles of glory against the same dreadful enemy. The manipulation of these more recent writers is still easily grasped because they repeat the same basic elements under different years. The duel of T. Manlius Torquatus with the Celtic warrior of prodigious size on the bridge of the Anio is related, e.g., under the headings of five different years: in 367 B.C.,[1] 366 B.C.,[2] 361 B.C.,[3] 358 B.C.,[4] and 357 B.C.;[5] or: Polybius states that the Gauls returned thirty years after their first attack in Latium and penetrated the Alban Hills (εἰς "Αλβαν, II 18, 6). Subsequent writers register their appearance in the *ager Albanus* in 367 B.C.[6] and again in 360 B.C.[7] Finally, we are informed that the Gauls, defeated by the Romans, fled across Campania to Apulia, looting and pillaging; this is first noted in 367 B.C. [8] and again in 361 B.C.; [9] Livy says they returned to Latium in the following year.[10] But here we have conclusive evidence that an annalist, contemporary with Sulla, simply expanded the second invasion of Polybius (Fabius Pictor) to six full years.[11]

---

[1] Claud. Quadrigarius fr. 10 a (H. R. Rel. 1², 207 Peter). Plut., *Camill.* 40, 1 sqq. and Polyaenus VIII 7, 2 (who give the thirteenth year after the capture of Rome as the date ; their common source confused this second inroad with the third one, as also Appian., *Celt.* 1, did by calling this invasion the "third." DH XIV 8 (12) has correctly ἐκ δευτέρου ἐπιστρατεύσαντες. Zon. VII 24, 11 (Cass Dio, ed. Boiss. 1, 86).

[2] Oros. III 6, 1-3.

[3] Licin. Macer in : Liv. VII 9, 4 ; cf. T. R. S. Broughton, MRR 1, 120. Cic., *De off.* III 31, 112. Liv. VII 9, 3-10, 14 (after Cl. Quadrigarius, cf. H. Peter, H. R. Rel. 1² 207 sq.). Eutr. 2, 5.

[4] *Vir. ill.* 28.

[5] Liv. VI 42, 5-6 : *bellatum cum Gallis eo anno* (367 B.C.) *circa Anienem flumen auctor est Claudius inclitamque in ponte pugnam, qua T. Manlius Gallum, cum quo provocatus manus conseruit, . . . tum pugnatam. pluribus auctoribus magis adducor, ut credam decem haud minus post annos ea acta.* This would be the thirtieth year after the Allia battle in the Greek chronology.

[6] Liv. VI 42, 6, DH XIV 8 (12) sq. App., *Celt.* 1. Zon. VII 24, 10-12 (Cass. Dio, ed. Boiss., *loc. cit.*). Mommsen, RF 2, 362 n. 112, goes too far.

[7] Liv. VII 11, 3.

[8] Liv. VI 42, 8.

[9] Claud. Quadrig. fr. 11 (H. R. Rel. 1², 210 Peter). Liv. VII 1, 3 ; 11, 1. 3.

[10] Liv. VII 11, 3.

[11] Claud. Quadrig. fr. 11 : *Quadrigarius Annali : ita per sexennium vagati Apuliam atque agrum Campanum, quod his per militem licebat, spoliabantur(sic).* Liv. VI 42, 8 follows him (in spite of his own doubts) relating the defeat of the Celts in 367 B.C. in *Albano agro (ibid.* 42, 6) : *palati alii Apuliam maxime petentes cum fuga se longinqua, tum quod passim eos simul pavor terrorque distulerant, ab hoste tutati*

Consequently, we are obliged to reduce the pretended number of Celtic invasions of Latium between 367 and 357 B.C. to the one mentioned in Polybius thirty years after the sack of Rome, when the Romans did not risk a battle. The later annalists, though multiplying the Celtic inroads and defeats around 360 B.C. (as reckoned in their chronology), preserved at the same time some most valuable information not contained in the abridged summary of Polybius. It is mainly the account of Livy, preserved in its entirety, which saved from oblivion the following features of the original account, extracted by Polybius:

a) The second arrival of the Gauls coincides with the war between Rome and Tibur.[1] Both enemies of Rome join in alliance against her.[2] Praeneste seems to have sided with Tibur—as she had often done previously—and the Celts.[3] In this war, Roman victories are announced in 360 and 358 B.C. near the *porta Collina* of the new city-wall of Rome,[4] another further on near Tibur,[5] and then somewhere around Pedum.[6] They are not historical, as we have seen. But the triumph of the plebeian consul Poetelius "over the Gauls and over Tibur," [7] based on some local success, seems to me historical.

b) It sounds reasonable, too, that the Gauls continued their drive across Latium toward the south, attracted by the greater riches of the Greek cities. This would make plausible the assumption that their return toward the north happened a year later than their arrival.

c) In the fifth century (we shall turn our attention to this below)

---

sunt. Further on, he notices to 366 B.C. (VII 1, 3) : *principio anni et de Gallis, quos primo palatos per Apuliam congregari iam fama erat, . . . agitata mentio.* Cf. Eutrop. 2, 5 and Oros. III 6, 3 (on the war of 358 B.C.). Another feature of this Celtic inroad narrated under different years is that the Roman general delays the battle, because he knows that the enemy loses discipline and eagerness to fight in a short lapse of time. Cf. DH 14, 8 (12). Zonaras VII 24, 10 sq. Oros. III 6, 1. Liv. VII 12, 10 sqq.

[1] T. Quinctius Poenus is declared dictator *belli Gallici causa* : Liv. VII 9, 5. War started in the same year against Tibur : *ibid.* VII 9, 1-2.

[2] The alliance against Rome, *ibid.* VII 11, 1-2 : *ut Gallorum exercitus, proxima nocte relictis trepide castris in Tiburtem agrum atque inde societate belli facta commeatuque benigne ab Tiburtibus adiutus, mox in Campaniam transierit. ea fuit causa, cur proximo anno C. Poetelius Balbus consul . . . adversus Tiburtes . . . exercitum duceret. ad quorum auxilium cum Galli ex Campania redissent,* etc.

[3] Liv. VII 12, 8.

[4] Liv. VII 11, 6.

[5] *Ibid.* VII 11, 7 ; cf. 11, 10.

[6] *Ibid.* VII 12, 9 and 15, 8.

[7] Liv. VII 11, 9. *Acta triumph.* ed. A. Degrassi 68 sq., 540.

Tibur and Praeneste were connected with the neighboring mountain tribes, whereas the Latin cities of the Alban Hills opposed them under the leadership of Rome. The same sort of partisanship divided the communities of the Alban region, where the Gauls wrought havoc and devastation,[1] from Tibur and Praeneste. At the same time the Celtic menace constrained the Latin states around the *mons Albanus* to join forces again with Rome. We must stress this point: this rapprochement did not mean the reestablishment of the Roman hegemony in Latium, dissolved by the collapse after the defeat on the Allia, as Fabius Pictor—on whose account the survey of Polybius is based—wished to make us believe. The view of the source of Livy, mentioning a renewal of the Latin-Roman coalition after an intermission of many years,[2] in the time of the Callic invasion about 360 B.C., is contradictory to the much more optimistic and rather illogical information in Polybius,[3] who states that in the thirty years after the sack of Rome, this city was again able to master Latium, and only the suddenness of the Celtic drive prevented her from rallying her allies to her support. We must follow Livy's version also because the Latins were once again rising in revolt against Rome within a few years' time: Rome certainly did recover rapidly after her resounding defeat, but the supremacy over the Latins was yet to be won.

The third Celtic invasion took place according to Polybius twelve years after the second, just discussed. The Roman Annals extend the fighting against the Gauls to two years, to 350 and 349 B.C., in contrast to a brief episode, as described in Polybius, which is agreed to be the more reasonable version.[4] But here again emerges the curious

---

[1] Liv. VII 11, 3 : *Tiburtes ... ad quorum auxilium cum Galli ex Campania redissent, foedae populationes in Labicano Tusculanoque et Albano agro haud dubie Tiburtibus ducibus sunt factae.*

[2] Liv. VII 12, 7 : *Gallici quoque belli fama increbrescebat. Sed inter multos terrores solacio fuit pax Latinis petentibus data, et magna vis militum ab iis ex foedere vetusto, quod multis intermiserant annis, accepta.* 8 : *quo praesidio cum fulta res Romana esset, levius fuit, quod Gallos . . .,* etc. Cf. Polybius II 18.

[3] Polyb. II 18, 5-6 : ἐν ᾧ καιρῷ (in the 30 years after the Allia-battle). Ῥωμαῖοι τήν τε σφετέραν δύναμιν ἀνέλαβον καὶ τὰ κατὰ τοὺς Λατίνους αὖθις πράγματα συνεστήσαντο. παραγενομένων δὲ πάλιν τῶν Κελτῶν εἰς Ἄλβαν στρατεύματι μεγάλῳ μετὰ τὴν τῆς πόλεως κατάληψιν ἔτει τριακοστῷ, τότε μὲν οὐκ ἐτόλμησαν ἀντεξαγαγεῖν Ῥωμαῖοι τὰ στρατόπεδα, διὰ τὸ παραδόξου γενομένης τῆς ἐφόδου προκαταληφθῆναι καὶ μὴ καταταχῆσαι τὰς τῶν συμμάχων ἀθροίσαντας δυνάμεις.

[4] B. Niese, *loc. cit.* Mommsen, RF 2, 364. G. De Sanctis, St. d. R. 2², 246 sqq. K. J. Beloch, RG 137 sq.

fact that though the original chronological framework of this event is the one found in the summary of the great Greek historian, the Roman annalists preserved nevertheless the authentic information with regard to the attitude of the Latins.

Polybius (II 18, 7-8) says that this time Rome was not taken by surprise but having been informed in time she was able to rally her allies' troops and marched resolutely against the Gauls; these latter did not venture to join in battle, but withdrew in the following night, panic-stricken. The opposite emerges from the account of Livy.[1] If we put together the events given under the headings of the consuls of 350 and 349 B.C., restricting them to one year only, it becomes evident that the Latins proceeded against Rome jointly with the Gauls upon the arrival of the latter's army in Latium and did not wait a year to revolt, as Livy stated.[2] The Senate made a supreme effort to raise ten legions—the largest army for a long time in the history of Rome [3]—so as to cope with the naval squadrons of Syracuse as well as their own rebellious tribesmen, allied with the Celts. This explains why the Celtic host marched again to the hilly section of the *ager Albanus*,[4] withdrawing to the citadel of Alba Longa,[5] and descended from the Alban hills toward the seashore for looting,[6] evidently supported by the neighboring cities. When pressed hard by the Romans, the Celtic forces fell back to the Pomptine plain,[7] and turned away from Latium toward the south,[8] apparently to enrich themselves in Magna Graecia.

---

[1] Liv. VII 23, 1 sqq. The other evidence reflects the same picture : Claud. Quadrig. fr. 12 (H. R. Rel. 1² 211 Peter). DH 15, 1. Val. Max. III 2, 6. Flor. I 8, 20. Zon. VII 25, 7-8. Eutr. 2, 6. Oros. III 6, 4-5. App., *Celt.* 2. *Fasti triumph.* (Inscr. Ital. XIII 1, p. 39 and the note by Degrassi, *ibid.* 540).

[2] Liv. VII 25, 5-6 : *inter hos longe maximus extitit terror concilia populorum Latinorum ad lucum Ferentinae habita responsumque haud ambiguum imperantibus milites Romanis datum, absisterent imperare iis, quorum auxilio egerent ; Latinos pro sua libertate potius quam alieno imperio laturos arma.*

[3] Liv. VII 25, 7-8.

[4] Liv. VII 23, 2 means this with *Gallorum exercitum in agro Latino castra posuisse,* because the Roman army convenes *extra portam Capenam* (23, 3).

[5] Liv. VII 24, 8 : *fusique per campos . . . . . quod editissimum inter aequales tumulos occurrebat oculis, arcem Albanam petunt.*

[6] Liv. VII 25, 3 : *Galli ex Albanis montibus, quia hiemis vim pati nequiverant, per campos maritumaque loca vagi populabantur.*

[7] Claud. Quadr., fr. 12. Liv. VII 26, 13.

[8] Liv. VII 26, 9 : *primo per Volscos Falernumque agrum dissipati sunt, inde Apuliam ac mare superum petierunt.* Cf. 32, 9 (with a rhetorical exaggeration).

This picture offers us the logical background for the great struggle between the Latin states and Rome in the next decade.[1] Rome's success was not spectacular, being still on the defensive; but it was great in its consequences. Celtic aggression was stopped for half a century; at the same time the Syracusan intervention failed to save Antium and the Volscians. The Latins lost their chance to shake off Roman supremacy with Celtic aid. The way to their final subjugation was laid open.

✌

THE WARS OF THE EARLY REPUBLIC WITH THE VOLSCIANS AND AEQUIANS

We have no explicit information about how and when the Volscians swept down from the mountains bearing their name to the Latin hills south of the *mons Albanus* and the adjacent coastal plain.[2] But different considerations allow us to determine at least the epoch in which this happened. First, it is certain that the Volscians, too, were previously subjugated by the Etruscans,[3] not only the Latins. Besides the clear statement of Cato, the early drainage of the Pomptine marshes bears witness to this, as do Etruscan geographical names and objects of Etruscan provenience found in the same region.[4] Since the conquest of Campania, as we have already seen,[5] it became vitally important for Etruria to have a firm grip on the communication lines between their main territory and their new Campanian cities and also to have coastal bases in that intermediate region for their shipping

---

[1] The question arises : who was the historian to whom Livy's sources owed this precious information—along with the story of the Greek fleet, blockading the coast of Latium—so much preferable to the orientation of Polybius? Perhaps the *annales maximi* contained it, and perhaps some early annalist found it there : the behavior of the Latins is not likely to be known to the Greeks.

[2] The last survey on ancient literary data and the archeological evidence is that of G. Radke, RE 9A, 773 sqq. 807 sqq.

[3] Cato, *Orig.* fr. 62 (H. R. Rel. 1² p. 73 Peter=Serv., *Aen.* 11, 567) : *Licet* (sc. Metabus) *Privernas esset, tamen quia in Tuscorum iure paene omnis Italia fuerat, generaliter in Metabum omnium odia ferebantur. Nam pulsus fuerat a gente Volscorum, quae etiam ipsa Etruscorum potestate regebatur, quod Cato plenissime exsecutus est.* Cf. Ed. Meyer, GdA 2², 1893, 706 and 5, 1902, 132 sq.

[4] M. Hoffmann, RE Suppl. 8, 1153 sq., brings the evidence ; we differ from him in its evaluation.

[5] Cf. above, p. 176 sqq.

ROME DURING THE EARLY REPUBLIC

toward the south. This necessity supports the conclusion that the Etruscan domination over the Volscians began more or less in the same epoch as over Latium; it is obvious that its end was connected too in some way with the events which enabled the Latins to get rid of their Etruscan overlords at the end of the sixth century B.C.

The struggle between Latins and Volscians [1] was the direct consequence of the breakdown of the foreign rule in their region, south and north of Monte Artemisio. According to our literary tradition the aggressors were—and we have no reason at all to disbelieve this— the Volscians with the Aequians, their relatives and neighbors; their warlike activity, however, was not aimed primarily at territorial gains after the conquest of the fertile plain of southern Latium, but consisted of annual looting expeditions,[2] the booty providing the basis of their primitive economic system.

The beginnings of the wars of Rome with the Volscians and Aequians are obfuscated, aside from the lack of information, by the tendency of the Roman Annals to illustrate the early ascent of Rome as a leading power by fictitious victories, continuing this practice after the disappearance of the kings.

The pre-annalistic report [3] of the capture of Suessa Pometia by Tarquinius Superbus is unhistorical: Pometia joined the League of Aricia as a Latin city in the last decade of the sixth century, and after the constitution of the League Superbus lost his realm. But were it historical, it could be only the enterprise of an Etruscan power,

---

[1] The literary sources were collected by A. Schwegler, RG 2, 1856, 691 sqq. Cf. Mommsen, RG 1⁷, 343 sqq. G. De Sanctis, St. R. 2², 98 sqq. K. J. Beloch, RG, 295 sqq., disregards the whole dossier of the Volscian wars of the fifth century B.C. as legendary or fictitious. This is, however, irresponsible and acritical.

[2] Liv. VI 12, 2-5 : *Non dubito, praeter satietatem tot iam libris adsidua bella cum Volscis gesta legentibus illud quoque succursurum, quod mihi percensenti propiores temporibus harum rerum auctores miraculo fuit, unde totiens victis Volscis et Aequis suffecerint milites, quod cum ab antiquis tacitum praetermissum sit, cuius tandem ego rei praeter opinionem, quae sua cuique coniectanti esse potest, auctor sim? simile veri est aut intervallis bellorum, sicut nunc in dilectibus fit Romanis, alia atque alia subole iuniorum ad bella instauranda totiens usos esse, aut non ex isdem semper populis exercitus scriptos, quamquam eadem semper gens bellum intulerit, aut innumerabilem multitudinem liberorum capitum in eis fuisse locis, quae nunc vix seminario exiguo militum relicto servitia Romana ab solitudine vindicant.* The true character of those wars is apparent, however, in Livy's reports on the Volscian and Aequian offensive, consisting merely of booty-collecting actions, and not of conquest, as the Roman counterstrokes.

[3] Cf. above, p. 139 sq. 324, and below, p. 367.

The Wars with the Volscians and Aequians

whose vassal Rome was at the time of her last king, and in no case a Roman conquest. All the rest of the accounts of Roman supremacy and success on Volscian soil are in the style of the freely invented glories of the regal age. Ancus Marcius punishes the Volscian raids in a victorious war;[1] King Priscus destroys Apiolae,[2] in truth the name of Pometia, translated by Pictor when duplicating the account of the building of the Capitoline temple; other writers, however, let the series of Volscian raids begin with Superbus only.[3] The Volscian centers of Ecetra and Antium are said to be subjects of this latter king,[4] who is also stated to have founded colonies in Signia and in Circeii, which became in fact Roman only much later.[5] The same king is victorious also against the Aequians in the Annals.[6]

The fictitious anticipation of the founding of colonies on Volscian soil, documenting forged Roman victories, does not stop with the establishment of the Republic. In 508 the colonization of Signia is again announced;[7] in 503-2 B.C. Pometia, allegedly destroyed by Tarquinius Superbus, reappears as a Latin colony, going over to the Auruncans with Cora, but recaptured[8] by the Romans. But this was a time when the victorious Latin cities, backed by Aristodemus, barred the way of the Romans to the south. In 495 the colony of King Superbus in Signia is reinforced, at least in the Annals.[9] In the same year, P. Servilius conquers Suessa Pometia once more,[10] and Ecetra becomes a Roman colony,[11] as do Velitrae in 494,[12] reinforced

[1] DH III 41, 5.

[2] DH III 49, 1-3. Liv. I 35, 7. Cf. above, p. 140.

[3] Liv. I 53, 2 : *is (sc.* Superbus*) primus Volscis bellum in ducentos amplius post suam aetatem annos movit, Suessamque Pometiam ex iis vi cepit.*

[4] DH IV 49, 1.

[5] DH IV 63, 1. Liv. I 56, 3. But cf. Liv. II 21, 7 and 39, 2, further on DH V 20, 1 and 58, 4. Plut., *Poplic.* 16, 3.—Circei recaptured by Coriolanus for the Volscians in 487: DH VIII 14, 1-2. Liv. II 39, 2. In reality it became a Roman colony only in 393 (Diod. XIV 102, 4), but revolted in 385 (Liv. VI 12, 6 ; 13, 8 ; 17, 7) and 383 B.C. (Liv. VI 21, 2).

[6] Strab. V 3, 4 (C. 231). Liv. I 55, 1.

[7] The *Signuria* in DH V 20, 1, and Plut., *Popl.* 16, 2 (cf. DH V 58, 4), can hardly be anything else than Signia ; cf. H. Nissen, It. Lk. 2, 650, n. 4.

[8] Liv. II 16, 8-17, 7. In 495 B.C., however, the Volscians were in the possession of both cities. Liv. II 22, 2.

[9] DH V 20, 1 ; VI 32, 1 ; Liv. II 21, 7.

[10] DH VI 29, 4 sq. Liv. II 25, 5 sq. Cf. G. De Sanctis, St. d. R. 2², 98 sq.

[11] Liv. II 25, 6. DH VI 32, 1, cf. 34, 4. But in 487 Ecetra appears in the hands of the Volscians (DH VIII 4, 4) as also in 464 (Liv. III 4, 2-3) and rises against Rome in 461 (Liv. III 10, 8) and again in 459 (DH X 28, 3).

[12] Liv. II 31, 4. DH VI 43, 1. Reinforced : Liv. II 34, 6. DH VII 12, 5 ; 13, 1.

in 492, Norba in the Pomptine plain in 492,[1] Satricum about the same time,[2] and Antium in 467.[3]

It will become apparent below, as G. De Sanctis and E. T. Salmon have already suggested, that Rome did not found citizen colonies at all in the fifth and fourth centuries, but all such foundations were then made by the Latin League. The key points just enumerated were on the strip of land between Volscians and Latins and, if historical, the new foundations could only be brought about by a great effort of the newly cemented *nomen Latinum* after the battle at Lake Regillus, in order to oppose new bastions to the aggressors. But the use of written Latin sources by Pictor is highly improbable, as it is also hardly imaginable that just after the victory of Rome against the League of Aricia, such an immediate, successful common effort against the Volscians would have been feasible. The offensive of the mountain tribes was in full swing till about 460 B.C.; no such great counterstrokes are credible before that turn of the tide.

The evidence quoted in our footnotes shows at a glance that the later Annals did not discard discrepancies which developed partly through the use of the sound *annales maximi* by the followers of Pictor, partly through additional fictions of these writers, flowing on in the transmissive channels of literary tradition along with other versions. In such circumstances, it is impossible to find an exact moment when the mystification ends and the events related become historical, because the two currents are intermingled; the make-up vanish slowly and the truth streams in only gradually. But a more general resolution of this problem is not hopeless at all.

First of all, we must consider a statement in the Annals which Diodorus found in his source: a remark made in connection with the invented victories of Camillus a year after the Gallic catastrophe. It is based on the assumption that the Volscian wars began not earlier than about 460 B.C.[4] Serious historians believed this to be correct,[5]

---

[1] DH VII 13, 5. Liv. II 34, 6. Cass. Dio fr. 18, 3.

[2] Liv. II 39, 3 : *Satricum Longulam Poluscam Coriolos, novella haec Romanis oppida* ; but *ibid.* 33, 5 : only Longula and Polusca are mentioned.

[3] DH IX 59, 1-2. Liv. III 1, 4-7. In truth, Antium was broken by Rome only in the middle of the fourth century, and it was colonized in 338 B.C. (Liv. VIII 14, 8. Strab. V 3, 5). On the sources : A. Klotz, Livius und seine Vorgänger, Berlin 1941, 253 sq. Soltau, Philol. 48, 1889, 282 sq.

[4] Liv. VI 2, 13 (a notice concerning the year 389 B.C.) : *Camillus ... ad deditionem Volscos septuagesimo demum anno subegit.* VI 5, 2 : *Pomptinus ager, tum primum post accisas a Camillo Volscorum res possessionis haud ambiguae.* Eutr. 2, 1

and such an assumption could be also supported by the official list of Roman triumphs, which lists in the fifth century an *ovatio* (the lesser triumph) over the Volscians in 462 B.C., a triumph in 459 *de Aequeis et Volsceis*, another in 458 *de Aequeis*, one in 449 *de Aequeis*, one in 443 *de Volsceis*.[1] Nevertheless, everything points to the fact that the offensive activity of the mountain tribes was raging in Latium for a long time, until the Romans were able to hit back. The pretended overwhelming superiority of the Romans over those peoples is vanishing in the Annals as early as 487 B.C., when an indecisive battle is admitted.[2] Volscian victories are acknowledged in 484,[3] in 478,[4] in 471;[5] heavy battles are recorded in 468,[6] and 464.[7] The inability of Rome to take action in 463, when Latins and Hernicans are defeated, is confessed.[8] Setbacks are the most unlikely thing the annalists would invent, and we must therefore take for granted that the continuous series of annual looting campaigns of Volscians and Aequians really began about 494 B.C., as our sources state.

Fabius Pictor had this chronology in mind when he inserted in his

---

(on the events of 389 again) : *Nam Camillus eo anno Volscorum civitatem, quae per septuaginta annos bellum gesserat, vicit.* Oros. III 3, 4 : *Interea Romani, qui per septuaginta annos ab urbe Volscorum, praeterea Faliscorum Aequorum et Sutrinorum subacti et adtriti adsiduis bellis conficiebantur, tandem in suprascriptis diebus Camillo duce easdem cepere civitates et redivivo finem dedere certamini.* Diod. XIV 117, 3 : . . . . εἰς μέσον ἀποληφθέντες οἱ Οὐόλσκοι σχεδὸν ἅπαντες κατεκόπησαν. διόπερ τὸν ἔμπροσθεν χρόνον ἰσχυροὶ δοκοῦντες εἶναι διὰ τὴν συμφορὰν ταύτην ἀσθενέστατοι τῶν περιοικούντων ἐθνῶν ἐγενήθησαν. The resplendent victory of Camillus is, of course, a fake invented for the purpose of reducing the effect of the catastrophic collapse of Rome in the previous year to a passing tempest. Fabius Pictor seems to me to have created it, and Polybius' κατάσπασμα is, I think, a neutralizing expression for the immediate recovery of Rome which was unbelievable for him. The continuation of the Volscian wars in the next years demonstrates that the Volscians were not at all broken, but their aggressiveness was rather revived when the Romans were knocked out by the Gauls : ταπεινῶν δ'ὄντων τῶν 'Ρωμαίων διὰ τὴν προειρημένην συμφοράν, οἱ Οὐόλσκοι πρὸς αὐτοὺς πόλεμον ἐξήνεγκαν (Diod. XIV 117, 1). The *fasti triumphales* have no Volscian triumph in the fourth century before 346 B.C. !

[5] O. Clason, RG 1, Berlin 1873, 72 sqq.
[1] Degrassi, Inscr. It. XIII 1, p. 67 sq.
[2] Liv. II 40, 14. The same event is accounted for in DH VIII 64, 3 ; 67, 1-10 as a Roman victory.
[3] DH VIII 84, 1-86, 2.
[4] DH IX 16, 1. 4. 5 ; 17, 4. 5. ; 18, 4.
[5] DH IX 50, 1-7 ; 53, 5. Liv. II 58, 3-60, 3.
[6] DH IX 57, 3 sqq. Liv. II 64, 5-65, 7. III 1. 4 ; 8, 7-15.
[7] DH IX 62, 1-66, 4. Liv. III 4, 2 sqq.
[8] DH IX 67, 1 sqq. Liv. III 6, 4 sqq.

narrative the story of the terrible devastation of Latium by the renegade Coriolanus in the years 491-89.[1] The enumeration of the Latin cities destroyed at this time by the Volscians, though interpolated with the names of Circeii, Satricum, and other strongholds then already in Volscian hands, can certainly be accepted as authentic for the towns in and around the Alban Hills.[2] Consequently, the seventy years counted back from the alleged decisive victory in 389 B.C. go back not to the start of the Volscian raids but to a previous great Roman success against them recounted under the year 462 B.C.[3]

The Volscian immigration in Southern Latium is most clearly reflected in our sources in the fate of the cities situated on the Pomptine plain. The Theogony of Hesiod knows Circeii in southernmost Latium as a Latin center.[4] Farther to the north, Cora and Pometia were still Latin in the last decade of the sixth century B.C., when they appear as members of the Latin League of Aricia.[5] The fertile plain between Campania and the Alban Hills was, consequently, then still Latin. The cities just mentioned are Volscian in the fifth century; they could have changed hands only about 500 when the Etruscan rule broke down there. The clash between the warlike shepherds of the central Apennine range and the Latins established in the coastal plain evidently began with this invasion.

The spectacular Roman progress in Volscian territory between 495 and 491 B.C.—in this year Rome is said to have humiliated Antium, calling up only her own troops [6]—seems to have been invented to mitigate the effect of the following ordeal of Latium inflicted by the Volscians under Coriolanus. A reliable entry in the Annals reveals the truth: in 492 B.C. the Pomptine territory is firmly held by the Volscians.[7] Another passage of the same sort—mentioning pestilence and hunger—shows that in 434 B.C. that fertile district

---

[1] Cf. E. T. Salmon, Cl. Q. 24, 1930, 96 sqq., and above, p. 155 sqq.

[2] Cf. A. Piganiol, Mél. 38, 1920, 302 n. 2.

[3] DH IX 69, 2 sqq. Liv. III 8, 3 sqq., especially *ibid.* 10 : *ibi Volscum nomen prope deletum est.*

[4] Hesiod, *Theog.* 1011 sqq. Cf. my comments in the paper "Die trojanischen Urahnen der Römer," Basel 1957, 24 sq.

[5] Cf. above, p. 49 sqq.

[6] DH VII 37, 3-5.

[7] DH VIII 1, 3 ; 2, 2. Liv. II 34, 4. Reliability is indicated partly by the fact that the items on *annona cara* and pestilence belonged to the oldest kernel of the *annales maximi*, partly by the connection of the events in question with the Cymean story analyzed in our second chapter.

The Wars with the Volscians and Aequians

still belongs to these enemies of Rome.[1] But after 406 B.C. this region is the object of an assiduous Roman offensive.[2] Though the overwhelming victory of Camillus in the year after the Gallic raid cannot be historical and the Pomptine plain could not yet have become "an undisputed possession"[3] of Rome, the struggle for it was quickly taken up again by the Roman state, soon regaining its strength, and the establishment of two Roman tribes in this area in 358 B.C.[4] could not be resisted by the Volscians.

The ceaseless series of Volscian raids and Roman counterstrokes from the days of Coriolanus on must not be reviewed here again in detail.[5] The Roman triumphs and ovations over the Volscians and Aequians in 462, 459, 458, 449, 443 must be accepted as historical. The substantial successes about 460 signalize the first turn of the tide in favor of the Latins and of Rome. A generation later, in 431, another decisive Roman victory followed after heavy fighting.[6] Dangerous wars began again in 424 B.C.,[7] but the place-names of conquered cities demonstrate that now Latins and Romans were step by step gaining the upper hand in this bitter struggle. At the same time, these geographical names illustrate how real history is emerging from the mist of the previous vague accounts. In 419 the Latin Labici joins the Aequians, but defeated with them in the next year, she becomes a Latin colony, besieged again in 397.[8] The neighboring Bola is captured and recaptured in 415 and 414 B.C.;[9] in 413 the Hernican Ferentinum is taken from the Volscians.[10] Carventum was seized in 410 by the two mountain tribes, but won back again. Changing hands once

[1] Liv. IV 35, 4.

[2] References to the sources given most recently by M. Hoffmann, RE Suppl. 8, 1155 sqq.

[3] Liv. VI 5, 2 ; cf. 6, 4.

[4] Liv. VII 15, 11.

[5] The sources are collected in A. Schwegler, RG, 2, 691 sqq. and analyzed in G. De Sanctis, St. d. R. 2¹, 1907, 104 sqq. K. J. Beloch, RG 302. E. T. Salmon, Phoenix 7, 1953, 126, etc.

[6] Diod. XII 64, 1-3. Liv. IV 26, 1 sqq. ; 30, 1-2. Plut., *Camill.* 2, 1. Ovid., *Fast.* 6, 721 sqq. G. De Sanctis, St. d. R. 2², 114.

[7] Liv. IV 36, 4 ; 37, 4 sqq. ; 42, 10.

[8] Diod. XIII 6, 8. Liv. IV 45, 3 sqq. ; 47, 1 sqq. V 16, 2. E. T. Salmon, Phoenix 7, 1953, 93 sqq., proved that all the colonies until 338 B.C. were Latin federal foundations, not Roman ones, as the annals pretend ; cf. also below, p. 391 sqq.

[9] Diod. XIII 42, 6. Liv. IV 49, 3 sqq.

[10] Liv. IV 51, 7 sq ; 56, 6. Cf. K. J. Beloch, RG 200.

more in 409, it was besieged without success by the (Latins and) Romans.[1] They, however, won back the fortress of Verrugo, which, lost again two years later, was conquered finally in 395 or 394.[2] There were Roman victories near Antium, the leading Volscian city, in 408 and between Ferentinum and Ecetra in 404.[3] In this latter year the Volscian city of Artena is captured.[4] In the source of Diodorus (XIV 34, 7) the reinforcement of the number of Roman colonists in Velitrae is recorded: in truth this could well be the initial date of this foundation of the League, taken from the *annales maximi*.

In 393 B.C. the federal colony of Vitellia on Aequian soil is revolting along with the Volscian Satricum and Velitrae.[5] But in the meantime, the Romans and Latins broke through across the Pomptine plain to the Campanian border and captured Anxur-Tarracina in 406, which changed hands again in 402 and 401.[6] Circeii becomes a colony in 393.[7] The very fact itself that in these years of the deadly struggle with Veii, Rome with her Latin allies was able to maintain successfully the high pressure of war in the north and in the south alike, demonstrates that she had begun to overshadow completely her neighbors from Southern Etruria down to the Cap of Circe.

The mutual pressure of the Latins and the Volscians-Aequians on each other resulted in the Volscians joining their forces throughout the fifth century with the Aequians.[8] This coalition had its natural counter-reaction on the Latin side: Tusculum—after some initial hesitation [9]—held firmly to Rome with the cities of the Alban Hills, whereas Praeneste and Tibur, hemmed in between the intruders and their own tribesmen, sought their own solutions, allowing the Aequians to protrude through their territory from the original homes of this tribe to the Algidus Pass, and these two important

---

[1] Liv. IV 53, 1 sqq. ; 55, 4. 8.

[2] Liv. IV 55, 8. Diod. XIV 11, 6. Liv. IV 58, 3. Diod. XIV 98, 5.

[3] Liv. IV 56, 4 sqq. 57, 7 ; 61, 6 sqq.

[4] Liv. IV 61, 6 sqq.

[5] Liv. V 29, 3. Diod. XIV 102, 4.

[6] Diod. XIV 16, 5. Liv. IV 59, 2 sqq. V 8, 2-3 ; 10, 2 ; 12, 6 ; 13, 1 ; 16, 2. Vell. I 14, 4.

[7] Diod. XIV 102, 4 ; cf. Liv. V, 24, 4.

[8] First mentioned, if I am not mistaken, in 488 B.C. in DH VIII 16, 3 ; 4-6. The data on the Aequians collected in A. Schwegler, RG 2, 700 sqq. Cf. G. De Sanctis, St. d. R. 2², 109 sqq., 112 sq. A. Klotz, Livius und seine Vorgänger, Berlin 1941, 284 sqq. R. M. Ogilvie, JRS 48, 1958, 42.

[9] Diod. XI 40, 5.

The Wars with the Volscians and Aequians

Latin cities did not join the Latin League in fighting the Aequians and the Volscians. It has been stressed already by others that in the same way the aggression of the Apennine shepherds cemented the tribal ties of the Latins: [1] though this is valid only with the relevant exceptions of Tibur and Praeneste just mentioned, the revival of the tribal alliance was nevertheless the vehicle of the gradual preeminence of Rome, proving herself by far the toughest in the long protracted strain of the Volscian and Aequian wars on the manpower and endurance of the Latin cities.

The warlike tension between the Latins and the Volscian-Aequian coalition in the fifth century B.C. also forced the other peoples in this area to take one side or the other. So the Hernicans,[2] too, were constrained to enter the network of alliances. The Roman Annals note under the year 486 B.C.[3] that the Hernicans were vanquished along with the Volscians, and that they were admitted as allies of Rome under the same conditions as the Latins. This is an anticipation of much later developments, as Mommsen realized and other scholars recognized after him.[4] The allegation that two-thirds of their territory was taken from them in 486 is refuted by the fact that the *ager Romanus antiquus*, as we have seen, did not reach the upper valley of the Liris in the fifth century. As the Hernicans served still in later times in separate national troop contingents in the wars of Rome, and had still a tribal council of their own, such a non-Latin tribe could not have been incorporated in the Latin League as early as 486 B.C.[5] On the other hand, the hard pressure of the Aequians on the Hernicans, the compliance of Praeneste with these invaders, and the opposition of Tusculum against them gave to the Hernicans no long respite in which to remain undecided: there was little choice but to march along with Tusculum and Rome; it was their interest as well as that of Tusculum "to break the chain of enemies from the Aequian

---

[1] E.g., G. De Sanctis, St. d. R. 2¹, 1907, 105. F. Altheim, Epochen der römischen Geschichte 1, Frankfurt/M. 1934, 104. A. N. Sherwin-White, R. Citiz., Oxford 1939, 20 sqq.

[2] The historical data concerning the Hernicans are collected in A. Schwegler, RG 2, 1856, 330 sqq.

[3] DH VIII 68, 4 ; 69, 2. Liv. II 41, 1 ; III 22, 4. Val. Max. VI 3, 1 b. *Fasti triumph. ad a.* 486 with the remarks of A. Degrassi, Inscr. It. XIII 1, 1947, 537.

[4] Mommsen, RF 2, Berlin 1879, 160 sqq. Ed. Meyer, GdA 5, Stuttgart 1902, 134. K. J. Beloch, RG 197 sqq. G. De Sanctis, St. d. R. 2², 1960, 96 sqq. F. Altheim, Epochen der röm. Gesch. 1, Frankfurt/M. 1934, 104, n. 33.

[5] A. N. Sherwin-White, R. Citiz., 24 sqq., maintains the opposite view.

mountains to the Volscian coast," [1] even if they became not yet incorporated in the League of the Latins and were not yet subjected to Rome.

In the course of the fifth century the ever growing political and military preponderance of Rome, exhausting the hostile neighbors, conquering more territory at the expense of allies and enemies alike, brought all of them to the verge of subjection. About 400 B.C. their fate seemed to be sealed. But when the Celts shattered the Roman power, they strove to free themselves once and for all from the fetters of the Roman superiority, as even the Latins did.

The wedge driven by the Romans and Latins in the Pomptine plain reaching Circeii in the south cut the Volscian cities in two isolated groups,[2] and it is perfectly obvious that they did not miss the great opportunity of 390 B.C. to expel the intruders. With the other resounding victories of Camillus in 389—a fiction introduced in all likelihood by Fabius Pictor to alleviate the burden of blame for the great fiasco—the defeat inflicted by him upon the Volscians (or Aequians) near Lanuvium [3] also must be dismissed as unhistorical; so too must the alleged Roman attack against the Aequians in 388 [4] and the distribution of the *ager Pomptinus* as early as 387 [5] among Roman citizen-colonists. Even the recapture of Velitrae by the Romans in 380 (Liv. VI 30, 6) cannot have been a lasting success because this Latin colony is one of the Volscian bases of the wars against Rome some few years later.

More credible are the assaults of the Volscians. The main base of their onslaught against Rome is the important harbor city Antium, whose assumed capture and submission in the fifth century are refuted by the great strength and vitality she displays in the decades after the Gallic assault.[6] In 386 B.C. the Volscians of Antium are reported rising against Rome, concentrating their forces around Satricum.[7] In 385 they are helped by Latins and Hernicans, their steady enemies in the past century; the Latin colonies of Velitrae and

[1] A. Piganiol, Mél. 38, 1920, 300 sqq.
[2] As G. De Sanctis, St. d. R. 2², 233, observed it.
[3] Diod. XIV 117, 1-4. Liv. VI 2, 2. 8-14 ; 5, 2 ; 12, 6.
[4] Liv. VI 4, 8.
[5] Liv. VI 6, 1.
[6] Cf. also J. H. Thiel, A History of Roman Sea-Power, Amsterdam 1954, 50.
[7] Liv. VI 6, 4-5. 10; 7, 1 sqq.; 9, 6 ; 10, 7-8. *Fasti triumph.*, Inscr. It. XIII 1, 61. Frontin. *Stratag.* II 8, 4.

Circeii, whose settlers consisted of Volscians and Latins alike, go along with them.[1] The same anti-Roman coalition appears again in 383 B.C.[2] In 379 B.C. the Volscians defeat the Romans;[3] mutual depredations of their fields are announced in 378.[4]

It is to be stressed that now Rome was standing indeed virtually alone; and also that she was able not only to bear the brunt of the assault but also to break its force alone, in no more than a decade after the total defeat of her army and the wholesale destruction of the living quarters of her inhabitants. This amazing achievement is the real basis of her ascent to power in Italy.

In 377 B.C. the Volscians, helped again by the Latins, clash with the Romans near Satricum. They are now beaten; the Antiates dissociate themselves from their Latin allies and give themselves up to Rome.[5] In one of the next few years Velitrae attacks Tusculum and raids the suburban district of Rome; the Romans besiege this city without success.[6] After the second Gallic assault Privernum joins the Veliterni in devastating the rural environs of Rome;[7] a triumph over Privernum was celebrated in 357 B.C.[8]

The Roman conquest of the Volscians is now on its way. In 358, as already stated, two new agrarian districts are added to Roman territory on the Pomptine plain: the *tribus Pomptina* and the *Poblilia*.[9] Desperate attempts of the Volscians followed to save their national existence. One raid on Latin territory is mentioned in 353 B.C.[10] Satricum, which was destroyed by the Latins, is fortified again by the Volscians of Antium [11] in 348 and destroyed by the Romans in 346 B.C.[12] In 341 Privernum and Antium try again to liberate themselves but the former stronghold was taken, and the latter was soon on the defensive.[13] The last chance for freedom emerged in 340,

[1] Liv. VI 11, 2. 9 ; 12, 1-13, 8 ; 15, 7 ; 16, 5 ; 17, 7-8.
[2] Liv. VI 21, 2.
[3] Liv. VI 30, 3-8.
[4] Liv. VI 31, 3-8.
[5] Liv. VI 32, 4-11 ; 33, 1-3.
[6] Liv. VI 36, 1-6 ; 37, 12 ; 38, 1.
[7] Liv. VII 15, 10-11.
[8] Liv. VII 16, 3-6. *Acta triumph.*, Inscr. It. XIII 1, 68 sq., 540.
[9] Liv. VII 15, 11.
[10] Liv. VII 19, 6-9.
[11] Liv. VII 27, 2.
[12] Liv. VII 27, 5-8.
[13] Liv. VIII 1, 1-6.

376

when the Latins and their federal colonies on Volscian soil, Setia, Signia, Velitrae, and Circeii, rose against the conqueror. The Volscians, joining them, are defeated with them.[1] In 339 B.C. Velitrae and Antium try again to regain their liberty in alliance with the Latins, but in 338 they share the fate of the subjugated Latins.[2] Though in this great war every hope must have vanished, Privernum rebelled in 330-29 against the ruling city;[3] in 320 Satricum went over to the powerful Samnites;[4] in 304-3 the Aequians rose against Rome.[5] All those upheavals were crushed. These peoples were no more a match for Rome, whose power completely outgrew the local proportions.

The exasperation over the Roman conquest can be measured from the fact that the former faithful allies of Latium, the small people of the Hernici, were also stubbornly rising against it[6] after the collapse in 390. Their defection is noticed in 386 B.C.[7] and 385 B.C.;[8] but it is easy to understand that only much later was Rome able to proceed against them. The declaration of the Hernican war, which proved to be not an easy enterprise, is given under the year 362 B.C.;[9] in 361 the capture of Ferentinum, one of their leading cities, is mentioned.[10] A Roman success over them in 360 B.C.[11] did not break their resistance, but only their defeat in 358.[12] Their last upheaval in 306 B.C.[13] was condemned a priori to failure.

The dry enumeration of well-known events on these pages was necessary to make it plain for the general reader that we know quite enough of the real progress and achievements of the Roman conquest,

[1] Liv. VIII 3, 9 sqq. ; 11, 9-10. 13-14.
[2] Liv. VIII 12, 7 ; 13, 4. 12 ; 14, 5-8.
[3] Liv. VIII 19, 4 sqq.; 20, 1 sqq.; 37, 8. *Acta triumph.*, ed. Degrassi 68 sqq., 541. Val. Max. VI 2, 1 ; IX 10, 1.
[4] Liv. IX 12, 5 ; 16, 3. Cf. T. R. S. Broughton, MRR 1, 154.
[5] Diod. XX 101, 5. *Acta triumph.*, ed. Degrassi 541. Liv. IX 45, 5 sqq.
[6] Cf. G. De Sanctis, St. d. R. 2², 241, who rightly stresses the point that invented details coloring the annalist tale does not effect the historicity of the basic facts.
[7] Liv. VI 6, 2. 13 ; 7, 1 ; 8, 8.
[8] Liv. VI 12, 6 ; 13, 7.
[9] Liv. VII 6, 7 ; 7, 1-8, 7.
[10] Liv. VII 9, 1. *Fasti triumph.*, ed. Degrassi p. 540. Cf. K. J. Beloch, RG 200.
[11] Liv. VII 11, 8-9. *Fasti triumph.*, *l.c.*
[12] Liv. VII 15, 8-9. *Fasti triumph.*, *l.c.*
[13] Cic., *Phil.* VI 5, 13. Liv. IX 43, 22. *Fasti triumph.*, ed. Degrassi p. 542. Cf. L. R. Taylor, Vot. Distr. 52.

reaching in 338 B.C. the doors of Campania, for the first time, of course.

᠅

THE LATIN CITY-STATES AND THE ROMAN REPUBLIC UNTIL THE CONQUEST OF LATIUM IN 338 B.C.

The reader of Livy is struck by the uncertainty and the varying content of the expression "Latins" in his narrative. In 383 Rome suspects that *Latium* will rise in arms against her: besides it Lanuvium is specially mentioned.[1] In 380 a tribune of the plebs complains that a war is intended, besides others, against the Latins *and* the Praenestines,[2] whereas later the Praenestines are called—correctly— "Latin foes," [3] who violated the time-honored alliance.[4] Livy notices, as Polybius does,[5] the accommodation with the "Latins" when the Celts again invaded Latium; [6] but his text also betrays the fact that Tibur and Praeneste do not belong to the Latin group joining Rome in that hour of anxiety.[7] This inexactitude is not that of Livy, who inherited it from his predecessors who were not eager to reveal the enmity of some important Latin cities against Rome; but it is also due to the continuous strife of the members of the tribe among themselves, which, however, did not entirely disrupt the ties of relationship amid this homogeneous group. Even the culturally incomparably more advanced Greek states tried to wipe out each other, and it is no wonder that the archaic structure of the Latin societies, the economy of which was still based on continued looting of neighbors rather than a peaceful exchange of goods with them, could not abstain from the use of weapons. The most honored occupation, even more than cattle-rearing and hunting, was combat; the virile ideal was superiority in hand-to-hand fighting. Even in the late fourth century feuds with local adversaries persisted within the exten-

---

[1] Liv. VI 21, 2 : *Hostes novi praeter Volscos* ..... *Circeiosque et Velitras colonias* (they were colonies of the Latin League as we shall see) .... *et suspectum Latium Lanuvini etiam* .... *subito exorti.*

[2] Liv. VI 27, 7 : *Latinis, Hernicis, Praenestinis iam intentari arma.*

[3] Liv. VI 28, 7 : the Praenestines cursed as a *Latinus hostis.*

[4] Liv. VI 29, 2 : *di testes foederis* invoked against the same.

[5] Polyb. II 18, 5.

[6] Liv. VII 12, 7.

[7] Liv. VII 11, 2 and 12, 8.

sive association of peoples already in existence in that epoch.[1] There can be no doubt that earlier the particularism was even more pronounced, though the lack of information largely prevents us from demonstrating this in detail.

There is no doubt either that all the Latins continued to participate in the celebration of the *Latiar* in the Alban Hills and also in the annual sacrifices in Lavinium prior to 338 B.C. In the same way, the Latin League, even if some states stood apart from it, was still theoretically the representative of the *nomen Latinum*, of the totality of the tribe, as of old.

If we now try to weigh the importance of the collective organization against that of the individual cities inside and outside of it, we observe a marked difference between the fifth century, in which the primary role in Latin politics belonged to the League, and the half century after the shock of the Celtic storm, when the coalition was overshadowed by the ambitions and the strife of the most powerful single states, whose rivalry did not stop until the bitter end. These two periods are, naturally, not separated by a gulf, but are characterized by a constant change and evolution, pointing increasingly more clearly toward the final result, the Roman conquest of Latium.

ૐ

SOME ASSOCIATES AND RIVALS OF THE RISING ROMAN POWER: GABII AND TUSCULUM, TIBUR AND PRAENESTE

Gabii

Midway between Rome and Praeneste was situated Gabii. Her significance in the archaic epoch—mainly in the sixth century—was certainly due to the fact that she was a station on the Etruscan communication line, going from the Tiber to the Anio and continuing across Gabii to Praeneste, Cales, and Capua. An old Roman formula of solemn execration, still preserved, attests that Gabii was once a dreadful enemy for Rome,[2] a fact also otherwise not forgotten there.[3] The

[1] Liv. VIII 19, 4 sqq. (the case of Fundi).

[2] Macrob., *Sat.* III 9, 13 : *in antiquitatibus autem haec oppida inveni devota : (Hi)stonios, Fregellas Gavios Veios Fidenas.*

[3] Fest. p. 402, 5 sqq. : *Suburam Verrius ... a pago Succusano dictam ait : hoc vero maxime probat eorum auctoritatem, qui aiunt, ita appellatam et regionem Urbis*

Romans remembered the Gabii of olden days as a populous city,[1] superior to them in culture,[2] which they could not conquer with arms.[3] They knew this from a very old treaty of alliance between Gabii and Rome, still preserved in the Augustan age in the temple of Semo Sancus Dius Fidius.[4] This sanctuary was dedicated in 466 B.C., and the seductive guess of E. Pais, that the agreement in question must be dated after that date of consecration,[5] seems to be correct: though the sacred grove of the god on the same spot was certainly much older, the cowhide, on which the text of the treaty was written, was certainly not meant to be exposed to sunshine and rain in the free air, but to be sheltered under a roof. The latest possible date for this *foedus Gabinum* is determined by the fact that on the occasion of the organization of the new zone of gentile tribes soon after 426 B.C.[6] a piece of land was cut away by the Romans from the territory of Gabii; it is also relevant that the demarcation line agreed upon at that moment was subsequently not changed again. In this span of time, between 466 and ca. 420 B.C., an early date has a better chance to be correct, for the following reasons. A revealing clause of the treaty between Rome and Gabii has been preserved among

et tribum a stativo praesidio, quod solitum sit succurrere Esquilis, infestantibus eam partem Urbis Gabinis.

[1] DH IV 53, 1 : νῦν μὲν οὐκέτι συνοικουμένη πᾶσα, πλὴν ὅσα μέρη πανδοκεύεται κατὰ τὴν δίοδον, τότε δὲ πολυάνθρωπος εἰ καί τις ἄλλη καὶ μεγάλη. τεκμήραιτο δ'ἄν τις αὐτῆς τὸ μέγεθος καὶ τὴν ἀξίωσιν ἐρείπια θεασάμενος οἰκιῶν πολλαχῇ καὶ τείχους κύκλον. ἔτι γὰρ ἔστηκεν αὐτοῦ τὰ πλεῖστα. Propert. IV 1, 34, on cities in olden times : *Et qui nunc nulli, maxima turba Gabi.*

[2] It can be deduced from the invented story, that Romulus and Remus received a higher education in Gabii : DH I 84, 5. Plut., *Rom.* 6, 2 and *De fort. Rom.* 8. *Origo gentis Rom.* 21, 3 (from Valerius Antias). Steph. Byz., *s.v.* Τάβιοι (instead of Γάβιοι). On the *cinctus Gabinus* : Man, RE 3, 2558 sqq.

[3] DH IV 53, 2 sqq. Liv. I 53, 2 sqq. Ovid., *Fast.* 2, 690 sqq. Zonaras VII 10, 6 sqq. (Cass. Dio vol. 1, 27 sq. Boiss.). Florus I 1, 5-7.

[4] DH IV 58, 4 : τούτων ἐστὶ τῶν ὁρκίων μνημεῖον ἐν Ῥώμῃ κείμενον ἐν ἱερῷ Διὸς Πιστίου, ὃν Ῥωμαῖοι Σάγκον καλοῦσιν, ἀσπὶς ξυλίνη βύρσῃ βοείᾳ περίτονος τοῦ σφαγιασθέντος ἐπὶ τῶν ὁρκίων τότε βοός, γράμμασιν ἀρχαϊκοῖς ἐπιγεγραμμένη τὰς γενομένας αὐτοῖς ὁμολογίας. Paul. Fest. p. 48, 19 L. : *Clipeum antiqui ob rotunditatem etiam corium bovis appellarunt, in quo foedus Gabinorum cum Romanis fuerat descriptum.* Hor., *Epist.* II 1, 24 sq. : *foedera regum vel Gabiis vel cum rigidis aequata Sabinis.* Cf. the Augustean coin-types of C. Antistius Vetus and of C. Antistius Reginus, H. Mattingly, BMC Emp. 1, 1923, 19 and 24 with pl. 3, 16 and 4, 10.

[5] DH IX 60, 8. Ovid., *Fast.* 6, 213 sqq. E. Pais, St. d. R. I 1, 357. *Contra* : G. De Sanctis, St. d. R. I², 355 n. 73 ; cf. *ibid.* 377 sq. Mommsen, St. R. 3, 598 n. 4. Ed. Meyer, GdA 5, 1902, 136.

[6] Cf. above, p. 311.

the prescriptions of the augural practice. For the faultless observation of the flight of a certain kind of bird, announcing the will of divinity —and to seek this was the obligatory prerequisite for every governmental action in peace and war—hostile and foreign territory was excluded, whereas the territory of Gabii was declared suitable in addition to that of Rome. This unique, juridically valid equation proves that the *foedus* was concluded on the basis of equal rights between the two partners, hardly imaginable after the first crushing defeat of the mountain tribes about 460 B.C., when the preeminence of Rome over her neighbors started growing fast. In the first half of the century the relatively ample size of Gabii could still lend her a certain weight, but thereafter she no longer played a relevant role in the Volscian-Aequian wars: the only thing we hear is that in 462 she suffered from a raid of those enemies of Rome [1] with whom she sided in 382, opposing Praeneste.[2] A glance at the map is enough to show that she had not much choice other than to rely on Rome, going along with Tusculum and the neighboring cities south of her, whereas Praeneste acted in concert with the Aequian foe.

The equal rights of Gabii with Rome certainly did not last long in reality: she soon became an outpost of the Roman state. But this does not alter the fact that toward the middle of the fifth century B.C., Rome was not yet able to swallow up such a community of moderate size, but was content to have her as an ally: the distribution of the old agrarian tribes has shown us that Gabii was not incorporated in the Roman territory and preserved her autonomy. The first steps of the Romans aiming at gaining ground toward the east were still endeavoring to remove obstacles just outside their own threshold, where Gabii was situated. Not even the annalists, heralds of the invented conquests of regal Rome, dared to assert that Gabii was subject to their city before the treaty, which gave them the basis for spinning out of it the story of Sextus Tarquinius, treacherous son of King Superbus.

Tusculum

This Latin state, with Aricia,[3] was the center of Latin resistance against Porsenna; but defeated along with the Tarquins near their

[1] Liv. III 8, 6.
[2] Liv. VI 21, 9.
[3] Cf. above, p. 47 sqq.

own city at Lake Regillus, by the Romans, Tusculum joined the Aequians, only to be defeated again with them by Rome. The source of Diodorus related her capture on this occasion, but as she remained outside the perimeter of the Roman state [1] and was not incorporated in Roman territory, this cannot be true. After this event, Tusculum became the most reliable ally of Rome against the Aequians, whose attacks were again and again launched across her territory, with stubborn battles fought east of her in the difficult hilly ground of the Algidus. In 460 B.C., when a social revolution almost overcame the ruling patriciate of Rome, the aristocracy of Tusculum saved their Roman peers.[2] Who the "banished" were who captured the Capitol with the help of masses of slaves is not clear: the partisans of the Tarquins were ousted a generation earlier, and the leader was a Sabine, Appius Herdonius; but it is utterly unlikely that exiles from other Latin cities would have tried to take over the city which gave them refuge. In any case, a similar situation in Ardea, where in an internal feud [3] not long afterward the populace called on the Volscians for assistance, and the aristocracy invoked the help of the Romans, shows the political collaboration between the ruling classes of the Latin cities. This political behavior did not remain restricted to the Latins. In 431 B.C. the Volscian and Aequian prisoners of war were all sold into slavery, except the aristocrats among them: *hostes praeter senatores omnes venum dati sunt* (Liv. IV 29, 4). The case of the *Campani*, whose aristocracy was rewarded by Rome for not participating with the rest of the population in the great revolt of the Latins shows the further extension of this political attitude beyond the frontiers of Latium. Roman protection of the ruling class of Volsinii attests its later continuation.

The cooperation between Rome and Tusculum lasted henceforward without interruption throughout the fifth century B.C. In 459 the

---

[1] Cf. above, p. 305. Diod. XI 40,5 (to the year Ol. 75, 4): Ἅμα δὲ τούτοις πραττομένοις Ῥωμαίοις πρὸς Αἰκολανοὺς καὶ τοὺς τὸ Τοῦσκλον κατοικοῦντας συνέστη πόλεμος, καὶ πρὸς μὲν Αἰκολανοὺς μάχην συνάψαντες ἐνίκησαν καὶ πολλοὺς τῶν πολεμίων ἀνεῖλον, μετὰ δὲ ταῦτα τὸ Τοῦσκλον ἐξεπολιόρκησαν καὶ τὴν τῶν Αἰκολανῶν πόλιν ἐχειρώσαντο. Who were the allies of Rome at this time is not hinted at. Cf. E. Pais, St. crit. 2, 165 n. 3. A. Klotz, Livius und seine Vorgänger, Berlin 1941, 275. A. Piganiol, Mél. 38, 1920, 297 sqq.

[2] DH IX 16, 3. Liv. III 8, 1- 11 ; 19, 7-8. The story was known to Cato the Elder, a native of Tusculum ; cf. Fr. Münzer, Adelsp. 65 sq., and *idem*, RE 8, 618 sqq.

[3] Liv. IV 11, 1-7.

382

ROME DURING THE EARLY REPUBLIC

Annals report that the Aequians captured the citadel of Tusculum and that the Romans liberated the city from the intruders.[1] In 455 the Romans, we are told, beat the Aequians after a raid on the rural districts of Tusculum,[2] and again in 449,[3] though suffering a setback. In 443 B.C. the Tusculans are said to have annihilated the remnants of a Volscian host, defeated by the Romans.[4] The accounts of this fighting certainly contain a kernel of truth, though the share of the Latin League in it is obscured or simply replaced by actions of Rome—as will be illustrated below in the discussion of the foundation of colonies. Later on, when the cities of the Alban Hills were beleaguered again by the Aequians, who had in their grip besides the narrow pass of the Algidus on the eastern rim of the natural mountain wall also the strong places of Labici and Bola north of Tusculum, it had no other choice than to go along with its neighbors and with Rome, becoming more and more preponderant by her sheer size. Labici, in Aequian hands in 419, was captured in 418 and became a federal colony, as Bola did in 414 B.C.[5] Tusculum was by now well protected from the north; the position of the Aequians on the Algidus was made untenable and the contact with the Hernicans safe. But the events of the following decades leave no uncertainty about the burden imposed by the ascendancy of Rome, threatening even her most faithful companion of arms. The rupture came not at once. In 394 B.C., after the capture of Veii, Tusculum still persists in remaining on the Roman side.[6] Even after the collapse of the Roman army at the Allia, when the bulk of the Latins turned away from the Romans, Tusculum, Gabii, and Labici seem still to have held on with them until 381 B.C.[7] In that year, however, the allegiance of Tusculum became shaken too: it helped in somewhat disguised form the Praenestines, who prepared war against Rome with the assistance of Velitrae and the Volscians. But it was pardoned under the condition that it accepted

[1] Liv. III 23, 3-5. DH X 20, 1-21, 1.
[2] Liv. III 31, 3-4. DH X 43, 1 sqq.
[3] Liv. III 38, 5 ; 40, 13-14 ; 42, 3-7. DH XI 3, 3 ; 4, 3 ; 23, 2. 4-6.
[4] Liv. IV 10, 4-5.
[5] Liv. IV 45, 3 sqq.; 46, 6, 12; 47, 4-7 ; 49, 4-5.
[6] Liv. V 28, 11-13.
[7] Liv. VI 21, 9 : *De Praenestinorum quoque defectione eo anno primum fama exorta ; arguentibusque eos Tusculanis et Gabinis et Labicanis, quorum in fines incursatum erat, ita placide ab senatu responsum est, ut minus credi de criminibus, quia nollent ea vera esse, appareret.*

the Roman citizenship and became consequently an appendix of the Roman state.[1]

This annexation of Tusculum was something new and momentous in Roman politics, which deserves closer examination. It was thought [2] that Tusculum was then simply incorporated geographically in the Roman territory. We know now, however, that this was not the case: it remained outside the boundaries of Rome,[3] which were never extended after ca. 420 B.C. in the direction of any of the Latin cities. Consequently, the Roman citizenship granted to the Tusculans in 381 was the very first example of the franchise given to a group outside of the Roman territory, to a community which preserved her *ager* and autonomy. The citizens of Tusculum had henceforth civic privileges and obligations both locally and with regard to the ruling power—a principle which, once introduced, spread increasingly with the growth of the empire. At the same time, the Roman citizenship of the Tusculans is also the start of the transformation of the voting districts from administrative units of the Roman territory to a juridical attribution of conquered peoples on a theoretical basis, a spiritualization of the frontiers. For the Tusculans this formula meant that the *ager Romanus* was not swallowing them up; they had their own *ager* and did not lose their identity and existence; they retained their self-government, as the case of L. Fulvius Curvus, discussed below, shows.

This concession was in 381 B.C. the smallest possible one calculated to compensate the Tusculans for the loss of their self-determination. The association with Rome was certainly advantageous for Tusculum, but only if there were no loss of independence, as was implied in the Roman citizenship; the attempts to shake off this yoke in the following decades demonstrate the desperation of the Tusculans,[4] as do the corresponding revolts of the Hernicans, or the rising of the insignificant Aequicoli against the same subordination, as late as

---

[1] Plut., *Camill.* 38, 5. DH XIV 6, 2-3. Cass. Dio fr. 28, 1-2 (vol. 1, 84 Boiss.). Val. Max. VII 3, *ext.* 9. Liv. VI 25, 1 sqq.; 26, 8. Cf. Cic., *Pro Balbo* 13, 31: *Itaque et ex Latio multi, ut Tusculani, ut Lanuvini . . . . . in civitatem sunt receptae* (the date of the citizenship of Lanuvium is unknown). The submission of Tusculum was certainly not so idyllic as depicted by Livy ; cf. A. Momigliano, Secondo contributo 91.

[2] G. De Sanctis, St. d. R. 2[1], 244 n. 3=2[2], 231 sq., with n. 5-6, 8. A. N. Sherwin-White, R. Citiz. 27, 29, 31, 32 sq., 56, 60 sq.

[3] Cf. above, p. 304 sqq.

[4] G. De Sanctis, St. d. R. 2[2], 231 sq.

ROME DURING THE EARLY REPUBLIC

304 B.C.[1] Praenestine troops in the Roman army decline even in 216 to accept Roman citizenship.

A free-born Latin who wished to migrate to Rome had already been free to do this, in the same way as a Roman could settle down in a Latin city if he liked; the full citizenship was in such cases only a question of registration.[2] But the Roman *civitas* of the Tusculans in 381 involved the obligation to serve in the legions of Rome, whether they were willing to do it or not. It is obvious, therefore, that they accepted this heavy obligation only under constraint. On the other hand, their aristocracy gained enormously by this union with Rome. The reader must be reminded of the fact that citizenship in itself did not entitle anybody in Rome to obtain a magistracy; this privilege was reserved since the fall of the monarchy for the families of the nobleman-cavalry.[3] The Tusculan aristocracy, favored already by the ruling class of Rome, as we saw, was from now on admitted to this very exclusive ruling circle. As early as 322 B.C., only one and a half decades after the final subjugation of Latium, the first Tusculan aristocrat became a Roman consul, followed by many others.[4] This extraordinary concession to the leading Tusculan families in 381 is also explained by the common aims and interests of the foreign policy of the two states: to drive the Aequians and the Volscians from the Algidus, the pass across the outer ring of the Alban Hills in the east, controlling the direct route to the Hernicans; to eliminate the Volscian stronghold of Velitrae on the route of the Latins to the Pomptine plain; and finally, to break the power of Praeneste.[5] In 377 B.C. the

[1] K. J. Beloch, RG 421 sq. A. N. Sherwin-White, *op. cit.* 39. On the Praenestines : Liv. XXIII 20, 2.

[2] Mommsen, St. R. 3, 635 sqq. ; cf. *ibid.* 48 sq. L. M.Hartmann, *De exilio apud Romanos*, Berlin 1887, 1 sqq. A. N. Sherwin-White, *op. cit.* 57. E. T. Salmon, Phoenix 7, 1953, 125.

[3] Cf. my study, Der frührömische Reiteradel, Baden-Baden 1952.

[4] Plin., *N.h.* VII 42, 136 (with details perverted for rhetorical effect, but sound otherwise) : *fuit et Balbus Cornelius maior consul, ... primus externorum ... usus illo honore, quem maiores Latio quoque negaverint. est et L. Fulvius inter insignia exempla, Tusculanorum rebellantium consul, eodemque honore, cum transisset, exornatus confestim a populo Romano, qui solus eodem anno, quo fuerat hostis, Romae triumphavit ex iis quorum consul fuerat.* Cic., *Pro Planc.* 8, 19 : *Tu es e municipio antiquissimo Tusculano, ex quo sunt plurimae familiae consulares, ... tot, quot ex reliquis municipiis omnibus non sunt.* Cf. G. De Sanctis, St. d. R. 2², 231 sq. Cf. Fr. Münzer, *Adelsp.* 64 sq., 72, 209. *Idem*, RE 7, 231. 236 (no. 46). Not only the Fulvii, but the Mamilii, descendants of the ancient kings of Tusculum, transferred their residence to Rome in the same epoch ; cf. Fr. Münzer, *Adelsp. l.c.*

[5] As pointed out by A. Piganiol, Mél. 38, 1920, 304 sq.

coalition of the Latins strikes at Tusculum as the ally of Rome; the citadel of the city is already in the hands of the aggressors when the Roman counterattack disposes of them.[1] Another attack on Tusculum by Velitrae with the same outcome is reported from 370 B.C.[2] In 360 B.C. Tusculum suffers again with Labici from raids of the enemies of Rome.[3] During the final upheaval of the Latin nation against Roman domination, however, Tusculum also rose against her mistress, including the noble clans treated with such a marked distinction by Rome.[4] The resentment of the Tusculans against the victorious power instigated them even after 338 B.C. to assist revolting neighbors: in 322 they barely escaped severe punishment for this.[5] They had to acquiesce in the irrevocable sovereignty of their old companions in arms.

Praeneste and Tibur

The Roman version of the history of Latium in the fifth century B.C., on which our acquaintance with that epoch is almost exclusively based, is curiously reticent about an important circumstance: namely that in this century there were two other Latin states besides Rome overshadowing their neighbors and attaining preeminence in their local environment in the same time as she did. This omission was observed long ago by modern scholars, and the truth established. "Tibur and Praeneste," writes A. N. Sherwin-White,[6] " . . . are barely mentioned in the fifth-century records. Yet in the fourth century they emerge as powers capable of sustaining a war with Rome by themselves, each with a little league of incorporated cities . . . . This seems to represent a development of the period. Like Rome, these two states emerge from the period of the invasions with an increase of lands and power. But this increase, like that of Rome, must have been at the expense of the remaining . . . *populi* which contracted the *foedus Cassianum*." By this development the smaller cities lost their liberty of action, and their manpower was increasingly exploited by their mightier neighbors, whose struggle for power

[1] Liv. VI 33, 6-12.
[2] Liv. VI 36, 1-6.
[3] Liv. VII 11, 2.
[4] Liv. VIII 7, 2.
[5] Liv. VIII 37, 8-12.
[6] A. N. Sherwin-White, R. Citiz. 29 sq.

paved the way for the unification of Latium under the leadership of the strongest of them.

About 400 B.C. this struggle was not yet decided. Praeneste was ruling then over eight Latin *oppida* in her surroundings,[1] and the extent of the conquest of Tibur could be hardly inferior,[2] especially as the size of her territory was superior to that of the other Latin cities, and was not much less than the Roman one.[3] We owe to Th. Ashby [4] the discovery that the settlements around Tibur were systematically fortified; as watchtowers and strong places were not lacking either in the outskirts of Rome, the same can be assumed for Praeneste. The consciousness of their past animated both the Praenestines and the Tiburtines also in times when this was only a glory gone forever. The Romans were annoyed by their proud spirit,[5] and certainly not without reason: as late as 216 B.C., when the Roman citizenship was offered as a reward along with other distinctions to the heroic Praenestine warriors who defended Casilinum against Hannibal, these Praenestines refused to accept it.[6] So as to satisfy at least to some extent their unbroken desire for independence, the Romans granted them some privileges in 338 B.C., which once marked the equal and mutual rights of the sovereign Latin states between themselves: Roman political refugees enjoyed the protection of exterritoriality in Praeneste and Tibur even in later centuries,[7] and the youth of these cities were allowed to fight in the wars of Rome under the command of their own magistrates, in their own cohorts.[8]

The Volscian and Aequian invasions did not force at once upon these two cities the political attitude which later became prevailing. As Tusculum first joined the Aequians and subsequently turned

---

[1] Liv. VI 29, 6. Cf. K. J. Beloch, RG 168.

[2] Liv. VII 18, 2 ; 19, 1.

[3] Beloch, RG 178. G. De Sanctis, St. d. R. 1², 376 n. 158. St. Weinstock, RE 6 A, 821.

[4] Th. Ashby, PBSR 3, 1905, 132 sq.

[5] Plaut., *Bacch.* 18. Verg., *Aen.* 7, 630 with the note of Servius. Liv. XLII 1, 7.

[6] Liv. XXIII 20, 2.

[7] Polyb. VI 14, 8. Liv. III 58, 10 ; IX 30, 5 ; XLIII 2, 10. Suet., *Tib.* 4, 2. App., *B.C.* 5, 21, 82. Cass. Dio XLVIII 10, 3, etc. Cf. Mommsen, St. R. 3, 48 sq. 635 sqq. L. M. Hartmann, *De exilio apud Romanos*, Berlin 1887, 1 sqq. G. Crifò, Ricerche sull' "exilium" nel periodo repubblicano, I, Milano 1961.

[8] Liv IX 16, 17 : *Praenestinus praetor . . . ex subsidiis suos duxerat in primam aciem*. Plin., *N.h.* XVII 11, 81 and Cass. Dio, fr. 36, 24 (vol. 1, p. 103 Boiss.), reproduce the same anecdote from 319 B.C. For Tibur, general considerations afford the same concession.

against them, so Praeneste detached herself from the Latin cities of
the Alban Hills in 499 B.C., enabling the Romans to attack them,[1]
and seems to have still maintained her goodwill when the Romans
clashed with the Hernicans in their surroundings.[2] In 462 B.C. marauding bands of the mountain tribes pillaged along with the rural
districts of Gabii and Tusculum the fields of the Praenestines;[3]
there is no reason to deny the historicity of a popular tradition in
Tibur of the celebration of a victory over the Volscians,[4] apparently
some time in those same decades.

But the reticence of the Roman Annals could not keep hidden the
fact that Praeneste and Tibur turned away from the League of the
Alban Hills and Rome at a certain moment and made their lasting
accommodations with the invaders. Did this happen about 460 B.C.,
when the first decisive victory over the Volscians upset the balance
of power in Latium? We do not know; but we found Praeneste in
462 still on the Latin side, and it is hard to imagine a still later date
for this development.

This new turn of affairs becomes obvious, as B. G. Niebuhr has
observed in considering the following geographical and military
situation. The territories of Praeneste and Tibur are hemmed in
between the original seats of the Aequians on the upper Anio and
the Fucinus on the one hand, and the Algidus, the vital passage on the
eastern rim of the Alban Hills then also in Aequian possession, on
the other. If the communications between the Aequian homeland
and their strategic base on the Algidus had been cut or endangered
by the two Latin cities in question, the Aequians would never have
been able to hold out on the Algidus until the beginning of the fourth
century B.C.; furthermore the battles would be fought—as K. J.
Beloch perceived—not around Tusculum and Labici, but in the region
of Praeneste and Tibur. So the last named two cities evidently came
to terms with the mountain tribes; and when these tribes were pushed
back by the Latin League, Praeneste and Tibur emerge in their
place as the main enemies of that League.[5]

[1] Liv. II 19, 2 : *Praeneste ab Latinis ad Romanos descivit. nec ultra bellum Latinum
. . . dilatum.*
[2] DH VIII 65, 1-66, 3.
[3] Liv. III 8, 6-7.
[4] Serv., *Aen.* 8, 285 : *salii sunt, qui tripudiantes aras circumibant. saltabant autem
ritu veteri armati post victoriam Tiburtinorum de Volscis.*
[5] B. G. Niebuhr, RG 2³, 1800, 650 sq. As G. De Sanctis, St. d. R. 2², 113 sq.,

ROME DURING THE EARLY REPUBLIC

It was certainly not without their connivance that the Aequians mobilized their forces against Rome in 389 B.C. after her collapse; but as this people does not appear again among the many hostile states rising against Rome in the fourth century, they seem to have been really defeated, as the Annals maintain, perhaps only a year or so later.[1] Some years later, the exasperation of the Volscians and of several Latin states was mounting to open war; [2] but Praeneste is said to have begun hostilities against her neighbors, who were faithful to Rome, only in 382 B.C. The Senate delayed in meeting the challenge.[3] The next year Praeneste energetically assisted the Volscian-Latin population of Velitrae against the Romans, who were constrained to proceed against them. One year later again, Praeneste with her Volscian allies captured Satricum[4]—recaptured again in heavy fighting; in 380 B.C. her army is raiding the outskirts of Rome, and withdrawing northward is beaten by the Romans at the Allia. The victors conquered her subject *oppida* and she was herself forced to surrender,[5] only to stir the Latins to rebellion at the end of 379.[6]

rightly stresses, this situation does not justify to assume with Niebuhr, O. Clason (RG 1, 79), and K. J. Beloch (RG 294 sq.) that Praeneste and Tibur were in the possession of the Aequians. Cf. also K. J. Beloch, *op. cit.* 181. G. De Sanctis, *op. cit.* 153 sqq., 236 sq., 275 sq. A. Piganiol, Mél. 38, 1920, 297 sqq. A different view by A. N. Sherwin-White, *op. cit.* 26 sqq.

[1] Diod. XIV 117, 4 (Camillus): ἀκούσας ὁ αὐτοκράτωρ πορθεῖσθαι Βώλας ὑπὸ Αἰκουλανῶν, ... ἀγαγὼν τὴν δύναμιν τοὺς πλείστους τῶν πολιορκούντων ἀνεῖλεν. Liv. VI 2, 14: *victor ex Volscis in Aequos transiit et ipsos bellum molientes*; *exercitus eorum ad Bolas oppressit, nec castra modo, sed urbem etiam adgressus impetu primo cepit*; cf. VI 4, 8. G. De Sanctis, St. d. R. 2², 236. This victory seems to have belonged to the historical kernel of the Camillus legend.

[2] Liv. VI 21, 2-3.

[3] Liv. VI 21, 9 (see p. 382 n. 7 above!).

[4] Liv. VI 22, 2-4; 27, 7. 9. Plut., *Camill.* 37, 2-6.

[5] Liv. VI 28, 1 sqq. *Ibid.* 29, 8-9. *T. Quinctius semel acie victor, binis castris hostium, novem oppidis vi captis, Praeneste in deditionem accepto Romam revertit triumphansque signum Praeneste devectum Iovis Imperatoris in Capitolium tulit. dedicatum est inter cellam Iovis ac Minervae tabulaque sub eo fixa, monumentum rerum gestarum, his ferme incisa litteris fuit: 'Iuppiter atque divi omnes hoc dederunt, ut T. Quinctius dictator oppida novem caperet.'* Festus, p. 498, 4 L.: *Trientem tertium pondo coronam auream dedisse se Iovi donum scripsit T. Quintius dictator cum per novem dies totidem urbes et decimam Praeneste cepisset. Id significare ait Cincius in* Μυσταγωγικῶν *lib. II.* I suspect that also Livy's text just quoted is based on Cincius. Cf. also G. De Sanctis, St. d. R. 2², 237 n. 31. A. Klotz, Livius und seine Vorgänger, 1941, 281. Diod. XV 47, 8: ʽΡωμαῖοι πρὸς Πραινεστίνους παραταξάμενοι καὶ νικήσαντες τοὺς πλείστους τῶν ἀντιταξαμένων κατέκοψαν. Eutrop. 2, 2. *Fasti triumph. Capit.* (broken away), cf. A. Degrassi, Inscr. It. XIII 1, 1947, 539.

[6] Liv. VI 30, 8.

In the following two decades, she apparently persevered in her opposition to Rome, even if she avoided major clashes. Yet about 360 B.C., when the Gauls appeared again in Latium, and the cities of the Alban Hills renewed their alliance with Rome to protect themselves against them,[1] Praeneste and Tibur joined the invaders.

We mentioned, when discussing the second Celtic inroad, that the tradition for this inroad was stretched out in the Annals over a series of years, and embellished with invented victories with details chronologically confused. We regard as sound the following basic facts. The Gauls devastate Latium, push on to Campania, and return on the same route home unharmed with their booty. On their way across Latium, Tibur—already estranged from Rome—gets help from them: the size of the operations described points rather to a smaller force, hired by the Tiburtines, than to the main body of the Celtic host. An abortive Tiburtine surprise attack on Rome provokes a Roman counteraction; the triumph celebrated for this victory in 360 B.C. over the Celts and the Tiburtines seems to be historical.[2] Praeneste is mentioned only incidentally, but she was punished later for her collusion with the Celts along with Tibur.[3] In 356 B.C. the capture of Empulum, a Tiburtine stronghold, by the Romans is recorded;[4] two years later Tibur with all her subject cities surrendered

[1] Cf. above, p. 360 sq.

[2] Liv. VII 9, 1-2 : . . . . *cum C. Sulpicius et C. Licinius Calvus consules in Hernicos exercitum duxissent . . . . . revertentibus inde eis Tiburtes portas clausere. ea ultima fuit causa, cum multae ante querimoniae ultro citroque iactatae essent, cur . . . bellum Tiburti populo indiceretur.* 11, 1 : . . . *ut Gallorum exercitus . . . in Tiburtem agrum, atque inde, societate belli facta commeatuque benigne ab Tiburtibus adiutus, mox in Campaniam transierit. Ea fuit causa, cur proximo anno C. Poetelius Balbus consul . . . adversus Tiburtes iussu populi exercitum duceret. ad quorum auxilium cum Galli ex Campania redissent, foedae populationes in Labicano Tusculanoque et Albano agro haud dubie Tiburtibus ducibus sunt factae.* 6-7 : *pugnatum haud procul porta Collina . . . . . avertitur tandem acies Gallorum. fuga Tibur sicut arcem belli Gallici petunt ; palati a consule Poetelio haud procul Tibure excepti, egressis ad opem ferendam Tiburtibus simul cum iis intra portas conpelluntur.* 9 : *Poetelius de Gallis Tiburtibusque geminum triumphum egit.* 12, 1-4 : *Itaque insequenti anno . . . primo silentio noctis ab Tibure agmine infesto profecti ad urbem Romam venerunt . . . . duabus portis egressi consules utrimque aciem subeuntium iam muros adgrediuntur . . . ., vix primum impetum Romanorum sustinuere.* Acta triumph. a. 360 a. Chr. n. : *De Gallis et Tiburtibus.*

[3] Liv. VII 12, 8 : *quod Gallos mox Praeneste venisse atque inde circa Pedum considisse auditum est.* Liv. VIII 14, 9 : *Tiburtes Praenestinique agro multati, neque ob recens tantum rebellionis . . . crimen, sed quod taedio imperii Romani cum Gallis, gente efferata, arma quondam consociassent.*

[4] Liv. VII 18, 2 : *Empulum eo anno ex Tiburtibus . . . captum.*

390

at discretion.[1] Praeneste, left alone, was constrained then to conclude an armistice with the Romans.[2] Finally, in 340 B.C. both cities rose again in arms with almost all the Latins against the Roman domination, and persevered in their resistance even after the setbacks of their associates. In 339 the Romans launched an offensive against them along the highway to Gabii and Praeneste. Midway between these cities, under the walls of Pedum,[3] the forces of Tibur and Praeneste were encamped, assisted by contingents from Lanuvium, Velitrae, and Antium. They were more than a match for the attacking army.[4] In 338, however, when their allies just named attacked by the Romans southeast of the Alban Hills, Tibur and Praeneste fought another valiant battle in front of Pedum, but could not prevent the capture of this stronghold. They now lost forever their independence with part of their territory.[5]

One more remark. Rome, faithful to her general policy, tried hard before and after her final victory to win over the aristocracy of these powerful states. Fr. Münzer was first to observe [6] that the clan of the Plautii, who gave consuls to Rome in 358, 347, 341, and in later years of the same century, were from Tibur and Praeneste. Their alliance

---

[1] Liv. VII 19, 1-2 : *cum Tiburtibus usque ad deditionem pugnatum. Sassula ex his urbs capta ; ceteraque oppida eandem fortunam habuissent, ni universa gens positis armis in fidem consulis venisset. Triumphatum de Tiburtibus.* Cf. *Fasti triumph. ad a.* 354 a. Chr. n. Chron. Oxyrh. ad Ol. 106, 3 (F. Gr. Hist. 255=2 B, p. 1153): κατὰ δὲ τὸν <τρί> τον Τιβουρτεῖνοι ὑπὸ <‘Ρωμαίων> καταπολεμηθέ<ντες> ἑαυτο>ὺς παρέδοσαν.

[2] Diod. XVI 45, 8 : ‘Ρωμαῖοι πρὸς μὲν Πραινεστίνους ἀνοχάς, πρὸς δὲ Σαυνίτας συνθήκας ἐποιήσαντο.

[3] Apparently the modern Gallicano, as Cluver and Nibby guessed and H. Dessau, CIL XIV p. 288 n. 6, accepted from them.

[4] Liv. VIII 12, 6-8 : *Aemilius ad Pedum exercitus duxit. Pedanos tuebatur Tiburs, Praenestinus Veliternusque populus ; venerant et ab Lanuvio Antioque auxilia. ubi cum proeliis quidem superior Romanus esset, ad urbem ipsam Pedum castraque sociorum populorum, quae urbi adiuncta erant, integer labor restaret, bello infecto repente omisso consul . . . Romam rediit.*

[5] Liv. VIII 13, 4-7 : *neque tamen nisi admodum a paucis populis Pedani adiuti sunt, Tiburtes Praenestinique, quorum ager proprior erat, Pedum pervenere ; Aricinos, Lanuvinosque et Veliternos Antiatibus Volscis se coniungentes ad Asturae flumen Maenius . . . adortus fudit. Camillus ad Pedum cum Tiburtibus, maxime valido exercitu, maiore mole, quamquam aeque prospero eventu pugnat. Tumultum maxime repentina inter proelium eruptio oppidanorum fecit, in quos parte exercitus conversa Camillus non compulit solum eos intra moenia, sed eodem etiam die, cum ipsos auxiliaque eorum perculisset, oppidum scalis cepit.* 14, 9 : *Tiburtes Praenestinique agro multati.* Cf. A. Rosenberg, Hermes 54, 1919, 125 sqq. *Acta triumph. Capit. ad a.* 338 a. Chr. n. : *de Pedaneis et Tiburtibus.* Eutr. 2, 7.

[6] Fr. Münzer, *Adelsp.* 36 sq., 44 sq.

with the Roman nobility began, of course, not just with the year of their first consulate, but was certainly older still. Q. Anicius of Praeneste, who earlier fought the Romans, became a curule aedile in Rome in 304 B.C.[1] The Caecilii from Praeneste had already attained the Roman consulate. This trend in Roman policy we have already noted in connection with the close allies of their city. They applied it also to their adversaries.

෯

THE LATIN LEAGUE FROM THE BATTLE AT LAKE REGILLUS TO ITS DISSOLUTION (338 B.C.)

In the survey of the relations of Rome with her neighbors we saw that the two largest Latin cities were opposing her throughout a century or longer; further, that she could rely only on the small cities of the Alban Hills. From the north, the east, and south—with the sole exception of the Hernicans east of the Algidus—potential or real enemies surrounded her and her allies, and in the west, the sea was closed to her. In such circumstances it is amazing that such a little group of states not only survived the concentric strangling pressure but was able to react violently and expand. To achieve this, the cohesion of this small confederation must have been extraordinary in the fifth century. The convincing proof of this extraordinary vitality of the Latin League and of her consequent policy of well organized expansion is provided by the spread of her colonial foundations.

It is essential for the correct understanding of the great achievements of the League in the fifth century that the reader should not lose sight of what we established in our earlier chapters concerning the relationships of the League with Rome. We saw that Rome stood not a priori above the League but was one of its members; that the League had its annual heads, electing them in rotation from all the member-cities; that the League alone decided upon common enterprises, not the Romans. The Latin triumph on the Alban mountain, the reward

---

[1] Plin., *N.h.* XXXIII 1, 17 : *ut aedilis curulis crearetur cum Q. Anicio Praenestino, qui paucis ante annis hostis fuisset.* The *pauci anni* is a rhetorical exaggeration, the "few" being 34 years ! Nevertheless, there is no reason to deny the historicity of this aedileship, *pace* H. Dessau, CIL XIV p. 288 n. 8.

ROME DURING THE EARLY REPUBLIC

of the federal leaders, was certainly the prototype of the Roman triumph, not vice versa, as the Annals would have us believe.[1]

An important feature in the structure of the Latin League of the fifth century is the sovereign right of every member. This autonomy of the old Latin states is still mirrored in the constitution of the later Latin colonies, which were established as independent communities with sovereign rights, as for instance in the coinage.[2] The silver coins struck in Cora and Signia, in the years of the outbreak of the first Punic war attest this. It is evident that this independence was far greater in the original Latin colonies before 338 B.C. than that of the Latins in the third century,[3] and further, that the autonomy of the newly founded Latin cities simply reflected the sovereign character of the mother cities of the colonists. This individual sovereignty enabled the Latin states to make war and to make special agreements with whom they liked: this latter capacity gave Rome the opportunity to swallow them up, one by one, when the time of her superiority arrived. These sovereign communities, however, had within the frame of their League important common rights such as, in peacetime, the freedom of their citizens to move to the territory of any other member-city, and in war, to participate in the booty and the land seized in common enterprises and from the enemy, collectively and individually.[4]

These common rights are the base of the foundation of new cities by the League, the so-called *coloniae Latinae*. It has been often pointed out by modern scholars that Livy calls *coloniae Romanae* such cities as Circeii, Setia, Norba, and Signia,[5] which are known later as Latin foundations, and certainly were such from the beginning. Though

---

[1] B. G. Niebuhr, RG 2², 42, observed for the first time that the Roman triumph on the Alban Mountain was not a new invention, but it revived an old custom. Though his opinion was rejected or passed in silence by excellent scholars (Mommsen, St. R. 1³, 134. Aust, in Roscher's Lex. 2, 693 sq., etc.), it is proved to be correct by the fact that also in Rome the Alban triumph had a legal validity (Mommsen, *loc. cit.*), which could not have been there without such antecedents. Cf. also G. Wissowa, RuK 2², 125. H. Müller-Karpe, Vom Anfang Roms, Heidelberg, 1959, 40.

[2] E. Pais, Mem. Acc. Lincei, sc. mor. 5. ser., 17, 1924, 323.

[3] Of these old colonies Signia and Cora struck coins ; cf. A. Sambon, Les monnaies antiques de l'Italie 1, Paris 1903, 100, no. 164-65. The reason why such foundations have no coins of their own is the very late beginning of the coinage in Latium (in the fifth and fourth centuries B.C. still no evidence).

[4] E. T. Salmon, Phoenix 7, 1953, 98 sqq.

[5] Liv. VII 42, 8. VIII 3, 9 ; 5, 3. XXVII 9, 7.

some excellent scholars refrained from drawing the necessary con-clusion from this,[1] others did take this step.[2] If the Ferentinates in 187 B.C. assumed that they had the right to join in Roman colonial foundations,[3] how much more natural was this before 338 B.C.!

But if we extend the examination of the early colonization to all the other cases known to us, it becomes manifest that not only the foundations mentioned above but all belong until the conquest of Latium by the Romans to the same category. G. De Sanctis wrote in 1907: "Colonies of Roman citizens provided with real communal rights were not established till the Latin war of 340-338 B.C., and also then, in general, only on the sea-shore." [4] This is an insight of great consequence, reached also by A. Rosenberg in 1919,[5] but exploited for the history of the Early Republic only quite recently by E. T. Salmon.[6] He rightly stresses the point that all those newly founded towns did not form part of the Roman state, as it is generally believed. These colonies of the League, as also the Roman colonies modeled on the same pattern after 338 B.C., had undoubtedly a strategic purpose—as he points out well [7]—implanted on strong sites, "usually intended to serve as defensive bastions rather than as offen-sive springboards, although presumably they were useful in either capacity. The principal role envisaged for them appears to have been that of immovable road-blocks, barring the advance of any enemy into the territory of Rome or her allies." In fact, this is a concept developed by the League in its fight against the Aequians and Volscians, in an extreme danger necessitating a comprehensive strategy; a danger which through its pressure forced great cohesion on this confederacy.

---

[1] As, e.g., M. Gelzer, RE 12, 958 sq.

[2] As, e.g., J. Beloch, Der ital. Bund 135 sq. J. Marquardt, St.-V. 1², 48. E. Kornemann, RE 4, 514, H. Nissen, It. Lk. 2, 26. E. Pais, St. crit. 3, 361 (all these historians think that both the League and Rome gave half of the colonists to the new foundations, an idea based on the pretension of the Roman Annals). A. Piganiol, Mél. 38, 1920, 297 sq. 301 sq. *Idem*, La conquête romaine, Paris 1927, 82. E. Pais, *op. cit.* (p. 392 n. 2 above) 318 sq. A. N. Sherwin-White, R. Citiz. 22 sq., 34 sq.

[3] Liv. XXXIV 42, 5. A. N. Sherwin-White, *l.c.*

[4] G. De Sanctis, St. d. R. 2¹, 1907, 248 : 2², 233.

[5] A. Rosenberg, Hermes 54, 1919, 161 sqq.

[6] E. T. Salmon, Phoenix 7, 1953, 93 sqq., 123 sqq. ; cf. *ibid.* 9, 1955, 63 sqq. I could not consult P. Frezza, Studi U. Paoli, Roma 1956, 305 sq., nor A. De-grassi, Guida allo studio della civiltà Romana antica 1², Napoli 1959, 301 sq.

[7] E. T. Salmon, Phoenix 9, 1955, 64 sq.

ROME DURING THE EARLY REPUBLIC

We have seen that the colonial foundations at the end of the regal epoch and the beginnings of the Republic are unhistorical. The Latins were then disunited and soon forced into the defensive: the sites of the federal colonies in themselves situated at key positions recently taken from the enemy (at a much later date than assumed) betray at least this much, that before the decisive victories of ca. 460 and 430 B.C. no such natural strongholds could be selected. Such a strategical planning as this systematic colonization needs a great deal of freedom of decision, reached only when the Latins were already recovering from the blows that they had suffered and were taking over the initiative from the Volscians and Aequians.

The first well-attested case is the Latin colony [1] of Ardea, founded by the League in 442,[2] after the old Latin settlement itself could not deal with the Volscian menace, aggravated by the collusion of the lower strata of the population with the enemy. Well inside the reduced Latin territory, this foundation is a purely defensive expedient, different in this from all the subsequent acts of this kind.

The full swing of the colonizing activity of the League was setting in about the time when the belt of gentile tribes around Rome was established. First, on the Aequian front, the protection of Tusculum was improved by the *deductio* of a federal colony to Labici, just north of this city, in 418 B.C.[3] This measure was hotly contested by the Aequians in the next decades.[4] They tried to balance the Latin action in 414 with the establishment of a colony of their own in the neighborhood, in Bola, which changed hands several times in the following quarter of a century.[5] Another colony instituted to hold in check the Aequians was Vitellia in the same region. We know only that it already existed in 393 B.C.,[6] but its beginnings could easily reach back to the same years in which Labici got her Latin settlers.

On the Volscian front, the stronghold Velitrae was founded in 401 B.C.[7] The next steps of advance in the region of the present-day

---

[1] DH XIII 5, 3. Plut., *Camill.* 23, 2. Liv. IV 11, 4 (the Rutuli admitted). XXVII 9, 7. XXIX 15, 5. App., *Ital.* 8, 5.

[2] Diod. XII 34, 5.

[3] Liv. IV 47, 1 sqq. Cf. Diod. XIII 6, 8.

[4] Liv. V 16, 2 (397 B.C.). *Ibid.* V 28, 6 sqq. (394 B.C.). Labici faithful to Rome in 383 and 360 B.C. : Liv. VI 21, 9. VII 11, 3.

[5] Liv. IV 49, 7 sqq. Diod. XIII 42, 6. XIV 117, 4. Liv. VI 2, 14 ; 5, 2.

[6] Liv. V 29, 3-5. Cf. Suet., *Vitell.* 1, 3. Liv. II 39, 4.

[7] This is the date which Diod. XIV 34, 7, gives for a reinforcement of the colonists by new ones. DH VI 4, 2 ; 43, 1 and Liv. II 31, 4 call her, as habitually

Monti Lepini were Cora and Norba, though we know only that the first was colonized before 340 B.C.,[1] and the second before 342 B.C.[2] It is obvious, too, that they must have been in Latin hands before Satricum and Setia, south of them. The last federal colony constituted before the Celtic storm seems to be Signia, protecting the lifeline of the Hernican territory, the valley of the Tolerus (Sacco), from the Volscians.[3] As the Hernicans were at war with Rome from 389 B.C., the federal colonization of Signia must be earlier; yet it cannot be much earlier. Of course, the city as such was flourishing as early as 500 B.C.[4]—whether it was an early Latin or a new Volscian settlement in that epoch, we cannot decide. But most of the federal colonies were established in towns already existing, captured from the enemy. Even the Latin Ardea was reinforced by new Latin settlers, because she could not withstand the aggression alone:

et nunc magnum manet Ardea nomen, sed fortuna fuit

in Vergil's words.[5] The case of Signia is similar.

The establishment of a federal colony in 393 B.C. in Circeii [6] demonstrates the offensive power of the League: the Latins broke through almost the whole length of the Volscian territory toward the south, and were now holding watch over the passage to Campania.

Most revealing is the continuation of the federal colonization on the same scale in the 380's of the fourth century, when Rome, humiliated by her breakdown against the Celts, made great concessions to an expansive federal policy of the Latins, though this hurt her own

most of the others, a Roman colony. Her Latin colonists and Volscian inhabitants were rebelling against Rome exasperatedly from 385 to 338 B.C. Liv. VI 12, 6 ; 13, 8 ; 17, 7 ; 21, 2-3 ; 30, 6 ; 36, 1-6 ; 37, 12 ; 38, 1. VII 15, 10-11. VIII 3, 9 ; 12, 7; 13, 5 ; 14, 5. She became a Roman colony in fact in 338 B.C. : Liv. VIII 14, 7.

[1] Liv. II 16, 8-17, 7 : *duae coloniae Latinae, Pometia et Cora.* The beautiful early didrachm of Cora in Paris (A. Sambon, Les monnaies antiques de l'Italie 1, Paris 1903, 100 no. 165) is the only specimen preserved; how many related coins of other federal colonies may have been lost for us!

[2] DH VII 13, 5 (Latin colony). Liv. VII 42, 8 (342 B.C.).

[3] Liv. VIII 3, 9, mentions her as a "Roman" colony in 340, but her coinage (A. Sambon, *op. cit.* 100 no. 164) proves that she was a sovereign city, i.e., a federal colony.

[4] R. Delbrueck, Das Kapitolium von Signia, Rom 1903. A. Rosenberg, Hermes 54, 1919, 158.

[5] Verg., *Aen.* 7, 410 sqq.

[6] Diod. XIV 102, 4. Latin colony : Liv. VIII 3, 9. XXVII 9, 7. XXIX 15, 5.

ambitions.[1] The outstanding problem was the occupation of the rich wheat-growing Pomptine plain, captured from the Volscians. The wishes of the Romans would be to distribute it among their citizens.[2] They indeed retained part of it, which was incorporated in 358 B.C. in their state, when one of the two new rural districts, the Pomptina, was established there.[3] Two new federal foundations were made in the same region: Satricum in 385 B.C.,[4] and Setia in 382, reinforced in 370.[5] As Mommsen observed long ago,[6] a good deal of the Pomptine region belonged to this latter city, so that the Roman *tribus Pomptina* was necessarily only a small piece of land before the Latin war.

It is equally important and characteristic for the prevalence of the League over Rome in these years that Rome ceded part of the territory conquered from Veii[7] to the Latins for the constitution of two federal colonies. In 383 B.C. Sutrium was founded [8] and Nepet either in the same year or some years later.[9] But at this juncture, the Latins and Rome were standing at the parting of ways. It is, I think, fair to characterize the new turn of events with the words of the scholar [10] who keenly observed it: "The first Roman counter-move came in an area which they had always regarded as sensitive and with which their connections had been of the closest ever since the Aequian

[1] Cf. E. T. Salmon, Phoenix 7, 1953, 130.

[2] Liv. VI 5, 1 ; 6, 1.

[3] Liv. VII 15, 11. Already in 383 B.C. *quinqueviros Pomptino agro dividendo . . . creaverunt.* Liv. VI 21, 4. L. R. Taylor, Vot. Distr. 51 sqq., accepted reasonably E. Pais' view that the *Poblilia* was placed on Hernican territory ; fortunately enough, there is no doubt on the situation of the *Pomptina.*

[4] Liv. VI 16, 6. The Volscian population was not expelled : Liv. VI 32, 4-10. There was still a lot of bitter fighting for the possession of Satricum (Liv. VI 22, 5 ; 32, 4-10 ; 33, 4. VII 27, 7-8) which revolted as late as 320-19 (Liv. IX 12, 5 ; 16, 3).

[5] Vell. I 14, 2. Liv. VI 30, 9. VII 42, 8. VIII 1, 1 ; 5, 7 ; 19, 4-5. Latin : Liv. VIII 3, 9.

[6] Mommsen, CIL X p. 640. Besides the passages quoted by him, it is also worth while to mention Martial. IV 64, 31, sqq. : *Vos nunc omnia parva qui putatis, centeno gelidum ligone Tibur, vel Praeneste domate pendulamque uni dedite Setiam colono : dum me iudice praeferantur istis Iuli iugera pauca Martialis.*

[7] Cf. Ed. Meyer, Kleine Schriften 2, Halle 1924, 311.

[8] Vell. I 14, 2. Diod. XIV 98, 5 ; 117, 4. XX 35, 1. Liv. VI 3, 2. IX 32, 1. Both Sutrium and Nepet are *coloniae Latinae* : Liv. XXVII 9, 7 ; 10, 7. On the divergencies on the date of foundation : K. J. Beloch, RG 305 sq. E. Pais, Mem. Acc. Linc. cl. mor. 5. ser. 17, 1924, 321 sq.

[9] Liv. VI 21, 4. Vell. I 14, 2.

[10] E. T. Salmon, Phoenix 7, 1953, 131 sq.

threat at the Algidus Pass: *viz*. Tusculum. This town was annexed in 381 B.C., becoming part of the Roman State ... Thereby a solid block of Roman territory from the Tiber to the Algidus Pass was created, splitting the Latins and rendering it extremely difficult for them to concert any joint move in the future. It is not surprising that Polybius (II 18, 5) is able to assert that the Romans recovered from the effects of the Gallic Raid in less than thirty years. Simultaneously the Latin policy of sending out colonies came to an abrupt halt: after the annexation of Tusculum colonization by the Latins ceased completely; Setia was the last of the *priscae Latinae coloniae*. Any later colonies came after the Latin war and were planted by the Romans. On the other hand, the Roman policy of viritane allotments was now resumed, as we shall see."

It is also true, I firmly believe, that "once it is realized that, prior to 338 B.C., it was the Latin League that founded colonies, while the Romans confined themselves to the practice of viritane allotments, a logical and connected account of the history of early Latium can be given." [1] These federal foundations were essentially different from the later Roman ones. They were not annexes, dependent on the mother city, without autonomy and independence, but sovereign communities, members of the Latin League, quite as the original homes of the colonists. Though a certain number of lots in their territory must have fallen to Roman citizens, their proportion was not large, because they were joining the Latins instead of Rome after the end of the federal collaboration in the early fourth century. [2] Antium, Velitrae, Signia, Setia, Satricum, Circeii were in upheaval against Rome—the Volscian elements of these states must also be taken into account, of course, in explaining this behavior—until the final subjugation of Latium, sometimes even longer.

The raids of the mountain peoples spent their first wrath in striking on the ring of the Latin states in the Alban Hills in the fifth century, seldom reaching the outskirts of Rome [3] behind them; this protective wall was extended and reinforced between 420 and 380 B.C. by the chain of the federal colonies. Rome profited greatly from the alliance of old and new Latin states alike. But in the forty years after the suspension of the federal expansion, she no longer needed their associa-

---

[1] *Ibid*. 104. Cf. also his short account, 123 sqq.
[2] A. N. Sherwin-White, R. Citiz. 22 sq., 34 sq. E. T. Salmon, *op. cit*. 129.
[3] A. N. Sherwin-White, *op. cit*. 20 sq.

tion as equals, but enforced their collaboration as subjects to her will and aims.

The attacks of the Syracusan fleet and the hostility of the Volscians of Antium led the Romans to introduce a new form of coastal defense in Latium. This was to guard the open coastline of this region by settlements of Roman citizens who had no independent communal organization, as had the previous federal foundations, but remained *cives Romani*, depending directly on the capital. They held watch in Ostia (from some time just after the middle of the fourth century),[1] in Antium (from 337 B.C.), and in Circeii (from 329 B.C.). This fertile idea spread rapidly to continental areas after the conquest of Latium throughout the whole new Empire, where the *coloniae civium Romanorum* became everywhere the backbone of control, defense, and cultural assimilation.

୫

THE ROMAN ASCENDENCY OVER LATIUM

The Etruscan domination was, as its final outcome shows, a brilliant school for the military and political education of the Latins. The Etruscan overlords neither ruined the social structure and the peculiar character of the Latin communities, nor did they destroy their tribal ties and national feelings. This is an amazing achievement in that early period of interstate relations in Italy: the great Roman principle to take care of and foster the conquered and strike only at the stubborn opponents—*parcere subjectis et debellare superbos*—seems to have its antecedents in the Etruscan statesmanship.

The ruling Etruscan dynasts and their retainers in the sixth century mingled with the local aristocracies in Latium. After they lost power, apparently the pattern of government that they established continued in the Latin cities, as we can still grasp in the case of Rome. A closed ring of noble families usurped the royal privileges of the *auspicium* and *imperium*, i.e., the government and its religious legalization by a

---

[1] F. Altheim, RG 2, Frankfurt 1953, 112, stresses correctly the point that if Ostia had existed at the time of the first treaties with Carthage, she would have certainly been mentioned in them as were Ardea, Antium, Circei, and Tarracina, the other Latin towns of the coastal plain, which were especially protected against raids by Carthage in those agreements. This fact reveals an important date : the foundation of Ostia is later than 343 B.C.

monopolized ritual technique. This common pattern found in all cities of fifth-century Latium certainly facilitated the reaching of common decisions in the revived tribal alliance.

The preponderant role of this ruling oligarchy was based on its efficiency and daring in fighting on horseback. The disregard of personal safety was coupled in these warriors with political insight and diplomatic skill in Rome as well as in Tusculum, Praeneste, or Tibur. Toward the end of the fifth century in consequence of the pressing military demands of their time, they admitted a second cavalry group to the mounted service, without sharing with them their governmental privileges, and established a heavily armored infantry— granting to both groups unavoidable political concessions: a belated repetition of Greek developments, and one not merely owing to chance.[1]

The unremitting attacks of the new invaders from the east and the south forced upon the Latins the revival of their tribal League. The "Latin name" became again under their pressure an efficient national entity. The only way to get rid of the perpetuated menace was to subjugate the raiders. Not a preconceived idea of planned conquest—as with the Etruscans—but bitter necessity pushed the Latins into the path of expansion. Their concentration on war had tremendous consequences for the future. The permanent readiness for fighting—fighting for their very existence—forged a weapon of adamant steel from their manpower, which proved itself to be superior to anything nearby and far away: when Rome succeeded in turning this formidable tool of conquest outward against foreign foes, nothing could stop her march of advance.

We must consider again the violent shocks which after the flight of the Tarquins upset the old and established the new balance of power in Latium. First, Rome was overwhelmed around 504 B.C. by the expedition of the King of Clusium. A year later the defeat and death of his son brought the collapse of the Etruscan rule in that region. Aricia and Tusculum are now the leading Latin powers, relying on Cyme. Tusculum is harboring the Tarquins [2] and their

---

[1] A. Piganiol, Histoire de Rome[1], Paris 1939, 48 sq. Cf. my study, Der früh-römische Reiteradel, *passim*.

[2] Fr. Münzer, Adelsp. 66, assumes the historicity of the relationship of the Tusculan Mamilii with the Tarquins of Rome. This cannot be proved, but it is not impossible. On Lake Regillus : A. Schwegler, RG 2, 60 sqq. M. Zoeller, Latium und Rom. Forschungen über ihre gemeinsame Geschichte und gegen-

retinue. Porsenna makes his peace with the new patrician rulers of Rome, who win in 499 or 496 B.C.,[1] apparently with the backing of the Etruscan invader, the battle at Lake Regillus (Pantano Secco) near Tusculum. The Tarquins flee to Cyme; their rule is over. The temple vowed in the battle to the heavenly patrons of the Roman patrician cavalry and consecrated in 484 B.C. on the *forum*, preserved the memory of that baptism of fire of the now ruling aristocracy.[2] Not long afterward their statues, partly recovered in excavations (Frontispiece and pl. II),[3] were erected at the *Lacus Iuturnae*, where the divine youths with their sweat-covered horses were believed to have miraculously appeared to announce the victory, as they did that of Locri at the river Sagra.[4]

This victory certainly did not mean the overpowering of all the Latin tribes by Rome, and the ensuing peace treaty, identified in the Annals with the *foedus Cassianum*, could not be, consequently, the *magna charta* of the hegemony of Rome over Latium. We know by chance that before the clash Praeneste detached herself from the League of Aricia; how many other communities did the same we do not know. Nor were Tusculum or other cities captured or broken in this war. The success was a much more restricted one than the Annals pretend. Yet it nourished nevertheless the aspirations of Rome to replace Tusculum and Aricia in the leadership of their League: the federal sanctuary of Diana on the Aventine, founded in some year before 456 B.C.,[5] proves that this aspiration existed, even if the Aventine cult failed in the role intended for it.

Soon after Lake Regillus the Aequians were capturing the Algidus Pass, and the Volscians inundating the Pomptine Plain. In the protracted defensive struggle as well as in the decisive Latin victories of 460 and 430 B.C., Rome had an important share. The first concrete

seitigen Beziehungen bis zum Jahr 338 v. Chr., Leipzig 1878, 208 sqq. Ed. Schwartz, RE 5, 950 (on the source-tradition). K. J. Beloch, RG 292 sq. G. De Sanctis, St. d. R. 2¹, 96 sq.

[1] The uncertainty of the exact date, stressed by Livy II 21, 4, does not change the reliability of the general chronological attribution.

[2] T. Frank, Mem. Am. Ac. 5, 1925, 79 sq. Th. Ashby, JRS 19, 1929, 161 sq. G. Lugli, Roma antica, il centro monumentale, Roma 1946, 179 sqq.

[3] W. Amelung, Neue Jahrbücher 5, 1902, 379 n. 1. G. Lugli, *op. cit.* 184. E. Nash, Arch. cl. 11, 1959, 227 sqq. The palm trunks supporting the body of the horses are later additions.

[4] Cf. A. Oldfather, RE 13, 1326 sq.

[5] Cf. above, p. 85 sqq.

indication of her elevated position in the League is that she was entrusted after 451 B.C. with the organization of the Latin Festival.

In 443-42 B.C. are reported two events, whose correlation, given in the Annals, must have been different in reality: a federal colony is established at Ardea, to eliminate the Volscian menace; and a special treaty is concluded between Ardea and Rome.[1] Was this double procedure a concerted action or a compromise solution between the League and Rome, as analogous combined actions in the near future suggest?

After the decisive victory of A. Postumius Tubertus over the Volscians, the Latin League and Rome gain the initiative. In 426 Fidenae is captured;[2] soon thereafter the belt of gentile tribes is added to the Roman territory, followed by the *tribus Crustumina*.[3] In 419 B.C. Labici, only a step north of Tusculum, becomes a federal colony, established to oppose the Aequians.[4] As we have seen, a series of additional colonies of the League followed on territory until then held by the Volscians. Naturally a substantial contingent of Romans must have been included among the colonists of the new foundations. Besides these federal actions, and simultaneously with them, Rome begins soon to appropriate new territory to herself on a large scale in every direction. A common strategy in both these expanding activities cannot be denied. It would otherwise have been quite impossible to begin in 406 B.C. the very serious war with Veii[5] in the north, and achieve also the great breakthrough to Campania with the capture of Anxur-Tarracina[6] in the south. The share of the League in the liquidation of the Veientan, Capenate, and Faliscan property through the colonies of Sutrium and Nepet demonstrates her full collaboration in the Roman enterprise. Nevertheless, the Roman acquisitions were so much superior in size that the Roman potential and resources at once overshadowed the League.[7] After the capture of Veii, when Rome got a free hand again toward the south,

---

[1] Liv. III 71, 2-72, 7. IV 1, 4 ; 7, 1-12 ; 9, 1-14 ; 10, 1-7 ; 11, 1-7. DH XI 54, 1 sq. K. J. Beloch, RG 164 sq.

[2] Cf. Mommsen, Hermes 13, 1878, 306 sqq.

[3] Cf. above, p. 310 sq.

[4] Liv. IV 45, 3 sq.; 46, 6. 9. 12; 47, 4-7 ; cf. 49, 8-9. Diod. XIII 42, 6. As a federal colony, Labici—contrary to the customary view—was *not* incorporated in the *ager Romanus* ; cf. our map, p. 297.

[5] Cf. A. Momigliano, Cl. Q. 36, 1942, 111 sqq.

[6] Liv. IV 59, 3 sqq.

[7] E. T. Salmon, Phoenix 7, 1953, 128.

ROME DURING THE EARLY REPUBLIC

the mountain tribes beg for peace,[1] to prevent her attack. Nothing could make more obvious the overwhelming Roman superiority than the behavior of their allies after 390, when a unique chance seemed to have arrived to shake off her dangerous preponderance.

About 400 B.C., the extension of the sovereign territory of Rome already surpasses so much that of most Latin states [2] that they can no longer be compared individually with her. The area of the city of Rome in the same time is precisely known to us by the circuit of the "Servian" wall, built after the Celtic storm. This enclosed, according to the calculation of K. J. Beloch, 426 hectares. Of the Greek harbor cities of the South, only Syracuse, Akragas, Kroton, and Tarentum exceeded this size; and it was neither equaled nor surpassed by any other city on the Italian mainland with one exception: only Veii of all the Etruscan cities occupied an even larger area than Rome.[3] Her growing splendor is illustrated by the dates of foundation of new state sanctuaries,[4] which continue to be erected throughout the first century of the Republic—in the same way as the import of Attic ceramics continued during this period.[5] These respectable dimensions of Rome were present in the mind of Antiochus of Syracuse, writing in the last decades of this century, when he represented the Sicels as migrating from *Rome* to their historical homes.[6]

The roots of this spectacular growth of Rome reach back, there can be no doubt, to the prosperity of the sixth century, when the flourishing Etrusco-Campanian trade enriched this important junction. But a glance to the modest circumference of the *ager Romanus antiquus* makes it evident that as yet no substantial base existed there for great developments. The towns of the Alban Hills, Aricia and Tusculum above all, which stood dwarfed beside Rome about 400 B.C., were a hundred years before still a match for her: the disparity between them came into existence, evidently, in the interval. The reasons for it were already touched upon above. The communities of the Alban Hills were exposed immediately to the Volscian and Aequian

[1] Liv. V 23, 12.
[2] The statistics of K. J. Beloch, RG 178, must be reworked for Rome (cf. our map, p. 297), but we do not have any more modern computations.
[3] H. Nissen, It. Lk. II 2, 502 sq.
[4] R. Bloch, R. Et. Lat. 37, 1959, 121.
[5] Cf. above, p. 333.
[6] Antiochos of Syracuse, Fr. Gr. Hist. 555 F 6 (III B, p 546 Jac.). We follow H. Nissen, *op. cit.* 495.

raids. Their prosperity was strangled; they survived but were bled dry. Rome, at a distance behind them, was rarely struck by massive attacks; her relative safety was favoring her growth and importance. As a strategic center she had all the qualifications to outgrow her partners.

This situation was inverted by the Celtic storm, it is true: Rome was subjected first to this devastating tempest. But the crushing defeat of their army and the laying in ashes of the roofs over their heads did not break the spirit of the Romans. Their manpower could be gathered again and harbored in Veii, as we saw; this saved the future. The terrors and anxieties of the months immediately following the ruinous collapse still vibrate vaguely in the popular tale of the brave maid Tutula-Philotis.[1]

The Annals do not veil the fact that after the great crisis the city "was encircled by the envy and hatred of the neighbors," [2] despising the burned out wreck.[3] Livy reports in the year after the sack of Rome the defection of the Latins and Hernicans.[4] Unable to cope with them, the Senate shuts its eyes to their disobedience.[5] Certain Latin cities—it is not clear which and how many of them—unofficially help the Volscians of Antium in their uprising against Rome, in encouraging their men to join the Antiates privately, as volunteers.[6]

[1] Varro, LL 6, 18 : *dies Poplifugia videtur nominatus, quod eo die tumultu repente fugerit populus : non multo enim post hic dies quam decessus Gallorum ex urbe, et qui tum sub urbe populi, ut Ficuleates ac Fidenates et finitimi alii, contra nos coniurarunt. aliquot huius d(i)ei vestigia fugae ex sacris apparent, de quibus rebus antiquitatum libri plura referunt.* Plut., *Rom.* 29, 4 sqq. *Idem, Camill.* 33, 3 sqq. Macrob., *Sat.* I 11, 35 sqq. Polyaen. 8, 30. Auson., *De fer.* 9. Cf. G. De Sanctis, St. d. R. 2², 229 sq.

[2] Liv. VI 6, 11.

[3] Flor. I 9, 1.

[4] Liv. VI 2, 3 : *novus quoque terror accesserat defectione Latinorum Hernicorumque, qui post pugnam ad lacum Regillum factam per annos prope centum nunquam ambigua fide in amicitia populi Romani fuerant.* The idyllic touch of unbroken fidelity is colored by the tendency demonstrated in our second and third chapters.

[5] Liv. VI 6, 2 : *et de Latino Hernicoque bello mentio facta in senatu maioris belli cura, quod Etruria in armis erat, dilata est.*

[6] Liv. VI 6, 4-5 (386 B.C.) : *Principio anni aversae curae hominum sunt a bello Etrusco, quod fugientium ex agro Pomptino agmen repente inlatum in urbem attulit Antiates in armis esse Latinorumque populos iuventutem suam misisse ad id bellum, eo abnuentis publicum fuisse consilium, quod non prohibitos tantummodo voluntarios dicerent militare, ubi vellent.* Cf. VI 6, 13. VI 7, 1 :. . . . *Furius ac Valerius ad Satricum profecti, quo non Volscorum modo iuventutem Antiates ex nova subole lectam sed ingentem (vim) Latinorum Hernicorumque conciverant ex integerrimis diutina pace populis.* 8, 8 : *Signo deinde receptui dato nox insecuta quietis Romanis perfecit bellum. Latini*

The allegation that in 386 B.C. the Senate called to account the Latin League as well as the Hernican League for not having sent Rome soldiers in the preceding years, and that the two Leagues gave evasive answers,[1] cannot be true. The more so as we know that a considerable group of Latin states took the side of Rome in these crucial years: Tusculum, Gabii, and Labici,[2] apparently with Aricia, Lavinium, Ardea, Cora, Norba, Satricum, and Signia.[3] The cooperation of Rome with the League is proved by the foundation of federal colonies in regions where the Romans acquired new territories just in these years. The Roman policy was rather to single out her enemies, subjugating them one by one, than to provoke them as a group. And the League was pursuing a vigorous policy of expansion in these years; it was most useful for Rome to cooperate with it.

However, though the League did not do so as a group, some Latin communities unofficially did help the Volscians in 385 B.C. against Rome.[4] The Romans, though victorious, made a conciliatory gesture

namque et Hernici relictis Volscis domos profecti sunt malis consiliis pares adepti eventus, etc. Cf. 11, 2. 9. Plut., *Camill.* 33, 1-2, speaks already in 389 B.C. of the Latins joining the Volscians and Aequians : ... ἐπιπίπτει πόλεμος, Αἰκανῶν μὲν ἅμα καὶ Οὐλούσκων καὶ Λατίνων εἰς τὴν χώραν ἐπιβαλόντων, Τυρρηνῶν δὲ πολιορκούντων Σούτριον, συμμαχίδα ῾Ρωμαίων πόλιν. ἐπειδὴ δ᾽οἱ τὴν ἡγεμονίαν ἔχοντες χιλίαρχοι στρατοπεδευσάμενοι περὶ τὸ Μαίκιον ὄρος ὑπὸ τῶν Λατίνων ἐπολιορκοῦντο καὶ κινδυνεύοντες ἀποβαλεῖν τὸ στρατόπεδον εἰς ῾Ρώμην ἔπεμψαν, ἀποδείκνυται τὸ τρίτον Κάμιλλος δικτάτωρ. But Livy VI 2, 5 sqq., relating the same events from the same source (2, 8 *nec procul a Lanuvio, ad Mecium is locus dicitur* is the Μαίκιον ὄρος of Plut.) does not involve the Latins, nor Frontinus II 4, 15, Eutr. 2, 1, Oros. III 3, 4 ; only Zon. 7, 24, has this version, too : πόλεμοι προσέπεσον διαφόρων ἐθνῶν, Αἰκουῶν τε καὶ Οὐλούσκων καὶ Λατίνων. We have to dismiss this as unhistorical.

[1] Liv. VI 10, 6-9 : *Eodem anno ab Latinis Hernicisque res repetitae quaesitumque, cur per eos annos militem ex instituto non dedissent. responsum frequenti utriusque gentis concilio est nec culpam in eo publicam nec consilium fuisse, quod suae iuventutis aliqui apud Volscos militaverint ; eos tamen ipsos pravi consilii poenam habere, nec quemquam ex iis reducem esse ; militis autem non dati causam terrorem adsiduum a Volscis fuisse, quam pestem adhaerentem lateri suo tot super alia aliis bellis exhauriri nequisse. quae relata patribus magis tempus quam causam non visa belli habere.* The concept that the Latins are obliged to send soldiers *ex formula togatorum* is, of course, anachronistic before 338 B.C. On the abusive generalisation of the term *Latini*, cf. above, p. 377.

[2] Liv. VI 21, 9.

[3] G. De Sanctis, St. d. R. 2², 232 sq.

[4] Liv. VI 12, 6 : *ingens certe, quod inter omnes auctores conveniat,* ... *Volscorum exercitus fuit. Ad hoc Latini Hernicique accesserant Cerceiensium quidam et coloni etiam a Velitris Romani.* 13, 7-8 : *pars maxima captivorum ex Latinis Hernicisque fuit, nec hominum de plebe, ut credi posset mercede militasse, sed principes quidam iuventutis inventi, manifesta fides publica ope Volscos hostes adiutos. Cerceiensium quoque*

in handing over to the Latin and Hernican communities concerned their captured men.[1] In 383 even Lanuvium revolted. Velitrae and Circeii persisted in their hostility and with the help of Praeneste, they destroyed in 381 the pro-Roman Satricum.[2] The Roman predominance must have become unbearable, if her closest ally, Tusculum, reinforced secretly the Latino-Volscian enemies of Rome all in vain.[3] Even Praeneste is subjugated in 380 B.C.,[4] along with Velitrae.

In these toilsome years, Rome undisturbed was incorporating the rich soil of Veii, Capena, and Falerii as four new agrarian districts,[5] and prepared allotments to be distributed to her citizens on the fertile Pomptine plain.[6] Besides these tremendous increases, upsetting the balance of power in her favor, Tusculum was absorbed, becoming part of her citizen-body. A decade after she was brought to the brink of annihilation by the Celts, she stood mightier than before. The cessation of the colonizing activity of the League demonstrates that its collaboration with Rome came to an end. The two new agrarian districts of Rome on the Pomptine plain finally established in 358 B.C. were a hindrance and a nuisance to the League. No wonder that in the following decades the Latin states try hard to shake off the ever-growing Roman menace to their liberty. Rome continues to deal at any one time with as few as possible, to tie them to herself individually by special treaties of alliance, undermining in this way the power of the League.

Our data are scarce and even those that we have are obscured sometimes by the misleading practice of calling any insurgents

quidam cogniti et coloni a Velitris ; *Romamque omnes missi percunctantibus primoribus patrum eadem, quae dictatori, defectionem sui quisque populi, haud perplexe indicavere.* Cf. 14, 1.

[1] Liv. VI 17, 7-8 : *Per eosdem dies Latinis et Hernicis, simul colonis Circeiensibus et a Velitris, purgantibus se Volsci crimine belli captivosque repetentibus ... tristia responsa reddita . . . . non negatum itaque tantum de captivis,* etc. Cf. *ibid.* 21, 3.

[2] Liv. VI 21, 2 (Lanuvium) ; 21, 9 (Praeneste) ; 21, 1-3, 6-8 (Circei and Velitrae) ; 22, 1-4 (destruction of Satricum). K. J. Beloch, RG 316 sq., may be quite right that the temple of Mater Matuta was saved only once from destruction in Satricum; but the Volscian war of 385 B.C. can be nevertheless historical.

[3] Liv. VI 25, 1 sqq.

[4] Liv. VI 22, 4. 7. ; 27, 10 ; 28, 1-29, 6. For further information and details cf. above, p. 385 sq.

[5] Liv. VI 5, 8. On the site of *Arniensis, Tromentina, Sabatina, Stellatina* cf. L. R. Taylor, Vot. Distr. 48 sqq.

[6] Liv. VI 5, 2 ; 6, 1 ; 21, 4.

against Rome "Latins." In 379 B.C. we hear of the collusion of "Latins" with the Volscians again.[1] Praeneste rebels once more, stirring up the "Latin peoples."[2] The reinforcement of the federal colony of Setia in this year is the last sign of concord between the League and Rome. In 377 B.C. "Latins" concentrate their forces against the Romans in conjunction with the Volscians of Antium and Satricum. The Antiates surrender after their defeat; the "Latins" continue the struggle. They burn down Satricum and capture Tusculum, relieved promptly by Rome.[3] This time, however, the Latin League stands behind the states fighting the Romans.[4] In 371 B.C. Velitrae is on the attack, besieging Tusculum, which is again relieved by a Roman army. Rome exerts herself to capture Velitrae. The long siege is, however, unsuccessful.[5] In 362 B.C. the Hernicans had certainly been estranged from Rome for many years;[6] in 361 Ferentinum is captured from them. Rome declares war against Tibur.[7] The second Celtic inroad intervenes: Tibur joins the Gauls (probably along with Praeneste), whereas the Latin cities of the Alban region and the Latin colonies in the south submit themselves in this dangerous situation to the Romans again.[8] In the thirty years after the sack of Rome the city completely recovered—writes Polybius[9]—and regained her ascendency over Latium. Yet in fact twenty more years were needed till the Latin states became her obedient satellites.

The surrender of the Latins around 358 B.C. did not include the most powerful Latin opponents of Rome. The war with Tibur lasted —with intermissions—from 361 to 354 B.C., when it surrendered.[10]

[1] Liv. VI 30, 4.

[2] Liv. VI 30, 8.

[3] Liv. VI 32, 4-33, 12.

[4] Liv. VI 33, 6: *Incensos ea rabie impetus Tusculum tulit ob iram, quod deserto communi concilio Latinorum non in societatem modo Romanam, sed etiam in civitatem se dedissent.*

[5] Liv. VI 36, 1-6 ; 37, 12.

[6] Liv. VII 6, 7-8, 7.

[7] Liv. VII 9, 1-2 ; 11, 2 sqq.

[8] Liv. VII 12, 7 : *Sed inter multos terrores solacio fuit, pax Latinis petentibus data et magna vis militum ab his ex foedere vetusto, quod multis intermiserant annis, accepta.* Cf. for details above, p. 360 sqq. Different views in G. De Sanctis, St. d. R. 2², 238 sqq., and E. T. Salmon, Phoenix 7, 1953, 131 sq.

[9] Polyb. II 18, 5: ἐν ᾧ καιρῷ 'Ρωμαῖοι τήν τε σφετέραν δύναμιν ἀνέλαβον καὶ τὰ κατὰ τοὺς Λατίνους αὖθις πράγματα συνεστήσαντο.

[10] Liv. VII 9, 1-2 ; 11, 1 sqq.; 12, 1 sqq.; 17, 1-2 ; 18, 2 ; 19, 1. *Acta triumph. Capit.* ad a. 360 a. Chr. n. = Inscr. It. XIII 1, 68 sq. and 540. Chronicle of Oxyrh., F. Gr. Hist. 255, 1 (2B, p. 1153 Jac.).

Praeneste was constrained at the same time to beg for a truce.[1] The Hernici are defeated in 360 and 358 B.C.[2] Velitrae and Privernum are making raids on Roman territory in their neighborhood; the latter is captured in 357 B.C.[3]

The unrest and tension in Latium were rising to the boiling point. Rome is resolved to make the Latin tribe her own tool of war; the Latins are not willing to accept the yoke. The Latin League or Rome—one of the two must lose the contest forever. Both parties look for allies outside. Rome settles her account with the states in Southern Etruria that rose against her in a conciliatory way: Tarquinii, Falerii, and Caere, vanquished, obtain favorable long-term armistices in 353-52 B.C. It was vitally important for Rome that they kept peace in the following decades.[4] In 354 Rome concludes an alliance with the most powerful confederation in Italy, the Samnites.[5]

It was in this tense atmosphere that the Celts arrived the third time in Latium. As we saw, the Latin communities of the Alban Hills must have joined the invaders, who could establish their base of operations against Rome only by their cooperation in their region.[6] The Romans stood the test, though the strain was still more aggravated by the appearance of a Greek fleet, helping Antium against her.[7] Rome mobilized ten legions in a supreme effort to match all the challenges alike: *inter duo simul bella externa defectione etiam sociorum senatus anxius cum cerneret metu tenendos quos fides non tenuisset, contendere omnes imperii vires consules dilectu habendo iussit* (Liv. VII 25, 7). The Celts did not risk a pitched battle [8] and turned to the South. The Roman answer to the powerful Syracusan naval action for the relief of Antium was the first treaty with Carthage. It is manifest that neither the Romans nor the confederated Latins had any regard to national sentiment in choosing their associates for the final decision.

---

[1] Diod. XVI 45, 8.

[2] Liv. VII 11, 2. 8-9. *Acta triumph.* p. 68 sq. 540 Degrassi. Liv. VII 12, 6 ; 15, 9.

[3] Liv. VII 15, 11 ; 16, 6. *Acta triumph. l.c.*

[4] Liv. VII 20, 8 ; 22, 5. Cf. G. De Sanctis, St. d. R. 2², 243.

[5] Liv. VII 19, 4. Diod. XVI 45, 8.

[6] Cf. above, p. 363 sq.

[7] Cf. above, p. 344 sqq.

[8] The triumph of M. Popillius Laenas, attributed to the year 350 B.C. (Liv. VII 25, 1. *Acta triumph.*, p. 68 sqq. 540 Degrassi. App., *Celt.* 1, 4), must be due to some local success against a Celtic detachment.

ROME DURING THE EARLY REPUBLIC

The open rupture of the League with Rome is noted under the year 349 B.C. in the Annals.[1] The details available for the protracted struggle ensuing in the following decade are rather disconnected bits than a coherent survey. Yet we are in the fortunate position of having some additional authentic information on the Romano-Latin military situation in the first and second treaties with Carthage,[2] as given in the third book of Polybius.

The recurrence of a Syracusan naval action against Latium is envisaged, with the participation of a Carthaginian squadron in warding it off, in the clause prescribing that if Carthaginians go ashore in Latium as foes—of course not foes of Rome with whom they just became linked by alliance—they must spare the country going aboard during night (22, 13). Another wartime provision is that if the Carthaginians should capture a Latin city which is not subject to Rome, they should deliver it unimpaired to the Romans (22, 12). In the second treaty this clause is modified: the capturing force is allowed to retain the looted money and the prisoners and deliver only the captured city (24, 5).

Otherwise Rome provides in these two treaties for the whole of Latium as her own domain. Carthage is not allowed to establish strongholds on Latian soil (22, 13). The coastal towns of Latium down to the Campanian border (22, 11) are protected by her against suffering harm from Carthaginian raiders; if other cities there, not subject to Rome, should be captured, they must be handed over to the Romans, as we saw.

Highly relevant is the fact that among the city-states which recognized the suzerainty of Rome (in written accords) and are mentioned by name in Polybius, there is an old community of the *prisci Latini*, Laurentum-Lavinium; there are among them also federal colonies such as Ardea, Antium, Circeii; and finally, there appears Tarracina, which certainly had a garrison, but did not yet become a regular Latin colony (22, 11). All these communities had, consequently, a special agreement with Rome, which undermined the strength of the Latin League.

---

[1] Liv. VII 25, 5-6: *inter hos longe maximus extitit terror concilia populorum Latinorum ad lucum Ferentinae habita responsumque haud ambiguum imperantibus milites Romanis datum, absisterent imperare iis, quorum auxilio egerent ; Latinos pro sua libertate potius quam pro alieno imperio laturos arma.*
[2] Cf. above, p. 354 sqq.

Besides these coastal towns just mentioned, there existed still others that also had such special alliances with Rome, acknowledging her domination (ὅσοι ἂν ὑπήκοοι, ibid.).[1] This means that Rome is constructing a network of alliances, binding to herself directly the Latin communities, one by one, disregarding completely the League. However, she was not enforcing the clause of sovereignty on the most powerful of the Latin cities, but concluded treaties with them on formally equal terms. This explains why we find in the second treaty two different sorts of Latin states not subject to Rome: those which had not yet an individual arrangement with Rome, i.e., which were not yet conquered; and those which did have a written accord with her, guaranteeing their autonomy (τίνας πρὸς οὓς εἰρήνη μέν ἐστιν ἔγγραπτος ῾Ρωμαίοις, μὴ ὑποτάττονται δέ τι αὐτοῖς, 24, 6). The paragraph providing that if Carthaginians make prisoners from these cities these men cannot be sold as slaves in Latium, or if they are sold, their freedom can be immediately restored by Romans, shows that only Latins can be meant here. Such an alliance on equal footing, *foedus aequum*, existed after 338 B.C. between Tibur and Rome as well as between Praeneste and Rome. Nobody doubts that already in the second treaty these two states are meant primarily.

If we possess in the treaties of 348 and 343 B.C. a reliable picture of the results achieved and of the aims pursued by the Romans in Latium, we must not forget that the League was still defying the Romans and that the spirit of independence was also still alive in communities already subdued. In 346 B.C. Rome struck at Satricum, repeopled by the Antiates, to prevent the latter from drawing in the Latins in their war against her.[2] The same threat of a general upheaval of the

---

[1] M. Gelzer, RE 12, 960, pointed out correctly that the special treaties, by which Latin states became dependent on Rome (ὑπήκοοι), are of the kind defined by Proculus in Dig. XLIX 15, 7 as follows : *liber autem populus est is, qui nullius alterius populi potestati est subiectus : is foederatus est item, sive aequo foedere in amicitiam venit sive foedere comprehensum est, ut is populus alterius populi maiestatem comiter conservaret. hoc enim adicitur, ut intellegatur alterum populum superiorem esse, non ut intellegatur alterum non esse liberum.* M. Gelzer quotes also Cic., *Pro Balbo* 16, 35 on the *foedus* between Rome and Gades : *Adiunctum illud etiam est, quod non est in omnibus foederibus : 'maiestatem populi Romani comiter conservanto'. Id habet hanc vim ut sint illi in foedere inferiores.* The first treaty mentions in this category Antium then rebelling, evidently assuming that the revolt will be quelled before long, and not willing to omit the important harbor from the coastal places to be protected from Carthaginian raids.

[2] Liv. VII 27, 5 : *Tertio anno post Satricum restitutum a Volscis M. Valerius Corvus iterum consul cum C. Poetelio factus, cum ex Latio nuntiatum esset legatos ab*

Latins made it urgent for Rome to quell the rising of the Auruncans in the following year.[1]

At this juncture, the balance of power in Central Italy suddenly was upset, partly by the Roman power radiating far outside the frontiers of Latium, partly by the parallel expansion of the Samnite confederation south of it. Peoples and city-states between the two were compelled by the coming clash to join one or the other of the two powers, so that their spheres of influence at once became contiguous and their interests colliding. The Latin League—their leaders overestimating their own abilities as well as the strength of their organization, as the outcome has shown—acted as a third power with the same expansionistic ambitions and imperialistic aims as the Romans and the Samnites.

The first Samnite-Roman war[2] arose from a chain reaction of events in Campania released by the dynamics of this situation. The Campanians, pressed hard by the Samnites, surrender their rich country to Rome as their last chance for survival. Rome, though recently bound by an alliance with the Samnites, and disregarding the mobilization of the Latin League preparing war against her, boldly takes the risk. The consuls of 343 B.C. gain the upper hand in heavy fighting in Campania and Samnium. The Latin League changed its mind under the impression of these victories and attacked instead of Rome the Paelignians, linked with the Romans.[3] In the next year

Antio circumire populos Latinorum ad concitandum bellum, priusquam plus hostium fieret, Volscis arma inferre iussus ad Satricum exercitu infesto pergit.

[1] Liv. VII 28, 2 : *Auruncum inde bellum ab repentina populatione coeptum, metuque, ne id factum populi unius, consilium omnis nominis Latini esset, dictator velut adversus armatum iam Latium L. Furius creatus magistrum equitum Cn. Manlium Capitolinum dixit ; et cum, quod per magnos tumultus fieri solitum erat, iustitio indicto dilectus sine vacationibus habitus esset. legiones, quantum maturari potuit, in Auruncos ductae.*

[2] Mommsen, RG 1[8], 356 n., found it inconsistent or impossible that the Antiates were rebelling in spite of their previous surrender, that the Latin League was making war on its own responsibility against the Paelignians, that the Roman army was marching to Campania in 340 across the Marsian-Paelignian territory, turning the flank of the hostile Latins, and finally that a Roman military revolt broke out in 342. But all these things are the more credible the more odd they look : they are easily understood as logical consequences of a complicated and difficult situation. Cf. also G. De Sanctis, St. d. R. 2[2], 255 sqq. W. Schur, Hermes 59, 1924, 460. B. Niese-E. Hohl, Grundl. d. r. G.[5], 1923, 55. G. Wissowa, Hermes 50, 1915, 5 ff. K. J. Beloch, RG 369 sqq. A. Klotz, RhM 1937, 211 sq. A. Afzelius, Die römische Eroberung Italiens (Acta Jutland. 14, 3), Aarhus-København 1942, 136 sqq. E. T. Salmon, Phoenix 7, 1953, 132 sqq. E. Ferenczy, Acta Antiqua 1, 1951-52, 145.

[3] Liv. VII 38, 1 : *Huius certaminis fortuna . . . . . Latinos iam exercitibus comparatis ab Romano in Paelignum vertit bellum.* Cf. VIII 4, 8. DH XV 3, 2. *Vir. ill.* 26, 1-3.

the discipline of the Roman garrisons in Campania broke down; their mutiny paralyzed Rome.[1] She lost some allies; the Latin League persisted in its hostility.[2] In 341 B.C. Rome is victorious against the Volscians of Privernum, Satricum, and Antium,[3] but makes peace with the Samnites, giving them a free hand against the Sidicini, but retaining under her sway the Campani. The alliance between Rome and the Samnites was renewed,[4] and as a result the Romans were in a position to come to grips with the Latin League.

The reaction of the opposite side promptly set in. The Sidicini, abandoned by Rome to the mercy of the Samnites, won over to their cause the Campanians and the Latin League, who immediately proceeded to raid Samnite territory with a powerful army.[5] Rome promises the Samnites to curb the Campani as their subjects, but gives them no definite answer in view of the Latin League. She had indeed no formal rights to interfere with the confederation,[6] though she was perfectly aware that the war preparations of the Latin alliance were primarily aimed at herself; [7] the League would strike first at the Samnites only to have its back protected when turning against Rome.[8]

In 340 the Latin League started the war against Rome.[9] With very

[1] Liv. VII 38, 4 sqq. DH XV 3, 2 sqq. App., *Samn.* 1, 1-3.

[2] Liv. VII 42, 8 : *Et huius fama seditionis et susceptum cum Samnitibus grave bellum aliquot populos ab Romana societate avertit, et praeter Latinorum infidum iam diu foedus Privernates etiam Norbam et Setiam, finitimas colonias Romanas, incursione subita depopulati sunt.* Cf. G. Radke, RE 23, 15.

[3] Liv. VIII 1, 1-6.

[4] Liv. VIII 1, 7 sqq ; 2, 13 ; 4, 9 ; 5, 2. Cic., *De div.* I 24, 51. Frontin., *Strat.* I 5, 14 ; IV 5, 9.

[5] Liv. VIII 2, 5-8 : *Samnites copiis iisdem, quibus usi adversus Romanum bellum fuerant, contra Sidicinos profecti . . .* ; *tum ab Sidicinis deditio prius ad Romanos coepta fieri est* ; *dein, postquam patres ut seram eam . . . . . . aspernabantur, ad Latinos iam sua sponte in arma motos facta est. ne Campani quidem . . . his se armis abstinuere. ex his tot populis unus ingens exercitus duce Latino fines Samnitium ingressus plus populationibus quam proeliis cladium fecit* ; *et quamquam superiores certaminibus Latini erant, haud inviti, ne saepius dimicandum foret, agro hostium excessere.*

[6] Liv. VIII 2, 13: *itaque Campanos, seu velint seu nolint, quieturos ; in foedere Latino nihil esse, quo bellare, cum quibus ipsi velint, prohibeantur.* Cf. ibid. 2, 9-12.

[7] Liv. VIII 3, 1-3 : *Quod responsum . . . . . Latinos, velut nihil iam non concedentibus Romanis, ferociores fecit. itaque per speciem adversus Samnites belli parandi crebra concilia indicentes omnibus consultationibus inter se principes occulte Romanum coquebant bellum. Huic quoque . . . . bello Campanus aderat.*

[8] Liv. VIII 3, 3 : *priusquam moverentur Romani, tolli ab tergo Samnitem hostem volebant.*

[9] Liv. VIII 6, 4. 7-8.

ROME DURING THE EARLY REPUBLIC

few exceptions, the whole nation followed its call. The later annalists thought that the cities which after the Roman victory preserved their allied Latin status and autonomy got this as a reward because they did not participate [1] in the rising. This is, however, an error in most cases. It is very likely that the federal colonies of Sutrium and Nepet, isolated from the bulk of the Latins amid a rather hostile Etruscan environment, stuck to Rome. We do not know the attitude of Cora and Ardea. Yet, the most stubborn antagonists of Rome, Tibur and Praeneste, preserved later on their restricted autonomy, as well as Signia, Setia, and Circeii of whom we also know that they fought against Rome,[2] along with Velitrae and the neighboring Volscian communities. It is obvious that in the final settlement Rome had no sentimental considerations but dealt with the most stubborn adversaries in the most accommodating spirit, so as not to drive them to exasperation. And even the most faithful allies of Rome, Tusculum [3] and Lavinium,[4] participated in the upheaval.

It can be safely assumed that the Latins made their plans in the belief that Rome would attack them directly. The consuls, however, making a considerable detour north and east, marched across Marsian and Paelignian territory to Campania, joining up with the allied Samnite forces.[5] The Roman historiography tried to minimize or eliminate the share of the Samnites in the victory,[6] which was of vital significance for Rome at that moment.[7] The decision in a battle near Mount Vesuvius fell in favor of the Romans, but only after extremely heavy fighting against the Latins and Campanians.[8] A second battle at Trifanum between Sinuessa and Minturnae made the last hopes of the Latins and their allies fade away; they surrendered to the conqueror.[9] They rise again, however, when Rome takes away part of

[1] Also E. T. Salmon, Phoenix 7, 1953, 133.

[2] Liv. VIII 3, 9 ; 5, 3 ; 11, 9. 10.

[3] Liv. VIII 7, 2.

[4] Liv. VIII 11, 3. *Acta triumph.* ad a. 338 B.C. Cf. A. Degrassi, Inscr. It. XIII 2, p. 541, and my remarks in : Die trojanischen Urahnen der Römer (Rektoratsprogramm, Basel 1956) 1957, 47 n. 131.

[5] Liv. VIII 6, 8. Flor. I 9, 1.

[6] DH XV 7, 2-3. Liv. VIII 10, 7 ; 11, 2.

[7] Chron. Oxyrh. Fr. Gr. Hist. 255 (II B, p. 1154 Jac.) ad Olymp. 110 : τούτων κατὰ τὸν πρῶτον (Σα)υνεῖται ('Ρωμα)ί(οι)ς π(αρ)ε(τά)ξαντο.—κατὰ δὲ τὸν δεύτερον Λατεῖ(νοι ἐπὶ τοὺ)ς 'Ρωμαίους συν(στάντες ἐ)πέβησαν.—κατὰ δὲ τὸν τρίτον.... καὶ 'Ρωμαῖοι ἐπὶ Λατείνους ἐστράτευσαν. Cf. A. Afzelius, *op. cit.*150 sqq.

[8] Liv. VIII 8, 19.

[9] Diod. XVI 90, 2. Liv. VIII 11, 10-12.

their territory for her own citizens.[1] Also the Volscians of Antium are devastating the agrarian districts of Rome, penetrating to the Tiber.[2] In 339 B.C. an army of the Latin cities was defeated again at the unknown site of the *Campi Fenectani*; [3] those communities which suffered the reverse gave themselves up.[4] A decisive advantage for Rome was that the League was not able to unite all the Latin forces again; it was easier for Rome to strike down the smaller groups, one by one. Also in 339, Tibur, Praeneste, Lanuvium, Antium, and Velitrae fought a pitched battle against the Romans at Pedum. They were overcome, but Pedum was taken only in 338 B.C., after another defeat of Tibur and Praeneste in the same region.[5]

In this third year the Latin cities were too weak to mobilize again a great army; but the loss of an important part of their fields embittered them so much that they would not give up.[6] They intended not to attack, but if one of them should be assailed, the others were to come to her help. This strategy did not work: while Tibur and Praeneste were tied down at Pedum, another Roman army took the forces of Aricia, Lanuvium, Velitrae, and Antium by surprise at the river Astura, dispersing them.[7] No other Latin army took the field; the Romans went around and forced every community to surrender, including the Volscian Antium.[8] The League and with her the common privileges of all the Latins were dissolved forever. The loose federal system of the tribal League, with its parliamentary liberties, with members enjoying their individual freedom, with widely diverging interests, without a permanent central government and long-range political planning, showed itself unable to contend with such a closely knit organization as the Roman state, directed by a governing class highly trained in diplomacy, highly skilled in generalship and hand-to-hand fighting, highly efficient in administration and politics. The human material used by both was the same; the superior leadership won the contest.[9]

---

[1] Liv. VIII 11, 13 ; 12, 5.
[2] Liv. VIII 12, 2-3.
[3] Liv. VIII 12, 5. *Acta triumph.* a 339 a. Chr. n.
[4] Liv. VIII 12, 6.
[5] Liv. VIII 12, 6-9 ; 13, 6-7. *Acta triumph.* a 338 a. Chr. n.
[6] Liv. VIII 13, 2 : *ad bellum opes deerant ; pacem ob agri adempti dolorem aspernabantur.* VIII 14, 9.
[7] Liv. VIII 13, 3-5.
[8] Liv. VIII 13, 8-9. 12.
[9] Cf. A. Heuss, Römische Geschichte, Braunschweig 1960, 45.

Excellent scholars thought until quite recently that in 338 B.C. the majority of the Latin states were simply deleted from the map, their communities broken up and incorporated in Rome. But this did not happen. We saw in our previous chapter that they retained the greater part of their territory and local administration; also that their aristocracy gained admission to the governing class of the ruling city. The ordinary members of the Latin communities had the prospect of sharing the booty and of obtaining landed property in the ensuing wars of Rome; the new Latin colonies gave them new opportunities for social ascent and prosperity. The great success of Rome was the conciliation of the vanquished Latins after 338 B.C., conceding her the leadership: *concedentibus Romam caput Latio esse.*[1] It was not by chance that the Romans were still praying to their gods centuries after their victory for the obedience of the Latins: *uti . . . semper Latinus obtemperassit.*[2] This was the secret of their unheard-of growth in the following decades.

๛

THE RELATIONS OF THE LATINS WITH ROME DURING THE EARLY REPUBLIC: POLITICAL, LEGAL, AND SOCIAL ASPECTS

About 600 B.C., when the settlements of the Latin cattle-rearing peoples were transformed into modern city-states by their Etruscan overlords, their tribal ties were not disrupted. The interrelations of these new urban communities were based partly on their time-honored customs, partly on their actual power. Their annual gatherings gave them the possibility to discuss and promote common interests, to elect the annual magistrates, to pay hommage to their ancestral gods for the welfare of the nation. Their tribal alliance was certainly modernized to some extent in the fifth century B.C. But the archaic features in her structure did not disappear by this adaptation to the changing times. When God's Peace was announced for the days of the *Latiar* every year, there were certainly fewer local feuds than centuries before; but the complete liberty to make

[1] Liv. VIII 4, 5.
[2] Cf. E. Diehl, Rh. Mus. 53, 1934, 255 sqq. L. R. Taylor, A. J. Ph. 55, 1934, 108 sqq. E. Norden, Aus altrömischen Priesterbüchern, Lund 1939, 104 sqq.

war against whom the member-states liked was not curtailed until the last breath of this organization.[1] This unrestrained freedom of action allowed the strongest to outgrow and enslave the others in the end.

Tibur and Praeneste were growing in size and power outside the confederation, as we saw; Rome undermined it from inside. Yet before that, she cooperated with the *nomen Latinum* throughout a century. A remarkable sign of this coordination is the circumstance that Rome ceased to extend her immediate territory in the direction of her Latin neighbors around 420 B.C., after the constitution of the gentile tribes, though she incorporated after this date more and more adjacent areas toward the Sabines, Etruscans, and Volscians. Even in much later times the supervision of scattered smaller citizen-groups began *ultra decimum milliarium*,[2] i.e., just outside the outer perimeter of the original gentile *tribus*. At the same time, we observed a systematic coordination of the expanding activity of the League and the Romans, especially between 420 and 380 B.C., when the increase of the Roman territory was accompanied by the foundation of new federal colonies. Of course, "the viritane allotments on seized enemy lands meant a steady increase in the size of a single political unit, whereas a Latin policy of sending out Latin colonies had merely meant an increase in the number of members in a military league.[3]

The Romans, impeded in their direct territorial expansion by the tribal confederation, soon discovered various other possibilities for the extension of their power and possessions within the League: by the decisive role of their army on the battlefields, by the weight of their vote in the tribal assembly, by their extensive participation in federal colonization, by military actions against Latin communities. By all these means and by building up another confederation in Latium through special alliances, they attained prominence and leadership step by step in the course of the fifth century.

This struggle for power between the Latin League and Rome, and its outcome to the advantage of Rome, was also sharply reflected in the interstate juridical position of every Latin individual. We saw in the first chapter that in the course of the fifth century the mutual privileges of the Latins in regard to relations with free persons of

---

[1] Cf. A. N. Sherwin-White, *op. cit.* 22, 24 sq., and above, p. 36. 121 sq.
[2] Liv. XL 37, 4.
[3] E. T. Salmon, Phoenix 7, 1953, 129.

other Latin communities became legally established rights, enforceable by the executive organs of each and every Latin state: to make commercial contracts between members of different Latin communities; to legalize a marriage between a man and a woman residing in any two Latin towns, with full protection of paternity rights and testamentary provisions; the liberty to transfer domicile to any other Latin state and not only to enjoy the privileges of a citizen in the new home-city, but also to have full legal protection and rights in the case of arriving in another Latin city as a political refugee; and finally, the right of the voluntary exile or former prisoner of war, to recover his civic rights and possessions when returning to his original place of residence (the so-called *postliminium*).[1] This means that these privileges offered to a Roman or a man from another Latin town much more liberty than a local citizenship could grant. It was a heavy interference with the Latin rights when a considerable group of Latin states lost these prerogatives in 338 B.C.[2]

We must stress this point: until 338 B.C. to be a *homo Latinus* meant infinitely more for a Latin than to be a *civis Romanus*. Nevertheless, the enrollment in the list of Roman citizens became one of the means by which the Romans increased their manpower, at least after the Gallic storm. In 389 B.C. they gave citizenship and land allotments to those Etruscans of Veii who, with Faliscans and Capenates, abandoned their home-cities battling with Rome and took the side of the enemy.[3] In 338 B.C. the Antiates, who wished to stay on, were granted the citizenship and the same land allotments as the Romans sent to the new maritime colony.[4] As the Latin League also freely admitted in newly founded colonies the local elements—mostly Volscians—this practice was no novelty. In 381 B.C. Tusculum was punished for her defection [5] with the obligation to become part of the Roman citizen-body, though not incorporated in the *ager Romanus*

---

[1] Mommsen, RG 1[8], 1888, 101 sq. A. N. Sherwin-White, R. Citiz. 32 sq. We could not yet utilize the new book of G. Crifò on *exilium* published in 1962.

[2] Liv. VIII 14, 10 : *ceteris Latinis populis conubia commerciaque et concilia inter se ademerunt*. At the same time, the Hernican communities which did not rebel against Rome were allowed to retain their autonomy and legal intermarriage between themselves, Liv. IX 43, 23.

[3] Liv. VI 4, 4 : *Eo anno in civitatem accepti qui Veientium Capenatiumque ac Faliscorum per ea bella transfugerant ad Romanos, agerque his novis civibus adsignatus.*

[4] Liv. VIII 14, 8.

[5] Liv. VI 25, 1 sqq.

and with some local self-government. This city, which had great advantages from her association with Rome, again and again revolted against her after this bestowal of *civitas Romana,* forced upon her. The value of *Roman* citizenship was then very different from what it became after the conquest of the world: a Latin city lost her individuality and independence by it, and her sons became obliged to fight for foreign interests in ever more distant regions. Tusculum was transformed from an equal partner to a subordinated appendix of Rome. In 338 B.C., however, the bestowal of full Roman citizen rights was restricted to the old allies of the Alban district: to Lanuvium, Aricia, Nomentum, Pedum, in addition to Tusculum.[1] Political reliability was considered, consequently. It is a pity that we are not allowed to identify those Latin cities, who lost the liberty of intermarriage, commercial freedom, and direct political contact with each other: this prohibition seems to me to be meant to prepare the way for the grant of citizenship: the same advantages were not excluded via Rome, and this could make the Roman citizenship more acceptable to those Latins. The third group, which retained the autonomy, were—except Ardea—the Latin antagonists of Rome, or at least noncooperative with her: Tibur, Praeneste, Cora, Norba, Signia, Circeii, Setia, with Sutrium and Nepet. Their allied status lent them more freedom and independence than the assimilation to Rome.

In 338 B.C., the non-Latin peoples subjected to Rome received the Roman citizenship without the right of participation in the political life of Rome:[2] this discrimination may have helped the Latins to overcome their bitterness over the loss of their autonomy. For the peoples incorporated in this way, limited citizenship was not a reward for fidelity, but a punishment after surrender.[3] At the very end of the fourth century the insignificant Aequicoli and the little Hernican communities were struggling hard against the compulsion "to become Romans."[4]

---

[1] Liv. VIII 14, 2-4. Cf. K. J. Beloch RG 377 (against Mommsen).
[2] Cf. K. J. Beloch, RG 380 sq.
[3] Liv. VIII 21, 1 sqq. (Privernum in 328 B.C.).
[4] Liv. IX 45, 5-8: *Ad Aequos inde ... versa arma Romana, quod .... post Hernicos subactos universa prope gens sine dissimulatione consilii publici ad hostes desciverat ; et postquam icto Romae cum Samnitibus foedere fetiales venerant res repetitum, temptationem aiebant esse, ut terrore incusso belli Romanos se fieri paterentur, quod quanto opere optandum foret Hernicos docuisse, cum, quibus licuerit, suas leges Romanae civitati praeoptaverint ; quibus legendi, quid mallent, copia non fuerit, pro poena necessariam civitatem fore. ob haec vulgo in conciliis iactata populus Romanus bellum fieri*

The enormous impetus of the Roman conquest in the next generations proves that the Latins were compensated by their share in it for their lost independence. Their coalescence with Rome engendered the solid nucleus of the great power emerging to rule the Mediterranean world.

In 381 and 338 B.C., when despite the grant of Roman citizenship the territories of the states in the Alban Hills—except the part lost as a punishment in 338—were preserved with local autonomy instead of being totally absorbed in the *ager Romanus*, a new development started. Even in the new Roman colonies some sort of self-government was soon conceded. In 317 B.C. the colonists of Antium complained in Rome about the lack of a lawful organization and of magistrates of their own; the Senate sent high-ranking men to regulate their status.[1] These procedures "set free the idea of the town within the state, to develop as it would." The "notion of a dual patria, possessed by all *cives Romani*" started the municipal system of the growing Empire.[2]

We do not need to proceed any further. The reader realizes, I hope, that despite all the scarcity of our information, and despite all the false embroidery obscuring the events in the Annals, there is still enough reliable source material to let us grasp at least the bare outlines of the developments ending in the conquest of Latium by the Romans. We have no reason whatsoever to suppose that this immensely arduous and complicated struggle for power lasting one and a half centuries, the outcome of which was not decided, in spite of the ever-growing Roman superiority, till the last battle of the great war in 338, would be nothing else than the repetition of the same process of expansion, accomplished already once before in a nebulous past, as the Annals pretend.

The difference between that picture of pure light without shadows under the kings on the one hand and the protracted severe trial of the

---

Aequis iussit. Liv. IX 43, 22- 24 (306 B.C.) : *Marcius de Hernicis triumphans in urbem rediit, . . . Hernicorum tribus populis, Aletrinati, Verulano Ferentinati, quia maluerunt quam civitatem, suae leges redditae, conubiumque inter ipsos, quod aliquamdiu soli Hernicorum habuerunt, permissum. Anagninis quique (alii) arma Romanis intulerant civitas sine suffragii latione data, concilia conubiaque adempta.* More in K. J. Beloch, RG 421 sq. A. N. Sherwin-White, R. Citiz. 46 sq.

[1] Liv. IX 20, 10. A different explanation in A. N. Sherwin-White, R. Citiz. 77. But the *ipsius coloniae patroni* are—at least for me—not local people, but Roman nobles.

[2] A. N. Sherwin-White, R. Citiz. 67.

young Republic on the other, is nothing else than the obvious discrepancy between the ideal happiness, easily lost, of the fairy tale and the lasting results of a wearisome human effort. The Roman greatness, gleaming undiminished even today across a past of more than two thousand years, is due, of course, to the real, prosaic effort we have just reviewed, redolent with sweat and blood. It has no support in the invented victories of Romulus and his imaginary successors. It is, however, an achievement of greatest consequence in the history of mankind.

Appendix

L'OCCUPAZIONE ETRUSCA DI CAMPANIA

W. JOHANNOVSKY

Fino a meno di un decennio fa sembrava che la Campania fosse da comprendere tutta quanta, durante la prima e la seconda età del ferro, sia pure con sfumature, nell'ambito di quel tipo di civiltà cui il G. Kaschnitz ha dato il nome, ormai invalso, di "Fossakultur".[1] I pochi oggetti villanoviani e protoetruschi di sicura provenienza Campana allora conosciuti[2] non cambiavano comunque nulla al quadro della situazione e la loro presenza si poteva anche spiegare con normali scambi commerciali lungo il litorale. La ceramica di bucchero pesante piuttosto abbondante già nella prima metà del VI secolo in alcune località campane (Capua, Pompei, Ponte Fratte e varii luoghi della valle del Sarno)[3] veniva invece messa in rapporto

[1] G. Kaschnitz-Weinberg, in Studi Etruschi, 7 (1933) pp. 150 s. e Handbuch d. Archäologie, Abt. 6, Textb. 2, München 1954, pp. 370 s.

[2] V. G. Buchner, Bull. Paletnologia Italiana, n.S., 1 (1936-37), pp. 820 (da Ischia e da Cuma). Altri vasi di tipo villanoviano, praticamente inediti, vengono da Suessula (collezione Spinelli) e dalla Valle del Sarno.

[3] Fondamentale è tuttora l'articolo del Patroni in Milani, Studi e materiali di archeologia e numismatica I (Firenze 1896) il quale per l'esistenza di qualche forma non comune nel bucchero propriamente Etrusco ha supposto l'esistenza di officine campane. V. inoltre A. Maiuri in Saggi di varie antichità, Venezia 1954, pp. 120 s. pp. 241 s. P. C. Sestieri in Not. d. Scavi 1949, pp. 178 ss.

con la fondazione di Capua da parte degli Etruschi su cui le fonti sono unanimi. Delle due tradizioni relative alla cronologia di tale avvenimento era giudicata più accettabile quella accolta da Catone,[1] riferita però, anzichè alla conquista nel 211, come apparirebbe più logica dal solo esame del testo, alla *deditio* del 340 a.C. Tale tesi che poneva la conquista etrusca della Campania interna verso gli inizi del VI sec. si conciliava in apparenza meglio con i dati archeologici conosciuti e divulgati che non l'altra, sostenuta dal Patroni e basato, oltrechè sulla scoperta a Capua di materiale più antico rimasto inedito, sulla cronologia più alta di Velleio, il quale in polemica con Catone pone la fondazione di Capua nell'VIII sec. a.c.[2]

In netto contrasto con alcuni dati di fatto appariva invece l'opinione espressa dallo J. Heurgon, e siamo al 1942, secondo la quale invece l'espansione etrusca verso il Sud sarebbe avvenuta verso il 524, epoca in cui Dionigi di Alicarnasso pone l'inizio del conflitto con Cuma[3] e Capua sarebbe stata preceduta sullo stesso posto da un villaggio osco, per la cui esistenza egli non fornisce peraltro alcun dato sicuro.

A questo punto stava la questione, quando a Padula e a Pontecagnano apparvero insospettatamente tombe ad incinerazione dell' VIII sec. a.C. con suppellettile di tipo villanoviano, che aveva maggiore affinità con la facies analoga dell'Etruria e del Bolognese che non con la Fossakultur.[4] Tale fatto, che isolato creò notevoli perplessità, trova ormai la sua logica spiegazione in seguito ai ritrovamenti di questi ultimi mesi nella Campania settentrionale soprattutto a Capua (S. Maria Capua Vetere). Quì, in seguito a lavori edilizi e a scavi regolari sono state scoperte ad occidente della città antica numerose sepolture appartenenti a tre fasi distinte fra le quali però non c'è quasi soluzione di continuità. Le più antiche, in parte ad incinerazione in qualche caso ad inumazione, ma molto spesso sconvolte da quelle successive, hanno corredi di tipo villanoviano costituiti generalmente da un ossuario, da una ciotola monoansata o biansata, da qualche anforisco sferoidale e da qualche attingitoio ad ansa bifora. Tale

---

[1] Apud Vell. Paterc. I 7, sulla questione A. Maiuri, op. cit. p. 251 s. con precedente bibliografia.

[2] Vell. Paterc. I 7.

[3] *Recherches sur l'histoire, la religion et la civilisation de Capoue préromaine*, Parigi 1942, pp. 59 ss.

[4] P. C. Sestieri, in Studi Etruschi 28 (1960) pp. 73 ss., M. Napoli, B. D'Agostino, G. Voza, *Mostra della Preistoria e della Protostoria nel Salernitano*, Napoli 1962, pp. 63 ss.

composizione dei corredi è quella solita in Etruria e le forme, fra cui
è particolarmente frequente, oltre all'ossuario biconico, quello sferoidale con labbro espanso, coincidono soprattutto con quelle in uso
nell' Etruria centrale, alla quale ci riconducono anche alcuni vasi
italo-geometrici di tipo conosciuto soprattutto da Bisenzio e da
Vulci.[1] Fra questi ultimi sono tre coppe di tipo argivo-cicladico, che
insieme alle fibule, di cui alcune sono ancora ad arco ingrossato, fanno
datare questa fase più antica, all'incirca fra la metà dell'VIII sec.a.C.
e primi decenni del VII sec.

Della fase successiva solo due tombe sconvolte contenevano ceramica di bucchero sottile mentre, abbondano quelle con bucchero di
transizione e pesante. Nella terza fase, dell'ultimo quarto dell VI e
agli inizi del V sec. a.C. il bucchero è ormai completamente assente.

Una seconda necropoli arcaica con tombe ad incinerazione dell'-
VIII se.a.C. e corredi analoghi a quelli più antichi di Capua, di Pontecagnano e di Padula è stata localizzata nel territorio Capuano a S.
Angelo in Formia, presso il Santuario di Diana Tifatina. Infine
nella necropoli di Cales è stata esplorata una tomba ad inumazione
con cumulo di pietre che conteneva, fra l'altro, vasi di bucchero sottile, di cui uno con figurazione incisa e un aryballos tardo-proto-
corinzio, per cui il corredo può essere datato fra il terzo e l'ultimo
quarto del VII sec. a.C.

Riassumendo, possiamo ormai dire che già nella seconda metà
dell'VIII sec.a.C. troviamo oramai a Capua, Pontecagnano e Padula
una facies di civiltà di tipo villanoviano etrusco e diversa dalla
Fossakultur, la quale tuttavia, con maggiori o minori influssi esterni,
persiste in altre località campane.[2] Anche se alcuni punti rimangono
oscuri,[3] quel che conosciamo è sufficiente per porre il problema su
nuove basi.

Oltre che per Capua infatti proprio per la zona intorno a Salerno
le fonti parlano di stanziamenti etruschi.[4] Inoltre sappiamo di rapporti

---

[1] A. Åkerström, Der geometrische Stil in Italien, Lund 1943, pp. 51 ss.

[2] P. es. a Suessula, a Calatia, nella Valle del Sarno e a Stabia.

[3] Non conosciamo, p. es. salvo dalla necropoli preellenica di Cuma (e da
Ischia C. Castiglione) quasi nulla della prima metà dell'VIII sec. e dei secoli
precedenti. Rimane inoltre da chiarire meglio, fra l'altro, la facies cui appartiene
la necropoli ad incinerazione di Capodifiume nell'agro Pestano (P. C. Sestieri,
Studi Etruschi, op. cit. pp. 75 ss., Napoli, D'Agostino, Voza, op. cit., pp. 79 ss.

[4] Strab. V, 4, 13, Plin. N.H. III, 70. Su alcuni toponimi v. A. Maiuri, op. cit.
p. 113, con bibliografia.

diretti fra gli Etruschi e Sibari,[1] e la sola via di comunicazione terrestre più o meno agevole dalla Campania verso il territorio di quest'ultima passava per il Valle di Diano, il cui centro economico è anche oggi Sala Consilina.

Da tutto ciò risulta più attendibile la tradizione cui attinge Velleio che non quanto sostiene Catone, il quale poi scrisse in un periodo di particolare animosità contro Capua. Rimane da spiegarsi il perchè di una così profonda penetrazione etrusca nel Meridione già nell'VIII sec. a.C. Può darsi che sia una consequenza diretta della fondazione di Cuma da parte degli Etruschi e Calcidesi e che il timore di una successiva espansione greca verso l'interno abbia indotto parte delle populazioni osche a provocare l'intervento etrusco. D'altra parte è evidente che lo scopo principale di tale penetrazione è quello di dominare le vie commerciali per l'Italia centrale e il Tirreno meridionale e il versante ionico e d'inserirsi con gli stanziamenti sul golfo di Salerno anche nel traffico marittimo a Sud di Cuma. Che i rapporti con quest'ultima siano stati all'inizio tutt'altro che pacifici può essere comunque dedotto dall'assenza totale di importazioni greche pervenute attraverso Cuma nelle più antiche tombe di Capua e di Pontecagnano.

[1] Athen. XII, 519.

Index

Aborigines, 57

Aefulae, 13

Aeneas, 19-20, 27, 57, 125-26, 134, 159, 189, 201, 240, 247-48, 251 sqq., 267, 273 sq., 278-88

Aeneas Indiges, 252

Aequians, 28, 107, 110, 138 sq., 237, 305, 322, 334, 338, 365-78, 380-82, 384, 387 sq., 393-94, 396 sq., 400-1

Aequicoli, 417

ager Albanus, 244 sq., 304, 306, 364; *Antias*, 305; *Ardeas*, 305; *Bolanus*, 305; *Crustuminus*, 304, 317; *Gabinus*, 302; *Labicanus*, 305; *Lanuvinus*, 305; *Laurens*, 308; *Pomptinus*, 374; *Praenestinus*, 305; *publicus*, 315; *Pupinius*, 308; *Romanus antiquus*, 297 sqq., 317, 373; *Solonius*, 306; *Tusculanus*, 305; *Vaticanus*, 310, 312, 316; *Veiens*, 305; *Veientanus*, 323

Agonalia, 253

Agrios, 238, 239 n. 1

Agylla, see *Caere*

aediles, see Rome

Alalia, battle of, 189, 211

Alba Longa, 10-11, 13, 16, 19, 20, 24-25, 30-32, 35, 101 sq., 129, 134-35, 139, 147, 190, 233, 236-46, 247-50, 260 sq., 274-75, 280, 312, 364

Alban League, 6; dynasty, 20, 126, 238, 247; monarchy, 243; magistrates, 242 sq.; priesthoods, 240 sq.; ritual, 240 sq., 261, 265; time-reckoning, 244; families in Rome, 146, 238, 250; *populi Albenses*, 13, 21, 53, 103, 250; *coloniae Albanae*, 102, 104, 126; terracotta figurines from the Alban region, 269

Alban Mountain, Alban Hills, *mons Albanus* 2-4, 21 sqq., 29 sqq., 34, 42, 53, 105, 119, 146, 237, 240, 246, 250, 260, 312, 328 sq., 330, 337, 360 sq., 365, 370, 372, 382, 387, 391, 397, 402, 406-7, 417

Alcibiades, 340, 346

Alcimus, 249, 279

Algidus, pass, 372, 381-82, 384, 387, 391, 397, 400

Allia, battle at the, 322, 356, 363

Amata, 257

Ambarvalia, 296 sqq.

Amulius, 126 n. 3

Anchises, 286 sq.

Ancona, 342, 359

Ancus, see *Marcius*

Q. Anicius, 391

Anio, 231-32, 302, 313, 361, 387

annales maximi, 107, 133-34, 156, 165

n. 1, 167 sq., 170 sq., 368, 372
annalist fiction, 10, 12, 29 sq., 82, 84, 101 sqq., 108, 111 sqq., 117, 169, 290, 292, 332, 360 sq., 363, 366, 400, 418
Annals, Roman, 136, 144-45 sqq., 150 sq., 153, 159, 195, 210, 230, 318, 323-24, 356 sq., 403
Antemnae, 129
Antium, 12, 55, 187, 339, 345, 348-49, 352, 364, 367, 368 n. 3, 370, 372, 374, 376, 390, 397-98, 403, 406-9, 411-13, 416
Anxur-Tarracina, 191, 339, 352 n. 4
Aphrodite, 256 n. 7, 280
Apiolae, 140, 367; see also *Pometia*
Apollo, 96, 167, 169, 341, 347
apotheosis by strangulation, 253
Apulia, 358 sq., 361
Ardea, 3, 12 n. 4, 14-15, 21, 49, 53-55, 121, 140, 153, 190, 210, 245, 256 n. 7, 270, 352 n. 4, 381, 394 sq., 404, 408, 412, 417
area Capitolina, 33 n. 6, 327
Aricia, 3, 12 n. 4, 15-16, 30, 48 sqq., 63 sqq., 74, 78, 107, 114, 121, 132, 140, 193, 235, 245, 337-39, 366, 368, 370, 380, 399, 400, 402, 404, 413, 417
Aristodemus, 50 sqq., 56 sqq., 62 sqq., 68 sqq., 337, 339, 367
Aristotle, 357
Arruns of Clusium, 157 sq.; son of Porsenna, 59, 66, 69, 72
Artemis Ephesia, 86 sq.
Ascanius, 249, 263
Astura river, 413
augurium, augural practice, *auspicium*, 37, 44, 78 sq., 81, 91, 120, 160, 380, 398
Aulus (Olus), see *Vibenna*
Aurunci, 107, 142, 367, 410
Aventine hill, 85 sqq., 96 sqq., 105, 136, 141, 146, 321

Baebius, Egerius, 49, 53
boar, female, *see* sow; boar clan, 280
Bola, 13, 371, 382
Bovillae, 12 n. 4, 15, 22, 241 sq., 302
Brutus, 77, 82, 83, 147, 351
Bubentum, 12 n. 4

Cabum, 12 n. 4, 15, 240; *Cabenses sacerdotes*, 240

Cacus, 228 sqq.
caducei, 285 n. 3
Caecilii, 391
Caeles, see *Vibenna*
Caelius mons, 197, 213
Caenina, Caeninenses, 15, 129, 132, 240 n. 2
Caere, 178, 187-88, 203-4, 209 sqq., 231, 279-80, 317, 330, 340 sqq., 359, 407
calendar, Roman, 304
Cales, 185, 187, 378, 422
Callias, 251
Callimachus, 156 sq.
Calpurnius Piso Censorius, 152
Cameria, 129
Camillus, M. Furius, 356, 368, 371, 374
Camitlnas, Marce, 222, 227
Campania, Campani, 138-40, 143, 182 sqq., 189, 193, 199, 229, 232, 240, 279, 358, 361, 365, 370, 381, 395, 401, 410 sqq., 420 sqq.
Campi Fenectani, 413
Capena, 191, 233, 401, 405, 416
Capitoline temple, 32, 51, 72, 78 sq., 84, 98 sq., 105, 128, 133, 139, 141-42, 166, 175, 195, 217 sq., 265, 320, 323 sqq., 351, 354, 367; Hill, 33, 151, 197, 201, 217, 322, 337, 352, 356, 381
Capitolium vetus, 199
Capua, 183 sq., 187-88, 193, 202, 206, 279, 340, 378, 420 sqq.
Caput aquae Ferentinae, 34 sq., 38, 105-6
Caput Oli, 217 sqq.
Capys, 279
carnem petere, 21 sqq., 53
Carthage, Carthaginians, 116, 121, 125, 159, 171, 185, 189, 210-11, 291, 304, 331, 339, 342 sq., 345 sq., 349-55, 407 sqq.
Carventum, 12 n. 4, 13, 371 sq.
casa Romuli, 274
Cassius, Spurius, 93, 112 sqq.
Castor, 269; see also *Dioscuri*
Castrimoenium, 13
Cato the Elder, 49, 126, 152, 174, 183 sq., 209-10, 248, 262, 331
Celtic immigration, invasions, wars, 64, 68, 96, 99, 107, 143, 148, 157 sq., 167, 169, 285 sq., 321 sq., 325 sqq., 338, 341 sq., 349, 355-65, 368, 374; assistance to the Latins, 116, 342, 345, 362, 364 sq., 371, 378, 389, 395, 403, 406-7

centuriate organization, 128, 315
Ceres, 92 sqq., 166, 268, 304
chronology, 56 sqq., 71, 78 sqq., 125
sqq., 154, 159, 166 n. 6, 167-68, 183
sq., 351, 355
Cincius, the antiquarian, 119 sqq.
Circe, 240
Circeii, 12 n. 4, 13, 16, 139-40, 187,
238-39, 367, 370, 372, 374 sq., 376,
392, 397, 398, 404, 408, 412, 417
cista, with Trojan relics, 286 sq.; Pasinati, 257; with the triumph of Aeneas, 45 n. 2
Claudii, Appii, 152, 154, 159-64
Claudius I., 212 sq., 215, 217 sq., 225
clavis annalis, 44, 78 sq., 167, 325, 351
clientela, 315
Cloaca maxima, 133, 195, 198, 320
Cloelia, 74, 82, 155
Clusium, 52, 59, 73, 75-76, 155, 157 sq.,
204, 214, 234 sq., 337 sq., 399
cognomina, 83
commercium, conubium, 38, 40-41, 116,
263, 312, 416-17
Conon, 249
Cora, 12 n. 4, 15-16, 49, 54, 367, 392,
395, 404, 412, 417
Corbintae, the people of *Corbio*, 12 n. 4
Coriolanus, 156, 370 sq.; the mother of,
155 sq.
Corioli, 12 n. 4
Corne, 89
Corsica, 189, 211, 340, 343, 348
Cortona, 279
Cremera, 132, 232, 293, 302, 312, 315,
338
Creusa-Eurydice, 285, 287 sq.
Crustumerium, 54, 132, 233, 317
curiae, 6, 17, 23, 129; *see also* Rome
Cyme, Cymaean chronicle, — chrono-
logy, 50 sqq., 56 sqq., 60 sqq., 68
sqq., 74 sq., 79, 185 sq., 189, 208,
231, 234, 337, 339, 351, 399-400

Daunians, 64
Dea Dia, 298, 300
decemviri, decemvirate, 31, 89, 94, 134,
154, 162, 245, 296, 306, 314, 322
Delphi, 2, 167, 169, 211, 296, 341, 346
Demaratos, 58
Deus Indiges, 252
Diana Aventinensis, 3, 50, 85 sqq., 95,

141, 166, 321, 400; *Nemorensis*, 3, 15,
48 sqq., 56, 271
dicator, see *dictator*
dictator as normal magistrate, 81, 115;
feriarum Latinarum causa, 32; *Latinus*,
see Latins
Dido, 158 sq.
Diodorus, 353, 368, and *passim*
Dionysius I. of Syracuse, 342 sqq., 358
sq.; II. of Syracuse, 249, 344 sqq.;
of Halicarnassus, 5, 11, 56 sqq., 85
n. 3, 94, 142 sq., 266 sq., 343, and
passim
Dioscuri, 93, 258-59, 268 sqq., 400
doliolum, Doliola, 284 sqq.
Domitius, Cn. Ahenobarbus, 261
Dorians, 2, 7 n. 1, 23

eagle, 277 sq.
Ecetra, 12, 367, 372
Egeria, 87
Egerius, see *Baebius*
Elba, 339, 344
Empulum, 389
engraved gems, 218 sqq., 226 sqq.
Ennius, 82, 126, 137, 145, 166, 170, 249
equites (noblemen-cavalry), 81, 92 sq.,
98
equus October, 172
Etruria, 132, 145, 169, 211, 213, 223,
227, 235, 279, 337-41, 344, 407
Etruscans, 128, 137-39, 142, 147, 157,
172, 249, 415-16
Etruscan immigration, 176 sq.; kingship, kings, 178 sq., 190, 192, 197,
281, 329, 331; oligarchy, 316; fasces,
27 sq.; League, 26 sq., 42, 76, 142
177 sqq., 204, 231, 338; *sacerdos Etruriae*, 26, 42, 53, 179; *praetor Etruriae,
ibid.*; boundary, 26; sea power, 55,
67, 339; colonization, 179 sq., 191,
233; dodekapoleis, 26, 338; cities,
105, 178 sq., 340; domination in Latium, 25, 27, 36, 42, 55, 176 sqq.,
208, 210 sqq., 240, 245 sqq., 378 sqq.,
318, 334, 366, 370, 398, 414; in Campania, 26, 54 sq., 177, 179, 182 sqq.,
340, 420 sqq.; in the Po valley, 26,
177, 179, 283 sq., 334; over the
Volscians, 365 sq.; over Picenum,
187; influence, 25 sqq., 48, 189 sqq.,
234, 254, 278 sqq.; culture, 25, 189

sqq., 234; town-planning and urbanization, 180 sqq., 195; hydrotechnics, 181, 191, 244; road-system, 232, 294 sqq.; religion, divinities, 189, 201, 269; votive terracottas, 268, 287 sqq.; soothsayers, 218 sqq., 228 sqq.; *saeculum*, 135; temples, 189, 198, 325; art, 221 sqq., 227 sqq., 234, 280 sqq., 287 sq., 323, 330; epic poetry, 228 sqq.; education, 201; commerce, 202 sqq., 240, 282 sqq., 293 sqq., 330, 337, 340, 402; names, nomenclature, 201, 214, 280, 365; families in Rome, 76; siege of Aricia, 59 sqq.; invasion against Cyme, 50 sqq., 64 sqq., 68 sqq., 74 sq.; inscriptions, 184, 191, 201, 221 sq., 281; gems, 226 sq., 286 sq.; vases, 284 sq.; bucchero, 184 sqq., 198, 420 sq.; coins, 276

Fabius Pictor, 56, 70 sq., 82, 107, 123-75, 207, 215 sqq., 220, 232, 243, 248-49, 274, 324, 338, 345 n. 3, 352, 355 sq.; Ambustus, 148; *Fabii*, 45, 132, 148 sq., 161, 163, 302, 312, 315, 338
Falerii, Falsicans, 191, 203, 233, 291, 295, 330, 338, 348, 401, 405, 407, 416
familiae Troianae, 255
fasces, 27 sq., 43 n. 2
fasti consulares, 72, 78 sqq., 115, 125, 134, 165 sqq., 173, 217, 351
Ferentina, see *caput; Ferentinum*, 371-72, 376, 393, 407
Feronia, 28
Festi (place-name), 298
Festus, Pompeius, 216
Ficana, 291
Ficulea, 132
Fidenae, 13, 129, 132-33, 191, 231-33, 302, 314, 317, 338, 341
Flavius, Cn., 78, 94, 167, 217, 327, 351
foedus aequum, 112 sq.; *Cassianum*, 112 sqq., 385, 400; *Gabinum*, 313, 379
Forcti, 13 n. 2
Fortinea, 12 n. 4
Fortuna muliebris, 300 sq.
Fossae Cluiliae, 244, 300
Fosso Galeria, 295-96
fox, see *Rutuli*
fratres Arvales, 297 sqq.; *Atiedii*, 23, 299

Fregenae, 212, 293, 317
Frutis, 201, 256 n. 1, 280

Gabii, 12 n. 4, 15, 22, 54, 107, 140, 187-88, 194, 302, 313, 331, 378-80, 382, 387, 390, 404
Gauls, *see* Celtic
Gellius, Cn., 229
Graecus ritus, 95-97
Greece, Greeks, 8, 146, 168, 170-72, 174, 188, 192, 211, 226 sq., 228 sq., 240, 341, 355, 362, 377, 402
Greek naval force, 344 sqq., 353, 407; influences, 96 sq., 105, 135, 153, 155 sq., 177, 181, 211, 240, 270, 276, 284; cults, 95 sqq., 269; synchronisms, 127; inscriptions, 321; pottery, imported, 185, 198 sq., 211, 266, 283 sq., 287, 320 n. 6, 330, 332 sq., 341

Hadria, 342, 359
Hannibal, 308
Hecate, 48, 87
Hellenistic literary techniques, 147 sqq., 171, 174
Hercules, 24, 163, 172, 201, 210, 228 sqq., 280
Herdonius, Appius, 381
Herminius, T., 76, 82, 337
Hernicans, 4 n. 1, 12, 28, 105, 107 sqq., 118, 145, 334, 369, 371, 373 sq., 376, 382, 384, 387, 391, 403-5, 407, 417
Hesiod's Theogony, 188 sq., 191, 238, 240, 251, 370
Hieron, 339
hirpus, Hirpini, 275
Horatius, Cocles, 74, 82
Horatius, M. cos. 509, 78 sq., 82; *tr. mil. cons. pot.* in 378, 327 sq., 351
Hostilius, Tullus, king, 34, 103, 111, 129, 132, 135-36; *C. Mancinus*, 261
hut urns, 274

Ianiculum, 73, 293, 303
Iguvium, tablets from, 23, 25, 299 sq.
Ilia, 158 sq., 247
Imperialism, Roman, 103 sqq., 131 sqq., 172 sq.
imperium, 44, 81, 91, 120 sq., 157, 160, 200, 398
Indiges, 27, 206, 253-56, 267
insignia of power, 27 sq., 138, 147, 200, 222 sq., 331

investiture of the executive, 44, 78 sq., 120 sq.

Ionian League, 2, 26, 86

Iunii, 114, 351

Iunius, M., see *Brutus*

Iuppiter Indiges, 31, 252; *Latiaris*, 11, 19 sq., 31, 33, 45, 377; *Terminus*, 220; *Imperator*, 388 n. 5; Iuppiter, 210

ius exilii, 38-39; *sedis mutandae*, 38 sq.; see also *commercium, conubium*

Iuturna, 270

kalias, 274

kings, Roman, 126, 134, 146, 164, 168, 172, 212 sq., 217 sq., 223, 231, 254, 290, 303, 323; kingship, 153, 214, 259, 291; first king and divine ancestor, 19 sq.; see also *Romulus, T. Tatius, Numa Pompilius, Tullus Hostilius, Ancus Marcius, Tarquinius Priscus, Servius Tullius, Tarquinius Superbus, Olus Vibenna*

Labici, 12 n. 4, 15, 22, 54, 371, 382, 385, 387, 394, 401, 404

labyrinth-pattern, 281 sq.

lacus Albanus, 244; *Iuturnae*, 93, 270, 400; *Regillus*, battle at, 53, 88, 111, 113, 116-17, 227, 270, 337, 368, 381, 399 n. 2, 400

Lanuvium, 15, 21, 31, 49, 54, 260, 264, 273 n. 3, 330, 374, 377, 390, 404, 413, 417

lapis niger, 214, 266

Lar Aineias, 255; *Lares*, 201, 255, 300; *Lares Grundules*, 277; *Praestites*, 277 n. 2

Larcius, Sp. and *T.*, 76, 81 sq., 337

Laris Papathnas, 221, 223, 227

Lars Arruns, 55; see also *Porsenna*

Larth Ultes, 221, 223-24

Latin League, 1, 4-5, 10, 25 sq., 36 sq., 41, 44, 48 sqq., 74, 78, 105, 107, 111, 116, 118, 132, 145-46, 233, 305, 322, 337, 368, 382, 391 sqq., 399, 401, 403 sqq.; partial leagues, 3, 48 sqq., 75, 85 sqq., 89, 105, 140; assemblies, 5, 26 sq., 45; *concilium Latinorum*, 37 sq., 40; annual meetings, 34 sqq., 40, 88, 116, 119, 221; army, 35-38, 44, 109, 120; executive organs, 42 sqq., 119 sqq., 188, 243; *dictator La-*

tinus, 5, 42 sq., 53, 101, 119, 243; praetors, 37, 43, 45, 111, 119; Latin triumph, 45, 391; *census*, 38; sovereign right of the members, 392, 397-408; legislation, 27, 116; federal territory, 38; *coloniae Latinae*, 10, 16 sq., 110 sq., 113, 140, 233, 368, 371, 374, 376, 382, 408-9, 414-15; distribution of booty, 116; Latin festival, 6, 26 sq., 29 sqq., 33, 42, 240, 250, 329, 377, 401; tribal worship, 264; *feriae Latinae*, 21, 29 sqq., 245, 265; *Latiar*, 29, 33, 379, 414; federal cult of *Iuppiter Latiaris*, 19, 31, 45, 377; of *Iuppiter Indiges*, 31, 265 sqq.; of *Diana*, 48 sqq., 85 sqq., 245, 322; *sacra principiorum nominis Latini*, 262; extraterritorial rights of the federal sanctuaries, 89, 99, 266 sq.; God's peace, 30, 40, 116, 121, 414; federal sacrifices, 3, 6, 18, 21, 38, 261 sq.; banquet on the Alban Mountain, 20 sqq.

Latin migration, 2, 8, 19, 102, 118; cattle-rearers, 2, 5 sq., 14, 176 sq., 239 n. 1, 243, 275, 315, 331, 377; myth of origin, 237, 239 n. 1, 250 sqq., 271 sqq.; ancestral king, 5, 14, 19, 101-2, 118, 237, 245, 260, 278 sqq.; tribal kingship, *ibid.*, and 189, 192, 246, 247; tribe, 1, 5 sqq., 24, 237, 407; tribal epoch, 7, 111, 118; tribal organization, 1, 27, 40, 42, 146, 277, 309, 414; *populi*, 2, 10, 13, 21, 25, 43, 55, 85, 119; *prisci Latini*, 10; *nomen Latinum*, 3, 24 sq., 37, 53, 105-7, 119, 264, 378, 399; thirty peoples, 6, 10 sqq., 16 sq., 24 sq., 53, 102, 104, 107, 135-36, 139, 238, 250, 271, 278; tripartite organization, 5-6, 17 sq., 48; fortified *oppida*, 336; city-states, 7, 26, 31, 36 sq., 53, 85, 116, 119 sq., 121, 129, 189 sq., 208, 245, 263, 277, 304 sq., 312, 314, 318, 354, 377 sq., 397, 402, 406 sqq., 413; aristocracy, 37, 122, 146, 381, 384, 390 sq., 398 sq., 414; municipal territories, 314, 380, 383, 386, 392, 414, 418; treaties between Latin states, 4, 24, 36, 103-4, 106-7, 109, 111 sqq., 115, 121, 263, 401; wars between Latin states, 2, 30, 36, 115, 121, 177,

377, 392, 415; revolting against Rome, 383, 403, 405 sqq., siding with the Volscians, 379 sqq.; assisted by Gauls, 116, 342, 345, 362, 364 sq., 371, 378, 389, 395, 403, 406-7; local autonomy under Roman rule, 305; Roman subjects, 101 sqq.; *socii Latini*, 25, 103 sq., 108 sq., 122; relations with Rome, 414 sqq.; script, 202, 266; inscriptions, 49, 192, 202, 207, 234; statuary groups, 271 sqq., 277 sq.; coinage, 392; Etruscan influences, 26 sqq., 48, 189 sqq., 398

Latins, 135 sq., 141, 142, 169, 175, 209, 247, 272, 278 sqq., 303, 312, 337, 355, 366, 369, 372 sqq., 374, 377 sqq., 396 sq., 406, 418

Latinus, king, 19-20, 112, 238, 251, 257, 260, 263

Latium, 1-2, 7, 26, 30, 45, 50, 55, 85, 117 sq., 141 sqq., 182, 186, 188, 191-93, 199, 206, 210, 234 sq., 237, 240, 249, 265, 270, 278, 305-6, 319, 329, 332 sqq., 337 sqq., 352, 354 sq., 358, 366, 377, 385, 408; *ius Latii*, 27, 31, 38, 272 sq.; *sedis mutandae*, 38, 384, 416; *exilii*, 38 sq., 386, 409, 416; *commercii*, 39 sq.; *conubii*, 40

Laurentes, Laurentum, see *Lavinium*

Lavinia, 251, 257

Lavinium, 3-4, 12 n. 4, 15-16, 19, 21, 30-32, 35, 41-42, 49, 89, 118, 134, 139, 172, 187 sqq., 192-93, 210, 232, 238, 240, 246-88, 295, 378, 404, 408, 412; federal cult in L., 249, 265 sqq.; sacred precinct of the Latins, 265 sqq.; annual treaty with Rome, 263, 265; the altars of the Latins, 265 sqq.; priesthoods, 264; *Laurentes Lavinates*, 241, 264; *mensae paniciae*, 252; private religiosity in Lavinium, 268

leges regiae, 147; *Valeriae-Horatiae*, 94; *XII tabularum*, see Twelve Tables

lex Icilia, 95

Liber et Libera, see *Ceres*

Licinius Stolo, C., 148

Liris, 54, 140, 187, 373

Livy, 56, 94, 110, 124, 127 sq., 142 sq., 147 sq., 362, 377, 392, and *passim*

Longula, 368 n. 2

Lucilius, 308

Lucretia, 82, 140, 152, 154

lucumo, 137, 157, 179, 200

lucus Deae Diae, lucus Dianius, 49, 89; *Ferentinae*, see *caput*; *Solis Indigetis*, 252

lupa, 277 sq., 302 (wolves of Mars)

Lupercalia, 20, 24, 45, 254, 315

lusus Troiae, 281 sqq.

Maesia silva, 288

magister populi, 43, 81, 84; *equitum*, 81, 83

Magni dii, 269

Manios, 192

Manlius Torquatus, T., 361

Marce, see *Camitlnas*

Marcius, Ancus, 104-5, 129, 132-33, 136, 139, 144, 290 sq., 291 n. 4, 294, 367; see also *Coriolanus-Marcii*, 114, 156

Mars, 299 sqq., 302 sq.

Marsian territory, 412

Mastarna, 133-34, 213 sqq., 225

Mediolanium, 272 n. 4

Metabus, 210

Mezentius, 188, 209 n. 1, 210

monkey, 282 sq.

Mount Vesuvius, battle at, 412

Mucius, see *Scaevola*

myth of origin, 5-6, 18 sq., 24, 250 sqq., 271 sqq., 278 sqq.

Naevius, 126, 159, 164-65, 170, 233, 249

Nanos-Nanas, 279

Neapolis, 349

Nepet, 233, 396, 401, 412, 417

noblemen-cavalry, 81, 92, 160, 270, 281, 331, 384, 398 sq.

Nola, 187

nomen = "nation", 3-4, 37, 53, 178, 264

Nomentum, 12 n. 4, 13, 54, 417

Norba, 12 n. 4, 16, 368, 392, 395, 404, 417

Numa, see *Pompilius*

Numasios, 192

Numic(i)us, 253, 257

Numitor, 126 n. 3, 247

Odysseus, 240, 279

Olus (Aulus), see *Vibenna*

Ostia, 54, 61, 144, 190, 212, 233, 290 n. 4, 291, 293, 295, 398

Paelignians, 410, 412

Palatine, 40, 57, 196-97, 201, 323
Pater Indiges, 252, 255
patricians, patriciate, 80 sq., 90 sq., 93, 98, 146, 148, 154, 160, 165, 167, 315-16, 400
Pedum, 12 n. 4, 54, 362, 390, 413, 417
penates publici, 112, 247, 249, 252, 255, 257, 261, 265, 267-69
perimeter of the *regio suburbana*, 314
Pesna Arcmsnas, 221, 223
Phocaeans, 189
Phoenician ware, 185
Picentes, Picenum, 187, 275, 338
Picus, 275
Pinarii, 315
Piso, see *Calpurnius*
Pithekusai, 339
Plautii, 390
plebs, plebeian names in the *fasti*, 80-82, 90 sq., 93, 97 sq., 114, 148, 154, 156, 160 sqq., 167, 169, 321 sq., 351
Politorium, 13
Polusca, 368
Polybius, 135, 150, 352, 355, 360, 364
Polydeukes, Poldoukes, Podloukes, Poloukes, Pultuke, 269 sq.
Pometia, Suessa, 15, 49, 54, 128, 139-40, 324, 366
Pompilius, Numa, 135, 147, 263
Pomptine plain, 61, 140, 191, 364-65, 368, 370 sqq., 374, 384, 396, 400, 405
Poplicola, Valerius, 84
populus (as the entire nation), 43, 81, 84
Porcius Cato, M., see *Cato*
Porsenna, 15, 51, 53, 59, 69, 72 sqq., 77 sq., 92, 133, 137, 142, 147, 168, 186, 208, 214, 234 sq., 289, 327, 337, 340, 351, 380, 400
Postumius, pirate captain, 346; *P. Albus, A.*, 92 sq., 115
Potiti[i], see *Valerii*
Praeneste, 12 n. 4, 41, 54, 187 sq., 190, 192, 194, 232, 270, 330, 362 sq., 372 sq., 377, 380, 382, 384, 385-91, 400, 405-6, 409, 412 sq., 415, 417
primeval giant, 254
private armies, 315 sq.
Privernum, 191, 210, 375-76, 407, 411
Punicum, harbor, 211
Pyrgi, 211, 340, 343, 359
Pyrrhus, 349
Pythagoras, statue of, 346

Querquetulum, 12 n. 4, 14
Quinctii, 45, 315
Quirinal, 40, 196, 199, 264
Quirinus, 301

Rasce, 221
Rea, 253
regia, 258
regio suburbana, 314
revolution of the *plebs*, 90 sq., 94, 98, 321
Rhome, 158 sq.
Robigalia, Robigus, 301
Romilius Rocus Vaticanus, T., 295, 310
Roman, Romans, Rome: myth of origin, 132, 134, 171, 190, 250; one of the 30 Latin units, 10, 13-15, 104; foundation of Rome, 134, 166 n. 6, 168, 173, 238; geographical position, 187, 193 sqq.; *ager Romanus*, 296 sqq., 317, 373; territory, 402, 415-16; *intra pomerium*, 49 sq., 303; *extra pomerium*, 89, 93-94, 99 sq., 321; Latine and Sabine elements, 196 sqq.; twofold organization, 196; tribus, 127, 129, 159 sq., 198, 244-45, 303, 306, and *s.v.*; curiae, 6, 17, 23, 129; *gentes maiores, minores*, 161; Etruscan families, 197 sqq., 337; *comitia curiata*, 6, 44; constitution, 149; treaties of alliance, 146, 263, 349 sqq., 379, 405, 408-9; associates and rivals, 378 sq.; end of the monarchy, 30, 59, 77 sq.; republic, 75, 78, 134; magistrates, 32, 97, 113, 115, 160, 223, 261; dictators, 43, 92, 120, 250, 337; *magister populi*, 43; *m. equitum*, 43; consuls, 29, 32, 148 sq.; censorship, 163; *tribuni plebis*, 91, 94, 98, 163; *aediles*, 92, 94 sqq., 167, 391; senate, 94, 163, 174; pontiffs, 125, 165, 168, 261, 298, 352; *flamines*, 261; Vestals, 250, 285 sq.; priesthoods, 241, 261, 263; *sacra principiorum p. R. Quiritium*, 263 sq.; festivals, 296 sqq., games, 33 n. 6, 99, 327; calendar, 200 sq.; census, 128 sq., 144; army, 98, 128 sq., 201; navy, 348 sqq.; citizenship, 41, 349, 383, 386, 416-18; *civitas sine suffragio*, 348 n. 2, 417; colonization, 102, 111, 139-40, 233, 272, 367-68, 374, 394, 397, 418; maritime colonies,

394, 398, 416; sea trade, 348-49, 355; coinage, 147, 260, 272-74, 349; topography, 289 sq.; urbanization, 195 sqq., 198 sq.; *Forum Boarium*, 198 sq.; *regia*, 196, 258; *arx*, 322, 326; Capitol, *s.v.*; sanctuaries, 198 sq., 270, 323 sqq., 326, 329, 331; famines, 61, 75, 338, 343, 370 sq.; ascendancy over the Latins, 25, 29-31, 45, 101 sq., 107, 122, 131 sqq., 135, 138, 141 sqq., 218, 263, 305, 331-419; Rome and Southern Etruria, 337-41; Rome and the Volscians, 319 sqq.; on the seashore, 347 sqq., 398; sea power, 347 sqq.

Romulus, 34, 127-29, 131-32, 133, 135-36, 146-47, 151, 172-73, 215, 247, 253, 263, 266, 289, 293

Rutuli, 14, 49, 53, 210, 277 sq.

Sabines, 28, 127, 129, 136 sq., 139, 141-42, 145, 151-52, 159, 161, 193, 196 sq., 232-33, 237, 293, 381, 415

salt-transport, salt-works, *salinae*, 132, 193, 232 sqq., 288 sqq., 292 sq., 313, 316, 341

Samnites, 28, 143, 184, 275, 346, 354, 376, 407, 410 sq.

Sanates, 13 n. 3

Sardinia, 347, 349

Sassula, 13

Satricum, 12 n. 4, 16, 191, 330, 368, 370, 374 sq., 376, 388, 395, 397, 404-6, 409, 411

Scaevola, 74, 84

Scaptia, 12 n. 4

Semo Sancus Dius Fidius, 379

Septem pagi, 73, 288 sq., 303, 313, 316

Servian wall, 99, 193, 320 sqq., 402

Servius, see *Tullius*

Setia, 12 n. 4, 16, 122, 376, 392, 395-97, 406, 412, 417

Sibyl of Cyme, 57; Sibylline books, 96, 124

Sicily, 61, 95, 177, 210, 287, 339, 342 sqq., 349, 353, 358

Sidicini, 411

Signia, 139-40, 367, 376, 392, 395, 397, 404, 412, 417

Silvia, 247, 280; *Silvii*, 239

Silvius, 20, 126 n. 3, 239 n. 1

Sol Indiges, 252 sq., 265

Solonium, 190, 233, 304

Sovana (*Svetimach*), 221

sow (female boar), 5, 18 sq., 247, 250, 271-78

Sparta, 152, 270

Stesichoros, 279

Suessa, see *Pometia*

Sulpicius, Servius, 148

Sutrium, 233, 396, 401, 412, 417

Syracuse, 339-40, 342 sqq., 353, 358, 364, 398, 402, 407-8

Tarchetios, 190, 280

Tarchon, 207, 228 sq., 279

Tarpeia, 151

Tarquinii (city of), 76 sq., 187, 203-4, 206 sqq., 231, 290, 325, 348, 407

Tarquinius Collatinus, L., 77, 147; *Priscus*, 29, 34, 58, 73, 104-6, 111, 132-42, 147, 213, 215, 220, 324, 367; *Superbus*, 12, 27, 29, 34, 59 sqq., 74 sqq., 77, 79, 104, 110, 133-36, 138, 140, 145, 153, 207, 213, 234 sq., 245, 296, 324, 327 sqq., 337, 351, 366-67, 380; *Cn. T.* (*Cneve Tarchunies*), 134, 217 sqq., 222 sq., 225, 230, 324, 327; *Sextus T.*, 380

Tarquins, 12, 55, 74, 144, 153-54, 160, 195, 206, 208, 231, 303, 320, 329, 331 sqq., 380, 399-400; their fall, 30, 59, 79, 84, 91, 107, 198, 234, 333

Tarracina, 187, 191, 352 n. 4, 372, 401, 408

Tatius, Titus, 146, 215, 263, 266 sq.

Telephus, 279, 280

Tellenae, 12 n. 4

Terentius Varro, M., 135, 191, 248, 261

Terminalia, 300

Thetis, 280

Tiber, 187, 193-94, 202, 212, 231 sqq., 289 sqq., 303, 313, 330, 338, 345, 397, 413

Tibur, 12 n. 4, 41, 49, 54, 187, 190, 194, 362 sq., 372 sq., 377, 385-90, 406, 409, 412 sq., 415, 417

Timaeus, 68, 125-26, 134, 147, 157, 159, 171 sq., 174, 248-51, 271, 273, 279, 285 sq., 343 n. 3

Timoleon, 345 sq.

Toleria, 12 n. 4, 13 n. 3

Tolerus, 54, 140, 187

tomba François, 221 sqq.

Tragliatella, jug of, 280 sqq.

tribus: the original 3 gentile tribes, 6, 17, 106; *urbanae*, 127, 306; *rusticae*, 127, 306 sqq., 313, 405; collective property of the tribes, 307 sq., 310; tribes with geographical names, 307 sqq., 316; but void of geographical meaning, 318, 383; with gentile names, 307, 310 sqq., 316-17, 394, 401; *Aemilia*, 313; *Arnensis*, 405; *Camilia*, 309 sq., 317; *Claudia*, 311, 314, 317; *Clustumina*, 307, 317, 401; *Collina*, 317; *Cornelia*, 313; *Esquilina*, 317; *Fabia*, 312; *Horatia*, 312; *Lemonia*, 307, 317; *Menenia*, 313 sq.; *Palatina*, 160, 317; *Papiria*, 313; *Poblilia*, 375; *Pollia*, 307 sq., 317; *Pomptina*, 375, 396; *Pupinia*, 308 sq., 317; *Quirina*, 159; *Romilia*, 295, 304, 310 sq., 312 sq., 317; *Sabatina*, 405; *Sergia*, 311, 313; *Stellatina*, 405; *Suburana*, 317; *Tromentina*, 405; *Voltinia*, 309, 317; *Voturia*, 313

Trifanum, battle at, 412

Troy, Trojans, 125-26, 158, 168, 172, 224, 227, 239 n. 1, 247-65, 273, 278 sqq.; Trojan game, 280 sq.; relics, 284 sqq.

truia, truials, truare, 281

Tuder, 272

Tullia, 152 sq.

Tullius, Servius, 49, 85 sqq., 90, 105-6, 127-30, 133-35, 142, 144, 146, 212 sqq., 320 sq.

Tullus, see *Hostilius*

Turnus (Tyrrhenus), 190, 210

Tusculum, 12 n. 4, 15, 30, 35, 54, 89, 106, 114, 193, 244 sq., 270, 308, 313, 372 sq., 375, 380-85, 387, 394, 397, 399 sq., 401-2, 404-6, 412, 416 sq.

Tutula-Philotis, 403

Twelve Tables, 39, 41, 295, 330 sq.

Tyrrhenia, 279

Tyrrhus, 280

Tyrsenos, 279

Umbrians, 64

Valerii Potiti, 315; *V.*, 161

Valerius Antias, 111, 127, see also *Poplicola*

Varro, see *Terentius*

Vaticanus, collis, 292; *ager*, 295, 303

Veii, Veientanes, 73, 76 sq., 96, 128-29, 131-33, 141, 167, 191, 193, 203-4, 208, 212, 231-34, 287 sq., 288 sq., 303, 312, 316 sq., 321-24, 338, 340-41, 347, 356-57, 372, 382, 396, 401-3, 405

Veiovis, 241

Vel Vibe, 230 n. 1, 233

Velienses, 13

Velitrae, 12 n. 4, 16, 191, 330, 367, 372, 374-76, 382, 384, 388, 390, 394, 397, 404, 406 sq., 412 sq.

Velleius Paterculus, 183 sq.

Veneti, 356-58

Venthi Cau[le]s, 222 sq.

Venus, 210

Verginia, 153 sqq., 159

Verrugo, 372

Vesperna, 268

Vesta, Vestals, 196, 241, 247, 255, 257 sq., 265, 267, 269, 271, 341

Vetulonia, 203

Veturii, 192

Vetusia, 192

via Appia, 302; *Campana*, 294, 299, 310; *Claudia*, 301, 310; *Latina*; *Praenestina*, 302; *Salaria*, 232, 293, 307

Vibenna, Aulus, 141, 215-31; *Caeles*, 141, 215-31

vicus Tuscus, 60, 197, 205, 331, 337

Villanova civilization, 185, 195, 199, 294, 421 sq.

Vitellia, 13, 372, 394

Volscians, 4 n. 1, 12, 14, 16, 28, 61, 105, 107-8, 110, 118, 122, 138-40, 142, 145, 156, 187, 237, 240, 305, 322, 324, 334, 337-39, 365-78, 380-82, 384, 386-88, 393-95, 397 sq., 400-402, 404-6, 411, 413, 415

Volsinii, 205, 221, 381

Voltumna, 26, 204 sq.; *Volturnus*, 205 sq.; *Vortumnus*, 204 sq.

Vulcanus, 279

Vulci, Vulcentanes, 76, 133, 141, 178, 203-4, 208, 212-31, 284 sq.

Wine, 157, 210 sqq.

Xenokrite, 58-59, 62, 72, 157, 210 sqq.

Plates

PLATE I

The cult image of Diana in Aricia on denarii of the year 43 B.C.

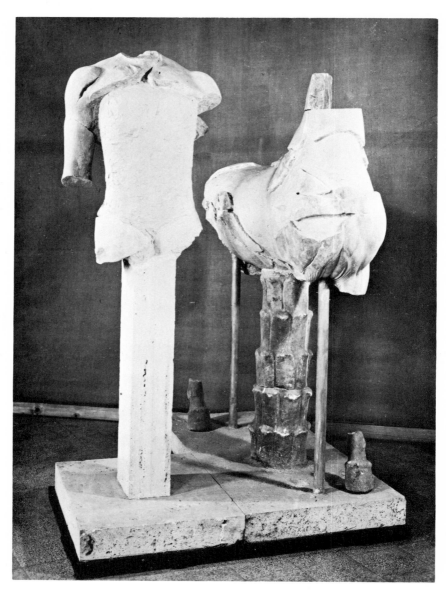

PLATE II

Marble group of the Dioscuri found in the Forum Romanum.

PLATE III

1. Roman silver coin from last decades of the third century B.C. 2. Terra-cotta herm, Tarquinia. 3. Roman silver coin. 4. Bronze coin struck in Capua under Hannibal. 5. Gold coin from 209 B.C. 6. Reverse of the same type. 7. Heavy cast, found in Lago di Nemi.

PLATE IV

1-2. Denarii of C. Sulpicius, about 100 B.C. 3. Bronze coin of Tuder in Umbria, late third century B.C. 4. Denarius of Vespasian. 5. Relief sculpture.

PLATE V

Marble group of the sow with the thirty piglets.

PLATE VI

Bronze medallions of Antoninus Pius.

PLATE VII

1-4. Bronze coins and medallions of Antoninus Pius. 5. Denarius of a Cornelius
Cetegus. 6. Intaglio. 7. Glass paste. 8. Bronze coin in commerce.

PLATE VIII

Wall painting from the "tomba François" in Vulci: Mastarna frees Caeles
Vibenna.

PLATE IX

Wall painting from "tomba François": Larth Ulthes stabs Laris Papathnas.

PLATE X

Wall painting from "tomba François": Rasce kills Pesna Arcmsnas.

PLATE XI

Wall painting from "tomba François": Aulus Vibenna kills Venthi Caules.

PLATE XII

Wall painting from "tomba François": Marce Camitlnas kills Cneve Tarchunies.

PLATE XIII

1-14. Engraved gems and glass pastes. 15-18. Denarii of L. Papius Celsus.

1.

2.

3.

8.

9.

10.

11.

4.

5.

6.

7.

PLATE XIV

Engraved gems and glass pastes.

PLATE XV

1-4. Carthaginian tetradrachms struck in Magna Graecia. 5-7. Roman didrachms.

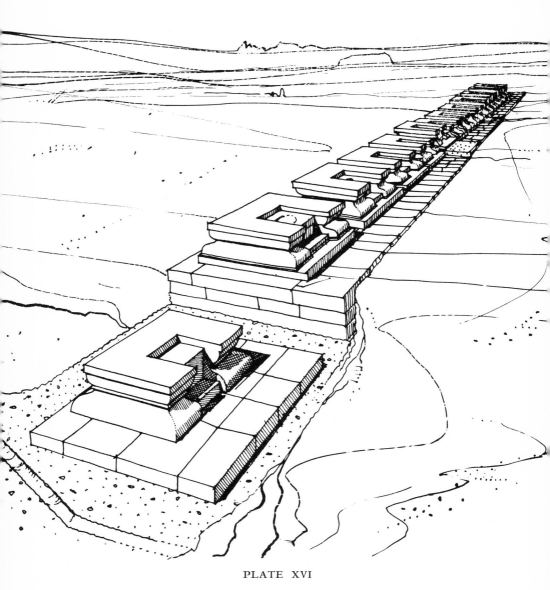

PLATE XVI

The great altars found outside Lavinium.

PLATE XVII

The cista Pasinati.

PLATE XVIII

1. Roman bronze coin. 2. Bronze coin of Capua. 3. Etruscan silver coin. 4. Roman ingot money. 5. Archaic Latin dedication from Lavinium.

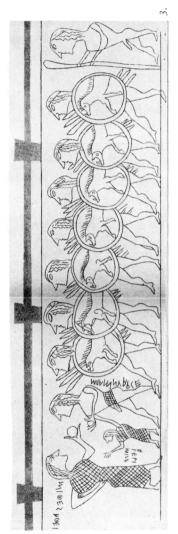

PLATE XIX

Drawings of a Caeretane jug, found at Tragliatella near Caere.

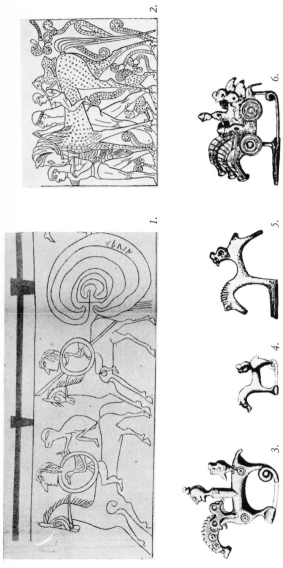

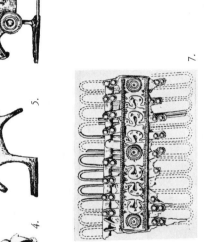

PLATE XX

1. Drawings from Caeretane earthenware jug. 2. Wall painting from the "tomba Campana" in Veii. 3. Bronze fibula from Marzabotto. 4. Fibula from Tarquinia. 5. Bronze fibula from Bologna. 6. Bronze fibula from Este. 7. Gold ornament from Marsiliana

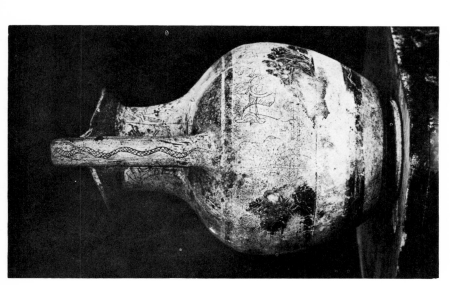

PLATE XXI

The Tragliatella jug.

PLATE XXII

The Tragliatella jug.

PLATE XXIII

Attic red figure vase.

PLATE XXIV

Attic black figure vase.

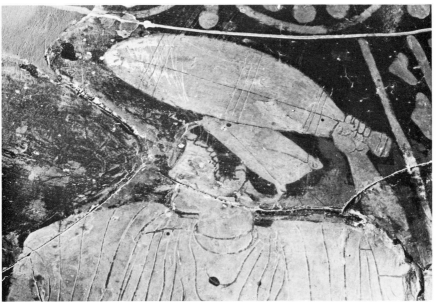

PLATE XXV

Etruscan red figure vase from Vulci.

Date Due

Demco 293-5